# An Introduction to the Geography of Tourism

# An Introduction to the Geography of Tourism

Third Edition

VELVET NELSON

ROWMAN & LITTLEFIELD
Lanham • Boulder • New York • London

Published by Rowman & Littlefield
An imprint of The Rowman & Littlefield Publishing Group, Inc.
4501 Forbes Boulevard, Suite 200, Lanham, Maryland 20706
www.rowman.com

6 Tinworth Street, London, SE11 5AL, United Kingdom

British Library Cataloguing in Publication Information Available

**Library of Congress Cataloging-in-Publication Data**
Names: Nelson, Velvet, 1979– author.
Title: An introduction to the geography of tourism / Velvet Nelson.
Description: Third edition. | Lanham, Maryland : Rowman & Littlefield, 2021. | Series:
    Exploring geography | Includes bibliographical references and index.
Identifiers: LCCN 2020052083 (print) | LCCN 2020052084 (ebook) | ISBN 9781538135167
    (cloth) | ISBN 9781538135174 (paperback) | ISBN 9781538135181 (epub)
Subjects: LCSH: Tourism—Environmental aspects. | Geographical perception.
Classification: LCC G156.5.E58 N45 2021 (print) | LCC G156.5.E58 (ebook) | DDC
    338.4/791—dc23
LC record available at https://lccn.loc.gov/2020052083
LC ebook record available at https://lccn.loc.gov/2020052084

For Dr. Brian Cooper
Your support made much of this work possible.

# Brief Contents

# Contents

# Illustrations

## Boxes

# Figures

# Maps

# Tables

# Preface to the Third Edition

I first started working on this project in 2010, and I started working on this edition at the beginning of 2020. It is hard to express just how much has happened in tourism in that decade. Tourism has been changing at an unbelievably fast pace. Even some of the things I had written in the second edition only four years ago seemed outdated. Then, as the COVID-19 pandemic unfolded, things started changing on a daily basis. Temperature checks were initiated at airports, passengers were quarantined on cruise ships, flights took off with only a handful of passengers, anyone who had traveled anywhere was asked to self-quarantine, all sorts of meetings and events were canceled, people canceled future trips, hotels were converted into makeshift hospitals, an airline started performing rapid coronavirus blood tests as part of their pre-boarding procedures, people lost their jobs, countries closed their borders, entire populations were locked down, and by the time I finished writing, over half a million people had died.

By the time you read this book, I hope that life has returned to some semblance of normal. However, the tourism landscape has most assuredly changed. The impact of the pandemic on travel and tourism was immediately felt around the world. At the same time, there were many questions about the long-term effects. Would travel and tourism-related businesses survive the pandemic to serve tourists in the future? Would it reduce demand for tourism for the foreseeable future due to new restrictions, economic crisis, or fear? Would it create a pent-up demand that would explode as soon as travel opened up again for those who remain financially able? Would this disruption provide an opportunity for stakeholders to reshape patterns of tourism to be more sustainable and resilient? Or would they be in such a rush to regain tourism income that it would be a return to business as usual? I do not know how this situation is going to play out. But I do know that tourism is a very real part of the world we currently live in that has real consequences for peoples and places, both when it occurs and, as we now see, when it does not.

Tourism is a dynamic system, and the geography of tourism is an exciting field of study. My goal for this textbook is to provide a broad overview of tourism from a geographic perspective. I want it to help students in geography use the foundation they have been building to learn about a new topic and to help students in tourism look at their topic from a new perspective. I draw from the ever-growing literature on tourism in general, and tourism geography specifically, and cover a wide range of subjects and approaches. But there is much more that could be done. This book is just a place to start. I encourage students to use this introduction as an opportunity to decide what part of the topic interests them most and learn more about it. For additional secondary research, begin by checking out the sources listed at the end of each chapter. A pandemic is not the time for primary research, but the time will come again when you can get out there and experience aspects of tourism for yourself.

There are many people to thank for their invaluable contributions to this project. In particular, I would like to thank Susan McEachern, editorial director at Rowman & Littlefield, for her work on this third edition and Brian Cooper for continuing to support my work. Big thanks go to Carolyn Nelson and Tom Nelson for being my first readers. I am indebted to Gang Gong for producing the maps used in this edition as well as Scott Jeffcote for supplying me with many of the photographs and for editing the rest. Special thanks go to the River Road research team (Derek Alderman, Candace Bright, David Butler, Perry Carter, Stephen Hanna, Arnold Modlin, and Amy Potter) for giving me permission to reproduce their map of Southern plantation and slavery museum sites. I am grateful for all of the family and friends who shared their stories with me and for Carolyn Nelson, Ava Fujimoto-Strait, and Pamela Rader who helped connect me with those who had stories to tell. These experiences—sometimes typical and sometimes extraordinary—help me, and hopefully the readers of this book, to think about things in new ways. Thanks also to the reviewers of the second edition, whose comments guided my approach to this edition. I also owe thanks and love to Kai Nelson Bailey, my self-appointed cheerleader for when I finished a chapter and task manager for when I didn't, as well as Barret Bailey who took on the role of educator/entertainer while we were quarantined at home so that I was able to continue writing.

# Abbreviations

| | |
|---|---|
| AAG | American Association of Geographers |
| AR | augmented reality |
| CDC | Centers for Disease Control and Prevention |
| CITES | Convention on the Trade in Endangered Species |
| CLIA | Cruise Lines International Association |
| CRS | Customer Reservation System |
| CSR | corporate social responsibility |
| CTO | Caribbean Tourism Organization |
| eVTOL | electronic vertical take-off and landing |
| eWOM | electronic word-of-mouth |
| FAA | Federal Aviation Administration |
| FSC | full service carriers |
| GDP | gross domestic product |
| GIS | geographic information system |
| GSTC | Global Sustainable Tourism Council |
| HSR | high-speed rail |
| IGU | International Geographical Union |
| IOC | International Olympic Committee |
| ISIL | Islamic State of Iraq and the Levant |
| LCCs | low-cost carriers |
| LNG | liquefied natural gas |
| MDGs | Millennium Development Goals |
| MICE | meetings, incentives, conventions, and exhibitions |
| MSA | metropolitan statistical area |
| NASA | National Aeronautics and Space Administration |
| NCGE | National Council for Geographic Education |
| NGO | nongovernmental organization |
| NGS | National Geographic Society |
| OHCHR | Office of the High Commissioner for Human Rights |
| P2P | peer-to-peer |

| | |
|---|---|
| PATA | Pacific Asia Travel Association |
| PPT | pro-poor tourism |
| RAISA | robots, artificial intelligence, and service automation |
| RGS | Royal Geographical Society |
| SABRE | Semi-Automated Business Research Environment |
| SDGs | Sustainable Development Goals |
| SIDS | small island developing states |
| SWOT | Strengths, Weaknesses, Opportunities, and Threats |
| TALC | tourist area life cycle |
| TGV | Train à Grande Vitesse |
| TIES | The International Ecotourism Society |
| TRA | tourism resource audit |
| TSA | Transportation Security Administration |
| UGC | User-Generated Content |
| UNESCO | United Nations Educational, Scientific, and Cultural Organization |
| UNODC | United Nations Office on Drugs and Crime |
| UNWTO | United Nations World Tourism Organization |
| VFR | visiting friends and relatives |
| VR | virtual reality |
| WOM | word-of-mouth |
| WTTC | World Travel & Tourism Council |

# Part I

# THE GEOGRAPHY OF TOURISM

While the study of tourism has at times been dismissed as the study of fun, tourism has an undeniable economic, social, cultural, political, and environmental impact on the world today. In fact, tourism has never been more important. The value of the tourism industry continues to increase. In 2018, international tourism receipts exceeded US$1.451 trillion. At the same time, more people are participating in tourism than ever before. In the same year, international tourist arrivals reached 1.401 billion and domestic tourists were estimated at eight to nine billion. This perhaps surprisingly complex global phenomenon is naturally a topic of geographic inquiry, and geography has much to contribute to our understanding of tourism.

Part I establishes the framework for our examination of the geography of tourism. Chapter 1 introduces the relationship between geography and tourism and outlines the thematic approach that will be used throughout the text. Chapter 2 lays the foundation for our discussion of tourism: it discusses the basic terminology of tourism and key concepts from the perspective of both the demand side of tourism and the supply side. Chapter 3 explores the concept of tourism products and introduces several products that will be referenced in the remaining sections.

# CHAPTER 1

# Geography and Tourism

Tourism is increasingly a part of our lives. Not only are more people traveling more frequently than ever before, but we see it and read about it more often as well. Travel and tourism are a staple in many people's social media feeds. These topics make their way into news stories from wildfires in Australia to the global spread of the novel coronavirus (SARS-CoV-2) and the disease it causes (COVID-19). They have even been the subject of comedy shows from Last Week Tonight with John Oliver's take on mountain climbing at Mount Everest (2019) to Patriot Act with Hasan Minhaj's look at the cruise industry (2019). The incredible growth of tourism worldwide is forcing us to think beyond the trips we would like to take to consider the potential for social media to bring thousands of people to a place, for vacation rentals to bring widespread changes to communities, or for the voracious demand for travel to contribute to climate change. And this just scratches the surface. Dig deeper and we can begin to appreciate that tourism is far more complicated than we ever realized.

While geography rarely factors into these conversations, it should. Now, more than ever, we need to work toward an understanding of tourism and the role it plays in shaping places and lives. Geography provides a powerful approach to this astonishingly complex phenomenon. Simply put, tourism is the subject of this textbook, and geography is the approach. In the chapters that follow, we will make an in-depth examination of tourism. We will first introduce the subject and then break it down with the use of different geographic themes or topics.

## Geography

While the question "What is geography?" seems simple enough, the answer often proves surprisingly elusive. We have heard the term "geography" all our lives. It is typically part of the primary school social studies curriculum. It is inherently tied to the popular *National Geographic* media. It is often a category in trivia games. Yet, ideas that come from these sources, among others, do not make it any easier to answer the question. In fact, the more you know about the topic, the harder it becomes to produce a neat, concise definition that encompasses everything geography is and geographers do.

From the literal translation of the original Greek word, *geography* means "writing about or describing the earth." People have always had a desire to know and understand the world they live in. Particularly during the ages of exploration and empire, there was a distinct need for the description of new places that people encountered. People wanted to know *where* these new places were, but they also wanted to know *what* these places were like. This included both the physical characteristics of that place and the human characteristics. They wanted to know how these new places were similar to and different from those places with which they were familiar. Therefore, the description of places—where they were and what was there—provided vast amounts of geographic data.

Thus, geography and travel have long been interconnected. The fundamental curiosity about other places, and the tradition of travel to explore these places, continued with scientific travelers of the eighteenth and nineteenth centuries. Although Charles Darwin is the most famous of these, the German Alexander von Humboldt (1769–1859) was one of the most notable geographers. Geographic historian Geoffrey Martin argues that von Humboldt was one of the figures who played an important role in the transition between the classical era of geography and what geography would become in the modern era.[1] Von Humboldt traveled extensively in Eurasia and the Americas and produced a tremendous body of work based on his observations. Through his descriptions of traveling in and experiencing new places, he generated significant interest in geography and inspired subsequent generations of travelers, including Darwin himself.

By the contemporary period, geography had outgrown the classical tradition of description. There were few places left in the world that were uncharted. Although the need for description was diminished, the need to understand the world persisted. In fact, this need seemed greater than ever before. The world was changing. Countless new patterns were emerging, new problems had to be faced, and new connections were forged between places. Having established the where and the what, geographers turned their attention to the *why*. Today, geographers continue to seek an understanding of the patterns of the world, everything from the physical processes that shape our environment to the various patterns of human life, and all of the ways in which the two—the physical and the human—come together, interact, and shape one another. Obviously, this is an enormous undertaking that involves an incredible diversity of work by geographers on topics like the processes of chemical weathering in the Himalayas, spatial modeling of deforestation in West Africa, natural resource management in Australia, the effect of extreme weather events on Central American coffee growers, the quantification of India's urban growth through the use of remote sensing data, American immigration patterns, the geographical dimensions of global pandemics, and more.

When we look at it this way, it is hardly surprising that there are no definitions that summarize all of this in a few words. Over time, geographers and geographic associations have proposed various definitions and frameworks to provide a mechanism for organizing the field. In one example, the Joint Committee on Geographic Education of the National Council for Geographic Education (NCGE) and the American Association of Geographers (AAG) proposed the five themes of geography, including location, place, human-environment interactions, movement, and regions.[2] This framework highlighted important concepts in geography and provided a starting point for discussing the ways in which geographers view the world.

More recently, a contingent of geographers has focused less on what geography *is* than what it can *do*. This movement has its origins in the concept of powerful knowledge, proposed by British sociologist of education Michael Young. In his view, powerful knowledge is knowledge that is produced within disciplinary communities and represents the best current understanding of phenomena. When taught in schools, this knowledge is powerful because it allows students to understand and explain phenomena that are often beyond their direct experience. This can shape the questions we ask, the issues we investigate, and even patterns of behavior. Such knowledge therefore provides the foundation for both intellectual and personal growth.[3]

This concept clearly resonates with geographers, as it allows us to express what we already know: geographic knowledge is powerful. Geography encourages us to think about the world in new ways. It allows us to gain insight into places that are beyond our direct experience, which can inspire us, help us understand our interconnectedness, and foster a sense of global citizenship. Geography provides us with the tools to analyze, explain, and understand the world—its physical phenomena, human phenomena, and the interactions between the two. This gives us power over our own knowledge in that we are better able to evaluate knowledge and to think critically and independently. Thus, we are better able to understand important current, and future, issues such as globalization, population growth, climate change, sustainability, and more. We are better able to engage in debate about these issues, to make informed decisions, and to work toward solutions, which is extraordinarily powerful.[4]

Some geographers have argued that Young's ideas about the origin of powerful knowledge are too narrow when applied in the context of geography. We all have personal geographies of place, space, and environment. This is based on our own knowledge and understanding of the world from our own experiences. Such knowledge can also be powerful because it is the lens through which we see the world, and it allows us to contextualize academic geography.[5]

The framing of powerful geography does not seek to displace geographic concepts. Such concepts, such as place, continue to provide the foundation for geographic ways of thinking. For example, **place** generally refers to parts of the earth's surface that have meaning based on the physical and human features of that location. This concept shapes the way we think about the world. It reminds us that we need to understand these features to be able to explain what happens and how it happens in a particular place. This helps us to recognize that similar issues may have very different outcomes in two places, requiring different strategies or solutions. We will further consider how geographic concepts and powerful geography apply to the geography of tourism below.

# Tourism

The United Nations World Tourism Organization (UNWTO) glossary of terms considers **tourism** to be the activities of visitors, referring to travelers taking a trip to a destination, outside of their usual environment for less than a year for any purpose (business, leisure, or other personal purpose) other than to be employed in the country or place visited. The glossary further identifies a tourist as an overnight visitor, or a visitor whose trip includes an overnight stay. This is in contrast with a same-day visitor, or an excursionist.[6] Taken together, these definitions broadly include movement from one geographic location to another, activities undertaken, and potentially accommodation in the place of destination. It also accounts for different purposes. Leisure activities are most commonly associated with tourism and indeed account for the majority (56 percent) of international tourism. However, this definition allows for business to be the primary motivation for travel, as well as "other personal purposes," which may include health, education, or visiting family and friends. While any of these may be the explicit reason for travel, there are also secondary reasons for both travel and any tourism activities undertaken at the destination.

These definitions make the distinction between those visitors who travel outside their usual environment for at least a day (but not more than a year) and those visitors who return home in the same day. These local and day trip activities are classified as part of normal recreation activities undertaken in our **leisure time**, or the free time that we have left over after we have done what is necessary, from work to household chores to sleep, and during which we can do what we choose. Nevertheless, these "same-day visitors" are often participating in the same activities as the "tourists" coming from farther away. Depending on one's starting location, day trips can even take place over international borders.

In addition, these definitions focus on tourists and their activities—essentially the demand side of tourism. Borrowed from economics and adapted in the context of tourism, **tourism demand** is defined as "the total number of persons who travel, or wish to travel, to use tourist facilities and services at places away from their places of work and residence."[7] This is a fundamental component of tourism: essentially tourism would not exist without tourists and the demand for tourism experiences. **Tourism supply** is defined as "the aggregate of all businesses that directly provide goods or services to facilitate business, pleasure, and leisure activities away from the home environment."[8] Just as demand is a fundamental component of tourism, so is supply. Tourism necessarily involves the production of services and experiences. Although we are generally familiar with this side of tourism from participating in tourism in one form or another, we may not give it much thought beyond our own interests and experiences. In fact, the very nature of tourism often means that we do not *want* to have to think about all of the things that comprise the supply side of tourism and make our experiences possible. However, both are fundamental components of tourism contingent upon and shaped by each other, and therefore both must be considered if we are to understand the whole of tourism.

# Geography and Tourism

Tourism is inherently geographic. Fundamentally, tourism is based on the temporary movements of people across space as well as their interactions with and effects on peoples, places, and environments. Basic concepts and approaches in geography have the potential to inform our thinking and can contribute to our understanding of tourism. We will take a brief look at some of these below.

## GEOGRAPHIC CONCEPTS

As discussed earlier, place refers to parts of the earth's surface that have meaning based on the physical and human features of that location. This basic geographic concept is also fundamental to the geography of tourism. Destinations are the places of tourism. The ideas and meanings attached to these places create a demand for experiences in these places. For example, we could reduce Paris to an absolute location at 48°50'N latitude and 2°20'E longitude, but it is, of course, far more than that. As a place, it is associated with specific physical features (e.g., the Seine River, famous landmarks such as the Eiffel Tower and Notre Dame Cathedral, figure 1.1) as well as the human features of a well-known tourism destination (e.g., culture, history, an atmosphere for romance). These same features will shape how tourism occurs in a destination.

We can also consider the **relative location** of the destination, or the position of a place in relation to other places and how such places are connected. A destination that has a good location relative to large tourist markets has a distinct advantage over one that is much farther away. However, accessibility can help equalize this factor. **Accessibility** is the relative ease with which one location may be reached from another. For example, a direct flight or a high-speed train increases the accessibility of a place. Yet, it is often the case that remote locations are harder to get to and from because of fewer transportation connections, longer travel times, and frequently higher transportation costs. As such, remote places are less likely to develop into large destinations in terms of the quantity of tourists received. That does not mean these locations cannot develop tourism, just that they are likely to develop in a different way than one that is more accessible. Such destinations may receive smaller numbers of tourists who stay at the destination for longer periods of time and spend more money on average.

Think, for example, of the difference between the Bahamas and the Seychelles. Both are small tropical island destinations with attractive beach resources, among others. Just off the coast of Florida, the Bahamas are strategically located relative to the large North American tourist market and well connected via transportation networks. As such, the islands have a well-developed tourism industry (figure 1.2). In 2018, the destination received 6.62 million international visitors (including 1.63 million overnight visitors and 4.49 million same-day visitors, primarily cruise passengers), and the majority of these visitors came from the United States and Canada. Tourist spending accounted for US$3.38 billion. The length of stay for overnight visitors has increased slightly over the past two decades, from an average of just over five nights to just under seven nights. In contrast, the Seychelles, located nearly 1,000 miles off the

**Figure 1.1. Tourism destinations are more than locations. They are places that have meaning based on their physical and human features, such as well-known landmarks like the Eiffel Tower in Paris, France.** *Source:* Kim Sinkhorn

coast of eastern Africa in the Indian Ocean, is far from the principal tourist markets in North America, Europe, and even East Asia. Despite significant tourism resources, these islands received just 405,000 international visitors in 2018 (including 362,000 overnight visitors and 43,000 same-day visitors, all cruise passengers), and US$611 million in tourism revenue. The length of stay has remained relatively steady, with overnight visitors averaging around ten nights.[9]

Tourism occurs at different geographic scales. **Scale** generally refers to the size of the area studied. Increasingly, we think of tourism in global terms. The tourism industry has become globalized with things like global airline alliances and multinational hotel chains. As a result, tourism activities have also become more global. In 2018, international tourist arrivals exceeded 1.4 billion,[10] a number that has been steadily increasing (with some temporary fluctuations) since the mid-twentieth century. Yet, this movement of people across space creates connections between places, and tourism involves distinctly local, place-based activities. These activities depend on the unique physical and/or human features of that place.

There has been much debate about the effect of **globalization** on local places and the increasing interconnectedness of the world. One argument maintains that places are becoming more similar with the forces of globalization, such as the diffusion of

Figure 1.2. The Bahamas are a highly accessible destination for the North American tourist market. In 2018, the islands received 6.62 million international visitors. *Source:* Scott Jeffcote

popular culture through media and the standardization of products from large multinational corporations. Yet another argument suggests that, in light of globalization, it is more important than ever to create or reinforce a sense of distinctiveness at the local or regional scale. Tourism has been recognized as an extraordinarily important component in creating and/or promoting a sense of distinctiveness to raise awareness about that place or enhance its reputation.

Tourism provides unique opportunities for interactions between tourists and the peoples, places, and environments they visit. Tourism may be considered one of the most significant ways in which people know places that are not their own. It creates connections between geographically distinct groups of people, people who otherwise might have little direct knowledge of or contact with one another. It also offers people the potential to explore new environments that are different from the ones with which they are familiar. At the same time, these interactions between tourists and places have specific effects for both peoples and places. Tourism actively plays a role in shaping the world in which we live. This can no longer be ignored, as it so often was in the past. We see massive overcrowding in tourist hotspots like Rome, Italy's Trevi Fountain; read about extreme pollution prompting closures in places like Boracay, Philippines; and hear about anti-tourism protests in cities like Barcelona, Spain.

The framework of powerful geography encourages us to use geographic concepts to better understand and work toward solutions for important issues such as these. Although sustainability and sustainable development are not exclusively geographic concepts, they have an important role to play in powerful geography. Sustainable development requires a holistic perspective—one that geography can provide—to consider the economic, social (and cultural), and environmental implications of development. According to the UN-WTO, **sustainable tourism development** is "tourism that takes full account of its current and future economic, social and environmental impacts, addressing the needs of visitors, the industry, the environment and host communities."[11] Such an approach is crucial as stakeholders work to address current problems in tourism destinations such as Rome, the Philippines, and Spain (among many other examples) as well as find ways to better manage tourism growth to prevent future problems. These issues are at the forefront of current discussions about tourism and will be an ongoing theme throughout this textbook.

The interconnectedness between these geographic concepts and tourism is also reflected in the geotourism, or geographical tourism, approach. Although there has been confusion about geotourism, which can also refer to geologic tourism, places have looked to this approach as a means of promoting a sustainable form of tourism that protects and represents unique place-based resources in light of increasing globalization and homogenization (see box 1.1). An example of this can be found at the Teton Geotourism Center, the world's first geotourism center located in Driggs, Idaho.

## REGIONAL GEOGRAPHY

**Regions** have long been used in geography as a means of effectively organizing and communicating spatial information. Essentially, regions help us break down the world into more manageable units. We can determine those areas of the earth's surface that have some commonality—based on a specific physical or human characteristic, like climate or religion, or a combination of characteristics—that distinguishes them from other parts of the world. We conceptualize the world in regional terms (e.g., Europe or Southeast Asia), and it is organized regionally as well (e.g., the European Union or the Association of Southeast Asian Nations). **Regional geography** studies the varied geographic characteristics of a region.

Regions are applied in the context of tourism in a number of ways. For example, regions may be used to explain patterns or trends in tourism. **Tourist-generating regions** are source areas for tourists, or where the largest numbers of tourists are coming from. We can identify characteristics of these regions that stimulate demand for tourism, such as an unfavorable climate or a high level of economic development. Likewise, we can identify characteristics of regions that would facilitate demand, such as a good relative location and a high level of accessibility. Tourist-generating regions are important in helping us understand why certain people may be more likely to travel and to where. Theoretically, this information may be used to create new opportunities for people to travel. Specifically, if we understand the barriers to travel for a particular region, we can begin to develop strategies to overcome these barriers. In practical terms, tourism marketers use this information. If a destination identifies its largest potential tourist market, then it will be able to develop a promotional campaign targeted at that audience.

Conversely, **tourist-receiving regions** are destination areas for tourists, or where the largest numbers of tourists are going. We can identify characteristics of these regions that contribute to the supply of tourism. Again, a good relative location and a

## Box 1.1.  In-Depth: Geotourism

The geotourism concept has evolved over more than two decades and across two disciplines. In the mid-1990s, English geologist Thomas Hose first proposed the idea of geotourism as "the provision of interpretive and service facilities to enable tourists to acquire knowledge and understanding of the geology and geomorphology of a site (including its contribution to the development of the Earth sciences) beyond the level of mere aesthetic appreciation."[a] This geologic tourism is recognized internationally and facilitated by the 147 United Nations Educational, Scientific and Cultural Organization (UNESCO) Global Geoparks that encompass geologically significant landscapes in forty-one countries.[b] From this tradition, geotourism is viewed as one of the special interest tourism products that have emerged with the expansion of the global tourism industry (see chapter 3). However, such a product has the potential to support sustainable tourism through local economic development, varied social benefits, and conservation of geologic heritage and diversity.[c] For example, the Global Geoparks initiative is connected to eight of the seventeen global Sustainable Development Goals (SDGs), including those addressing economic growth, education, and sustainable consumption.[d]

Jonathon Tourtellot, founding director of National Geographic's former Center for Sustainable Destinations, proposed the second idea of geotourism as an *approach* to tourism rather than as a specific product. This tradition defines **geotourism** as "tourism that sustains or enhances the distinctive geographical character of a place—its environment, heritage, aesthetics, culture, and the well-being of its residents."[e] Geotourism should bring together the geographic characteristics of a place (physical and human) in environmentally and culturally responsible ways to create a meaningful travel experience. This version of geotourism explicitly supports the tenets of sustainable tourism through its thirteen guiding principles. These are as follows:

1. *Integrity of a place* (i.e., highlight and enhance the things that make the destination unique)
2. *International codes* (i.e., adhere to internationally accepted guidelines, such as the Global Sustainable Tourism Council's (GSTC) criteria for sustainable destinations)
3. *Community involvement* (i.e., incorporate local people in the planning, development, execution, and evaluation of tourism)
4. *Community benefit* (i.e., ensure that local people benefit through business opportunities, employment, cultural enrichment, etc.)
5. *Tourist satisfaction* (i.e., provide high-quality experiences that tourists will want to share with others)
6. *Conservation of resources* (i.e., promote sustainable use of resources such as water and energy)
7. *Protection and enhancement of destination appeal* (i.e., manage tourist numbers and behaviors to prevent erosion of unique characteristics)
8. *Planning* (i.e., consider both short- and long-term impacts from tourism and adopt appropriate policies)
9. *Land use* (i.e., manage tourism development to prevent environmental degradation)
10. *Market diversity* (i.e., offer a range of options for different socioeconomic and demographic categories of tourists)
11. *Interactive interpretation* (i.e., encourage both local people and tourists to learn about and appreciate the place)
12. *Market selectivity* (i.e., focus on tourism market segments that will appreciate the unique aspects of place)
13. *Evaluation* (i.e., conduct regular evaluations and make necessary adjustments)

To bring the geotourism concept to life, the National Geographic program combined global sustainable tourism expertise with local knowledge (via local Geotourism Stewardship Councils) to create an approach to tourism that met these principles at the destinations. This led to the publication of Geotourism MapGuides for more than twenty destinations around the world. The Four Corners Region, at the intersection of Colorado, Utah, New Mexico, and Arizona, offers one example. Geotourism is considered a fitting approach for this area with its distinct geographic character, from the unique landscape of the Colorado Plateau to the rich Native American cultural heritage. Many of the region's sites, protected under the auspices of the national park service, exemplify this combination of physical and human characteristics of place. The MapGuide features an interactive map based on a geographic information system (GIS). This tool allows potential visitors to explore the area's natural and cultural attractions, events, and even opportunities to get involved in the community through volunteering. In addition to well-known attractions, area residents have a chance to nominate their favorite sites for inclusion in the guide. This approach allows local people to play an active role in representing what they feel makes that place unique. It also helps visitors learn about little-known attractions, get "off the beaten path," and experience place in a way they would not be able to on their own.

Despite the potential confusion, the two ideas of geotourism are not incompatible. The principles of geographic tourism can also serve as a guide for the development of geologic tourism in a place. At the same time, the geology and geomorphology of a place have a part to play in geographic tourism. Moreover, both geotourism as a tourism product and as an approach to tourism inherently recognize the need to protect the resources on which tourism depends and support sustainable tourism development.

*Discussion topic*: If geotourism, as an approach to tourism, is intended to highlight the unique geographic character of a place, do you think all tourism might be considered geotourism? Why or why not?

*Tourism online*: National Geographic, "Four Corners Region Geotourism MapGuide," at www.fourcornersgeotourism.com

---

[a] Thomas A. Hose. "Selling the Story of Britain's Stone." *Environmental Interpretation* 10 (1995): 16–17.

[b] United Nations Educational, Scientific, and Cultural Organization. "List of UNESCO Global Geoparks (UGGp)," *Earth Sciences*, accessed March 2, 2020, http://www.unesco.org/new/en/natural-sciences/environment/earth-sciences/unesco-global-geoparks/list-of-unesco-global-geoparks/.

[c] Ross Dowling and David Newsome, "Geotourism: Definition, Characteristics and International Perspectives," in *Handbook of Geotourism*, eds. Ross Dowling and David Newsome (Cheltenham: Edward Elgar Publishing Limited, 2018), 3.

[d] United Nations Educational, Scientific, and Cultural Organization. "UNESCO Global Geoparks and Their Contribution to the Sustainable Development Goals," *Earth Sciences*, accessed March 2, 2020, http://www.unesco.org/new/en/natural-sciences/environment/earth-sciences/unesco-global-geoparks/sustainable-development-goals/.

[e] National Geographic Society, "Geotourism," accessed March 2, 2020, https://www.nationalgeographic.com/maps/geotourism/.

---

high level of accessibility are important, as well as the attractions of the region and a well-developed tourism infrastructure. Tourist-receiving regions are important in helping us understand why certain places have successfully developed as destinations. This information may be used as an example for other places also seeking to develop tourism.

International agencies such as the UNWTO use regions to examine trends in the global tourism industry. The UNWTO identifies Europe as both the single largest tourist-generating region and the largest receiving region. As of 2018, the European region accounted for approximately 48 percent of international tourists and 51 percent of international tourist arrivals (map 1.1).[12] This is attributed to a range of factors, including a diverse set of attractive destinations, high levels of accessibility, a well-developed tourism infrastructure, and a long tradition of travel. Yet, long-standing trends in international tourism have been changing in recent years. The importance of Europe as both a generating and a receiving region has been declining with the emergence of new tourists and new destinations.

Destinations also use regions to present information to potential tourists and to create unique tourism experiences (see box 1.2). A national destination may use the concept to organize smaller destination regions. This allows tourists searching for a destination to match their interests or requirements to a particular place within that country. For example, the official website of India's Ministry of Tourism, Incredible India, invites potential visitors to discover destinations in six distinct geographic regions of the country based on different resources and experiences. In other cases, several nations will work together to generate interest in and awareness of themselves as a destination region. For instance, the mission of the Pacific Asia Travel Association (PATA) is to act "as a catalyst for the responsible development of travel and tourism to, from, and within the Asia Pacific region."[13]

The regional approach has been applied to the geography of tourism and is particularly useful for examining cases of tourism within different regional contexts. However, as we move toward a powerful geography perspective, we need to ensure that we have the framework to analyze, explain, and understand the world in terms of physical phenomena, human phenomena, and the interactions between the two. As such, we will be using a topical approach throughout this textbook.

## TOPICAL GEOGRAPHY

**Topical geography** studies a particular geographic topic in various place or regional contexts. Figure 1.3 provides a graphic illustration of the discipline of geography. This diagram demonstrates a hierarchy of just some of the topics studied in geography. Geography as a whole is broken down into two principal subdivisions. **Human geography** is the subdivision that studies the patterns of human occupation of the earth, while **physical geography** is the subdivision that studies the earth's physical systems. These subdivisions are further broken down into the topical branches of geography. The subjects addressed by each of these topical branches, including everything from climate to culture, may be examined through the key concepts in geography.

Fitting the geography of tourism into this picture is no easy task. If pressed, most geographers would probably consider the geography of tourism to be a branch of human geography. Certainly tourism is a human phenomenon, and much of the focus in the geography of tourism is on human ideas and activities. Likewise, the majority of geographers who study the geography of tourism are, in fact, human geographers. This

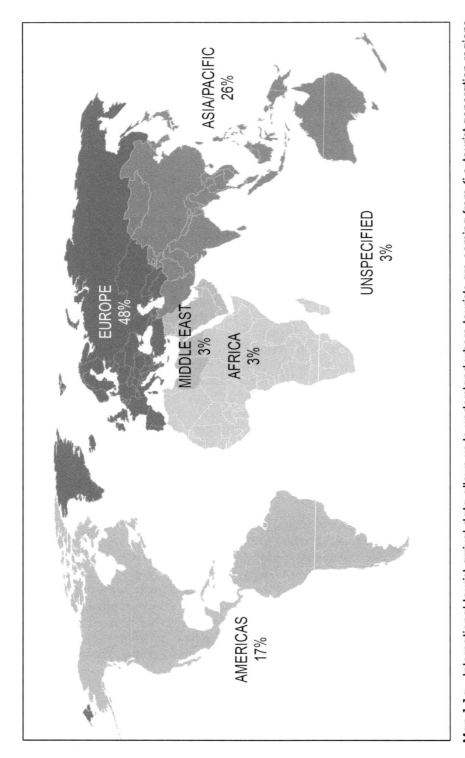

Map 1.1a. International tourist arrival data allows us to understand where tourists are coming from (i.e. tourist-generation regions shown here) and where they are going (i.e. tourist-receiving regions shown in Map 1.1b). Europe continues to be the world's most significant tourist region with a majority of both international tourists and international tourist arrivals. *Source:* Gang Gong

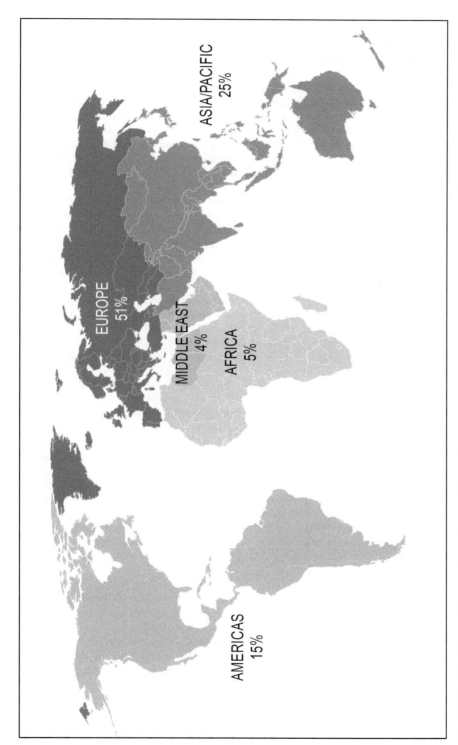

**Map 1.1b.** Tourist-receiving regions. *Source:* Gang Gong

# Box 1.2. Case Study: The Crown of the Continent Cross-Border Destination Region

The concept of regions has a very long tradition in geography. If we apply the definition of a region to tourism, we could consider destination regions to be those areas of the earth's surface with similar resources for tourism, whether this is a specific characteristic in the physical or human geography of that place or a combination of characteristics. For large countries, destination regions play a significant role in organizing and coordinating tourism efforts in different geographic areas. For diverse countries, regions provide an important means of communicating information about distinct areas and helping potential tourists match their interests with what the destination has to offer.

The areas of the earth's surface with similar resources for tourism may also span two or more countries. In the past, this would have been a barrier to cooperation, but countries are increasingly recognizing the value of working together to improve the position of both. Cross-border tourism projects raise the profile of a region and the destinations within the region as well as create a sense of differentiation from other destinations. This increases the destinations' competitive advantage by appealing to special interests (e.g., specialized routes or itineraries throughout a region) and creating distinctive experiences (e.g., the opportunity to participate in activities in more than one country). Complementary destinations that might once have been seen as competitors become partners as they seek to bring in visitors who might be interested in both places. These destinations further benefit from sharing knowledge, expertise, and resources, which reduces redundancies and allows for innovation. In addition, this cooperation improves resource management and supports a more sustainable regional tourism system.[a]

Tourism is an attractive strategy for places in often-peripheral border regions, but small destinations can struggle to compete on their own. Countries have viewed projects to establish cross-border destination regions as an opportunity in recent years. Nonetheless, any project involving international collaboration has potential challenges. In some cases, the extent of "cooperation" is a basic exchange of information. However, integration and innovation are key to fully achieving the competitive advantages of cross-border destination regions. Geography provides insight in every step of the process.

The Crown of the Continent offers one example of a cross-border destination region. This 28,000-square-mile region at the heart of North America spans the US-Canadian border between the state of Montana and the provinces of Alberta and British Columbia. Physically, the cross-border region lies at the narrow "waist" of the Rocky Mountains and is considered to be one of the most diverse and intact ecosystems in the temperate zones. Culturally, the region has a rich indigenous history with intertribal connections and cooperation.[b]

The "jewel" in the center of the "crown" is Waterton-Glacier International Peace Park. Glacier received national park status in the US in 1910; Waterton Lakes National Park received similar status in Canada in 1930. Rangers recognized that their parks were part of a greater ecosystem. They felt strongly that the border separating the two parks was artificial and first proposed international cooperation to understand and protect the region. Local Rotary Clubs on both sides of the border further advocated for the idea. In 1932, Waterton-Glacier International Peace Park was established by the US Congress and Canadian Parliament. The designation is intended to facilitate stronger shared management of park resources and to promote peaceful relations between the two countries. Waterton-Glacier was the first international peace park in the world and has provided an example for cross-border parks and projects around the world. In 1995, the Peace Park was officially designated as a UNESCO World Heritage Site in recognition of both its ecological significance and its model of cooperation.

Park stakeholders have also played an instrumental role in the Crown of the Continent Managers Partnership. This interagency forum brings together local, state, provincial, tribal, and federal resource management agencies throughout the wider Crown region that surrounds the Peace Park. This partnership helps raise awareness among gateway communities about the unique characteristics of the region that should be both protected and celebrated. It also educates stakeholders on common issues across the region and opportunities to support collaborative initiatives.[c]

Currently, one of the greatest issues is the threat to the region's glaciers posed by climate change. Over the past 100 years, Northwest Montana has warmed at about twice the average global rate. Clearly the glaciers have symbolic value for the Peace Park and the wider Crown region; however, reduced winter snowpack and melting glaciers will contribute to significant hydrologic changes.[d] There are many potential barriers to cooperation,[e] but cross-border partnerships will continue to be important as stakeholders adapt to changes, work to improve resilience, and promote economic, social, and environmental sustainability throughout the region.

*Discussion topic*: What do you think might be some of the challenges associated with cross-border tourism projects?

*Tourism online*: National Geographic, "Crown of the Continent," at https://crownofthe continent.natgeotourism.com

---

[a] Ksenija Vodeb, "Cross-Border Regions as Potential Tourist Destinations along the Slovene Croatian Frontier," *Tourism and Hospitality Management* 16 (2010): 219–21.

[b] National Geographic Society, "Crown of the Continent: About the Region," accessed March 17, 2020, https://crownofthecontinent.natgeotourism.com/info/about-the-region/cote7f04525dd3fbc235.

[c] National Geographic Society, "Waterton-Glacier International Peace Park," accessed March 17, 2020, https://crownofthecontinent.natgeotourism.com/content/waterton-glacier-international-peace-park/cot4c671f8692e2cf66a.

[d] National Park Service, "Glacier National Park: Climate Change," accessed March 17, 2020, https://www.nps.gov/glac/learn/nature/climate-change.htm.

[e] Dallen J. Timothy, "Cross-Border Partnership in Tourism Resource Management: International Parks Along the US-Canada Border," *Journal of Sustainable Tourism* 7, nos. 3&4 (1999): 185.

---

would suggest that we could insert a new "wedge" into the pie for tourism geography, and it would largely go unquestioned (figure 1.4).

This kind of conceptualization may be useful in showing that the geography of tourism is a topical branch that coexists with the others at the center of geography. However, it is less useful in helping us understand how to approach its study. As a new space for the geography of tourism is created, it may be tempting to come to the conclusion that the topic can stand alone. To some extent, overlap exists between the topical branches. Yet, this goes beyond mere overlap in the case of the geography of tourism. All of these other areas—cultural geography, economic geography, population geography, political geography, etc.—have much to contribute to the study of tourism through the lens of geography. By tracing the geography of tourism through the human side, we lose some

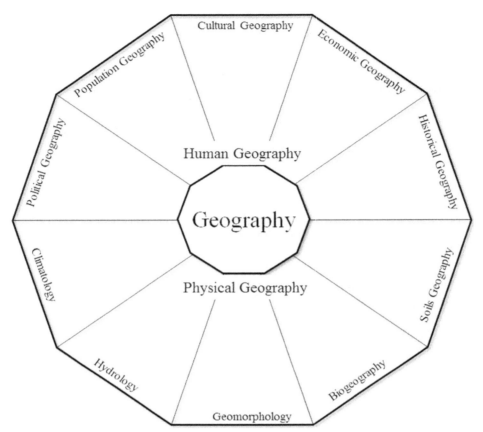

**Figure 1.3. This graphic representation of geography illustrates the topical approach in which the discipline is broken down based on various topics in human and physical geography. Topical geography allows us to understand a particular aspect of the world.** *Source:* Velvet Nelson

of the components in physical geography—geomorphology, climatology, hazards, etc.—that also play extraordinarily crucial roles in shaping tourism destinations and activities. Furthermore, we cannot truly separate the human and physical divisions, as much of tourism involves interactions between people and the environments of the places they visit.

Rather than thinking of the geography of tourism as part of this hierarchy of topics, it may be more productive for our purposes to think of the geography of tourism in the same way geography as a whole is conceptualized. With the geography of tourism in the center of the schematic, we can recognize that there are both human and physical components at work in tourism, and each of the topical branches can help us understand a different part of the complex phenomenon that is tourism (figure 1.5).

For example, we can use the tools and concepts of climatology to help us understand tourism. Patterns of climate provide insight into things like tourism demand and supply and, by extension, tourist-generating and tourist-receiving regions. Winter

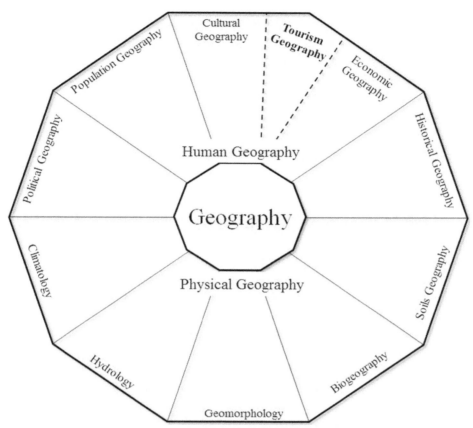

**Figure 1.4.** We can try to fit the topical branch of tourism geography into our graphic representation of the discipline. The argument is often made that tourism is a cultural and economic activity; thus, the geography of tourism has a place in between the major topical branches of cultural geography and economic geography. *Source:* Velvet Nelson

vacations are often popular among people who live in the higher latitudes because long, cold winters generate a demand for the experience of a warm, sunny place. As such, cold climates are significant source areas for tourists, while tropical climates have long been significant destinations. Likewise, we can use the framework of political geography to provide insights into patterns of tourism. On a routine basis, politics and international relations create barriers to tourism between two places through visa requirements, complicated permits, and so on. Conversely, the removal of these barriers can create new opportunities. While geopolitical events like terrorism and armed conflicts will obviously have a direct impact on tourism for that destination, they can also have ripple effects on tourism throughout the world. After the events of September 11, 2001, there was an immediate decline in tourism to New York City and Washington, DC, as well as a general decline in travel globally.

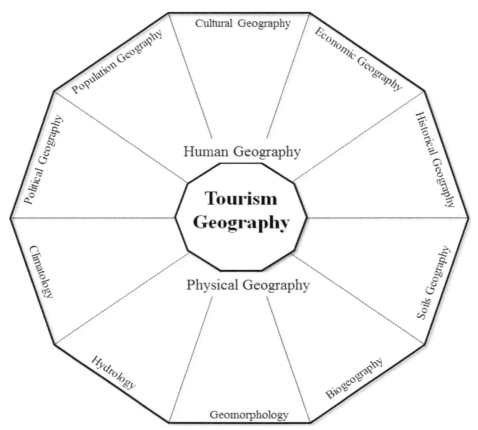

**Figure 1.5.** If we adapt the graphic representation of geography for the geography of tourism, we can begin to appreciate all the components of tourism. Likewise, we can see how the topical structure of geography will allow us to break down and investigate this complex phenomenon. *Source:* Velvet Nelson

# Tourism Geography

While the geography of tourism is not a new field, the incredible growth of tourism worldwide has generated increasing interest in this topic. Major academic geographic associations now have special groups or commissions devoted to the topic, including the Recreation, Tourism, and Sport specialty group of the American Association of Geographers (AAG), the Geography of Leisure and Tourism research group of the Royal Geographical Society (RGS), and the Commission on the Geography of Tourism, Leisure, and Global Change of the International Geographical Union (IGU). Research on topics in the field is published in journals across both geography and tourism studies, including the dedicated journal *Tourism Geographies*.

In a review of tourism geography publications, Dieter Müller identified seven interrelated clusters of research topics (see table 1.1). The largest cluster was "heritage,

---

## Box 1.3.  Terminology: Affect and Effect

*Affect. Effect.* The two words may sound the same when they are pronounced. There is a difference of only one letter in the spelling. It probably does not help that one is often used in the definition of the other. But that does not mean they can be used interchangeably. They do, in fact, have different meanings, and they have distinct implications for our purposes in the geography of tourism.

We will be using *affect* as a verb. To **affect** is to act on or produce a change in something. We can use the topical branches of geography—on both the human and physical sides—to understand the factors that affect the tourism industry. For example, our understanding of climatology or political geography can help us understand how climatic hazards (e.g., hurricanes and cyclones) or geopolitical events (e.g., war and terrorism) have the potential to affect the tourism industry—that is, to act on or produce a change in tourism. Any of these events have the potential to destroy the tourism infrastructure and prevent people from visiting a destination, at least for a while.

We will be using *effect* as a noun. An **effect** is something that is produced by an agency or cause: it is a result or a consequence. Again, we can use the topical branches of geography to understand what kinds of effects the tourism industry has. For example, our understanding of economic geography or environmental geography can help us understand the effects of tourism—that is, the results of tourism. The flow of income and investment into a place from the tourism industry may act as a catalyst for other types of development, or increased tourism development in fragile natural environments may cause environmental degradation.

*Discussion topic*: Pick a tourism destination and identify three factors that you think might *affect* tourism at that destination and three *effects* that you think tourism might have on that destination. What topical branches of geography would you use to examine each of these factors and effects?

---

image and identity." This cluster consisted of traditional tourism geography research topics on heritage and culture related to issues of image, identity, and authenticity. Newer foci in this area include tourist experiences and tourism representations with associated questions of power (e.g., What/who is remembered? How is it/are they remembered?) The second cluster was "impacts." This, too, is a long-standing theme with topics with strong current interest in climate change, vulnerability, risk, and adaptation. The third cluster was "protected areas and sustainability." This is attributed to human-environment interactions as a key geographic theme and includes the burgeoning interest in sustainable tourism. The fourth cluster was "primary industries

**Table 1.1.  Thematic Research Clusters in Tourism Geography**

| |
|---|
| Heritage, image, and identity |
| Impacts |
| Protected areas and sustainability |
| Primary industries and land use |
| Rural areas and accessibility |
| Industry and economic development |
| Israel |

and land use." Topics include agriculture, forests, and land use and change. In this case, tourism may not be the focus but a related or complementary activity. The fifth cluster was "rural areas and accessibility." In light of the ongoing trend toward urbanization, this represents an interesting trend in research. Much of the attention in this cluster is on the disadvantages of rural locations and rural development concerns, along with the trend toward second homes. The sixth cluster was "industry and economic development." This relates to tourism as a business, economic activity, and economic development strategy. The final cluster was "Israel" based on its unique circumstances.[14]

There are many key themes in geography present among these topics; however, Müller noted that basic geographic concepts such as space and place appear less frequently. Topics increasing in frequency are those in the second and third clusters: climate change, vulnerability, and sustainability. This may reflect the wider changes taking place in geography. Such fundamental concepts continue to shape geographic thinking and our understanding of tourism geography. Jarkko Saarinen succinctly reminds us: "Tourism changes places, and places have a different influence on tourism and its impacts on communities and environments."[15] The powerful geography approach seeks to apply this thinking to understand and work toward solutions for important issues, such as climate change and sustainability.

In addition, China has grown as a research topic in recent years. This focus is also important in understanding contemporary, and future, trends in tourism. In 2018, China was the fourth largest destination with 63 million international tourist arrivals. China was the world's largest spender, accounting for one-fifth of international tourism spending (US$277 billion). Perhaps more significantly, only about 10 percent of China's 1.4 billion inhabitants currently travel internationally. That proportion is projected to double by 2027.[16] Clearly this will have widespread implications for tourism and places around the world.

Tourism is changing rapidly, thus the field of tourism geography is also changing. This means that it is an exciting time but also a challenging one. We have a monumental task ahead of us, but geography is powerful. It provides us with powerful tools as we try to understand tourism in the world today and work toward a sustainable tourism future.

# Tourism Geographers

Tourism geographers are geographers. Geography provides us with the flexibility to study an incredible diversity of topics from a variety of perspectives. Geography provides the framework, or lens, through which we can view, explore, and understand various phenomena of the world in which we live. This framework encourages us to think holistically. The topical branches in geography do not stand alone.

For some geographers, tourism is the primary theme in their research (box 1.4). Yet, these researchers will draw on various perspectives from different topical branches. For example, a geographer studying issues associated with heritage tourism will likely have a foundation in cultural geography, or one studying the relationship between tourism and climate change will necessarily have an understanding of climatology.

In his 2008 progress report, Chris Gibson found that common tourism geography research themes overlapped with environmental geography, historical geography, and cultural geography.[17]

For others, tourism may not be the primary theme or object of their work, but it is a relevant issue nonetheless. This is the trend Müller identified in the "primary industries and land use" cluster. In today's world, tourism is a far-reaching phenomenon with implications on more places and more aspects of life than is generally recognized. Geographers studying these topics may never be called tourism geographers: however, their contributions to the geography of tourism should be considered important nonetheless. Gibson argued that geography is a discipline that allows researchers to work on particular aspects of tourism, as it is situated within wider issues such as sustainability, poverty, changing patterns of land use, the rights of indigenous peoples, and others.

Finally, Gibson's study explored where this research is coming from. He found that the United Kingdom and the United States dominated published geographic research, with Canada a distant third. In Müller's study ten years later, the same three countries appeared at the top of the list. However, countries such as South Africa, Sweden, China, Finland, Germany, and Spain have experienced the greatest increases

## Box 1.4.  Experience: The Life of a Tourism Geographer

*Dr. Dieter Müller is a tourism geographer and Deputy Vice-Chancellor of research and postgraduate education in the social sciences and humanities at Umeå University in Sweden. He is also a past chair of the Commission on the Geography of Tourism, Leisure, and Global Change of the International Geographical Union. He reflects on the changes in travel and tourism over the course of his life and the importance of tourism geography research.*

Growing up in Germany in the 1970s, my favorite book was an atlas. Together with some of my family's coffee table books and books from the public library, the atlas enabled me to travel the world in my thoughts. At that time, it did not seem realistic to think that one day I would actually be able to travel the world. There were high travel costs, language barriers, and practical hurdles to international travel such as visa requirements. Still, the world came to my hometown through television shows portraying foreign countries, books, and geography lectures in school that were mandatory from fifth grade onward. I was happy to enjoy a good geography education that taught me about foreign places, and I was eager to learn more and to see them for myself. I am also grateful to my dad, who never stopped taking me on excursions to experience places in both cities and the countryside.

At that time, long-distance traveling was not a part of the everyday life for an average family, nor were there many visitors from elsewhere. Life was rather local, and trips longer than 20 miles were the exception. For international travel, our family had their summer holidays in neighboring Austria, just some 200 miles away from home, that seemed exotic. I had heard that other kids in school had been to Italy, some 350 miles away, and some had even been to the US, where they had aunts, uncles, and cousins. This was because the small town where I grew up, with 20,000 citizens, had a US Army airport at the time. In its heyday, about 13,000 US soldiers and their families were stationed there, which eventually entailed marriages and emigration. Even in my high school class, one of my comrades married a US Army officer and moved to Colorado Springs.

During the course of my life, increasing wealth and declining travel costs have meant that traveling abroad has become an almost routine activity for many people in Central and Northern Europe. Initially, many households added winter skiing holidays in the Alps to their annual summer vacations at Mediterranean coasts. Later on, weekend trips and short breaks to events and shopping in urban destinations and getaways and nature activities in the countryside were also added. Borders increasingly played a minor role, particularly in Europe. While we were thoroughly checked when entering Austria in the 1970s, the European political integration implied that border controls now are obsolete, and traveling around Europe even without a passport is possible for almost everyone.

Contrary to my childhood expectations, globalization and my career as an academic have enabled me to travel the world, and today I have visited all continents except Antarctica. It is, however, important to remember that Europeans and North Americans are privileged in that they are allowed to travel almost everywhere without any major restrictions. At the same time, many travelers from elsewhere in the world are prevented from crossing borders, seen as potential intruders or risks. This becomes obvious at many border crossings where race and national profiling is employed in order to sort out the "unwanted" tourists. This makes me feel uneasy and reminds me of the uneven distribution of wealth and opportunities.

However, this also underlines the importance of tourism to different stakeholders. Indeed, it shows that tourism is a very desirable activity and for many households the annual holiday trip is the greatest expense during the year. Hence, people long for their vacations; they plan the trip and save money to pay for it. Today, social media enables them to share impressions and experiences with friends and relatives, which makes tourism an important form of symbolic consumption showing who you are or want to be.

To me this is an important reason to engage in tourism geographies; tourism matters to people who travel and to those who would like to travel. However, it also matters to hosts as well as communities and environments in various destinations. I find it fascinating that many regions put great efforts in attracting tourism to change the course of a place, and I am even more triggered by regions where people think they can ban or stop tourism and see it as evil. Hence, from having been a relatively marginal phenomenon tourism has increasingly turned into a power that influences the economic, political, and social development of cities and regions.

This became very obvious in 2020 when the COVID-19 pandemic entailed that states and regions enter lockdown mode in order to avoid diffusion of the lethal virus. Consequently, leisure and business tourism were paused more or less all over the world. Besides being irritating for those who wished to travel, this tragic situation uncovered how important tourism has become for communities and economies everywhere. It showed how labor markets are dependent on tourism consumption, and the decline of flight networks affected businesses as well. Moreover, families were kept apart, and people could not maintain physical contact, such as attending weddings, celebrations, or funerals of friends and relatives elsewhere.

Even though I am convinced that tourism will bounce back to a similar state as before the pandemic rather quickly, the true challenge is how tourism can be practiced and organized in the future considering major global threats such as climate change and uneven economic development. This is a major issue for tourism geographies research, and it certainly will require more practitioners in industry and public administration who are educated to address these topics and contribute to creative solutions.

Against this background, I am convinced that tourism geographies are a very important tool to understand and manage not only the tourism industry but also communities and society. Indeed, I find tourism geographies one of the most exciting, timely, and relevant branches of geography, and personally, I have never regretted that I entered and stayed within this dynamic field of research.

*—Dieter*

in research output. These are countries that have experienced considerable growth in tourism, like China, or significant problems resulting from tourism, like Spain.

## Conclusion

Geography has a long tradition based on the fundamental human desire to understand the world, and the modern discipline provides us with the tools and concepts to explain the patterns and phenomena that comprise the world. Although geography and tourism may not automatically be associated with one another, the relationship is undeniable. As such, geography is particularly well suited to provide the framework for exploring the massive worldwide phenomenon of tourism. In particular, we will use a topical approach in geography to break this complicated concept down into more manageable pieces.

This textbook is intended to be precisely what it says it is: an introduction. It is not, and cannot be, comprehensive. Any one of the topics discussed in the chapters of this text could very well merit an entire text of its own. In fact, there are many excellent examples available that discuss such specific topics in much greater depth than what has been done here. At the same time, there are many other topics that could have just as easily been included. The fact that they were not is more a function of a lack of space than a lack of importance. This text is but a beginning, a starting point.

This first chapter briefly discussed geography and tourism for the purpose of introducing this idea of a "geography of tourism." The remaining chapters in part I continue to develop a basis in tourism that will allow us to subsequently examine key issues through the framework of geography. Specifically, chapter 2 ("Basic Concepts in Tourism") introduces some of the terminology and ideas in tourism that will provide the foundation for discussions in the remaining chapters, while chapter 3 ("Overview of Tourism Products") provides a brief overview of the types of tourism experiences (i.e., the "products" of the tourism industry) that are offered by destinations around the world.

## Key Terms

- accessibility
- affect
- effect
- geotourism
- globalization
- human geography
- leisure time
- physical geography
- place
- region
- regional geography
- relative location

- scale
- sustainable tourism development
- topical geography
- tourism

- tourism demand
- tourism supply
- tourist-generating regions
- tourist-receiving regions

# Notes

1. Geoffrey J. Martin, *All Possible Worlds: A History of Geographical Ideas* (New York: Oxford University Press, 2005).

2. David A. Lanegran and Salvatore J. Natoli, *Guidelines for Geographic Education in the Elementary and Secondary Schools* (Washington, DC: Association of American Geographers, 1984).

3. Alaric Maude, "Applying the Concept of Powerful Knowledge to School Geography," in *The Power of Geographical Thinking*, eds. Clare Brooks, Graham Butt, and Mary Fargher (Chaim: Springer, 2017), 27–8.

4. Alaric Maude, "What Might Powerful Geographical Knowledge Look Like?" *Geography* 101, no. 2 (2016): 72–5.

5. Margaret Roberts, "Powerful Knowledge and Geographical Education," *The Curriculum Journal*, 25, no. 2 (2014): 192.

6. United Nations World Tourism Organization, "Glossary of Tourism Terms," accessed March 5, 2020, https://www.unwto.org/glossary-tourism-terms.

7. Alister Mathieson and Geoffrey Wall, *Tourism: Economic, Physical, and Social Impacts* (London: Longman, 1982), 1.

8. Stephen L. J. Smith, "Defining Tourism: A Supply Side View," *Annals of Tourism Research* 15, no. 2 (1988): 183.

9. United Nations World Tourism Organization, *Compendium of Tourism Statistics Dataset [Electronic]* (Madrid: UNWTO, 2020).

10. United Nations World Tourism Organization, *International Tourism Highlights 2019 Edition* (2019), 2, accessed March 5, 2020, https://www.e-unwto.org/doi/pdf/10.18111/9789284421152.

11. United Nations World Tourism Organization, "Sustainable Development," accessed April 3, 2020, https://www.unwto.org/sustainable-development.

12. United Nations World Tourism Organization, *International Tourism Highlights*, 6, 15.

13. Pacific Asia Travel Association, "About PATA," accessed March 6, 2020, https://www.pata.org/about-pata/.

14. Dieter K. Müller, "Tourism Geographies: A Bibliometric Review," in *A Research Agenda for Tourism Geographies*, ed. Dieter K. Müller (Cheltenham: Edward Elgar Publishing, 2019), 18–20.

15. Jarkko Saarinen, "Not a Serious Subject?! Academic Relevancy and Critical Tourism Geographies," in *A Research Agenda for Tourism Geographies*, ed. Dieter K. Müller (Cheltenham: Edward Elgar Publishing, 2019), 34.

16. United Nations World Tourism Organization, *International Tourism Highlights*, 9, 15.

17. Chris Gibson, "Locating Geographies of Tourism," *Progress in Human Geography* 32, no. 3 (2008): 409–13.

# CHAPTER 2

# Basic Concepts in Tourism

The concept of tourism means different things because we have different perspectives and experiences. People in significant tourist-generating regions may think of tourism as something they have done in the past and they would like to do again in the future. This is a demand-side perspective. In contrast, people in significant tourist-receiving regions may associate tourism with all of the tourists who come and go during the course of a season. This is a supply-side perspective. Both are fundamental in understanding tourism.

In this chapter, we will discuss some of the key terms (box 2.1) and concepts from the perspective of both the demand side of tourism and the supply side. In particular, we will consider what tourism means from the demand side, who tourists are, and what geographic factors motivate them and affect their demand for travel and tourism. We will also examine what types of tourism are provided on the supply side, what characteristics of places create tourism attractions, and what comprises the tourism system.

---

### Box 2.1. Terminology: Tourism

In chapter 1, we discussed the UNWTO definition of tourism. But because tourism can be approached from different perspectives, some additional terminology is useful. **Inbound tourism** comprises the activities of a nonresident visitor within the destination or country on a tourism trip. **Outbound tourism** comprises the activities of a resident visitor outside the destination or country on a tourism trip. Additionally, there is a distinction between **domestic tourism**, which comprises the activities of a resident visitor within their own country on a tourism trip, and **international tourism**, which comprises the activities of resident visitors outside their country on a tourism trip. Additional distinctions may be made between short-haul tourism and long-haul tourism. This is based on either distance or travel time by a particular mode, or type, of transport. For example, a short-haul flight is generally considered to be less than three hours, while a long-haul flight takes longer than six hours. However, there is no standardized measure for how these categories are actually defined. For additional terminology, see the UNWTO Glossary of Tourism Terms.[a]

*Discussion topic*: Plan an itinerary for a short-haul international trip and a long-haul domestic trip.

---

[a] United Nations World Tourism Organization, "Glossary of Tourism Terms," accessed March 5, 2020, https://www.unwto.org/glossary-tourism-terms.

# The Demand Side

One approach to tourism is from the demand side, with a focus on tourists. This is, of course, a fundamental component of tourism: tourism would not exist without tourists and the demand for tourism experiences. The demand side has important implications for our understanding of geographic patterns in tourism. The first half of this chapter introduces some of the theories and concepts that have been put forth to help us understand tourism from the demand side.

## TOURISM

When we think about our past and future experiences, we are thinking about the demand side of tourism. Therefore, one of the easiest ways for us to conceptualize tourism is as a process with a series of stages (figure 2.1). This process begins in the

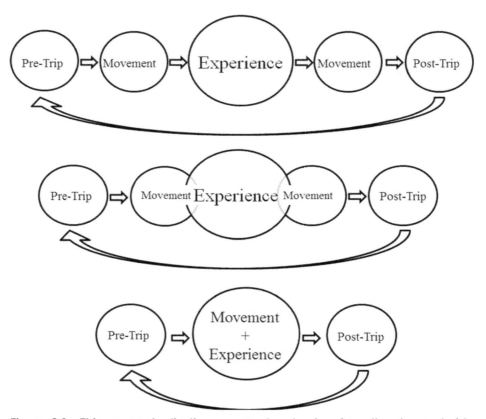

**Figure 2.1. This conceptualization approaches tourism from the demand side and takes into consideration the stages that contribute to the overall process of tourism. These stages do not necessarily occur in a linear fashion but may overlap and influence the others. *Source:* Velvet Nelson**

**pre-trip stage**, when we think about traveling and consider our options. We evaluate different destinations in terms of the resources and attractions of each place, the tourism products (i.e., the type of experiences), the level of infrastructure (e.g., types of accommodations or transport accessibility), and how these things match up with our interests and expectations. Most of us will also consider the overall cost of a trip to these places in relation to our budget. We have access to a tremendous amount of information to aid us in this evaluation and decision-making process. We draw from our experiences and those of family and friends, the images of places that come from popular media, and social media. As people around the world gained access to the Internet, they began to research and book their own travel. Yet, travel agents still have a role to play. Some tourists preferred to have a travel agent do most of the work in the pre-trip stage due to a lack of knowledge about trip planning or simply a lack of interest in the often time-consuming process. Recently, others have become disaffected with the information overload of online trip planning and are once again turning to an agent to save time and even money.[1]

The next three stages comprise the trip itself. For many trips, these stages will occur one after the other. In the **movement stage**, we use some form of transportation to travel to a destination. At the destination, the **experience stage** is the main component in the process, in which we participate in a variety of activities. Then we repeat the movement stage as we return home again. For example, the Midwestern family taking a trip to Disney World may fly from their nearest airport to Orlando, Florida (movement), spend a few days at a resort and/or theme parks (experience), and then fly home (movement). In this case, movement is simply a means to an end to get to the destination and the experience stage. However, these stages are not always distinct, and the act of traveling can be an integral part of the experience stage. For example, a Midwestern family on a road trip may take a scenic route and visit any number of tourist attractions over the course of their trip. In this case, the movement stage lasts the duration of the trip, from the time they leave home to the time they return. The experience stage takes place concurrently with the movement stage.

The final stage is the **post-trip stage**, which occurs after we return from our trip. We relive our trip through memories and conversations about the trip, as well as through tangible products of the trip, like pictures and souvenirs. These memories can be positive or negative, depending on what happened during the three principal stages of the trip. This stage is typically most intense in the period immediately following the trip, and although it diminishes over time, many things can trigger memories for a long time afterward. The tourism process then becomes circular, when we tap into these memories and past experiences to help us make decisions as we start planning our next trip (i.e., the pre-trip stage).

One of the principal advantages of this demand-side conceptualization of tourism is that it is readily understood and does not complicate something that should be relatively straightforward. In addition, it takes into consideration the role of pre-trip planning and the decision-making process, which are neglected in typical definitions of tourism that focus only on travel to a destination and activities undertaken there.

## TOURISTS

From the United Nations World Tourism Organization's (UNWTO) definition, "a visitor (domestic, inbound or outbound) is classified as a tourist (or overnight visitor), if his/her trip includes an overnight stay, or as a same-day visitor (or excursionist) otherwise."[2] Such definitions are used to identify tourists for the purpose of record keeping and statistics. However, it does little to help us conceptualize who tourists are, as it is broad enough to encompass anything from children on vacation with their parents to adults traveling for work, from week-long spring break partiers to students spending a semester studying abroad. Popular ideas and stereotypes have long been more influential in shaping our ideas about tourists.

The term *tourist* came into widespread use in the nineteenth century, and even then there were clear—and not always flattering—connotations. Up to this time, explorers were recognized to be individuals who traveled to places that had not previously been extensively visited or documented by others from their society. Likewise, travelers were considered to be those who traveled for a specific purpose, such as business enterprises or official government functions. The new category of "tourists" was different from either of these. Unlike travelers, tourists were regarded as individuals who did not travel for any purpose other than the experience of travel itself and the pleasure they derived from that experience.[3] Unlike explorers, tourists were often criticized for traveling to the same places and having the same experiences as all of the explorers, travelers, and even other tourists who came before them.[4]

From this time, highly satirized representations of tourists began to appear in various media, from newspapers to novels. The "ugly American tourist" is a long-standing stereotype in which visitors from the US are characterized as loud, ignorant, and obnoxiously dressed. Today, national tourist stereotypes are as diverse as the major tourist markets. Other stereotypes focus on types of behavior as opposed to nationality. For example, one travel writer identified seven tourist stereotypes: social media addict, guidebook hugger, disillusioned old hand, package tourist, backpacker, deluxe tourist, and tour group member. He asks readers to consider in which category they belong, although none is particularly flattering.[5]

These gross generalizations range from funny to offensive, and we know in reality there is tremendous variation in the billions of tourists in the world. To accommodate the differences that exist between tourists, scholars have proposed **tourist typologies** to identify categories (or types) of tourists. These typologies are based on different variables, such as motivations and behavior as well as demographic characteristics, lifestyle, personality, and more. This type of framework should be understood as a spectrum or continuum of tourists, across which several key categories are identified and defined. These categories merely identify some of the characteristics of tourists at certain points on the continuum. Not all tourists will be grouped into these defined categories but instead will fall at various points along the continuum between categories.

While many different typologies have been proposed over the years, Erik Cohen's framework has long been used as a summary of key categories. To some extent, this framework is similar to the earlier distinctions made between explorers, travelers, and tourists (although the different use of terms may be confusing). This typology divides tourists into four broad types based on factors such as the types of places and experience sought through travel.[6]

The **drifter** occupies one end of the spectrum. Drifters often do not consider themselves tourists (figure 2.2). Like explorers from an earlier era, this category of tourists likes to be seen as a pioneer who is the first to "discover" new destinations. Such places may have little in the way of a dedicated tourism infrastructure or tourism services. As a result, these tourists may stay in local guesthouses or private homes, use local transportation, shop at local markets, and eat at local restaurants and kitchens. Whether it is out of interest—or necessity, given the nature of these destinations— drifters immerse themselves in the local culture. For some, this is a process of education and self-exploration. For others, it is about doing something different, something not usually done.

The **explorer** bears resemblance to the earlier definition of a traveler. This category of tourists has motivations for travel other than simply diversion, whether education, religious enlightenment, mental or physical well-being, or other specific types of experiences at the destination. These tourists look for unusual types of experiences and greater contact with the local population than just interacting with the people who

**Figure 2.2.** In Erik Cohen's typology of tourists, "drifters" prefer to travel to "off-the-beaten-path" places with little tourism infrastructure and few tourists. *Source:* Velvet Nelson

hold service positions in the tourism industry, such as front desk clerks, restaurant serv-ers, or housekeeping and maintenance staff. Explorers typically make their own travel arrangements and rely on a combination of both the tourism infrastructure and the local infrastructure. For example, these tourists may arrive at the destination by the same means as other categories of tourists, but instead of taking a tour bus to explore the destination, they use the local transportation infrastructure.

In this typology, the traditional "tourist" category is divided into two different types. The next type along the continuum is the **individual mass tourist**. For these tourists, the primary motivation is typically some form of relaxation, recreation, or diversion, and they have some desire for things that are familiar and comfortable. They are generally dependent on the tourism infrastructure for getting to and staying at the destination, and they may use tourism industry services for at least part of their trip, such as taking a guided tour at the destination. However, these tourists are also interested in having experiences at the destination that would not be available to them in their home environment, and they will seek the opportunity to explore the destina-tion, albeit in a relatively safe manner.

Finally, the **organized mass tourist** occupies the position at the opposite end of the continuum. These tourists are primarily interested in diversion and escaping the boredom or repetition of daily life. They place a high emphasis on rest and relaxation and enjoying themselves with good food and/or entertainment. These tourists are less interested in unique experiences of place and are more likely to travel to destinations that are familiar or have characteristics that are familiar. Therefore, even if they travel to a foreign destination, they will stay in recognized brand name (i.e., multinational) resorts. These facilities are designed to provide the standard of accommodation, ser-vices, or types of food that such tourists are accustomed to at home. Organized mass tourists are highly dependent on the tourism infrastructure and services to structure their vacation. This may be a package that bundles services together at competitive prices, whether it is a comprehensive guided tour (with all transportation, accommo-dation, most meals, and tour services included) or a resort package (accommodation, some or all meals, and airport transfers included). As a result, little additional planning for the trip is necessary, there is little uncertainty about what will happen on the trip, and there may be little incentive to stray from the confines of the tour bus or resort complex. Thus, there is little to no interaction with the people or the place of the destination.

This kind of framework helps us to contextualize not just tourist demand but also supply in terms of the different levels of infrastructure and service provision. Yet, it is incredibly difficult to describe the vast and ever-changing global tourist market in a few simple categories. Tourism has undergone many changes in recent years that can make it harder to understand how modern patterns fit within this traditional model. For example, in the past a tourist staying in a private home would most likely be a drifter who wanted to have greater interaction with local people or because the chosen destination had little to no accommodation infrastructure. Today, we would not necessarily make those assumptions. More than 500 million people have stayed in private houses or apartments (or treehouses) through Airbnb in more than 100,000 cities around the world.[7] Certainly not all of these tourists would fall on the drifter end of the spectrum. In light of concerns about overtourism, cultural erosion, and/or environmental degradation, off-the-beaten-path destinations are putting restrictions on independent travel. Tourists interested in these places are typically drifters, but due to the restrictions, they may be forced to visit on the type of guided package tour that would normally be associated with organized mass tourists.

Typologies give us a place to start contextualizing tourism patterns in this introduction. However, throughout our discussion, we also need to consider how new trends are reshaping these patterns and possibly think about what a typology of tourists will look like in the future.

## TOURIST MOTIVATIONS

The above types of tourists have different motivations for and interests in tourism experiences. As geographers, we should be interested in what factors cause people to temporarily leave one place for another. If we understand these factors, we can begin to explain why certain places developed, or are currently developing, as significant tourist-generating regions and why others became, or are currently becoming, significant receiving regions. This has a practical significance; destinations need to be able to identify potential markets by understanding how demand matches up with their supply. However, motivations may be complicated, and often it is a combination of factors that cause people to seek tourism experiences.

The motivation that has long been most commonly associated with tourism is the pursuit of pleasure. However, implicit in this motivation is the real or perceived need for a temporary change of setting. This may be considered a geographic **push factor**, or something that impels people to temporarily leave their usual environment to travel somewhere else. This may be an escape from the routine of daily life with associated home and work issues, or boredom with familiar physical and social environments. Correspondingly, it is assumed that there is something that can be obtained at the destination that cannot be obtained at home. This may be considered a geographic **pull factor**, or something that attracts people to a particular destination. The pull may be something tangible that may be obtained at the destination, like being able to buy certain types of local products or eat authentic local cuisine. In most cases, however, it is an intangible, like having the opportunity to interact with new people, escaping a crowded city to enjoy rural landscapes and amenities (box 2.2), or gaining social capital from Instagramming a new place. For both the push and the pull, this "something" will be different for everyone.

Borrowing from one of geography's related disciplines, anthropology, we can see how these motivations have been laid out in Nelson Graburn's concept of **tourist inversions**.[8] In this theory, the experience we seek in our temporary escape is one of contrasts. Much of this involves a shift in attitudes or patterns of behavior away from the norm to a temporary opposite. A common example is the inversion from work and stress to peace and relaxation. For example, when we spend a long period of time working hard at school or at a job (or, in some cases, both simultaneously), tourism becomes our means of seeking the opposite: going on vacation for a period of rest and relaxation

# Box 2.2.  Case Study: A Rural Wine Trail for Urban Visitors

The definition of tourism allows for various motivations for visitors to take a trip outside of their usual environment. While motivations can be complex, geographic factors have the potential to offer some insight. We can consider geographic push and pull factors such as climate, landscape, or community type. For example, urban areas have widely varied attractions and have strong pull factors for many people, but they may also have push factors for residents. Rural areas can capitalize on this by providing corresponding pull factors.

The Houston-The Woodlands-Sugar Land metropolitan statistical area (MSA) spans nearly 10,000 square miles in southeast Texas, bordering the Gulf of Mexico. With a population of over 6.9 million in 2018, the MSA was the fifth largest in the United States. If the MSA were a state, it would have the fifteenth largest population. The median age was 34.4 years, and pretax per capita personal income was $52,765, which was 2.2 percent higher than the US average (2017).[a] Stakeholders across the MSA have worked to promote a vibrant culture with a wide range of urban amenities including visual and performing art venues, museums, award-winning restaurants, sporting events, convention centers, events, and more. Yet, Houston is not without its detractions. The MSA is often described as a sprawling urban jungle with issues such as traffic congestion and poor air quality.

Communities around MSAs interested in tourism as a rural development strategy try to highlight their resources to attract urban visitors for short trips (i.e., day or weekend trips). For example, local wineries offer attractive landscapes that can be visited year-round for vineyard tours as well as wine tastings and romantic weekend getaways at associated bed-and-breakfast facilities. Wineries also host scheduled events such as grape crushing, cooking classes, and wine dinners and accommodate special events such as weddings. While a winery may not exert a significant enough pull factor to motivate urban residents to make a trip, a wine trail might. Tourist trails raise the profile of destinations and attractions, allowing them to generate more interest than a single attraction. They can be appealing to visitors by providing a trip structure and giving them the opportunity to make the most of limited time by visiting multiple sites.[b]

Stakeholders established the Texas Bluebonnet Wine Trail in communities northwest of Houston (map 2.1) to target visitors from the MSA.[c] This trail includes eight local wineries that are all located within roughly an hour of the city. Grouped together, the trail encourages visitors to plan stops at multiple wineries during the course of their trip, with further recommendations for area restaurants or shopping. In addition, member wineries work together to produce seasonal wine trail events such as the fall wine and sausage trail. The Texas wine country may not exert the same national or international pull as renowned wine regions, such as California's Napa Valley, but it does provide Houston-area residents an opportunity to escape urban push factors, if only for a little while.

*Discussion topic:* What do you think are the most significant geographic push factors for tourism from major urban areas such as Houston? What do you think are the corresponding pull factors for rural tourism attractions such as the wineries located on the Texas Bluebonnet Wine Trail?

*Tourism online:* Texas Bluebonnet Wine Trail, "Welcome to the Texas Bluebonnet Wine Trail," at https://www.texasbluebonnetwinetrail.com

---

[a] Greater Houston Partnership, "Houston Facts 2019," accessed March 18, 2020, https://www.houston.org/sites/default/files/2019-08/Houston%20Facts%202019%20Final_3.pdf.
[b] David Ward-Perkins, Christina Beckmann, and Jackie Ellis, *Tourism Routes and Trails: Theory and Practice* (CABI: Oxfordshire, 2020).
[c] Texas Bluebonnet Wine Trail, "Welcome to the Texas Bluebonnet Wine Trail," accessed March 18, 2020, https://www.texasbluebonnetwinetrail.com.

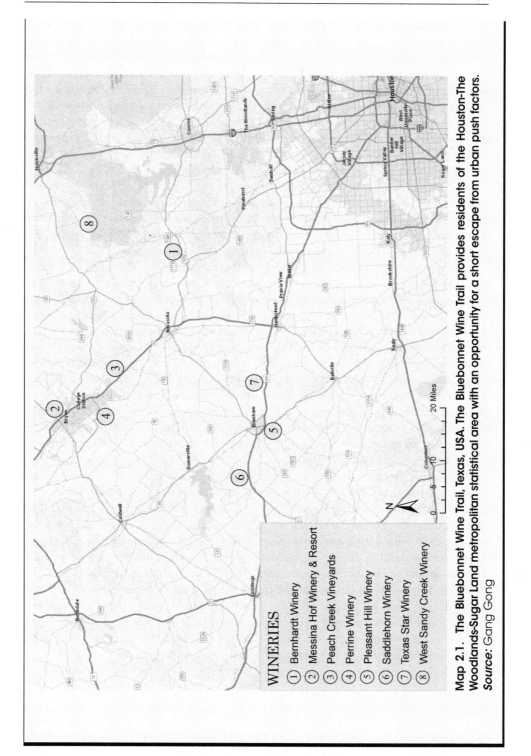

**Map 2.1. The Bluebonnet Wine Trail, Texas, USA. The Bluebonnet Wine Trail provides residents of the Houston-The Woodlands-Sugar Land metropolitan statistical area with an opportunity for a short escape from urban push factors.** *Source:* Gang Gong

WINERIES

1. Bernhardt Winery
2. Messina Hof Winery & Resort
3. Peach Creek Vineyards
4. Perrine Winery
5. Pleasant Hill Winery
6. Saddlehorn Winery
7. Texas Star Winery
8. West Sandy Creek Winery

away from the stresses in our daily lives. Likewise, we might feel that our daily lives have become routine and mundane. Tourism gives us the opportunity to do something exciting for a change, have an adventure. Another common inversion is the shift from economy to extravagance. We may have to budget our money in the course of our daily lives, but we will save up to splurge on a vacation. During these few days, we may spend more on food, drinks, entertainment, and other activities than we normally would.

In some cases, these inversions in behavior contribute to the generally poor reputation of tourists in many parts of the world. In particular, many inversions go from moderation to excess. Graburn suggests that overindulgence in food is the product of one tourist inversion. The same idea applies to overindulgence in alcohol and drugs. This inversion, as highlighted by popular media, is the one that gives spring break tourists—and, by extension, spring break destinations—a bad name. In the case of this inversion, students who usually go to class, study, work, party occasionally, and generally live within the norms of society travel to a spring break hotspot during the designated semester break and party to excess, with all that it entails.

There is also a geographic dimension to tourist inversions, in terms of a shift away from the tourist's home and community toward a temporary opposite. This shift is much more locally contingent, and the inversions may work both ways. One of the most common inversions of this type involves the movement from cold climates to warm ones. People in middle and upper latitudes who experience long, cold winters may seek to escape that weather and the associated symptoms of seasonal affective disorder for a short time by traveling to a warm, sunny place in the lower latitudes. At the same time, people in warm climates may travel to colder ones to be able to participate in winter sports, such as skiing. People in densely populated urban areas may seek to escape the congestion, noise, and pollution of the city for expansive natural areas such as the national parks, although people living in rural areas or small towns may look to big cities for the wide array of shopping, dining, and entertainment options that they do not have at home (figure 2.3).

These inversions continue to provide a significant motivation for travel. However, scholars suggest that, in the modern era, tourism is increasingly becoming a part of a lifestyle rather than a contrast to daily life.[9] For example, Richard Florida describes the "creative class" as a new social class of workers in science, technology, and the arts who seek out cities with a high quality of place. This includes distinctive urban amenities, diverse peoples, and a vibrant atmosphere—in essence, the same characteristics that make an attractive destination for tourism. For this creative class, there may be little difference between expectations for the places they live and the places they visit.[10] In addition, a segment of tourists prioritize travel as a part of their lives. They look for the next opportunity, wherever that may be, as opposed to seeking out specific types of places or experiences. One study found that 83 percent of Millennials prefer to take more short breaks throughout the year as opposed to one longer trip.[11]

## TYPES OF DEMAND

In the previous chapter, our definition of demand included those who travel and those who wish to travel. Consequently, we need to distinguish between different types of

Figure 2.3. Times Square in New York City is known for its bright lights and crowded streets. While this type of experience may not appeal to everyone, it may exert a strong pull force on someone from a rural or small-town area looking to "get lost" in the big city. *Source:* Scott Jeffcote

demand, including effective demand, suppressed demand, or no demand. **Effective demand** is the type of demand we typically think of, as it refers to those people who wish to and have the opportunity to travel. We can measure effective demand relatively easily with tourism statistics like visitation rates and participation in certain tourism activities.

However, this does not give us a complete picture, as participation is not always reflective of desire. **Suppressed demand** refers to the people who wish to travel but do not. It is much more difficult to measure the number of people who simply *want* to travel. Moreover, there are many reasons why people who wish to travel do not, so we can break this category down even further. **Potential demand** is a type of suppressed demand that refers to those people who want to travel and will do so when their circumstances change. For example, students often have a potential demand for tourism. This means that they may have an interest in (or a perceived *need* for!) tourism experiences, but they may not have the **discretionary income** (i.e., the money that is left over after taxes and all other necessary expenses of life like rent, food, transportation, clothing, tuition, and books have been taken care of) to travel. While we would like to think that we will be able to convert that potential demand to effective demand after getting a job, that does not always happen. Twenty-three percent of Americans have no paid vacation days, and 55 percent of Americans with paid vacation days do not use all of them. For some, budget issues continue to be a significant constraint, but it may also be part of our culture. One survey found that 54 percent of US workers felt guilty about taking vacation time.[12]

**Deferred demand** is a type of suppressed demand that refers to those people who want to travel but have to put off their trip, not because of their own circumstances but because of some problem or barrier in the supply environment. This could be a problem—or even a perceived problem—at the desired destination. For example, in 2017 major hurricanes Irma and Maria caused extensive damage in the Caribbean and caused thousands of deaths. Places such as Barbuda, Dominica, and Puerto Rico (among others) were devastated. Due to widespread media images of the damage, tourists canceled or postponed trips to destinations throughout the region—not just those that were seriously affected. As a whole, the Caribbean lost more than US$1 billion in tourism revenues.[13] Deferred demand could also be attributed to a problem in the tourism infrastructure that would prevent tourists from reaching or being able to stay at their intended destination. In April 2010, the eruption of Iceland's Eyjafjallajökull volcano and the subsequent ash cloud shut down airports across Europe and created a massive backlog of travelers. Many people who had plans to travel to a number of different destinations during this time were forced to cancel their trips. Finally, while disease outbreaks can cause deferred demand for specific destinations, we have now seen how it can defer global demand for travel. At the time of writing (March 2020), we are under a US Department of State Global Level 4 Health Advisory: Do Not Travel (the highest level) due to the COVID-19 pandemic.[14]

It is important to understand what factors are going to allow demand to be fulfilled as well as what factors will prevent it. If tourism stakeholders understand those factors, then they can begin to see what strategies might help people with suppressed demand get past any barriers and have the experiences they are looking for. At least theoretically, suppressed demand can be converted into effective demand if the right opportunities are presented.[15] This might involve offering discounts to students with limited discretionary income, such as Eurail discounted Youth Passes for people aged sixteen to twenty-four. Or it might involve targeted promotional campaigns. In early 2018, the Puerto Rico Tourism Company knew they had to overcome months of media images of devastation to encourage spring bookings. They worked with media groups to use advanced strategies to target potential tourists visiting travel websites, searching for Caribbean vacations, social media posts, and so on, and to communicate the message that the island was ready for visitors.[16]

It may seem like it should be easy to assess demand because we often assume that if people are not already traveling, they probably want to. However, there is one additional category of demand: **no demand**. This refers to people who for various reasons really do not want to travel.

## FACTORS IN DEMAND

A person's demand for tourism may be shaped by the nature of the society in which he or she lives. For example, a country's government can help generate effective demand by creating opportunities for people to travel. The lack of mandated paid vacation or holidays in the US contributes to suppressed demand. In contrast, Austria creates opportunities for effective demand by mandating 25 paid workdays off in addition to 13 paid holidays.[17]

The level of development in a society also shapes demand. Higher levels of development will lay the foundation for more people in a society to translate their desire for travel and tourism experiences into effective demand. Higher levels of economic development bring an increase in both discretionary income and leisure time. Higher levels of social development bring improvements in the health, well-being, and education of the population. These things give more people within that society greater means, interest, and opportunity to travel. While the countries of Europe continue to account for the largest proportion of international tourists, Asian countries have been experiencing conditions that allow more people to travel. Asia and the Pacific is the world's second largest tourist-generating region, and countries like China and India are quickly becoming major markets.

At the same time, individual factors—such as a person's view of the world and his or her childhood influences and experiences—as well as personality type play a distinct role in determining whether he or she has a strong desire to travel or prefers to spend his or her leisure time at home. Personal biases and even phobias, such as a fear of flying, will also shape an individual's demand.

A person's stage in the life cycle affects demand. In the youth stage (i.e., children who have not yet reached the age of legal adulthood), interest in travel and tourism experiences varies. Younger children are most likely to have a demand for experiences that are specifically promoted to this demographic, like a Disney experience. Beyond this, demand is shaped by the travel patterns of their family. If parents make travel a priority, children will grow up with, and come to expect, these experiences. However, many children have no demand for travel because they lack opportunity; such experiences may not even be a part of their consciousness. Demand for travel may increase during the teenage years with greater awareness, but whether demand is effective or potential is still determined by parents/guardians.

In the young adult stage (i.e., individuals who are legally of age but do not yet have the responsibilities associated with adulthood), there is typically a higher demand for travel because of the pent-up desire for freedom and independence from the youth stage. Students, in particular, have long designated holidays between terms that provide the opportunity for travel. However, a significant barrier to travel during this stage is financial. This may result in potential demand, where they will travel in the future if/when their circumstances change, but many may still be able to translate their desire into effective demand by using their limited discretionary income to take short trips and travel cheaply by using public transportation and staying in hostels.

The adult stage (i.e., individuals with responsibilities but not children) can be associated with a complex set of variables that may contribute either effective or potential demand. Working individuals with an income, or a combined income for partners/spouses, and accumulated vacation time have both the time and money to travel. However, as they develop careers and set down roots in their home environment (buy a house, acquire pets, get involved in community activities, etc.), they may find it increasingly difficult to get away for extended periods of time.

The family stage (i.e., couples or single parents with dependent children) presents many barriers to effective demand. Families have household, childcare, educational, and other expenses and therefore less discretionary income for travel. At the same time, the cost of travel increases with more transport tickets, larger hotel rooms, more activities, and so on. Between parents' work schedules and the children's school/activity schedules, it may be difficult to find a time when everyone is free to travel. Family trips often require more coordination and preparation (packing drinks and snacks, entertainment, favorite toys or blankets, various first aid supplies in case of illness or accidents, etc.). Thus, to make demand effective, families may choose destinations closer to home, trips of shorter durations, or trips to visit family, such as grandparents.

Initially, effective demand can increase in the empty nest stage. Once children no longer require financial support, individuals may experience an increase in discretionary income. Leisure time continues to increase with retirement. Thus, empty nesters may translate any potential demand into effective demand. As this stage transitions into the elderly stage over time, effective demand decreases again. Retirees on a fixed income may have to make choices about the experiences they can afford. Travel may become physically more difficult (e.g., getting tired more easily), and health concerns can present a distinct challenge. Ultimately, suppressed demand transitions into no demand as the individual feels that the experience of tourism is no longer worth the effort of traveling.

While there are, of course, always exceptions to these general patterns, the life cycle variable provides some insight into why demand might be effective for some people within a society and potential for others. This helps **tourism stakeholders**, the various individuals or organizations that have an interest (or stake) in tourism, to develop strategies to translate potential demand into effective demand. For example, destinations have recognized that families are a significant potential market with a demand for travel, if the right opportunities are presented. As a result, stakeholders encourage family travel with family-friendly resorts that offer activities for children and/or babysitting services to allow parents some quiet time as well as specially priced family packages to make a vacation more affordable.

There are clearly connections between lifecycle factors and generational ones. Baby Boomers are in the empty nest stage (and beyond) and are not as dependent on budget. Much of the Generation X cohort is in the family stage and travel is generally family-centered. They are established in the workforce often with strong earning potential, but time presents the most common constraint. While debt can be a constraint for Millennials, this generation prioritizes travel. They are more likely to save for trips and to take more trips than the other generations, although they are typically shorter in duration. Some of this cohort are entering the family stage, but many continue to travel with their young children to a range of destinations, including those not previously associated with family travel.[18] Stakeholders need to understand these patterns to attract or accommodate new markets.

Considerable attention is currently being given to Generation Z. As this generation moves from the youth stage to the young adult stage, they are the newest entrants to the market (box 2.3). Many have grown up with travel as a part of their lives. Those starting to travel independently of their families are budget-conscious, but many tourism businesses are looking to earn the loyalty of this increasingly powerful consumer group now. These digital natives have global lives and prioritize new experiences while traveling. Studies suggest they are environmentally conscious.[19] They are likely to consider sustainability in their travel choices, and for some, efforts to reduce emissions will affect decisions about how to travel and how frequently.[20]

# Box 2.3.   Experience: A Generation Z Perspective on Travel and Tourism

*Generation Z is the newest generation of tourists. Tourism stakeholders are looking for ways to connect with this increasingly powerful consumer group. Certain factors play a shaping role in each generational group. In the case of Gen Z, these factors include the pervasiveness of technology and the looming threat of climate change. Yet, members of a generational group are still individuals with their own perspectives. In the following, Prezley, a Gen Zer at the start of his college career, shares his perspective.*

I was born in New Hampshire but have lived most of my life in Texas. I have family scattered across the country, and many of my earliest memories come from the experiences of traveling to visit relatives in places like Hawaii, Maryland, Virginia, and Ohio. The climate and geography of these places was so different from Texas. Traveling up north to much colder weather and snow was always an exciting experience, but my favorite place to visit has always been Hawaii. The islands are extremely unique places, home to ten different climate zones and an extraordinary culture that always seemed magical to me. I love enjoying local food and adventuring around the islands, creating everlasting memories with my family.

I am also fortunate that my parents are professors, and I have been able to tag along on their field courses to places like Spain, Italy, and Morocco. International travel has been much different than traveling within the US and has significantly broadened my horizons and experiences. I have enjoyed trying new foods, visiting cultural and historical sites, and interacting with local people. Although I may be unable to speak their language, there is much more to be taken away from interactions with individuals that reveals a great deal about their culture.

Morocco made a big impression on me. The art and architecture of Moroccan cities was amazing. Every single mosque, and many buildings, shared very intricate details with geometric designs, reflecting Islamic culture. The layout of the cities was also fascinating. Many had a "medina" containing narrow streets reminiscent of a labyrinth. This was typically the oldest and most historic section of the city. It was lots of fun exploring the cities and observing how local people go about their daily lives. In many areas, restrooms had holes in the ground instead of toilets. This didn't bother me, but it did make me appreciate the things I have access to in America that many people around the world do not. Being able to learn about people and their cultures while learning more about myself has been the greatest reward of my traveling experiences thus far.

I definitely have a desire to travel more in the future, and social media plays a big role in this. I follow Instagram travel accounts that post pictures and videos of countries from all over the world. This often sparks my interest in specific destinations. I think the aesthetic of the travel photography that appears on social media easily attracts people and encourages travel. My mom and I will see photographs people take while on hikes in Hawaii on top of mountains and ridges that overlook the island, and we become inspired to do the hike ourselves and recreate the same photo. However, social media does have the potential to foster unrealistic expectations of travel destinations, which can cause people to travel to places without proper knowledge or preparations. People see videos of others cliff jumping in Hawaii, swimming at a beautiful green sand beach, or hiking to lava flows and think they should do it as well. When people undertake these activities blindly, with no attention to safety, they could injure themselves, others, or the land. I have seen people recklessly swim far out in dangerous currents, walk on coral reefs, get up close to a lava flow for a picture, or trespass on sacred lands. This is why it's important for travelers to have a better understanding of the places where they travel and to be mindful of their actions.

I think I will take advantage of travel experiences whenever possible, although at this time, money is going to be a big constraint. If I do travel in the near future, it would have to be some place cheap, or I would have to plan a trip with a tight budget. If money wasn't an issue, I would probably base my decision on the geography of places. I enjoy more natural environments, especially tropical and coastal places, and some places that I'd like to visit include Greece, Fiji, and New Zealand. I'm also interested in large cities like New York, Paris, and Tokyo. On the contrary, I am not interested in places with an abundance of resorts that seem artificial, like Disney. Places like this are often extremely wasteful and awful for the environment.

I try to be conscious of my own environmental footprint while traveling. Some things I can do include picking up trash and recycling, avoiding bottled water, and using as many eco-friendly products as possible, such as reef-friendly sunscreen. Additionally, as a traveler, I know I am a consumer, so I feel that it is important to give back to the places I visit through volunteering. Volunteering can be extremely helpful to communities and nonprofit social and environmental organizations that require physical labor. In the past, I have volunteered for Pōhāhā I Ka Lani, a nonprofit environmental and cultural organization that operates out of Waipiʻo Valley in Hawaii. They work to restore ancient taro fields, sacred to native Hawaiians. The volunteer work usually consists of removing invasive species, clearing trees, planting and harvesting taro plants, or rebuilding the stone structure of the taro fields. Giving back is extremely rewarding and is often one of my favorite and most memorable parts of the trip. As the saying goes, "For it is in giving that we receive."

—*Prezley*

# The Supply Side

Tourism may also be approached from the supply side with a focus on the mechanisms that support tourism. This, too, is a fundamental component of tourism: tourism necessarily involves the provision of services and experiences. Geography has generally had more to contribute to this side of tourism because of the discipline's focus on the places and place-based resources that play an important role in the supply of tourism. While issues of tourism resources will be the focus of chapters in part II, the remainder of this chapter introduces some of the theories and concepts that have been put forth to help us understand tourism from the supply side.

## TOURISM

From the supply-side perspective, a distinction we can make to help us understand patterns in tourism is that of mass tourism and niche tourism. The concept of mass tourism is explained through Fordism, or the system of mass production and consumption, typically linked back to Henry Ford and the changes made in automobile manufacturing. Fordism refers to the manufacture of standardized goods in large volumes at a low cost. Thus, **mass tourism** is the production of standardized experiences made available to large numbers of tourists at a low cost.

At mass tourism destinations, the infrastructure is well developed to handle large quantities of tourists. There are typically good transportation links that allow people to easily reach the destination, whether it is interstate highway access, a major international airport, or a cruise terminal. There may be a spatial concentration of hotels and resorts to accommodate these tourists, as well as restaurants and entertainment facilities to meet their needs. Large multinational corporations often dominate these service providers. Whether tourists visit Jamaica or Singapore, they can stay at a Hilton. When they are in Liechtenstein or China, they can get a coffee at Starbucks. To some extent, tourists can expect similar experiences at these places regardless of where they are actually located. Because the emphasis of mass tourism is on quantity, low-cost packages may be offered to make these destinations accessible to medium- and lower-income groups. In addition, the standardization of experiences means that destinations may be considered interchangeable. This leads to competition between destinations, which contributes to a further reduction in prices.

The most prominent mass tourism destinations have traditionally been in warm climates and coastal areas. The idea of mass tourism is also associated with key inversions discussed above, like relaxation and partying. As a result, mass tourism is often seen as the worst of tourism, characterized by stereotyped tourists. Yet, mass tourism has existed since the early eras of tourism and will continue to exist because it meets certain needs. The well-developed infrastructure facilitates tourism for large numbers of people, while the competition and economies of scale allow more people to participate in tourism than would otherwise be possible. Moreover, it provides the type of experiences that many tourists continue to demand. However, with the increase in global travel, more destinations are receiving high quantities of tourists, some of which were not developed to handle such numbers. This has led to concerns about overtourism (see box 2.4).

Mass tourism is contrasted with **niche tourism** (also called "alternative" or "special interest" tourism), which is based on the concept of post-Fordism. This concept reflects changes in the ways in which production and consumption are understood. Post-Fordism recognizes that there is not always a single mass market in which all demands may be met through mass production. As a result, there is a need for differentiated or specialized products targeted at specific markets. Particularly as the tourism industry has developed and more people have had the opportunity to travel to different places, there has been a growing demand for new types of experiences outside the mainstream. Niche tourism allows destinations to exploit a particular resource that they possess and create a sense of distinction so that tourists feel they must visit that destination to have that experience. It also allows tourists to choose a vacation experience that is more tailored to their specific interests rather than a one-size-fits-all package.

Many destinations become characterized by either mass tourism or niche tourism, although a destination has the potential to tailor its offerings to meet the demands of different types of tourists. Some tourism products that will be discussed in the next chapter lend themselves more toward one type of tourism over the other, and each type will affect tourists and tourism destinations in different ways.

# Box 2.4.   In-Depth: Overtourism

Literary scholar James Butler noted that, at the end of the eighteenth century, English poet William Wordsworth demonstrated very modern attitudes toward tourists in his writings. War on the continent had brought a significant increase in tourism to the Lake District in the 1790s. Wordsworth lamented the effects of tourism that he felt had changed the people and places he remembered from his childhood, even as he himself toured the district in 1799.[a] Although the term "overtourism" would not emerge for another two centuries, Wordsworth—among others in various times and places—would probably find the concerns expressed through this idea familiar: too many tourists, poorly behaved tourists, conflicts between tourists and residents, deterioration of both tourists' experiences and residents' quality of life, and more[b] (figure 2.4).

Overtourism dominated conversations about tourism in the late 2010s, but we are reminded, "Like a volcano, overtourism has been threatening to erupt for a very long time."[c] In the past few years, scholars have proposed various definitions for **overtourism**. A UNWTO report defined it as "the impact of tourism on a destination, or parts thereof, that excessively influences perceived quality of life of citizens and/or quality of visitors' experiences in a negative way."[d] While it may be tempting to equate overtourism with mass tourism, mass tourism does not necessarily result in the problems associated with overtourism. Instead, these problems are primarily attributed to poor planning and management. Thus, a mass tourism destination that is well planned and managed may have fewer negative economic, social, and environmental

**Figure 2.4.   While the term "overtourism" is new, tourism destinations have long experienced issues with overcrowding. This photograph, dated in the 1930s, shows the crowds at Jones Beach State Park in New York.** *Source:* New York State Archives. Jones Beach photographs, ca. 1937. Series B1836-04, Box 1.

effects per capita than a niche tourism destination that is ill equipped to handle even relatively small numbers of visitors.[e] Overtourism can therefore occur in destinations from major urban areas to rural heritage sites, from coastal resort areas to mountain peaks.

Although the circumstances of overtourism are place specific, there are certain factors that generally contribute to the phenomenon. On the demand side, more people are enabled to travel due to improving socioeconomic conditions and declining relative cost of travel with low-cost air carriers, cruise packages, and accommodation rentals. In particular, more people are traveling from large countries like China and India. On the supply side, destinations have been unable or unwilling to control tourist numbers. Stakeholders from governments to transport operators (e.g., airlines and cruises) have prioritized tourism growth with a short-term focus on economic gain while neglecting social and/or environmental considerations. Other voices, such as those of residents and communities, often go unheard until the situation has deteriorated.[f]

In the foreword of a 2019 volume on overtourism, Tony Wheeler (co-founder of Lonely Planet) concluded, "Finally, remember that time-worn truism that what goes up can equally easily come down."[g] Certainly no one could have anticipated that just a year later tourism would come to an unprecedented halt due to the COVID-19 pandemic and, in the midst of the economic devastation of the industry, it would seem almost strange to talk about the problems of overtourism. Yet, tourism will return. It may take time, but it will return. As we move forward, it is important that we learn from the past. We will continue to take a closer look at both the causes and effects of overtourism in the following chapters.

*Discussion topic:* Do you think "overtourism" is a new phenomenon or simply a new word to describe long-standing issues? Explain.

---

[a] James A. Butler, "Tourist or Native Son: Wordsworth's Homecomings of 1799–1800," *Nineteenth-Century Literature* 51, no. 1 (1996), 1, 5.

[b] Rachel Dodds and Richard W. Butler, "Introduction," in *Overtourism: Issues, Realities and Solutions*, eds. Rachel Dodds and Richard W. Butler (Berlin: De Gruyter, 2019), 1.

[c] Justin Francis, "Overtourism: It's Time for Some Answers," in *Overtourism: Issues, Realities and Solutions*, eds. Rachel Dodds and Richard W. Butler (Berlin: De Gruyter, 2019), v.

[d] UNWTO, "'Overtourism'? Understanding and Managing Urban Tourism Growth Beyond Perceptions," accessed April 8, 2020, https://www.e-unwto.org/doi/pdf/10.18111/9789284420070.

[e] Rachel Dodds and Richard W. Butler, "Conclusion," in *Overtourism: Issues, Realities and Solutions*, eds. Rachel Dodds and Richard W. Butler (Berlin: De Gruyter, 2019), 262.

[f] Rachel Dodds and Richard W. Butler, "Enablers of Overtourism," in *Overtourism: Issues, Realities and Solutions*, eds. Rachel Dodds and Richard W. Butler (Berlin: De Gruyter, 2019), 6.

[g] Tony Wheeler, "Foreword," in *Overtourism: Excesses, Discontents and Measures in Travel and Tourism*, eds. Claudio Milano, Joseph M. Cheer, and Marina Novelli (Oxfordshire: CABI, 2019), xvii.

## TOURISM ATTRACTIONS

**Tourism attractions** are aspects of places that are of interest to tourists and provide a pull factor for the destination. Attractions can include things to be seen, activities to be done, or experiences to be had. Some tourism attractions seem "given." For example, the most spectacular scenes of natural beauty, impressive architectural constructions, and places where significant historic events occurred are those that are natural for people to want to experience. However, these sites are attractions because they have been given meaning. This meaning may be given by the tourists themselves and the types of things they demand, but it may also be given by the tourism industry. Each potential destination has to find the attraction (or attractions) that makes it unique and will cause people to want to visit that place instead of another.

There are four broad categories of tourism attractions: natural, human (not originally intended for tourism), human (intended for tourism), and special events.[21] Natural attractions are obviously based on the physical geography of a place, such as the coast, mountains, forests, caves, inland water sources, flora, fauna, and so on. The first category of human attractions includes those places or characteristics of places that had some other purpose or function but have since become an attraction for tourism, such as historic structures, religious institutions, and aspects of local culture. The second category of human attractions includes those places or aspects of places that were specifically designed to attract visitors, such as amusement parks, casinos, shopping centers, resorts, and museums. Finally, special events is a diverse category that can include religious and secular festivals, sporting events, conferences and conventions, and even social events such as weddings and reunions.

Almost anything can be made into a tourist attraction, including a whole array of oddities and curiosities (figure 2.5). Even objects of dubious origins can be turned into an attraction. The Blarney Stone of Blarney Castle in Ireland is a well-known tourism attraction visited by an estimated 400,000 people annually. Legend has it that those who kiss the Blarney Stone will gain the gift of eloquence, and visitors have reportedly gone through this ritual for more than two hundred years. Early visitors were held by their ankles and lowered head first over the battlements to perform this act, but safety

**Figure 2.5.** *Shuttlecocks* **is an outdoor art installation by Claes Oldenburg and Coosje van Bruggen at the Nelson-Atkins Museum of Art in Kansas City, Missouri, and identified as one of America's unusual attractions.** *Source:* Scott Jeffcote

measures have since been put into place so that visitors only have to lean backwards while holding onto an iron railing with the help of a guide. The origins of the stone—and this ritual—are much debated, and some reports suggest that the stone was, in fact, once part of the castle's latrine system. Regardless of its original purpose, the Blarney Stone has been called the most unhygienic tourism attraction in the world.[22]

Not all attractions are created equal; some have greater pull forces than others. There are a few prominent international sites that people all over the world would like to have the opportunity to see or experience at least once in their lifetime, whether it is the Eiffel Tower or the Great Wall of China. These attractions have the greatest pull force. Essentially, they are one of the most important reasons people choose to visit that destination. These sites are often featured on lists like the "new wonders of the world," compiled in 2007. This type of designation only increases the desirability of such sites as tourism attractions.

A secondary tier of tourism attractions also exerts some pull. These attractions may factor into tourists' decisions to visit a particular destination and will certainly be experienced when tourists visit that place, but they are not the primary reason. In the example given above, few people are likely to visit Ireland solely because of Blarney Castle, but clearly many tourists make a point to have this experience when they are there.

There are also other attractions that may exert little pull or have little influence on tourists' decision to visit that destination. These may be attractions that people only learn about once they arrive at the destination and may be experienced only by tourists who spend more time at the destination. These tourists have the opportunity to explore the destination in greater depth and visit sites beyond those that are well known. Mount Rushmore is a high-profile stop on road trips, but visitors who stay in the area for a longer period of time will explore other scenic and historic places in the Black Hills National Forest and Wind Cave National Park.

## THE TOURISM SYSTEM

Attractions play an important role in creating the demand for travel, but they cannot exist alone. The services provided by the tourism industry facilitate travel to and experience of these attractions. For example, Stonehenge is a well-known United Nations Educational, Scientific, and Cultural Organization (UNESCO) World Heritage Site attraction that draws tourists from all over the world to the English county of Wiltshire. Yet, English Heritage, the organization that owns and manages the site, is not in the business of organizing trips to Stonehenge. The site itself offers only minimal options for food and drink and does not offer visitors a place to stay. Thus, other service providers in the surrounding area must meet the needs of tourists visiting Stonehenge.

Correspondingly, attractions may account for only a small proportion of income at a destination. Some attractions operate on a pay-for-participation basis, but there are just as many attractions that are free or have only a minimal admission fee. As such, it is various tourism industry service providers that generate revenues. This can be so significant that travel and tourism is one of the world's largest economic sectors, accounting for one in ten jobs and approximately 10 percent of global GDP.[23] However, there is not always hard data regarding all aspects of the various travel, tourism, and hospitality-related economic activities ranging from transportation to accommodation, food and beverage, tours, entertainment, retail, and more. In addition, there is overlap between the services provided to tourists and those provided to nontourists, and only part of tourism services takes place in the formal sector of the economy. The remainder is provided in the unregulated informal sector of the economy (e.g., tourists purchasing goods from vendors they encounter on the street or at the beach) that may not be accounted for in official statistics. The collaborative or sharing economy, in which people use their own resources (e.g., cars or apartments) to provide services for tourists, further complicates matters.

To help us appreciate the complexity of tourism, scholars suggest conceptualizing tourism as a multifaceted and dynamic system. This recognizes that there are many interrelated elements in tourism, from tourists to places, from public sector organizations to nongovernmental organizations, and from private businesses to members of the community. Because of the interrelationships between all of these, changes in one part of the system will have implications for others—and tourism is always changing. Thus, we need a holistic view of the system to understand what is involved in tourism and how new destinations and products, technological innovations, and changing consumer preferences are continuously reshaping tourism.

Peer-to-peer exchanges (P2P) are one example of a change that has generated many other changes throughout the tourism system. Airbnb and other P2P accommodation platforms may be viewed as a "disruptive innovation," in which the disruptive product has the potential to transform a market.[24] These platforms facilitate the process of connecting those with available living spaces—whether it be a spare room, apartment, house, or castle—with potential guests in a way that was previously unfeasible. Although Airbnb continues to face legal issues related to regulation in cities from New York to Barcelona (who can rent, what spaces can be rented, how many nights per year can be rented, etc.), the company operates in more than 190 countries. Many tourists now view them as an alternative to traditional hospitality service providers. In just a few years, this has affected particularly the lower-end leisure hotel market, reduced hospitality jobs and tax income, transformed residential spaces into commercial ones, and diminished residents' well-being.[25] Ripple effects throughout the tourism system such as these will be discussed in subsequent chapters.

## Conclusion

Tourists are often lumped into a single (typically stereotyped) category, yet there is an incredible diversity in terms of who they are, where they are coming from, where they are going, and what motivates them to temporarily leave home. The demand-side perspective offers us insight into these variables. This plays a crucial role in helping us understand the supply side, as peoples and places around the world seek to meet tourism demand. Both sides are part of the larger tourism system. This chapter discussed some of the key concepts that will help us understand both demand and supply, which will provide the foundation for our examination of tourism throughout the rest of the chapters in this book.

# Key Terms

- deferred demand
- discretionary income
- domestic tourism
- drifter
- effective demand
- experience stage
- explorer
- inbound tourism
- individual mass tourist
- international tourism
- mass tourism
- movement stage
- niche tourism
- no demand

- organized mass tourist
- outbound tourism
- overtourism
- post-trip stage
- potential demand
- pre-trip stage
- pull factor
- push factor
- suppressed demand
- tourism attractions
- tourism stakeholders
- tourist inversions
- tourist typology

# Notes

1. Elizabeth Becker, *Overbooked: The Exploding Business of Travel and Tourism* (New York: Simon & Schuster Paperbacks, 2013), 381.

2. United Nations World Tourism Organization, "Glossary of Tourism Terms," accessed March 5, 2020, https://www.unwto.org/glossary-tourism-terms.

3. James Duncan and Derek Gregory, "Introduction," in *Writes of Passage: Reading Travel Writing*, ed. James Duncan and Derek Gregory (London: Routledge, 1999), 6.

4. Derek Gregory, "Scripting Egypt: Orientalism and the Cultures of Travel," In *Writes of Passage: Reading Travel Writing*, ed. James Duncan and Derek Gregory (London: Routledge, 1999).

5. Tim Pile, "Seven Tourist Stereotypes—Which One Fits You?" *Post Magazine*, August 23, 2017, accessed March 18, 2020, https://www.scmp.com/magazines/post-magazine/travel/article/2107837/seven-tourist-stereotypes-which-one-fits-you.

6. Erik Cohen, "Toward a Sociology of International Tourism," *Social Research* 39, no. 1 (1972): 167–8.

7. Airbnb Newsroom, "Fast Facts," accessed March 18, 2020, https://news.airbnb.com/fast-facts/.

8. Nelson Graburn, "The Anthropology of Tourism," *Annals of Tourism Research* 10 (1983): 21–2

9. Greg Richards, "Creativity and Tourism: The State of the Art," *Annals of Tourism Research* 38 (2011): 1233.

10. Richard Florida, *The Rise of the Creative Class, Revisited* (New York: Basic Books, 2012).

11. Alex Butler, "Millennials Would Rather Take Shorter Trips Than One Long Vacation, Says Survey," *Lonely Planet*, May 9, 2016, accessed March 19, 2020, https://www.lonelyplanet.com/articles/millennial-vacation-trips.

12. Hannah Sampson, "What Does America Have Against Vacation?" *The Washington Post*, August 28, 2019, accessed March 19, 2020, https://www.washingtonpost.com/travel/2019/08/28/what-does-america-have-against-vacation/.

13. Sarah Peter, "Hurricanes Cost Caribbean $1 Billion in Tourism: Industry Group," *Reuters*, June 14, 2018, accessed March 20, 2020, https://www.reuters.com/article/us-storm-tourism/hurricanes-cost-caribbean-1-billion-in-tourism-industry-group-idUSKBN1JA2IA.

14. US Department of State, "Global Level 4 Health Advisory—Do Not Travel," accessed March 20, 2020, https://travel.state.gov/content/travel/en/traveladvisories/ea/travel-advisory-alert-global-level-4-health-advisory-issue.html.

15. Brian Boniface and Chris Cooper, *Worldwide Destinations: The Geography of Travel and Tourism*, 4th ed. (Amsterdam: Elsevier Butterworth Heinemann, 2005).

16. Brad Adgate, "An Advanced Media Ad Campaign for Puerto Rico Tourism," *Forbes*, February 5, 2019, accessed March 20, 2020, https://www.forbes.com/sites/bradadgate/2019/02/05/an-advanced-media-ad-campaign-for-puerto-rico-tourism/#13c0e5492820.

17. Sampson, "What Does America Have Against Vacation?"

18. Expedia and The Center for Generational Kinetics, *Generations on the Move: A Deep Dive into Multi-Generational Travel Trends and How Their Habits Will Impact the Future of the Industry*, January 2018 (2017), accessed March 20, 2020, https://viewfinder.expedia.com/wp-content/uploads/2017/12/Expedia-Generations-on-the-Move.pdf.

19. Hamed Haddouche and Christine Salomone, "Generation Z and the Tourist Experience: Tourist Stories and Use of Social Networks," *Journal of Tourism Futures* 4, no. 1 (2018), 70, 73.

20. Louis Cheslaw, "Gen Z Are Pressuring the Travel Industry in All the Right Ways," *Condé Nast Traveler*, July 29, 2019, accessed March 20, 2020, https://www.cntraveller.com/article/gen-z-travel-industry.

21. John Swarbrooke, *The Development and Management of Visitor Attractions*, 2nd ed. (Burlington, MA: Butterworth-Heinemann, 2002).

22. Paul Thompson, "Blarney Stone 'Most Unhygienic Tourist Attraction in the World,'" *Daily Mail*, June 16, 2009, accessed March 20, 2020, https://www.dailymail.co.uk/news/article-1193477/Blarney-Stone-unhygienic-tourist-attraction-world.html.

23. World Travel & Tourism Council, "Home," accessed March 20, 2020, https://www.wttc.org.

24. Daniel Guttentag, "Airbnb: Disruptive Innovation and the Rise of an Informal Tourism Accommodation Sector," *Current Issues in Tourism* 18, no. 12 (2015), 1194.

25. Anna Farmaki and Dimitrios Stergiou, "Impacts of P2P Accommodation: Neighbourhood Perspectives," *e-Review of Tourism Research* 16, no. 2/3 (2019), 46.

# CHAPTER 3

# Overview of Tourism Products

Eating, partying, praying, shopping, swimming, sightseeing, gambling, getting cosmetic surgery, hiking, helping, and having sex—although these things may seem to have nothing in common, they are all activities people participate in through tourism. Tourism is not a one-size-fits-all experience. People have different reasons for traveling, and they want different things from their experiences. Consequently, there is a distinct need for different types of **tourism products**. As a service industry, the primary "products" of tourism are not tangible goods but experiences. With more people traveling than ever before, the tourism industry has developed to provide an array of increasingly diversified and specialized experiences to meet the demands of tourists across the spectrum, from organized mass tourists to drifters.

This chapter provides a brief introduction to some of the types of products that comprise the modern tourism industry. It is a selection of tourism products that crosses different types of tourism and tourists. Many of these products overlap and share the characteristics of other products but have a unique emphasis or appeal to a specific market. Each product involves different resources and affects destinations in distinct ways. We will explore these issues further in the context of the thematic chapters throughout the rest of this text.

## Beach Tourism or Sun, Sea, and Sand (3S) Tourism

Perhaps the most widespread and recognizable tourism product around the world is beach tourism. This is often referred to as "3S tourism" in reference to the three key resources for the product: sun, sea, and sand. Sometimes more S's are added to the mix—including sex and spirits—but for our purposes, we will consider sex tourism as a separate (albeit often related) tourism product. Obviously, the focal point of 3S tourism is the beach, which has served as an attraction since an early era in the modern tourism industry (see chapter 4). Yet, 3S tourism is more than just the beach. Beyond any other, this product has been used to characterize the tourism industry.

Every major world region has 3S tourism destinations. Some of the largest, best-known, and most popular destinations are based on this product. Moreover, 3S tourism appeals to some of the most basic tourist motivations, including the pursuit of pleasure and self-indulgence.

Typical 3S tourism is mass tourism, which accounts for the temporary movements of large numbers of tourists from the more developed countries in the northern climates to well-established coastal destinations, often developing countries with warmer, tropical climates. This product is highly dependent on a well-developed tourism infrastructure to facilitate the mass movement of people and create the desired experience at the destination. Resorts are often a fundamental component of these destinations. They offer the comforts of home and the facilities to enjoy the three S's, including beachfront access, swimming pools, lounge chairs, water-sport equipment, and so on. Because a key goal of this product is relaxation and leisure, related facilities include restaurants, nightclubs, and other venues offering entertainment. Given these amenities, there may be little incentive to leave the resort to experience other aspects of the destination.

Characteristic of mass tourism, these destinations are relatively standardized, so there is a certain degree of interchangeability among similar destinations in different parts of the world. However, not all tourism oriented around the beach is synonymous with organized mass tourism. Destinations with beach resources may not have the capacity to develop this type of large-scale industry, and they may not want to. Correspondingly, individual mass tourists and explorers interested in vacationing at the beach may not want this type of experience. The demand–supply match allows some destinations to maintain the natural quality of their beaches with limited infrastructure to accommodate a smaller number of tourists who appreciate the quieter, more intimate experience. In contrast with major destinations in the Caribbean basin characterized by mass 3S tourism, some of the islands with less developed tourism industries, such as Grand Turk—an island in the Turks and Caicos—offer this brand of beach tourism.

## Sex and Romance Tourism

Sex tourism is a product that takes place in destinations all over the world in a variety of forms. The most commonly recognized sex tourism product involves travel to a place to engage in commercial sex (i.e., prostitution). This brand of sex tourism tends to be associated more with male tourists than female. For many destinations, sex is considered to be a by-product of travel rather than the primary motivation (e.g., business travelers hiring prostitutes at the destination during the course of their trip). However, other destinations have become known for the availability of commercial sex, a particular type of commercial sex (e.g., homosexual or child sex), or other opportunities to experience things that might not be available to them in their home environment. Therefore, destinations attract tourists specifically for this purpose. Well-known destinations for this brand of sex tourism are in Southeast Asia, predominantly Thailand and the Philippines. Locals may also be engaged for extended periods, perhaps as a travel companion for the duration of the tourist's vacation. For example, in Kenya, this may be referred to as romantic safaris.[1]

Sex tourism has grown with the tourism industry and expanded into new destinations around the world. The nongovernmental organization (NGO) Equality Now also expressed concern that #MeToo had the potential to further increase sex tourists coming from countries where the movement had strengthened awareness of and opposition to sexual harassment and exploitation.[2] The demand generated by sex tourists has become a driving force in the commercial sex trade and consequently trade in women and children. In addition to sexual exploitation, trafficked persons often suffer from extreme violations of their human rights, such as the right to not be held in slavery or involuntary servitude, the right to be free from violence and cruel or inhumane treatment, and the right to health. The Office of the High Commissioner for Human Rights (OHCHR) estimates that the profit made from the sexual exploitation of children for tourism could be up to US$20 billion per year.[3]

#MeToo also has the potential to increase awareness about exploitation in sex tourism and allow victims' voices to be heard, which has an important role to play. Governmental and nongovernmental organizations as well as private companies have worked to develop codes of conduct for both tourism stakeholders and tourists (for more on codes of conduct, see chapter 11). Furthermore, countries like the United States have passed child sex tourism laws under which tourists who engage in sex with minors, even outside of the country, can face up to thirty years in a US prison. Human rights organizations are also now trying to harness the power of tourism to try to fight sex trafficking. For example, TraffickCam encourages travelers to take photos of hotel rooms and upload them to their website or mobile application. When traffickers post photos of victims in online advertisements, investigators can search the resulting database of images to try to determine the victim's location.[4]

Sex tourism that does not involve commercial sex is harder to define and is therefore less commonly recognized. This may be framed as seeking romance and/or a relationship rather than sex (e.g., "romance tourism"). Money may not be exchanged for sex, but there still may be an economic motivation as tourists offer partners drinks, meals, entertainment, and/or gifts during the course of their time together. Popular 3S destinations like Jamaica and the Dominican Republic became associated with this phenomenon, where typically white female tourists were involved with black "beach boys." It became so common that women traveling without a male companion at these destinations were assumed to be sex tourists.

Romance, as well as sex, between tourists also occurs. The atmosphere of popular 3S destinations, where the focus is on relaxation and pleasure, lends itself to this form of sex tourism (see box 3.1). Clothing may be minimal (perhaps even optional), alcohol and/or recreational drugs may be present, and inhibitions may be lowered. However, this is not the only type of destination associated with such patterns. Far from the beach, the scenic and historic city of Lijiang in China's Yunnan Province has become known as a destination for *yanyu*—romantic encounters—among young Chinese tourists (figure 3.1). Yanyu does not necessarily imply sexual relations but more generally the interactions that take place between male and female tourists.[5]

**Figure 3.1.  Lijiang, China is known as a destination for *yanyu*, or romantic encounters, among young Chinese tourists. *Source:* Velvet Nelson**

Perhaps not surprisingly, research has shown that, although many people have reported engaging in any one of the above behaviors, few would describe themselves as sex tourists.[6]

# Box 3.1. Case Study: Mass S Tourism in the Mediterranean

*"You will either have the holiday of your life or a holiday from hell, all depending on your outlook on life."*[a]

As this travel guide suggests, much of tourism experiences comes down to perspective. While some tourists avoid prototypical sun, sea, sand, sex, and spirits tourism, it clearly holds appeal for many tourists around the world, as evidenced by the tremendous popularity of resorts providing these experiences. In this case, the guide is describing Magaluf, one of the principal resorts on the Mediterranean island of Palma de Mallorca (map 3.1) and a destination often cited as having all of the excesses of S tourism in the region. Like many S destinations, Magaluf was once a small island fishing village. During the 1960s, the Mallorcan municipality of Calvià experienced significant investment in mass tourism infrastructure and high-rise resort development in both Magaluf and neighboring Palmanova. Today, the resort has little appearance of or connection to the rest of the island or the Spanish mainland. The municipality receives large numbers of the 19 million tourists who visit the Balearic Islands annually.

Most tourism promotions highlight Magaluf's beaches, with the promise of beautiful sand, clear water, and the relaxation of sunbathing during the day. While these S's may be the primary attraction for neighboring Palmanova, they are often only secondary considerations for Magaluf. Also known as "Shagaluf," this resort is better known for its other S's and the multitude of bars and nightclubs, cheap alcohol, the twenty-four-hour party atmosphere, and casual sex. In fact, tourism researcher Hazel Andrews found that there was an "expectation that sexual activity was a reason, if not *the* reason, for being there."[b] The principal tourist market for Magaluf tends to be young adult (from age 18 to the 30s) British working-class singles. Most arrive in groups on package tours, sometimes for stag and hen parties.

The atmosphere tends to be sexually charged, with references to and an abundance of naked bodies, from topless sunbathers to exposure during bar crawl drinking games. Tourists are warned about the issues associated with large quantities of inebriated tourists during the peak summer months. Females in particular are warned about unwanted attention, potential harassment, and drink spiking. Although a subset of tourists returns to the resort year after year, its negative reputation has been growing with reports of muggings, stabbings, sexual assaults, and tourist deaths attributed to excessive consumption of alcohol and/or drugs. "Balconing," which involves climbing between (usually hotel) balconies or jumping from a balcony into a swimming pool, has been a scourge for years, causing serious injuries or death. In addition, a 2018 report warned that young Britons working at bars and clubs in the resort were at risk of becoming victims of modern slavery.[c]

Mallorca's tourism stakeholders have become increasingly frustrated that Magaluf's reputation for 5S tourism predominates over its other natural, cultural heritage, and agricultural tourism products. The destination initiated a process to rejuvenate, rebrand, and possibly even rename the resort. In 2015, local officials sought to impose restrictions on the notorious pub crawls, drinking in the streets, and public nudity.[d] Unfortunately, five years later, the conversation remains much the same. In 2020, the Balearic Island Government banned pub crawls and placed further restrictions on alcohol sales and party boats in an effort to combat "excess tourism." The new law also bans balconing. Fines for these activities range from 6,000 to 600,000 Euros. The government argues that this legislation is the first of its kind in Europe, intended to force real change and promote a more responsible tourism.[e]

In addition to the issues raised here, Mallorca experienced anti-tourism protests in 2018 and 2019. Local groups argue that tourism on the island is unsustainable and has created both

**Map 3.1. Palma de Mallorca, Spain. Popular resorts at this Mediterranean destination like Palmanova and Magaluf are based on tourism's S's.** *Source:* XNR Productions

social and environmental crises. While the problem is bigger than Magaluf, the bad behavior of "booze tourists" has the potential to act as a flashpoint. Change is clearly needed.

*Discussion topic*: Do you think Magaluf can change its primary tourism product (from 5S) and its poor reputation? What factors will facilitate or hinder this change?

*Tourism online*: Balearic Agency for Tourism Strategy, "Mallorca" at https://www.illes-balears.travel/en/mallorca/

---

[a] Islas Travel Guides, "Welcome to Our Guide to Magaluf," accessed March 9, 2020, http://www.majorca-mallorca.co.uk/magaluf.htm.

[b] Hazel Andrews, "Feeling at Home: Embodying Britishness in a Spanish Charter Tourists Resort," *Tourist Studies* 5, no. 3 (2005): 251.

[c] Chris Creegan and Kieran Guilbert, "Slavery Risk for Young Brits taking Mallorca Seasonal Party Jobs," *Global Citizen*, June 1, 2018, accessed March 9, 2020, https://www.globalcitizen.org/en/content/britons-modern-slavery-uk-mallorca-party-jobs/.

[d] Tracy McVeigh, "Magaluf's Days of Drinking and Casual Sex Are Numbered—Or So Mallorca Hopes," *The Observer*, April 18, 2015, accessed March 9, 2020, https://www.theguardian.com/travel/2015/apr/18/vodka-sex-magaluf-tourists-spain-mallorca-shagaluf.

[e] Hugh Morris, "Majorca and Ibiza Ban Pub Crawls and 'Happy Hour' in New Crackdown on Boozy Tourists," *The Telegraph*, January 20, 2020, accessed March 9, 2020, https://www.telegraph.co.uk/travel/news/alcohol-laws-magaluf-ibiza/.

# Nature Tourism

Nature tourism is a product that represents a diverse group of activities set in or based on the appreciation of natural attractions. These attractions may be protected as parks and preserves; in particular, the national park designation plays a role in the creation of opportunities for nature tourism, as both domestic and international tourists make it a point to visit these places. Nature tourism may be the primary tourism product for a trip or one type of activity participated in during the course of a trip. For example, birding is a specialized nature tourism product that has been growing in recent years. The practice of bird watching and listening is particularly popular among older, affluent tourists, traditionally from more developed countries such as the United States and the United Kingdom, who enjoy traveling to new places in search of opportunities to observe different species. Dedicated tour companies provide entire trips oriented around the practice.

Although nature tourism may be positioned as niche tourism in opposition to mass tourism such as 3S, this product can also provide a diversionary activity for mass tourists. In the case of the Caribbean, islands depend on sun, sea, and sand to attract tourists. However, these destinations also promote nature tourism as an activity tourists can participate in for a day, or part of a day, during their vacation. This is not the primary motivation for the trip, but it allows tourists to experience more of an island than simply resort areas on the coast. These products may be packaged as nature walks or hikes, in which guides highlight local flora and fauna.

As the global tourism industry has been growing, more destinations around the world have utilized their natural attractions and developed a nature tourism product. There are good examples of nature-based tourism activities in which tourists have the opportunity to learn about and experience unique environments and/or wildlife. At the same time, there are bad examples of nature being exploited and degraded for the purpose of tourism. The ecotourism concept evolved out of debates about how nature tourism should take place (see box 3.2).

# Box 3.2.  In-Depth: The Ecotourism Concept

The term **ecotourism** is frequently used as a synonym for nature tourism. In theory, there is overlap between the two products; in practice, there may be little distinction between them. However, the concept of ecotourism is intended to go beyond activities in nature and/or appreciating nature. The International Ecotourism Society (TIES) defines ecotourism as "responsible travel to natural areas that conserves the environment, sustains the well-being of the local people, and involves interpretation and education."[a] The concept is based on the principles of sustainable development where natural areas are managed to be economically, socially, and environmentally sustainable. The argument may be made for tourism if it is shown to be as profitable as other, more environmentally destructive activities, such as logging or commercial development. This depends on the preservation of the physical resources that provide the basis for tourism, as well as human resources. Local people should be involved in activities to ensure that the tourism developed fits within their values and lifestyles. They should directly benefit from tourism, not only to improve their quality of life but also to ensure that they have a stake in it and will provide the necessary support.

Destinations around the world have attempted to translate the ecotourism concept into a tourism product, with varying results. Places such as Costa Rica and Kenya have become associated with ecotourism, while others offer some type of experience called ecotourism. As such, researchers argue that it may be useful to make a distinction between hard and soft variations of ecotourism that exist in practice.[b] In this model, "hard ecotourism" is a niche product involving small numbers of tourists who are explicitly interested in wilderness experiences as well as ensuring the sustainability of their actions. Typically categorized toward the drifter end of the spectrum, these tourists visit more remote destinations where there are few other tourists and tourist services. Ecotourism is the primary focus of the trip, which may be physically and/or mentally demanding. This may be done as part of a specialized tour package through an operator or booking platform, but it may also be undertaken independently with the use of informal local resources.

"Soft ecotourism" has been criticized as just a different label for nature tourism, with little of the concept behind ecotourism. This variation provides mass tourists with an opportunity to have an "ecotourism" experience as part of their larger trip. These tourists have a more superficial interest in environmental issues. Their experiences are shorter and may be even just a day trip to a natural area that is relatively close to the principal destination region and has the appropriate infrastructure (e.g., paths, bathrooms, refreshments) to accommodate a large number of tourists. Interactions with nature are facilitated by a guide, but they tend to be more superficial. These hard and soft positions are, of course, two ends of a spectrum, and there are many examples of experiences that fall somewhere in between.

Thus, while ecotourism was intended to provide a sustainable framework for nature tourism, it has, to some extent, become just another buzzword to generate interest in tourism. This has led to the development of certification programs to help ensure that products being labeled ecotourism are, in fact, environmentally sustainable. For example, Ecotourism Australia is one of the most long-standing ecotourism accreditation systems. This organization developed a set of guidelines for various levels of environmentally sustainable tourism, from nature tourism that uses specific measures to minimize the impact of tourists' activities on the environment to an advanced form of ecotourism in which operators are highly committed to best practices, environmental conservation, and local support. Businesses can then use this certification to support their claims of sustainability to knowledgeable tourists.

*Discussion topic*: Search for an ecotourism product (e.g., tour, experience, accommodation). Do you think the product described should be considered nature tourism or ecotourism? Explain.

*Tourism online*: Ecotourism Australia, "Home: Ecotourism Australia," at https://www.ecotourism.org.au

---

[a] The International Ecotourism Society, "What Is Ecotourism?," accessed March 10, 2020, https://ecotourism.org/what-is-ecotourism/.

[b] David A. Fennell, *Ecotourism*, 4th ed. (London: Routledge, 2015), 12.

# Sport, Adventure, and Adrenaline Tourism

Sport tourism, adventure tourism, and adrenaline tourism are related products centered on physical activity with varying degrees of intensity. Sports and other physical activities may be the primary motivation for a trip or simply one activity. These products encompass a range of activities, seasons, environments, and infrastructural requirements. The activity may be one that the tourist is involved in at home during his or her leisure time. Avid golfers often plan trips where they travel to play different courses, including famous ones associated with major professional golf tournaments such as Augusta National in Georgia. The activity may also be something that the tourist has limited opportunity to enjoy in their home environment. In the subtropical states of the American South, people will have to plan a trip to a resort in places like Colorado to fulfill their demand for winter sports.

Alpine skiing, cross-country skiing, and snowboarding are popular winter recreation activities that provide the basis for winter sport tourism. Some ski resorts in Europe date back to the late nineteenth century, while the oldest resorts in North America date back to the early twentieth century. Summer sport tourism, or warm weather sport, includes diverse activities, ranging from kayaking to horseback riding. Water sport tourism is also immensely popular at coastal destinations and includes swimming, snorkeling, scuba diving, surfing, wind surfing, jet skiing, water skiing, sailing, fishing, and more. While these activities may take place at any number of coastal destinations, some have particularly been associated with water-sport tourism. For example, Bonaire, in the Netherlands Antilles, is a prime destination for divers.

Adventure tourism is more likely to be a physical activity that tourists would not participate in at home and is more dependent on the natural resources of a place. These activities may require specialized equipment and training or skill, and there is some degree of excitement and/or perceived risk. Examples of adventure tourism might include zip lining in rain forest canopies, kite boarding, whitewater rafting or kayaking, and mountain biking (figure 3.2) or trekking. Soft adventure tourism may be an activity for mass tourists close to well-developed destination areas, while hard adventure tourism transitions into adrenaline or extreme tourism with activities such as rock climbing, spelunking, bungee jumping, and skydiving. This product is more likely to be the focus of a trip that takes place in remote,

**Figure 3.2. Adventure tourism often involves physical activities in spectacular natural environments. Mountain biking provides adrenaline-inducing excitement, while the scenery enhances the experience. *Source:* Scott Jeffcote**

possibly even dangerous, locations. The activities are intense and the risk greater, but the adrenaline rush is part of the attraction.

# Rural and Urban Tourism

Rural tourism and urban tourism offer distinctive experiences based on their particular sets of resources. While there is some overlap between rural tourism and nature tourism, the former is more specifically associated with the general sensibility of "rural" that pertains to life in the countryside. Rural recreation activities such as scenic drives, country picnics, hunting, or fishing may be included in this product.

Farm tourism or agricultural tourism (agritourism/agrotourism) is a specialized product that has evolved out of rural tourism. Activities within this product vary widely. Tourists may participate in activities set in the farm environment, such as horseback riding or hiking farm trails (figure 3.3). They may consume farm produce,

**Figure 3.3. Farm or agricultural tourism is a tourism product that encompasses a wide range of activities. At Chá Gorreana tea plantation in the Azores, visitors can tour the factory, sample teas, and hike trails through the fields.** *Source:* Velvet Nelson

such as eating at a farm restaurant, purchasing items at a farm market, or even doing the "pick-your-own" option. Tourists may also participate in farm activities. Some activities are simulated, such as tourist cattle drives and cowboy cookouts hosted by dude ranch resorts, but there are also working farms and ranches on which the tourist learns about and assists in daily chores or harvests. For these activities, tourists will stay on the farm in facilities converted to serve as a bed-and-breakfast or specially constructed facilities such as cottages. Farm tourism has a particularly strong tradition in Europe.

Likewise, urban tourism is an overarching product that may encompass cultural and heritage tourism or event tourism (below). Towns and cities have an array of attractions upon which urban tourism may be based, and some of the largest tourism destinations in the world are major cities, such as Paris, New York City, Bangkok, and Dubai. Attractions may be spatially concentrated in particular parts of the city, such as historic neighborhoods, shopping and entertainment districts, or waterfront developments.

Attractions include historic buildings, from ancient ruins to churches and cathedrals or castles and palaces. Although these places were not originally intended for tourism, they may be preserved as attractions. In other cases, places are transformed to become attractions. For example, the Meatpacking District in Manhattan developed based on the spatial concentration of slaughterhouses and packing plants. This area has been redeveloped into one of New York's most fashionable neighborhoods with diverse restaurants, trendy clubs, stylish boutiques, and luxury hotels. This, combined with historic district designations, has given rise to walking and guided tours of the area. Other urban amenities, such as upscale or boutique shopping, museums, art galleries, theaters, concert venues, sports arenas, restaurants, bars, nightclubs, and more, serve the dual purpose of providing a desirable living environment for residents and an attractive environment for tourist visits.

# Cultural and Heritage Tourism

Cultural tourism is arguably one of the oldest tourism products, as many of the earliest tourists traveled for the experience of other cultures and cultural attractions. As the tourism industry began to develop specialized products, cultural tourism was considered a niche tourism product oriented toward a small subset of affluent and educated tourists interested in authentic experiences of other cultures. Today, however, cultural tourism is recognized as one of the broadest tourism products, which encompasses a vast range of attractions and activities and has extensive overlap with other products.

Cultural tourism is based on human attractions, and in particular, elements of a society's culture. For the most part, cultural tourism pertains to the unique cultural patterns that have evolved in a specific place over time to serve a purpose for that group of people, not to attract tourists. This includes the patterns of lifestyles, cuisine, clothing, art, music, folklore, religious practices, and more that make a place distinct. In the modern world, with globalization and the perception of uniform contemporary lifestyles, there is an interest in and a demand for experiences of different cultures. Although many of these patterns no longer have a role in the daily lives of these people, this demand means that elements of traditional culture may be maintained when they might otherwise be lost.

There is considerable overlap between cultural tourism and heritage tourism. Heritage tourism as a distinct tourism product is a relatively recent development and is considered one of the fastest growing. Heritage tourism encompasses travel to varied sites of historic (and often cultural) importance such as the Parthenon or the Taj Mahal, sites where important historic events occurred such as Independence Hall in Philadelphia or the D-Day landing beaches in Normandy, and sites that represent the stories and people of the past such as the National Museum of Cultural History in Pretoria, South Africa or Mozart's Birthplace museum in Salzburg, Austria. Prominent heritage tourism attractions are designated United Nations Educational, Scientific, and Cultural Organization (UNESCO) World Heritage Sites. Using a specific set of selection criteria, the organization identifies places with outstanding universal value.[7] While these places would likely serve as tourism attractions regardless, the World Heritage Site designation raises the site's profile and increases visits.

Contemporary culture also plays a role in tourism. Elements of contemporary culture may be used to attract tourists, but tourism may also be a side effect of cultural activities. This brand of cultural tourism may be associated with some aspect of high culture, such as artistic works and performances. England is particularly known for its literary destinations—places specifically associated with a well-known writer or referenced in a widely read work. This may also be associated with popular culture. For example, major film and television projects, such as *Harry Potter*, *Game of Thrones*, and *Downton Abbey*, have all generated significant tourism to film sites.

Although attractions developed specifically for the purpose of tourism do not fit traditional ideas of cultural tourism, they are nonetheless shaped by and represent aspects of contemporary culture. For example, Disneyland and Disney World are widely visited tourism destinations that have been described as epitomizing American culture. Similarly the theme park–like environment of Las Vegas is distinctly part of popular American culture. In contrast with tourism related to elements of traditional culture that may be associated with rural areas, these activities are more often associated with cities and overlap with urban tourism.

# Food and Beverage Tourism

The food and drink of a place is a fundamental tourism resource. In the past, these items played a supporting role in tourism, providing tourists with sustenance while they were away from their home environment. However, in recent years, the popularity of food in the media and the expansion of ethnic restaurants have exposed more people to the foods of places they have not yet had the opportunity to visit.[8] This creates a demand for the experiences of those places and their foods.

This has given rise to a relatively new tourism product. Although the terms culinary tourism and gastronomic tourism are also used, often with more specific implications, food and beverage tourism provides a simple and comprehensive label. Food and beverage tourism describes travel motivated by, or involving an interest in, learning about and experiencing the food and drink of a place. This can include the experience of everyday foods served by street vendors and local restaurants; it can also include elaborate tasting menus served by restaurants with a Michelin star or featured on the S. Pellegrino and Acqua Panna World's 50 Best Restaurants list (figure 3.4). For some, food has become the primary reason for traveling to a particular destination, but for many tourists today, enjoying the food of a destination is simply one part of the expectations they have for their trip.

This product is often considered a subset of cultural tourism in which tourists can observe, participate in, and gain an understanding of other cultures through food and eating experiences.[9] Food is a part of the culture of a place. Some destinations, like France and Italy, have a well-known reputation for quality food and eating experiences. Countless others around the world are currently engaged in the process of defining, or redefining, a food culture that can increase its pull factor for potential tourists. Peru is one of the most successful examples. The country has won World's Leading Culinary Destination from the World Travel Awards every year since the category was created in 2012 (as of 2019).[10]

While food and beverage are often considered part of an overall package, beverage tourism is an increasingly popular special interest tourism product in its own right. Wine tourism—in the form of wine trails, vineyard and winery tours, and wine tastings—has been the most developed product that has often overlapped with rural and agricultural tourism (see, for example, box 2.2). However, interest in craft beers,

**Figure 3.4. Food and beverage tourism is an increasingly popular tourism product. In one example, people from all over the world visit a highly ranked restaurant in Lima, Peru to try its tasting menu featuring dishes from each of the country's geographic regions.** *Source:* Velvet Nelson

ciders, liquors, and even tea and coffee has been growing. These products are often connected to specific places that aficionados might wish to visit (e.g., the Kentucky Bourbon Trail). Others signify local or regional connections and therefore become a part of the experience of those places (e.g., the Great Lakes Brewing Company in Cleveland, Ohio).

# Drug Tourism

Drug tourism is typically defined by an individual's interest in a destination due to the ability to consume licit or illicit drugs in that place. However, tourists may also travel to a destination without prior knowledge or intention of consuming but may ultimately participate in drug tourism. Studies show different motivations for participating in drug tourism. For some tourists, this is part of the inversions discussed in chapter 2. In their daily lives, these people operate within the legal frameworks and established norms of society; on vacation, they seek to escape from routine and break free from these restrictions. For other tourists, this is part of the experience of place and an opportunity to participate in local culture.[11] Still others seek self-actualization with the aid of substances not available to them in their home environment.

Amsterdam is perhaps the most well-known example of a drug tourism destination. Cannabis is an illicit drug in the Netherlands, but an official policy of tolerance allows "coffee shops" to sell small quantities to patrons. This has been a significant attraction for the city. The Dutch government has made several attempts to ban tourists from coffee shops, but none have been turned into law. Still, other policies have made it more difficult to obtain the product, leading some to proclaim Barcelona as the "new Amsterdam."[12] In another example, drug tourists have visited Amazonian Peru and Brazil with the intention of trying ayahuasca. Indigenous people have traditionally used this mixture of psychedelic plants for ceremonial and healing purposes. Studies have shown that local dealers posing as shamans exploit tourists seeking enlightenment through religious ceremonies or simply an unusual experience.[13] The tourist demand for ayahuasca experiences has been increasing in recent years, raising concerns about deforestation due to expanding commercial plantations as well as the use of dangerous or deadly alternatives.[14]

In 2014, Colorado and Washington became the first American states to legalize recreational sales of marijuana. By the beginning of 2020, this had expanded to eleven US states. However, there can still be challenges for drug tourists. Vendors are prohibited from traditional advertising. In addition, smoking marijuana in public is still illegal, and the majority of the traditional hotel infrastructure is also smoke-free. Therefore, it may be difficult for visitors to know where to go to both purchase legitimate (i.e., not black market) products and consume them. This has given rise to a drug tourism industry. In addition to helping tourists shop and find marijuana-friendly lodging, companies offer opportunities to visit growers and learn about products, take cannabis cooking classes, and receive cannabis-related spa treatments.[15]

While drug tourism can provide an attraction for a destination and make a significant economic contribution, there are nonetheless many potential issues depending on the nature of the product. Businesses involved in drug tourism need to ensure they are in compliance with the laws of the places in which they operate and maintain any necessary permits and insurance. Communities may be concerned about unacceptable public behavior, an increased burden on public health systems, and potentially even drug trafficking and drug-related crime. Tourists should be aware of any potential legal and/or health consequences to their activities. Each year, drug-related tourist deaths occur.

# Dark Tourism

Dark tourism is the term used to describe a range of experiences whereby people visit sites of death or attractions/exhibits that represent death. Thanatourism is a lesser-used term derived from Greek mythology in which Thanatos was the personification of death. Interest in death is by no means a modern phenomenon; some scholars argue that public consumption of suffering and death in the Roman gladiatorial games or medieval executions were precursors to dark tourism.[16] Nonetheless, sites of—and associated with—natural disasters (e.g., Hurricane Katrina), human-caused disasters (e.g., Pripyat, Ukraine, the city that was abandoned after the Chernobyl nuclear meltdown, now an official tourist attraction), human atrocities (e.g., the Nazi concentration camp at Auschwitz), and death (e.g., Hiroshima Peace Memorial Park, figure 3.5) have had an increasing presence in modern tourism. Tourists have a variety of motivations for visiting such sites, ranging from a fascination with death to a desire to connect with their identity or heritage.

Philip Stone, Executive Director of the Institute for Dark Tourism, argues that there is a spectrum of dark tourism.[17] Some sites sensationalize events to entertain visitors (e.g., Jack the Ripper tours in London's East End), while others seek to educate visitors and to engage them with persistent issues (e.g., the International Slavery Museum in Liverpool that not only examines issues associated with slavery but also the legacies of racism and discrimination). Some sites are accidental, in that they naturally attract curiosity because of the death that occurred there (e.g., the site of the car crash in which Princess Diana was killed). Other sites are purposefully constructed for commemoration (e.g., the National September 11 Memorial and Museum).

Evidence, artifacts, and memorials constitute the tangible heritage, or markers, associated with disasters or atrocities. They can be used as tools to articulate and promote remembrance of the event, but they are not always sufficient to engender empathy among visitors. Thus, memories of the event, such as testimonials of survivors, constitute the intangible heritage and an equally important component of these sites.[18] Still, geographers remind us that places of memory are selective, often contested

**Figure 3.5. Dark tourism refers to a range of experiences whereby people visit sites associated with death. The Hiroshima Peace Memorial Park in Hiroshima, Japan is such a site that receives over one million visitors a year. The park is intended to recognize the site of the first city in the world to experience a nuclear attack, to remember the victims, and to promote peace. *Source:* Velvet Nelson**

or politicized, interpretations of the past, and must be viewed critically.[19] Consider, for example, the different viewpoints on memorial sites associated with civil wars around the world. While many such sites are intended to promote reconciliation and healing, narratives and counternarratives of events can be contentious and foster resentment.

# Slow, Digital-Free, and Wellness Tourism

Slow tourism evolved from the slow food and slow cities movements, both coming out of Italy. The slow food movement supported local and traditional foods as well as sustainability. The slow cities movement focused on the development of places with a good quality of life, healthy environments, and sustainable economies. Slow tourism is primarily an approach to travel. For some, travel has become an extension of fast-paced modern life. They feel the need to see and do as much as possible to maximize their limited vacation days that they often return home more exhausted or overwhelmed than before they left. In terms of inversions, slow tourism experiences are the opposite of fast-paced modern life. These experiences allow tourists to slow down and relax. Slow tourism often involves slow travel (e.g., trains, bicycling, walking) that promotes a more leisurely pace and more opportunities to interact with people (traveling companions and locals alike) and places. While perhaps less explicit than slow food and cities, sustainability is also a part of slow tourism through support for local businesses, aspects of social relations and wellbeing, and reduced environmental footprints.[20]

The idea of digital-free tourism has been connected to slow tourism and wellness tourism. Our lives are more connected now than ever before, which makes it harder for tourists to "get away" from family, friends, followers, work, etc. and to effectively engage with people and places. In other words, some may find it difficult to achieve the objectives of slow tourism if they remain connected. Thus, there is growing interest in digital-free tourism (or disconnected tourism). While some may choose to leave devices at home, many tourists remain concerned about the potential vulnerabilities of being truly disconnected (e.g., getting lost, not being able to get help if it is needed, etc.). Others may try to leave devices turned off or specifically travel to destinations that have limited to no connectivity. It is worth noting that digital-free tourism can have very different outcomes depending on the individual, from liberating to anxiety-inducing.[21]

Finally, wellness tourism is one of the most significant trends in recent years. Health is one of the oldest motivations for travel, but modern lifestyles have given rise to a host of mental and physical conditions for which tourists seek various types and degrees of treatments. As with many other products, this may be the focus of a trip or simply one aspect, and destinations are increasingly incorporating this into their messaging. Wellness experiences now range from traditional spa pampering to a type of adventure tourism that is mentally and physically demanding to promote fortitude and soul-searching.[22] This product is clearly connected to slow tourism (e.g., retreats centered around connecting with people and places), digital-free tourism (e.g., digital detoxes), and even medical tourism (e.g., thermographic technology that creates visual heat maps to reveal areas of pain for more targeted treatments).

# Medical and Birth Tourism

Medical tourism describes travel to a different country to access health care facilities and services. There are around fifty countries around the world in which medical tourism is a national industry developed jointly by national health and tourism offices. The range of services provided to medical tourists span dental procedures, joint replacements, cosmetic procedures, fertility treatments, and cardiac surgeries. For the majority of medical tourists, cost is the primary motivation. Low costs for these services mean that, even including travel expenses, tourists pay a fraction of the costs they would be charged at home. Moreover, patients are able to recover from their procedures in comfortable and attractive environments, from Brazil to Malaysia. In some cases, the savings is so significant that health insurance companies may cover the cost of both treatments and the travel to approved destinations. Other motivations for medical tourism include reduced time to receive care, access to services that may not be available in the home country, or the privacy afforded for more sensitive procedures.

While some hospitals may have international accreditation, currently, there is no single international accreditation program for medical tourism, raising concerns about how to ensure quality of care. Recovering patients may be vulnerable to diseases not present in their home environment (e.g. tropical diseases), and additional illnesses can delay healing. There can be further risks of complications associated with long-haul flights as the patients return home. Additionally, medical tourism can lead to shortages of available medical care for potentially lower income residents of the destination country.[23]

Birth tourism (or maternity tourism) is a form of medical tourism. Pregnant women may cross international borders to receive maternity care and give birth for many reasons. However, the potential for birth tourism to provide a legal route to citizenship for not only the newborns but also their families has entangled the topic in contentious immigration debates. The topic occasionally makes its way into national news, for example, with raids on southern California's "maternity hotels" for Chinese birth tourists.[24] In 2020, the US Department of State amended visa regulations in an effort to crack down on birth tourism. The new policy allows consular officers overseas to deny nonimmigrant visa applications for persons they believe will travel to the US for the purpose of giving birth to obtain citizenship for their child.[25] At the time of writing, there are still many questions about how this policy will be carried out.

# Event and MICE Tourism

Event tourism is based on special events as a category of tourism attractions. Special events have long been an attraction for localized markets and have often generated day trips, for example, as people travel to neighboring towns to participate in local festivals. However, as more people are enabled to travel farther distances, this product has exploded. It now encompasses a diverse set of events that are global in nature or highly localized, always in the same location or at various locations, religious or secular, annual or one time only (see box 3.3).

India's Kumbh Mela is the world's largest gathering of people. In 2013, more than 120 million people participated in the riverside Hindu religious festival over the course

## Box 3.3.   Experience: Spain's La Tomatina Festival

*The events that attract tourists come in all forms. La Tomatina Festival happens once a year when 20,000 tourists from around the world come to Buñol, Spain to participate in what is described as the world's largest food fight. Lopa had seen La Tomatina in a Bollywood movie, so when she and her husband decided to go backpacking in Europe, she planned the trip around the festival.*

My husband, Omkar, and I spent six months planning a backpacking trip through Europe. We wanted it to be fun, organic, and authentic. You can imagine our excitement and that beautiful sense of nervousness we felt as we packed our one backpack each and set out on our once-in-a-lifetime journey. We felt totally free and detached from our normal busy lives. This was exactly what we had been looking for. We traveled through Brussels (Belgium), Amsterdam (the Netherlands), Hamburg and Berlin (Germany), and finally Barcelona and Valencia (Spain).

By this time, I was really starting to crave some restaurants from home—mostly Taco Bell. To my surprise there was a Taco Bell in Valencia! When we arrived in the city around 10:30 am, we walked straight to the Taco Bell. Unfortunately, it didn't open until noon and we were forced to wait. We walked to our Airbnb to drop off our things, and about an hour later, we made our way back just in time for the restaurant to open. Omkar was excited that they served french fries, beer, and ice cream there. The meal definitely hit home.

That night, we did our last-minute prep for La Tomatina. Visitors are required to bring passports and printed tickets, which we put in Ziploc bags. We hadn't booked the special bus service since it was kind of pricey at €60 per person. Instead, we found that we could take a couple trains to Buñol for much less, and our festival ticket was just €10 per person. Omkar and I enjoy doing things the hard way sometimes, so we decided to find our own way to Buñol.

Our alarm went off at 4:30 a.m. Omkar wore swim trunks with a shirt, and I put on my swimsuit with shorts and a tank on top. I had gotten a pair of Crocs sandals for the trip since they had a strap around the heel. This was a good decision since Omkar wore some cheap flip-flops that broke halfway through the festival. We got dressed quickly and grabbed the Ziploc bags with our passports, tickets, money, and camera (which was actually double-bagged). We did not take our phones. It was pitch dark when we silently left in the morning, so as not to wake our Airbnb host. On our walk to the train station, we were surprised to see so many people making their way to either the train station or the buses, and mostly everyone was wearing white. We missed the 5:13 a.m. train by three minutes, so we waited for the 5:45 a.m. train.

At the next station, the ticket counter wasn't open yet, so we waited in line behind a couple of people. Within fifteen minutes, the line had grown to a queue of around 200 people. When the doors opened, there was a mad dash for the ticket counter. While we were waiting for the first train to Buñol, the platform filled up with people of all ages wearing white shirts. When the train arrived, there was another mad dash, and within a few minutes all the seats were full. We started chatting with the guy sitting in front of us who was an international student studying in Germany. He had already started on a bottle of sangria. It was 6:40 a.m.!

The train reached Buñol an hour later. We walked towards this small, quaint town on a winding, downhill path until we got to the ticket counter. On the way, there were stalls with people selling beer and sangria. We made our way to the town square with everyone else and waited. While we drank sangria and met new people, the townsfolk threw water on us from the rooftops. At first, we were annoyed, but as it got hotter and hotter we found ourselves waiting for them to throw the next bucket of cool water on us.

The organizers brought in an enormous wooden pole. They covered it in lard, hung a piece of ham at the top, and secured it in the ground. At about 9 a.m., people started attempting to climb the pole. Traditionally, the tomato throwing starts once someone reaches the top and gets the ham. Initially, we thought that this would be a pretty easy task, but it was not, which provided hours of entertainment! Pole climbers began taking chunks of lard from the pole and throwing it into the crowd. A chunk fell on my neck, which grossed me out! People were climbing on top of each other and devising pyramids to reach the top. When they were about three-fourths of the way to the top, some guy took off his clothes and started climbing the pyramid in the nude! I've never seen a group of people disperse that quickly.

Attempts at reaching the ham lasted for two hours. At 11 a.m., a siren went off signaling the start of La Tomatina. By this time, the street was so filled with festivalgoers that we were shoulder to shoulder. Trucks filled with tomatoes arrived. To make room for them, we all had to squeeze onto the sidewalks. The people on the truck started throwing tomatoes at the crowd, and the locals were throwing water from above. It was chaos! The tomatoes would rest on our shoulders because there was no room for them to fall to the ground. We were instructed to crush the tomatoes before throwing so they weren't as hard. Not everyone followed that rule. Omkar got whacked in the face with a tomato so hard he shouted and tried to lean down. When he finally looked up, I could see his left eye already starting to bruise. After that, we put on our sunglasses to save our eyes from any other flying tomatoes.

We were quickly covered with tomato, water, and lard. Ten minutes was about enough for me, but Omkar was having a blast, even with his black eye. After about 50 minutes, we started making our way out. On the way, people would use their sangria/beer glasses to scoop up tomato-and-lard puree and dump it on your head. The event ended shortly after that. As we slowly made our way back to the train state, locals hosed us off. We got hosed off at three different places and were still covered in tomato! Once we finally got on the train, we realized how exhausted we were and slept all the way to our stop. By the time we got to our Airbnb, I went straight into the shower. A 45-minute shower and 3 shampoos later, I was sure I got all the tomato out of my hair—and everywhere else. By the time Omkar got out of the shower, we were starving. We had only eaten croissants in the morning before we left for Buñol. We went back to Taco Bell, and it was delicious. By 6:45 p.m., we were both passed out.

La Tomatina was an amazing experience. We walked away with some great memories, new experiences, and a black eye. Omkar can now proudly say he got his first black eye in Spain in the middle of a fight; he leaves out the part about who—or should I say *what*—gave it to him!

—*Lopa*

of 55 days. At least as many, if not more, were projected for the 2019 event. Secular festivals are based on a range of attractions, from popular culture to local heritage or even local produce. Oktoberfest, held in Munich over a sixteen-day period at the end of September and the beginning of October, is one of the most famous of these events. In 2019, the event drew in 6.3 million visitors who consumed an estimated 7.3 million liters of beer.[26] The Sauerkraut Festival started as a small local festival in Waynesville, Ohio, a town with around three thousand residents, and has grown into a major event attracting approximately 350,000 visitors from all over the country. More than thirty food vendors offer everything from traditional pork and sauerkraut dishes to sauerkraut ice cream.[27]

Major sporting events are some of the most widely known forms of event tourism. In some cases, these are annual events that occur in the same place. As a result, these destinations are often closely associated with the event. For example, the Kentucky Derby is a world-famous thoroughbred horse race held in May at Churchill Downs in Louisville, Kentucky, that attracts approximately 150,000 visitors each year.[28] In other cases, events take place at certain intervals and are hosted at different venues around the world. The Olympic Games are a global event held every two years, alternating between the summer and winter games. Major cities compete to host the games, not only to bring international attention to the city and country but also to bring investment and tourism. Rio de Janeiro, host to the 2016 Summer Olympic Games, received over 11,000 athletes and 500,000 spectators, while half of the world's population watched coverage of the events.[29]

Tourists are also increasingly traveling to places for personal events. This type of event tourism is related to the Visiting Friends and Relatives product discussed below. For example, with dispersed family networks, reunions may be held at vacation destinations to take advantage of the tourism infrastructure as well as maximize the limited time and money many families have available for travel. Likewise, the rise of destination weddings has generated a type of event tourism where the couple, as well as friends and family, travel to a tourism destination for the ceremony as well as related activities.

MICE tourism refers to Meetings, Incentives, Conventions, and Exhibitions. These events have become so important that major cities all over the world have developed extensive convention facilities and actively compete to host organizations' events. These events range from just a few hundred participants to tens of thousands. For example, the 2019 Annual Meeting of the American Association of Geographers (AAG), held in Washington, DC, saw 8,500 participants from seventy-eight countries.[30] The majority of these participants must travel to and stay at the event site, and they may bring partners or children with them. The primary financial gain is often not from the event itself but from expenditures at hotels, restaurants, evening entertainment activities, shopping, and so on. In addition, events can help sustain tourism revenues by bringing in visitors during nonpeak times of the year.[31]

During the COVID-19 outbreak in 2020, events from local festivals to the Tokyo Olympic Games were postponed or canceled. In the meetings sector, many organizations experimented with virtual events. For example, the 2020 Annual Meeting of the AAG, scheduled to be held in Denver, Colorado, was canceled, but organizers coordinated a virtual conference with more than 130 sessions and panels.[32] Those concerned about the impact of travel on climate change used this opportunity to argue that such virtual meetings are, in fact, a viable alternative to large-scale travel for face-to-face meetings. Whether this will have a long-term effect on MICE tourism remains to be seen.

# Visiting Friends and Relatives (VFR) and Roots Tourism

Visiting friends and relatives (VFR) is one of the most common tourism products in which people participate. This product developed significantly in the second half of the twentieth century with increased mobilities. People in many parts of the world experienced greater abilities to move to new locations, within their own country or abroad, based on a variety of opportunities for school, work, or otherwise. This created dispersed networks of family and friends. At the same time, people experienced greater abilities to travel to visit these family and friends. VFR is often domestic tourism; however, this is also one of the largest tourism products for places with high rates of emigration. This form of international tourism links the place of origin, whether it is a small Caribbean island like Trinidad or a large country like India, with the places to which people have migrated.

Still, VFR tourism is a product that generally receives little attention. Many people do not consider VFR trips to be tourism because it may be seen as an obligation rather than a vacation or simply "going home" rather than "going away." Moreover, VFR tourists are often seen as existing "outside" the normal tourism industry. Their patterns of behavior might be determined by different factors than those of other tourists. For example, their destination choice is based on where friends or relatives live as opposed to the attractions of a place. They may be less reliant on the tourism infrastructure. They may stay in and eat at people's homes as opposed to staying in hotels or other accommodations and eating at restaurants. They may rely on their hosts' personal cars rather than renting one or using local transportation, and their hosts may serve as their guides rather than hiring one or taking a tour. Although these tourists may contribute less to the tourism industry at a destination, they are nonetheless contributing to the local economy.

There may be overlap between this product and others in terms of motivations. For example, people may travel to their birthplace for events such as weddings or reunions. In addition, there will be overlap with other products as people participate in tourism activities during the course of their visit with family and friends. Because of the tremendous variations within this product, some researchers have argued for it to be broken down into smaller segments, including domestic and international, short-haul and long-haul, or visiting friends and visiting relatives.[33]

VFR has some overlap with roots tourism. For example, migrants may return to their places of origin to renew their sense of identity that may feel lost the longer they are away. Much of roots tourism involves the descendants of migrants who may travel as tourists to their ancestral lands to meet relatives or to discover the culture of their ancestral society. Roots tourists' itineraries are often personal as they visit the places with which their ancestors were connected as opposed to typical destinations. Some scholars have likened this type of tourism to a secular pilgrimage involving a physical journey to the ancestral place as well as an emotional journey with the search for identity.[34] Particularly for descendants of immigrants, such journeys may ultimately reinforce tourists' ideas of homeland as the place in which they were born and raised.[35]

# Service Tourism

Service tourism involves traveling to another place to volunteer one's time providing aid, assisting with local development, contributing to conservation efforts, participating in research projects, and more. We may not think of service work that takes place outside of the home environment as tourism because of the traditional association of tourism with leisure activities and the pursuit of pleasure. However, interest in volunteering in other places—and companies or organizations providing opportunities to do so—has been growing in recent years. This trend has given rise to the term "voluntourism."

Typically, service tourism involves the movement of tourists from more developed countries to less developed ones. Service tourism destinations may also be impoverished areas of developed countries (e.g., parts of the Appalachian region) or those devastated by a natural disaster (e.g., the hurricane-ravaged Gulf Coast region). Although the potential market for service tourism includes everyone, experiences are often oriented toward young people, particularly students or recent college graduates. Service tourists still pay for their travel, accommodation, and other daily expenses in addition to donating their time and labor. They may actually pay more for their experiences—while receiving fewer services—than they would for a traditional holiday.[36] For-profit companies may additionally require a fee for organizing the experience.

This product is sometimes considered "alternative tourism" in that it presents tourists with an alternative to other products that appeal to traditional touristic motivations. For example, the "alternative spring break" is targeted at students looking for something other than the typical spring break trip that covers all of the S's. Suppliers market these experiences as opportunities for adventurous, sophisticated, and thoughtful travelers, in opposition to indulgent, self-absorbed, and insensitive mass tourists.[37] Thus, tourists interested in this product generally have characteristics in common with drifters and explorers: they wish to visit out-of-the-ordinary places, interact with local people, and have a deeper experience of place. Unlike typical drifters and explorers who create their own experiences, service tourists must rely on a company or organization to create opportunities for service and facilitate their experience. However, this may open more doors for service tourists, allowing them to more effectively penetrate the back regions of a place than even drifters. In particular, these tourists have the opportunity to experience life as it is lived in that place by staying, eating, and socializing with local people.

Proponents of service tourism claim that there are both short- and long-term benefits of such experiences, although most center on tourists (e.g., personal development) rather than local communities. However, arguments cite an increase in intercultural awareness as well as social, political, or environmental consciousness. This can have an impact that lasts beyond the trip if it leads to greater global citizenship and activism to continue to learn about key issues and be involved in promoting change. Critics claim that service tourism not only has few benefits for host communities, but it can actually harm them. At the least, tourists may not have the skills to complete the tasks they are assigned (e.g., construction), and the resulting products may be subpar.[38] At the very worst, children are separated from their families and kept in poor conditions at orphanages to attract visitors (i.e., "orphanage tourism") who not only pay fees but may be motivated to donate additional money.[39]

Categorizing service tourism as good or bad is too simplistic. Instead, scholars propose a spectrum of experiences, including the harmful, the egocentric (i.e., providing for the self-centered interests of typically affluent youth), the harmless (i.e., offering little impact, positive or negative, for the host community), the helpful (i.e., offering constructive assistance), the educational (i.e., providing opportunities for greater cross-cultural understanding), and social action (i.e., leading to long-term involvement).[40] In addition to critically reflecting on one's own motivations, potential service tourists should fully research the organization with which they seek to travel and to consider the potential consequences of their involvement in that place.

# And More

This chapter introduces some of the big categories of tourism products as well as some of the more controversial products. However, tourism is constantly evolving with ever-more specialized products to meet the demands of tourists. The potential for new, sometimes ultra-niche and sometimes just strange tourism products is limitless. Here are just a few more examples.

Astrotourism involves travel to places with unpolluted night skies based on an interest in stars and phenomena such as eclipses and meteor showers. The International Dark-Sky Association defines six categories of dark skies places, from communities where planning actively promotes natural skies to International Dark Sky Sanctuaries as the most remote and darkest places in the world (e.g., Pitcairn Islands in the South Pacific).[41] Although interest in astrotourism has been growing in recent years, concerns include the influx of visitors to remote places that lack the infrastructure for tourism and the impact that more cars (and headlights) will have on night sky quality.

Terminal tourism refers to the practice of visiting airports to watch airplanes as well as experience airports' various amenities including restaurants, microbreweries, wine bars, shopping, entertainment, art exhibits, and more. While terminal tourism is still prohibited at most airports, some airports like Pittsburgh International allowed it (pre-COVID-19), and other airports were also considering such policies to increase revenues. The idea of terminal tourism raises concerns from parking to security to competition for scarce resources like seating.[42] Airplane enthusiasts' demand for terminal tourism might be better suited to small airport restaurants, already frequented by pilots looking for a "$100 hamburger" (referring to the cost of the trip as opposed to the cost of the meal), which is often just an excuse to fly.

# Conclusion

The primary "products" of tourism are not tangible goods but a set of wide-ranging experiences. These experiences can be grouped into large categories, like nature tourism and culture tourism, but they can also be subdivided into tourism products that reflect more specific interests, activities, or experiences (e.g., golf tourism as a part of summer sport tourism). Although each category was addressed only briefly, this overview contributes to our broad understanding of demands in tourism and how those demands are met in the supply side. It also provides the necessary context for discussions of the geographic foundation for and the effects of tourism, since tourism products rely on different resources and have varied effects.

# Key Terms

- ecotourism
- tourism products

# Notes

1. Rose Kisia Omondi and Chris Ryan, "Sex Tourism: Romantic Safaris, Prayers and Witchcraft at the Kenyan Coast," *Tourism Management* 58 (2017), 217.

2. Egle Gerulaityte, "Can #MeToo Help Stop Sex Tourism?" *Equality Now*, accessed March 10, 2020. https://www.equalitynow.org/can_metoo_help_stop_sex_tourism?locale=en.

3. Office of the High Commissioner for Human Rights, "Combatting Child Sex Tourism," April 10, 2013, accessed March 10, 2020, https://www.ohchr.org/EN/NewsEvents/Pages/ChildsexTourism.aspx.

4. Exchange Initiative, "About TraffickCam," accessed March 10, 2020, https://traffickcam.com/about.

5. Honggang Xu and Tian Ye, "Tourist Experience in Lijiang—The Capital of Yanyu," *Journal of China Tourism Research* 12, no. 1 (2016): 8.

6. Martin Oppermann, "Sex Tourism," *Annals of Tourism Research* 26, no. 2 (1999): 256.

7. United Nations Educational, Scientific, and Cultural Organization, "The Criteria for Selection," accessed March 11, 2020, https://whc.unesco.org/en/criteria/.

8. Athena H. N. Mak, Margaret Lumbers, and Anita Eves, "Globalisation and Food Consumption in Tourism," *Annals of Tourism Research* 39, no. 1 (2012): 184.

9. Barbara Santich, "The Study of Gastronomy and Its Relevance to Hospitality Education and Training," *Hospitality Management* 23 (2004):20.

10. World Travel Awards, "2019 Winners—World Travel Awards," accessed March 11, 2020, https://www.worldtravelawards.com/winners/2019.

11. Natan Uriely and Yniv Belhassen, "Drugs and Tourists' Experiences," *Journal of Travel Research* 43 (2005): 239, 242–3.

12. Winston Ross, "Holland's New Marijuana Laws Are Changing Old Amsterdam," *Newsweek*, February 22, 2015, accessed March 11, 2020, https://www.newsweek.com/marijuana-and-old-amsterdam-308218.

13. Marlene Dobkin deRios, "Drug Tourism in the Amazon," *Anthropology of Consciousness* 5, no. 1 (1994): 18.

14. Max Opray, "Tourist boom for ayahuasca a mixed blessing for Amazon," *The Guardian*, January 24, 2017, accessed March 11, 2020, https://www.theguardian.com/sustainable-business/2017/jan/24/tourist-boom-peru-ayahuasca-drink-amazon-spirituality-healing.

15. Julie Weed, "Book Your 'Bud and Breakfast', Marijuana Tourism Is Growing in Colorado and Washington," *Forbes,* March 17, 2015, accessed March 11, 2020, https://www.forbes.com/sites/julieweed/2015/03/17/book-your-bud-and-breakfast-marijuana-tourism-is-growing-in-colorado-and-washington/#33a7884864d4.

16. Philip Stone and Richard Sharpley, "Consuming Dark Tourism: A Thanatological Perspective," *Annals of Tourism Research* 35, no. 2 (2008): 574.

17. Philip R. Stone, "A Dark Tourism Spectrum: Towards a Typology of Death and Macabre Related Tourist Sites, Attractions and Exhibitions," *Tourism* 54, no. 2 (2006): 145–60.

18. Myriam Janse-Verbeke and Wanda George, "Reflections on the Great War Centenary: From Warscapes to Memoryscapes in 100 Years," in *Tourism and War*, ed. Richard Butler and Wantanee Suntikul (London: Routledge, 2013), 273–5.

19. Derek H. Alderman, "Surrogation and the Politics of Remembering Slavery in Savannah, Georgia (USA)," *Journal of Historical Geography*, 36 (2010): 90.

20. Simone Fullagar, Erica Wilson, and Kevin Markwel, "Starting Slow: Thinking Through Slow Mobilities and Experiences," in *Slow Tourism: Experiences and Mobilities*, eds. Simone Fullagar, Kevin Markwell, and Erica Wilson (Bristol: Channel View Publications, 2012), 3–5

21. Wenjie Cai, Brad McKenna, and Lena Waizenegger, "Turning it Off: Emotions in Digital-Free Travel," *Journal of Travel Research*, https://doi.org/10.1177/0047287519868314.

22. Daisy Finer, "Biomarkers, Sweat Lodges, and Shamans: Today's Wellness Retreats Go Far Beyond a Detox," *Condé Nast Traveler*, August 26, 2019, accessed March 16, 2020. https://www.cntraveler.com/story/whats-next-for-destination-spas-and-wellness-retreats.

23. Sukanya Banerjee, Siddhartha Sankar Nath, Nilanjan Dey, and Hjime Eto, "Global Medial Tourism: A Review," in *Medical Tourism: Breakthroughs in Research and Practice* (Hershey, PA: IGI Global, 2018), 2–3.

24. Sean H. Wang, "Fetal Citizens? Birthright Citizenship, Reproductive Futurism, and the 'Panic' over Chinese Birth Tourism in Southern California," *Environment and Planning D: Society and Space*, 35, 2 (2017): 265.

25. United States Department of State, "Birth Tourism Update," January 23, 2020, accessed March 12, 2020, https://travel.state.gov/content/travel/en/News/visas-news/20200123_birth-tourism-update.html.

26. Oktoberfest, "The Official Oktoberfest Review 2019," accessed March 11, 2020, https://www.oktoberfest.de/en/magazine/oktoberfest-news/2019/the-official-oktoberfest-review-2019.

27. Ohio Sauerkraut Festival, "About," accessed March 11, 2020, https://sauerkrautfestival.waynesvilleohio.com/about/history-of-the-sauerkraut-festival-4/.

28. Churchill Downs Incorporated, "What to Expect at the Kentucky Derby," accessed March 11, 2020, https://www.kentuckyderby.com/visit/what-to-expect.

29. The International Olympic Committee, "How Do We Know that Rio 2016 Was a Success," accessed March 11, 2020, https://www.olympic.org/news/how-do-we-know-that-rio-2016-was-a-success.

30. American Association of Geographers, "AAG 2019 Annual Meeting—Washington, DC," accessed March 11, 2020, https://www2.aag.org/aagannualmeeting/AAGAnnualMeeting/AAG2019DC.aspx.

31. Calvin Jones and ShiNa Li, "The Economic Importance of Meetings and Conferences: A Satellite Account Approach," *Annals of Tourism Research* 52 (2015): 117.

32. American Association of Geographers, "AAG to Facilitate Virtual Meeting," accessed March 23, 2020, https://www2.aag.org/aagannualmeeting/.

33. Gianna Moscardo, Philip Pearce, Alastair Morrison, David Green, and Joseph T. O'Leary, "Developing a Typology for Understanding Visiting Friends and Relatives Markets," *Journal of Travel Research* 38, no. 3 (2000): 251–9.

34. Paul Basu, "Route Metaphors of 'Roots-Tourism' in the Scottish Highland Diaspora," in *Reframing Pilgrimage: Cultures in Motion*, eds. Simon Coleman and John Eade (London: Routledge, 2004), 155–8.

35. Naho Maruyama and Amanda Stronza, "Roots Tourism of Chinese Americans," Ethnology, 49, 1 (2010): 24.

36. Stephen Wearing, *Volunteer Tourism: Experiences That Make a Difference* (Wallingford, UK: CABI, 2001), 2.

37. Keri Vacanti Brondo, "The Spectacle of Saving: Conservation Voluntourism and the New Neoliberal Economy on Utila, Honduras," *Journal of Sustainable Tourism* 23, no. 10 (2015): 1407.

38. Brondo, "The Spectacle of Saving," 1407.

39. Joseph M. Cheer, Leigh Mathews, Kathryn E. van Doore, and Karen Flanagan, *Modern Day Slavery and Orphanage Tourism* (Oxfordshire: CABI, 2020), xv.

40. Regina Scheyvens, *Tourism and Poverty* (New York: Routledge, 2011), 98.

41. International Darky-Sky Association, "International Dark Sky Places," accessed March 12, 2020, https://www.darksky.org/our-work/conservation/idsp/.

42. Audrey Farnsworth, "No One Wants to Hang Out at an Airport—So Stop Trying to Make it a Thing," *Fodor's Travel*, September 4, 2019, accessed March 11, 2020, https://www.fodors.com/news/airlines/no-one-wants-to-hang-out-an-airport-so-stop-trying-to-make-it-a-thing.

# Part II

# THE GEOGRAPHIC FOUNDATION OF TOURISM

Tourism is not simply a product of the modern world. People have been traveling for various reasons since ancient times. However, patterns of tourism have historically been spatially concentrated. Certain places became destinations for tourists, because those places were accessible based on the transportation systems available at the time and because they possessed the physical and/or cultural resources that were valued by people in the principal tourist-generating societies during that period. Today, we see the dynamic reshaping of tourism patterns. Places all over the world are more accessible than ever, and new tourist markets are demanding different types of experiences. Trying to understand these ever-changing patterns in places with widely varied circumstances can seem overwhelming. Yet the framework of geography—with its diverse set of topical branches across both physical and human geography—provides us with the means of exploring all of these issues.

This section begins our examination of tourism through the topical branches of geography. In particular, these chapters consider the geographic foundation of tourism. Chapter 4 discusses the historical geography of tourism. While we cannot make a comprehensive study of the historical geography of tourism in this introductory text, this chapter examines some of the geographic factors that contributed to the development of the modern tourism industry and some of the factors that presented challenges in this process. Chapter 5 discusses the transport geography of tourism. It examines the components of the transport system and some of the fundamental issues in tourism transport. Chapter 6 discusses the physical geography of tourism. This chapter illustrates how we can use the tools and concepts of branches in physical geography to understand the physical resources that provide the basis for tourism at destinations around the world and the physical factors that present a barrier to tourism. Finally, Chapter 7 discusses the human geography of tourism. It draws on the tools and concepts in some of human geography's most prominent branches to understand the human resources used in tourism, as well as human-created barriers.

# CHAPTER 4

# The Historical Geography of Tourism

Some of us may daydream about hopping in our car and driving across the American West, cruising the Caribbean for a few days, or getting on a plane and flying to New Zealand. Of course, we may never take these trips, for any number of reasons. But it is easy for us to imagine because we *can* do these things, which is something we often take for granted. If we look back, say, two hundred years, it is an entirely different story. At that time, the first expeditions across the West had only just been completed by explorers like Lewis and Clark. The round-trip journey took over two years of difficult travel on foot, on horseback, and in small boats. A sailing trip to and around the Caribbean would take many months, dependent on wind and weather conditions. It could be a dangerous journey, with threats of hurricanes, tropical diseases, slave revolts, pirate attacks, or naval battles. Traveling to New Zealand would have been virtually unthinkable for an American.

Nevertheless, tourism was already a well-established phenomenon in the world. Clearly there are significant differences between this early tourism and today, but there are surprising parallels as well. Thinking about the past is not just a matter of idle curiosity; it is essential if we are to truly understand modern tourism in all of its complexity.

**Historical geography** is a topical branch of geography. Like the other branches, historical geography uses the framework of geography to examine topics in and that contribute to the study of a particular field—in this case, history. Therefore, we can consider historical geography to be the study of the geography and geographic conditions of past periods. Yet, historical geography has another vital role to play. Geography is a means of understanding the world. However, as we examine current patterns and circumstances of places, we cannot truly understand them if we do not understand how they came to be. Thus, historical geography can also be used to examine the processes of change that have taken place over time so that we might better understand the geography of the present. Perhaps taken a step further, if we understand this evolution over time, we might be able to project the geography of the future. As such, historical geography has a part to play in all geography, including the geography of tourism.

Research in tourism studies generally focuses on contemporary issues, and tourism has typically been a neglected topic in historical research. Likewise, there has been little relationship between tourism geography and historical geography, despite the fact that the latter framework clearly has potential to contribute to both the study of tourism in past periods and the evolution of tourism over time. Consequently, historical tourism research has been somewhat uneven, focusing on tourism during specific time periods or in particular places. Yet, the evolution of tourism as a mass phenomenon is considered one of the most significant social developments in recent history. The importance of studying the past to understand the factors that allowed the development of tourism, and the origins of many of the patterns we see today, should be clear.

This chapter continues to lay the foundation for our discussion of the geography of tourism. It provides an overview of tourism in key past periods and the development of the modern tourism industry. The framework of geography can help us understand the factors that allowed this development to take place. We will consider some of these factors here so that we may begin to develop an appreciation for broad patterns and trends in tourism; however, we will continue to examine these issues as they pertain to the topical branches discussed in the following chapters.

# Premodern Travel

Travel has taken place throughout human history, leading some scholars to argue that we can trace this history back to the Sumerians some six thousand years ago.[1] Most scholars do not go back so far, as little is known about this period. Some scholars point to evidence found in the ancient Mediterranean world among the Greek and Roman civilizations as some of the earliest examples of tourism. Others consider health-related travel and religious pilgrimages as important predecessors of tourism. There are often few sources of data available that could afford us insight into patterns of travel and tourism in these premodern time periods. Additionally, little research has focused on these patterns in non-European contexts.[2] For example, there is comparatively little English-language literature on travel within Asian cultures, including China, Japan, and India, although these cultures have a rich legacy of travel writing. Given this context, the following discussion is necessarily selective.

## ROMAN TOURISTS

Although examples of travel for health, culture, or even pleasure may be found in other ancient civilizations, such as Greece, the Romans may be considered the first true tourists based on a number of parallels with later—even modern—eras of tourism. We do not have the benefit of historical sources, such as letters and diaries, to provide in-depth perspectives on tourists and their activities during this era; however, information can be obtained from archaeological evidence and the writings of scholars and social commentators that have survived the passage of time.

There were several key factors that laid the foundation for tourism in the Roman Empire. One of the most important was the two-hundred-year long period of peace and stability that the empire enjoyed (called the Pax Romana—from the end of the first century BCE to the end of the second century CE), which is typically a precondition for tourism. This helped create a prosperous society that was able to develop an interest in traveling to other places for health or pleasure without fear of having to cross hostile territory.[3]

The Roman Empire also had a well-developed transportation infrastructure. This extensive network of paved roads was built for military purposes and to connect the empire's vast land area, as well as providing the basis for commercial trade. Increased patterns of movement within the empire also generated new developments in public transportation, with organized relays of horses at five- or six-mile intervals, by which a person could travel up to 100 miles per day. Likewise, inns were established along the roads to accommodate traveling government officials and merchants. This infrastructure also facilitated travel for pleasure.[4]

The Romans had various motivations for travel, many of which had a distinctly practical basis. For example, one motivation was military tourism. Soldiers had explicit reasons for traveling, but these expeditions could also be combined with pleasure. Women and children might be allowed to travel with husbands and fathers, and families could visit attractions along the way. The Romans had developed an appreciation for leisure and entertainment activities. This meant that at least part of the population had free time outside of work and necessary daily chores and that they enjoyed celebrations that were distinct from religious rituals or ceremonies.

Health tourism was also widely practiced among the Romans. Some invalids traveled to places with distinct physical properties, such as mineral waters or hot springs, that would be beneficial to those with certain health conditions. Perhaps more significantly, people traveled to escape places with conditions that would be detrimental to their health. All but the poorest citizens left Rome during the summer due to extreme heat and the rampant spread of disease among the crowded urban population. These middle- and upper-class citizens would retreat to the surrounding countryside in lower altitudes of mountainous regions, where temperatures would be cooler and the air fresher.[5] Similarly, seaside resorts in the coastal region between Rome and Naples became popular destinations for those seeking to get away from the city. These fashionable resorts replicated the best parts of social life from Rome and offered entertainments including baths, dining, concerts and theater performances, and even gladiator games.[6]

Only a few privileged groups had the time and resources to be able to travel farther afield in the Mediterranean region. This included the most affluent families, high-ranking government officials, and young men from the upper class in the process of completing their education. Cultural attractions such as temples and ancient monuments formed the basis of many destinations. Most cities had temples that not only represented a god or goddess but also served the function of museum with collections of statues, paintings, and artifacts. The list of the Seven Wonders of the World created some of the most sought-after destinations and formed the basis for an early version of the Grand Tour. This was a tourist itinerary, typically through Greece, Asia Minor, and Egypt, comprising the most important sights. Egypt, in particular, boasted of wonders such as the Pyramids of Giza and the Lighthouse of Alexandria, as well as landscapes and a culture that would have seemed different and exotic to Roman tourists. In contrast, the mountainous landscapes of the Alps were generally avoided, as they were considered barriers to travel rather than attractions.[7]

Roman tourism has been described as being "typically modern" and having "nearly all of the trappings of its late-twentieth century counterpart."[8] Roman tourists visited many of the same sites popular among tourists today. They had the benefit of guidebooks to instruct them on what they were to see; however, they had to read about the sites before their travels because the books were expensive, large, heavy, leather-bound volumes of papyrus sheets. During the course of their travels, Roman tourists would hire guides. To remember their experiences, they would sketch the scenes they saw or purchase souvenirs, such as paintings, artifacts, or miniature replicas of statues or monuments.[9]

## PILGRIMS

Despite the apparent familiarity of the type of tourism seen during the Pax Romana, it was not to last. The collapse of the Roman Empire brought an end to these patterns. The transportation infrastructure fell into disrepair, and traveling became a dangerous proposition with the poor condition of roads, closed inns, and various threats of wild animals, thieves, and hostile territories. As such, there was little thought of traveling for pleasure. Only the most adventurous, the most determined, or those who absolutely had to would risk travel.

One of the most common forms of travel in Europe during the Middle Ages (from the fifth to the fifteenth centuries) was undertaken by devout individuals with strongly held spiritual beliefs. Some of the best-known and frequently visited shrines included Santiago de Compostela in Spain (as early as the ninth century) and Canterbury in England (from the twelfth century). Pilgrimages were also undertaken to the Holy Land, although this was a much more difficult, time-consuming, expensive, and dangerous journey for those traveling from Europe.[10] At this time, travel for health reasons became intertwined with religious pilgrimages. The Roman Catholic Church had an extremely powerful influence over life during the Middle Ages, and people increasingly turned to faith healing. They traveled to shrines with the express purpose of appealing to the patron saint for miraculous cures. Given the generally poor living conditions during this period, with high rates of malnutrition and disease, this became a relatively common practice.[11]

Pilgrimages have taken place in Asian societies over an even greater scope of time than in Europe.[12] Buddhist monks would often travel to learn from renowned teachers. Particularly between the fifth and eighth centuries, there was significant religious traffic between India and China. Pilgrimages were long, typically spanning a period of years, and overland journeys involved crossing much difficult terrain.[13] For example, over the course of eighteen years (627–45), the Buddhist pilgrim Xuanzang traveled approximately 16,000 miles through modern-day Kyrgyzstan, Kazakhstan, Uzbekistan, Afghanistan, Pakistan, Kashmir, and India and returned to China with over 600 religious texts.[14] Likewise, Indian and subsequently Japanese monks traveled to China.

In the seventh century, the Hajj was established as one of the five pillars of Islam. Caravan routes to Mecca were established from several origins, including Kufa (Iraq), Damascus (Syria), and Cairo (Egypt). Starting in the eighth century, the ruling Abbasids, who made multiple pilgrimages themselves, subsidized improvements to the 900-mile pilgrim route from Kufa. These included wells, rest stations, milestones, fire beacons, and forts. Although the journey became easier, pilgrims were still vulnerable to predatory nomads.[15] Al-Abdari, an educated religious scholar and poet, left a narrative of his pilgrimage to Mecca and Medina (1289–90) that describes his journey through North Africa into the Arabian Peninsula.[16]

## EXPLORERS AND TRAVELERS

Exploration provided another significant motivation for travel during this era. Explorers' written accounts and detailed descriptions of peoples and places encountered offer some of the most significant records of premodern travel. These writings range from Gerald of Wales' *Topographia Hibernica*, first published in 1188 based on the author's journey to Ireland, to what is thought to be the sole surviving anonymously written journal from Vasco da Gama's journey to India (1497–9).

Exploration has often been associated with the European age of expansion and colonization, but people all over the world have had a curiosity about and a desire to experience other places. Exploration flourished during the Ming dynasty (1368–1644) in China. In the early years of the dynasty, Zheng He made seven large-scale, officially sponsored overseas journeys that extended as far as the eastern coast of Africa. Although these costly expeditions were short lived, exploration within China continued. Its size and diversity in both landscapes and people offered ample opportunities for journeys, and explorers sought ever more remote regions. Many of these explorers were officials who held posts throughout the country, but others came from wealthy backgrounds and were able to travel without the need for an official position.[17] For example, Xu Xiake is considered one of the greatest Chinese travelers and a prolific travel writer. From 1609 to 1636, he traveled extensively throughout China, primarily on foot, with a particular interest in physical geography research.[18]

One of the best known African travelers was Ibn Battuta. He was a North African Muslim scholar who began his travels with a pilgrimage to Mecca at the age of twenty-one. After that, he continued to both visit famous places and to hold official positions. From 1325 to 1354, Ibn Battuta traveled through forty-five modern-day nations in Africa and Asia. Upon his return to Morocco, dictations of his experiences produced more than twenty-five manuscripts.[19] Iraqi priest Ilyas Hanna al-Mawsuli began his journey to Europe in 1668. He then obtained a permit from the Spanish king to travel to South America. Although little is known about who he was, his manner of travel (e.g., a private cabin while crossing the Atlantic, litters and coaches while traveling in Peru, an entourage of slaves, servants, and dogs) indicates that he was wealthy or well sponsored. Based on his account, al-Mawsuli followed the same general route and visited the same "attractions" as other travelers to the region at that time.[20]

# The Evolution of Modern Tourism

The origin of tourism is a subject of debate among scholars. This is partially attributed to the lack of a clear definition and what motivations and/or activities should (or should not) be considered tourism. The beginning of modern tourism development is commonly placed in eighteenth-century Western Europe. The verb *tour* had come into usage in the English language in the seventeenth century, and by the eighteenth century, the noun *tourist* had developed to describe those who traveled, typically for pleasure or culture.[21] At this time, tourism became a popular activity among the elite upper classes who had sufficient disposable income and leisure time. In particular, Britain is cited as not only one of the first nations to develop tourism but also one of the largest sources of tourists during this early era. With new innovations in transportation, tourism was increasingly expanded to the middle classes as well. As a result, the greatest quantity of research has focused on the emergence and expansion of tourism that started in Europe in the eighteenth century and accelerated throughout the nineteenth and twentieth centuries.

## THE GRAND TOUR

The European Grand Tour represents a key component in the evolution of tourism. A variation of the Grand Tour took place as early as the Elizabethan era in the sixteenth century and evolved into the traditional Grand Tour era from the mid seventeenth century through the eighteenth century. This was originally intended to provide young British men from the aristocratic class with a classical education. Often traveling with tutors, they would visit the cultural centers of Renaissance Europe and sites of classic antiquity. Italy, above all, was the focal point of such a tour, with destinations such as Venice, Florence, Rome, and Naples.[22]

The average length of the Grand Tour was forty months, and the journey often followed a designated route through France, Italy, Germany, Switzerland, and/or the Low Countries (modern Belgium, the Netherlands, and Luxembourg). Few tourists strayed from this route into other areas. Particularly early in this era, traveling conditions were difficult, so the route was distinctly shaped by geographic conditions and available transportation technologies. As with Roman tourism, the Alps were considered a barrier to be crossed en route to the highlighted destinations rather than an attraction in themselves. A widespread, efficient network of transportation that met the needs of these tourists was slow to develop. Likewise, there were few accommodations. Although some of the main cities on the tour developed hotels, these Grand Tourists generally had to use the same inns, hostels, and post houses as other travelers.[23]

Toward the end of the eighteenth century, the Grand Tour began to experience a number of changes. The demographics of the Grand Tourists steadily expanded to include aristocrats from other Northern European countries as well as the sons of the growing class of affluent but not titled British families. The territory of the tour expanded, as tourists searched for newer and more exclusive destinations, such as Greece, Portugal, and Turkey. The focus of the Grand Tour also began to shift. Education continued to play a role, but sightseeing gained in importance. Tourists visited archaeological sites, museums, and art galleries, and they attended concerts and theater performances. Socialization and the development of social contact with others in the same class at assemblies and balls also came to be a part of the Grand Tour. Given the increasing importance of these latter activities, some critics argued that the Grand Tour had become nothing more than the pursuit of pleasure.[24]

The onset of the French Revolution in 1789, followed by the conflict surrounding the Napoleonic Wars, effectively halted Continental travel. While this interval brought a boost in British domestic travel, it also created a pent-up demand for experiences abroad. Napoleon's defeat at Waterloo and the Second Treaty of Paris in 1815 created a host of new opportunities for international travel. Many of the changes to the Grand Tour that had begun before the Napoleonic Wars continued after travel resumed. This effectively ended the Grand Tour era and ushered in a new era of international tourism in the nineteenth century in which more people participated than ever before (box 4.1).

In this era, more adults and families began to travel. This expanded females' participation in travel, a trend that would continue with an increasingly organized tourism infrastructure. Members of the middle class also began to participate, which generated further changes in the nature of the experience. Middle-class tourists did not have the advantage of invitations from local nobility, so they had to rely on the developing tourism infrastructure (e.g., hotels). They were less likely to travel with servants and household staff, which created a demand for local serving staff at the places of destination. These tourists had less time and money available to travel, so before the middle of the nineteenth century, the average length of a European tour had been reduced to four months. As tourists had less time to spend at the destination, seeing

---

## Box 4.1.  In-Depth: The Rise of Organized Mass Tourism and the End of an Era

Thomas Cook (1808–92) is often referred to as the father of modern organized mass tourism because of the role he and his company played in organizing tourism services that made tourism easier and more accessible to more people.[a] Cook was a bookseller and a Baptist preacher who got his start by organizing a train trip for 570 people to attend a temperance meeting in 1841 England. This event has been described as the beginning of an era.[b] Cook began to organize excursions for other groups, which quickly evolved into organizing low-cost pleasure trips primarily utilizing rail transport and the growing accommodation industry. Within a few years, Cook's Tours had opened up new opportunities for tourism among the working classes, as well as for females traveling without male companions. Travel by rail was quick, cheap, and generally considered safe. The company preplanned all aspects of the trip. The tourists did not have to know anyone at the destination, and they did not have to worry about whether the accommodations would be suitable.

Based on the existing popularity of seaside resorts, they were one of the key destinations for Cook's Tours. However, as preferences changed, and demands for new experiences arose, Cook's Tours were responsive. The company offered trips to new destinations in England, such as the Lake District, as well as new destinations in Wales, Scotland, and Ireland. These destinations were quickly followed by Continental tours. By the middle of the 1850s, Cook was organizing tours in France and Germany, followed by Switzerland and Italy. Thus, a new generation and a new class of tourists could experience many of the same places as the Grand Tour, albeit on a far more compressed time frame and with ever more of the comforts of home.[c] A century later, Thomas Cook & Son Ltd. remained at the forefront of organized mass tourism when the company launched a new type of packaged trip. Instead of traveling by chartered rail transport, this trip was based on chartered air transport. The company began with trips from Britain to Corsica and continued to expand into new destinations.[d]

Thomas Cook was an innovator, but his railway excursion was not the first of its kind nor was his company the only one providing similar services. One tourism historian acknowledged, "[Cook] did not do it all himself. He had competitors—and he had the good sense to learn from them. But the firm he established outlived nearly all its British rivals."[e] Indeed, the endurance of the company bearing his name has played a role in maintaining his legacy. Thomas Cook was one of the oldest travel companies in the world and one of the most widely recognized travel brands. They served an estimated nineteen million tourists a year who traveled to more than eighty destinations worldwide.[f]

The end of the era came abruptly on September 23, 2019, when the Thomas Cook Group announced that it was ceasing all operations effective immediately. The action left an estimated 600,000 tourists stranded around the world. The British government undertook a massive effort—the largest peacetime repatriation in the country's history—to bring home 150,000 of its citizens. Others were forced to pay high prices to purchase new return plane tickets. Countless more tourists had their upcoming vacation plans canceled. Furthermore, more than twenty thousand employees lost their jobs, and destinations faced the potential collapse of their tourism industries. In the case of the Canary and Balearic Islands, 3.2 million of the 3.6 million annual international visitors arrived on planes owned or chartered by Thomas Cook.[g]

This news generated considerable discussion about what went wrong. Some of the factors involved in the collapse were beyond the company's control, including political unrest in some of its popular destinations such as Turkey and Egypt, the 2018 summer heat wave that reduced demand for warm-weather winter trips, and the uncertainty of the Brexit process that kept many UK tourists from booking European trips. However, one of the most significant factors was that the one-time innovator failed to adapt. As travel booking moved online, the company continued to generate most of its business from nearly 600 physical stores. Peer-to-peer accommodations brought about a shift in the way many people traveled, and Millennial tourists were simply less interested in package holidays.[h]

Tourism is changing rapidly. Thus, while it is valuable to understand the processes of change that have taken place over time, tourism stakeholders cannot lose sight of present patterns and future directions.

*Discussion topic*: What do you think was the most significant development of Cook's Tours in the evolution of modern tourism? What do you think the Thomas Cook Groups could have done to stay relevant in the present market?

---

[a] Freya Higgins-Desbiolles, "More than an 'Industry': The Forgotten Power of Tourism as a Social Force," *Tourism Management* 27 (2006): 1193.

[b] Fred Inglis, *The Delicious History of the Holiday* (London: Routledge, 2000), 47.

[c] Orvar Löfgren, *On Holiday: A History of Vacationing* (Berkeley: University of California Press, 1999): 163; Jack Simmons, "Railways, Hotels, and Tourism in Great Britain 1839–1914," *Journal of Contemporary History* 19 (1984): 208.

[d] Gareth Shaw and Allan M. Williams, *Critical Issues in Tourism: A Geographical Perspective* (Malden, MA: Blackwell Publishing, 2002), 227.

[e] Jack Simmons, "Thomas Cook of Leicester," *The Leicestershire Archeological and Historical Society, Transactions* 49 (1973), 31.

[f] Shannon Sims, "How Could Travel Giant Thomas Cook Fail?" *The New York Times*, September 23, 2019, accessed March 26, 2020, https://www.nytimes.com/2019/09/23/travel/why-thomas-cook-travel-collapsed.html.

[g] Ceylan Yeginsu and Michael Wolgelenter, "Thomas Cook Travel Company Collapses, Stranding Thousands," *The New York Times*, September 23, 2019, accessed March 26, 2020, https://www.nytimes.com/2019/09/23/travel/thomas-cook-airline-collapse.html.

[h] Sims, "How Could Travel Giant Thomas Cook Fail?"

the sights took precedence over learning about them. Many continued to follow the same route and visit the same cities for their well-known attractions.[25]

During this same period in the nineteenth century, European tourists also began to extend their reach into new regions. Explorers and travelers had already been in Africa, Asia, and the Americas, but the new generations of tourists visited these places for pleasure. Transatlantic travel had become safer following the end of the Napoleonic Wars, as well as easier and faster with the development of steamships. Lingering concerns, however, focused on the hazards of tropical storms and the fear of diseases such as yellow fever and malaria. Scholars have argued that this wave of European tourists arriving in other parts of the world was a new form of colonialism. Soon after the arrival of the first tourists at a destination, the subsequent numbers of tourists at that destination steadily increased. On one hand, this had the positive effect of creating a demand for new businesses to cater to the needs of these tourists. On the other hand, local residents and even other tourist groups complained about negative effects ranging from increased use of European languages to higher costs of living. Such debates about the growth of tourism and the nature of its effects occurred in countless places throughout the world and continues to this day.

European Grand Tour travel is significant in that it is the first era of tourism in which there is considerable source material for analysis.[26] In that era and since, a tremendous number of documents—including tourists' personal diaries, letters, and published narratives, as well as travel company literature and promotions—were produced that provide us with insights into why people traveled, where they went, how they got there, and what their experiences were. We do not always have access to this same type of data about travel in other periods or places. Even the information that we do have is limited in perspective. Most of the sources from the Grand Tour era come from tourists. Considerably less data are available from a supply-side perspective, including from individuals providing services to these tourists.

## RESORT TOURISM

The development of spas and resorts also played a role in the evolution of modern tourism. Health had long been a primary motivator for travel. Physicians put forth many theories about which environments possessed the best curative properties for various conditions, most notably tuberculosis. Spas—places usually possessing mineral springs—had been used intermittently over time as destinations for invalids seeking cures for different ailments. The role of faith healing during the medieval era led to a decline in early spas, but by the seventeenth century these places experienced a resurgence with visits from members of royal and noble families. There was a growing interest in balneotherapy, or water therapy, and physicians widely promoted cures from either drinking or bathing in mineral waters. Thus, spas had the dual benefit of possessing health-giving properties and providing an escape from the poor environmental conditions of the increasingly polluted industrial cities. As a result, by the eighteenth century, English spas such as Bath and Tunbridge Wells had become immensely popular.[27]

Although spas were initially developed for those seeking cures, and in some cases prevention, they soon became known as fashionable and exclusive resorts. As the socialization function became more important, resorts built promenades and assembly rooms and offered theater performances, concerts, dances, receptions, card parties, and gambling. Eventually, "seasons" developed in which the upper classes would converge on spa towns for the entertainment and to both see and be seen.[28]

The earliest English resorts were located around mineral springs in areas that were inland and relatively accessible to London. At this time, the coast and the sea were seen as dangerous places to be avoided if possible. It was a wild landscape full of hazards, from unpredictable weather to pirates and smugglers. However, by the late eighteenth century, several factors contributed to a change in attitudes and allowed new spa resorts to emerge. First, a new appreciation began to develop for rugged natural scenery and the forces of nature that had formerly generated fear. Second, physicians began to advocate the health advantages of the seaside, including taking brisk walks along the beach and sea bathing. Sea bathing was a carefully regulated activity, typically undertaken with the aid of bathing machines. These wooden structures allowed the bather to be gradually immersed in the water safely and privately, the latter being especially important for ladies.[29]

Initially, seaside spas provided a complement to inland resorts. Visits to the seaside would take place at different times of the year than the social season at the fashionable inland destinations. However, the seaside spas were increasingly developed into resorts with the same comforts and entertainments and thus started to compete with inland resorts for status and clientele. As with the inland resorts, the most successful spas, such as Brighton, were those that were relatively accessible from London. Transportation by stagecoach often made farther resorts impractical because this mode was expensive, and poor roads made travel both slow and uncomfortable.[30]

The development of seaside spas changed the nature of the coastline, which had once been characterized by scattered fishing villages.[31] These resort towns began to be connected by new modes of transportation, including steamships and passenger trains. Such innovations shortened travel time and reduced the expense of travel, allowing more people from the middle classes to make the trip. This brought further changes in the nature of the resorts. The earlier, upper-class tourists rented houses for the season and established a temporary residence complete with its own serving staff.[32] The increase in middle-class tourists, who spent shorter amounts of time at the destination, created a demand for accommodation facilities such as hotels and boardinghouses.

By the second half of the nineteenth century, faster and more reliable rail service allowed day trips to the seaside. This meant that even the working classes, who were not able to get away for extended periods of time or did not have the money to stay in a hotel, were also able to enjoy the resorts. By this time, less emphasis was placed on curing illnesses and more on promoting well-being. Sea bathing with the use of expensive bathing machines fell out of favor, and tourists were encouraged to get out and enjoy the fresh sea air. Perhaps the most important component of a seaside holiday was the pursuit of pleasure, as these tourists sought to emulate the life of leisure displayed by the upper classes—at least for a short time.[33]

Once these resorts were seen as less exclusive, the upper class, followed by the middle class, began looking for new destinations, often abroad. The same transportation innovations that made resorts at home more accessible also helped open up new resorts across Europe. These tourists particularly looked to the new winter resorts developing in the Mediterranean region, such as the Côte d'Azur in France. As with coastal resorts in England, these areas were previously underutilized for tourism. However, with the development of spa tourism, the region's mild climate was highly desirable among northern tourists and was popularized by the British royal family. Likewise, members of the Austrian royal family made other resorts fashionable, particularly within their own empire, such as Opatija on the Istrian Peninsula (Croatia).

Although these resorts provided relief from the cold, damp northern winters, they were generally to be avoided during the summer. In the Victorian era, tanned skin was highly unfashionable and considered a sign of the working classes. In addition, clothing styles were tight and made from heavy materials that would have been unsuitable for the Mediterranean summer heat.[34] By the early twentieth century, however, physicians began recommending heliotherapy, based on exposure to sunlight. Clothing styles became less restrictive and hot, which allowed people to spend more time outside. As more people swam freely in the ocean, swimwear also was needed. Suntans became fashionable, as the upper classes had time to spend at resort destinations in the sun, while the working classes were stuck inside factories.

Thus, a new tourism product, based on the combination of sun and sea, became enormously popular. The Mediterranean was at the heart of this new trend. Developments in air transport and relatively inexpensive foreign package vacations made the Mediterranean more accessible. New and exotic resorts developed in places such as the Caribbean. At the same time, the original coastal resorts in England declined. Upper- and middle-class tourists had the opportunity to visit new resorts, which left the old resorts to day-trippers and lower-income tourists who could not afford to travel abroad. With little new investment, the infrastructure became outdated. For example, at some of the early resorts where tourists had once arrived by train, there were few parking facilities to accommodate those now arriving by car.

Spa and seaside resorts were among the first modern tourism destinations to emerge in many parts of the world. English beliefs about the curative properties of mineral waters carried over to American society; therefore, some of the earliest destinations here were also spas. Ballston Spa in Saratoga County, New York, was one of the first resorts around the turn of the nineteenth century. It boasted the first hotel in the country built outside one of the major cities. New accommodations and entertainments drew ever more tourists, who came for leisure and socialization rather than health. Then, as these spas became overrun with visitors, the original and wealthy tourists sought newer, more exclusive resorts, and they were replaced at existing resorts by the middle classes.[35] Seaside resorts also gained in popularity. Atlantic City in New Jersey dates back to the mid nineteenth century. Tourism development began in Florida toward the end of the century and continued to grow as rail, and then auto, transport made the state more accessible (figure 4.1).

**Figure 4.1.** Seaside resorts have long been popular tourism destinations. In 1952, this Midwestern family traveled to Miami, Florida to enjoy the beach. *Source:* Tom Nelson

# Twentieth-Century Tourism

This brief discussion establishes some of the key factors in the evolution of tourism. Over the course of the twentieth century, new developments allowed tourism to continue to expand, while also maintaining many patterns of the past. For example, new modes of transport brought more changes to both destinations and experiences. With increased automobile ownership and highway construction in the interwar years, "autotouring" became popular, especially in the United States. In the years after World War II, air travel was opened up for mass passenger transport. Particularly as the price of air travel came down, destinations around the world were suddenly far more accessible. This contributed to a surge in international tourist arrivals. In 1950, there were an estimated twenty-five million international tourists. By 1999, that number had grown to 664 million.[36] One tourism historian summarized:

> So it was with holidays. Every social class in its turn followed the example of those "above", first to the spas, then to the seaside and holidays abroad. Merchants and tradesman followed the aristocracy to Bath and Cheltenham by stagecoach, the lower middle class in turn followed them to the seaside by rail, and finally, the working class went by air to Majorca and Benidorm, which became the most popular holiday resort in Spain.

He argued that it was increasingly difficult for the vanguard to find exclusive destinations. "The most privileged hideouts have now to be shared with the cosmopolitan world of tourists who travel in their millions."[37] Written in the 1990s, the antecedent to present concerns about overtourism can clearly be seen.

Despite this incredible growth, tourism did not come easily to all places or equally to all peoples as a result of various barriers, often political or economic in nature. For example, we could look at the Cold War era to understand the political policies that restricted patterns of travel for people in countries behind Europe's "Iron Curtain." Likewise, we could look at different periods of economic development for countries, such as China, to understand when more segments of the population gained the disposable income and/or leisure time to travel for pleasure (box 4.2). In the United States, we need to take a closer look at the Jim Crow era of racial segregation. This period reshaped patterns of travel and tourism for African Americans and left a legacy that can be seen today.

## TOURISM IN THE JIM CROW ERA

In the late nineteenth century, there was a relatively small (approximately 10 percent), affluent segment of the African American population that was able to travel for pleasure. These doctors, lawyers, entrepreneurs, and politicians visited newly developed resorts such as Saratoga Springs (New York) and Atlantic City (New Jersey) along with white tourists.[38] However, this was relatively short lived. Geographers Derek Alderman and Joshua Inwood state:

> The term "Jim Crow" refers to a racial caste-like system that began as early as 1877 with the end of Reconstruction and operated primarily, but not exclusively, in the southeastern United States. While Jim Crow is often identified with rigid laws that marginalized and excluded African Americans, it actually represented a broad array of formal and informal social, economic, and political practices that segregated blacks and whites and justified rampant racism, intimidation, and violence toward African Americans.[39]

With the Jim Crow system of segregation, African American tourists, regardless of means or status, increasingly found these resorts and other facilities closed to them. Travel in general became more difficult and even perilous.

## Box 4.2.  Experience: Travel and Tourism in China

*The baby boomer generation, referring to those individuals born in the years after World War II, has experienced many changes in the world in their lifetime. While not necessarily known as baby boomers, the same generation in China has seen extensive changes—politically and economically as well as in travel and tourism. Xia is part of this generation.*

I was born in Jiangsu province, China in the late 1940s. When I was a child, most people did not travel. It was not easy to travel; it took time and money. When people did travel, it was generally to go to the places to which they were assigned to work or to visit immediate family members who were assigned to work in other places. I traveled for the latter reason. My father served as the head of a county, but we lived in a different county. I remember traveling with my mother to visit him. However, it was a difficult trip. My mother was in one of the last generations to undergo foot binding. This is where young girls' feet were bound to change the shape and size. As a result, she was unable to walk very far. Public transportation was restricted to travel between larger towns. Most people did not have their own vehicles. Only people who needed to transport produce to market would have a sort of cart or rickshaw. So, we had to depend on people who would allow us to ride on one of these carts as far as the county seat. From there we could take a bus to the city in which my father worked.

The Cultural Revolution began in 1966. For a short time, in that year and the next, young people, mostly students but also some workers, were able to participate in a state-sponsored "Red pilgrimage." Essentially, Chairman Mao encouraged us to travel to historical sites and places associated with China's Communist Party Revolution. The government would pay for the trips, with transportation, accommodation, and meals included. I was a teenager at the time. When I first heard about it, I did not see how this was possible. Then my classmates and I heard from the first group to take these trips, and we decided to try it ourselves. In the fall of 1966, I traveled for about a month with two friends from our home in Jinan to several places, including Mao Zedong's hometown, Shaoshan, in Hunan province (figure 4.2). Some people took full advantage of these trips as a way to go to other places, sightsee, visit people, and so on.

When my older sister finished college in 1968, she was assigned to work in Liuzhou, in the Guangxi autonomous region. This remote, mountainous region was far from our home, in the south of the country bordering Vietnam. When she first reported to work, I traveled with her. We traveled by train, but there were no direct routes, so it took several days on multiple trains. We traveled in early spring. I remember this because farmers were plowing their fields, and as they uncovered snakes hibernating in the ground, they would hang them from the trees.

I had finished high school, but colleges were shut down during this time and young people were sent to work. Those who already lived in rural areas generally stayed in those areas for work. Those who lived in urban areas, like me, were sent to rural areas to learn from the farmers. People had some ability to choose their assignment, and like my sister, I wanted to go somewhere far from home. I was assigned to Hubei Province, and I moved there to teach high school. As an unmarried woman, I was allotted a week to visit my family, so I was able to travel home to see my parents. After I was married, I had fewer days. Because it took three days to travel home, and it wasn't cheap, it simply wasn't feasible to make the trip every year. I had to accumulate my days, and money, over the course of a couple of years so I would eventually have a longer period to travel and spend at home.

By the early 1980s people were traveling more. I think people started to have more time and money. In particular, at this time it was the fashion for newlyweds to take a honeymoon trip. Of course, the couples who didn't have much money traveled to places that were relatively close to where they lived. Those who were more affluent were able to travel farther or to the more famous destinations such as cities in Yunnan province in mountainous western China. In the 1990s, my school occasionally organized trips, paid for by the state, for the teachers as a benefit of work. Most of these trips involved only short travel, but some were multiday trips. On one of these trips, we traveled to Dalian, a sort of tourist city in Liaoning province.

For me, travel changed after 2002. My husband and I traveled from China to the US to visit our son in Boston, Massachusetts. Over the two months that we spent there, our son took us to many places in the US, from Acadia National Park in Maine to some of the country's historic cities like Washington, DC, Philadelphia (Pennsylvania), and Williamsburg (Virginia). This opened our minds about the experience of travel. By this time, we had also retired, so when we returned to China, we began to travel more frequently. In particular, almost every year, we would travel from our home in northern China to places in the south. This allowed us to see new places—and to avoid the cold, harsh winter. We would rent a house or apartment and stay there for several months, depending on how much we liked it. We have now been to most of the cities in southern China.

Today, travel in China is great. The rail system is fast and convenient. We can go most places comfortably within a day so we don't have to sleep on the train anymore. For most people, trains are generally affordable as well. One change that we have not adopted, however, is the digital revolution. Now, most people use mobile applications linked to their bank accounts to do things like buy train tickets. It is far less common, but we still prefer to go to an outlet to buy our tickets with cash like we have always done.

—*Xia*

**Figure 4.2.  In 1966, Xia and her friends traveled over 1,200 kilometers from their home in China's Shandong Province to visit Mao Zedong's hometown in Hunan Province.** *Source:* Xia Liu

Because African Americans suffered from various expressions of discrimination using public transportation, many welcomed the freedom afforded by the automobile (figure 4.3). Still, African Americans faced significant barriers to traveling beyond familiar places. Segregation practices could vary considerably from town to town, so travelers never knew what to expect. On the road, they faced constant apprehension about whether they would be able to find a place to eat or to spend the night.[40] The latter was particularly serious, because they might encounter "sundown towns" that prohibited African Americans from being out after nightfall.[41] Defying such laws and practices, even if unknowingly, could lead to violent reprisals.[42] Even if they were able to obtain products and services while traveling, they often faced poor quality, rude treatment, and inflated prices. Essentially, travel for African Americans could be harder, longer and less direct, and more expensive than that for their white counterparts.[43]

Increasingly, African American–owned businesses provided the necessary services for African American travelers and tourists. In 1936, Victor Green, an African American postal worker in Harlem, produced the first edition of *The Negro Motorist Green Book*. It began as a local guide for New York City, using his experiences and those of other postal workers, to provide a listing of businesses that welcomed African American

**Figure 4.3. Although automobiles offered African Americans freedom from the discrimination and harassment common on public transportation, they still faced many barriers to travel. *Source:* Al Stephens**

customers. This included private residences that lodged African American travelers in the absence of other available accommodations. The guide was eventually expanded to include cities in locations across the United States as well as several international destinations. In this process, he relied on an early form of user-generated content (UGC) by asking African American travelers to submit the names of suitable businesses they encountered.[44] Still, the majority of such businesses were spatially concentrated in the eastern United States; few facilities were available in the West.[45] African Americans also developed their own resorts where they could enjoy the same leisure activities as other vacationers without fear of discrimination (box 4.3).

## Box 4.3. Case Study: Michigan's Black Eden

According to one historian, in the Jim Crow era "blacks could almost never achieve total relaxation, but ... they came closest to doing so when there were no whites around. It is hardly surprising that successful blacks did all they could to *insulate* themselves, and particularly their children, from unpleasant confrontations with whites."[a] In the early twentieth century, entrepreneurs began to recognize the need to establish resorts for middle-class, urban African American professionals and business owners. Like their white counterparts, these peoples sought to escape the summer heat, poor environmental conditions, and social pressures associated with cities at the time. To avoid potential problems, these resorts needed to be developed in relatively remote places.[b] In rural Michigan, Idlewild offered a place that was a reasonable driving distance from Midwestern cities like Detroit (Michigan), Cleveland (Ohio), Chicago (Illinois), Indianapolis (Indiana), and even St. Louis (Missouri), but far enough from the racism and discrimination present in these cities.[c]

In 1912, four white couples purchased 2,700 acres of land in the northwestern part of Lower Michigan near Idlewild Lake and founded the Idlewild Resort Company (map 4.1). With the intention of appealing to the African American community, they organized train and bus tours to bring people from key cities to see the area and sell lots.[d] Development at the resort occurred slowly and facilities were initially limited, but vacationers enjoyed its simplicity and rusticity.[e] After World War I, development accelerated. Popular activities included hiking, horseback riding, swimming, boating, and fishing as well as relaxing, reading, and playing cards in the clubhouse. With the establishment of entertainment venues and jazz clubs, such as the Flamingo Club and the Paradise Club, the resort gained a reputation as a cultural mecca. In addition to regular acts that ranged from magicians to showgirls, many well-known and up-and-coming African American entertainers performed in Idlewild, including Duke Ellington, Louis Armstrong, B.B. King, Sarah Vaughn, Dinah Washington, Della Reese, the Four Tops, and the Temptations.[f]

In its heyday, Idlewild was known as the Black Eden of Michigan. When it reached its peak in the 1940s, the resort's summertime population exceeded twenty thousand. It was a place to see and be seen. In the post–World War II era, Idlewild began to attract African American vacationers from the working middle class; however, after the Civil Rights Act of 1964, the community began to decline. African Americans faced fewer restrictions in terms of where they could vacation and began to explore new destinations. Entertainers had the opportunity to perform at other resorts with bigger audiences and more money. Over time, little new investment was made in the tourism infrastructure, and the resort failed to remain competitive.[g] The economy collapsed, and the population plummeted.

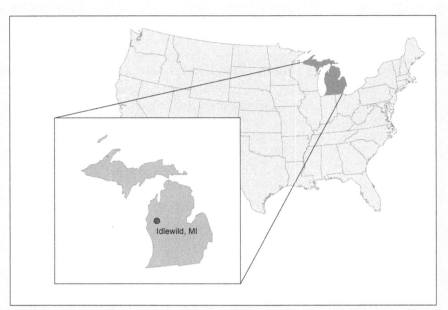

**Map 4.1.   Idlewild, Michigan, USA. During the Jim Crow era, Idlewild became a popular African American resort that drew visitors from cities like Detroit, Cleveland, Chicago, Indianapolis, and St. Louis. Source:** Gang Gong

Then a growing number of retirees chose to settle in the community. Many of these retirees had visited the area during its prime and wanted to see its history preserved. Revitalization efforts began in the 1990s, and the Idlewild Music Festival was established in the early 2000s to help connect modern tourists with the resort's heritage.[h] In 2012, the community hosted its centenary. While no one expects to recreate the Idlewild of the past, its significance should not be forgotten. Idlewild is considered to be one of the oldest, most famous, and most memorable African American resort communities in the United States.[i] More than that, it was one of the few places of retreat for middle-class African Americans during the Jim Crow era, a place where they could relax and enjoy the same leisure opportunities available to white Americans.

*Discussion topic*: What factors led to the development of Idlewild as a tourist resort? Do you think these factors are specific to this time and/or place?

*Tourism online*: Lake County Chamber of Commerce, "Idlewild," at https://lake countymichigan.com/about/idlewild/

---

[a] Mark S. Foster, "In the Face of 'Jim Crow': Prosperous Blacks and Vacations, Travel and Outdoor Leisure, 1890–1945," *The Journal of Negro History*, 84, no. 2 (1999): 131, original emphasis.

[b] Foster, "In the Face of 'Jim Crow'," 140.

[c] Ronald J. Stephens, *Idlewild: The Black Eden of Michigan* (Charleston, SC: Arcadia, 2001), 10.

[d] Kathlyn Gay, *African-American Holidays, Festivals, and Celebrations: The History, Customs, and Symbols Associated with Both Traditional and Contemporary Religious and Secular Events Observed by Americans of African Descent* (Detroit, MI: Omnigraphics, 2007), 223.

[e] Myra B. Young Armstead, "Revisiting Hotels and Other Lodgings: American Tourist Spaces through the Lens of Black Pleasure-Travelers, 1880–1950," *The Journal of Decorative and Propaganda Arts* 25 (2005), 145.[f] Foster, "In the Face of 'Jim Crow'," 139–40.

[g] Stephens, *Idlewild*, 10, 119.

[h] Gay, *African-American Holidays*, 224.

[i] Stephens, *Idlewild*, 8.

In the early 1940s, one journalist concluded that African Americans would have an easier time traveling abroad than in the United States.[46] Foreign travel was still limited at this time, but those with sufficient means who were able to do so often reported that they experienced less discrimination. Still, they were conscious of their appearance and behavior. Some noted that they seemed to be curiosities in the places they visited. Others felt that, as they were the first African American many people had encountered, they bore the responsibility of shaping these peoples' opinions about the group as a whole.[47]

In the introduction to the 1949 edition of the *Green Book*, the author wrote:

> There will be a day sometime in the near future when this guide will not have to be published. That is when we as a race will have equal opportunities and privileges in the United States. It will be a great day for us to suspend this publication for then we can go wherever we please, and without embarrassment. But until that time comes we shall continue to publish this information for your convenience each year.[48]

Indeed, Green continued to publish his guide until the mid-1960s. The Civil Rights Act of 1964 outlawed discrimination and opened up greater opportunities for African American travel and tourism. Yet, discrimination and racism continued to affect African American tourists. This will be discussed further in chapters 13 and 14.

## THE DIGITAL REVOLUTION

As air travel opened up for passenger transport (figure 4.4), airlines struggled to manage both their inventory and passenger reservations. Airline agents took reservations in person or over the phone, hand wrote them on cards, and organized them in filing carousels. With this inefficient and often inaccurate system, flights could be over- or underbooked, which created problems for both the airlines and their passengers. To address this issue, American Airlines entered into an agreement with IBM to build the industry's first computerized airline reservation system, known as SABRE (Semi-Automated Business Research Environment). By 1964, the system was fully operational.[49] This launched the first major wave of information technology in travel and tourism, as other airlines worked to establish their own Customer Reservation Systems (CRS). In the first decade, SABRE was the world's largest private real-time data-processing system. It served more than 10,000 travel agents around the world, but it remained inaccessible to individual consumers.[50]

The introduction of the worldwide web provided the basis for the second major wave of information technology in travel and tourism. In 1995, a small business called Internet Travel Network used a web-based booking tool to facilitate the first online airline ticket booking. In the following year, Microsoft launched its online travel agency, Expedia. By 2000, another small business started TripAdvisor to allow tourists to leave reviews of hotels and other tourists to use these reviews to make their decisions.[51] TripAdvisor was the first social travel site and is still the largest.

**Figure 4.4.** By the 1970s, international air transport was becoming increasingly accessible, allowing more people to travel than ever before. This group of international tourists is preparing to board a plane in Columbus, Ohio for a European tour in 1971. **Source:** Carolyn Nelson

As consumers became more familiar and comfortable with online booking systems, they also began to use this method for hotels, trains, car rentals, tours, and so on. Online travel agents increasingly competed with the traditional "high street" (or brick-and-mortar) agents. An academic journal article from 2009 cautions, "Businesses that have not made use of the Internet cannot compete and therefore they must grasp the opportunity before they are out-competed by those that have."[52] Ten years later, the world's oldest travel company collapsed, this advice apparently having gone unheeded (see box 4.1).

Arguably, we are in the midst of a third major development of information technology in travel and tourism, but this will be considered in chapter 13.

# Conclusion

Research on tourism in past periods has focused on several key eras considered instrumental in the evolution of modern tourism. In particular, the Grand Tour is often cited as the origin of modern international tourism. In fact, some scholars argue that the Grand Tour lives on:

> The true descendants of … the Grand Tour tradition, however, consist of the young interrailers who roam the city in search of other interrailers and the groups of American and Japanese college students doing the modern version of the Grand Tour. Just as in the seventeenth century, they are here with the blessing of their parents. A season of interrailing or a European tour is still supposed to be a good investment in a middle class education.[53]

The historical geography of tourism is a fundamental component in our investigation of the geography of tourism. Historical geography provides the framework for examining the geographic patterns of tourism in past periods, and the changes that have taken place over time. This is the foundation for the patterns that we see today. Although it may be hard for us to imagine tourism in earlier periods, clearly many parallels may be seen. Moreover, starting from the early nineteenth century, we can trace the evolution of infrastructure, organization, experiences, and even many of the problems of tourism directly to the patterns that we see today and will be exploring in greater depth in the remaining chapters.

# Key Terms

• historical geography

# Notes

1. Charles R. Goeldner and J. R. Brent Ritchie, *Tourism: Principles, Practices, Philosophies*, 9th ed. (Hoboken, NJ: Wiley, 2006), 41.
2. John Towner, "What Is Tourism's History?" *Tourism Management* 16, no. 5 (1995): 340.
3. Maxine Feifer, *Tourism in History: From Imperial Rome to the Present* (New York: Stein and Day, 1986), 9.
4. Feifer, *Tourism in History*, 9–10; Bruce Prideaux, "The Role of the Transport System in Destination Development," *Tourism Management* 21 (2000): 53; Loykie Lomine, "Tourism in Augustan Society (44BC–AD69)," in *Histories of Tourism: Representation, Identity and Conflict*, ed. John Walton (Clevedon: Channel View Publications, 2005), 84; Goeldner and Ritchie, *Tourism*, 44.
5. Simon Kevan, "Quests for Cures: A History of Tourism for Climate and Health," *International Journal of Biometeorology* 37 (1993): 114.
6. Lomine, "Tourism in Augustan Society," 78.
7. Lomine, "Tourism in Augustan Society," 73–7.

8. Lomine, "Tourism in Augustan Society," 69; Feifer, *Tourism in History*, 8.

9. Feifer, *Tourism in History*, 16; Lomine, "Tourism in Augustan Society," 74; Goeldner and Ritchie, *Tourism*, 44.

10. Jack Simmons, "Railways, Hotels, and Tourism in Great Britain 1839–1914," *Journal of Contemporary History* 19 (1984): 207; Goeldner and Ritchie, *Tourism*, 50.

11. Kevan, "Quests for Cures," 115.

12. Goeldner and Ritchie, *Tourism*, 49.

13. Tabish Khair, Martin Leer, Justin D. Edwards, and Hanna Ziadeh, *Other Routes: 1500 Years of African and Asian Travel Writing* (Bloomington: Indiana University Press, 2005), 32–3.

14. Julian Ward, *Xu Xiake (1587–1641): The Art of Travel Writing* (London: Routledge, 2001), 8.

15. F. E. Peters, *The Hajj: The Muslim Pilgrimage to Mecca and the Holy Places* (Princeton, NJ: Princeton University Press, 1994), 73–4.

16. Khair et al., *Other Routes*, 281–2.

17. Ward, *Xu Xiake*, 14–5, 20.

18. Khair et al., *Other Routes*, 184–5.

19. Khair et al., *Other Routes*, 289–91.

20. Khair et al., *Other Routes*, 299–300.

21. Simmons, "Railways, Hotels, and Tourism," 207; Marguerite Shaffer, *See America First: Tourism and National Identity, 1880–1940* (Washington, DC: Smithsonian Institution Press, 2001), 11.

22. John Towner, "The Grand Tour: A Key Phase in the History of Tourism," *Annals of Tourism Research* 12 (1985): 301; Feifer, *Tourism in History*, 64; Kevan, "Quests for Cures," 116; Tom Baum, "Images of Tourism Past and Present," *International Journal of Contemporary Hospitality Management* 8 (1996): 25; Orvar Löfgren, *On Holiday: A History of Vacationing* (Berkeley: University of California Press, 1999), 157; Goeldner and Ritchie, *Tourism*, 51.

23. Towner, "The Grand Tour," 321–2.

24. Feifer, *Tourism in History*, 98; Goeldner and Ritchie, *Tourism*, 51; Löfgren, *On Holiday*, 161; Towner, "The Grand Tour," 301; Stephen Williams, *Tourism Geography* (London, Routledge, 1998), 44.

25. Towner, "The Grand Tour," 301, 316–17; Baum, "Images of Tourism," 25, 28; Rudy Koshar, "'What Ought to Be Seen': Tourists' Guidebooks and National Identities in Modern Germany and Europe," *Journal of Contemporary History* 33 (1998): 326; Williams, *Tourism Geography*, 44; Löfgren, *On Holiday*, 163.

26. Towner, "The Grand Tour," 298.

27. John Beckerson and John K. Walton, "Selling Air: Marketing the Intangible at British Resorts," in *Histories of Tourism: Representation, Identity and Conflict*, ed. John Walton (Clevedon: Channel View Publications, 2005), 55; Williams, *Tourism Geography*, 23.

28. Goeldner and Ritchie, *Tourism*, 54; Löfgren, *On Holiday*, 160; Williams, *Tourism Geography*, 23.

29. Kevan, "Quests for Cures," 116; Löfgren, *On Holiday*, 113–16; Williams, *Tourism Geography*, 23.

30. Beckerson and Walton, "Selling Air," 55; Löfgren, *On Holiday*, 112; Williams, *Tourism Geography*, 23–4.

31. John K. Walton, "Prospects in Tourism History: Evolution, State of Play and Future Development," *Tourism Management* 30 (2009): 787.

32. Baum, "Images of Tourism," 27–8.

33. Beckerson and Walton, "Selling Air," 55–6; Feifer, *Tourism in History*, 205; Goeldner and Ritchie, *Tourism*, 54; Kevan, "Quests for Cures," 118; Löfgren, *On Holiday*, 120; Williams, *Tourism Geography*, 26.

34. Kevan, "Quests for Cures," 118–19; Löfgren, *On Holiday*, 163; Williams, *Tourism Geography*, 44–5.

35. Richard H. Gassan, *The Birth of American Tourism: New York, the Hudson Valley, and American Culture, 1790–1830* (Amherst: University of Massachusetts Press, 2008), 5, 13–14.

36. World Tourism Organization, "Tourism Highlights 2000, 2nd ed.," August 2000, accessed March 27, 2020, https://www.e-unwto.org/doi/pdf/10.18111/9789284403745.

37. Bill Cormack, *A History of Holidays, 1812–1990* (London: Routledge, 1998), 5.

38. Myra B. Young Armstead, "Revisiting Hotels and Other Lodgings: American Tourist Spaces through the Lens of Black Pleasure-Travelers, 1880–1950," *The Journal of Decorative and Propaganda Arts* 25 (2005): 137–8.

39. Derek H. Alderman and Joshua Inwood, "Toward a Pedagogy of Jim Crow: A Geographic Reading of *The Green Book*, in Teaching Ethnic Geography in the 21st Century," in *Teaching Ethnic Geography in the 21st Century*, ed. Lawrence E. Estaville, Edris J. Montalvo, and Fenda A. Akiwumi (Washington, DC: National Council for Geographic Education, 2014), 68.

40. Mark S. Foster, "In the Face of 'Jim Crow': Prosperous Blacks and Vacations, Travel and Outdoor Leisure, 1890–1945," *The Journal of Negro History* 84, no. 2 (1999): 140–1.

41. Alderman and Inwood, "Toward a Pedagogy of Jim Crow," 70.

42. Armstead, "Revisiting Hotels and Other Lodgings," 140.

43. Alderman and Inwood, "Toward a Pedagogy of Jim Crow," 73; Foster, "In the Face of 'Jim Crow'," 136.

44. Jacinda Townsend, "How the Green Book Helped African-American Tourists Navigate a Segregated Nation," *Smithsonian Magazine*, April 2016, accessed October 10, 2016, http://www.smithsonianmag.com/smithsonian-institution/history-green-book-african-american-travelers-180958506/?no-ist.

45. Foster, "In the Face of 'Jim Crow'," 137.

46. Armstead, "Revisiting Hotels and Other Lodgings," 140.

47. Foster, "In the Face of 'Jim Crow'," 132.

48. Victor H. Green, *The Negro Motorist Green Book, 1949 Edition* (New York: Victor H. Green & Co., Publishers, 1949), 1.

49. Sabre Corporation, "The Sabre Story," accessed March 30, 2020, https://www.sabre.com/files/Sabre-History.pdf.

50. Farrokh Mamaghani, "Impact of E-Commerce on Travel and Tourism: An Historical Analysis," *International Journal of Management* 26, no. 3 (2009): 367.

51. Kevin May, "How 25 Years of the Web Inspired the Travel Revolution," *The Guardian*, March 12, 2014, accessed March 30, 2020, https://www.theguardian.com/travel/2014/mar/12/how-25-years-of-the-web-inspired-the-travel-revolution.

52. Mamaghani, "Impact of E-Commerce on Travel and Tourism," 365.

53. Löfgren, *On Holiday*, 160.

# CHAPTER 5

# The Transport Geography of Tourism

Improvements in transportation modes and infrastructure were among the most important factors in allowing modern tourism to develop on a large scale and become a regular part of the lives of billions of people around the world. Technological advances provided the basis for the exponential expansion of local, regional, and global transportation networks and made travel faster, easier, and cheaper. This not only created new tourist-generating and tourist-receiving regions but also prompted a host of other changes in the tourism infrastructure, such as accommodations. As a result, the availability of transportation infrastructure and services has been considered a fundamental precondition for tourism.[1] With growing concerns about important issues like climate change and sustainability, however, the availability of *sustainable* transport infrastructure and services may be an increasingly significant factor in tourism in the future.

**Transport geography** is a topical branch of geography that is concerned with the movement of goods and people from one location to another, including the spatial patterns of this movement and the geographic factors that allow or constrain it. Transport is inherently geographic, and transport geography is firmly based on geographic concepts like movement and location. Additionally, place reminds us that we need to examine the specific physical and human features of the location to understand how movement occurs. Scale allows us to examine transportation networks at local and regional scales but also consider how these networks are connected into a global system. Geography provides the tools that allow transport geographers to explain, predict, and plan for a variety of transport issues, including those that relate to travel and tourism.

There is a distinct and reciprocal relationship between transport and tourism. Tourists constitute an important source of demand for transportation services, and the consistent growth of travel and tourism has been a key topic in transport geography studies.[2] At the same time, transportation is a vital component of tourism and our study of the geography of tourism. We need to understand the means of connection between the people who demand tourism experiences and the places that are able to supply those experiences. As tourism is based on the temporary movements of people across space, the transportation that facilitates these movements is key in converting suppressed demand to effective demand. Beyond getting tourists to a destination, transportation also facilitates their experience of that destination.

While the understanding of this relationship is important, the intersection of transport and tourism geography research increasingly focuses using knowledge from both areas to work toward solutions for current issues, in line with the powerful geography framework. This chapter continues our exploration of the geographic foundation of tourism by examining transportation as a fundamental component of tourism. Transport geography provides us with the framework to examine the transport system, particularly the role of different transportation modes in tourism, the geographic factors that shape patterns of movement, and key issues in tourism transport sustainability. In addition, we will look at some of the ways researchers are examining the intersection between tourism and transport.

# The Evolution of Transportation and Tourism

As we saw in the last chapter, historical geography plays an important role in helping us to understand how current patterns came about. Thus, it is worth taking a brief look at how the transport system evolved and shaped tourism. The ancient Romans were among the earliest societies to travel, and an extensive road network—combined with an organized system of horse-and-cart transport—was one of the key factors in this development. Likewise, the deterioration of these roads after the collapse of the Roman Empire was one of the issues that brought all nonessential travel to a halt.

Over time, new transportation systems developed throughout Europe that allowed greater opportunities for travel. From the mid to late Middle Ages, while roads remained poor, water transport provided some means for travel. Major river systems such as the Rhine, Danube, and Loire, as well as canal networks, formed the basis for transportation within the region and provided regular passenger services. New options for travel over land also gradually developed and expanded across the region. In the fifteenth century, the post system was developed in France, where travelers could change horses at relay stations established at regular intervals. This evolved into a widespread network of coach services by the middle of the eighteenth century.[3]

The innovations with the greatest impact on tourism came at the beginning of the nineteenth century with the development of commercially successful steam locomotion. Regular steamboat service offered faster, more reliable, and increasingly comfortable transportation.[4] Steamboats operated along river systems and supplanted earlier, slower, riskier oceanic sailing vessels. Steam packets traveling regular transatlantic routes were the most efficient means of travel throughout much of the nineteenth century. Originally intended for transporting the mail, they also began carrying cargo and passengers. Then, as rail service developed and expanded, it trumped all previous means of transportation. Although railways were originally intended for carrying heavy freight, like coal, they also proved extremely successful for passenger travel. Not only were railroads faster and more efficient than other available modes, they could also routinely carry ten times the number of passengers as a horse-drawn coach.[5] In addition, the typical charge of one penny per mile for rail travel was substantially lower than coach fares.[6]

Both forms of steam locomotion (boats and trains) reshaped patterns of tourism in a myriad of ways. Due to decreased travel time and cost, more people from the middle and lower classes were enabled to participate. This increase in tourism raised concerns among the earlier generations of tourists. In some cases, these earlier tourists sought new destinations in previously distant or inaccessible places. In other cases, they fought to limit the changes that were taking place at existing destinations. English poet William Wordsworth, one of the early voices to express concerns about the negative effects of tourism, strongly objected to the proposed rail development in the Lake District. He felt that increased tourism development would destroy the natural beauty of the area that was the primary attraction. Although this line was not built, rail stations on the periphery of the area nonetheless brought substantial numbers of tourists, who traveled into the area on foot or by coach.[7]

The invention of the sleeping car provided greater opportunities for long, uninterrupted train trips. This idea evolved into the Pullman car—luxury sleeping cars that effectively served as a hotel on wheels and allowed the upper classes to travel longer distances in comfort. However, rail travel created new challenges as well. For example, where it formerly took weeks for a tourist to travel from locations in Northern Europe to destinations in Southern Europe, trains reduced the trip from London to Nice to just one-and-a-half days. Prominent physicians claimed that this was not enough time for passengers, particularly those traveling for health reasons, to adjust to changing environmental conditions. To avoid potentially serious health complications, these physicians argued that travelers should break the journey down into intermittent stages.[8]

Steam-based transportation also changed the ways people experienced places. Tourists had the opportunity to see different landscapes in locations farther afield and to see them in a new way. Instead of stopping at strategic vantage points, tourists viewed the landscape through glass windows on scenic cruises and railroads, and they had to learn to focus on a moving landscape. These tourists were also somewhat restricted in what they saw along transportation corridors, whether it was a river, canal, or rail line.[9] Additional modes of transport were necessary for further exploration. Tourists would have to take horse-drawn carriages or buses to nature sites and scenic vistas. Secondary transport was even needed to reach downtown centers, as rail stations were typically located outside of town. Consequently, enterprising innkeepers invested in shuttle services and opened inns near the station to capture the in-transit market.

At the beginning of the twentieth century, the automobile further reshaped and expanded tourism (figure 5.1). Widespread personal car ownership played an important role in the development of modern mass tourism. In the United States, this—combined with the expansion of the interstate highway system—allowed tourists increasing freedom to visit multiple destinations during the course of a single trip and to explore new areas of the country. New attractions and destination regions emerged, leading to the development of new types of accommodations, such as the motor hotel (motel), to meet tourists' needs.[10]

Air transportation created ever more opportunities for tourism—especially mass international tourism—in the second half of the twentieth century. Air travel had been made available to a select group of affluent tourists following the end of World War I, but it was greatly expanded in the years following World War II. Innovations in air transportation, such as the jet engine and wide-bodied passenger jets, allowed planes to increase both the distance traveled and the numbers of passengers carried. As such, all

**Figure 5.1. Personal car ownership played an important role in the development of modern mass tourism in the United States.** *Source:* Tom Nelson

parts of the world have been opened up to tourism, including many destinations that are almost entirely dependent on air transportation for international tourist arrivals.

While these innovations in transportation were not driven by tourism, the tourism industry directly benefited from improvements in safety and efficiency as well as reductions in cost. The framework of historical geography helps us examine these changes that have taken place over time to better understand the interconnections between transport and tourism. This gives us valuable insight as the transport industry continues to evolve with new issues as well as new innovations.

# The Transport System

Transport geography recognizes transport as a complex system that involves networks, nodes, and modes and is based on demand. A **transportation network** is the spatial structure and organization of the infrastructure that supports, and to some extent determines, patterns of movement.[11] The transportation infrastructure has been expanding at both the local and global scales, becoming an ever-more intricate web of interconnections. At the same time, the relative cost of transportation has declined. These factors have allowed more movement to take place than ever before. The nature of the network can encourage people to travel along one route or discourage them from traveling along another.

These networks may be highly dependent on geography. For example, the physical geography of a place will affect patterns of transportation, whether it is physical features like mountains, river systems, and ground stability; atmospheric conditions such as wind directions; or oceanic conditions such as currents. The human geography of a place, such as the circumstances of political geography, also can have an effect on transport. National boundaries may affect the ability to create a transportation network and efficiently connect places, either on the ground or in the air through no-fly zones. For example, heightened geopolitical tensions between the US and Iran led the Federal Aviation Administration (FAA) to ban US carriers from flying through Iranian airspace in June 2019. As a result, United Airlines suspended its direct flight from Newark, New Jersey to Mumbai, India and global carriers also rerouted flights to avoid the area.[12]

**Transportation nodes** are the access points to the network. These nodes may be **terminals**, where transport flows begin or end, or **interchanges** within a network.[13] Population geography often plays the most significant role in determining the location of nodes. In general, nodes are likely to be situated in areas with high population densities, and terminals in particular will be located in or near major cities. **Transportation modes** are the means of movement or the type of transportation. Broadly, there are three categories of modes based on where this movement takes place—over land (surface), water, or air—with different types within each category (see table 5.1).

For tourism, the primary function of this transport system is to facilitate the movements of passengers to and from destinations. Secondary functions include getting tourists to the transport terminal and supporting the movements of tourists within the destination. Since tourism is typically considered to be nonessential travel, transport services must be safe, relatively convenient and comfortable, and competitively priced to support tourism. However, the networks, nodes, and modes of this system will not be solely used for the purposes of tourism. Instead, the tourism industry generally takes advantage of existing transport systems, with the exception of new destinations that were specifically planned for the purpose of tourism. Although there are also examples of dedicated tourism transport at a destination or specific attraction, tourists are typically only one group of users of transportation facilities and services. Generally, no distinction is made between tourists and other transit passengers, which means it is often difficult to clearly identify specific usage patterns, economic impacts, environmental effects, and so on related to tourism.

Modes serve different roles in tourism, and trips frequently require the use of multiple modes. For example, personal cars, taxis and ride-share services, or inner-city train systems may be used to get to and from the terminal node (i.e., a train station, airport, or seaport). Likewise, tourists may rent a car, take taxis and tour buses, or use public transportation systems to reach and get around their destination. It is important that destinations seek to develop a comprehensive transportation system in which the networks of the different modes used in tourism are integrated. This will allow tourists to change from one mode to another as seamlessly as possible.

As tourists, we typically evaluate our options instinctively, with little reflection; therefore, these issues often seem self-evident. However, there are many factors that determine the appropriate mode(s) of transportation for a trip. There are both practical considerations involved (i.e., what modes are available for a trip) and a variety of perceptual considerations (i.e., personal preferences and constraints).[14]

Distance is one of the most important practical considerations that may automatically eliminate one or more modes. Greater distances require longer travel times and/or higher transportation costs. Monetary cost is one of the most important perceptual

**Table 5.1. Summary of the Advantages and Disadvantages Associated with the Modes and Types of Tourism Transport**

| Mode | Tourist Considerations | Destination Considerations | |
|---|---|---|---|
| **Surface** | | | |
| Walk | Free<br>Flexibility<br>Required in traffic-free zones | Used only for short distances<br>Dependent on physical condition | Reduces traffic congestion and pollution<br>Increases access to businesses | Requires investment in some infrastructure (e.g., paths, sidewalks, signs) |
| Rail | Well suited for short- to medium-haul travel<br>Ease of navigation versus driving<br>May facilitate tourism experiences (e.g., historic or scenic trains) | Constrained by schedules and routes<br>Costs vary by destination | Schedules and routes can be modified based on demand<br>May serve as an attraction | May require investment in infrastructure, new technology, and/or maintenance |
| Personal car | Flexibility<br>Privacy<br>Well suited for short- to medium-haul travel | Associated with varied costs (e.g., fuel, tolls, parking)<br>May be difficult to navigate unfamiliar roads | Increases accessibility of destinations not served by mass transit | May require investment in roads and parking facilities<br>Brings fewer visitors per vehicle<br>May generate congestion and pollution |
| Scheduled bus | Low cost<br>Ease of navigation versus driving<br>May be used for short- or medium-haul travel | Constrained by schedules and routes<br>Lack of privacy, personal space, and security | Requires little additional investment<br>Schedules and routes can be modified based on demand | May be subject to significant perceptual constraints (e.g., location of stations, prevalence of crime) |
| **Water** | | | |
| Ferry | Provides access to small destinations<br>Offers the ability to take personal cars | Slow<br>Not used for long-haul travel | Increases access to small destinations | Requires docking and terminal facilities |
| Cruise | Allows travel to multiple destinations<br>Provides a vacation experience | Requires travel to port<br>Slow<br>Not well suited for long-haul travel | Increases access to island/coastal destinations<br>Has the potential to bring large quantities of tourists | Requires a deepwater harbor or ferry service, docking and terminal facilities<br>Generates pollution (e.g., air, water) |
| **Air** | | | |
| Scheduled | Provides access to more destinations<br>Well suited for long-haul travel | May have high costs<br>May contribute to increased stress levels<br>May have health risks (e.g., jet lag, deep-vein thrombosis) | Increases access to remote or hard-to-reach destinations<br>Has the potential to bring large quantities of tourists | Requires space for/investment in runway and terminal facilities<br>Must be regulated<br>Generates pollution (e.g., air, noise) |
| Sightseeing | Offers a unique experience | May have high costs | Facilitates access to large-scale attractions | May be disruptive |

considerations. Transportation accounts for some of the largest expenditures in tourism. For many trips, the experience stage begins when the tourists reach the destination; thus, they are interested in reaching their destination as quickly and efficiently as possible. However, for tourists with a limited budget for a trip, it may come down to a choice: spend more money on transportation or on the experience at the destination. For example, a direct flight may be the option that requires the shortest amount of travel time, and, by extension, often the least amount of hassles and potential problems in the form of lines, security screenings, delays, lost luggage, and so on. This allows the maximum amount of time spent at the destination. Yet, a flight with multiple connections or even other modes of transport, such as a personal car, may be lower-cost options that are longer or less convenient but could allow the tourists to spend an additional day at the destination, participate in a particular tourism activity, or make other expenditures. Likewise, if transportation cost is a significant factor, tourists may need to consider a second- or third-choice destination as an alternative.

Personal goals and preferences also play a role in transportation decisions. Rather than being primarily concerned with getting from point A to point B in the fastest manner possible, tourists might be interested in seeing things along the way, where the movement stage is as important as the experience stage in the tourism process. Consequently, they might choose to drive a personal car to get a better view of the landscape through which they are passing, as well as to have the freedom to make stops or take intentional detours along the way. Additionally, tourists who are afraid to fly will take an alternative mode of transportation to get to their destination, regardless of whether air transport is the quickest, easiest, or cheapest mode.

This choice of mode affects the level of interaction tourists will have with both people and places. The development of new modes of transportation changed the ways in which people experienced places. The faster the mode, the less of the passing landscape is seen. For air transportation in particular, observing the landscape is generally not considered a part of travel; therefore, tourists only have the opportunity to experience the place of the destination as opposed to the places of travel as well. The choice of mode also has the potential to create opportunities for interaction with other people or limit it. Personal cars tend to isolate tourists, both from locals and from other tourists. Specialized tourism transport, such as charter and sightseeing buses, fosters interaction with other tourists, while walking and taking public transportation often allows tourists the greatest opportunities to interact with local people.

Destination stakeholders must also consider the use of different modes. In cases where the majority of tourists travel by personal car, stakeholders need to identify transport flows and places where traffic is concentrated at a destination. This information can help planners formulate effective strategies to eliminate potential bottlenecks or alleviate problems with congestion and overcrowding during peak seasons. These solutions may include designating alternative routes, directing tourists to alternate attractions, or creating new policies such as the establishment of restricted or traffic-free zones. This will help reduce the negative impacts on the destination created by traffic and pollution and improve the visitor experience.[15]

Tourists at major urban destinations may be reliant on public transportation systems due to prohibitive costs (e.g., car rental, insurance, parking, congestion charges for driving in the city center, and the like) or unfamiliarity with roads and traffic patterns. In these cases, stakeholders must consider usage patterns and competition for mass transportation resources. During the high tourist season, mass transportation may run at or over capacity. If the supply of transport services is not expanded to meet the increased demand, systems can become congested. All users experience decreased access to and quality of transportation services. Tourists' usage can complement commuters' usage when they visit on weekends and holidays. However, during peak times (e.g., the summer months), tourists compete with residents.[16] For tourists, this can have a negative impact on their ability to visit the desired attractions and their overall satisfaction with the destination. For residents, this is another factor that can lead to animosity toward tourists.

Surface transport has traditionally accounted for the highest proportion of tourist travel. However, air transport has steadily increased its share of international tourism trips. According to UNWTO data, the share of air travel for international trips was 58 percent in 2018, while surface travel was 39 percent and water was just 3 percent.[17] The following sections will take a closer look at the geography and sustainability of modes of tourism transport.

## SURFACE TRANSPORT

In comparison with the other primary categories of mode, surface transport is more dependent on geography because the development of a network is restricted by land area, infrastructure, and possibly even national boundaries. Yet, surface transport is clearly a widely used mode of tourism transport throughout the tourism process and may claim a higher proportion of travel again in the future due to concerns about flying in light of climate change or even a post-COVID-19 decline in airlines and routes (see below).

Self-powered surface transport, such as walking or cycling, is one of the most basic forms of surface transport that can be used to get around a destination or as a form of transportation-as-experience. While they are generally used for short experiences (e.g., a nature hike), longer trips have gained attention in light of movements toward slow and sustainable tourism. Such trips have the potential to bring economic benefits particularly to rural communities, social benefits in terms of improved health and community relations, and environmental benefits as a low-carbon transport option. However, one of the most significant barriers to this form of tourism is infrastructural; walking and cycling tourists require long-distance networks of safe roads or paths.

Particularly in urban areas, personal transport has become increasingly accessible to tourists as well as residents. Bicycles and electric scooters can be rented at shops, kiosks, and via mobile apps (figure 5.2). In addition, cities have seen a rise in bicycle, scooter, and Segway sightseeing tours; however, these have been controversial. Such vehicles compete with pedestrians for often limited space on sidewalks or narrow streets. Residents complain about the congestion created by large tour groups and express concerns about safety with the speed of the vehicles often combined with users' inexperience and/or inattention as they take in the sights. Tied into wider problems with overtourism, various cities have imposed restrictions and bans on these vehicles or tours.

**Figure 5.2. Bicycle rentals are an increasingly popular option for easily getting around and experiencing a destination.** *Source*: Scott Jeffcote

The use of rail transport in tourism is highly uneven. Countries like the United States that placed an emphasis on expansion of road networks have seen some of the greatest declines in passenger rail transport. Few developing countries have invested in creating rail networks. However, throughout Europe and parts of East Asia, extensively developed rail networks continue to be used on a wide scale. Some countries have even made new investments in infrastructure and technological advances to improve rail transport and provide a competitive means of getting to or from a destination.

France's Train à Grande Vitesse (TGV) is an intercity high-speed rail service (HSR). Based on the success of the TGV, other countries in the region such as Germany, Spain, and Italy developed their own high-speed rail services. High-speed rail service is relatively new in China, but the country now has the longest network in the world and the most riders. HSR has the potential to increase the accessibility and therefore the attractiveness of a destination, yet studies suggest that existing rather than developing destinations are most likely to benefit from this added value. Additionally, HSR does not necessarily lead to an increase in tourism as it primarily functions as a substitute for or competitor to air transportation, especially for medium distances.[18]

With concerns about climate change, there are increased calls for travelers to choose rail over air to reduce greenhouse gas emissions. In 2019, #trainbrag began trending on social media, particularly in Europe (from #tågskryt in Swedish). People post pictures from their rail trips online to highlight the ways in which they are reducing their carbon footprint and to encourage others to do the same. This movement shows the interest in traveling more sustainably, but there are still challenges in terms of time and money. In places with existing rail networks, government-subsidized prices could increase the cost competitiveness of rail trips. Companies could also be incentivized to make sustainable choices for business travel and offer paid "travel" days in addition to vacation days for employees who choose to travel sustainably. However, for places that must develop or expand rail networks, concerns include financial costs as well as environmental costs in terms of habitat and biodiversity disruption or loss.

Road transport plays an important, yet diverse, role in tourism. Personal cars continue to be a significant mode for travel to a destination, while personal, rented, and even shared (through P2P exchanges like Uber or Zipcar) cars are used for getting around at the destination. Recreational vehicles (RVs) offer a unique form of tourism contingent upon transport. Scheduled bus services account for a small amount of tourism transport to and from destinations, and local bus services may be used to reach a major transport node (e.g., an airport) or for travel within a destination. Charter bus services are used in package tours and excursions from a resort area, and specialized tourism transport, such as sightseeing and hop-on hop-off buses that stop at major attractions, provides an additional option at major destinations.

The use of personal cars represents a key area of concern for sustainable tourism transport. Reductions in tourism transport emissions could be achieved through a shift from cars to energy-efficient public transport. This has the potential to provide economic (e.g., local jobs) and social (e.g., opportunities to interact with local people) benefits as well. However, many destinations simply lack well-developed public transportation networks. In general, rural destinations are poorly connected by public transport, so the majority of visitors arrive by cars. This contributes to traffic congestion, reduced air quality, and diminished visitor experiences. Most solutions are implemented locally, such as prohibiting car use and/or providing free local public transport services at the destination.

Autonomous vehicles have the potential to change tourism transport. Time spent traveling could be used for sightseeing, entertainment, or work. The vehicles could offer tourists a safer alternative to driving in unfamiliar settings or under suboptimal conditions such as when they are tired. Autonomous vehicles are also projected to produce less emissions; however, this benefit may be offset by increased demand. Although autonomous transport is still largely in the future, applications are already being tested. In 2018, the Lake District National Park (England) participated in a feasibility study to use driverless vehicles as a sustainable transport option to ease problems associated with personal cars in the park.[19]

## WATER TRANSPORT

Developments in other modes, particularly air, have changed the role of water transport in tourism. Nonetheless, water transport continues to play an important role in tourism with the cruise ship industry, where transportation constitutes the tourism experience rather than serving as a means to an end. In 2018, there were 28.5 million cruise passengers globally, with 11.3 million of them traveling in the Caribbean region alone (figure 5.3). The Mediterranean region also has experienced significant growth, and new routes are being developed all over the world. North Americans overwhelmingly account for the largest cruise market with 14.2 million passengers, followed by Europeans (6.7 million) and Asians (4.2 million).[20] Cruises were once marketed to older age groups, but many lines have expanded their target markets by offering various price options; attractions for younger markets, such as families with small children; new experiences like cooking classes or music festivals; and trends like wellness tourism.

Despite this popularity, the cruise industry has experienced widespread criticism. Average cruise ship size has been increasing, with many new ships carrying over 5,000 passengers. With the potential to off-load this many people at a destination at one time, cruise ships have become enmeshed in concerns about overtourism. For example, Dubrovnik, Croatia attracted international attention when the World Heritage Site's mayor instituted a policy that only two ships per day with no more than 5,000 total passengers would be permitted to dock in an effort to ease the pressures of overcrowding. Recent reports have also raised concerns about crimes aboard cruise ships, particularly sexual assault, as well as labor issues, including demanding schedules and low base wages with a high dependency on tips from guests.

Environmental sustainability is another significant issue that has gained widespread attention. Cruise ships are considered to be one of the most energy-intense forms of tourism on a per person, per trip basis.[21] This has particular implications for cruise ports. Cruise ships also produce large quantities of sewage and graywater from sinks, showers, and laundry facilities. Ineffective treatments can allow contaminants such as nutrients or bacteria to be discharged into the water. In addition, cruise ships have knowingly discharged waste. In 2016, Princess Cruise Lines, a subsidiary of Carnival Corporation, was fined US$40 million for dumping oil-contaminated waste into the sea. In 2019, the company was fined an additional US$20 million for violating probation terms by dumping plastic.[22] The cruise industry has prioritized changes to improve its sustainability and its reputation (see box 5.1).

**Figure 5.3.  Cruises are a significant part of the tourism industry, with 28.5 million people traveling by cruise ship in 2018.** *Source*: Scott Jeffcote

## Box 5.1.   Case Study: Cruises, Sustainability, and the Galápagos Islands

In recent years, the cruise industry has experienced significant growth, accompanied by increased concern about its environmental impact. In particular, the industry has focused on its contributions to climate change. In its *2020 State of the Cruise Industry Outlook*, Cruise Lines International Association (CLIA) reported, "Our members have committed over $22 billion in new, energy-efficient ships and technologies to minimize our environmental impact and make progress towards our goal of reducing the rate of carbon emissions by 40% by 2030 as compared to 2008."[a] Companies are experimenting with a variety of strategies including capping seagoing speeds, using liquefied natural gas (LNG), investing in exhaust gas cleaning systems, and developing clean energy capacity at ports to allow ships to turn off engines.

While these are important steps, cruises have wider impacts that must also be considered. The Galápagos is an archipelago of volcanic islands in the Pacific Ocean west of Ecuador (map 5.1). It is a highly sought-after destination for its exceptional biodiversity and therefore constitutes a particularly important case study to examine these impacts. Galápagos National Park and Marine Reserve is a UNESCO World Heritage Site visited by over 72,000 cruise tourists.[b] With high annual growth rates, the destination was on the list of World Heritage Sites in Danger from 2007 to 2010. The Ecuadorian government implemented new regulations, but concerns about tourism (the increasing land-based tourism as well as the traditional live-aboard cruises) remain.[c] The government limits the size of and routes of ships, but ongoing issues include the introduction of invasive species, human interactions with wildlife that could create stress or change patterns of behavior, and increased waste (particularly plastic).

In recognition of these place-based concerns, some cruise companies are making further changes to their ships and practices for their Galápagos tours. In 2019, the *Celebrity Flora*, a 100-passenger luxury ship, was built specifically to address the environmental impacts of cruising these islands. Consistent with current industry initiatives, the ship is designed for fuel efficiency and reduced emissions. More specifically, the ship uses anchorless technology, which helps maintain its position and protect the sensitive seabed in the marine reserve. Plastic cups and water bottles are replaced with a reusable metal bottle and filtration stations, and waste management practices recycle or reuse other materials.[d] The *M/Y Conservation*, an eighteen-passenger ship, was projected for launch in 2020. The ship's Ecuador-based operator aimed for it to be the most sustainable to cruise the islands. Plans included a new type of engine to reduce emissions and water pollution, and it would run quietly to minimize the disturbance of marine life. A treatment system would filter water to prevent ocean contamination, and onboard amenities and cleaning products would be nontoxic and biodegradable. Waste would be reused or taken back to the mainland for recycling. The company has stated its intention to make its design freely available for others in the Galápagos.[e]

Tourism plays an important role in preserving the Galápagos, but the stakes are high. For some operators, this creates an incentive to innovate, to develop better technologies and policies. It will be interesting to see what effects these innovations have over the next few years.

*Discussion topic*: Do you think such changes made to cruise ships and policies will become the norm in the Galápagos Islands? Do you think these changes could also be implemented throughout the global cruise industry? Explain.

*Tourism online*: Galapagos Conservancy, "Sustainable Tourism in Galapagos," at https://www.galapagos.org/travel/travel/sustainable-tourism/

---

[a] Cruise Lines International Association, "2020 State of the Cruise Industry Outlook," accessed April 13, 2020, https://cruising.org/-/media/research-updates/research/state-of-the-cruise-industry.pdf.

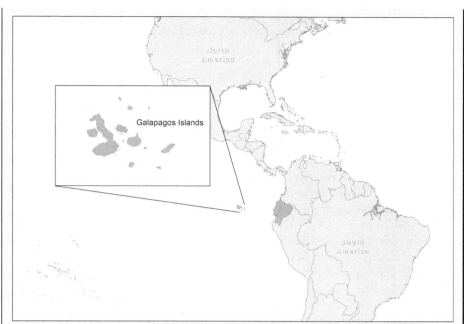

**Map 5.1. The Galápagos Islands, Ecuador. The Galápagos Islands Park and Marine Reserve is a UNESCO World Heritage Site visited by over 72,000 cruise tourists annually.** *Source*: Gang Gong

[b] Cultural & Natural Heritage Tours—Galapagos, "20% Growth in Land-Based Tourism Last Year—Can this Continue?" February 1, 2019, accessed April 14, 2020, https://www.cnhtours.com/news/2019/2/1/20-growth-in-land-based-tourism-last-year-can-this-continue/.

[c] Kerstin K. Zander, Angelica Saeteros, Daniel Orellana, Veronica Toral Granda, Aggie Wegner, Arturo Izurietah, and Stephen T. Garnett, "Determinants of Tourist Satisfaction with National Park Guides and Facilities in the Galápagos," *International Journal of Tourism Sciences* 16, nos. 1–2 (2016): 61.

[d] Rana Good, "5 Cool Eco-Friendly Features on the New Celebrity Flora," *Forbes*, July 29, 2019, accessed August 14, 2020, https://www.forbes.com/sites/ranagood/2019/07/29/eco-friendly-features-celebrity-flora/#5fd890c623f3.

[e] Mary Holland, "The Cruise Ship That Could Preserve the Galapagos Islands," *Condé Nast Traveler*, August 30, 2019, accessed April 14, 2020, https://www.cntraveler.com/story/the-cruise-ship-that-could-preserve-the-galapagos-islands.

In 2020, the cruise industry experienced further damage to its reputation. In the first and most publicized case, a *Diamond Princess* passenger who had disembarked in Hong Kong on February 1 tested positive for COVID-19. Two days later, the ship was quarantined upon arrival in Japanese waters with 3,711 passengers and crew members. In the confined space, the virus spread to more than 700 of them. By the end of March, thirty-two cruise ships had been affected with passengers or crew members who tested positive for the virus or by ports prohibiting them from docking due to fears about the virus.[23] The Centers for Disease Control and Prevention (CDC) issued a No Sail Order that would require cruise ships to cease operations for the duration of the crisis. Industry experts predicted that cruises would be one of the slowest tourism sectors to recover because of the negative press during this time. To reassure customers, cruise companies may need to retrofit ships to create areas that can be quarantined if necessary as well as establish better screening protocols (e.g., temperature checks upon boarding) and contingency plans.[24]

## AIR TRANSPORT

Air transport is the most recently developed mode and has primarily been used in tourism as a means of reaching the destination. In fact, this mode has been vital in increasing the accessibility of remote and poorly connected destinations (figure 5.4). Due to high costs, air travel has been unavailable for much of the world's population. However, recent developments such as the introduction of low-cost carriers have started to make changes in the way airlines do business.

Low-cost carriers (LCCs), also known as discount, budget, or no-frills airlines, concentrate on reducing operating costs to offer lower ticket prices to passengers. These carriers often run out of secondary airports that not only charge lower airport fees but also allow quicker operations. Traditionally, they have offered point-to-point services (i.e., limited or no connections to other places) on shorter routes to maximize the number of trips in both directions, and they maintain fast turnaround times to increase aircraft utilization.[25] Carriers benefit from little competition on these routes. However, there has also been an increase in long-haul, low-cost airlines.

**Figure 5.4. Air transport provides the means of reaching destinations that are isolated by poor surface transportation networks—in this case, Dangriga, Belize.** *Source*: Tom Nelson

LCCs operate with minimal personnel, and staff tend to work the maximum hours legally allowed with relatively low pay and few benefits. These factors allow a cost advantage over full-service carriers (FSC) of up to 60 percent.[26] Most LCCs have only one seating class, no seat assignments, and limited personal space to maximize the number of seats. Price is the primary consideration for passengers traveling on LCCs. These passengers are willing to accept fewer and lower-quality services as a trade-off for these low prices, and they are willing to travel farther to access airports serviced by LCCs. Air transport, and LCCs in particular, have been connected to overtourism. The LCCs allow more people to travel, creating overcrowding issues in major destinations, although they also have the potential to redirect tourists to lesser-known destinations.

Recently, fly-share and semiprivate jet companies have attracted attention. These companies primarily focus on short-haul, regional trips that are presented as a faster and easier alternative to driving. Operating with annual or monthly memberships, services promote private terminals with no security lines as well as other business class amenities. Routes were initially concentrated on the West Coast of the US, with increasing East Coast options.[27] In addition, flying taxis have been discussed as the future of transportation. Uber Air proposes using a network of small electric vertical take-off and landing (eVTOL) vehicles. The technology is intended to be energy efficient as well as space efficient by making use of existing infrastructure to create an extensive network of "skyports." The company set a launch date of 2023 in Dallas (Texas), Los Angeles (California), and Melbourne (Australia).[28]

Like other modes, air transport has come under scrutiny for its emissions. The precursor to #trainbrag, #flightshame (#flygskam), originated in Sweden to push for reductions in air travel due to its environmental impact. In 2018 and 2019, domestic travel in that country declined. As the movement expanded, some viewed it as a way of inducing shame in others to get them to change their behavior, which gave rise to att smygflyga (to fly in secret). In response, the industry is more actively promoting their efforts to reduce emissions (see box 5.2).[29]

Air transport currently faces a number of challenges. With a growth in airline fleets combined with retirements, a pilot shortage has been looming. As of 2019, Boeing projected a demand of 804,000 new civil aviation pilots as well as 914,000 new cabin crew, and 769,000 new maintenance technicians to support commercial aviation, business aviation, and civil helicopter industries over the next twenty years.[30] Airplane capacity became another issue after two deadly crashes grounded nearly 400 Boeing 737 Max jets in March 2019. This took 40,000 seats out of service in the US every day. Thousands of flights were canceled, remaining flights were more crowded, and airlines saw lower profits.[31] By the end of 2019, more than twenty airlines (primarily regional and LCCs) went bankrupt. Just a few months later, COVID-19 grounded approximately 80 percent of the world's fleet. At the time of writing, the International Air Transport Association is projecting a global air transport revenue loss of US$252 billion,[32] and there is an incredible amount of uncertainty about how many airlines (most likely those receiving government support) will survive (see box 5.3).

## Box 5.2.   In-Depth: Airlines, Emissions, and Offsets

Air transport accounts for approximately 2 percent of global human-induced carbon emissions. To reduce this carbon footprint, airlines around the world are considering mitigation strategies. **Climate change mitigation** is defined as the technological, economic, and sociocultural changes that can lead to reductions in greenhouse gas emissions. One solution is to reduce air travel, which seemed unrealistic until the COVID-19 pandemic grounded most flights. Prior to that, more promising solutions included innovations or practices to reduce emissions and offsetting emissions.

Various strategies are used to reduce emissions. As airlines replace the older aircraft in their fleet with newer, more efficient ones, they will reduce fuel consumption and emissions. The replacement process may be accelerated by COVID-19 shutdown. Likewise, outdated air traffic control systems were rife with inefficiencies. The Federal Aviation Administration (FAA) is in the process of transitioning to the NextGen satellite-based system to improve not only safety but also efficiency. Pilots also work to maximize efficiency within the constraints of the aircraft, air traffic control, and the weather. Sustainable aviation fuel is thought to hold the greatest potential for reducing emissions. Sustainable aviation fuels are derived from cooking oil, plant oils, municipal waste, waste gases, and agricultural residues and can be used with existing jet engine technology. This fuel reduces overall lifecycle emissions by as much as 80 percent compared to fossil fuels.[a] US-based JetBlue had plans to begin purchasing sustainable aviation fuel for flights from San Francisco International Airport in 2020. Delta invested in a facility to produce sustainable fuel for its flights in the same year. At this time, the extent to which these plans will be set back by the COVID-19 crisis is unknown.

Since the mid-2000s, tourists have been able to purchase offsets approximately equivalent to the emissions incurred in their travel. The money generated by offsets would be invested in projects to reduce global emissions, such as providing cleaner and safer cooking stoves to families in the least developed parts of the world. However, such programs were not widely known, nor were they convenient when they had to be purchased from a third party instead of as part of the booking process. It was often difficult for individuals to verify how the money was spent or if the projects actually resulted in the anticipated reductions. In addition, critics argued that offsets provided wealthy tourists with a means of easing their guilt without having to change their behavior. Perhaps there is a measure of truth to this, as offsets gained renewed attention in light of flight shame.

While most airlines now offer this option to passengers, some offset their emissions at certain times or on specific routes. In 2019, the UK-based LCC EasyJet became the world's first major airline to offset emissions for all flights.[b] Shortly thereafter, JetBlue announced that it would begin offset emissions for all US flights starting in July 2020. Based on beginning-of-the-year forecasts, the company projected their offsets would be the equivalent of removing more than 1.5 million passenger vehicles from the road.[c] As with individual offsets, critics express concerns that this will allow airlines to continue business as usual, although both EasyJet and JetBlue stated that offsets are simply a stopgap solution while they continue to develop other measures to reduce emissions.

*Discussion topic*: Do you think the responsibility for offsetting flight emissions should lie with the airline or the individual? Explain.

*Tourism online:* JetBlue, "JetBlue Is Going Carbon Neutral on All Domestic Flights," http://blog.jetblue.com/offset-jan-2020/

---

[a] Air Transport Action Group, "Beginner's Guide to Sustainable Aviation Fuel, Edition 3," November 2017, accessed April 15, 2020, https://aviationbenefits.org/media/166152/beginners-guide-to-saf_web.pdf.

[b] Jessica Puckett, "EasyJet Will Now Pay for Carbon Offsets on All its Flights," *Condé Nast Traveler*, November 19, 2019, accessed April 15, 2020, https://www.cntraveler.com/story/easyjet-will-now-pay-for-carbon-offsets-on-all-its-flights.

[c] JetBlue, "JetBlue Prepares Its Business for a New Climate Reality," January 6, 2020, accessed April 15, 2020, http://blueir.investproductions.com/investor-relations/press-releases/2020/01-06-2020-131859289.

## Box 5.3.  Experience: Flying During COVID-19

*In the spring of 2020, COVID-19 brought the travel industry nearly to a halt. While countless flights were canceled, the world saw eerie images of empty Transportation Security Administration (TSA) screening areas and airplanes parked on runways. Harrison, a commercial pilot for a US regional carrier, continued to fly a drastically reduced schedule. He offered his thoughts on the situation as it was unfolding.*

For the past two years, we have been facing a pilot shortage. The mandatory retirement age for commercial pilots is sixty-five, and many senior pilots at major airlines were getting close to that age. By 2023, it was predicted that we would have the fewest number of pilots for the anticipated amount of flights. Now, with an 80 to 90 percent decrease in flights, there is an oversupply of pilots. For many carriers, pilots within five years of retirement age have been offered an early retirement package, which will hopefully allow younger pilots to remain active during this time. However, it is likely that a lot of furloughs are still coming. We are an industry that is heavily dependent on demand—and demand for a "luxury" item at that. Until travel comes back, we have to expect to see reductions.

Airports are empty (figure 5.5). All of the restaurants and stores in the airports are closed. Our planes have a capacity of 76, and most flights have ten passengers or less. There are very

**Figure 5.5. At the peak of the global COVID-19 pandemic, flights were drastically reduced. Those who did travel during this time encountered an unfamiliar site: empty airport terminals. *Source*:** Harrison Caubble

few regular fliers. Recently, our passengers have consisted of exchange students from universities trying to get back to their home countries. We are considered essential workers, and I am not afraid to continue flying. We are taking precautions to keep our remaining passengers and ourselves healthy. Crews are fogging the plane with a disinfectant and wiping down seats, tray tables, and so on. There are sanitizer wipes everywhere. Crew members aren't usually allowed to wear masks or gloves, but that is now permitted. Yet, so far I have only flown into one airport where law enforcement was checking temperatures on arrival and ensuring that those staying in the state would quarantine.

Airplanes need to fly regularly. Having all of these planes parked can cause maintenance issues. Some carriers were already in the process of phasing out older and less profitable planes. Many won't be brought back into service. Fleets will be leaner going forward, but the aircraft with newer technologies will be more efficient. Getting them flying again will take time. Each plane will need to undergo significant inspections, maintenance, and possibly even repairs. In addition, flight crews will need to retrain on simulators. Gate agents, baggage handlers, and other staff who were laid off need to be brought back and (re)trained. It is likely to be a six- to eight-month process. It would be hard to see much of a return before the end of 2020, if not early 2021.

As of now, three regional carriers have already shut down. More will probably face bankruptcy, even potentially one of the major carriers. Airlines are very expensive to operate, and the industry can't sustain these kinds of losses. US carriers aren't subsidized by the government like they are in other countries (e.g., Qatar Airways), but as a result of the Coronavirus Aid, Relief, and Economic Security Act (CARES Act), the government will get a stake in airlines in exchange for financial aid. This aid was necessary, and it may still take more for the airlines to survive. Travel is an essential part of today's world, and we need US carriers to transport people within the US. We also need to get international travel back up and running when it is possible so that we are able to capture that revenue here at home as opposed to ceding it to another international carrier.

Ultimately, there is still an incredible amount of uncertainty about how long this pandemic will last and how we respond to it. I think my carrier is likely to make it through this time. Our leadership is very strategic and is already looking at where the opportunities will be for us in the coming months. Hopefully we all get through this first of all, but hopefully we can get through this on the path to something better.

*—Harrison*

## SPACE TRANSPORT

The final category—space—is much discussed and anticipated but at least at this time is still impractical for all but a few very wealthy individuals. Interest in space tourism has existed since the space race. In 1989, Pan American Airways reportedly had a wait list of over 93,000 people for its first passenger flight to the moon. The company folded in 1991. Ten years later, the world saw its first space tourist. American Dennis Tito traveled on a Russian spacecraft to the International Space Station. Over the next decade, six additional tourists paid an estimated US$20–35 million for an orbital trip.[33] In 2010, the Russian Space Agency suspended orbital space tourism and has not resumed it since then. In 2019, the National Aeronautics and Space Administration (NASA) announced plans to allow private companies to send space tourists to the International Space Station beginning the following year. Costs were estimated at US$35,000 per night in addition to the cost of travel, thought to be around $US60 million.[34]

Virgin Galactic initially planned to start offering suborbital space trips in 2009, but the project experienced numerous delays. The company's *VSS Enterprise* was destroyed during a test flight in 2014. Seven hundred seats had already been reserved for its first commercial flight scheduled for the following year. Tickets cost US$200,000.[35] Prior to the COVID-19 shutdown, the company restated their commitment to launching in 2020 and announced plans to increase to 270 flights a year by 2023. Virgin Galactic is now competing with Jeff Bezos' Blue Origin and Elon Musk's SpaceX projects.[36] In addition, several companies have proposed construction of variations on space hotels, from an addition to the International Space Station to a new space station with a capacity of 100 guests per week and cruise ship–type amenities[37] perhaps not unlike the vessel in the science fiction comedy series *Avenue 5* (2020).

The idea of space tourism was initially dismissed by agencies such as NASA due to safety hazards as well as the amount of time and resources involved; however, with recent developments, it is now regarded as a possibility to generate revenues for space agencies. Still there are many areas of research on the potential for space tourism. For example, actual demand for the experience needs to be determined. While surveys conducted over the years show a high level of interest in space tourism, the idea is still considered hypothetical for most due to technological and/or financial barriers. One study found that at least one-quarter of respondents would be unlikely to participate in space tourism, even if cost were not a consideration. Perceived risk was the primary reason given. Other issues pertain to health and training of participants; regulation, liability, and insurance; socioeconomic impacts of space tourism at spaceport locations; and environmental impact and carbon footprint.[38] Using carbon calculators, one travel site estimated that emissions from one trip on a SpaceX vessel would be the equivalent of 395 transatlantic flights.[39]

Space tourism is a captivating idea. According to one set of scholars, "Space appears to be the next natural step in satisfying people's need for exploration, adventure and new recreation activities."[40] Indeed, with more places facing issues of overtourism, those who can afford to do so will look for ever-more exclusive destinations despite the costs. This prompts the question: even if we can go, should we?

# Directions in Research

Issues associated with sustainability in tourism transport, including some of those discussed here, constitute a key area of research. Yet, researchers explore the intersection between tourism and transport in other ways and work to address other current issues. For example, the rise of products like nature, rural, and sport tourism has at times strained the relationship between tourism and transport. These products typically involve the transfer of tourists from an urban market or a centrally located terminal node (e.g., an airport) to remote locations that are not well served by public transportation. In addition, tourists participating in various sports activities may be carrying heavy or bulky equipment, such as golf clubs, skis, surfboards, and bicycles.[41] These items are difficult to take on public transportation, if in fact they are permitted at all. As such, these tourism products are heavily reliant on private cars. Tourists must either be able to reach the destination in their own vehicles or rent a car upon their arrival at the terminal, and destination stakeholders must plan accordingly to manage vehicles in an area that is perhaps unaccustomed to high volumes of traffic.

Other researchers are considering issues of access to tourism transport and inequality. Tourism is dependent on transport to facilitate experiences. As such, tourism becomes unavailable to people without ready access to or the ability to pay for transportation, such as lower-income groups in inner-city areas, populations living in remote rural areas, or large segments of the population in developing countries. Tourism transport can become a symbol of inequality and a means of segregating tourists from residents. For example, the modes used for tourists are typically modern, safe, and comfortable, whereas the public transportation used by residents may be old, deficient, and overcrowded. Tourist transport does not generally serve the needs of residents and may, in fact, be off-limits to them.

Finally, researchers examine the relationship between tourism, transport, and health. Although early health concerns about the faster speeds of rail travel proved to be unfounded, the increase in long-distance air transport associated with tourism has generated new risks. This can range from the comparatively mild effects of jet lag to traveler's thrombosis, which, in the most serious cases, can result in a potentially fatal pulmonary embolism. In addition, new attention is being given to the increased levels of stress that can result from anxiety about flying, the threat of terrorism, missed flights, lost baggage, and more.[42] While this can lead to occasional (and well-publicized) incidents of aggression or violence, it also can exacerbate existing medical conditions, resulting in in-flight emergencies. Geographers have been involved in studying the rapid diffusion of infectious diseases, from severe acute respiratory syndrome (SARS) to Ebola, by air travel, and we can expect considerable new research on COVID-19.

# Conclusion

Transport is a fundamental component in tourism, as it facilitates the movement of tourists from their place of origin to their destination. Transportation systems were a precondition for tourism, and innovations helped usher in several key eras in tourism. In particular, transport was one of the factors in the development of modern mass tourism, which allows more people—in more parts of the world—to travel than ever before. At the same time, transportation can distinctly shape the tourism experience. As transport geography provides the means of exploring the spatial patterns of movement and the geographic factors that allow or constrain this movement, we can apply the concepts of this topical branch to contribute to our understanding of the role transport plays in tourism.

# Key Terms

- climate change mitigation
- interchange
- terminal
- transport geography
- transportation mode
- transportation network
- transportation node

# Notes

1. Bruce Prideaux, "The Role of the Transport System in Destination Development," *Tourism Management* 21 (2000): 54.

2. Richard D. Knowles, "How the Journal of Transport Geography has Evolved since 1993," *Journal of Transport Geography* 81 (2019): 2.

3. John Towner, "The Grand Tour: A Key Phase in the History of Tourism," *Annals of Tourism Research* 12 (1985): 322.

4. Marguerite Shaffer, *See America First: Tourism and National Identity, 1880–1940* (Washington, DC: Smithsonian Institution Press, 2001), 13.

5. Jack Simmons, "Railways, Hotels, and Tourism in Great Britain, 1839–1914," *Journal of Contemporary History* 19 (1984): 207.

6. Charles R. Goeldner and J. R. Brent Ritchie, *Tourism: Principles, Practices, Philosophies*, 9th ed. (Hoboken, NJ: Wiley, 2006), 56.

7. Simmons, "Railways, Hotels, and Tourism," 212.

8. Simon M. Kevan, "Quests for Cures: A History of Tourism for Climate and Health," *International Journal of Biometeorology* 37 (1993): 118.

9. Orvar Löfgren, *On Holiday: A History of Vacationing* (Berkeley: University of California Press, 1999), 43.

10. Gareth Shaw and Allan M. Williams, *Critical Issues in Tourism: A Geographical Perspective*, 2nd ed. (Malden, MA: Blackwell, 2002), 216–17.

11. Jean-Paul Rodrigue, Claude Comtois, and Brian Slack, *The Geography of Transport Systems*, 4th ed. (London: Routledge, 2017), 10.

12. Mahita Gajanan, "The FAA Just Banned Flights over Iranian Air Space. Here's What Fliers Need to Know," *Time*, June 21, 2019, accessed April 10, 2020, https://time.com/5611991/faa-iran-air-space-tensions-ban/.

13. Rodrigue, Comtois, and Slack, *The Geography of Transport Systems*, 10.

14. Alan Lew and Bob McKercher, "Modeling Tourist Movements: A Local Destination Analysis," *Annals of Tourism Research* 33 (2006): 407.

15. Lew and McKercher, "Modeling Tourist Movements," 420.

16. Daniel Albalate and Germà Bel, "Tourism and Urban Public Transport: Holding Demand Pressure under Supply Constraints," *Tourism Management* 31 (2010): 432.

17. United Nations World Tourism Organization, *International Tourism Highlights 2019 Edition* (2019), 7, accessed March 5, 2020, https://www.e-unwto.org/doi/pdf/10.18111/9789284421152.

18. Daniel Albalate, Javier Campos, and Juan Luis Jiménez, "Tourism and High Speed Rail in Spain: Does the AVE Increase Local Visitors?" *Annals of Tourism Research* 65 (2017): 72–3.

19. Scott A. Cohen and Debbie Hopkins, "Autonomous Vehicles and the Future of Urban Tourism," *Annals of Tourism Research* 74 (2019): 34–5.

20. Cruise Lines International Association, "2020 State of the Cruise Industry Outlook," accessed April 13, 2020, https://cruising.org/-/media/research-updates/research/state-of-the-cruise-industry.pdf.

21. Morten Simonsen, Stefan Gössling, and Hans Jakob Walnum, "Cruise Ship Emissions in Norwegian Waters: A Geographical Analysis," *Journal of Transport Geography* 78 (2019): 87.

22. Sarah Mervosh, "Carnival Cruises to Pay $20 Million in Pollution and Cover-Up Case," *The New York Times*, June 4, 2019, accessed April 13, 2020, https://www.nytimes.com/2019/06/04/business/carnival-cruise-pollution.html.

23. Brittany Chang, "32 Cruise Ships around the World Have Been Affected by the Coronavirus So Far, Leaving Passengers Infected, Dead, or Stranded—See the Full List," *Business Insider*, March 25, 2020, accessed April 13, 2020, https://www.businessinsider.com/cruises-that-have-been-affected-by-coronavirus-2020-3.

24. Katherine Alex Beaven, "A Futurist Predicts How You'll Be Traveling after Coronavirus," *Fodor's Travel*, April 1, 2020, accessed April 13, 2020, https://www.fodors.com/news/coronavirus/a-futurist-predicts-how-youll-be-traveling-after-coronavirus.

25. Juan L. Eugenio-Martin and Federico Inchuasti-Sintes, "Low-Cost Travel and Tourism Expenditures," *Annals of Tourism Research* 57 (2016): 142.

26. Sven Gross and Louisa Klemmer, *Introduction to Tourism Transport* (Oxfordshire: CABI, 2014): 34.

27. Jason Sheeler, "How to Fly Private without Breaking the Bank," Condé Nast Traveler, January 10, 2020, accessed April 14, 2020, https://www.cntraveler.com/story/how-to-fly-private-semi-private-jets.

28. Uber Elevate, "Uber Air," accessed April 27, 2020, https://www.uber.com/us/en/elevate/uberair/.

29. Tommy Lund, "Sweden's Air Travel Drops in Year When 'Flight Shaming' Took Off," *Reuters*, January 10, 2020, accessed April 15, 2020, https://www.reuters.com/article/us-airlines-sweden/swedens-air-travel-drops-in-year-when-flight-shaming-took-off-idUSKBN1Z90UI.

30. Boeing, "Pilot & Technician Outlook 2019–2038," accessed April 15, 2020, https://www.boeing.com/commercial/market/pilot-technician-outlook/.

31. Jim Zarroli, "Boeing 737 Max Grounding Takes Toll on Airlines and Passengers," National Public Radio, July 29, 2019, accessed April 15, 2020, https://www.npr.org/2019/07/29/746345317/boeing-737-max-grounding-takes-toll-on-airlines-and-passengers.

32. International Air Transport Association, "Deeper Revenue Hit from COVID-19," March 24, 2020, accessed April 15, 2020, https://www.iata.org/en/pressroom/pr/2020-03-24-01/.

33. Sam Cole, "Space Tourism: Prospects, Positioning, and Planning," *Journal of Tourism Futures* 1, no. 2 (2015): 132.

34. Stefanie Waldek, "You Can Soon Vacation in Space for $35,000 Per Night," *Condé Nast Traveler*, June 10, 2019, accessed April 10, 2020, https://www.cntraveler.com/story/you-can-soon-vacation-in-space-for-dollar35000-per-night.

35. Cole, "Space Tourism," 133.

36. Ruqayyah Moynihan and Thomas Giraudet, "Richard Branson Wants Virgin Galactic to Send People to Space Every 32 Hours by 2023," *Business Insider*, September 10, 2019, accessed April 10, 2020, https://www.businessinsider.com/branson-virgin-galactic-people-space-every-32-hours-2019-9?r=US&IR=T.

37. Jessica Puckett, "What Spending a Night at a Space Hotel Looks Like," Condé Nast Traveler, September 6, 2019, accessed April 10, 2020, https://www.cntraveler.com/story/what-spending-a-night-at-a-space-hotel-looks-like.

38. Maharaj Vijay Reddy, Mirela Nica, and Keith Wilkes, "Space Tourism: Research Recommendations for the Future of the Industry and Perspectives of Potential Participants," *Tourism Management* 33 (2012): 1095–7.

39. Champion Traveler, "One SpaceX Rocket Launch Produces the Equivalent of 395 Transatlantic Flights Worth of $CO_2$ Emissions," accessed April 10, 2020, https://championtraveler.com/news/one-spacex-rocket-launch-produces-the-equivalent-of-395-transatlantic-flights-worth-of-co2-emissions/.

40. Reddy, Nica, and Wilkes, "Space Tourism," 1101.

41. Jennifer Reilly, Peter Williams, and Wolfgang Haider, "Moving Towards More Eco-Efficient Tourist Transportation to a Resort Destination: The Case of Whistler, British Columbia," *Research in Transportation Economics* 26 (2010): 71.

42. Stephen Page and Joanne Connell, "Transport and Tourism," in *The Wiley Blackwell Companion to Tourism*, ed. Alan A. Lew, C. Michael Hall, and Allan M. Williams (Malden: Wiley Blackwell, 2014), 163.

# CHAPTER 6

# The Physical Geography of Tourism

Tourists routinely evaluate the physical geography of potential destinations. For most tourists, this is not something that is done scientifically, systematically, or even consciously; they simply want to know if a place has the physical setting they are looking for, if its physical conditions will provide them with the opportunity to participate in the activities they want, or if its conditions might keep them from doing those things. Some rely on stereotypes about places, but those tourists who do a little research into the physical geography of a place are able to make informed decisions about where to go as well as when. This type of research is going to become more important in the future with changing environmental conditions that will make it more difficult to rely on assumptions.

Tourism stakeholders also consider the physical geography of their destinations. In the planning stage, stakeholders must assess the physical resources that will provide the foundation for tourism in that place, the physical barriers to tourism, and increasingly the physical changes and processes that have the potential to disrupt tourism. Then, they must devise strategies that will allow them to use resources sustainably and to manage the challenges presented by barriers as well as "shocks" such as natural disasters. These stakeholders, consisting of various community members, business owners, and/or government officials, may not have the knowledge or expertise they need to do this on their own. The work of physical scientists and environmental consultants, many of whom come from a background in geography, can provide stakeholders with the information they need to develop a tourism destination, manage it, and plan for future environmental changes. The powerful geography approach provides an important means of preparing geographers to address these issues.

Because tourism is a human phenomenon, greater emphasis has been placed on examining tourism through the topical branches of human geography. Nonetheless, it is clearly important to consider the physical side of geography as well. Physical geography is the subdivision of geography that studies the earth's physical systems. Physical geography is organized into topical branches, such as meteorology and climatology, hydrology and oceanography, geomorphology, and biogeography. This chapter introduces each of these topical branches and examines how the elements in the earth's physical system *affect* (see box 1.3) tourism, either as a resource that provides the basis for tourism or as a barrier that prevents tourism. In addition, it considers how climate change is also affecting tourism. As summarized by one geographer,

> Given tourism's strong dependence on natural resources such as weather and climate, biodiversity, or pristine landscapes, it is clear that climate change has the potential to both negatively and positively influence this economic sector. Assessing potential impacts of climate change on the tourism sector is vital for adapting tourism products and destinations to a changing tourist demand and availability of natural resources.[1]

First, however, we will discuss the concept of resources as applied in the context of tourism.

# Resources, Barriers, and the Tourism Resource Audit

Resources generally refer to products that are perceived to have value and may be used to satisfy human needs and/or wants. Resources are relative and subjective; what is considered a resource depends on the cultural, political, economic, and/or technological circumstances of a society at a given point in time.[2] Consequently, something that might be considered a resource for one group of people might not be for another due to different cultural values, political priorities, economic conditions, or levels of technology. Likewise, what is considered a resource in one time period might not be in another due to changes in any of these factors. We typically think of physical or natural resources that are elements in the earth system. The availability of these resources is dependent on physical processes but also on human efforts.

Applied to the context of tourism geography, **tourism resources** are those components of a destination's environment (physical or human) that have the potential to facilitate tourism or provide the basis for tourism attractions. Physical tourism resources are considered to be "an invaluable tourism asset and ... fundamental to the development of tourism for virtually all destinations. They tend to be the foundation from which other resources are developed, and thus often play both a principal and key supporting role in tourism."[3] Moreover, tourism activities are contingent on not one but a combination of resources. These resources may be tangible features in the geography of a place that can be readily used or appreciated (e.g., scenic mountains as an attractive backdrop for a wellness resort). Destinations may also need to develop these resources for use in tourism (e.g., creating ski lifts and runs on mountains to allow people to participate in winter sport tourism).

The presence of resources can allow a destination to develop; however, the presence of barriers can prevent or disrupt tourism in that place. A barrier refers to something material in the environment that constitutes a physical impediment or something immaterial that creates a logistical or perceptual impediment. As with resources, what is considered a barrier—and the extent to which it functions as one—varies with different cultural norms, political policies, economic circumstances, or technological advancement. Elements in the earth–ocean–atmosphere system can present distinct physical barriers but also perceptual barriers.

In tourism, both physical and perceptual barriers may prevent tourists from visiting certain destinations. These barriers also have the potential to shape the ways in which destinations develop. Thus, destination stakeholders need to evaluate its physical geography not only for potential resources but also for any barriers and to find ways of overcoming them—whether it is grading the landscape, installing artificial snowmakers, or convincing potential tourists that the weather is really not as bad as they think it is going to be.

Tourism stakeholders, especially those at emerging destinations, frequently fail to fully understand the conditions of their own resource base. With economic benefit as the goal, stakeholders may take shortcuts in the development process. They may choose to model their industry on that of a successful destination, even though circumstances are different for each place. They may conduct only a superficial analysis of the area's resources, or they may assume that they already have all of the information they need. Yet, it is hardly ever that simple. Some resources are attractions in themselves; these are the ones that are often easy to spot (e.g., Half Dome, Yosemite National Park). Others, however, simply provide the framework that allows for tourism. It can be much more difficult to understand how the quality, quantity, distribution, accessibility, seasonality, and so forth of these resources are going to affect tourism in that place.

The **tourism resource audit** (TRA) is a tool that can be used by destination stakeholders to systematically identify, classify, and assess all of the features of a place that will impact the supply of tourism. Because resources are subjective, however, this can be tricky. Typically, a range of stakeholders, coming from different perspectives, should be involved to create the most comprehensive and appropriate dataset. This will include experts to provide scientific data and analysis, community members to contribute local knowledge, industry analysts to assess market potential, and even tourists to offer the demand-side perspective. A variety of strategies can be used to create an exhaustive list of resources that are critically evaluated to understand how they might affect tourism. Geographic information systems (GIS) are used to manage the often-large datasets created by a TRA. Analysis of this data allows stakeholders to determine the strengths and weaknesses of tourism at the destination, improvements that need to be made, and strategies that should be put in place for both immediate and long-term development.

Although this process is, perhaps, less exciting than other aspects of tourism development and promotion, it is fundamental. According to the authors of *The Tourism Development Handbook*, "The effort put in at this stage should be well rewarded later on with the development of a more successful and sustainable tourism destination."[4] Still, a TRA only captures the condition of resources at a given time. Resources, and what are considered resources, are not static. Consequently, the TRA database should be updated regularly, and tourism strategies reevaluated accordingly.

# The Physical System, Physical Geography, and Tourism

The systems view is an important organizing concept in physical geography, as the earth is made up of interrelated physical systems, including the abiotic systems (i.e., the overlapping, nonliving systems consisting of the atmosphere, hydrosphere, and lithosphere) that provide the basis for the biotic system (i.e., the living system made up of the biosphere). Specifically, the atmosphere is the thin, gaseous layer surrounding the earth's surface. The hydrosphere encompasses the waters that exist in the atmosphere, on the earth's surface, and in the crust near the surface. The lithosphere includes the solid part of the earth. Finally, these three spheres form the basis for the biosphere, which is the area where living organisms can exist.

Each of these spheres can be studied through different but ultimately interrelated topical branches in geography, including meteorology and climatology (atmosphere), hydrology and oceanography (hydrosphere), geomorphology (lithosphere), and biogeography (biosphere). Table 6.1 provides a summary of the resources and barriers associated with each of these branches of physical geography, and the issues are discussed below. There have generally been fewer links between tourism and these topical branches of geography in comparison with those on the human side of geography. Nonetheless, physical geography plays a crucial role in our understanding of the earth and our place in it, and geographers recognize that these physical systems have distinct impacts on all aspects of human life. Particularly with the powerful geography framework, there is clear potential for greater research applying knowledge from physical geography to better understand and work toward current issues in tourism.

## METEOROLOGY, CLIMATOLOGY, AND TOURISM

While it may seem like the atmosphere is beyond the scope of geography, it is still an integral part in the earth system. Not only do atmospheric processes affect what happens in other spheres, these phenomena also affect human life every day. Geographers are interested in both weather and climate to understand how patterns vary from place to place, how they shape those places, and how they affect human activities on the earth's surface. Meteorology and climatology are interrelated atmospheric sciences. **Meteorology** is the study of weather, which refers to the atmospheric conditions (e.g., air temperature and pressure, humidity, precipitation, wind speed and direction, cloud cover and type) for a given place and time. Because these conditions are dynamic, in an almost constant state of change, there is a distinct focus on short-term patterns. **Climatology** is the study of climate, which refers to the aggregate of weather conditions for a given place over time. Climatology expands upon meteorology by considering longer-term trends, generalizing about average weather conditions, and identifying variations or extremes.

In one introduction to physical geography, the distinction between weather and climate is bluntly put in this way: the idea of a place's climate is what attracts people to that place, but it is the reality of day-to-day weather conditions that makes them leave.[5] While simplistic, this raises an important consideration for the demand perspective in the geography of tourism. Tourists depend on information about the climate of a destination to try to make an informed decision about whether or not that place generally has the right conditions for the desired tourism activities at the time of year in which they intend to visit. Yet, climate data do not predict specific weather conditions. Forecasts become increasingly unreliable beyond just a few days, and most trips

**Table 6.1. Summary of How Features in Each of the Topical Branches of Physical Geography Can Become Resources for or Barriers to Tourism**

| Branch | Resources | Barriers |
|---|---|---|
| Meteorology and climatology | Attraction<br>In general, good weather conditions<br>Perceptual depending on individual and cultural preferences and desired activities<br><br>Basis for activities<br>Moderate temperatures<br>Sun (e.g., sunbathing)<br>Precipitation (e.g., skiing)/lack of precipitation (e.g., most outdoor activities)<br>Wind (e.g., windsurfing)/lack of wind (e.g., swimming) | Detraction<br>Perceptual depending on individual and cultural preferences and desired activities<br><br>Disrupt activities<br>Extreme temperatures<br>Precipitation/lack of precipitation<br>Wind/lack of wind<br>Natural hazards (e.g., thunderstorms, hurricanes, blizzards) |
| Hydrology and oceanography | Attraction<br>Unique water features (e.g., waterfalls, geysers)<br>Specific characteristics (e.g., meandering rivers for floating, rapids for whitewater rafting and kayaking)<br>Distinct properties (e.g., thermal or mineral springs for medical treatments)<br>Foundation for attractive tourism landscapes (e.g., green golf courses, landscaped resorts, decorative fountains)<br><br>Basis for activities<br>Swimming and bathing<br>Boating and rafting<br>Watersports<br>Fishing<br><br>Necessary quantity and quality<br>Drinking and bathing<br>Cooking and cleaning | Detraction<br>Perceptual (e.g., lack of available water to create attractive tourism landscapes)<br>Physical (e.g., poor water quality)<br><br>Disrupt activities<br>Lack of available water to participate in tourism activities<br>Health risks from poor water quality<br>Natural hazards (e.g., flooding, tidal surges, tsunamis) |

*(continued)*

**Table 6.1. (continued)**

| Branch | Resources | Barriers |
|---|---|---|
| Geomorphology | Attraction<br>Unique landforms (e.g., islands, mountains, canyons, caves)<br>Cultural values (e.g., sacred landscapes)<br>Landform processes (e.g., erupting volcanoes) | Detraction<br>Perceptual (e.g., cultural and personal perceptions of uninteresting or ugly landscapes) |
| | Location for resorts<br>High-altitude summer retreats and health resorts | Prevent accessibility<br>Physical (e.g., landforms that cut a destination off from major markets and/or make transportation difficult) |
| | Basis for activities<br>Mountain hiking/climbing<br>Winter sports | Disrupt activities<br>Natural hazards (e.g., earthquakes, volcanic eruptions) |
| Biogeography | Attraction<br>Distinct biomes (e.g., tropical rainforest, temperate rain forest, desert)<br>Attractive vegetation (e.g., flowering plants, fall colors)<br>Unique, rare, or endangered plant and animal species | Detraction<br>Lack of expected vegetation (e.g., barren instead of lush)<br>Deforested landscapes<br>Diminished wildlife populations due to habitat loss, overhunting, and poaching |
| | Basis for activities<br>Nature hikes, canopy tours<br>Fruit picking, truffle hunting<br>Bird watching, wildlife safaris | Disrupt activities<br>Natural hazards (e.g., wildfires)<br>Outbreaks of animal diseases (e.g., foot-and-mouth disease) |

will be planned well in advance of that. Consequently, tourists may find that the actual weather conditions at the destination during their vacation are not what they expected. This can be simply an inconvenience or prompt small changes in their plans, but it can also fundamentally alter or even cancel a trip.

One tourism scholar notes: "It is generally accepted that climate is an important part of the region's tourism resource base, but the role of climate in determining the suitability of a region for tourism or outdoor recreation is often assumed to be self-evident and therefore to require no elaboration."[6] Another argues that tourism planning rarely considers anything more than "simple, general descriptions of the climate, which are often unconnected to the needs of tourism."[7] When we consider all of the ways in which weather and climate affect tourism, we should begin to realize that this cannot be taken for granted.

## WEATHER AND CLIMATE AS A RESOURCE AND A BARRIER FOR TOURISM

Weather and climate arguably have a greater influence over what can and cannot be done in a given place than any other physical feature, which is clearly relevant to tourism. These elements determine the time and length of the tourism season, the products that can be developed, the location of activities and infrastructure, and more. Generally speaking, climate is the feature that a destination is least able to manipulate to provide the desired conditions for tourism. There are exceptions; for example, winter sport destinations use snowmakers to ensure that tourists have the experience they came for, even though natural conditions (i.e., a day of sun with sufficient fresh powder) would still be preferred.

Whether it is nature-based or in an urban area, much of tourism takes place outside. As such, elements of weather and climate can be a resource that provides the conditions that allow for tourism activities to take place. These elements of weather and climate can also be the resource on which tourism depends. Obviously, sun is a vital resource for sun, sea, and sand tourism. For these elements of the physical system, though, what is considered a resource for or a barrier to tourism is variable, depending on the activity and perceptions. This means that the same feature can, in fact, be both. For example, in the case of Tarifa, Spain, located between the popular 3S resorts of Costa del Sol and Costa de la Luz, the presence of high winds was a barrier to the development of sun, sea, and sand tourism. However, stakeholders turned this feature into a tourism resource by promoting the destination as the "capital of wind" and developing niche tourism activities like windsurfing.[8] Likewise, fog and mist might present a barrier to viewing scenic landscapes, but it could also add to the mystique of the place or increase the feeling of wonder as a scene suddenly presents itself to the viewer (figure 6.1).

Destinations seek to reassure potential tourists in target markets of their conditions, but even destinations with notoriously poor weather conditions for tourism activities try to make the most of it. For example, Scotland's National Tourism Organization website, Visit Scotland, reads: "We've all heard plenty of jokes about the Scottish weather—but most of them aren't true! Scotland's climate

**Figure 6.1. The Castle of Lousã, set in the mountains of Portugal, is "veiled in mystery and myth." The mountain mist creates a fitting setting for such a place.** *Source*: Tom Nelson

is actually quite moderate and very changeable, although on occasion we get really hot or really cold weather. As the old Scottish saying goes, 'there's no such thing as bad weather, only the wrong clothes!'"[9] Rather than shying away from their bad weather, they make light of it while highlighting other attractions. The site playfully itemizes their reasons why rain is actually a good thing, from providing the foundation for the country's lush natural vegetation and waterfalls to creating opportunities for visiting museums and drinking whiskey.

In addition to permitting or preventing tourist activities, weather conditions affect tourists' comfort and mood.[10] Tourists who were wet, cold, and miserable while visiting a destination or participating in an activity will have negative associations with that experience. This may have nothing to do with the characteristics of the site the tourists visited or the quality of the activity in which they participated. Their memories of the experience will be tied to their emotions. If they choose to share their experiences in online forums, their posts, reviews, or blogs will reflect these emotions. Other potential tourists who read negative accounts may be deterred from the destination, even though they might have a different set of conditions and therefore a completely different experience. In this case, weather can become a perceptual barrier.

Finally, extreme weather events such as hurricanes (box 6.1) or blizzards present a barrier to tourism. As a perceptual barrier, tourists may avoid destinations when

# Box 6.1.  Case Study: Hurricane Impacts on Caribbean Tourism

In a recent volume on tourism in the Caribbean, the author wrote, "For many, the Caribbean is synonymous with tourism."[a] The Caribbean region is primarily comprised of small island developing states (SIDS) that are among the most tourism-dependent places in the world. For example, over 90 percent of employment in Antigua is related to the tourism industry.[b] The Caribbean is also associated with natural hazards, from the annual threat of hurricanes to earthquakes and even volcanic eruptions. Indeed, frequent hazards present a distinct challenge to this tourism-dependent region.

A natural hazard is defined as a naturally occurring geophysical, atmospheric, or hydrologic event that has the potential to harm or damage. A natural disaster is the occurrence of an extreme hazard event that affects communities through disruption or loss of life and damage or destruction of places and property. However, it is important to note that a disaster is as much the outcome of economic (e.g., poverty), social (e.g., population densities), and environmental (e.g., deforestation) vulnerabilities as it is the hazard itself.[c] A tropical cyclone is an example of a naturally occurring atmospheric–hydrologic event that can be destructive with strong winds and intense rainfall. Such an event is classified as a hurricane with sustained winds over 74 miles per hour. The Saffir–Simpson scale categorizes hurricanes on a scale of one to five based on sustained wind speeds and the storm surge, or the sudden rise of water levels that carry ocean water inland. A Category 1 storm is likely to bring minimal damage, while a Category 5 storm will have catastrophic damage.[d]

Every year, from June through November, Caribbean destinations are always at risk for tropical storm and hurricane strikes. Yet, the past few years have seen a high number of severe storms. The 2017 Atlantic hurricane season was one of the most active seasons with seventeen named storms, ten of which were hurricanes, and six of which were major hurricanes classified as a Category 3 or higher. In September of that year, Hurricane Irma made landfall on several Caribbean islands as a Category 4 and 5 storm and caused 37 deaths in the region. In just a few examples, 95 percent of structures were damaged on Barbuda, and the damages on Saint Martin/Sint Maarten were estimated at US$1.5 billion. In the same month, Hurricane Maria, another Category 5 storm, caused over 100 direct deaths in the region and an estimated 3,000 more in its aftermath. Maria devastated Dominica, causing US$1.3 billion infrastructural damages, while also destroying much of the lush rainforests that characterized the "Nature Island." Puerto Rico and the US Virgin Islands sustained US$65–90 billion in damages, making it one of the costliest hurricanes in the US.[e] The 2018 and 2019 seasons were also above average. In particular, 2019's Category 5 Hurricane Dorian became the worst natural disaster in Bahamian history, causing 70 deaths and at least US$1.5 billion in damages.

These damages included housing and basic infrastructure as well as considerable damage to the tourism infrastructure. With this damage to airports, cruise terminals, roads, resorts, and more presenting a tangible barrier, destinations also faced lost income from tourism in the impending season and potentially long recovery periods. Overall, tourist arrivals to the region in 2018 declined by 2.3 percent, while destinations most affected by the 2017 hurricanes experienced extreme declines. Puerto Rico saw a decrease of 45.6 percent, while Saint Martin/Sint Maarten decreased by 79.0 percent.[f] In the former, it took nearly two years for roads through key tourist areas to be cleared and the majority of hotels to be reopened. In the same time, the latter's airport was still undergoing repairs, and the hospitality sector was slower to reopen. With more than 700 islands and cays, the majority of the Bahamian islands were able to host tourists in the 2019–2020 tourist season until the COVID-19 shutdown.

The media images of the storms battering islands and the devastation can be powerful and act as a deterrent for potential tourists. Even places that are not directly affected by events often experience declines. Significant marketing efforts must be undertaken, by individual destinations and the regional tourism organization (Caribbean Tourism Organization), to communicate to major markets in North America and Europe that visits are still possible, even desirable as places seek to rebuild their economies (see chapter 2). However, some studies suggest that first-time visitors are more likely than repeat visitors to view this as a perceptual barrier.[g]

*Discussion topic*: Consider the ways in which the tourism industry in the Caribbean is affected by hurricanes. How could destinations try to reduce their vulnerability to this natural hazard?

*Tourism online*: Discover Puerto Rico, "Puerto Rico Travel Guide," https://www .discoverpuertorico.com

---

[a] Andrew Spencer, *Travel and Tourism in the Caribbean: Challenges and Opportunities for Small Island Developing States* (Cham: Plagrave Macmillan, 2019): 1.

[b] Spencer, *Travel and Tourism in the Caribbean*, 10.

[c] C. Michael Hall, Girish Prayag, and Alberto Amore, *Tourism and Resilience: Individual, Organisational and Destination Perspectives* (Bristol: Channel View Publications, 2018), 17.

[d] Alan Strahler, *Introducing Physical Geography*, 6th edition (Hoboken: John Wiley & Sons, Inc., 2013): 209–10.

[e] Eric S. Blake, "The 2017 Atlantic Hurricane Season: Catastrophic Losses and Costs," *Weatherwise* 71, no 3 (2018): 28, 35, 37.

[f] Ryan Skeete, "CTO Caribbean Tourism Performance Report 2018 & Outlook for 2019," February 13, 2019, accessed April 22, 2020, https://www.onecaribbean.org/wp-content/uploads/Ryan-Skeete-CTO-State-Industry-Report-2019 .pdf.

[g] Hugues Seraphin, "Natural Disaster and Destination Management: The Case of the Caribbean and Hurricane Irma," *Current Issues in Tourism* 22, no. 1 (2019): 25.

---

and where there is the potential for a hazard to occur (e.g., the low tourism season for destinations in the Caribbean corresponds to the hurricane season). As a physical barrier, these events have the potential to prevent tourists from reaching a destination or participating in the desired activities at a particular time. In addition, the damage and destruction caused by an extreme weather event has a long-term effect on the destination. It will face not only the cost of repairs but also the lost revenues while it is partially or completely closed to tourists. Additionally, the destination may have to work to recover those tourists who went elsewhere for the duration by advertising that they are open again or by offering discount specials.

## CLIMATE CHANGE IMPACTS

The relationship between climate and tourism has gotten increased attention due to climate change. Part of this new research agenda considers the ways in which the tourism industry is contributing to climate change (see box 5.2). Additional research considers the ways in which climate change is affecting patterns of tourism and will continue to do so in the future. The tourism industry is considered to be highly sensitive to changing climatic conditions, and some of the world's most popular tourism destinations are considered among the most vulnerable places (e.g., islands, other coastal areas, and mountains). Even protected UNESCO World Heritage Sites—ranging from Australia's Great Barrier Reef to the Glacier-Waterton International Peace Park on the border between the United States and Canada (see box 1.2)—are considered threatened by the effects of climate change.

These effects—direct and indirect—have the potential to dramatically reshape patterns of tourism. The direct effects of climate change may create new opportunities, new challenges, or simply changing conditions with little net gain or loss for destinations. Warmer temperatures may present an opportunity for places at higher latitudes or in higher elevations to develop or expand their summer tourism offerings. This could represent a shift in destination regions. As existing summer resorts in tropical and subtropical locations experience even hotter temperatures and heat waves that are uncomfortable at best and deadly at worst, they will become less desirable. At the same time, tourists from the significant tourist-generating regions in Northern Europe, North America, and parts of Asia may find places closer to home more attractive.[11] This type of shift would have a significant economic impact on highly dependent tourism regions like the Mediterranean.

While there are real implications for tourists' comfort and well-being associated with high temperatures, this may be more of a perceptual barrier based on media representations of climate change. For instance, one much-cited article in the online edition of *The Guardian* refers to a study predicting that Mediterranean summers could become too hot for tourists after the year 2020.[12] The article offers little indication of what, exactly, is deemed "too hot" for tourists. In reality, thresholds for heat are both personal (i.e., what the individual is accustomed to and prefers) and contextual (i.e., what the same temperature feels like in different locations).[13] Prior to the collapse of Thomas Cook (see box 4.1), the company saw decreased profits during the 2018 summer heatwave. Rather than citing temperatures in destination regions like the Mediterranean though, they attributed the decline to more people staying home to enjoy the warm, sunny weather in the UK as opposed to booking last-minute holidays.[14]

Warmer temperatures could also lead to a shift in tourism seasons. The expansion of warm-weather tourism activities in traditionally cold-weather destinations may be offset by declines in winter tourism. Winter sport tourism is particularly vulnerable to changing climatic conditions. Many popular ski resorts, such as those in New England, are facing increased average temperatures, shorter winter seasons, and increasingly unreliable snowfalls. If these resorts are unable to supply snow artificially due to water or energy constraints or even sufficiently cool temperatures, winter sport tourism may become unfeasible in the future. As stakeholders at these destinations refocus on summer offerings (e.g., hiking trails, mountain bike trails, zip lines, ropes courses, Frisbee golf courses), their efforts are to maintain tourism in that place as opposed to expanding it for greater benefit.

Climate change also has the potential to magnify existing barriers. Warmer temperatures are projected to contribute to an increase in the frequency and severity of extreme weather events. Destinations affected by these events will experience an increase in operating costs from higher insurance premiums and investments in emergency infrastructure such as backup water and power systems.[15] As tourism is disrupted more regularly, however, these destinations will also suffer from lost income, not only during and after each event but also over the long term as tourists begin to avoid places perceived to be risky.

## HYDROLOGY, OCEANOGRAPHY, AND TOURISM

The hydrosphere includes the surface water in oceans, lakes, and rivers; subsurface water; frozen water; and even water vapor in the atmosphere. As a result, there is significant overlap between this sphere and the others. Broadly, **hydrology** is the science of water and considers the properties, distribution, and circulation of water in the hydrosphere. Modern hydrology is specifically concerned with fresh water.[16] Fresh water is incredibly important in shaping human activities; consequently, the study of hydrology provides us with the means of understanding the availability of fresh water so that this fundamental resource can be appropriately managed to provide people with both the quality and quantity of water that they need. At its most basic, oceanography is the study of processes in oceans and seas and is therefore concerned with saline water. The global ocean is the most extensive feature of the hydrosphere. Covering 71 percent of the earth's surface, oceans make up approximately 97 percent of the earth's surface water.[17]

### WATER AS A RESOURCE AND A BARRIER FOR TOURISM

Water is a tremendously significant resource for tourism. Combined with the environments surrounding it, this feature provides the basis for countless tourism attractions and activities around the world. Features such as waterfalls are often scenic attractions, while thermal and mineral springs have long provided the basis for health resorts. Rivers and lakes allow for recreational activities, such as boating, fishing, rafting, kayaking, and more. The beach, in particular, is considered to have a powerful appeal to the physical senses.

Knowledge about these environments is important for stakeholders in the development and maintenance of a destination. Depositional coastlines characterized by beaches are common mass 3S destinations, while the more rugged erosional coastlines can be a resource for scenic tourism. The calm waters of sheltered coves may be an important resource for mass tourism but not for niche tourism based on adventure and sport. Stakeholders also need to be aware of the physical processes at work along coastlines that can affect these resources and other infrastructure. Sea level rise, wave action, and coastal flooding contribute to coastal erosion in which soil, rocks, or sand is displaced. Beach nourishment projects are frequently used to artificially replace lost sand, improve sand quality, protect against erosion, and improve beaches for recreation. According to the American Shore and Beach Preservation Association's National Beach Nourishment Database, the US coastline has had nearly 500 projects from 1923 to 2020 with costs exceeding US$7.9 billion (map 6.1).[18]

Finally, stakeholders need information about these resources to provide a safe and suitable environment for tourism activities. Data about tides, currents, and waves

**Map 6.1. Beach Nourishment Projects, USA. Between 1923 and 2020, the US coastline saw 476 nourishment projects. Florida has had the greatest number of projects (80), followed by Massachusetts (56) and California (44).** *Source*: Gang Gong

should be used to identify the optimal times to participate in water sports (e.g., swimming, snorkeling, scuba diving, surfing) and to provide tourists with warnings about potentially hazardous conditions.

A lack of water—in terms of appropriate quality or quantity—can present a tangible barrier to tourism development. This can be overcome, but there may be economic, social, or environmental costs. Water is a necessary precondition for tourism because it is a fundamental human resource. A destination needs to ensure adequate levels of water quality for both tourism resources (e.g., quality of surface water for aesthetic purposes and tourism activities) and human resources (e.g., quality of water for drinking and bathing). At the same time, stakeholders must understand the constraints of water supply at the destination and consumption patterns to balance the needs of local economic activities, the resident population, and tourists. Las Vegas, a desert destination that received over 42.5 million tourists in 2019,[19] is unable to provide enough water to support this demand from locally available surface and groundwater reservoirs and must import water with expensive diversion systems.

Small island destinations (e.g., Curaçao, Cyprus, and Mauritius), as well as dry coastal destinations (e.g., Australia, Dubai, southern California), are increasingly looking to desalination of seawater to meet their needs, yet there are some concerns about the process and its outcomes. The desalination process may not produce bacteriologically safe water for drinking, which can create a health risk for international tourists.[20] Desalination yields approximately 30 percent drinking water and 70 percent brine, which contains all of the salt. This brine cannot be discharged back into the sea because of the effect it would have on ocean ecosystems. Instead, the brine is discharged back into the aquifer by injection wells, which increase the groundwater salinity over time.[21] The process is also energy-intensive. Recent research has investigated the potential for small-scale desalination systems powered by renewable energy sources to provide fresh water to these areas without increasing local air pollution or contributing to global climate change.[22]

Water also presents a barrier to tourism in the form of hazards, although this is tied to meteorological or geomorphic hazards (box 6.2). Coastal destinations are affected by tidal surges caused by hurricanes or tsunamis as a result of earthquakes. One of the most devastating disasters in recent times was the 2004 Indian Ocean tsunami that killed approximately 230,000 people across fourteen countries, including an estimated 9,000 tourists enjoying a beach vacation. In the case of Sri Lanka, this disaster was estimated to have cost the tourism industry US$250 million and 27,000 tourism-related jobs. Across the region, countless small and medium-size tourism businesses did not have insurance that would allow them to rebuild.[23] In addition, many tourists stayed away from these popular beach destinations out of fear due to the traumatic and highly publicized nature of the event.

---

## Box 6.2.  Experience: Physical Geography, Travel, and Research

*Travel is an important part of geography. Physical geographers immerse themselves in landscapes around the world to better understand the processes that have shaped the planet. Many of the spectacular landscapes and landforms we study are also important resources for tourism. For Dr. Ross Guida, travel and tourism experiences have long been intertwined with his interest in physical geography. Today, he studies river-related issues in the US and in Europe.*

Earth's dynamic physical processes result in many tourism opportunities. Growing up in Wisconsin, near Lake Michigan (one of North America's five Great Lakes), I observed a post-glacial landscape, coastal processes, and the numerous people that would visit beaches during the summer and take out their boats for fishing and recreation. As a kid, I experienced the Chicago River and the commercial attractions along it that bring many US and international travelers to downtown Chicago. My early interests and experiences near water led to me study physical geography, rivers, and hydrology.

Each river I've spent time around presents different tourism opportunities and challenges. In Northwest Wisconsin, the Chippewa River flows free (without dams) from Eau Claire to its confluence with the Mississippi River. During the summer, we would float the river on tubes to cool off, much like other rivers around the world that are popular recreation destinations. While canoeing the river, we observed river terraces and old channel deposits in eroded banks, demonstrating that the river has migrated back and forth across its floodplain since glaciers receded thousands of years ago. Although summer on the river was great, the tourism and recreation season on the Chippewa is limited by ice and Wisconsin's frigid winter temperatures. When the river is high during flooding in spring and early summer, some physical features are under water, and it is dangerous to be on the river in canoes and rafts.

In the US Southwest (e.g., Utah, Nevada, and Arizona), I've taken multiple trips along the Colorado River, a highly managed river system that provides water for multiple uses in an arid environment. I've looked up through slot canyons on Lake Powell and seen the rocky walls that line Lake Mead. Hoover and Glen Canyon Dams, that create these two reservoirs, also attract numerous visitors themselves. The Grand Canyon, carved out by the Colorado over millions of years, is a spectacular location to observe biogeographic and temperature differences across the elevation gradient from the Rim down to the river a few thousand feet below. As you hike into the canyon, and down toward the river where you can camp and raft, the exposed rock is a physical geographer and geologist's dream. Each layer transports visitors back through Earth's history. However, popular areas for tourists along the Colorado are under threat as water availability declines due to climate change, extended drought, and overuse. As water levels fall, marinas are left high and dry, and some canyons that were accessible from the water are only reached with longer drives and hiking. The Colorado's big dams also hold sediment back, reducing bars for camping along the lower river.

Along the Mississippi River, I've spent time in small towns with famous frontier sites and big cities that started as major economic and river navigation hubs. In Minneapolis, Minnesota, I've visited St. Anthony Falls and talked about historic mill production that was possible due to the river's available power thanks to the knickpoint (waterfall) that formed naturally and eroded upstream post-glaciation. In St. Louis, Missouri, I've looked down on the Mississippi from the famous Gateway Arch. Just upstream of the Arch, the Missouri River empties into the Mississippi, and the Missouri has its own physical geography to experience from the North Dakota Badlands to the Rockies in Montana. Heading downstream from the Arch, you ultimately wind up in New Orleans, Louisiana, a city with culture and tourism at its heart. New Orleans is located where it is thanks to the Mississippi connecting the continent's interior drainage to the Gulf of Mexico. While the Mississippi presents many opportunities, including waterfront views and recreation, each year it floods, threatening the livelihood of residents and businesses in the floodplain. Levees and flood walls have largely held up along the most densely populated reaches of the river, allowing for tourism to persist. However, some smaller river towns are not as lucky during large floods, and Hurricane Katrina reminds us that large flood events test the resilience of tourism even in New Orleans.

Past studies on flooding and river dynamics also took me to Central Europe to work on issues related to the Danube River, the "most international basin in the world," with water flow contributed from 19 basin countries. Spending time on a Danube River cruise takes you past many historic sites and landscapes from southern Germany through Austria, Hungary, along the Croatian border, into Serbia, and finally Romania. Along the Danube's course, the physical geography changes from steep headwaters in the Alps to the extensive, fertile soils of the Hungarian Plain below the Carpathian Mountains. As the river approaches the Black Sea, it spreads out into its delta, a UNESCO World Heritage Site. Each year, there is at least one flood on the Danube, and some result in more problems than others. In 2013, while I was living in Hungary, a record-breaking flood worked its way downstream from Germany and Austria. Tourists were stranded as the water was too high for cruise boats to safely navigate, and some roads and rail lines were also flooded.

River cities and towns are great places to visit thanks to the landforms and landscapes that result from fluvial processes. From large bluffs to waterfalls and canyons, spectacular views and opportunities abound. But rivers are constantly evolving, and their dynamic nature poses challenges for the resilience of river communities and tourism. As physical geographers, studying how we can make communities more resilient to flooding (and droughts) by gaining a better understanding of the climatology, hydrology, and hydraulics of the system will ensure future generations get to visit river-related sites as well.

*—Ross*

## CLIMATE CHANGE IMPACTS

The impacts of climate change go beyond the direct effects on patterns of weather and climate. Climate change will affect other physical resources for tourism and exacerbate conditions that constitute barriers. Sea level rise poses a threat to various coastal tourism resources. Destinations are projected to see increased beach and coastal erosion as well as damage to, or destruction of, coastal infrastructure and beachfront real estate. Stakeholders will have to make investments in projects to both minimize and repair the damage to maintain its attractiveness to tourists and investors. These destinations may experience a heightened risk of coastal flooding and potentially the intrusion of saline water into fresh water aquifers.[24] This can negatively impact a destination's ability to meet local and tourist water requirements. In the worst-case scenarios, sea-level rise could submerge low-lying coastal areas and islands (figure 6.2).

Dry regions are projected to experience longer periods of drought, and desert and semidesert areas are projected to expand. This has the potential to create new, or exacerbate existing, problems of water shortages. This directly affects the tourism

**Figure 6.2.** Sea-level rise is threatening tourism resources and infrastructure at low-lying destinations such as the Maldives in the Indian Ocean. *Source*: Nick Wise

industry in terms of water availability, and the impacts are magnified by the fact that the high tourist season often corresponds with the dry season. It also affects related industries, such as agriculture, which provides not only consumable products but also experiences for tourists (e.g., agritourism). As competition for scarce water resources intensifies, this has the potential to generate resentment and hostility toward the tourism industry akin to the overtourism protests seen in major urban destinations.[25] At the same time, temperate regions are projected to experience wetter, as well as warmer, conditions. These conditions could allow an increase in the risk and geographic spread of vector-borne infectious diseases, such as malaria, West Nile virus, Zika virus, and Eastern Equine Encephalitis. More tourists may need to seek the advice of medical professionals regarding their risks associated with travel to these areas and use prophylactic pharmaceuticals. Some tourists may choose not to travel to these places at all.

## GEOMORPHOLOGY AND TOURISM

**Geomorphology** is the study of landforms, which refers to the shapes of the earth's surface. The study of geomorphology considers the characteristics and spatial distribution patterns of landforms, as well as the internal and external geographic processes that create and shape them. Landforms are changing constantly as a result of a variety of forces in the atmosphere, hydrosphere, and biosphere that are continuously at work on the surface of the lithosphere. The internal forces are generally constructive in nature, meaning that they increase the relief (the changes in elevation and slope) of the earth's surface, while the external forces are more likely to be destructive in that they wear features down and decrease the relief of the surface. Over time, the action of these forces has created the landforms that provide the basis of destinations we know today—for example, the Hawaiian Islands (formed by a hotspot or magma plume), the Alps (formed by compressional folding and faulting), or Arches National Park (formed by erosion).

### LANDFORMS AS A RESOURCE AND A BARRIER FOR TOURISM

As a resource, landforms and landform processes can be a natural tourism attraction. One of the most well-known examples of a landform-based natural attraction is the Grand Canyon, but others include Uluru (also known as Ayers Rock) in Australia, the Rock of Gibraltar on the Iberian Peninsula, or the "fairy chimney" rocks at Göreme, Turkey (figure 6.3). Cultural values are often attributed to these landforms, and they are visited for that reason (e.g., sacred mountains). Places where we can safely see the physical (internal) forces of landscape formation at work can also become tourism attractions. For example, volcano tourism is a niche tourism product that has been growing in popularity. Sakurajima, Japan is a popular destination. Visitors are likely to see smoke from the mountain from one of the scenic outlook points and may witness an eruption with large ash plumes. In addition, the area is known for volcanic hot springs to be enjoyed at a traditional onsen (hot spring) or

**Figure 6.3. The unique landforms of Göreme, Turkey are a distinct physical resource for tourism.** *Source*: David McTier

the public foot spa.[26] Likewise, landforms can also be a tourism resource by providing opportunities for tourism. Mountain resorts around the world are extraordinarily popular destinations for both the scenery and activities such as hiking, climbing, and winter sports.

Landforms can also present a barrier to tourism, primarily by preventing people from reaching the place of destination. Mountain destinations around the world have long had to manage accessibility issues. It can be a difficult and costly process to extend ground transportation lines to a resort or to construct the necessary infrastructure for air transport. Pakyong Airport, opened in 2018, was described as "a breathtaking piece of engineering on the roof of the world."[27] The airport significantly increased accessibility to India's northeastern state of Sikkim, located in the Himalayan mountains, particularly for tourists to this scenic region. However, at 4,593 feet, construction of the airport cost US$68.7 million and involved clearing mountains and building a steep embankment to create the runway.

At the same time, natural hazards caused by the dynamic processes of landscape formation have the potential to damage the tourism infrastructure and disrupt tourism activities. In 2019, Mount Agung on the Indonesian island of Bali erupted, spreading lava and rocks over a two-mile area. Although no tourists were evacuated, the eruption led to flight cancellations.[28] As the destination received a total of 15.7 million visitors in the previous year, a major eruption could be devastating to tourism.[29] Globally, the massive ash cloud from the eruption of Iceland's Eyjafjallajökull volcano in 2010 had a ripple effect, disrupting travel and tourism around the world.

Tourism stakeholders will benefit from the expert knowledge of geomorphologists during the TRA not merely to identify the potential features of interest but also to provide guidance on how these features can be developed for tourism. At the same time, scientific information about landform processes should be used to help the destination create an effective disaster response plan.

## CLIMATE CHANGE IMPACTS

Tourism depends on a high-quality landscape and natural attractions. Indirect climate-induced environmental changes have the potential to undermine this. For example, glaciers contribute to an overall landscape aesthetic and constitute an attraction for millions of tourists around the world. However, warming temperatures have accelerated glacial retreat. This has the potential to change the appearance of mountain scenery and to reshape landforms. In addition, this process could increase the risk of natural hazards. Slopes exposed by glacial retreat may be unstable and prone to landslides, especially with a trigger event such as an earthquake. There may be an initial increase in meltwater, but over time, retreating glaciers provide less water to the rivers downstream. This has further implications for the species, ecosystems, people, and economic activities that depend on the water from those rivers.

In addition, attention has also recently been given to the impact of glacier loss on mountain tourism (i.e., trekking and climbing). Trekking trails have often made use of glaciers as shortcuts across valleys. As the glacier surface lowers, crossing will become more difficult with a steeper descent to the surface and subsequent ascent. As the glaciers disappear, routes will have to be diverted. With warmer temperatures, the loss of snow cover will increase the risk of avalanches and rockfalls. This creates harder and more dangerous climbing conditions. As mountain tourism supports communities in popular trekking areas, destination stakeholders need to work with both scientists and the mountaineers/Sherpas who have specific local knowledge to understand changes and form appropriate solutions to ensure an enjoyable and safe experience for tourists.[30]

## BIOGEOGRAPHY AND TOURISM

**Biogeography**, combining principles from biology and geography, is the study of living things. Alexander von Humboldt, a leading figure in the development of modern geography, is widely considered to be the founder of biogeography. This topical branch considers the spatial patterns and physical processes of living things in the collection of ecosystems contained within the earth's biosphere. Biogeographers are interested in the extent of diversity among the earth's species, broadly described by the term biological diversity (biodiversity). Moreover, biogeographers are concerned with explaining the changes in these patterns and processes that have taken place over time and understanding the impact of human activities on diverse species and their habitats.

## BIODIVERSITY AS A RESOURCE AND A BARRIER FOR TOURISM

The biogeography of a place is primarily considered a resource for tourism. For example, the presence of unique animal species and/or plant species becomes a key resource for products such as nature and wildlife tourism. Tourists to eastern and southern Africa are interested in viewing distinctive animals in their natural habitat, such as the "Big Five" (e.g., African elephant, Cape buffalo, leopard, lion, and rhinoceros), among others (figure 6.4).

These characteristics of physical geography can present a barrier, often perceptual, to tourism. Consider destinations that lack the "right" kind of vegetation—or the vegetation that tourists expect. Tropical island destinations around the world have been subject to Western perceptions of an island paradise (i.e., lush, green environments typically epitomized by palm trees). Of course, not all of these islands exhibit these patterns. The comparatively flat "ABC" islands in the southern Caribbean (i.e., Aruba, Bonaire, and Curaçao) are characterized by desert scrub and cactus vegetation. To some extent, this barrier can be overcome as destinations, and particularly resorts, artificially plant nonnative trees and flowers in an effort to create the perceived desired appearance. However, this is often an unsustainable solution due to limited water resources in such environments.

**Figure 6.4. Wildlife is a vital resource for tourism at many African destinations. Tourists are particularly interested in seeing the "charismatic" species such as this cheetah in Kenya's Mara North Conservancy.** *Source*: Velvet Nelson

Tourism stakeholders will benefit from the knowledge generated by biogeographers about the factors that contribute to the success or failure of a particular species so that they may adequately protect these resources. In particular, research in biogeography has examined the potential for tourism to be used as a tool in environmental preservation with the goal of preventing habitat and/or species loss. Much of this work has focused on the ecotourism concept introduced in chapter 3. In addition, biogeographers have been instrumental in studying the effects of tourism on ecosystems. This will be discussed further in chapter 10.

### CLIMATE CHANGE IMPACTS

Loss of biodiversity is one of the key concerns associated with indirect climate-induced environmental change. Rising temperatures and shifting precipitation patterns will affect ecosystems. Plants and animals will have to adapt or migrate, and those that are unable to do so will become extinct. This may present a short-term opportunity for some nature-based destinations, as tourists travel with the intention of seeing endangered species in their native habitat while they still can (see last-chance tourism below). If species decline and loss cannot be prevented, the primary reason for tourism in that place may be eliminated. Species of pests may also migrate based on changing conditions. For example, infestations of nonnative insect species can cause further damage to ecosystems.

The expansion of dry areas and longer droughts also has the potential to increase the risk of wildfire. This will impact landscape (e.g., forests) and infrastructure, both of which can be detrimental to the tourism industry. In the Amazon, wildfires are more likely to occur in years with serious droughts, but the massive fires in 2019 were attributed to deforestation. The fires were considered ecologically devastating,[31] which undermines the tourism resource base. Sonoma County, in California's wine country, had a fire in the same year. Concerns about the increasingly hot, dry conditions combined with high winds also led to intentional power outages to prevent further fires. Although there were no active fires in Napa County, media attention contributed to a decline in the tourism industry nonetheless.[32] With a prolonged drought in Australia, the fire season started earlier than usual in 2020 and burned an estimated twenty million acres. Tourism industry loses were initially estimated at US$4.5 billion.[33]

# Climate Change and Tourism

Tourism geography research has prioritized issues associated with climate change, vulnerability, and adaptation.[34] As discussed in chapter 2, changes in one part of the tourism system will have ramifications on others. As destinations experience various impacts, revenues from tourism may become more unreliable, while operating costs are likely to increase. Depending on the type of changes experienced, a destination may have to rely more heavily on cooling systems for a longer period of the year, use snowmaking equipment more often, use irrigation and watering systems, and/or pay higher hazard insurance premiums. If these costs are passed on to tourists, travelers may have to reevaluate their decisions, not only about where they go but also whether they go. Those tourists who are able to continue to travel may be forced to choose different destinations for their desired activities or to participate at different times of the year. As such, tourists are considered to have the greatest ability to adapt; however, institutional changes may also be required to give tourists the most flexibility such as rescheduling school holidays.[35]

Climate change is predicted to have a negative impact on global economic growth by the middle of this century. As such, we could see a decrease in discretionary income. In addition, reduced access to vital natural resources has the potential to increase political instability and conflict. These factors would contribute to a decrease in effective demand for tourism.[36] This reduced demand will have a negative impact on people in tourism-dependent places. At the same time, these places are also likely to be confronting other challenges associated with climate-induced environmental change. Many areas projected to experience the greatest changes are the most dependent on tourism, including coastal areas and small island developing states (SIDS).

In light of media representations of environmental changes occurring in these places, there have been growing concerns that such places might be fundamentally changed or destroyed altogether. This has been viewed as an opportunity in tourism. Playing upon concerns, stakeholders have begun to encourage tourists—at least those who have the means—to see such places before they are "gone." This is sometimes referred to as disappearing tourism, doom tourism, or **last-chance tourism**.[37] Last-chance tourism provides individuals with the opportunity to see a particular place, geographic feature, or species in its natural habitat while they still can. It also allows them to witness the changes that are taking place and, ultimately, the end firsthand. For some tourists, last-chance tourism is a manifestation of their genuine interest in the specific resource and concern for its impending demise. Destinations may choose to promote their vulnerability as a means of generating attention and aid in efforts to protect their vanishing resources. In fact, there are positive examples in which tourism has contributed to the recovery of environments or species. Yet, for other tourists, this is considered to be an expression of egocentrism. Destinations may capitalize on these tourists' desire for exclusivity, and their willingness to pay for the privilege of rarity.

Nearly all of the types of resources discussed above have become the focus of last-chance tourism in various parts of the world. Although tourists have long visited the UNESCO World Heritage Sites, there is a new imperative to scuba dive on the Great Barrier Reef while it is still one of the world's most biodiverse ecosystems and to hike in Glacier-Waterton International Peace Park while there are still glaciers. Tourists are interested in skiing historic resorts under natural conditions and seeing endangered wildlife in their natural habitat, whether it is polar bears in Canada or mountain gorillas in Rwanda. They are increasingly visiting the Arctic and Antarctic regions for the experience of sea ice before it melts and possibly even to witness the drama of a calving glacier. They want to have the opportunity to sit on the beaches of small island destinations like Tuvalu or the Maldives before they are submerged. Yet, such tourists might ultimately be contributing to the demise of these destinations.

# Box 6.3.   In-Depth: Climate Change Vulnerability, Adaptation, and Resilience in Tourism

As destinations around the world face opportunities and challenges associated with climate change, we need to explore concepts that will help us better understand and address these issues. First, we need to understand a destination's vulnerability. **Vulnerability** refers to a system's sensitivity or susceptibility to shocks and disturbances.[a] As we have seen in this chapter, many destinations are highly dependent on their physical resources for tourism. These destinations are the most vulnerable to climate change impacts that will alter or damage those resources. This will have a ripple effect throughout the system, undermining economies that are based on tourism, creating challenges for resident populations, and possibly leading to further environmental changes. Too often, vulnerabilities are exposed by shocks to the system, such as a natural disaster. Thus, in addition to TRA, vulnerability assessments should be conducted periodically among a wide range of stakeholders (e.g., government officials, large and small business owners, community groups) to identify at-risk resources.[b]

Whether stakeholders are responding to shocks or taking a more proactive approach, they need to find ways to reduce vulnerabilities. Adaptation generally refers to actions intended to manage current or future predicted changes.[c] More specifically, **climate change adaptation** refers to the technological, economic, and sociocultural changes intended to minimize the risks and capitalize on the opportunities created by climate change.[d] Awareness of climate change impacts has been highest among stakeholders with the most vulnerabilities and the ones that have already experienced changing conditions. For example, stakeholders at winter sports destinations are not only aware of their risks but have taken a relatively proactive approach to adaptation. Strategies to maintain their viability as a tourist destination have involved both technological (e.g., enhanced snowmaking equipment) and economic changes (e.g., diversifying activities).[e]

Stakeholders across destinations need to assess adaptive capacity. This might include available technologies, resources (e.g., natural, human, financial), institutional support, and previous adaptive experience (e.g., developing and/or implementing a disaster response plan). Stakeholders should identify, evaluate, and select adaptation options. To determine whether a strategy is appropriate, stakeholders need to consider the following questions: How much does the strategy cost to implement and maintain? How easily can this strategy be implemented? What is the time frame for implementation and outcomes? Do we have the skills needed to implement this strategy or will we need education and training? Will it be effective in solving our problems? Who will benefit? Will there be any negative social or environmental impacts? Are we willing to accept it? The next step is to implement the chosen course of action, and the final step is to monitor and evaluate the strategies used.[f]

There are many challenges to climate change adaptation. While the need for it is widely recognized, local tourism stakeholders have received relatively little support from the scientific community, government organizations, or development agencies.[g] These stakeholders would benefit from technical expertise and financial assistance to help understand their risks and develop appropriate adaptation strategies that will minimize risks without affecting the quality of their tourism resources.[h] Adaptation is locally contingent; one place cannot simply replicate what was successful in another. Additionally, adaptation strategies cannot be based on past evidence because conditions are changing. This makes long-term planning difficult, and any strategies implemented now must be flexible to adjust for changes as they occur.[i]

Finally, the concept of resilience is increasingly applied to tourism. **Resilience** refers to the ability of a system to absorb shocks and disturbances and recover.[j] While resilience can be considered in a variety of contexts (e.g., destinations facing overtourism pressures), research has particularly focused on resilience in the face of climate change.[k] A resilience assessment will consider the strengths of a destination in coping with climate change impacts. Combined with the vulnerability assessment, this will help shape adaptation policies and increase their likelihood of success.[l] This concept is still developing in the tourism literature.

Stakeholders at the most vulnerable destinations are already experiencing impacts and are looking for ways to adapt before it is too late. For example, visit the link below to read about a program to promote climate change resilience through adaptation in tourism in the Maldives. Projects to coordinate adaptation efforts, and research on these projects, have been on the rise, but more work needs to be done in both regards to promote more systematic adaptation efforts in the tourism system in the future.

*Discussion topic:* What arguments would you use to convince a stakeholder to participate in adaptation for future climate change impacts?

*Tourism online:* United Nations Development Programme, "Increasing Climate Change Resilience of Maldives through Adaptation in the Tourism Sector," https://www.adaptation-undp.org/projects/ldcf-climate-resilient-tourism-maldives

---

[a] C. Michael Hall, Girish Prayag, and Alberto Amore, *Tourism and Resilience: Individual, Organisational and Destination Perspectives* (Bristol: Channel View Publications, 2018), 12.

[b] Tarik Dogru, Elizabeth A. Marchio, Umit Bulut, and Courtney Suess, "Climate Change: Vulnerability and Resilience of Tourism and the Entire Economy," *Tourism Management* 72 (2019): 293.

[c] Hall, Prayag, and Amore, *Tourism and Resilience*, 12.

[d] Daniel Scott, "Climate Change Implications for Tourism," in *The Wiley Blackwell Companion to Tourism*, eds. Alan A. Lew, C. Michael Hall, and Allan M. Williams (Malden: Wiley Blackwell, 2014), 474.

[e] Daniel Scott and Christopher Lemieux, "The Vulnerability of Tourism to Climate Change," in *The Routledge Handbook of Tourism and the Environment*, eds. Andrew Holden and David Fennell (London: Routledge, 2013), 247.

[f] Murray C. Simpson, Stefan Gossling, Daniel Scott, C. Michael Hall, and Elizabeth Gladin, *Climate Change Adaptation and Mitigation in the Tourism Sector: Frameworks, Tools and Practices* (Paris: UNEP, University of Oxford, UNWTO and WMO, 2008), 35–45.

[g] Scott, "Climate Change Impacts for Tourism," 474.

[h] Scott and Lemieux, "The Vulnerability of Tourism," 250.

[i] Wolfgang Strasdas, "Ecotourism and the Challenge of Climate Change: Vulnerability, Responsibility, and Mitigation Strategies," in *Sustainable Tourism & the Millennium Development Goals: Effecting Positive Change*, ed. Kelly S. Bricker, Rosemary Black, and Stuart Cottrell (Burlington: Jones & Bartlett Learning, 2013), 212.

[j] Rachel Dodds and Richard W. Butler, "Introduction," in *Overtourism: Issues, Realities and Solutions*, eds. Rachel Dodds and Richard W. Butler (Berlin: De Gruyter, 2019), 2.

[k] Hall, Prayag, and Amore, *Tourism and Resilience*, 106.

[l] Dogru, Marchio, Bulut, and Suess, "Climate Change," 293.

# Conclusion

As a place-based phenomenon, tourism is shaped by and to some extent dependent on the earth's physical features and processes. These things can be either a resource that allows for tourism to take place or a barrier that prevents it. The factors that determine whether something is a resource or a barrier vary between places, societies, and even periods of time depending on the particular circumstances, perceptions, and perhaps level of technology. The topical branches of physical geography provide the means of examining the earth's physical systems across the atmosphere, hydrosphere, lithosphere, and biosphere. The knowledge generated by meteorology, climatology, hydrology, oceanography, geomorphology, and biogeography can be used to better understand how elements in the physical system affect patterns of tourism. This knowledge will become even more important in the future in light of global environmental change.

# Key Terms

- biogeography
- climate change adaptation
- climatology
- geomorphology
- hydrology
- last-chance tourism
- meteorology
- resilience
- tourism resource
- tourism resource audit
- vulnerability

# Notes

1. Robert Steiger, "Tourism and Climate Change," in *A Research Agenda for Tourism Geographies*, ed. Dieter K. Müller (Cheltenham: Edward Elgar Publishing, 2019), 138.

2. Derek Gregory, Ron Johnston, and Geraldine Pratt. *Dictionary of Human Geography*, 5th ed. (Hoboken, NJ: Wiley-Blackwell, 2009), 649.

3. Kerry Godfrey and Jackie Clarke, *The Tourism Development Handbook: A Practical Approach to Planning and Marketing* (London: Cassell, 2000), 66.

4. Godfrey and Clarke, *The Tourism Development Handbook*, 72.

5. Tom McKnight and Darrel Hess, *Physical Geography: A Landscape Appreciation* (Upper Saddle River, NJ: Prentice Hall, 2000), 67.

6. C.R. De Freitas, "Tourism Climatology: Evaluating Environmental Information for Decision Making and Business Planning in the Recreation and Tourism Sector," *International Journal of Biometeorology* 48 (2003): 45.

7. Gómez-Martín, M. Belén, "Weather, Climate, and Tourism: A Geographical Perspective," *Annals of Tourism Research* 32, no. 3 (2005): 587.

8. Gómez-Martín, "Weather, Climate, and Tourism," 576.

9. Visit Scotland, "Climate & Weather in Scotland," accessed April 20, 2020, https://www.visitscotland.com/about/practical-information/weather/.

10. Jelmer H. G. Jeuring and Karin B. M. Peters, "The Influence of the Weather on Tourist Experiences: Analysing Travel Blog Narratives," *Journal of Vacation Marketing* 19, no. 3 (2013): 214–15.

11. Daniel Scott, "Climate Change Implications for Tourism," in *The Wiley Blackwell Companion to Tourism*, ed. Alan A. Lew, C. Michael Hall, and Allan M. Williams (Malden, MA: Wiley Blackwell, 2014), 469.

12. "Climate Change Could Bring Tourists to UK—Report," *The Guardian*, July 28, 2006, accessed April 20, 2020, https://www.theguardian.com/travel/2006/jul/28/travelnews.uknews .climatechange.

13. Daniel Scott and Christopher Lemieux, "The Vulnerability of Tourism to Climate Change," in *The Routledge Handbook of Tourism and the Environment*, ed. Andrew Holden and David Fennell (London: Routledge, 2013), 245–6.

14. "Thomas Cook Blames Heatwave for Profit Warning," *BBC News*, September 24, 2018, accessed April 20, 2020, https://www.bbc.com/news/business-45624215.

15. Scott, "Climate Change Implications," 469.

16. Tim Davie, *Fundamentals of Hydrology*, 2nd ed. (London: Routledge, 2002), xvii.

17. Steve Kershaw, *Oceanography: An Earth Science Perspective* (Cheltenham, UK: Stanley Thornes, 2000), 5, 17.

18. American Shore and Beach Preservation Association, "National Beach Nourishment Database," accessed April 20, 2020, https://gim2.aptim.com/ASBPANationwideRenourishment/.

19. Las Vegas Convention and Visitors Authority, "Las Vegas Historic Tourism Statistics," March 2020, accessed April 20, 2020, https://assets.simpleviewcms.com/simpleview/image/ upload/v1/clients/lasvegas/Historical_1970_to_2019_ada0164b-b599-4fac-8f7a-eb26bfe17187 .pdf.

20. Atef M. Diab, "Bacteriological Studies on the Potability, Efficacy, and EIA of Desalination Operations at Sharm El-Sheikh Region, Egypt," *Egyptian Journal of Biology* 3 (2001): 63.

21. Ramadan A. Awwad, T. N. Olsthoorn, Y. Zhou, Stefan Uhlenbrook, and Ebel Smidt, "Optimum Pumping-Injection System for Saline Groundwater Desalination in Sharm El Sheikh," *WaterMill Working Paper Series* 11 (2008): 8.

22. Faten Hosney Fahmy, Ninet Mohamed Ahmed, and Hanaa Mohamed Farghally, "Optimization of Renewable Energy Power System for Small Scale Brackish Reverse Osmosis Desalination Unit and a Tourism Motel in Egypt," *Smart Grid and Renewable Energy* 3 (2012): 43–4.

23. Andrew Holden, *Environment and Tourism*, 2nd ed. (London: Routledge, 2008), 222.

24. Holden, *Environment and Tourism*, 222.

25. Peter Burns and Lyn Bibbings, "Climate Change and Tourism," in *The Routledge Handbook of Tourism and the Environment*, ed. Andrew Holden and David Fennell (London: Routledge, 2013), 414–15.

26. Japan National Tourism Organization, "Sakurajima," accessed April 20, 2020, https:// www.japan.travel/en/spot/603/.

27. Maggie Hiufu Wong, "India's New Pakyong Airport Opens in Incredible Himalayan Surroundings," *CNN Travel*, September 25, 2018, accessed April 20, 2020, https://www.cnn .com/travel/article/pakyong-airport-india/index.html.

28. Emily Dixon, "Bali Volcano: Flights Canceled after Mount Agung Erupts," *CNN Travel*, May 25, 2019, accessed April 20, 2020, https://www.cnn.com/2019/05/25/asia/indonesia-bali-volcano-eruption-intl/index.html.

29. Bali Discovery Tours, "Strong Start to 2019 for Foreign Tourist Arrivals to Bali," accessed April 20, 2020, https://balidiscovery.com/news/strong-start-to-2019-for-foreign-tourist-arrivals-to-bali.

30. C. Scott Watson and Owen King, "Everest's Thinning Glaciers: Implications for Tourism and Mountaineering," *Geology Today* 34, no. 1 (2018): 19, 22.

31. Alejandra Borunda, "See How Much of the Amazon Is Burning, How It Compares to Other Years," *National Geographic*, August 29, 2019, accessed April 20, 2020, https://www .nationalgeographic.com/environment/2019/08/amazon-fires-cause-deforestation-graphic-map/.

32. Jennifer Huffman, "National Publicity about Fires and Blackouts has Impact on Napa Tourism," *Napa Valley Register*, November 1, 2019, accessed April 20, 2020, https://

napavalleyregister.com/news/local/national-publicity-about-fires-and-blackouts-has-impact-on-napa-tourism/article_19b31892-7bb8-5666-be78-a25255b3049d.html.

33. Tamara Thiessen, "Australia Bushfire Burns Tourism Industry: $4.5 Billion as Holidayers Cancel," *Forbes*, January 20, 2020, accessed April 20, 2020, https://www.forbes.com/sites/tamarathiessen/2020/01/20/australia-bushfires-hit-tourism-industry-as-holidayers-cancel/#1556876672c5.

34. Dieter K. Müller, "Tourism Geographies: A Bibliometric Review," in *A Research Agenda for Tourism Geographies*, ed. Dieter K. Müller (Cheltenham: Edward Elgar Publishing, 2019), 18.

35. C. Michael Hall, Girish Prayag, and Alberto Amore, *Tourism and Resilience: Individual, Organisational and Destination Perspectives* (Bristol: Channel View Publications, 2018), 7.

36. Scott, "Climate Change Implications," 469–71.

37. Raynald Harvey Lemelin, Emma Stewart, and Jackie Dawson, "An Introduction to Last Chance Tourism," in *Last Chance Tourism: Adapting Tourism Opportunities in a Changing World*, ed. Raynald Harvey Lemelin, Jackie Dawson, and Emma J. Stewart (London, Routledge, 2012).

# CHAPTER 7

# The Human Geography of Tourism

Tourists evaluate the human geography of potential destinations. As with physical geography, it may not be a scientific, systematic, or conscious evaluation. In some cases, tourists have a long-standing cultural interest. For example, a tourist who loves sushi has perhaps always wanted to visit Japan. In other cases, tourists instinctually gravitate toward certain places while automatically avoiding others based on their preferences. A tourist who loves the quaintness of small towns and finds big cities overwhelming or stressful might never consider a trip to New York City, New York but take a closer look at Clinton, New Jersey, a town of less than 3,000 that is about an hour's drive from the city. If a country is going through a bloody civil war, few tourists would be likely to even think of it as they consider potential destinations. From the demand perspective, the human characteristics of a place play an important role in shaping what tourists want or expect from the destinations they visit.

As established in the previous chapter, tourism resources are those components of *both* the physical and human environments of a destination that have the potential to facilitate tourism or provide the basis for tourism attractions. Thus, tourism stakeholders must also assess the human resources that will provide the foundation for tourism in that place, the human barriers to tourism, and increasingly the social changes and processes that have the potential to disrupt tourism. As with the physical resources, stakeholders must consider strategies that will allow them to use these resources sustainably and manage the challenges presented by barriers. This requires participation from many stakeholder groups, including the public and private sectors, nongovernmental and community organizations, researchers, and more. Once again, the powerful geography approach provides the foundation with which individuals from these groups can contextualize issues and work toward solutions.

Human geography is the subdivision of geography that studies the patterns of human occupation of the earth. Human geography is organized into many topical branches. In this chapter, we will introduce just a few of them—including cultural, urban, rural, and political geographies—for the purpose of identifying and examining the human resources that provide the basis for tourism as well as the human factors that present a barrier to tourism. These topical branches are clearly interrelated.

Many of the resources and barriers discussed through each of the branches below could easily be approached from a different perspective through the framework of another.

# Cultural Geography and Tourism

The concept of culture is hard to define and open to multiple interpretations. Culture is global and local, historic and contemporary, material and symbolic. It can be considered high (oriented toward a select audience educated to appreciate it), or it may be defined as mass or popular and consumed by a wide audience. It is dynamic and ever changing. Thus, we can think of culture as encompassing the way of life for a group of people, with its roots in the past but evolving with present circumstances. Everything, from their artistic expressions to their daily activities, contributes to this way of life and helps create and recreate the meanings and associations they have, as well as their values and identity. In geography, culture has long been an important topic as we try to understand the world. **Cultural geography** is a dynamic and widely recognized topical branch that studies a variety of issues pertaining to how societies make sense of, give meaning to, interact with, and shape places.

Given the vast scope of cultural geography, there has been considerable interconnection between this topical branch and the geography of tourism. Within the context of this discussion, we can use the framework of cultural geography to help us identify cultural resources for tourism, analyze potential barriers to tourism that exist between cultures, and current issues associated with authenticity. While the role of cultural geography is highlighted in this discussion, it is important to note that the branch also has a significant part to play in helping us understand the effects of tourism on culture and societies (discussed in part III) and factors that shape interactions between tourists and places (discussed in part IV).

## CULTURE AS A RESOURCE AND A BARRIER FOR TOURISM

The cultural resources for tourism are virtually limitless. Remnants and symbols of a place's cultural heritage have been some of the most significant resources for tourism throughout history. Ancient Roman and modern international tourists alike have been fascinated by the Pyramids of Giza, both for the spectacle of the archaeological site and for its mythology. Cultural heritage resources for tourism can be specific features within a place that hold significance or those that reflect different time periods and cultural influences. Religious sites, such as cathedrals, mosques, and temples, are recognized within their respective belief systems for their religious importance but also appreciated for their history and their aesthetic design. Thus, well-known sites like the La Sagrada Familia (Barcelona, Spain), the Blue Mosque (Istanbul, Turkey), or Kinkaku-ju (Kyoto, Japan) have become significant tourism attractions visited both by adherents of the particular belief system and other international tourists.

Not all elements of cultural heritage need to have a long history or be significant in the greater scope of world affairs to be considered a potential resource. For example, Harry Potter has become an integral part of England's cultural heritage and tourism today (see "Harry Potter locations" on VisitBritain's home page). Any place that has a part to play in his story—or which served as the inspiration for a place in the story—becomes a resource.

The characteristics of traditional cultures—such as distinctive appearances, clothing styles, livelihood patterns, housing types, cuisines, and more—can individually or collectively be considered tourism resources (box 7.1). These may be indigenous peoples, minority groups, or other populations that live outside of the wider society such as the Amish in parts of Pennsylvania, New York, and Ohio. At the same time, the characteristics of a modern society can be a resource, as international tourists seek to do things like experience a "typical" Irish pub or ride one of London's double-decker buses.

## Box 7.1.  Experience: Learning about Traditional Medicine from a Peruvian Shaman

*Elements of traditional culture can be a resource for tourism. Some tourists will travel specifically to learn about and experience traditional cultures firsthand. Dylan is a pharmacy student. He had the opportunity to travel to Peru with a group of students from his university to learn about traditional medicine from a local shaman.*

In March 2020, I had the amazing experience of traveling to Peru. We spent a day in the city of Iquitos, before heading to the Yagua village, located on the Amazon River. We spent four days there with Freddy, our local guide, Don Antonio, a shaman, and Connie, a US-trained pharmacist who has been Antonio's apprentice for more than 20 years.

We spent the first day primarily getting acclimated to the high temperatures and humidity of the jungle. Our group went pink dolphin sighting, and we were lucky enough to spot a pair of the dolphins on a lake in front of the lodge. According to Freddy and Don Antonio, these dolphins are treated with love and respect; to the locals, they are like guardian angels. In the local indigenous culture, the animals are sacred. Local people do not touch them or hunt them. It is believed that these dolphins have the ability to turn into handsome men. We were told that if a dolphin sees a beautiful girl at night, it will turn into a handsome man who will seduce the girl. He will take her back to the lake, and they will jump in as a "surprise." If she forgets her friends, family, and home during the next three days, she will become a dolphin. This serves as a warning to young girls.

After arriving back at the lodge, Don Antonio performed his first ceremony with us, a *limpia*. This ceremony welcomed us into the jungle and blessed us with good fortune during our time there. One by one, everyone in our group sat in front of Don Antonio and he poured flower water on top of us while he said some words of blessing. Each ceremony that we experienced with Don Antonio was used to heal the mind, body, and soul.

The next day, we went on a nature walk with Don Antonio. On this walk, he explained to us various plants that he uses to help his patients. For example, to help diagnose and treat diabetes for his patients, he would have them first urinate on the ground. If ants come to the urine, then Antonio knew that the patient was diabetic, since sugar was found in the urine. Then, he would instruct the patient to drink one tablespoon of boiled cocona juice (e.g., a type of South American fruit that can be compared to a cranberry), without added sugar, once a day for 15 days. After 15 days, he instructed the patient to go see a licensed physician to get their blood glucose levels tested. If the patient was within a normal range, he/she was instructed to keep drinking the boiled cocona juice.

Don Antonio also talked about the Ubos tree. This tree has many medicinal purposes. In particular, the sap of this tree is used to help treat uterine cancer in women. There are many requirements that the women would need to follow to maximize treatment, but Don Antonio said that he has seen it work. Don Antonio had a true passion about the plants we talked about during the walk, and he loved when we asked questions about the plants. Shamanism is dying out, and he wanted to spread his knowledge to as many people as he could. One quote that truly resonates with me is: "You must have the love and compassion for the medicine to work. If you do not believe, it will not work."

We also had the opportunity to have a "personal healing" session with Don Antonio, along with Freddy as the translator, during the week. The session was a spiritual healing, to heal and revitalize your spirit. Antonio used palm leaves, tobacco smoke, and rose water in the session. He started by rubbing the rose water all over our bodies. Then he used the tobacco to blow smoke on us, and finally he "hit" us with the palm leaves while chanting a song called *icaro*. For someone who lives in the realm of Western Medicine, this was clearly not something I was used to. It is truly hard to explain how I felt after the session. I was taken aback that he knew things about my life when he had never met me before. At the start of the session, he told me that I have potential in the world, great potential. He also told me that I must help myself, before anyone can help me. This really resonated with me. A sense of relief overcame me because it showed me that I must take care of myself. The healing session was a personal "restart," and I live by the lessons he taught me.

Later that evening, the group had a lesson with Connie regarding the use of ayahuasca in shamanism. People use this mixture of plants for its psychedelic effects. If Don Antonio is unsure what is wrong with his patient, he would use ayahuasca as an "x-ray" to see what is going on inside the person's body. Connie talked about the dangers of ayahuasca if it is not used properly and respected. She warned us that it is a very powerful drug, and a shaman must be there to help guide its use.

Our last journey on a tributary of the Amazon was to see the giant lily pads. We were blessed to have Antonio with us when we went to see them. They were nestled deep in the jungle, far from the fast-moving waters of the Amazon. When we arrived, Antonio told us of a legend that says that the lily pads sing to attract men. Once the men arrive, the lily pads turn into females who lure them back to the pond where the females turn into mermaids. When this happens, the man forgets about everything.

Before we left to go back to Iquitos, we had our closing ceremony with Don Antonio. This was to further bless us in our endeavors outside of the rainforest. The ceremony consisted of burning wood from the Paulo Santo tree and sap from the Copal tree. We stood around the fire in a circle and one by one, we had to stand in the center next to the fire and smudge ourselves in the smoke. While we were smudging ourselves, we had to say something that we were grateful for. It was a great opportunity to reflect upon the knowledge that we received during our time in the jungle.

Soon after our arrival back home, we found out that Don Antonio had passed away of natural causes. Hearing this news truly made me appreciate the knowledge and time that we were able to spend with him. We were the last group of students that he would ever meet and teach. He had such a great passion for sharing his knowledge with people who were truly interested in shamanism. Antonio's gentle and warm spirit still lives on with us today and like Antonio told us, "You're next! Put your toe to the line and step into your medicine!"

—Dylan

Various aspects of the arts, based on traditional or modern culture, can serve as a resource as well. While these resources may not be the primary attraction that draws tourists to a place, they constitute a part of the experience. Visual arts provide the basis for attractions: famous museums (e.g., the National Gallery of Art in Washington, DC), city-level art districts (e.g., the South Main Arts District in Memphis, Tennessee), and open-air sculpture parks (e.g., Laumeier Sculpture Park in St. Louis, Missouri). The production of arts and crafts—and these items themselves—can be a resource for tourism. Tourists may visit a traditional "factory" in Tunisia to watch the skilled craft workers make carpets and potentially purchase one to take home with them. The same applies to the performing arts. Tourists may seek to observe or even participate in cultural festivals (figure 7.1). They may try to see a well-known play or musical in a famous theater district, such as New York City's Broadway. In other cases, tourists may wish to see the performances that are specific to the place visited. For example, tourists to Chengdu, China, may attend a Sichuan opera, the highlight of which is typically *bian lian*, or face-changing. In this unique and highly protected art form, performers rapidly change a succession of brightly colored masks.

Less tangible elements of a place's culture can either contribute as a resource for tourism or constitute a barrier. For example, language is a basic element of culture.

**Figure 7.1.   While Mardi Gras is New Orleans's most famous cultural festival, others include the Jazz & Heritage Festival, French Quarter Fest, Wine and Food Experience, and Po-Boy Festival. *Source*:** Scott Jeffcote

A common language between the sending and receiving countries or regions may be considered a resource for that particular destination. In contrast, the lack of a commonly spoken language can become a barrier. This, of course, is perceptual. For many tourists, the idea of not being able to communicate with people at the destination is a source of anxiety and stress; thus, they will be more likely to choose destinations where they feel confident that they know the majority of people will be able to speak the same language.

The same can apply to religious beliefs or cultural value systems. Many societies are open to and tolerant of cultural differences in physical appearance, patterns of dress, or codes of behavior. However, this is not always the case. Tourists are often requested to observe the norms of the society they visit, which may involve changes in the ways they dress (e.g., wearing more conservative clothing) or the ways they act (e.g., refraining from holding hands with one's partner or other public displays of affection). Many tourists are willing to respect these practices so that they may have the experience of that place and culture. However, others may be reluctant to visit a place where they feel they are restricted or are concerned about reports of harsh punishments for those who, perhaps unintentionally, violate one of these social rules.

As new tourist-generating regions emerge and send increasing numbers of tourists around the world, stakeholders are recognizing the importance of trying to ease these barriers. For example, with the recent and predicted growth of the Chinese market (chapter 1), destination stakeholders post information in Mandarin and hire Mandarin speakers to ease the language barrier. Other changes based on culture are also made to welcome Chinese visitors, such as designing hotel rooms based on feng shui, creating adjoining rooms to accommodate multifamily groups, or offering rooms with multiple beds for business travelers expected to share a room.[1]

The Muslim population is both growing worldwide and growing as a tourism market segment. Islamic tourism or halal tourism refers to the design of and practices within the tourism industry that aim to follow the rules and principles of Shari'ah (Islamic law). Halal tourism is not necessarily tourism that is motivated by religious reasons; rather, it caters to the specific needs of Muslim travelers. Tours may ensure the availability of halal food or itineraries built around prayer timings. Hotels may offer certified halal toiletries, prayer mats and Qibla direction in rooms, or dedicated prayer rooms. Resorts may promote separate pool and spa facilities for men and women as well as the ability for women to wear "burkinis," or swimming suits that cover the whole body except face, hands, and feet. While the latter may sound like a straightforward cultural accommodation, places from French beaches to Hungarian spas have banned the use of such swimwear. Halal products and services are commonly found in places with large Muslim populations, but destinations from Japan to Brazil are increasingly offering Muslim-friendly options to attract these tourists.[2]

## AUTHENTICITY

In the 1960s, Daniel Boorstin bemoaned the decline of the traveler and the rise of the tourist. He elaborated that the tourist was someone who was satisfied with experiences that were contrived and inauthentic.[3] More than a decade later, Dean MacCannell argued that it was life in the modern world that was increasingly superficial, inauthentic, and inadequate. As a result, he claimed that people feel the need to search for authenticity, in other times or other places, and tourism aids this quest. However, even though tourists may be motivated by a desire for authentic experiences, they might not always achieve such experiences. He explained this through the concept of staged authenticity.[4]

MacCannell's concept was based on sociologist Erving Goffman's structural division of social settings. Goffman's theory stated that places have front regions and back regions. Front regions are those that are open to and intended for outsiders. This is the part of a place that is carefully constructed to present a certain image to outsiders. Back regions are those that are reserved for insiders. This is the part of the place that facilitates insiders' daily activities; it is where they can be themselves rather than putting on a show or providing a service. Because the back region is generally closed to outsiders, this helps maintain the illusions presented to outsiders in the front. As he applied this model to tourism, MacCannell expanded this dichotomy into a continuum of stages. While the first three stages are front regions in that they are intended for tourists, they are increasingly designed to give the appearance of a back region and therefore a more authentic experience. The final three stages are back regions in that they were not intended for tourists, but they make varying accommodations for tourists.[5]

The first stage begins with the **front region**, or places that have been entirely constructed for tourism. This consists of all-inclusive tourist resorts and theme parks. These sites have little, if any, relation to the character of the larger place in which they are situated. Fort Fun Adventure Park is an American Wild West–themed amusement park in Germany. People in such places are either tourists or employees doing a job. The second stage is used to describe a front region that is decorated in a style reminiscent of a back region. Although these places are not likely to be mistaken for the real thing, they are not intended to be. Patrons of a waterfront seafood restaurant with the façade and décor of a fishing boat may enjoy the atmosphere but will be under no illusions that they are on a working fishing vessel.

The third stage is still a front region, but it is designed to simulate a back region. Areas in the third stage may be intended to convince visitors that they are, in fact, visiting a back region. Tourist ranches may exist within the same type of setting as working ranches. This contributes to the appearance of authenticity, but the tourist ranches are romanticized—and most likely sanitized—versions that are recreated for visitors to experience. Tourists may not be aware of the difference between the actual and simulated experiences, either due to the provider's attention to detail or simply their own lack of knowledge. The fourth stage is a back region that has been opened up to outsiders. It was not explicitly constructed for tourism, but it has been altered in some ways to accommodate tourism. Working ranches that also provide experiences for tourists would fall into this category.

The fifth stage is nearer to Goffman's idea of back region, but under various circumstances, visitors are allowed into these places. Because of this, places might be "cleaned up" a bit. In some destinations with a poorly developed tourism infrastructure, there may be a lack of formal restaurants; therefore, tourists may take meals in residents' homes. Although this is typically done on an informal basis, there are some examples of destinations that recognize this practice and have legal regulations for such in-home "restaurants" (e.g., Cuba's *paladares*). The final stage is the true **back region**. These are places that are not intended for, or expected to receive, outsiders. As a result, the nature of the place and insiders' patterns of behavior remain largely unchanged by tourism. The home provides a refuge for individuals or families who live in a destination region and work in the tourism industry. It is a place of their own that need only meet their own expectations and allows them to do what they choose. On occasion, tourists who develop a relationship with local people may be invited to gain a glimpse into the back region.

Tourists have been criticized for being people who travel to another place without really experiencing it. In other words, tourists' experiences are in the first stages of the continuum. The parts of a place he or she experiences are staged for the benefit of tourists and do not reflect the real character of the place; thus, they are considered to be inauthentic. Some tourists, such as organized mass tourists, are content with these experiences. Their primary motivation for travel may be to escape their normal environment as opposed to experiencing a new place. Yet, other tourists, such as drifters, will find such experiences unsatisfying. They will continue to search for entry into back regions for more authentic experiences of place.

Authenticity is generally used to refer to the genuineness of something or the accuracy of the reproduction of that thing. In tourism, this is related to objects, attractions, and/or experiences. For many tourists, authenticity is equated with traditional culture. However, scholars point out that authenticity is a socially constructed and contested concept. People will have different ideas about what is authentic and what is not, and they will use different criteria to make those judgments. For some, authenticity may refer only to what is original (e.g., a structure from the period in which it was built, an artifact from the period in which it was used). For others, the idea may allow for people from the original ethnic/culture group to produce things in traditional ways (e.g., crafts made by people from that group using typical materials and tools, classic performances by people from that group). Still others may look for expert confirmation or external certification to tell them that something is authentic.[6] Additionally, authenticity is negotiable. Ideas about what is authentic may change over time. People may forget or romanticize the origins of a cultural practice.[7] They may simply accept that culture changes over time and with various influences. Something that was once viewed as inauthentic may eventually come to be seen as an authentic expression of culture.[8]

Some tourist scholars have argued that staged authenticity can play a role in tourism. It can help destination stakeholders control interactions with visitors and protect elements of their culture they do not want to see used for the purposes of tourism. Yet, recent trends in tourism are eroding the distinctions between front and back regions. In 2019, the UNWTO identified "travel to change" as its top consumer travel trend. This included the quest for authenticity as well as to live like a local.[9] Indeed, this idea has become very attractive to tourists, and vacation rentals have increasingly brought tourism into residential areas, in effect, the destination's back region. This changes residents' relationships with people and places, from not knowing their neighbors to not being able to enjoy the places where they would normally spend their free time (e.g., their favorite local coffee shop). Thus, locals may not be able to, in fact, *live like a local* anymore. This raises concerns for authenticity and cultural sustainability with regard to community well-being and sense of place. It also has implications for tourists' experiences as these back regions become more like front regions and perceived as inauthentic.[10] The effect of tourism on culture will be discussed further in chapter 9.

# Urban Geography, Rural Geography, and Tourism

Urban geography and rural geography are distinct topical branches of geography that study specific geographic areas. Yet, these areas—and the studies of them—are not unrelated. Ideas about and definitions of urban and rural areas are often contingent upon each other. They may be negatively defined (i.e., the definition of one is predicated on *not* being the other) or simply defined in opposition with one another (i.e., the characteristic of one is the opposite for the other). Using the 2020 US Census Bureau urban and rural classifications as an example, urbanized areas are those with 50,000 or more people and urban clusters are those with at least 2,500 but less than 50,000 people. Correspondingly, a rural area "encompasses all population, housing, and territory not included within an urban area."[11]

Urban geography and rural geography are topical branches in human geography that have clear ties to population and economic geographies. In addition, these branches deal with themes that are shared by social, cultural, political, and even environmental geographies. **Urban geography** may be defined as the study of the relationships between or patterns within cities and metropolitan areas,[12] while **rural geography** may be defined as the study of contemporary rural landscapes, societies, and economies. As long as the majority of the world's population lived in rural areas and was dependent on environmental resources for their survival, greater attention was given to these issues. Reflecting changing spatial patterns, urban geography emerged as a topic of inquiry in the mid-twentieth century. Subsequently, less attention was given to rural geography; however, specialists in this area continue to work to understand the changing nature of rural areas (e.g., changing patterns of rural production and consumption or rural poverty).[13]

Both urban and rural areas have long been sites for tourism. Urban tourism dates back to the Grand Tour in classical cities such as Paris, Vienna, Venice, and Rome. Interest in rural tourism developed with the pastoral ideal that was popularized in art and literature based on beautiful rural settings and romanticized country life. Interest in experiences of the rural gained even more momentum with the Romantic Movement, which was primarily a response to the tremendous rise in both industrialization and urbanization. Today, tourists consider the potential resources and barriers of urban and/or rural areas in their destination decision-making process.

## URBAN AREAS AS A RESOURCE AND A BARRIER FOR TOURISM

The urban tourism product is based on a wide range of resources. In fact, one of the strengths of this product is the tremendous extent of urban resources that can be made into various categories of attractions (human—not originally intended for tourism;

human—intended for tourism; and special events). Thus, urban tourism overlaps with many other products (e.g., cultural, heritage, VFR, MICE), and it draws from different tourist markets (e.g., leisure tourists, business tourists).

Many attractions are derived from the history of cities, from the ancient (e.g., the Acropolis in Athens, Greece, used as a fortress from the second millennium BCE, with the present temples dating back to the fifth century BCE, now a UNESCO World Heritage Site and major tourism attraction) to the more modern. These attractions are so significant that a city's historic district may also be the primary tourist district. The spatial concentration of attractions prompts the development of other tourist facilities and services. Markets or bazaars that were key places for residents to obtain needed products now serve as an attraction for tourists (e.g., Pike Place fish market in Seattle, Washington) and a place to buy souvenirs. Ethnic neighborhoods once served a distinct purpose for immigrants; today, they are highlighted in tourism as part of the city's unique and colorful character (e.g., Little Havana in Miami, Florida).

Cities all over the world have recognized the potential to create new attractions for tourism from existing resources.[14] Tourism has been seen as an important vehicle for urban revitalization, such as the redevelopment of a harbor or former industrial site into a fashionable shopping and/or entertainment district (e.g., the proposed redevelopment of an underutilized industrial space on the Chula Vista waterfront of San Diego Bay, California into a recreational and resort destination).[15] Tourism also stimulates new ways of looking at urban infrastructure. For example, Rio de Janeiro, Brazil, has been at the forefront of slum tourism, an offshoot of the urban tourism product that involves tours of the city's infamous favelas. Tourism can be a factor in cities' decisions to host special events, from local festivals to hallmark events like the Olympic Games.

Urban destinations depend heavily on their reputations, both nationally and internationally. A widespread reputation is a distinctly positive factor, as it creates a demand for the experience of that specific destination. However, based on reputation alone, cities may suffer from the perception that they have a finite number of resources to offer. Every major city has certain attractions that are well known; tourists to these destinations will be sure to see or experience them (e.g., the Statue of Liberty in New York City, New York, figure 7.2). However, these destinations are prone to one-time visits, where tourists feel that they have "been there, done that" and are ready to experience attractions in other cities. Destinations have to work to create new attractions, revitalize existing ones, or promote lesser-known and alternative attractions. The author of an alternative things-to-do article notes that London is a popular destination with many iconic attractions and then poses the question, "But what if you've already been there, done that, and got the T-shirt?" She continues,

> Don't get me wrong, Buckingham Palace, Big Ben, and co have their place—but it's not on this list. Instead, consider this your chance to delve deeper into London's characterful neighborhoods, get the lowdown on lesser-known things to do, and enjoy this global capital on a local scale—just like the natives do.[16]

The principal barriers to urban tourism are often perceptual, based on stereotypes of major cities, although there may be a real basis behind this. Tourists may feel that

**Figure 7.2. Urban destinations often have high-profile attractions that visitors make a point to see, such as New York City's Statue of Liberty. _Source_:** Velvet Nelson

pollution (e.g., smog) renders urban destinations unattractive. They may be put off by having to experience high-profile destinations with thousands of other tourists. In light of concerns about overtourism, urban destinations have begun to create "barriers" to control visitor numbers. Logistical barriers include capping visitor numbers, such as Dubrovnik, Croatia's limit on the number of cruise passengers permitted per day (see chapter 5) or Barcelona, Spain's attempts to limit the number of tourist beds. Other efforts to minimize the effects of overtourism may create additional perceptual barriers. Venice, Italy not only instituted a fee for day-trippers to visit, they have also created a long list of fineable offenses. For some, these measures are viewed as anti-tourist, and they will avoid visiting a place where they do not feel welcome.[17]

As discussed with reference to authenticity above, tourism has a direct impact on people and places. While we will consider these effects in Part III, the issue needs some consideration in this discussion of urban geography and tourism. Urban tourism is an agent of urban change, and urban geography can provide a useful framework for investigating these socio-spatial changes (box 7.2)

## RURAL AREAS AS A RESOURCE AND A BARRIER FOR TOURISM

Rural areas are not simply the homogenous spaces outside of cities. This category encompasses "fringe" areas that are located on the periphery of large urban areas, re-mote areas that are far from urban areas or difficult to access, and essentially all other places in between. Rural areas have diverse physical landscapes, varied population sizes,

# Box 7.2.  In-Depth: Touristification

Urban change is not a new subject to urban geographers. Yet, the role of tourism as an agent of urban change long went unrecognized.[a] Perhaps more significantly, cities seemed to lack the understanding of the issues associated with this tourism-driven change and the tools to manage the negative effects of these changes.[b] With the rapid growth of urban tourism in recent years, researchers, the media, and urban stakeholders have begun to pay more attention to the ways in which tourism affects cities.

The concept of gentrification is often used as a starting point in these discussions. Gentrification involves the reinvestment of capital, direct or indirect displacement of low-income groups by high-income groups, and the corresponding physical and social changes of urban areas.[c] From this, some authors describe a process of tourism gentrification in which commercial investment transforms a residential area into a tourism destination. The existing residential and commercial infrastructure of these typically older, working-class neighborhoods is replaced with tourist accommodations and entertainment, leisure, and nonessential shopping venues. This leads to the displacement of long-standing residents.

Others argue that the concept of gentrification is useful but ultimately falls short in its ability to explain contemporary patterns of tourism-driven change[d] (e.g., gentrification involves population replacement whereas tourism-driven change leads to depopulation[e]). The framework of "touristification" is offered as an alternative, although it is still evolving as we try to understand these processes as they unfold in different ways in different places.[f] For example, middle-class and even upper-class gentrified neighborhoods, as well as working-class neighborhoods, may be transformed into a place for tourist consumption.

There are some key concerns about the physical and social changes associated with touristification in urban destinations. Hotels expand into residential areas, high-income foreigners purchase vacation homes, and investors purchase property for short-term vacation rentals on platforms such as Airbnb. This decreases the availability of affordable residential housing, and particularly low-income residents are vulnerable to displacement.[g] Local retail shops are closed as shopping areas are converted to boutique shops, upscale international brands, or cheap mass-produced souvenirs for visitors. Such changes not only make it harder for residents to get necessities, they also disrupt long-standing cultural patterns. This has implications for remaining residents as well as for tourists looking for a more authentic experience of place.[h] The increase in restaurants, bars, and other entertainment venues can also lead to a decrease in community livability in terms of noise levels, street cleanliness, and even safety.[i] At the same time, community members may not be able to enjoy the new facilities or activities for financial reasons.[j]

There are many academic case studies examining touristification in cities around the world. Research cited here drew from case studies from Paris, France to Cape Town, South Africa. However, the popular media has also taken on the issue in its own way. Travel information company *Fodor's* identified the so-called Brooklyn Effect as one of the worst travel trends of the 2010s. This borough of New York City, New York experienced the processes of gentrification that converted former industrial buildings into fashionable lofts and upscale shopping that led to the creation of a "go-now, super-cool-and-artsy-but-still-a-little-gritty destination."[k] This is associated with the familiar problems of residential and small-business displacement due to skyrocketing prices. Yet, the author looks beyond the changes in Brooklyn to consider the effect its popularity has had on other destinations, such as Oakland, California (i.e., "Brooklyn by the Bay"), that seek to replicate Brooklyn's model with the same look and feel, the same types of restaurants and shops, and typically the same effects.

The rapid growth of urban tourism has led to many changes in city destinations that have been given greater attention in recent years. The COVID-19 pandemic will likely raise additional issues regarding the sustainability of places oriented around tourist consumption and possibly further physical and social changes in urban destinations.

*Discussion topic:* Do you think city officials should develop policies and actions to manage tourism-driven change? Explain.

*Tourism online:* New York City's Official Convention and Visitors Bureau, "Brooklyn, New York City," at https://www.nycgo.com/boroughs-neighborhoods/brooklyn/

---

[a] Tim Freytag and Michael Bauder, "Bottom-Up Touristification and Urban Transformations in Paris," *Tourism Geographies* 20, no. 3 (2018): 444; Gustav Visser, "The Challenges of Tourism and Urban Economic (Re)Development in Southern Cities," in *A Research Agenda for Tourism Geographies*, ed. Dieter K. Müller (Cheltenham: Edward Elgar Publishing, 2019): 107.

[b] Jorge Sequera and Jordi Nofre, "Debates Shaken, Not Stirred: New Debates on Touristification and the Limits of Gentrification," *City* 22, nos. 5–6 (2018): 844.

[c] Macià Blázquez-Salom, Asunción Blanco-Romero, Jaume Gual Carbonell, and Ivan Murray, "Tourist Gentrification of Retail Shops in Palma (Majorca)," in *Overtourism: Excesses, Discontents and Measures in Travel and Tourism*, eds. Claudio Milano, Joseph M. Cheer, and Marina Novelli (Oxfordshire: CABI, 2019): 42.

[d] Sequera and Nofre, "Debates Shaken: Not Stirred," 849–50.

[e] Jaime Jover and Ibán Díaz-Parra, "Who Is the City for? Overtourism, Lifestyle Migration and Social Sustainability," *Tourism Geographies* DOI: 10.1080/14616688.2020.1713878 (2020): 5.

[f] Freytag and Bauder, "Bottom Up-Touristification," 445.

[g] Jesús M. González-Pérez, "The Dispute Over Tourist Cities. Tourism Gentrification in the Historic Centre of Palma (Majorca, Spain)," *Tourism Geographies* 22, no. 1 (2020): 175.

[h] Blázquez-Salom et al., "Tourist Gentrification of Retail Shops," 43.

[i] Sequera and Nofre, "Debates Shaken: Not Stirred," 848.

[j] Visser, "The Challenges of Tourism," 113.

[k] Barbara Noe Kennedy, "These Are the 11 Best and Worst Travel Trends of the Past Decade," *Fodor's Travel*, October 25, 2019, accessed May 1, 2020, https://www.fodors.com/news/photos/these-are-the-11-best-and-worst-travel-trends-of-the-past-decade.

---

different economic activities, and wide-ranging potential for development.[18] Rural geography has an important role to play in giving us the tools to understand rural areas and the resources for and barriers to rural tourism.

The year 2020 was slated to be the UNWTO Year of Tourism and Rural Development. This was intended to bring attention to the opportunities for tourism to contribute to economic development in rural communities as well as preserve rural cultures.[19] Rural tourism serves as an umbrella for specialized tourism products based on diverse rural resources that range from farm settings and activities to small-town cultural festivals. Rural resources may also be used in different ways to meet the demands of a particular group of tourists. For example, both farm tourism and wine tourism are based on agricultural production, but tourists interested in farm stays are different from tourists interested in vineyard tours and wine tastings (figure 7.3). Rural areas may be attractive as an escape from the perceived problems of urban areas (e.g., pollution) or homogenization attributed to globalization. Thus, the opportunity to have an authentic experience of place can also be a perceived resource.

Figure 7.3.   Rural tourism resources are highly diverse. For example, this farm offers a quaint rural experience for urban residents as well as wine tastings and entertainment. *Source*: Scott Jeffcote

Each rural tourism experience is considered unique; tourists may participate in the same activity (e.g., pick-your-own produce) at different places. Similarly, the geographic scale of rural areas means that travel and activities are often time consuming, and tourists may only have the opportunity to experience a part of the landscape. If they are satisfied with this experience, they may be interested in returning to experience more. In fact, rural tourists often develop an attachment to place based on their experiences that lead them to return to the same places and possibly even purchase or build a second home in their preferred rural settings (e.g., a country house or a lake house).

While the diversity of activities has the potential to appeal to different tourist markets, rural tourism is limited by perceptual and logistical barriers. Perceptually, there may be biases against rural areas amongst markets who may not appreciate what places have to offer. Additionally, business and MICE tourism is less likely to occur in rural areas than urban ones, although opportunities exist (e.g., a corporate retreat or a small conference held at a rural winery). Logistically, rural tourism also tends to be highly seasonal in nature. Many activities take place out-of-doors and/or are dependent on the stages of agricultural production (e.g., planting or harvest).

Some of the greatest barriers to rural tourism relate to accessibility. With the exception of vast publicly owned spaces, found in areas such as the western United States, much of the rural landscape around the world is privately owned. Even when some owners are willing to give tourists access to their land, activities may be disrupted or even rendered impossible by owners who do not permit access. For example, in 2014, the US Supreme Court ruled in favor of a private landowner in Wyoming who fought the conversion of a disused rail line that crossed part of his land into a bicycle path.[20] Rural areas are also less connected than urban ones. It may be more difficult and more time consuming to reach these places, and it is dependent on transportation. Personal vehicles must be used to reach areas that are not served by public transportation, such as a rail network. This becomes a form of social exclusion, where certain groups, such as the lower socioeconomic segments of the population, are not able to participate.[21]

Although overtourism has been primarily associated with urban areas, there are important concerns for rural areas. Even a comparatively small number of people can create challenges in such places. Residents may feel overwhelmed by this influx of visitors. Limited facilities (e.g., parking) or services may be overburdened, and resources (e.g., paths) may experience overuse and degradation. Whereas overtourism can exacerbate existing urban problems, many of these issues in rural areas did not previously exist.[22] As such, renewed attention to rural geography—combined with political geography (see below)—could help destinations work toward appropriate management strategies.

## CREATIVITY

Creativity is an important topic in geography and tourism. One of the leading scholars on the subject, Richard Florida, identified a creative class comprised of individuals working in arts, media, culture, science, and technology that has been reshaping patterns of geography by seeking out urban centers.[23] This creative class has been drawn to cities for many reasons including access to urban amenities (e.g., restaurants, museums) and diversity. Places with people of different ages, races, ethnic backgrounds, religions, and sexual orientations are more likely to be tolerant and open-minded but also offer opportunities for new experiences.[24] These factors are considered "creative resources" and are important for cities, especially those that lack significant tangible resources for tourism (e.g., former manufacturing cities). Essentially, creativity becomes the basis for places to be considered "cool."[25] Austin, Texas is a prime example; city attractions include live music, diverse restaurants, and a generally distinctive (sometimes weird by their own admission) cultural environment.

The emergence of creative communities appeared to help drive urban regeneration.[26] Cities in North America, Europe, and Australia subsequently designated cultural quarters, defined spaces characterized by creativity, to stimulate this process. In many cases, this was seen as a means to an end—increased property values, investment, and tourism—rather than an opportunity to support creative livelihoods. The increased concentration of artists led to increased competition. At the same time, rising property values began to force out not only the local working classes but also the low-income artists. Only the most commercially successful artists were able to stay, which limited the creative synergy that such places generally depend on.[27]

In comparison to cities, small towns have generally been perceived to be homogenous and boring. However, in recent years, creative individuals have begun to reconsider small towns, which also reshapes patterns of geography. For those who could no longer afford to live in urban arts districts, this was initially for practical reasons. Yet, individuals have been able to find small-town places where people were open-minded and interested in embracing the creative industries. They found different types of amenities in these areas and new sources of inspiration. Visual artists adopted new materials from the environment; performing artists drew upon the issues of the rural working class.[28]

Arts towns attract urban residents on day trips and weekend getaways, and they serve as attractions for tourists to a larger region. For example, Manitou Springs, Colorado is easily accessible to Denver-area residents, but it is also a potential point of interest for tourists in the region for other attractions such as the Pike's Peak Cog Railway. Not all small towns or rural communities will be accepting of such change, but there are many examples of small towns that have benefitted from this type of arts-driven economic development and revitalization.

# Political Geography and Tourism

The study of political geography has evolved with the changing world. Today, globalization has become one of the greatest processes of change in the world and requires new ways of looking at the policies of and connections between places. Thus, we might consider **political geography** to be the study of the ways in which states relate in a globalized world. This topical branch has clear implications for many others in human geography, such as urban and rural geographies as well as economic, social, and environmental geographies, which we examine in Part III.

The relationship between tourism, geography, and politics has long been poorly recognized. Yet, tourism plays a role in major global issues today, from migration to climate change, and it is shaped by such issues as well. The discussion in this section continues the focus on resources and barriers for tourism, but we will need to keep the political geography framework in mind throughout the remaining chapters. Political decisions and actions have a distinct role to play in understanding the effects of tourism but also in the representations of destinations.

## POLITICAL FACTORS AS A RESOURCE AND A BARRIER FOR TOURISM

Many of the factors discussed in these two chapters have considered tourism resources as those components of a destination's (physical or human) environment that have the potential to provide the basis for tourism attractions. In some cases, political factors can also provide this basis, such as the political tourists who travel to participate in the spectacle of the Iowa caucuses, the first major event in the US presidential primary election season. However, we can consider those factors that have the potential to *facilitate* tourism, which is more often the case for political tourism resources. A government's policies at the national, regional, or local scale can shape tourism development. For example, Mexico's state-planned tourism development model led to the establishment of popular resorts such as Cancún and Los Cabos with the intention of creating benefits such as increased employment, economic development, and social well-being.[29] Governments can support tourism development by investing in the construction or upgrade of basic infrastructure (e.g., transportation facilities, electricity, water supply, sewage) and protection of the appropriate resources (e.g., natural, cultural, heritage). Governments can also create barriers to tourism development through bureaucratic red tape.

Good international relations between countries and open entry policies, such as eliminating visa requirements for some or all inbound international tourists, can improve accessibility. In 2020, Japan had the most "powerful" passport with visa-free or on-arrival access to 191 countries.[30] Open borders can be advantageous for tourism. The Schengen Area is a "borderless" region encompassing twenty-six European countries. Tourists entering the Schengen Area must pass through border control, but under normal circumstances any international travel within the area can be done without undergoing these procedures. This facilitates ease of travel, both for international tourists who are citizens of any of the member countries and for other tourists traveling between destinations in the area. Border controls were temporarily reintroduced in some Schengen countries as over one million migrants poured into Europe in 2015 (map 7.1), which also had implications for tourists. Borders were closed again during the COVID-19 pandemic in 2020.

Changing relations between countries can affect people's ability to travel, at least until negotiations can establish new policies (box 7.3). Poor relations between two countries may restrict travel from one to the other but not necessarily have an adverse impact on the industry as a whole. For example, American policies have restricted travel to Cuba (to varying degrees depending on the administration) since the Cuban Revolution; thus, the island has been deprived of this potentially large tourist market with a good relative location. Yet, Cuba nonetheless attracted 4.7 million visitors in 2018, primarily from other countries in the Americas and Europe (figure 7.4).[31] The "forbidden" nature of tourism under political restrictions still has the potential to generate tourist visits, even with the risk of fines, imprisonment, or death.[32]

Entry regulations and border controls can also effectively serve as a barrier to tourism. A country may prevent travel to their destination by barring tourists from certain countries, such as US President Trump's 2017 executive order prohibiting travelers from Iran, Iraq, Libya, Somalia, Sudan, Syria, and Yemen. A country may also discourage travel to their destinations by imposing strict policies, such as requiring tourists to check in with the police upon entry or traveling with a guide at all times. The same is true if the country has difficult procedures, long wait times, and/or high fees for applying for entry visas. In her examination of tourism, journalist Elizabeth Becker summarized the findings of a survey intended to understand a post-9/11 drop in foreign visitors:

> The would-be tourists were furious about the difficulty they now faced getting a visa to the United States and the treatment they received once they arrived at an American airport. Tourists were questioned on arrival in minute detail about why they wanted to visit… Foreigners not only did not feel welcome, they felt they had to prove they were innocent of unmentioned tendencies, to border guards who acted as if every foreigner could be the next terrorist.[33]

Facial recognition, the latest development in US border control intended to prevent terrorism, has also raised concerns about privacy and misuse. The technology was

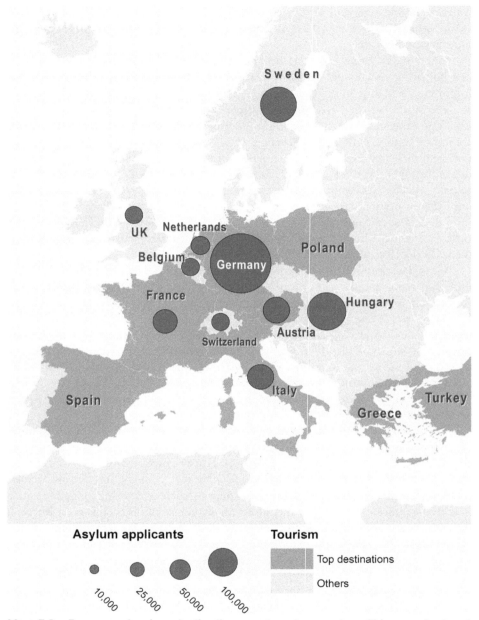

Map 7.1. European tourism destinations and asylum seekers. This map looks at the top ten European destinations for international tourist arrivals and the top ten European countries for asylum seekers during the 2015 migrant crisis. *Source*: Gang Gong

# Box 7.3.  Case Study: Tourism and Brexit

On June 23, 2016, over 30 million UK citizens voted in a referendum concerning the continuation of the country as a member of the European Union (EU). A slight majority (51.8 percent) voted for the UK's exit of the supranational organization (i.e., British exit or Brexit).[a] Although the original exit deadline was set for March 29, 2019, it was delayed twice before formally occurring on January 31, 2020. Negotiations were scheduled to continue during a transition period set to run through December 31, 2020, but at the time of writing, the process has been disrupted by the COVID-19 pandemic.[b]

Since the referendum, there has been a tremendous amount of financial and political uncertainty, which has had and will continue to have implications for travel and tourism. After the decision, the value of the UK pound sterling fell. As a result, travel costs for Britons increased approximately 22 percent.[c] Outbound tourists would face a variety of other costs as well. The weaker pound would increase costs for UK-based airlines, which would be likely to pass at least a portion of these costs on to consumers. UK travelers would no longer be covered by European Health Insurance Cards, so they would likely face higher travel insurance premiums. Brexit would also end surcharge-free mobile phone roaming in Europe. In our mobile-dependent society, many travelers would feel the need to purchase international wireless plans or pay roaming charges to continue to access data. Initial predictions suggested that, these factors combined with other constraints on discretionary income, outbound tourism would decrease by 5 percent, accounting for 4.7 million tourist trips once Brexit occurred.[d]

During the transition period, UK citizens would still be permitted to travel visa-free within the Schengen Area. Additional negotiations were required to establish new procedures starting in 2021. One option would be a visa waiver in which UK citizens would pay a fee to apply to travel in the Schengen Area without a visa. Surveys suggested Britons would support this policy, provided the fees were not too expansive and the procedure would not be too time consuming. Travelers would still be required to use different lines and procedures on arrival at airports and ferry terminals. Until additional infrastructure is established to handle an increase in traffic through these lines, travelers could face longer wait times on arrival.[e]

There is also uncertainty about how Brexit will affect the country's own travel and tourism industry. In 2018, the value of the UK tourism industry was £145.9 billion.[f] Some predictions suggested fewer domestic trips, accounting for a decline of US$5.6 billion, but potentially an increase in inbound tourism.[g] However, Brexit has the potential to further affect the industry through immigration policies. The proposed system is based on skills and/or salaries. The minimum salary requirement of £30,000 would be well above the industry averages of £23,000 for full-time workers and £17,000 for part-time workers. Yet, tourism and hospitality businesses are dependent on these foreign workers as tour guides, bus drivers, cleaning staff, and others. For example, tourism in the Lake District supports around 15,000 jobs, and approximately 59 percent of these workers come from the EU. With a local unemployment rate of 0.9 percent, there are significant concerns about how businesses would manage the labor shortage if the new policy went into effect.[h]

Finally, Brexit will not only affect British travel and tourism. Countries dependent on UK tourists are projected to experience declines. Proportionally, Ireland would see the largest visitor declines, while Spain would be the most affected in terms of volume with an estimated decline of around one million tourists.[i] The UNWTO notes, "uncertainty surrounding Brexit, the collapse of Thomas Cook, geopolitical and social tensions, and the global economic slowdown all contributed to slower growth in 2019, when compared to the exceptional rates of 2017 and 2018."[j]

Since the referendum, the unknowns about Brexit have created both real and perceptual barriers to tourism. The ongoing negotiations have the potential to create even more.

Stakeholders in destinations within and outside the UK will have to stay informed about and adapt to these changing circumstances.

*Discussion topic:* Consider the current or potential barriers to tourism created by the Brexit process and identify possible strategies to overcome these barriers.

*Tourism online:* VisitBritain, "The Official Tourism Website of Great Britain," at https://www.visitbritain.com/us/en

---

[a] Nikolaos Pappas, "UK Outbound Travel and Brexit Complexity," *Tourism Management* 72 (2019): 13.

[b] Alasdair Sandford, "Post-Brexit Guide: Where Are We Now—and How Did We Get Here?" *Euronews*, March 24, 2020, accessed May 2, 2020, https://www.euronews.com/2020/02/11/brexit-draft-deal-first-of-many-hurdles-to-a-smooth-exit.

[c] Pappas, "UK Outbound Travel," 13.

[d] Simon Kyte, David Goodger, and Helen McDermott, ""No-Deal" Brexit to Knock 2% off Travel and Tourism GDP," *Oxford Economics*, December 6, 2018, accessed May 2, 2020, https://www.oxfordeconomics.com/recent-releases/fdf4ac5f-5d3b-49c0-87a7-1b9578093b96.

[e] Joe Minihane, "What Brexit Will Mean for Travelers," *CNN Travel*, January 31, 2020, accessed May 2, 2020, https://www.cnn.com/travel/article/post-brexit-travel-advice/index.html.

[f] Antonia Wilson, "UK Tourism Industry Set to Struggle under Post-Brexit Immigration Plans," *The Guardian*, November 4, 2019, accessed May 2, 2020, https://www.theguardian.com/travel/2019/nov/04/uk-tourism-industry-struggle-post-brexit-immigration-plans.

[g] Kyte, Goodger, and McDermott, ""No-Deal Brexit."

[h] UK Inbound, "Two out of Three Tourism Businesses Fear Immigration Reforms May Cause Closures," October 10, 2019, accessed May 2, 2020, https://www.ukinbound.org/advocacy-news/two-out-of-three-tourism-businesses-fear-immigration-reforms-may-cause-closures/.

[i] Kyte, Goodger, and McDermott, ""No-Deal Brexit."

[j] United Nations World Tourism Organization, "International Tourism Growth Continues to Outpace the Global Economy," January 20, 2020, accessed May 2, 2020, https://www.unwto.org/international-tourism-growth-continues-to-outpace-the-economy.

launched in Orlando International Airport in 2018 and projected to be in use in all major international airports in the country by 2021.

In light of various issues at a destination, such as politically motivated protests or violence, countries may issue temporary travel alerts or warnings. In 2019, transportation strikes in Paris affected tourists' ability to get to and from the airport and get to certain sites. In the same year, demonstrations in Hong Kong led to canceled flights. Many countries warn their citizens considering travel to the US about gun violence, particularly following mass shootings. In 2019, the US State Department designated twenty-nine countries as Level 3—Reconsider Travel (e.g., Honduras) and Level 4—Do Not Travel (e.g., North Korea) based on high levels of crime, terrorism, and/or armed conflict.[34] It is worth taking a closer look at the relationship between these issues and tourism.

## CONFLICT AND TERRORISM

Logic dictates that a stable political environment is an important precondition for tourism; thus, an unstable political environment is a barrier to tourism. Most tourists will avoid any destination that is unstable or that they perceive to be unstable—at least until the situation changes. At best, tourists at destinations experiencing political

**Figure 7.4.** US policies have prevented Americans from traveling to Cuba under most circumstances. However, there is a perceived demand for the experience of the country, as many Americans have a vivid mental image of the destination based on things like music and vintage cars. *Source*: Velvet Nelson

instability may find their vacation disrupted; at worst, they may find themselves caught up in the middle of a conflict. When the long-standing conflict between India and Pakistan over Kashmir threatened to erupt again in 2019, the state's government ordered approximately 20,000 Indian tourists and Hindu pilgrims to leave the area. In addition, foreign governments, such as the UK and Germany, issued warnings for their citizens to avoid travel to Kashmir.[35]

The editors of a volume on tourism and war argue that the relationship between the two can be complicated.[36] Certainly it is expected that tourism in a place will decline during times of conflict, but global tourism continues, typically unabated, during that conflict. If that place previously received tourists, other destinations might benefit from its conflict. Tourists who might have chosen to visit that place will consider alternative destinations. The growth of these destinations may be short lived, as tourists return to the original place once the conflict is over. However, such destinations may benefit from increased exposure during that time as a result of new tourist visits and social media representations of their experiences.

Sites associated with past conflicts or incidents of terrorism can become dark tourism attractions (see chapter 3) due to curiosity or commemoration. There has also been a growing niche tourism market for places with active conflicts. Highly specialized tour operators create experiences in which tourists can see what is happening in these places. This is described as a hybrid product with elements of both adventure tourism and dark tourism. Tourists are motivated by the risk involved as well as the desire for unusual and "authentic" experiences. This is typically a high-end tour product due to the logistical planning for such an excursion and security precautions (e.g., armored vehicles, security guards) but can also appeal to a segment of the backpacker market looking for extreme experiences. There is considerable debate about this type of conflict tourism. Some argue that it is an educational experience in which participants gain a deeper understanding of the issues involved in the conflict. Others cite the ethical issues associated with the voyeurism in watching the devastation of other peoples and places.[37]

While such opportunities exist, conflict and terrorism have a negative impact on tourism. In fact, terrorist organizations may specifically target the tourism industry. In areas with tourists, terrorists are less likely to stand out as outsiders who may arouse suspicion. Tourists and the tourism infrastructure (e.g., attractions, hotels, shopping venues, cafés and restaurants) are viewed as "soft targets." They are relatively vulnerable, and attacks against them have the potential to generate maximum terror and chaos. Targeting tourists (especially foreign) and the tourism industry ensures a high level of publicity. Attacks on the industry have an immediate, and potentially long-term, economic impact.[38]

Places that face recurring issues with violence will struggle to retain a positive reputation and tourist confidence, while others are more resilient.[39] Since the mid-2000s, Turkey's tourism industry had experienced steady growth. In 2014, the country received 41.6 million international visitors and was among the largest international tourist destinations in the world.[40] Between June 2015 and January 2017, there were twenty major attacks, primarily linked to Kurdish militants and the Islamic State of Iraq and the Levant (ISIL) that resulted in the deaths of at least 435 people. Three of these attacks occurred in tourist areas of Istanbul, and one took place at the Istanbul airport.[41] Also in July 2016, a coup d'état was attempted against the government that resulted in the deaths of more than three hundred people. International tourist arrivals fell by 25 percent that year. Yet, by 2018, tourism in the country reached a new high with 46.1 million international visitors.[42] Researchers have recently questioned the future of this resilience, as both Millennials and Generation Z rank terrorism as a top concern.[43]

Tourism can play a role in conflict and terrorism. There may be a preexisting dispute between peoples or places that is exacerbated by tourism. Both parties may compete for the potential benefits of tourism, or one may react negatively to the perceived costs associated with tourism. For example, tourism geographer Dallen Timothy discusses the case of an eleventh-century Hindu temple complex and UNESCO World Heritage Site situated within a contested section of the border between Thailand and Cambodia. While there are other issues in this conflict, the economic implications of tourism at such an attraction cannot be discounted.[44] Finally, tourism may factor into conditions for conflict. When tourism development hurts local people, economically or socially, it may spark retaliation and violent confrontation. In 2017, "anti-tourism activists" in Barcelona vandalized tourist rental bicycles, slashed the tires of an occupied sightseeing bus, and spray-painted anti-tourism messages.[45] This was one of the more extreme examples but part of wider overtourism protests throughout Europe.

## Conclusion

Just as the physical features and processes of place shape tourism, so will the varied human features and processes of that place. There are countless factors that will act as resources for or barriers to tourism; these chapters have barely skimmed the surface. Nonetheless, we can begin to see how we can use a geographic framework to help us identify and explore these issues. In part III, we will build on this foundation by examining the geographic effects of tourism. The nature of these effects for any destination will undoubtedly be influenced by the characteristics of both the physical geography and the human geography of that place. Thus, we will continue to draw upon these topical branches that we have already discussed, even as we turn our focus to a few new ones.

## Key Terms

- back region
- cultural geography
- front region
- political geography
- rural geography
- urban geography

## Notes

1. Mark Ellwood, "How Chinese Tourists Are Changing the Travel Landscape," *Condé Nast Traveler*, November 2, 2018, accessed April 24, 2020, https://www.cntraveler.com/story/chinese-tourists-changing-travel.

2. Mohamed Battour and Mohd Nazari Ismail, "Halal Tourism, Concepts, Practises, Challenges and Future," *Tourism Management Perspectives* 19 (2016): 151–3.

3. Daniel J. Boorstin, *The Image: A Guide to Pseudo-Events in America* (New York: Vintage Books, 1961; 50th Anniversary Edition, 2012), 84–5.

4. Dean MacCannell, "Staged Authenticity: Arrangements of Social Space in Tourist Settings," *American Journal of Sociology* 79, no. 3 (1973): 597.

5. MacCannell, "Staged Authenticity"; Dean MacCannell, *The Tourist: A New Theory of the Leisure Class* (New York: Schocken Books, 1976; reprinted with foreword by Lucy R. Lippard; Berkeley: University of California Press, 1999).

6. Chris Halewood and Kevin Hannam, "Viking Heritage Tourism: Authenticity and Commodification," *Annals of Tourism Research* 28, no. 3 (2001): 568.

7. Deepak Chhabra, Robert Healy, and Erin Sills, "Staged Authenticity and Heritage Tourism," *Annals of Tourism Research* 30, no. 3 (2003): 706.

8. Erik Cohen, "Authenticity and Commoditization in Tourism," *Annals of Tourism Research* 15 (1988): 374.

9. United Nations World Tourism Organization, *International Tourism Highlights 2019 Edition* (2019), 5, accessed March 5, 2020, https://www.e-unwto.org/doi/pdf/10.18111/9789284421152.

10. Jillian M. Rickly, "Overtourism and Authenticity," in *Overtourism: Issues, Realities and Solutions*, eds. Rachel Dodds and Richard W. Butler (Berlin: De Gruyter, 2019): 53.

11. United States Census Bureau, "Urban and Rural," accessed April 26, 2020, https://www.census.gov/programs-surveys/geography/guidance/geo-areas/urban-rural.html.

12. David H. Kaplan, Steven R. Holloway, and James O. Wheeler, *Urban Geography*, 3rd ed. (Hoboken, NJ: Wiley, 2014), 7.

13. Michael Woods, *Rural Geography: Processes, Responses and Experiences in Rural Restructuring* (Los Angeles: Sage, 2005), 32.

14. T. C. Chang and Shirlena Huang, "Urban Tourism: Between the Global and the Local," in *A Companion to Tourism*, ed. Alan A. Lew, C. Michael Hall, and Allan M. Williams (Malden, MA: Blackwell, 2004), 227.

15. Port of San Diego, "Chula Vista Bayfront Project," accessed April 26, 2020, https://www.portofsandiego.org/projects/chula-vista-bayfront.

16. Kylie Maxcy, "Actually Cool Things to Do When You Visit London," *Thrillist*, November 28, 2018, accessed April 26, 2020, https://www.thrillist.com/travel/london/things-to-do-in-london.

17. Mark Ellwood, "The Other Side of Venice's Overtourism Problem," *Condé Nast Traveler*, October 24, 2018, accessed April 27, 2020, https://www.cntraveler.com/story/the-other-side-of-venices-overtourism-problem.

18. Rhonda L. Koster, "Why Differentiate Rural Tourism Geographies?" in *Perspectives on Rural Tourism Geographies: Case Studies from Developed Nations on the Exotic, the Fringe and the Boring Bits in Between*, eds. Rhonda L. Koster and Doris A. Carson (Cham: Springer, 2019), 6.

19. United Nations World Tourism Organization, "International Tourism Growth Continues to Outpace the Global Economy," January 20, 2020, accessed May 2, 2020, https://www.unwto.org/taxonomy/term/347.

20. Bill Chappell, "Family Trust Wins Supreme Court Fight against Bike Trail," *NPR*, March 10, 2014, accessed April 27, 2020, https://www.npr.org/sections/thetwo-way/2014/03/10/288584936/family-trust-wins-supreme-court-fight-against-bike-trail.

21. Richard Sharpley, "Tourism and the Countryside," in *A Companion to Tourism*, eds. Alan A. Lew, C. Michael Hall, and Allan M. Williams (Malden, MA: Blackwell, 2004), 380.

22. Richard W. Butler, "Overtourism in Rural Settings: The Scottish Highlands and Islands," in *Overtourism: Issues, Realities and Solutions*, eds. Rachel Dodds and Richard W. Butler (Berlin: De Gruyter, 2019): 199, 209.

23. Richard Florida, *The Rise of the Creative Class, Revisited* (New York: Basic Books, 2012), 11.

24. Florida, *The Rise of the Creative Class, Revisited*, 293–4.

25. Greg Richards, "Creativity and Tourism: The State of the Art," *Annals of Tourism Research* 38, no. 4 (2011): 1230.

26. Florida, *The Rise of the Creative Class, Revisited*, xiii.

27. Gordon Waitt and Chris Gibson, "Tourism and Creative Economies," in *The Wiley Blackwell Companion to Tourism*, ed. Alan A. Lew, C. Michael Hall, and Allan M. Williams (Malden, MA: Wiley Blackwell, 2014), 233–5.

28. Charlotte Higgins, "Art in the Countryside: Why More and More UK Creatives Are Leaving the City," *The Guardian*, August 26, 2013, accessed April 27, 2020, https://www.theguardian.com/artanddesign/2013/aug/26/art-countryside-uk-creatives.

29. Carlos Monterrubio, Maribel Osorio, and Jazmín Benítez, "Comparing Enclave Tourism's Socioeconomic Impacts: A Dependency Theory Approach to Three State-Planned Resorts in Mexico," *Journal of Destination Marketing & Management* 8 (2018): 416.

30. Maureen O'Hare, "Henley Index: Japan Tops 2020 List of World's Most Powerful Passports," *CNN Travel*, January 7, 2020, accessed April 28, 2020, https://www.cnn.com/travel/article/henley-index-world-best-passport-2020/index.html.

31. United Nations World Tourism Organization, *Compendium of Tourism Statistics Dataset [Electronic]* (Madrid: UNWTO, 2020).

32. Charlie Campbell, "Otto Warmbier's Death May Spell the End of American Tourism to North Korea. Sadly, That's About It," *Time*, June 22, 2017, accessed April 29, 2020, https://time.com/4824670/north-korea-otto-warmbier-kim-jong-un-torture/.

33. Elizabeth Becker, *Overbooked: The Exploding Business of Travel and Tourism* (New York: Simon & Schuster Paperbacks, 2013), 355.

34. Ellen Cranley, "The 29 Riskiest Countries for Americans to Travel to," *Business Insider*, June 12, 2019, accessed April 29, 2020, https://www.businessinsider.com/travel-warnings-us-state-department-2019-6.

35. "India Orders Tourists to Leave Kashmir over 'Terror Threat'," *BBC News*, August 3, 2019, accessed April 29, 2020, https://www.bbc.com/news/world-asia-india-49222571.

36. Richard Butler and Wantanee Suntikul, "Tourism and War: An Ill Wind?" in *Tourism and War*, ed. Richard Butler and Wantanee Suntikul (London: Routledge, 2013), 3.

37. Gada Mahrouse, "War-Zone Tourism: Thinking beyond Voyeurism and Danger," *ACME: An International Journal for Critical Geographies* 15 no. 2 (2016): 331–6.

38. Sevil F. Sönmez, "Tourism, Terrorism, and Political Instability," *Annals of Tourism Research* 25, no. 2 (1998): 424–5.

39. Shrabani Saha and Ghialy Yap, "The Moderation Effects of Political Instability and Terrorism on Tourism Development: A Cross-Country Panel Analysis," *Journal of Travel Research* 53 no. 4 (2014): 509.

40. United Nations World Tourism Organization, *Compendium of Tourism Statistics Dataset*.

41. "Wave of Terror Attacks in Turkey Continue at a Steady Pace," *The New York Times*, January 5, 2017, accessed April 29, 2020, https://www.nytimes.com/interactive/2016/06/28/world/middleeast/turkey-terror-attacks-bombings.html?_r=0.

42. United Nations World Tourism Organization, *Compendium of Tourism Statistics Dataset*.

43. Andres Coca-Stefaniak and Alastair M. Morrison, "City Tourism Destinations and Terrorism—A Worrying Trend for Now, But Could It Get Worse?" *International Journal of Tourism Cities* 4, no. 2 (2018): 409.

44. Dallen J. Timothy, "Tourism, War, and Political Instability: Territorial and Religious Perspectives," in *Tourism and War*, ed. Richard Butler and Wantanee Suntikul (London: Routledge, 2013): 17.

45. Karl McLaughlin, "Anti-Tourism Attacks in Spain: Who Is Behind Them and What Do They Want?" *The Conversation*, August 9, 2017, accessed April 29, 2020, https://theconversation.com/anti-tourism-attacks-in-spain-who-is-behind-them-and-what-do-they-want-82097.

# Part III

# THE GEOGRAPHY OF TOURISM EFFECTS

From the time the modern tourism industry began to take off in the middle of the twentieth century, peoples and places around the globe looked to tourism as a means of development. The promise of economic benefits from tourism, namely job creation and income generation, has been extremely alluring. With the evolution of the environmental movement, the potential for environmental preservation through tourism has also been a strong motivator. Today, these arguments for tourism can be heard in places all over the world, whether on a small island with chronic high unemployment rates or in a remote wilderness area under pressure from the extractive industries. Tourism has been held up as the panacea for all sorts of problems. Indeed, properly planned and developed, tourism can have a positive impact on both the peoples and the places involved. However, this is not always the case. Tourism has a wide range of effects or outcomes—economic, social, and environmental—and neither the benefits of tourism, nor the costs, are evenly distributed. We need to first understand each of the economic, social, and environmental effects of tourism, then consider the interrelationships between them. That holistic perspective is vital if tourism is to contribute to sustainable development.

This section examines the geography of tourism effects. In particular, chapter 8 discusses the economic geography of tourism. Chapter 9 considers the social geography of tourism, and chapter 10 explores the environmental geography of tourism. Each of these chapters uses the tools and concepts of the respective topical branches to help us understand both the benefits and the costs of tourism on the human and physical resources of the destination. In addition, they will address some of the factors that play a role in determining what the outcome of tourism will be for a particular place. Finally, chapter 11 brings all of these topics together as it looks at the relationship between tourism and sustainable development.

# CHAPTER 8

# The Economic Geography of Tourism

Tourism is big business. Until 2020, tourism growth had outpaced the global economy. It was the world's third largest export category, ahead of automotive and food products. It accounted for 10 percent of global gross domestic product (GDP) and employed one in ten workers around the world.[1] With figures like these, it is not surprising that the promise of positive economic impacts has been the primary driving factor behind tourism development.[2] However, neither the economic benefits nor the economic costs of tourism are evenly distributed between countries, communities, or even segments of the population. Consequently, who benefits from tourism and who is hurt by it are issues that need to be carefully considered.

The economic geography of tourism gives us the means to examine the economic effects of tourism at the individual, local, and national scales. **Economic geography** is a topical branch in human geography that is related to the field of economics and intersects with other branches such as social, political, and urban geographies. Broadly, economic geography is the study of the spatial patterns, human–environment interactions, and place-based effects of economic activities. Economic geography has a long-standing focus on issues of production. Traditionally, this has been used to describe production in the primary (e.g., agriculture) or secondary (e.g., manufacturing) economic sectors. Yet, with the tremendous rise of the tertiary sector (i.e., services) in the modern world, the study of economic geography has adapted to reflect this change.[3]

Industry and economic development is one of the key clusters of tourism geography research.[4] The potential economic benefits of tourism are extraordinarily important in the development of tourism destinations around the world. Yet, the promise of such benefits should not be adhered to blindly; they must be weighed against the potential costs to determine whether net benefits will, in fact, be received. This chapter utilizes the tools and concepts of economic geography to consider the potential for tourism to contribute to economic development at a destination, as well as the failure of tourism to live up to this potential or have other negative consequences for the destination. Additionally, it also discusses the factors that influence the outcome of these effects.

# Economic Benefits of Tourism

The UNWTO argues, "As one of the largest and fastest growing economic sectors in the world, tourism is well-positioned to foster economic growth and development at all levels and provide income through job creation."[5] **Economic development** is typically described as a process. It encompasses the various changes that create conditions for improvements in productivity and income and therefore the well-being of the population. Essentially, economic development has the potential to bring many changes to the economic geography of a place. For many less developed countries based on predominantly low-income primary sector activities, tourism has provided opportunities for economic diversification. Countries that were not considered to have a cost-effective location for industrial development were increasingly identified as having attractive locations and/or resources for tourism. This allowed the development of tertiary activities, which may be accompanied by an increase in income. As such, the benefits of tourism have primarily focused on job creation and the interrelated factors of income, investment, and economic development.

## TOURISM EMPLOYMENT

One of the principal benefits of tourism is job creation. This is particularly important for countries that have traditionally experienced problems with high unemployment rates, as well as rural and peripheral regions of countries where jobs are limited. For example, the Caribbean has a history of chronic unemployment and high rates of labor-based emigration. Thus, the creation of new jobs for tourism has been a distinct advantage for many islands.

There is considerable potential for direct employment in the tourism industry, which is considered to have a relatively high demand for labor. For example, Las Vegas Sands employs approximately 9,300 people at the Venetian Resort Hotel Casino in Las Vegas, Nevada (including the Venetian, The Palazzo, Venezia towers, and corporate offices), the largest hotel/resort complex in the United States in terms of number of guest rooms.[6] This one complex maintains a larger workforce than many traditional manufacturing facilities, which have been experiencing declines in labor demand as a result of increased mechanization. By way of comparison, Hyundai Motor Manufacturing Alabama employs three thousand people.[7] Because tourism employment is place-based, it cannot be outsourced in the same way as manufacturing jobs.

Direct employment in the tourism industry varies widely. Some people may be employed to facilitate destination planning, development, or promotion. Others provide services to tourists by working at local information offices or serving as guides. Hotels and resorts employ countless people; depending on the scale of the hotel and the services provided, these employees may function as valet parking attendants, bellhops, check-in clerks, concierges, housekeepers, groundskeepers, maintenance crews, security forces, bartenders, servers, kitchen staff, salespeople in in-house retailers, spa therapists, casino dealers, entertainers, and even the gondoliers in the case of the

Venetian. Tourist attractions also employ a range of staff to maintain facilities and to facilitate the tourism experience.

In addition, there is considerable potential for indirect employment generated by the tourism industry. These jobs may support tourism development, but workers are not directly involved in serving tourists. This includes jobs in the construction industry that are required to build both the general infrastructure that will allow tourism (e.g., airports or highways) and the specific tourism infrastructure (e.g., hotels). Likewise, this can include manufacturing jobs that produce the goods that are sold to tourists. These jobs may also be created in related service industries that both support and benefit from tourism but do not solely cater to the tourist market. This includes jobs in transport services, general retail businesses, local restaurants, or others (figure 8.1).

The tremendous diversity of services provided in the context of tourism constitutes an added benefit: it allows jobs to be created in a variety of capacities and at different skill or education levels. This opens up tourism employment to a wider range of people, rather than a subset of the population. For example, 54 percent of people employed in tourism are women compared to 39 percent of people in the overall economy.[8] Particularly in less developed countries, less skilled work is accessible to women, who may not have had the opportunity to obtain a formal education. In addition, the domestic nature of many of the services provided in tourism may be seen as an acceptable form of employment in parts of the world where women have not traditionally had a place outside of the home and in the formal economic sectors. The part-time and seasonal nature of some tourism employment can provide opportunities for students to earn money or gain work experience during or between academic terms.[9]

**Figure 8.1. Atlantis Paradise Island Resort in the Bahamas reportedly accounts for an estimated 8,000 direct jobs and contributes to another 10,000–12,000 jobs indirectly.** *Source*: Scott Jeffcote

## INCOME, INVESTMENT, AND ECONOMIC DEVELOPMENT

For most places, the potential financial benefits of tourism are one of the key factors driving tourism development. However, these benefits come in different forms with different effects. Tourism has the potential to bring investment to a place or region. A place may possess the resources for tourism, but varying degrees of development will be required before tourism can take place. This is typically infrastructural development to allow people to reach the destination, to stay there (if appropriate), and to appreciate attractions. The public sector is likely to invest in the basic infrastructure, such as transport systems and utilities, and some attractions, such as local/national parks, monuments, or museums. The private sector is likely to invest in specific tourist infrastructure, such as accommodations, as well as attractions. For many destinations, particularly those in poorer regions seeking to use tourism as a strategy to improve the economy and income levels, the local private sector may not have sufficient capital to invest in tourism development. As such, external—often foreign—investment may be a crucial catalyst for growth and starting the development process in that place, when it would not have been possible otherwise.

Tourism also has the potential to bring currency to a destination. Thus, tourism geographers are concerned not only with the movement of people from one place to another but also with money. In the case of domestic tourism, there may be a spatial redistribution of currency within the country. This is particularly significant when destinations are developed in poorer, peripheral regions of a country. Tourism is an important means of allowing some of the wealth that is concentrated in the country's primary urban area to be channeled into these destinations, thereby decreasing regional inequalities. In the case of international tourism, this indicates an influx of currency that contributes to the country's gross domestic product (GDP) and has the potential to improve its trade balance (i.e., increase its surplus or decrease its deficit). Similarly, this signifies a means of redistributing some of the wealth from the more developed countries of the world to the less developed ones. However, concerted efforts must be made to ensure that the poorer segments of the population are able to participate in tourism (box 8.1)

The **travel account** is defined as the difference between the income that the destination country receives from tourism and the expenditures of that country's citizens when they travel abroad. The trend toward tourism in less developed countries such as Nicaragua, Mozambique, or Cambodia has allowed these destinations to develop a positive travel account. In other words, such destinations receive international tourists and therefore derive income from these tourists, but because international tourism is beyond the financial means of much of their population, they send relatively few tourists to other countries. In contrast, more developed countries such as Germany and Japan have traditionally had a negative travel account. These countries are significant tourist-generating areas and send substantial numbers of tourists abroad every year who spend money in other countries. As smaller numbers of tourists visit these destinations, the income derived from them is less than the amount being spent abroad.[10]

The **direct economic effect** of tourism refers to the initial introduction of currency into the local economy by tourists themselves. This is in the form of **tourist dollars**, or the money that tourists bring with them and spend at the destination

# Box 8.1. Experience: Tourism and Economic Development in Africa

*Squack runs a tour operation business offering exclusive safaris in multiple countries across Sub-Saharan Africa. The main focus is on wildlife and photography, and the majority of his safaris include a private guide who is both tour leader and an expert on fauna and flora. He takes the approach that it is very important to give travelers a balanced and educated perspective with regard to tourism, conservation and local communities, as these are always interlinked. He discusses this below.*

In many African countries, tourism is vital to the economy. Not only is tourism one of the single most important revenue streams for foreign currency, but it is also a major sector for providing employment to the local populace. How can tourism be as responsible as possible? How can tourism link with conservation and ultimately lead to conservation success?

The local communities living side by side with wild animals suffer the direct consequences of human–wildlife conflict. Loss of human lives is one factor, but the most important aspect is the loss of livestock or loss of crops. To many of these communities, loss of livestock or crops means that they have lost not only their livelihoods, but also their only means of survival, especially considering that there is often no provision of social welfare. This is where tourism and conservation must interlink to provide direct benefits to the local communities. Communities receiving direct benefits from tourism are transformed into active conservation stakeholders. If the preservation of wildlife benefits the communities and human–wildlife conflicts are mitigated, then these communities can be very effective conservation foot soldiers. Communities suffering human–wildlife conflicts without any benefits or mitigation will not continue to share space and resources with the wildlife.

Benefits to communities can take many forms. First, there can be direct income benefits to the community. For instance, the fees that are charged for tourists to visit the area can either be disbursed among community members or channeled into community infrastructure such as health clinics and schools. Second, there can be employment for local community members in the tourism industry or increased education and qualification of local community members. Third, this can be some form of 'land rent' paid to the community land-owners so that land is set aside as habitat for wildlife instead of being used for agriculture or livestock.

The double-edged sword with all this is that with increased income and better infrastructure often people from elsewhere move into the area, resulting in increased human population pressure on resources. In some cases, local tradition dictates that abundance of livestock must be valued above all else. In such cases, increased income without education or without alternatives can lead to a substantial increase in livestock and agricultural development. This increases pressure on the wildlife and there is often direct competition for natural resources and space, since shrinking habitats is a major cause for wildlife population decline. Every area and community needs to have all these considerations taken into account in order to make sure that tourism has a net positive effect on both the community and the wildlife it is based on. Different areas and different communities need to be carefully assessed since a one-size-fits-all approach is not practicable.

Some areas would benefit hugely from increased tourism numbers, and with this in mind some areas need development in terms of infrastructure, in terms of accessing the areas as well as facilities for tourists to stay at, and unique drawcard activities or attractions. Some areas are already oversubscribed, and the environment and wildlife are beginning to see a negative impact. As such, a number of options could be looked into, such as raising entry fees or restrictions on the numbers of visitors allowed access. These options are fraught with difficulties, and unfortunately there is no easy answer. Stricter enforcement of regulations could also improve the situation, but there is often a disregard for the rule of law.

Some areas are so remote and expensive to access that tourist numbers will never be high. In places like these an open mind about alternative usage is needed. The preservation of habitat, and the survival of all the animal species living in this habitat, is possible only if there is value creation for the local community as well as the government. Unless better options can be found, value creation in some of these remote areas is possible only by allowing sustainable consumptive use, preferably high value to mitigate potential impact. Without value creation these areas will be turned over to farming and agriculture and the habitat will be lost, which is the ultimate end of the game. The issue of consumptive use raises highly emotional arguments, but the most important voice in these discussions is always lacking. The people on the ground must be given a voice and local government must be included in decision-making processes. Otherwise international organizations are simply forcing their ideologies onto the people who ultimately bear the cost of living side by side with wildlife.

The COVID-19 pandemic has brought further challenges. Poaching and other illegal resource extraction have seen an increase in these tough times. With tourism at a standstill, workers in the sector as well as communities living alongside the protected areas are directly affected and find themselves without income. Many African countries have very little to nothing in the way of social security, and if you don't work you have zero income. At this stage who can blame people for poaching bushmeat to feed their families, or in some instances turning to commercial poaching for the survival of their families? Moral compunctions and ethical considerations weigh nothing when it is a question of survival.

*–Squack*

on lodging, food, excursions, souvenirs, and more. The **indirect economic effect** of tourism refers to the second round of spending that is a direct result of the tourist dollars. The recipients of tourist dollars use this money to pay expenses, employees, taxes, and so on, as well as to reinvest in the tourism business. This involves buying goods and services demanded by tourists or new equipment that will allow them to better serve the tourist market. This round of spending is primarily intended to improve or expand the tourism sector in a way that will encourage future visitation and spending (i.e., greater direct effects) at the destination. As long as the additional spending takes place within the local economy (e.g., hiring local workers, buying locally produced goods), it can create additional economic benefits for the destination. Finally, the **induced economic effect** constitutes an additional round of spending. For example, recipients of tourist dollars pay taxes, licenses, or fees on their business; then the government may use this money to subsidize local development projects. Likewise, recipients may use tourist dollars to pay their employees, who then purchase the goods and services that they need for their own consumption.

This process of spending and respending may be quantified by the **multiplier effect**. This is typically expressed as a ratio. For example, the ratio of 1 to 1.25 means that for every tourist dollar that is spent directly on tourism, an additional 25 cents is created indirectly in the local economy. The multiplier effect may be used to estimate the economic benefits of tourism because it provides an indication of how the income from tourism is distributed throughout the economy. The greater the ratio, the more likely it is that money is staying within that economy. Consequently, the ratio will generally be higher at the national scale rather than at the local scale, where some money will necessarily be spent outside the community. Businesses will be required to pay federal taxes, which may not be reinvested in that particular place. Not all goods can be obtained locally, and not all employees live at the destination and spend their earnings there. The multiplier effect is criticized because it can be extremely difficult to calculate depending on a wide range of factors. As such, it should be considered with caution, as a general guide to describe the potential for additional economic benefits to the destination as opposed to a precise measure.[11]

The development of tourism has the potential to contribute to economic diversification as well as sustainable development and community resilience. Tourism businesses can take advantage of existing local economic activities or encourage the development of new ones to support tourism and provide the goods or services demanded by tourists. These are called **linkages** and are typically part of the indirect economic effects. For instance, tourism has the potential for strong linkages to local agricultural or fishing industries where foods are produced and prepared locally for tourist consumption at markets, restaurants, or resorts. Nearly all tourists must spend a portion of their budget on food, but many are interested in consuming local food and beverages as a means of trying something new or having an authentic

**Figure 8.2.** The Cadushy Distillery on the Caribbean island of Bonaire uses the locally grown Kadushi cactus to make its distinctive liqueur and tea. Visitors tour the distillery and purchase products to be taken home. *Source*: Velvet Nelson

## Box 8.2. Case Study: Tourism and Poverty Reduction in Peru's Sacred Valley

In 2015, world leaders adopted the 2030 Agenda for Sustainable Development. The document notes, "We recognise that eradicating poverty in all its forms and dimensions, including extreme poverty, is the greatest global challenge and an indispensable requirement for sustainable development."[a] The UNWTO argues that sustainable tourism development can be tied to national poverty reduction goals through support for small businesses and empowerment of disadvantaged groups.[b]

The idea of using tourism as a tool for poverty reduction is not new; the **pro-poor tourism** (PPT) approach was developed in the late 1990s. PPT is defined as tourism that results in increased net benefits for poor people and ensures that tourism growth contributes to poverty reduction. It seeks to expand the economic benefits of tourism to the poor by addressing those barriers that prevent them from participating in tourism.[c] Thus, tourism as mechanism for pro-poor growth can support sustainable development and increase community resilience.[d] PPT is not a specific tourism "product" like those discussed in chapter 3. The approach can be applied to ecotourism, agritourism, cultural tourism, indigenous tourism, rural tourism, urban tourism, and more.

Proponents of PPT argue that the tourism industry is better suited to contribute to poverty reduction than many other economic activities because it is a diverse, labor-intensive industry that often utilizes freely available resources (e.g., natural environments or elements of culture). Tourism has the potential to complement and supplement existing economic activities (e.g., agriculture or fishing), thereby increasing income-earning potential. Tourism brings the consumer to the producer, which opens up opportunities for poor people who may not have the ability to take their goods or services to a place of consumption.[e] PPT is also considered to be less culturally disruptive than traditional forms of tourism.[f]

Critics argue that PPT can be difficult to execute without private sector support, broader changes within the tourism industry, and/or broader structural changes.[g] With a focus on accruing net economic benefits, other social and environmental impacts may be overlooked, which undermines sustainable development.[h] In addition, wider tourism impacts are not considered. For example, PPT encourages travel from more developed countries to less developed ones. This typically takes the form of long-distance international air transport. The greenhouse gas emissions incurred in this travel contributes to climate change, and impoverished people in the less developed countries are highly vulnerable to the effects of climate change.[i]

Case studies offer useful insight into some of the opportunities and challenges associated with PPT. In Peru, the government actively began promoting tourism as a strategy for economic growth in 1993. In ten years, the country received 1.65 million international visitors. By 2018, that number had grown 326 percent.[j] Approximately one-third of these visitors travel to Machu Picchu, a UNESCO World Heritage Site and one of Latin America's top tourist destinations.[k] To capitalize on this market, rural communities in Peru's Sacred Valley (map 8.1) were specifically targeted for PPT through the Rural Community Tourism Program. The program was intended to assist communities with the sustainable development of existing physical and human resources for tourism.[l] One mayor in the region stated, "Tourism plays a very important role in poverty reduction for the people of Peru. It represents a great deal of economic opportunity for poor people living in the Cusco region, where few other forms of income exist"[m] (figure 8.3).

Tourism researcher David Knight examined the complexities of developing PPT in these communities. Community tourism association members typically cook and serve lunch for tour groups, using as many locally grown ingredients as possible. They also provide

**Map 8.1. The Sacred Valley, Peru. Approximately 500,000 visitors travel to the Sacred Valley to visit Machu Picchu.** *Source:* Gang Gong

'workshops' to allow visitors to learn about local livelihoods, from agriculture to craft work, and offer opportunities for visitors to buy locally made products. In the case of Chichubamba, Knight noted that community members were initially interested in hosting visitors, but when it took three years for them to actually receive visitors, many abandoned the idea. Association members keep the money from the lunches and workshops they host, but when the number of visitors varies between groups, some receive more than others, which has also discouraged participation. In Qorqor, visitors did not pay for workshops; hosts were dependent on visitors choosing to purchase items. Tour guides did not always provide sufficient notice about a visit for members to obtain and prepare food, and guides canceled as many as 50 percent of visits.[n]

While there were clearly challenges in the process of developing PPT, Knight noted that evidence of multidimensional poverty reduction could be observed. In addition to measures of income, multidimensional poverty encompasses various factors that affect peoples' quality of life, such as a lack of basic needs or a lack of community. In the Sacred Valley communities, subsistence farmers were able to earn income through complementary activities. Families were able to make improvements to their homes and living standards as well as educate their children. In particular, women had increased opportunities to work and earn income, be involved in the community, and gain respect.[o]

Pro-poor tourism, like other approaches to tourism, has negative effects as well as positive ones. Tourism stakeholders need to understand these effects and adapt as necessary to maximize the positive effects while continually working to minimize the negative effects. This is especially important for stakeholders working in or with impoverished communities that face a variety of constraints, from isolated and challenging physical environments to the lack of knowledge about or connections in tourism.

**Figure 8.3. There are many challenges to economic development in Peru's Sacred Valley. The Rural Community Tourism Program strives to promote pro-poor tourism as an economic opportunity in this rugged region.** *Source:* Velvet Nelson

*Discussion topic*: Conduct a SWOT (Strengths, Weaknesses, Opportunities, and Threats) analysis for pro-poor tourism in rural communities such as those in the Sacred Valley.

*Tourism online*: PromPeru, "Explore the Sacred Valley," at https://www.peru.travel/en/experiences/explore-the-sacred-valley

[a] United Nations, "Transforming Our World: The 2030 Agenda for Sustainable Development," accessed May 5, 2020, https://sustainabledevelopment.un.org/post2015/transformingourworld.

[b] United Nations World Tourism Organization, "SDG 1 – No Poverty," accessed May 5, 2020, http://tourism4sdgs.org/sdg-1-no-poverty/.

[c] Caroline Ashley, Dilys Roe, and Harold Goodwin, "Pro-Poor Strategies: Making Tourism Work for the Poor," *Pro-Poor Tourism Report* 1 (2001): viii.

[d] David W. Knight, "An Institutional Analysis of Local Strategies for Enhancing Pro-Poor Tourism Outcomes in Cuzco, Peru," *Journal of Sustainable Tourism* 26, no. 4 (2018): 631–2.

[e] Caroline Ashley, Charlotte Boyd, and Harold Goodwin, "Pro-Poor Tourism: Putting Poverty at the Heart of the Tourism Agenda," *Natural Resource Perspectives* 51 (2000): 1–2.

[f] David W. Knight and Stuart P. Cottrell, "Evaluating Tourism-Linked Empowerment in Cuzco, Peru," *Annals of Tourism Research* 56 (2016): 33.

[g] Richard Butler, Ross Curran, and Kevin D. O'Gorman, "Pro-Poor Tourism in a First World Urban Setting: Case Study of Glasgow Govan," *International Journal of Tourism Research*, 15 (2013): 443.

[h] Christian M. Rogerson, "Informal Sector Business Tourism and Pro-Poor Tourism: Africa's Migrant Entrepreneurs," *Mediterranean Journal of Social Sciences* 5, no. 16 (2014): 153–4.

i Jordi Gascón, "Pro-Poor Tourism as a Strategy to Fight Rural Poverty: A Critique," *Journal of Agrarian Change* 15, no. 4 (2015): 500.

j United Nations World Tourism Organization, *Compendium of Tourism Statistics Dataset [Electronic]* (Madrid: UN-WTO, 2020).

k The World Bank, "Peru: Easing Business Regulations in One of the World's Most Famous Tourist Destinations," November 1, 2016, accessed May 6, 2020, https://www.worldbank.org/en/results/2016/11/01/peru-easing-business-regulations-in-one-of-the-worlds-most-famous-tourist-destinations.

l United Nations World Tourism Organization, *Tourism and Culture Partnership in Peru – Models for Collaboration Between Tourism, Culture and Community* (Madrid: UNWTO, 2016), 72–5.

m The World Bank, "Peru."

n Knight, "An Institutional Analysis of Local Strategies," 638–41.

o David Warner Knight, "Poverty Alleviation Through Tourism? Community Perceptions of Intrepid Travel in Peru's Sacred Valley," *Intrepid Travel*, accessed May 6, 2020, https://www.intrepidtravel.com/sites/intrepid/files/teal/1.%20Peru%20Research%20Summary%2C%20David%20W%20Knight.pdf.

experience of place (figure 8.2). Thus, linkages may be used to create a sense of place-based distinctiveness and a competitive advantage for the destination. A subset of tourists is also interested in sustainability and more willing to visit those destinations or businesses that support local producers and/or minimize food miles.[12] Linkages can also be created with local craft industries (e.g., hotels using locally produced toiletries or linens). Tourists may be inspired to purchase such products to enjoy after they return home. The slow tourism trend is particularly well suited to the creation of local linkages.

Although some existing economic activities might have the potential for linkages as the tourism industry becomes well established, at least initially the local economy may not be sufficiently or appropriately developed to support the tourism industry. Existing activities may require adaptations to meet the specific demands of tourism. The local agricultural industry may make a transition from a single crop (e.g., rice) to more diversified agriculture to supply the range of products in demand by the tourism industry (e.g., avocados). Likewise, the local fishing industry may need to expand in order to supply the quantity of products demanded by the tourism industry. Additionally, activities may need to be wholly developed; until then, products must be imported. However, to maximize the economic (as well as social and environmental) benefits of tourism, local linkages should be created as soon as it is feasible to support the sustainable development of local communities.

# Economic Costs of Tourism

Places all across the globe would like to get a share of the tourism industry. Consequently, much emphasis is placed on the economic benefits of tourism. Yet, the *potential* for these benefits must be carefully considered to understand what the *actual* effect will be on a destination (i.e., who will receive the benefits and what will be the outcomes). As such, we need to take a closer look at the nature of the jobs created in the tourism industry at a destination, the extent of economic effects, and the changes that occur in the local economy.

## TOURISM EMPLOYMENT

The jobs created in the construction industry, the tourism industry, and the various supporting industries can attract immigrants from other regions of a country or from other countries. This is the case when tourism is developed in peripheral areas where there may not be a large enough local population to fill the new demand for labor or in areas where the local population is not interested in the type of work needed. This labor-induced migration can quickly outstrip available jobs and result in a labor surplus. In fact, areas with a high dependence on tourism may have higher levels of unemployment than surrounding regions. This is due to the number of people who move to the destination based on the promise of employment or with the hope of higher-paid employment than would be available to them in their home community.

In addition, tourism is both seasonal and cyclical, which has the potential to affect employment patterns. Even popular tropical destinations, such as the islands of the Caribbean, have a distinct tourist season. Higher rates of precipitation during the wet season, as well as the increased risk of hurricanes, are considered barriers to tourism (chapter 6). At the same time, the majority of tourists come from the Northern Hemisphere during the winter months for the inversion of cold to warm weather (chapter 2). Consequently, at these destinations, there is a high demand for labor during peak months, and tourism businesses may need to hire additional workers. Yet, during the low season, some of these workers may have to find temporary employment in other sectors if possible, emigrate in search of opportunities, or face unemployment.

Tourism employment is entirely based on the success of the industry. When a destination is experiencing growth, new jobs will be created in both tourism and related industries. For example, when a destination is developing or expanding, a tremendous amount of local and/or tourism infrastructure may be built, creating a boom in the construction industry. However, when the industry as a whole, or a specific destination, is experiencing a decline, jobs will quickly disappear. COVID-19 provided a vivid example of this. As of April 2020, the World Travel and Tourism Council (WTTC) estimated a loss of 100.8 million travel and tourism jobs due to the pandemic.[13]

While tourism is a labor-intensive industry, recent developments could lead to reduced employment opportunities. As more tourists choose peer-to-peer accommodations (e.g., Airbnb), there is decreased demand for hotel accommodations; however, hotels support more jobs.[14] Technology will also affect tourism employment in the future. A first wave of advances in robotic and artificial intelligence technology led to job losses in manufacturing. The second wave is going to lead to job losses in the service sector (box 8.3). In tourism, the accommodation, food service, and transport sectors are considered to have high automation potential.[15]

The types of employment in tourism and its related industries is one of the most common criticisms. Many jobs are unskilled and low-wage, which may have few benefits for the local population. Tourism businesses may seek to minimize costs by providing services to tourists on an on-demand basis. Instead of a staff of

# Box 8.3.  In-Depth: Robots, Artificial Intelligence, and Service Automation in Tourism

Technology is a part of our daily lives, so it should not be a surprise that it is increasingly part of travel, tourism, and hospitality as well. While some innovations still seem fantastical and far off, others are already accepted practices in tourism, such as the use of self-check-in kiosks at the airport and mobile boarding passes. Considering both current use and future applications, it is worth taking a look at the role of robots, artificial intelligence, and service automation (RAISA) in tourism and its implications for tourism employment.

Items like cleaning robots (e.g., vacuums) are not uncommon, but some places are taking it a step farther. In 2019, a new hotel in Copenhagen, Denmark advertised the use of self-disinfecting technology in guest rooms.[a] Robots also serve in a variety of other capacities. In 2017, LG Electronics trialed a guide robot at Incheon International Airport in Seoul, South Korea. The robot provided information about boarding times and the location of terminal services in Korean, English, Chinese, and Japanese.[b] Hotels now feature concierge robots to answer questions, butler robots that can deliver food or other amenities to guests, and even robot bartenders that make cocktails. In one experiment, the Henn-na Hotel in Japan was promoted as the world's first hotel staffed by robots, including two velociraptor robot receptionists and doll robot assistants in each room. Unfortunately, 243 robots were laid off in 2019 when it turned out they were not very good at their jobs.[c]

Tourism businesses use artificial intelligence for online customer service to provide prompt responses to inquiries as well as on site. For example, some hotels offer in-room assistants similar to Amazon Alexa and Google Home. Facial recognition software applications facilitate automated passport control programs like Clear or expedited customs and immigration programs like Global Entry. New models of airplanes will have sensors to provide flight crews with information such as available overhead bin space, seat belts left unbuckled, and even the number of people in line for the bathroom.[d] Self-service technologies, including self-service kiosks (e.g., airports, hotels, restaurants, tourist information offices), and mobile applications have a wide range of uses. Airports and tourist attractions (see chapter 5) are testing the use of autonomous transport, and in 2018, the concept of an autonomous travel suite won an innovation award. This proposed solar-powered, self-driving electric vehicle equipped with the features of a hotel room would combine transportation and accommodation to make travel more comfortable and efficient.[e]

For tourism businesses, adoption of technology involves a range of costs, including investment in the technology, operation and maintenance costs, information technology specialists, adaptations to infrastructure to allow the equipment to operate effectively, and even insurance in the event of damage caused by the technology. These costs have to be weighed against advantages. RAISA can save employees time and effort. For example, cleaning robots can reduce the amount of time spent cleaning hotel rooms as well as make the task less physically demanding or even safer. RAISA can reduce human error, which can have cost savings. RAISA can also work efficiently (e.g., serving multiple customers at once) without the constraints of labor laws. As technology reduces employee workloads or replaces employees (i.e., outsourcing jobs to RAISA), businesses can reduce labor costs, such as salaries/wages, retirement/pension contributions, and/or health insurance. In addition, RAISA can fill labor shortages in difficult or demanding jobs, jobs that require specific skill sets such as fluency in multiple languages, or in locations experiencing population declines. Innovative uses of RAISA can also create a competitive advantage for the business.[f]

Although reduced labor costs may be considered a positive for businesses, there are distinct concerns associated with decreased employment opportunities in tourism.

Although low-skilled and low-income positions are at the highest risk of automation, even more nuanced positions, like tour guides, could be replaced by mobile applications.[g] As opposed to seeing how RAISA could make their jobs easier, employees may see it as a threat.

Tourist perceptions of RAISA also need to be understood.[h] Some may prefer the hospitality traditionally provided by human employees in tourism or have concerns about privacy associated with the use of technology. Others are accustomed to technology in their lives, and the use of self-service technologies away from home may be considered an extension of this. Moreover, due to the social distancing practices implemented during COVID-19, tourism businesses began considering ways to create physical barriers between employees and guests and accelerate the transition to technology like mobile applications to minimize the need for human-to-human contact. Unfortunately, this may mean that many of the tourism jobs that were lost during the pandemic might not come back. This has the potential to create economic hardship in places dependent on tourism and increased resistance as places experience the negative effects of tourism without benefitting from it.

*Discussion topic:* Explain your willingness/unwillingness to accept the use of RAISA in your travel and tourism experiences. In this decision, would you consider the affect of RAISA on human employment?

*Tourism online:* Henn-na Hotel, "Brand Concept," https://www.h-n-h.jp/en/concept

---

[a] Caitlin Morton, "Would You Stay in a Hotel Room that Cleans Itself?" *Condé Nast Traveler*, February 26, 2019, accessed May 4, 2020, https://www.cntraveler.com/story/would-you-stay-in-a-hotel-room-that-cleans-itself.

[b] LG Electronics, "LG Airport Robots Take Over Korea's Largest Airport," July 21, 2017, accessed May 4, 2020, https://www.lg.com/sg/press-release/lg-airport-robots-take-over-koreas-largest-airport.

[c] Jessica Miley, "Japanese Hotel Fires Robot Staff after They Annoy Human Staff and Guests," *Interesting Engineering*, January 17, 2019, accessed May 4, 2020, https://interestingengineering.com/japanese-hotel-fires-robot-staff-after-they-annoy-human-staff-and-guests.

[d] Jessica Puckett, "New Airbus Planes Will Track Your Every Move through the Cabin," Condé Nast Traveler, September 13, 2019, accessed May 4, 2020, https://www.cntraveler.com/story/new-airbus-planes-will-track-your-every-move-through-the-cabin.

[e] Sasha Brady, "Self-Driving Hotel Suites Could Dramatically Change the Way We Travel," Lonely Planet, November 23, 2018, accessed May 4, 2020, https://www.lonelyplanet.com/articles/self-driving-hotel-suites.

[f] Stanislav Ivanov and Craig Webster, "Conceptual Framework for the Use of Robots, Artificial Intelligence and Service Automation in Travel, Tourism, and Hospitality Companies," in *Robots, Artificial Intelligence, and Service Automation in Travel, Tourism and Hospitality*, eds. Stanislav Ivanov and Craig Webster (London: Emerald Publishing, 2019); Stanislav Ivanov and Craig Webster, "Economic Fundamentals in the Use of Robots, Artificial Intelligence and Service Automation in Travel, Tourism, and Hospitality," in *Robots, Artificial Intelligence and Service Automation in Travel, Tourism and Hospitality*, eds. Stanislav Ivanov and Craig Webster (London: Emerald Publishing, 2019).

[g] C. Michael Hall, Girish Prayag, and Alberto Amore, *Tourism and Resilience: Individual, Organisational and Destination Perspectives* (Bristol: Channel View Publications, 2018).

[h] Ivanov and Webster, "Conceptual Framework for the Use of Robots"; Ivanov and Webster, "Economic Fundamentals in the Use of Robots."

---

full-time employees, businesses may rely on independent contractors who are paid an hourly wage or per job and who receive no benefits like health care or pension plans. For example, in 2012, Spanish labor reforms allowed hotels to outsource cleaning services. The outsourced contracts often pay less and require workers to clean a minimum number of rooms per shift. A national workers' organization, Las Kellys, argues that it is not possible to meet the quotas during their shift, so cleaners end up working longer hours, further reducing their hourly rate. The contract nature of the work leads to insecurity, and many workers come from vulnerable groups (e.g., single mothers). The physically demanding nature of the work leads to health problems such as back pain and arthritis, as well as mental health concerns such as anxiety. In 2018, Las Kellys attempted to convince booking platforms such as TripAdvisor to include a seal that would allow guests to choose hotels that support good practices.[16]

Highly paid and managerial positions represent a smaller proportion of overall tourism jobs. Women in particular are more likely to remain in low-paid, unskilled jobs due to fewer opportunities for training and advancement.[17] However, when tourism is developed in rural or peripheral regions of a country and/or less developed countries, the local population in general may not have the education, training, or experience to be able to hold these types of jobs. Additionally, multinational companies may prefer to import workers who are already familiar with company policies or who may be more likely to understand the needs of the targeted tourist market. Unless a concerted effort is made to develop the local resource base to be able to successfully hold higher-level tourism positions, a destination can become dependent on foreign expertise.

The growth of jobs in the tourism industry may have negative consequences in other areas of the economy. Jobs in the tourism industry may have higher wages than other local employment opportunities. They may be perceived to be less physically demanding than manual labor jobs or more stable than activities like agriculture that are highly dependent on unpredictable environmental conditions. As people choose tourism employment over others, this can contribute to labor shortages and declines in other parts of the local economy. Thus, tourism will not necessarily result in an increase in employment opportunities or produce a net gain in the local or national economy.

Despite the perception of tourism as anything but a serious business, there are significant concerns about human rights violations and even modern-day slavery. Regulations on labor, from pay to working conditions, vary widely between countries. In particular, concerns about the migrant labor that has facilitated tourism growth have gotten increased attention in recent years. For example, human rights organizations have brought attention to the situation of the nearly one million migrant construction workers who build luxury hotels in the United Arab Emirates. Workers, primarily from South Asia, incur large debts to pay high recruitment fees to obtain jobs but earn around US$190 a month. They work long hours in difficult climatic conditions and live in crowded and unsanitary camps.[18] Similar concerns have been raised about the migrant construction workers in Qatar building facilities to host the 2022 FIFA World Cup. A study found that heatstroke was likely the cause of the deaths of more than 1,300 Nepali workers from 2009 to 2017.[19]

## INCOME, INVESTMENT, AND ECONOMIC DEVELOPMENT

Tourism income plays an incredibly important role for individuals and economies. Yet, tourism is a sensitive industry that may be adversely affected by any number of unforeseen factors that destinations and workers have little or no control over. In addition to job losses, the WTTC claimed that tourism losses from the COVID-19 pandemic could reach US$2.7 trillion (April 2020 estimate).[20]

Tourism has the potential to support other economic activities, but in reality tourism often grows at the expense of other activities. Land traditionally used for agriculture may be sold, voluntarily or under coercion, for commercial tourism development. The potential for creating economic linkages between agriculture and tourism at the destination is diminished or lost altogether. Rather than promoting economic diversification, this can result in greater concentration in a single economic sector and an overdependence on tourism as the principal source of income in a local or national economy. As a result, the economy is more vulnerable to fluctuations in the industry.

Although foreign investment may initially provide an important source of income that allows for destination development, an overdependence on multinational companies can have a long-term impact on the nature of economic effects at the destination. The income these companies generate is more likely to be transferred out of the region or country instead of contributing to the multiplier effect. This is referred to as **leakages**. These leakages are the part of tourism income that does not get reinvested in the local economy. Some leakage occurs with each round of spending after tourist dollars are introduced into the economy, until no further respending can take place. The direct effect will be mitigated if the tourism businesses are externally owned, because profits will be transferred out of the region or country. The indirect effects will be reduced if tourism businesses seek external suppliers for their products. Likewise, the induced effects will be eliminated if local people spend their earnings outside the region or country or on imported goods.[21]

The classic example of leakage is seen in the all-inclusive package mass tourism resorts. Multinational companies based in the more developed countries of the world own these large-scale chain resorts. When tourists travel from these same countries and spend their tourist dollars at the resort, those dollars may, in fact, be returning to the country of origin. Take, for example, the context of food. In some cases, despite the higher transportation costs of importing food, the company may be able to obtain food items at a lower cost from a subsidized mass producer at home as opposed to the higher per-unit cost of a small-scale local producer (figure 8.4).[22] Whether it is true or not, the perception exists that mass tourists do not care where their food comes from or that they will have concerns about the quality and integrity of local foods. They may suspect that this food was produced and/or processed under unhygienic conditions or that it will not be up to the same standards they are accustomed to at home. These types of resorts may also assume that mass tourists prefer the types of foods eaten at home and will not try new types of foods for fear of getting sick.[23]

The result is that, although countries like Nicaragua, Mozambique, or Cambodia may have a positive travel account, they may not receive the full economic benefits of tourism. These less developed countries have little capacity to develop tourism on their own; therefore, they are likely to rely on multinational companies to do it for them. Even though they receive international tourists, there are typically high levels of leakages that reduce the multiplier effect. As a result, little money is retained or reinvested at the destination, and the goal of redistributing wealth between parts of the world remains unrealized.

Figure 8.4. **When tourism providers are unable or unwilling to work with small-scale agricultural producers, like this vegetable farmer in Guizhou, China, opportunities for creating local linkages are lost.** *Source*: Velvet Nelson

Moreover, rather than redistributing a country's wealth and economic opportunities, tourism may contribute to a further spatial concentration. This may be in an area that already has a stronger development base, such as a major metropolitan area, or it may be the development of a tourist zone. This can create or contribute to regional inequalities, as that area develops, modernizes, and experiences the economic benefits of tourism while other areas remain marginalized.

Likewise, tourism will not necessarily result in a redistribution of wealth among the population. Much of the money that is not leaked out of a region or country tends to stay in the hands of the upper- and middle-income groups. Despite concepts like pro-poor tourism and the potential for tourism to improve the economic well-being of traditionally marginalized populations such as rural and/or indigenous peoples, few of the economic benefits of tourism actually accrue to the poorest segments of a population. For the most part, tourism development does not incorporate poverty elimination objectives. This is because tourism is largely driven by the private sector and companies whose primary objective is profit.

In fact, tourism has the potential to further harm the local population, especially the poorest segments of that population. As a destination develops, it may experience increasing land costs and costs of living. Land is often assessed for tax purposes on its market value rather than its use. As land at an emerging destination is sold to tourism developers at a relatively high cost, the value of all of the land in the area may be reassessed, resulting in an increase in property taxes. This may make it increasingly difficult for landowners to be able to afford to live on and/or use their land as they had in the past. For example, a farmer may have a piece of land that has been in his family for generations. He would like to maintain this land for both the heritage it represents to him and its use as a working farm. However, his income from the farm may no longer be enough to support his family and pay the increased taxes to keep the land.

The value of goods and services may be adjusted based on the amount of money tourists will pay for such things as opposed to the local population. For example, property owners at a destination may have the opportunity to rent houses or apartments/flats to tourists at a high per-week price. As such, local residents might not be able to afford to rent living space within the destination area, and they will be forced to move elsewhere. Similarly, stores may cater to tourists who are able and/or willing to pay more for certain products. Again, residents might not be able to afford to buy these products, at least from these stores (see box 7.2). Consequently, they may have to travel outside the destination to obtain the products they need, and if this is not an option for them based on transportation constraints, they will have to find alternatives or go without.

Finally, a destination may experience a range of hidden economic costs associated with tourism. For example, there may be a financial cost associated with managing the social or environmental effects of tourism that will be discussed in the following chapters.

## Factors in Economic Effects

In some cases, we will be able to clearly see the effects of tourism on the economy. This is most likely in communities or countries with relatively undeveloped or undiversified economies. For example, small island developing states (SIDS), whether they are located in the Caribbean, the Mediterranean, the Indian Ocean, or the Pacific, face similar constraints to economic development (e.g., limited resource bases, lack of economies of scale, reduced competitiveness of products due to high transportation costs, few opportunities for private sector investment, little resilience to natural disasters).[24] The development of tourism in the SIDS can result in clearly identifiable economic impacts, such as an influx of foreign investment, a decrease in the unemployment rate, and an increase in the per capita gross domestic product. In other cases, the impact of tourism on a country's overall economy can be more difficult to determine. The development of tourism may reflect a redistribution of resources, such as an investment or employment in tourism instead of other economic activities.

The specific economic effects of tourism at a destination, and the extent of these effects, will likely vary widely. The often-interrelated factors that may determine these effects can include the nature of the local economy and the level of development at the destination, as seen in the example above. Similarly, the type of tourism, ownership in the tourism industry, and tourist spending patterns at the destination can have an impact on these effects.

For example, mass tourism destinations are more likely to be characterized by large-scale multinational companies that may use foreign staff and rely on imported supplies. As such, leakages are going to be high. In contrast, niche tourism destinations are more likely to be characterized by small-scale, locally owned tourism businesses with significant local linkages and therefore a higher multiplier effect. However, many destinations have a combination of both, typically a higher proportion of small local businesses (e.g., hotels or restaurants), but the large companies will have the greatest capacity (e.g., the most beds or tables).

Organized mass tourists typically contribute the fewest tourist dollars to the local economy. One of the most prominent examples can be seen in the cruise industry. The large quantities of cruise tourists notoriously contribute very little to the local economy at the visited ports. Cruise companies have invested in private islands where any money spent goes back to the company as opposed to the local economy. Some passengers never even leave the ship. In contrast, drifters and explorers, who spend longer at a single destination and rely less on the explicit tourism infrastructure, have greater opportunities to (although they do not always) support local businesses.

# Knowledge and Education

For the majority of tourists (actual and potential) around the world, money is one of the most important concerns. We may have a demand for tourism, but ultimately it is a nonessential expense. We must determine how much of our disposable income we can devote to travel and what experiences we can afford. There is a small, but growing, subset of socially conscious individuals who would be interested in supporting the local economy at the places they visit; however, they may be faced with a choice. If they cannot afford a niche destination (one with a higher cost due to the lack of economies of scale but strong local linkages), do they accept a cheaper vacation at a mass destination (one with a lower cost due to economies of scale but higher levels of leakages) or stay home?

Even if tourists are interested in and willing to pay more for destinations that are economically beneficial to local people, they may not be knowledgeable enough to make an informed decision. In contrast to fair trade commodities, there is little in the way of widely known or recognized certification of tourism products. There are a few examples, such as Fair Trade Tourism, which certifies that African tourism enterprises have fair wages and working conditions, fair purchasing and operations, an equitable distribution of benefits, and respect for human rights, culture, and the environment.[25] However, it often falls to individual tourism businesses to advertise their own policies on their website or other promotional literature, such as local ownership, fair wages, support of local farmers and craftspeople, and so on.

Tourism businesses must also weigh the higher cost of policies that support the local economy against the cost of not doing so. These are profit-oriented businesses, and paying higher wages or higher costs for locally produced supplies can reduce their profit margin. Alternatively, if these expenses are built into the price of the tourism product, the venture may become less competitive and lose business to other companies or destinations offering similar products. Yet, there can be value in promoting ethical business practices. Perhaps more significantly, the local population has the potential to undermine tourism if they feel they are not receiving enough benefits from the industry. Consequently, it is important to understand the nature and distribution of the economic effects at a destination.

## Conclusion

Tourism has emerged as one of the world's most significant economic activities. As such, a foundation in economic geography is a vital component in the geography of tourism. It can be easy to focus only on the positive economic effects of tourism. In fact, it is often the case that those who are better off to begin with are the ones who are most likely to benefit from tourism. As they have the greatest voice and power in decision making, the positive outcomes may be the only ones considered. Yet, it may be that a substantial proportion of the population will never see the benefits of tourism and may not want to see it take place. Ultimately, both the public and the private sectors should undertake efforts to see that more segments of the population are able to benefit from and therefore support the industry.

## Key Terms

- direct economic effect
- economic development
- economic geography
- indirect economic effect
- induced economic effect
- leakages

- linkages
- multiplier effect
- pro-poor tourism
- tourist dollars
- travel account

## Notes

1. United Nations World Tourism Organization, *International Tourism Highlights 2019 Edition* (2019), 3, 8, accessed March 5, 2020, https://www.e-unwto.org/doi/pdf/10.18111/9789284421152.

2. Marion Joppe, "The Roles of Policy, Planning and Governance in Preventing and Managing Overtourism," in *Overtourism: Issues, Realities and Solutions*, eds. Rachel Dodds and Richard W. Butler (Berlin: De Gruyter, 2019): 251.

3. Susan Hanson. "Thinking Back, Thinking Ahead: Some Questions for Economic Geographers," in *Economic Geography: Past, Present, and Future*, ed. Sharmistha Bagchi-Sen and Helen Lawton Smith (London: Routledge, 2006), 25–33.

4. Dieter K. Müller, "Tourism Geographies: A Bibliometric Review," in *A Research Agenda for Tourism Geographies*, ed. Dieter K. Müller (Cheltenham: Edward Elgar Publishing, 2019), 18–20.

5. United Nations World Tourism Organization, "SDG 1 – No Poverty," accessed May 5, 2020, http://tourism4sdgs.org/sdg-1-no-poverty/.

6. Joyce Lupiani and Jordan Gartner, "Las Vegas Sands to Pay Employees Amid Venetian, Palazzo Closures," *KTVN Las Vegas*, March 18, 2020, accessed May 7, 2020, https://www.ktnv.com/news/las-vegas-sands-closing-the-venetian-and-palazzo-hotel-casinos.

7. Hyundai Motor Manufacturing Alabama, "About HMMA," accessed May 7, 2020, http://www.hmmausa.com/our-company/about-hmma/.

8. United Nations World Tourism Organization, *Global Report on Women in Tourism, Second Edition, Key Findings* (2019), 3, accessed May 7, 2020, https://www.e-unwto.org/doi/pdf/10.18111/9789284420407.

9. Dimitri Ioannides and Kristina Zampoukos, "Exploring the Geographic Dimensions of Tourism Work and Workers," in *A Research Agenda for Tourism Geographies*, ed. Dieter K. Müller (Cheltenham: Edward Elgar Publishing, 2019), 93.

10. Stephen Williams. *Tourism Geography* (London: Routledge, 1998), 87–8.

11. Williams, *Tourism Geography*, 90–1.

12. Regina Scheyvens and Gabriel Laeis, "Linkages between Tourist Resorts, Local Food Production and the Sustainable Development Goals," *Tourism Geographies* (2019), DOI: 10.1080/14616688.2019.1674369

13. World Travel & Tourism Council, "WTTC Now Estimates Over 100 Million Jobs Losses In the Travel & Tourism Sector and Alerts G20 Countries to the Scale of the Crisis," April 24, 2020, accessed May 8, 2020, https://wttc.org/News-Article/WTTC-now-estimates-over-100-million-jobs-losses-in-the-Travel-&-Tourism-sector-and-alerts-G20-countries-to-the-scale-of-the-crisis.

14. Joan B. Garau-Vadell, Desiderio Gutiérrez-Taño, Ricardo Díaz-Armas, "Residents' Support for P2P Accommodation in Mass Tourism Destinations," *Journal of Travel Research* 58, no. 4 (2019), 551.

15. C. Michael Hall, Girish Prayag, and Alberto Amore, *Tourism and Resilience: Individual, Organisational and Destination Perspectives* (Bristol: Channel View Publications, 2018), 2–3.

16. James Badcock, "Spain's Hotel Chambermaids 'Las Kellys' Fight for Fair Pay," *BBC News*, October 18, 2017, accessed May 8, 2020, https://www.bbc.com/news/world-europe-41650252; Stephen Burgen, "Spanish Hotel Cleaners Seek Tripadvisor's Help to Fight Exploitation," *The Guardian*, July 2, 2018, accessed May 8, 2020, https://www.theguardian.com/world/2018/jul/02/spanish-chambermaids-seek-tripadvisor-help-to-fight-exploitation?CMP=Share_iOSApp_Other.

17. Stroma Cole, "Introduction: Gender Equality and Tourism – Beyond Empowerment," in *Gender Equality and Tourism: Beyond Empowerment*, ed. Stroma Cole (Oxfordshire: CABI, 2018), 1–2.

18. Human Rights Watch, "Migrant Workers' Rights on Saadiyat Island in the United Arab Emirates: 2015 Progress Report," February 10, 2015, accessed May 9, 2020, https://www.hrw.org/report/2015/02/10/migrant-workers-rights-saadiyat-island-united-arab-emirates/2015-progress-report#page.

19.  Human Rights Watch, "Qatar: Urgently Investigate Migrant Worker Deaths," October 10, 2019, accessed May 9, 2020, https://www.hrw.org/news/2019/10/10/qatar-urgently-investigate-migrant-worker-deaths#.

20.  World Travel & Tourism Council, "WTTC Now Estimates."

21.  Williams, *Tourism Geography*, 86.

22.  Konstantinos Andriotis, *Degrowth in Tourism: Conceptual, Theoretical and Philosophical Issues* (Oxfordshire: CABI, 2018): 158.

23.  Scheyvens and Gabriel Laeis, "Linkages between Tourist Resorts."

24.  United Nations Office of the High Representative for the Least Developed Countries, Landlocked Developing Countries and the Small Island Developing States, "About the Small Island Developing States," accessed May 9, 2020, http://unohrlls.org/about-sids/.

25.  Fair Trade Tourism, "About Us," accessed May 9, 2020, http://www.fairtrade.travel/About-Us/.

# CHAPTER 9

# The Social Geography of Tourism

Having long been ignored, the social effects of tourism began appearing in news headlines in the mid-2010s. Residents protested a host of issues from rising costs of living to tourists' anti-social behaviors. The previous chapter considered some of the ways in which the economic effects of tourism can impact peoples' lives directly (e.g., personal income from work in tourism or related fields) or indirectly (e.g., economic development at the destination due to tourism income). However, it is clear that tourism affects peoples and societies in far more ways than these.

The social geography of tourism gives us the means to consider how tourism impacts people and their lives. **Social geography** is a topical branch in human geography that encompasses a range of perspectives on the relationships between society and space. Society refers to the ties or connections between people either occupying a geographic space or connected by networks across space (e.g., common values, ways of life, political systems, or perceived identities). Thus, social geography might consider space as a setting for social interactions or the ways in which spaces are shaped by these interactions. In particular, the focus in studies of social geography is on issues of inequality.[1]

Social geography has an important part to play in our understanding of the geography of tourism. Tourism presents an opportunity for social interaction; it brings together groups of people who may have relatively little direct contact and/or little in common. Tourism can be a catalyst for social change; the development of tourism activities may reshape long-standing cultural patterns and ways of life. As such, this chapter continues our discussion of the geographic effects of tourism by utilizing the tools and concepts of social geography to consider the potential benefits of tourism for tourists and local peoples. It also considers the potential costs of tourism, particularly with regard to people in the community in which tourism is taking place. Finally, it discusses the factors that might determine the type and extent of these effects, as well as possible measures to maximize the positive effects while minimizing the negative.

# Social Benefits of Tourism

While the negative outcomes of the social interactions that take place in the context of tourism and the social changes that result from tourism attract the most attention, tourism can have positive outcomes as well. On a personal level, tourism has long been argued to contribute to psychological well-being.[2] On a global level, tourism has been conceptualized as a means of promoting global understanding and peace.[3] Peace parks, such as Waterton-Glacier International Peace Park (see box 1.2), are popular destinations that highlight the cooperation and good will relations between countries in cross-border regions. However, the idea of people-to-people diplomacy of tourism can be even more significant. The contact hypothesis suggests that contact through tourism has the potential to change peoples' perspective on the "other," such as an ethnic or racial group that has been negatively portrayed in the media. This could reduce prejudices and/or hostilities, assuming people approach the experience with civility and a willingness to learn about the other.[4]

Tourism may also be argued to have the potential for social development at a destination. Tourism can generate positive social changes at a destination, such as new opportunities for segments of the local community or new developments that could improve the quality of life for local people. At the same time, tourism development may serve as a catalyst for movements to protect against wider (negative) social changes by supporting traditional ways of life and reinforcing social identities.

## PERSONAL DEVELOPMENT

Tourism can provide the opportunity for interaction between peoples and places that might not otherwise occur. If this is undertaken with an openness and a sensitivity to other peoples and ways of life, tourism can be a beneficial experience for both tourists and local people at the destination visited. Tourists have the potential to not only meet other people but to also experience life in other societies firsthand. Approaches like slow tourism are most likely to create opportunities for tourists to have meaningful interactions with people in the places visited. These interactions allow tourists to gain a better understanding of, and even empathy for, that society. Conversely, experiences also have the potential to give tourists a new perspective on life in their own society and possibly even generate changes in their daily lives. These may be small changes, such as a desire to eat different kinds of foods, but it can also lead to major changes, such as inspiring one to lead a more sustainable lifestyle at home. In fact, some tourists—particularly explorers and drifters—participate in tourism because of the potential for such transformative experiences.

Residents at a destination also have the opportunity to interact with other groups of people. This is particularly applicable in the case of countries or communities that have a positive travel account (i.e., they have high rates of inbound tourism and low rates of outbound tourism). Although these people may not have the opportunity to travel to and experience other societies, they still have the opportunity to meet and learn about the tourists who visit their destination. Meaningful engagement with tourists can promote greater cross-cultural understanding beyond stereotyped images.

Social media has the potential to extend this interaction. When tourists connect with people they meet in other places on social media sites, they continue to learn about each other in ways that would not have been possible at the destination. For example, when connections are made with destination residents, those individuals have the opportunity to see what tourists' daily lives are like through the posts they make after they return home. When connections are made with other tourists, both individuals can see what life is like in places they may not yet have had the chance to visit. Additionally, all get to see how people in other places react to local or global events, which may help them to consider issues from other perspectives and gain a broader worldview.

Tourism can also promote a greater understanding of various issues and events. For example, tourists to a place like Jerusalem will have the opportunity to see significant historic and cultural attractions. However, for many tourists, an equally important part of their trip will be to gain a better understanding of this complex place. They may visit educational and cultural centers to learn about different groups of people and to hear about their experiences firsthand (figure 9.1). These tourists will return home with new perspectives on a geopolitical issue that is often in the news.

## SOCIAL DEVELOPMENT

Arguments for tourism have often cited the potential for new opportunities within a community. The economic benefits of tourism can lead to social benefits as well.

**Figure 9.1. This American tourist had the opportunity to talk to Palestinians in the Dheisheh Refugee Camp in the West Bank. The camp was created in 1949 after the Arab Israeli War as a temporary refuge for around 3,000 people. Today, estimates suggest there are as many as 15,000 people living in the camp.** *Source*: Larry Hardman

New types of jobs associated with tourism and the income from these jobs can provide local people with greater freedom to choose not only where they live but also how they live, although this is relative. Rural communities around the world have been experiencing declining opportunities for employment and livelihood. This creates a push factor, pushing people out of their communities. For some people, destination regions provide a pull factor, pulling people in with the promise of a more modern or vibrant community with access to jobs as well as other amenities and opportunities. However, others may wish to maintain their life with family and friends in their home community. The extension of tourism into rural areas might provide them with means to do so as opposed to having little choice but to emigrate.

Access to jobs and income can create opportunities for traditionally marginalized populations. In many parts of the world, women have had few opportunities for employment outside of the home and/or in the formal sector of the economy (i.e., their domain has been in the private sphere). The jobs created by tourism have generally been compatible with traditional roles for women (e.g., food preparation), while giving them the opportunity for employment in the public sphere, increased social interaction, increased income to support themselves and/or their families, and possibly even financial independence from their family or spouse (see box 8.2). As women gain a greater value in society and greater freedom, this can lay the foundation for additional social changes with the goal of reducing gender inequalities.

Tourism can enhance quality of life for residents. Amenities developed for tourism (e.g., restaurants, entertainment) can be enjoyed by local people. The creation or beautification of open-access public spaces to ensure an attractive environment for tourism can contribute to increased community pride and satisfaction for local people. Improved public transportation systems that will facilitate the movement of tourists at the destination can also increase the mobilities of local people. Expanded police protection and measures to reduce incidents of both petty and violent crimes promote a safe and stable environment for tourism investment and tourist visitation, but can increase security for local people as well.

In addition, there is potential for a destination to use the income from tourism to invest in local and/or domestic social development. Again, these improvements may support tourism, but local people can benefit nonetheless. For example, destination stakeholders might invest in the human resource base by building or expanding schools, education, and training programs to develop a strong tourism workforce. This increasingly well-educated population will have more opportunities to improve their lives and contribute to the local/national economy.

## PRESERVATION

Perhaps the most frequently cited argument for tourism is preservation—in this case, the preservation of local ways of life, traditions, and identities. Tourism is a distinctly place-based activity. The trend away from the standardization of mass tourism has emphasized the need for destinations to be able to offer the unique combination of physical and human attributes that constitute a place. Accordingly, stakeholders in a place seeking to develop this type of tourism will have an impetus to maintain these attributes. As such, stakeholders may resist the processes of globalization that contribute to a sameness between different parts of the world—a sense of placelessness (see chapter 12). Decision-makers might choose to limit the development of chain restaurants or big box stores and direct resources, as well as tourists, to support local businesses, like independent restaurants or mom-and-pop shops. This need for a sense of distinctiveness at destinations can also help reinforce or rejuvenate social identities that might otherwise be lost.

Tourism can support traditional ways of life or simply be more compatible with them than other forms of economic development. This might be in the form of the backward linkages with local farmers or fishermen who are able to continue their livelihood, with the tourism industry serving as a ready market for their produce. In the case of traditional societies, livelihood and culture may be linked. Therefore, if these societies can continue to practice long-standing patterns of livelihood, then they have greater ability to maintain their cultural heritage.

Tourism is cited as having the potential to maintain or even revitalize aspects of traditional culture, such as artistic performances or crafts. One of the criticisms of globalization is the loss of such traditions. However, some categories of tourists seek unique experiences of places and souvenirs of these experiences. As such, tourism can provide the motivation for local people to continue to practice rituals, songs, dances, or theatrical performances, when these things might otherwise be abandoned in favor of the patterns of modern global culture. Similarly, the production of local arts and crafts for tourists' consumption has the potential to keep traditions and skills alive when local craftspeople might otherwise find higher-wage industrial employment and local consumers have increased access to cheap, mass-produced merchandise. Even in light of the production of cheaper copies of traditional crafts, there is still likely to be a demand for high-quality, "authentic" items produced by local people using local materials (figure 9.2).

## CRISIS RESPONSE

The tourism system is highly vulnerable to shocks, from natural disasters to violent attacks and global pandemics. Yet, the tourism system also plays a role in helping communities respond to these shocks. In the wake of Hurricane Sandy in 2012, Airbnb hosts in New York offered their properties to those who were forced to evacuate their homes. Airbnb subsequently launched Open Homes to help provide people with a free place to stay in times of need. While there are many criticisms of Airbnb's practices, their network of rooms, apartments, and houses was well suited to provide a quick response to both natural and human disasters, including flooding in Central Europe (2014) and the mass shootings in Orlando, Florida (2016) and Las Vegas, Nevada (2017). The program also partnered with nonprofit organizations to help provide temporary housing for refugees and asylum seekers as they transition into their new community.[5]

Vacation rentals and hotels left empty by the COVID-19 shutdowns also provided housing for healthcare workers fighting COVID-19 so they did not expose their families at home to the virus. Hotels and cruise ships both provided space for isolating

**Figure 9.2.   When tourists demand high-quality products made at the destination, it allows skilled craftspeople to continue their work and carry on cultural traditions. This artist is working in a handicraft center in the old Tibetan quarter of Lhasa.** *Source*: Velvet Nelson

mild-case patients. Hotels put together care packages of essentials like food and toilet paper for workers that had been laid off and donated items to local charities trying to assist countless others without work. Commercial airlines flew medical volunteers and supplies to virus hotspots,[6] and furloughed flight attendants with first-aid training volunteered their services at hospitals to assist overwhelmed staff.[7] While those throughout the tourism system faced significant hardship during this time, some were able to take advantage of their resources to help support their communities.

## Social Costs of Tourism

The outcomes of tourism depend on how it is developed and managed at a given destination. In some cases, tourism may fail to fully achieve these potential social benefits due to missed opportunities. In other cases, tourism not only fails to achieve social benefits for peoples and places but also has clear social costs. Social interactions through tourism can result in culture clash and misperceptions about the other group. Tourism development can contribute to a decrease in the quality of life for a local community by marginalizing sectors of the population, introducing or exacerbating social problems, and limiting local peoples' access to places. Finally, tourism can also contribute to irreversible changes in traditional societies and cultural patterns or, ultimately, their destruction.

## MISSED OPPORTUNITIES

For many people, tourism is associated with relaxation and pleasure. To meet this demand, tourism stakeholders may seek to provide entertaining and enjoyable experiences rather than ones that facilitate geopolitical goals, challenges tourists' opinions, or prompts them to think about issues that might be difficult or uncomfortable. This represents a missed opportunity for tourism to promote peace or to act as a catalyst for personal development.

Although tourism between divided nations has the potential to reduce tensions and support peace, these outcomes may not materialize for a variety of reasons. For example, the Mt. Gumgang resort project, located in a scenic region of North Korea, was proposed with the intention of working toward improved relations between the North and South. However, the resort was developed as an enclave (e.g., a geographically isolated and spatially concentrated tourism facility) with no contact between North Korean citizens and South Korean tourists. Tourist demand was further hindered by a long list of things these tourists were not allowed to do and charges of spying against a tourist at the resort, in addition to continued geopolitical tensions.[8]

In another example, box 9.1 considers the missed opportunity for tourism at plantation homes in the American South to initiate a more open and honest discussion of slavery and its implications for modern race relations in the country.

---

### Box 9.1.  Case Study: Plantation Tourism in the American South

"As geographers, we are interested in understanding the process and politics of narrating the history of slavery through the South's museums, historical markers, and other places of memory."[a]

Heritage sites, such as museums, have the potential to engage the public with issues of the past that guide our understanding of the present. Despite the significance of slavery in American history, the issue has long gone unmentioned in the plantation museums that have become a distinct part of the Southern heritage tourism landscape (map 9.1). Slavery remains an uncomfortable subject for many people who do not want to be reminded of the inhumanity and trauma.[b] Heritage tourism stakeholders have relied on romanticized narratives of the plantation past to produce experiences that will best appeal to potential tourists.[c]

Critical research on the topic of slavery in plantation tourism began in the early 2000s. In line with broader trends in tourism geography (see chapter 1), this research particularly

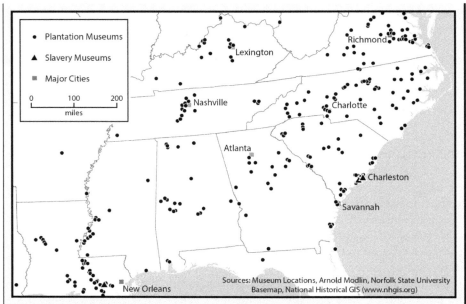

**Map 9.1. Plantation museums, USA. Plantation museums are a part of the heritage tourism landscape in the American South, while slavery museums are a relatively new addition. From "The Transformation of Racialized American Southern Heritage Landscape," NSF Award #1359780, Research Team: Derek Alderman, Candace Bright, David Butler, Perry Carter, Stephen P. Hanna, Arnold Modlin, and Amy Potter. *Source:* Stephen P. Hanna**

focused on issues of tourism representations. David Butler conducted a study of tourist brochures to understand what themes stakeholders were using to promote plantation sites to potential markets. He found that the brochures gave considerably more attention to the owners of the plantation, the architecture of the "Big House," the grounds, the crops, and the furnishings than to slavery. He described this as a process of "whitewashing."[d] Similarly, Jennifer Eichstedt and Stephen Small conducted a study of plantation tours. They found that the majority of plantations practiced "symbolic annihilation"; in other words, these sites ignored the institution and experience of slavery. This eliminates the significance of slavery and the enslaved to the region and its history. It implies that the topic is not important enough—to either stakeholders or visitors—to be acknowledged.[e]

Of the plantations that broached the topic, Eichstedt and Small described three additional categories. In the first of these categories, "trivialization and deflection," sites acknowledged slavery and/or the enslaved but primarily relied on romanticized narratives to control the discussion. While admitting that slavery was a part of the landscape, these narratives tap into visitors' ideas of the Southern plantation from popular culture (e.g., *Gone with the Wind*) and shield them from potentially unpleasant conversations. In the next category, "segregation and marginalization," sites offered representations of slavery and/or the enslaved but in separate spaces (e.g., tours of "slave cabins" in addition to those at the "Big House") or separate experiences (e.g., special interest tours with a different script than the standard tour). This also minimizes the subject as not important enough to be included in the typical visitor experience. Only a minority of visitors, generally those already interested in the topic, will undertake the extra effort required to visit additional sites or to plan a special tour in advance. In the final category, "relative incorporation," sites tried to address slavery but often failed to fully engage visitors with the issue.[f] Derek Alderman and Rachel Campbell argue that "incorporation" implies that slave histories are simply "added" to the existing narratives. Having been marginalized for so long, it is not that easy. They propose a "symbolic excavation" in which the identities of the enslaved and their contributions to the plantation and the economy need to be uncovered and possibly even reconstructed.[g]

In his original study, Butler asked the question, "Does it really matter?" The majority of tourists on vacation are looking for enjoyable experiences, and plantations are trying to provide those experiences, resulting in the processes described above. However, in answer to his own question, Butler reminds us that these heritage museums represent the past to visitors.[h] Ignoring slavery at these sites leaves this past unresolved; ignoring the enslaved disregards them as important historical actors. Thus, the issue is very much connected to current understandings of race and racism.[i]

Although change can be slow, there are signs of progress since those first studies of the millennium. For example, Oak Alley Plantation is a popular site in the River Road area of Louisiana that presented a romanticized image of the antebellum South to visitors. In 2013, the site opened the "Slavery at Oak Alley" exhibit with newly constructed replica slave cabins, period or replica furniture and artifacts, and a wall bearing the names of the enslaved on the plantation. Stephen Hanna notes that visitors' questions and criticisms about the absence of slavery on the plantation—both during tours and in online reviews on sites like TripAdvisor—played an important role in the decision to create this exhibit.[j] Matthew Cook discusses sites that employ "counter-narrative" strategies. These sites not only address slavery more directly but also work to emotionally engage visitors with the issue. One such site is Whitney Plantation, also in the River Road area. Opened in 2014, this plantation museum is dedicated to slavery.[k]

Plantations have an opportunity to critically address slavery and work toward a better understanding of how it has shaped the region and the nation. Geographers, like those mentioned here among others, demonstrate the powerful geography approach as they work to understand and raise awareness about these issues.

*Discussion topic*: What factors should plantation museums consider in deciding how to represent slavery and the enslaved?

*Tourism online*: Oak Alley Plantation, "Oak Alley Foundation: A National Historic Landmark," at https://www.oakalleyplantation.org; Whitney Plantation, "Guided Tours of Whitney Plantation Museum," http://www.whitneyplantation.com

---

[a] Derek H. Alderman and Rachel M. Campbell, "Symbolic Excavation and the Artifact Politics of Remembering Slavery in the American South: Observations from Walterboro, South Carolina," *Southeastern Geographer* 48, no. 3 (2008): 339.

[b] Derek H. Alderman, "Surrogation and the Politics of Remembering Slavery in Savannah, Georgia (USA)," *Journal of Historical Geography* 36, no. 1 (2010): 91.

[c] David L. Butler, Perry L. Carter, and Owen J. Dwyer, "Imagining Plantations: Slavery, Dominant Narratives, and the Foreign Born," *Southeastern Geographer* 48, no. 3 (2008): 299.

[d] David L. Butler, "Whitewashing Plantations," *International Journal of Hospitality & Tourism Administration* 2, no. 3–4 (2001): 166–7.

[e] Jennifer L. Eichstedt and Stephen Small, *Representations of Slavery: Race and Ideology in Southern Plantation Museums* (Washington, DC: Smithsonian Institution Press, 2002): 10.

[f] Eichstedt and Small, *Representations of Slavery*, 10–11.

[g] Alderman and Campbell, "Symbolic Excavation," 342.

[h] Butler, "Whitewashing Plantations," 173.

[i] Christine N. Buzinde and Carla Almeida Santos, "Interpreting Slavery Tourism," *Annals of Tourism Research* 36, no. 3 (2009): 441.

[j] Stephen P. Hanna, "Placing the Enslaved at Oak Alley Plantation: Narratives, Spatial Contexts, and the Limits of Surrogation," *Journal of Heritage Tourism* 11, no. 3 (2016): 224.

[k] Matthew R. Cook, "Counter-Narratives of Slavery in the Deep South: The Politics of Empathy Along and Beyond River Road," *Journal of Heritage Tourism* 11, no. 3 (2016): 304.

## CULTURE CLASH

Although tourism can have a positive effect on tourists and locals if both approach the experience with an openness and a respect for others, it can also have a negative effect if one or both groups are closed minded and/or hostile to the other. Tourists and local people alike have been guilty of this. Local people complain about tourists who make little attempt to familiarize themselves with the language or customs of the places visited. Tourists have often displayed a sense of entitlement in which they feel they have the right to act however they please, including in ways that they would not normally act, because they paid for the vacation.[9] These issues may be a source of annoyance to local people or a serious offense, and tourism may come to be viewed as a detriment to the community rather than an asset. Conversely, tourists complain about local people who do not treat outsiders with civility. This can have a significant impact on how tourists view the destination and represent the destination to other potential visitors. As such, a place can develop a poor reputation, which can affect future tourism.

When different social groups come together—especially groups with significant differences in languages, ethnicities, religions, or lifestyles—the potential exists for misunderstandings and culture clash. For tourists, culture shock may be as minor as a feeling of uneasiness in the unfamiliar setting of the destination or as significant as a sense of complete disorientation. Local people may also experience culture shock, especially as destinations continue to receive more visitors from more places. As locals have more sustained contact with a tourist culture, they are more likely to experience significant effects. The **demonstration effect** is a term used to suggest that local people will experience changes in attitudes, values, or patterns of behavior as a result of observing tourists. Although it may be argued that the demonstration effect can be positive (e.g., tourists' demonstrating sustainable livelihoods such as carrying reusable bottles, straws, or cutlery or picking up trash for proper disposal, see box 11.3), the demonstration effect has had significant negative social effects in destinations around the world.[10] In one study, an interview respondent described this process in the context of Cozumel, Mexico:

> People forget about their culture, they forget their traditions and adopt the dress style, the food styles of tourists, most of them Americans. It's not uncommon to see a young kid on the streets acting like an American. I don't know…their jeans, the shirts…they begin to adopt other people's way of life. Then tradition is lost, we are losing the normal way of life…we begin to be somebody else instead of ourselves.[11]

This loss of cultural identity can diminish the perceived authenticity and distinctiveness of a place, which may reduce the demand for tourism on which its economy may depend.

In addition, the image that is presented by tourists on vacation may be substantially different from their patterns of behavior and consumption at home. This can be seen in the tourist inversions discussed in chapter 2, where tourists may dress more casually, behave more freely, and spend more money on food, alcohol, or luxury items than they would at home. As such, local people may develop misconceptions about life in other parts of the world and, given the demonstration effect, may strive to emulate the worst parts of tourist culture.

Young people in a community are generally most susceptible to the demonstration effect, as they are quick to adopt outside values, dress codes, or lifestyles. This has the potential to cause conflict in the local community, where the new patterns contrast with traditional views held by older generations. Additionally, culture clash can occur between residents and migrants attracted by tourism employment. Differences in culture (e.g., religion) or perceived loss of cultural distinctiveness can be a source of tension; however, this is also likely to be tied up in concerns about migrants competing for resources (e.g., housing or water) and jobs.

## DECLINING QUALITY OF LIFE

While tourism can create new job opportunities when it is developed in a community, tourism developed outside a community can create a push factor for migration. This contributes to problems of brain drain, where these people are no longer contributing their human capital to their home community. Young people may be attracted to destination regions for the opportunities of new or higher-paying jobs, greater wealth, access to material possessions, or the ability to change their lifestyles. As a result, the remaining aging community may experience problems with stagnation and decline, further perpetuating the problem of emigration.

Tourism may introduce new preferences and patterns of behavior or consumption that can contribute to a decline in quality of life. A destination may experience an increase in fast-food restaurants and restaurants catering to Western tastes. As local preferences change accordingly, people may eat more of these high-calorie, processed foods as opposed to fresh, healthy local options. This can create new problems like obesity, type 2 diabetes, and heart disease. Likewise, tourism can create the conditions that allow social problems that may or may not already exist—such as alcoholism, the sale of illegal drugs, prostitution, and/or gambling—to flourish. The arrival of affluent tourists may provide the inducement for local people to get involved in the provision of one of these activities. Conversely, wage labor from tourism may give local people increased disposable income to participate in such activities.

While some destinations may take measures to improve security for tourists, tourism can also contribute to an increase in insecurity and crime. In a study of Boracay, Philippines, local respondents felt that what was once a small, tight-knit community had been changed by tourism and tourism-induced migration. Residents no longer knew people (i.e., tourists and migrants), which led to reduced perceptions of safety. They were also concerned about a rise in prostitution and the exploitation of women and children associated with organized crime. The authors described this as the "dark side" of the opportunities offered by tourism development.[12]

Although tourism development can lead to improvements at a destination, local people may not always benefit from these improvements. The construction of tourist facilities or the designation of parks or reserves can lead to the displacement of local people. In many countries, people, often ethnic minorities, may have lived in a certain area for generations without having modern, legal land ownership. As this land becomes targeted for tourism development, the lack of legal ownership allows the government to sanction their removal. Similarly, tourism developments may limit local peoples' access to certain sites or facilities, such as beaches or parks. Transportation infrastructure may be oriented around the needs of tourists without meeting the needs of local people. Shops oriented toward the tourist market, from cheap souvenirs to luxury items, may replace local shops. Even when daily goods are available, they may be sold at significantly higher prices.

Noise pollution takes place in areas with a dense concentration of tourism facilities and infrastructure, such as airports, roads, or entertainment districts. While this type of pollution can generate annoyance and dissatisfaction among tourists, it can lead to declining quality of life for residents and even contribute to serious physiological and psychological health concerns. This has become a growing problem with touristification (see box 7.2). The expansion of vacation rentals into residential neighborhoods has led to complaints about the noise from visitors coming and going at all hours of the day and inconsiderate behavior such as late-night parties on any day of the week. In addition, residents complained of increased anxiety and a decreased sense of community.[13]

Despite widespread shutdowns during the COVID-19 pandemic, some rural destinations were overwhelmed by visitors. People in Wales complained about a large influx of visitors fleeing cities. In March 2020, Snowdonia National Park Authority reported the busiest visitor day on record. In this case, residents were concerned about their physical well-being. These concerns were not insignificant, given the relatively high proportion of elderly people and the low health care capacity in the small communities.[14]

In general, the declining quality of life in tourism destinations has given rise to anti-tourism movements and "tourismphobia." The term tourismphobia was coined in 2008 in response to the processes of touristification occurring in Barcelona, Spain. However, the idea of tourismphobia has been evocative and liberally used. The Spanish media began to use it to broadly describe increasing dissatisfaction with the effects of tourism growth.[15] Others have taken it a step farther and used the term to refer to a dislike or hatred of tourists independent of other characteristics (e.g., race or ethnicity)[16] and a rejection of tourists in destinations around the world (figure 9.3).[17] Tourismphobia can be complicated. People in various destinations are clearly frustrated by the effects of tourism and tourists on their lives, but many people (and places) are economically dependent on tourism. Thus, they must be conscious of the ways they will be further affected if they push back too hard against tourism.

## CULTURAL EROSION

If efforts are not consciously made to preserve culture and ways of life, they can be eroded or even destroyed by tourism. The development of standardized mass tourism, particularly by multinational companies with globally recognized brands, can overwhelm and fundamentally alter the unique character of a place. Visual pollution can

**Figure 9.3.** The term tourismphobia has been used to describe local dissatisfaction with the effects of tourism growth and even the rejection of tourists in popular destinations such as Barcelona, Spain. This dissatisfaction is demonstrated throughout the city through messages such as this one affixed to a public trash bin. *Source*: Leo Zonn

result from tourism facilities that have been constructed without consideration for local environments, materials, and architectural styles. A rural area or village may become more urbanized or commercialized, and local businesses may be replaced by chains.

Elements of local culture may be lost as people adopt elements of the tourist culture. For example, it is typically unrealistic to expect that tourists will learn a significant amount of the language spoken at their intended destination. It is unrealistic to expect local people to learn all of the native languages spoken by the tourists they receive. As a result, there is a distinct need for a **lingua franca**, or a language that is used for the purpose of communication between people speaking different languages. As tourism becomes the major source of income in an area, families may choose to educate their children in the lingua franca to provide them with the greatest potential to gain well-paid employment in tourism. However, this often comes at the expense of local languages.[18]

The elements of culture that are intended to be preserved through tourism may also be destroyed by it, as they are changed to meet tourists' demands. Local cuisine may be made more palatable to tourists' tastes. Local objects that once had use and meaning within a society may be turned into something to be produced and sold as souvenirs (box 9.2). The mass production of these objects—possibly outsourced to

# Box 9.2.  In-Depth: Museumization, Commodification, and Cultural Sustainability in Tourism

Sustainable development has three main spheres or pillars: economic, social, and environmental. Yet, increased attention has been given to the role of culture in sustainable development. Some argue that culture is fundamental to each of the main spheres, while others argue that culture should be viewed as a fourth sphere.[a] Regardless, movements toward sustainable tourism need to consider the role of culture in tourism development (see chapter 7) and the ways in which tourism affects culture.[b]

One area of research looks at cultural change. Cultures are dynamic and evolve based on a variety of factors, which can include tourism. For example, an indigenous community expresses concern that its cultural heritage is eroding due to the processes of globalization. Tourism presents an opportunity for the community to ensure that traditions are maintained. Community members identify the aspects of culture they wish to recognize and the ways in which these aspects will be presented to tourists. However, even attempts to preserve culture can have negative consequences. In realizing the economic value of heritage tourism, the community may become museumized, with its culture essentially frozen at a point in time to match tourists' expectations.

Particularly with ethnic or indigenous tourism, tourists may hold a certain image of "traditional" culture (e.g., patterns of dress or lack of technology). These tourists may be looking for authentic experiences, but they may not have complete or accurate information about the culture to be able to make an effective judgment about its authenticity. Likewise, external tourism stakeholders seeking to create a unique experience for tourists may manipulate cultural aspects to emphasize differences with modern or mainstream culture. Aspects of culture that do not fit this image, such as those that are recent developments or influenced by other groups, may be suppressed. This museumization prevents cultures from evolving naturally and can result in dissatisfaction as local people may come to resent being viewed as "backward."[c]

This leads to additional questions about the use of culture in tourism. The term **commodification** is used to describe the way in which something of intrinsic or cultural value is transformed into a product with commercial value that can be packaged and sold for consumption (i.e., a commodity).[d] Although almost all aspects of a place—physical and human—may be commodified for the purposes of tourism, attention has particularly been focused on the commodification of culture. Commodification of culture can take place for many different reasons, but, as one scholar notes, "The most important characteristic is its *purposeful production* for tourism consumption."[e] In other words, a tourism company or a local community may deliberately make changes or adaptations to aspects of culture based on the potential economic benefits that can be derived from tourism.

Some scholars argue that tourism inevitably results in cultural commodification. This is seen as particularly applicable in cases of mass tourism, in which the emphasis is on mass production and consumption of both tangible goods and experiences.[f] As the objects or performances are commodified for tourists' consumption, they are irrevocably changed. Many scholars have viewed these changes as a loss of authenticity. Yet, others argue that this need not be the case. A society can use—and perhaps adapt—an element of their culture in tourism, to receive the economic benefits of the industry. At the same time, they will be able to keep the most important, closely guarded elements of culture for themselves, with their original meanings or for their intended purposes. Indeed, there are some cases in which communities have entirely created cultural works (e.g., items to be sold as souvenirs) or practices (e.g., festivals) for the purpose of tourism that have no traditional basis in the culture. These works or practices are empty of meaning, but they may be presented to tourists as authentic.[g]

Cultural sustainability therefore refers to the ability of a society to retain or adapt the parts of their culture that give them identity and distinguish them from other groups of people.[h] This includes both tangible and intangible culture. In particular, attention should be given to issues of cultural sustainability for low-income and marginalized groups in tourism destinations. These groups may no longer be able to access tangible culture (e.g., sacred sites) because it is transformed into a tourism attraction. These groups may also experience pressure to change aspects of intangible heritage (e.g., patterns of dress or language) to be able to participate in and receive the economic benefits of tourism.

Tourism's cultural impacts are complex, but stakeholders have generally given them little attention. To move toward sustainable tourism, diverse groups of people need to be involved in the processes of planning, developing, and managing tourism to minimize negative impacts on culture. Destination stakeholders may need to establish policies or dedicate resources to cultural sustainability. For example, stakeholders may offer local people free/discounted visits or dedicated access times (e.g., days or times reserved for local people) to cultural heritage sites that would allow them to participate in traditional practices without the presence of tourists. In addition, stakeholders may choose to allocate resources for cultural preservation (e.g., schools).[i] This will promote the continuation of and pride in customs among local people, which not only supports cultural sustainability but also has the potential to produce more distinctive and authentic cultural resources for tourism.

*Discussion topic*: Do you think culture should be turned into a saleable commodity? Explain.

---

[a] Theopisti Stylianou-Lambert, Nikolaos Boukas, and Marina Christodoulou-Yerali, "Museums and Cultural Sustainability: Stakeholders, Forces, and Cultural Policies," *International Journal of Cultural Policy* 20, no. 5 (2014): 568.

[b] Tazim Jamal, Blanca Camargo, Jennifer Sandlin, and Romano Segrado, "Tourism and Cultural Sustainability: Towards an Eco-Cultural Justice for Place and People," *Tourism Recreation Research* 35, no 3 (2010): 270.

[c] Philip Feifan Xie, *Authenticating Ethnic Tourism* (Bristol: Channel View Publications, 2011), 109–11, 239.

[d] Erik Cohen, "Authenticity and Commoditization in Tourism," *Annals of Tourism Research* 15 (1988): 380.

[e] Milena Ivanovic, *Cultural Tourism* (Cape Town: Juta, 2008), 121 (emphasis added).

[f] Robert Shepherd, "Commodification, Culture, and Tourism," *Tourist Studies* 2, no. 2 (2002): 185.

[g] Nicola MacLeod, "Cultural Tourism: Aspects of Authenticity and Commodification," in *Cultural Tourism in a Changing World: Politics, Participation, and (Re)presentation*, ed. Melanie K. Smith and Mike Robinson (Clevedon: Channel View Publications, 2006), 177–8.

[h] Martin Mowforth and Ian Munt, *Tourism and Sustainability: Development, Globalisation and New Tourism in the Third World*, 4th ed. (Abingdon: Routledge, 2016), 109.

[i] Jamal et al., "Tourism and Cultural Sustainability," 275.

---

factories with cheap labor—may result in a decline in the need for local skilled craftspeople. Rituals, songs, dances, or theater shows may be held for profit rather than for their original spiritual or social functions. Such events may be reformulated to make them easy to be performed for and understood by tourists. In some cases, they may be created specifically to fit tourists' preconceived ideas. Eventually, those within the society, including the craftspeople and performers, may lose their understanding of the original significance and/or meaning.

**Figure 9.4.  Tourist information often highlights churches, temples, or mosques as tourism attractions and encourages visitation for historic and/or cultural reasons. As such, these sites may be perceived as open for tourists' pleasure as opposed to a place with a specific function for local people. *Source*:** Tom Nelson

Finally, even those practices that continue to be undertaken by local people may be disrupted by the presence of tourists and tourism activities. For example, churches, temples, mosques, and other sacred sites may be presented to or perceived by tourists as attractions to be seen rather than places for practitioners to worship. These tourists may fail to respect religious ceremonies taking place or disturb those who came to pray (figure 9.4). Although these sites may not be logistically off limits to local people, they become effectively unavailable to people who wish to use them for their original purpose.

## Factors in Social Effects

There are some instances in which the effects of tourism on a community may be clearly identified. This is particularly the case when tourism activities are developed in relatively isolated and undeveloped communities. For example, the development of tourism in a remote indigenous community will bring a host of changes to their society. This might include the construction of new infrastructure to support tourism (e.g., roads) and the importation of new products for tourists' consumption (e.g., bottled water), which can create further problems like package waste. It might require minor changes, such as changes in traditional patterns of dress, but it might also bring devastating consequences, such as diseases. Yet, it can often be difficult to separate what effects are a direct result of tourism and what would have occurred as a result of large societal changes. These destinations may be experiencing an erosion of local culture and unique social identities, but tourism's contribution may be indistinguishable from the effects of multinational corporations and the global media.

The specific social effects of tourism at a destination, and the extent of these effects, will vary widely. The often-interrelated factors can include the type of tourists a destination receives, the number of tourists, the capability of the destination to handle these tourists, the spatial distance between tourists and local communities at the destination, the type of interaction that takes place between tourists and local people, and the duration of exposure to other cultures.

The typology of tourists discussed in chapter 2 (drifters, explorers, individual mass tourists, and organized mass tourists) may give us an indication of the number of each type of tourists a destination receives, the character of the destination, and/or the type of interaction that will take place between tourists and locals. Drifters and explorers typically arrive at a destination in relatively small numbers, whereas the categories of mass tourists account for large numbers of visitors at a destination. Thus, it might be anticipated that larger numbers of mass tourists will have more effects on the local community at the destination than smaller numbers of independent tourists. In some cases, this assumption might be accurate. For example, local residents in a small, emerging destination may be willing to welcome the drifters and explorers who seek to immerse themselves in the community and thereby have minimal negative impacts. In contrast, once that destination is "discovered" and increasingly visited by mass tourists who are less conscious of their impact on the destination, the community may begin to experience more negative social effects.

Number of tourists alone does not provide a complete picture. The character of the destination will affect its ability to handle the tourists it receives. In the example above, the emerging destination may have little infrastructure in place to accommodate even the slightest temporary increases in population associated with its tourism growth (e.g., overcrowding on local roads and public transport or at local restaurants and establishments). Tourists will be much more conspicuous, and local people may have little experience in dealing with outsiders. Consequently, the potential for incidences of culture clash is increased. A well-developed tourism destination may be able to receive larger quantities of mass tourists with fewer effects. Nonetheless, with more people traveling, even these destinations can be overwhelmed.

In addition, some mass tourism destinations were developed specifically to spatially isolate tourists from the local community. In this case, large quantities of tourists may visit the destination, but they will be concentrated within designated areas. Enclave resorts and self-contained hotel complexes, such as those characterizing many popular 3 and 5S destinations like the Dominican Republic, were constructed separate from existing communities. The only local people who have interactions with tourists are those who are employed in the resort community. As such, the effects of tourism are largely spatially contained, and local people may be able to live their lives as they choose and experience relatively few negative consequences from tourism. However, the potential for positive social exchange between tourists and locals is lost.

Tourists interact with locals in different ways. In the first category, interaction takes place as tourists purchase goods and/or services from local people. In the second category, tourists and local people visit and use the same facilities, including beaches, parks, restaurants, or other entertainment venues. This spatial proximity increases the opportunity for contact between tourists and locals but does not necessarily indicate that interaction will occur. Finally, in the third category, tourists and/or locals seek interaction for the purpose of talking to, getting to know, and exchanging ideas with the other. This might take place in a structured experience, for example, when tourists take a guided tour not only to experience a place but also to gain knowledge about that place from the perspective of a local guide. This can also be something far more intimate and personal, such as when a local person invites a tourist to his or her home for a meal.

Organized mass tourists are primarily motivated by relaxation and self-indulgence and less interested in experiencing the place visited. They are more likely to stay at large multinational resorts. Local people typically have very little presence at these resorts, with the exception of those who are employed by the resort, due to financial barriers as well as physical ones (e.g., walls and gates). With a range of amenities available to them, these tourists have little need or desire to leave the resort. As such, their opportunities for contact with local people are limited and most likely fall under the first category. Individual mass tourists and explorers may have greater interaction in the second category as they seek new places to experience outside of resort/tourist areas. In addition, the nature of the destinations visited by explorers and drifters lends itself much more to this type of interaction. Because these destinations are less developed with tourism infrastructure, tourists will necessarily share spaces and facilities with local people. This creates opportunities for interaction. Moreover, these tourists tend to be more interested in the experience of place, including experiences with people in the local community. Thus, they are most likely to seek out the type of interaction described in the third category.

One of the key differences between the impacts on tourists and locals is the duration of exposure to other peoples, cultures, and ways of life. The concept of **acculturation** is used to describe the process of exchange that takes place when two groups of people come into contact over time. Yet, this is rarely an equal exchange. One group is likely to have more of an impact on the other, and the second group will experience the greatest changes. Tourist–local interactions present an interesting case in acculturation. Although the potential exists for tourists to be influenced by what they experience at the destination, they are less likely to be affected and experience any real changes to their daily lives because each individual tourist experiences only short-term exposure to the destination culture. In contrast, local people experience more sustained exposure to tourists and their patterns. As a result, the local community is more likely to experience significant cultural changes.

## Box 9.3.  Experience: Study Abroad from Low to High Tourist Seasons

*Seasonality can be another factor in the social effects of tourism. Residents often have a very different relationship with place between the low and the high tourist seasons. Libby had the opportunity to spend a study abroad semester in Florence, Italy. It was the low season when she arrived, but the numbers of tourists steadily grew leading up to the high season. As she learned what changes she needed to make in her daily routine, she got a glimpse of what it is like to live in a tourism destination.*

In my junior year of college, I spent a study abroad semester, from January to May, in Florence, Italy. I was very fortunate to be able to travel to many different places in Italy during that time. However, I felt that the most amazing part of the experience was the ability to immerse myself in the city of Florence, getting to know its back streets and some of the business owners who lived there. I came to believe that study abroad students fall into a different category of tourist. While we may have been constantly in awe at the beginning, we quickly learned the ebb and flow of the city. Strangely enough, one of the adjustments I had the most trouble making was walking on sidewalks. They were so narrow that they typically only fit one person, so walking in the street became necessary. Another adjustment was trying to process that Italians dress for the season, not the weather, meaning it might be 20 degrees Celsius (around 68 degrees Fahrenheit) in February and they would wear parka coats.

At orientation, program leaders emphasized the importance of adapting to culture shock. International travel was not anything new to me and I hadn't experienced culture shock before, but this was the first time I had lived in any of those places for longer than two weeks. In reality, though, life in Florence was not extraordinarily different from life in Ohio. I can't recall having a problem communicating with the Italians while I was there. Along with my classmates, I volunteered at a local high school to speak to a class weekly about American culture and to help with their English classes. I was shocked to discover that these 15-year-olds were learning grammatical concepts that I couldn't fully understand. Meanwhile, my greatest point of pride while in Florence was my ability, at the end of the semester, to hold a conversation entirely in 5-year-old level Italian with a man selling paintings.

My friends and I had a favorite restaurant that was halfway down the street between our school and the Duomo. We affectionately called this restaurant Little David's, although I'm not sure that was the real name. We were there pretty much once a week, sometimes even more often, and the waiters learned our favorite orders. At one point about halfway through the semester, we noticed that Little David's had not been open for a few days and we were afraid it had closed permanently. When it did open about two weeks later, my friends and I went for dinner, only to discover they had changed the menu. Rather than just two pages like they used to have, they had what resembled a short novel. They began offering food that would appeal to American tourists, including fettuccini alfredo. Before going to Florence, we were given a long list of tips about what to expect, and chief among them was that fettuccini alfredo is (much to my disappointment) not real Italian food.

I'm grateful that I enjoyed the classic tourist sites at the beginning of my time there. Although "tourist season" began to reach its peak at the beginning of May, it was around mid-March that the many attractions that Florence had to offer became overcrowded. In February, the Galleria dell'Accademia, which houses the David statue, had no wait; in April, there was a line stretching around the building and down the block. While I had made it a habit of walking the longer way to school just so that I could pass the Duomo on my way, the beautiful view was not worth dealing with the intense crowds. I quickly learned that saying excuse me to every single person I bumped would be a waste of time because it was impossible to navigate through the streets without running into someone every couple of steps. What made things more difficult were the pickpockets and scammers we had to try to avoid. While I had been prepared for the pickpockets, they had not told us there would be men who laid posters on the ground just for the purpose of trying to get you to step on them so you would have to pay. In an effort to avoid these crowds, I began taking back roads more often. This allowed me to see a part of Florence that was untouched by tourists and that I had not given enough attention to.

Another popular tourist attraction in Florence was the leather market that circled the Mercato Centrale. The leather market was made up of at least a hundred individual vendors trying to sell leather goods including anything from keychains to suitcases. The easiest route to get to the Mercato Centrale from the city center required you to walk down one of the streets lined with these vendors. During tourist season, these streets were a nightmare for anyone with claustrophobia. Vendors would berate you from all sides, trying to pull you in to buy their wares, and all the while you are trying to weave through the crowds of people who are perusing the different items.

My time in Florence was the greatest learning experience I have ever had. Staying in Florence for a few months let me see how the city changed from calm and slow in January to loud and fast as it got warmer. Although there's nothing quite like getting to walk through the city streets when spring weather finally arrives, being able to have a quiet and unimpeded view of Florence's history was worth the cold.

*—Libby*

# Knowledge and Education

Concerns about overtourism, tourismification, and tourismphobia have drawn attention to the social effects of tourism; however, these effects cannot be separated from the economic effects discussed in the last chapter and the environmental effects discussed in the next chapter. For example, the economic success of a tourism destination depends on the support of the local community. These are the people who will have to deal with the consequences of tourism. If the local community is concerned about the negative social effects of tourism, they will not support its development. If the local community experiences these negative effects, they may actively undermine the tourism industry. Prior to the COVID-19 pandemic, the tipping point had been reached in many destinations, where people protested against the negative effects of tourism despite its economic significance.

Because the private sector is typically most concerned with economic effects, it has traditionally done little in the way of assessing the potential social effects of tourism development. If a private sector developer undertook any community assessment, it was likely mandated by the public sector.[19] Tourism businesses have slowly been paying more attention to sustainability, often through corporate social responsibility (CSR) programs. As originally conceptualized, CSR was used to refer to the obligations of businesses to act in accordance with the objectives and values of society. CSR has primarily focused on economic, social, and environmental initiatives, although it has been argued that culture is an important element in tourism CSR.[20] Benefits of CSR include maintaining the physical and human resources on which tourism depends, supporting local people to prevent disruption of the industry, and creating a favorable image and customer satisfaction. While such programs are a step in the right direction, more research is needed to understand their actions and outcomes.[21]

The public sector should have a stake in ensuring the social well-being of its population; however, it too has often neglected to consider the social effects. In some cases, governments actively support tourism development in spite of residents' opposition.[22] Government agencies need to consider a variety of issues related to tourism development such as land ownership and access to public lands, resources, or sites. Increasingly, governments are faced with difficult decisions about how to balance the need to keep visitor numbers to manageable levels with the economic dependence on tourism. Stakeholders may need to direct the circumstances in which interaction between visitors and locals takes place and establish policies to control tourists' behavior (e.g., dress codes, codes of conduct) to minimize the potential for culture clash.

Education can go a long way in preventing the negative outcomes of tourist–local interactions at a destination. One of the most common complaints levied against tourists is ignorance of the place, its people, and their customs, which contributes to the process of culture clash. At the same time, this ignorance can be one of the key contributors to culture shock. Tourists are almost always encouraged to learn about a place before they visit. This helps ensure that the tourists are able to make an informed decision that their chosen destination will meet their expectations, and it helps tourists understand what is expected of them. However, this is not a prerequisite to travel, and this lack of education has been cited as a contributing factor in poor tourist behavior and the resulting anti-tourism sentiments.

# Conclusion

In the midst of the COVID-19 pandemic, tourism scholars argued, "There is an opportunity—if not an outright necessity—not just to regain travel and tourism dollars and market position once the pandemic recedes, but to reform and repair the industry in meaningful ways."[23] Many places are economically dependent on tourism, but it has become clear that patterns in tourism are not socially sustainable. As stakeholders work to redevelop tourism, the perspective of social geography can provide a powerful basis for finding new ways to work toward a more sustainable and equitable system.

# Key Terms

- acculturation
- commodification
- demonstration effect
- lingua franca
- social geography

# Notes

1. Rachel Pain, Michael Barke, Duncan Fuller, Jamie Gough, Robert MacFarlane, and Graham Mowl, *Introducing Social Geographies* (London: Arnold, 2001), 1.

2. C. Michael Hall, Girish Prayag, and Alberto Amore, *Tourism and Resilience: Individual, Organisational and Destination Perspectives* (Bristol: Channel View Publications, 2018): 62.

3. Stephen Pratt and Anyu Liu, "Does Tourism Really Lead to Peace? A Global View," *International Journal of Tourism Research* 18 (2016): 83.

4. Alon Gelbman, "Tourism, Peace, and Global Stability," in *Handbook of Globalisation and Tourism*, ed. Dallen J. Timothy (Cheltenham: Edward Elgar Publishing Limited, 2019), 151, 156.

5. Airbnb Help Center, "What Is Open Homes?" accessed May 15, 2020, https://www.airbnb.com/help/article/2340/what-is-open-homes.

6. Sarah Firshein, "All the Ways the Travel Industry Is Helping with Coronavirus," Condé Nast Traveler, March 26, 2020, accessed May 15, 2020, https://www.cntraveler.com/story/how-the-travel-industry-is-helping-amid-coronavirus.

7. James Asquith, "Grounded Flight Attendants Are Being Redeployed to Hospitals in Coronavirus Battle," *Forbes*, March 30, 2020, accessed May 15, 2020, https://www.forbes.com/sites/jamesasquith/2020/03/30/grounded-flight-attendants-are-being-redeployed-to-hospitals-in-coronavirus-battle/#139f05a74eb6.

8. Samuel Seongseop Kim and Bruce Prideaux, "Tourism, Peace, Politics and Ideology: Impacts of the Mt. Gumgang Tour Project in the Korean Peninsula," *Tourism Management* 24 (2003): 676, 680–1.

9. Alastair M. Morrison, Xinran Y. Lehto, and Jonathon G. Day, *The Tourism System*, 8th edition (Dubuque: Kendall Hunt Publishing, 2018), 46.

10. Stephen Williams, *Tourism Geography* (London: Routledge, 1998), 152–3.

11. Tazim Jamal, Blanca Camargo, Jennifer Sandlin, and Romano Segrado, "Tourism and Cultural Sustainability: Towards an Eco-Cultural Justice for Place and People," *Tourism Recreation Research* 35, no 3 (2010): 274.

12. Lei Tin Jackie Ong, Donovan Storey, and John Minnery, "Beyond the Beach: Balancing Environmental and Socio-Cultural Sustainability in Boracay, the Philippines," *Tourism Geographies* 13, no. 4 (2011): 561.

13. Anna Farmaki and Dimitrios Stergious, "Impacts of P2P Accommodation: Neighborhood Perspectives," e-Review of Tourism Research 16, no. 2/3 (2019); 46.

14. "Coronavirus: 'Unprecedented' Crowds in Wales Despite Warnings," *BBC News*, March 22, 2020, accessed May 18, 2020, https://www.bbc.com/news/uk-wales-51994504.

15. Claudio Milano, Marina Novelli, and Joseph M. Cheer, "Overtourism and Tourismphobia: A Journey through Four Decades of Tourism Development, Planning and Local Concerns," *Tourism Planning & Development* 16, no. 4 (2019): 354.

16. Marco Martins, "Tourism Planning and Tourismphobia: An Analysis of the Strategic Tourism Plan of Barcelona 2010–2015," *Journal of Tourism, Heritage & Serivces Marketing* 4, no. 1 (2018): 3–7.

17. Hugues Seraphin, Vanessa Gowreesunkar, Mustafeed Zaman, Stéphane Bourliataux-Lajoinie, "Community Based Festivals as a Tool to Tackle Tourismphobia and Antitourism Movements," *Journal of Hospitality and Tourism Management* 39 (2019): 219.

18. Jamal et al., "Tourism and Cultural Sustainability," 274.

19. Michael C. Hall and Alan Lew, *Understanding and Managing Tourism Impacts: An Integrated Approach* (New York: Routledge, 2009), 58.

20.  Jeou-Shyan Horng, Hsuan Hsu, and Chang-Yen Tsai, "An Assessment Model of Corporate Social Responsibility Practice in the Tourism Industry," *Journal of Sustainable Tourism* 26, no. 7 (2018): 1085–7.

21.  Emma Hughes and Regina Scheyvens, "Corporate Social Responsibility in Tourism Post-2015: A Development First Approach," *Tourism Geographies* 18, no. 5 (2016): 472.

22.  Richard W. Butler, "Overtourism in Rural Settings: The Scottish Highlands and Islands," in *Overtourism: Issues, Realities and Solutions*, eds. Rachel Dodds and Richard W. Butler (Berlin: De Gruyter, 2019): 209.

23.  Stefanie Benjamin, Alana Dillette, and Derek H. Alderman, ""We Can't Return to Normal": Committing to Tourism Equity in the Post-Pandemic Age," *Tourism Geographies* DOI: 10.1080/14616688.2020.1759130.

# CHAPTER 10

# The Environmental Geography of Tourism

Tourism frequently gets linked to much-discussed environmental issues in the mass media. It is cited as an economic alternative to logging in the Amazon rain forest. It is used to argue against drilling for oil in the Arctic National Wildlife Refuge. It is considered to be the best chance for protecting rare and endangered wildlife species in sub-Saharan Africa. This connection between tourism and environmental issues brings together some of the topics that we have already discussed. In particular, it recognizes that the physical resources of a place can constitute very powerful attractions for tourism. It also recognizes that tourism is a viable economic activity that can be as profitable as or, in fact, more profitable in the long term than other, less environmentally sustainable economic activities.

The environmental geography of tourism allows us to explore this connection. Like tourism geography, **environmental geography** is a topical branch of geography that can be difficult to place within the field. Some scholars consider environmental geography to provide the geographic perspective on environmental science and therefore approach the topic as a "hard" science. Yet, this approach neglects a crucial component of environmental geography: people. Environmental geography is distinguished from other branches of physical geography in the recognition of and focus on the earth as the human environment. In other words, it considers the ways in which the environment affects people and people affect the environment. As such, environmental geography lies at the intersection of human and physical geography. Human-environment interaction is a long-standing theme in geography. Environmental geography provides the means of exploring this theme. While some geographers may approach the topic from a physical geography background (e.g., the science of human-induced climate change), others will do so from a human geography background (e.g., the human response to climate change).

Environmental geography has an important part to play in the geography of tourism. Natural attractions based on physical resources provide the basis for different tourism products in destinations around the globe. In the modern world, where billions of people live in highly urbanized areas, tourism provides a distinct opportunity for people to interact with the environment. To some extent, the relationship between tourism and the environment may be described as symbiotic: because tourism benefits from being located in high-quality environments, those same environments ought to benefit from measures of protection aimed at maintaining their value as tourism attractions. However, the incredible growth of tourism has made it difficult to sustain this symbiosis. While tourism does indeed have the potential for enhancement and protection of the environment, it has also, in many cases, become a major source of environmental problems that have threatened to destroy those resources on which tourism depends.

This chapter continues our discussion of the geographic effects of tourism. Specifically, this chapter utilizes the tools and concepts from environmental geography to consider the possibility for tourism to positively contribute to the maintenance of high-quality environments, as well as the potential negative environmental consequences of tourism. It also discusses the factors that shape the nature of these effects and the need for education to maximize the positive effects while minimizing the negative effects.

# Environmental Benefits of Tourism

There is a small, but slowly growing, segment of environmentally conscious tourists who seek not only to minimize their negative impacts but also to have positive impacts. For example, visitors may choose to participate in service tourism as a part of their overall experience, such as planting trees, cleaning up beaches, or other place-specific projects (figure 10.1). For the majority of tourists, however, their actions in a place are unlikely to result in any direct benefits for the environment. When we undertake any type of activity—including tourism—in an environment, we cannot help but impact it in some way. Environmental benefits from tourism more often come from conscientious tourism planning and development that works to improve the environmental quality of the destination, maintain environmental standards, and/or preserve the environmental resources of that destination.

## IMPROVEMENT

Tourism can provide a distinct impetus for cleaning up the environment of a place. The environment must be safe enough to allow tourist visits. Thus, the destination must ensure an appropriate level of environmental quality. The high-profile nature of event tourism has provided a strong motivator for places to reduce pollution. To address concerns about athletes' well-being, potential host sites for the Olympic Games must acknowledge issues and outline plans to address these issues. For example, in their bid to host the 2022 Winter Games, it was recognized that "Almaty [Kazakhstan] often experiences poor air quality, particularly in the winter months, and current levels of air pollution could impact athletes and Games participants. However, hosting the Games in Almaty could provide impetus for improvements in air quality, public transport, energy use, waste infrastructure and housing."[1]

The environment must also be attractive enough to encourage and sustain tourist visits. Stakeholders, particularly those who are economically dependent on tourism,

**Figure 10.1.  On a field course, students learn about and give back to the land by volunteering with a local environmental nonprofit to clear invasive species in an ancient loʻi in Waipiʻo Valley, Hawaii. *Source*:** Ava Fujimoto-Strait

have an incentive to maintain a clean environment. On Pico, an island in the Azores, one tour guide acknowledged the difficulty of trash removal efforts on Mount Pico. He reported that, when he leads groups on the mountain, he picks up trash and carries it back down for proper disposal.[2]

When an existing destination experiences damage or contamination as a result of, say, a natural disaster or an industrial accident, the economic benefits of tourism can provide a powerful motivator to get the affected sites cleaned up and/or restored as quickly as possible so that tourists can return. For example, in the aftermath of the 2004 Indian Ocean tsunami, affected destinations had to manage the disposal of debris and other solid wastes and to purify water sources that were contaminated by damaged septic tanks and sewage treatment infrastructure.

A potential destination must restore the environmental quality of a brownfield site (i.e., land previously used for industrial purposes that may have been contaminated by low levels of toxins or pollutants) before tourism can be developed. Mines, factories, warehouses, and other industrial facilities may be abandoned after their operations have been shut down. While these places are often considered a form of visual or aesthetic pollution, there may also be a correlation between such derelict facilities and physical pollution or contamination. The land itself may have been damaged by in-dustrial uses; hazardous chemicals may have leached into the soil or water sources; or the decaying infrastructure, such as buried or rusted pipes, may continue to contribute to environmental degradation. As long as the quality of the environment has not been irreparably damaged, these abandoned facilities may be reclaimed and redeveloped for tourism and recreation in a number of forms.

In some cases, the infrastructure may be preserved, essentially in its original state with some modifications to accommodate visitation, as a tourism attraction to highlight the heritage of the industry in that place. For example, mining in Cornwall and West Devon (United Kingdom) occurred from 1700 to the onset of World War I. This economic activity not only had a profound impact on the region and its culture, but its innovations influenced industrialized mining operations throughout the world. In recognition of this significance, the regional landscape has been granted UNESCO World Heritage status. The site extends across ten different areas and features a range of educational and recreational experiences.[3]

In other cases, some of the infrastructure may be maintained but adapted for new purposes. The Don Valley Brick Works and quarry in Toronto, Canada was shuttered in 1984 after a century in operation. The City of Toronto filled in the quarry and created wetland and meadow habitats, but the majority of the industrial buildings remained abandoned. The industrial heritage and geological significance of site provided the foundation for geotourism development. The farmers' market was one of the first projects to open in 2007. By the end of the year, the market ranked first on a national news' top things to do in the city list.[4] In 2010, the Evergreen Brick Works opened as a community environmental center that recognizes the site's natural, cultural, and economic heritage while showcasing innovative sustainable development practices and technologies.[5]

Rural industrial landscapes may also be cleared, leveled, contoured, and replanted to reestablish native flora, recreate habitat for native fauna, and develop an appropriate landscape for recreation, such as multiuse paths. Although landscape reclamation can be a costly process, laws require it in many parts of the world for environmental protection. In addition, grants and other resources may be made available for local communities to convert these areas for tourism as an alternative means of development once nonrenewable resources have been exploited by other economic activities. The Wilds provides an example of a tourist attraction on nearly ten thousand acres of reclaimed mine land in the US state of Ohio. In the 1980s, the Central Ohio Coal Company donated the land to a nonprofit organization. The organization redeveloped the land as a conservation center and open-range habitat for rare and endangered species from all over the world. Visitors to The Wilds can take a "safari" (i.e., an interactive wildlife tour), stay at the lodge, or participate in outdoor recreation activities like fly fishing.[6]

## MAINTENANCE

Tourism can provide the means of maintaining the environmental quality of a place. Tourism is often accompanied by infrastructure development. The development of hotels and resorts, as well as the corresponding influx of tourists that temporarily increases the size of the population at a destination, can overwhelm existing environmental quality systems. In one example, Andorra, a European microstate located between

France and Spain, has a population of around 77,000 but receives over eight million visitors per year.[7] Local governments may require tourism stakeholders to either construct or contribute to the construction of environmental management facilities. This may be a new facility that did not previously exist at the destination or an expanded facility better equipped to handle increased usage. This may also be an improved facility to ensure that the quality provided (e.g., water) meets the standards of foreign tourists. Although tourism is the explicit reason for these changes, local residents may benefit from them as well.

Tourism revenues may also be reinvested in an environment. As tourism activities will have an impact on the environment in which they take place, a portion of the income from these activities may be allocated for measures to minimize impacts or repair damage from tourism. Nature trails need to be adequately planned and subsequently maintained to limit the extent of erosion, especially in areas expected to receive large quantities of visitors (figure 10.2). Such practices include stabilizing

**Figure 10.2.  Boardwalks on nature trails can serve many functions, such as making the trail more accessible, allowing for drainage, protecting vegetation, and controlling foot traffic. *Source*:** Velvet Nelson

slopes, using natural vegetation to form buffers, and maintaining erosion control measures. These measures need not be expensive or high-tech: in the case of Grenada, the Caribbean island uses nutmeg shells—one of their primary agricultural products—as an organic means of mulching paths that are prone to get muddy and slippery with high traffic.

## PRESERVATION

Environmental preservation has been one of the most significant arguments for tourism development. Many places around the world would be lost to industrial, commercial, or residential development if they were not set aside for the purpose of tourism. Tourism constitutes a viable economic alternative to these other, often more damaging, forms of development. As a result, the land can be made economically productive while it is kept, more or less, in its original state. Trees are a resource that can be exploited by removing them from the land and selling them to paper and pulp mills, furniture manufacturers, the construction industry, and so on. However, the forest as a whole may be seen as a resource to be enjoyed by hikers, birdwatchers, and other nature enthusiasts. If tourism and recreation in a place is thought to be as valuable—or perhaps even more valuable in the long term—then the argument for preservation has greater weight, and the landscape can be maintained as a whole.

In some cases, private tourism stakeholders will recognize the potential for protecting the natural features of a place, and they will invest in nature tourism with the intention of ultimately generating a profit. The private sector has an important part to play in tourism. Particularly in less developed countries where local and/ or national governments may have few resources to devote to preservation efforts, private individuals and companies may be better able to achieve these goals. For example, the Makasutu Culture Forest in the West African country of The Gambia is a project that began in 1992, when two individuals initially purchased four acres of land to build a small backpackers' lodge. When the surrounding forest became the target of deforestation, they realized the need for preservation of a much wider area. Today, the forest is a thousand-acre private reserve and the site of nature-based tourism activities.[8]

In other cases, the public sector takes a leading role in the landscape preservation and resource protection that is needed to create the foundation for tourism. Local and/or national governments may invest in or subsidize preservation, and at the same time, income generated from operator licenses or visitor fees can help finance site maintenance, resource protection from developers or poachers, and additional preservation. There are many categories of **protected areas**. The International Union for Conservation of Nature's definition of a protected area is "a clearly defined geographical space recognised, dedicated and managed, through legal or other effective means, to achieve the long-term conservation of nature with associated ecosystems and cultural values."[9] The six overarching categories represent different levels of protection and allow for different types of activities. Category I includes strict

# Box 10.1.  Experience: Thirty Years in the National Parks

*In the US National Parks System, there are 419 units, including everything from national parks to historical parks, battlefields, monuments, recreation areas, seashores, scenic trails, and more. The different categories of protected areas within and between units provide diverse opportunities for tourism for the more than 327.5 million visitors a year. Some of these visitors will make a point to see major attractions, such as the Old Faithful Geyser in Yellowstone National Park, while others, like Kim, want to fully explore these places that have been recognized as important to our national heritage. She has made this her travel priority, and she has had some amazing experiences over the years.*

I have had the privilege of visiting 296 units in the National Park System. This number fluctuates as new units are added, while others are delisted. I'm glad that we, as a country, have protected our many unique and diverse environments but also our cultural heritage. I'm glad that I have had the opportunity to experience these places. There are so many simply wonderful parks, including places that few people know exist. I enjoy visiting all categories in the park system. Recently, I have started exploring my family history through the park system. I have an ancestor who arrived in the US in 1846 and less than twenty years later he fought in the Civil War. I was able to trace him to the Battle of Chickamauga at the Chickamauga National Military Park in Georgia. But I really love the big, wide-open backcountry parks in the West. These are the ones I will visit year after year.

Yellowstone National Park is one of my favorites. I've been there thirteen times in the past thirty years. I usually go for about a week and either camp in the park or stay in a lodge. A number of new lodges have been built, and you'll see huge numbers of tour buses in those areas. I try to make sure I stay in a different area just because I know that many people will put a strain on the place. I get up early to see the sunrise, and then I spend my days hiking on some of the backcountry trails. The landscape is so unique, with great opportunities to view wildlife, especially if you're willing to get off the main road. Some people think that they can see the whole park from the loop road, and they want to know when the animals will "come out." In all of my years visiting and exploring the trails—including some old trails that are no longer maintained or published—I know I haven't seen the entire park. But I've seen lots of animals, including mountain goats, bighorn sheep, deer, antelope, elk, moose, buffalo, and bears. In fact, one of the most amazing (and a little scary) moments was when we witnessed a herd of buffalo charging because they were being chased by a bear!

I've seen a lot of changes over the years. Some changes are cyclical, and you can definitely tell when there's money being spent on the parks and when there isn't. I've seen the infrastructure get run down and facilities closed, but then a few years later, things will be open and repaired again. I've seen places get understaffed, especially for the number of visitors they receive. In recent years, I've seen an increase in the number of private guides operating tours for small groups of people. I think this helps with congestion in the park, where not everyone is in private cars, but I also think it helps with education and visitor behavior. I've seen these guides let people know when they are doing something that could be potentially harmful to themselves or to the wildlife. This is important. I've watched people trying to take selfies without paying attention to their surroundings, which is just not safe.

Other changes reflect the development of new—and often better—policies. My mother has some pictures of Yellowstone from the 1960s where bears are being fed out of car windows. They had been allowed to feed out of the park's trash dumps since the nineteenth century, and this was considered a tourist attraction. It wasn't until the 1970s that Yellowstone implemented new policies that kept people from feeding the bears and required visitors to properly store and dispose of food in the park. Today they are very careful, and everything is recycled that can be.

I think there are more areas that are open for easy access, but more of the backcountry areas have been closed off to the general public. You have to have a permit to go into the backcountry, which makes sense. It keeps the casual person from going into areas that they really shouldn't be in, and it makes sure the park rangers know where people are in case anything happens. I also like the fact they get updates from rangers in the backcountry, so when I check in before a hike, I get some additional information about what's going on in that area. Some of these trails are closed during parts of the year as well. For example, I know that the Pelican Creek Trail is closed to hikers during the bears' mating season to prevent any interference or disruption of mating patterns.

I appreciate the ability to go into the backcountry. I am most interested in getting "off the beaten path," hiking and experiencing the quiet of nature. That's just me and my personality; I have to find my own way. However, there are places for everyone in the park; you just have to know where to go. At the big, easily accessible camping sites, you'll find lots of people and the big, luxury RVs. At the more primitive, remote sites, you'll find just a handful of hard-core campers. At the major entry points and scenic spots, you'll find tour buses unloading people from all over the world, but get a mile off the main road on a hiking trail, and you might be the only one out there.

—*Kim*

nature reserves and wilderness areas. These areas are considered the most ecologically fragile, and therefore activities within them are most restricted. The strict nature reserves (Ia) are generally limited to scientific study, service programs, and cultural/spiritual users (e.g., Ashmore Reef and Cartier Island Reserves, Australia); wilderness areas (Ib) preserve largely uninhabited and unmodified lands but may be managed to allow some visitation (e.g., Syltefjorddalen nature reserve, Norway). Category II consists of national parks, which are perhaps the most commonly recognized protected areas. These are typically areas with unique natural and/or scenic qualities that are intended to preserve natural heritage and may be managed for scientific, educational, and/or recreational use (e.g., Sunderbans National Park, India).

Category III is designated for natural monuments, which are intended to conserve specific features that have unique natural or cultural value (e.g., Devil's Tower National Monument, Wyoming). Category IV includes habitat and species management areas protected to prevent loss of biodiversity directly or indirectly due to the loss of habitat (e.g., Haleji Lake Wildlife Sanctuary, Pakistan). Category V comprises protected landscapes and/or seascapes and is intended to maintain the quality of human-environment interactions in that landscape that often take place in the form of tourism and recreation (e.g., Logarska Dolina Landscape Park, Slovenia). Finally, Category VI includes managed resource protection areas that have the least amount of restrictions. These areas need to be managed to allow for multiple uses that might combine sustainable resource harvesting with recreation activities (e.g., Tamshiyacu-Tahuayo Communal Reserve, Peru).

Each of these potential benefits—improvement, maintenance, and preservation—is just that: potential. Concerted efforts must be undertaken to recognize the value of the physical resources for tourism and to ensure the existence of a high-quality environment for tourism. Although this may be considered a necessary prerequisite for tourism, these efforts require knowledge, planning, and financial resources that destinations do not always have. Thus, it is important to carefully consider what efforts are being undertaken at a destination and how they weigh against the negative effects—or environmental costs—of tourism.

# Environmental Costs of Tourism

The majority of research on the environmental effects of tourism has focused on costs, as the interactions between tourists and the environments of the places they visit are far more likely to have negative consequences. This includes resource consumption, pollution, and landscape destruction.

## RESOURCE CONSUMPTION

In an introduction to a volume on overtourism, the authors argued, "Based on the use and consumption of local resources and common goods, tourism could also be considered an equivalent extractive industry, having repercussions on the natural environment and on local livelihoods and well-being."[10] Tourism—particularly large-scale mass tourism—can place a heavy demand on local resources. These demands are likely to be in competition with other local economic activities and/or residential uses, and tourism may be given priority. In the worst-case scenario, the high demand for resources from tourism activities depletes that resource, not only to the detriment of future tourism but to the detriment of all activities undertaken in that environment. This can include land, construction resources, water, fuel, and/or power supplies, among others.

Land is a resource that is needed for tourism infrastructure, which can be extensive, including airports, roads, accommodation facilities, entertainment venues, and more. While this extent of infrastructure may not necessarily be a prerequisite for tourism, it accompanies tourism development and facilitates tourism activities. As a result, local people may be displaced and other economic activities supplanted in prime tourism development land. Competition for land between tourism and local uses is typically most intense in small island destinations, such as those in the Caribbean or the South Pacific, where land is a scarce resource. This is something that may be taken for granted by the tourists who visit that destination and do not consider how that land was used before tourism or how it might otherwise be used. Yet, as an economic activity, tourism must create enough jobs to compensate for lost jobs in agriculture or other traditional activities. New jobs must provide sufficient wages for local people to purchase from external suppliers the food that they need to support their families to compensate for the loss of the food they once produced for themselves.

Various types of construction resources are consumed in the development of tourism infrastructure. Local lumber resources may be used in hotel/resort construction. As such, this resource is no longer available for local construction or other uses (e.g., as a source of fuel). Sand may be mined from beaches to make concrete, for building construction, or for construction of roads and airport runways. In both cases, trees and sand may additionally have the potential to serve as a tourism resource. If they are removed from the environment to be used as a construction resource, they will no longer contribute to the tourism base.

Water is a resource that is used in high quantities in tourism. The accommodation sector accounts for some of the greatest water demands at tourism destinations. Water may be used on the hotel/resort property in decorative fountains and to maintain green vegetation and flower gardens, even at destinations that have a dry climate. Likewise, water may be used in swimming pools and spa facilities. Guests account for a proportion of accommodations' water usage. Western tourists, in particular, have reportedly high water uses with baths, long showers, and in some case multiple showers per day. Guest services also constitute a source of water consumption. This includes kitchen and restaurant facilities but is primarily accounted for with laundry facilities, as the guests' sheets and towels are typically washed daily. In addition, tourism attractions and activities utilize varying quantities of water resources, including water parks, golf courses, botanical gardens, and ski resorts that rely on snowmakers. Given the economic importance of tourism, these activities may receive priority access to water resources. Other local economic activities and residential uses may then face restrictions or shortages.

The situation is similar for local fuel and/or energy resources. Accommodations and tourism attractions may require high electricity consumption to power their operations. This can put a strain on the destination's electricity-generating capacity. To prevent shortages that would affect tourists and tourism activities, thereby creating dissatisfaction with the destination experience, power may be cut to local business and/or residential customers at peak times.

In cases where tourism is already developed, local resources may be exploited for tourists' consumption. Economically, a high demand for locally made souvenirs would be considered a positive. However, to meet this demand, local residents may mine coral to make craft items and jewelry or remove trees and grasses to make boxes, baskets, and mats, and so on.

## POLLUTION

Although tourism has been described as a "smokeless industry,"[11] it can either contribute to or directly result in all types of pollution at both the local and global scales (box 10.2). Water and air pollution are considered the most severe problems, but other types of pollution—such as noise or visual pollution—can also be problematic for tourism destinations.

Because many tourism activities are located in coastal areas or on lakes and rivers, water pollution is one of the most significant types of pollution associated with

## Box 10.2.  Case Study: Environmental Effects of Tourism on Mount Everest

With growing interest in adventure tourism, the most mountainous regions in the world have experienced an increase in tourists and tourism development. Mount Everest, located on the border of Nepal and China, is the world's highest mountain at over 29,000 feet (map 10.1). In Nepal, Mount Everest is known as Chomolangma to the local Sherpa and Sagarmatha to the Nepalese. The region has considerable prestige as a destination for trekking and mountaineering.[a]

In 1953, Tenzing Norgay Sherpa and Sir Edmund Hillary made history with the first successful ascent of Mount Everest. Ten years later, only twenty tourists visited Nepal's Everest region. In 1976, the Nepalese government established the Sagarmatha National Park. In addition to Mount Everest and the spectacular scenery of the Himalayas, the area is known for high levels of biodiversity, including rare wildlife species such as snow leopard. In 1979, the park was designated a UNESCO World Heritage Site. Visitor numbers steadily increased, with the exception of periods of political instability and natural disasters. By 2017, the park received over 45,000 foreign tourists.[b]

The number of climbing permits has also increased steadily, including a record of 381 permits issued for the 2019 spring season (April to May). Guides, porters, and other support staff are not included in this number.[c] Because there is a relatively small window of good weather, expedition teams are often climbing at the same time, creating the widely shared photos of long lines of climbers awaiting their turn at the summit. Thus, despite comparatively low numbers, Everest has been cited as a case of overtourism. This has direct human

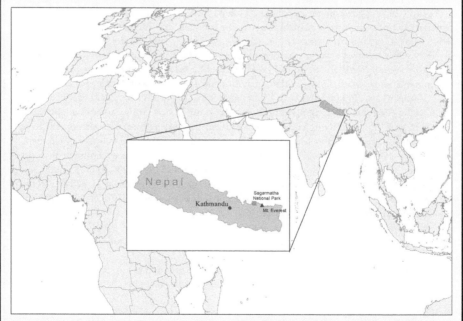

**Map 10.1.  Mount Everest, Nepal. A dramatic increase in visitors to Sagarmatha National Park and climbers seeking to summit Mount Everest has led to significant environmental concerns. Source:** Gang Gong

costs, as climbers waiting in line exhaust their oxygen supply. It also has environmental costs and further ramifications on human health.

Key environmental effects of tourism include landscape degradation, deforestation, loss of biodiversity, waste disposal, and pollution. Foot traffic has led to degradation and erosion of mountain paths. Tourism development increased the demand for wood for the construction of tourism-related facilities and as a source of fuel due to the expense of other imported fuels. This been a driver of deforestation, which has implications for biodiversity.[d]

While waste disposal is not a new issue, it is an increasingly urgent one. The Sagarmatha Pollution Control Committee, a community-based nongovernmental organization, was established in 1991 to develop waste management infrastructure, sustainable waste management strategies, and promote waste reduction, reuse, and recycling.[e] However, Mount Everest has been described as the world's highest garbage dump with discarded tents, oxygen canisters, food packaging, human feces, and even the bodies of many of the 200 climbers who have lost their lives on the mountain.[f] Melting glaciers and snow are exposing layers of waste, and climbers contribute more every year. This waste poses a health risk for diseases such as cholera and hepatitis A to climbers and support staff at Base Camp who use melted snow for drinking water as well as thousands of people living in the Everest watershed.[g]

Several cleanup efforts have been conducted, but there are significant challenges to cleanup efforts. This includes low oxygen levels, subzero temperatures, and treacherous terrain.[h] The task gets more difficult in the higher altitudes. One National Geographic writer and climber noted that cleanup efforts have had little impact above Base Camp and described Camp II at 21,240 feet as "particularly disgusting."[i] In 2019, a fourteen-member team collected ten tons of waste over a six-week period. It is estimated that some thirty tons of waste remain.[j] While waste removal is clearly needed, there are ethical questions about sending local people to retrieve waste generated by foreign tourists.

In 2014, the government instituted a policy in which climbers were required to return eighteen pounds of waste, not including oxygen cylinders and human waste, to the Sagarmatha Pollution Control Committee at Base Camp. If they failed to do so, they would lose a US$4,000 deposit. However, there were questions about whether that policy was being monitored or enforced.[k] An additional proposal would involve scanning and tagging climbers' equipment. They would, again, forfeit a deposit if they returned without all of their items.[l]

Tourism is an important source of income for Nepal. It has brought positive changes, such as the development of modern infrastructure in the Everest region, increased household incomes, and improved living conditions.[m] Tourism has also had negative effects that have led to calls to increase permit fees and issue fewer permits to reduce the number of climbers, and impose (as well as enforce) stricter waste removal procedures. The government is working toward these policies, such as increasing permit fees from US$11,000 to US$35,000 and ensuring climbers have experience summiting at least one other peak above 21,325 feet in the country.[n] Still, others feel that the economic benefits of mountain tourism and the hubris of tourists will continue to take precedence.[o]

*Discussion topic*: How do the environmental effects of tourism on Mount Everest affect the economic and social outcomes? How could stakeholders work toward a more sustainable tourism?

*Tourism online*: Nepal Tourism Board, "Trekking, Mountaineering & More in Everest Region Nepal," at https://www.welcomenepal.com/places-to-see/everest.html

---

[a] Sanjay K. Nepal, "Tourism and Change in Nepal's Mount Everest," in *Mountain Tourism: Experiences, Communities, Environments and Sustainable Futures*, eds. Harold Richins and John S. Hull (Oxfordshire: CABI, 2016), 285.

[b] Government of Nepal, "State of Conservation Report Sagarmatha National Park (Nepal) (N120)," November 2017, accessed May 25, 2020, https://www.google.com/url?sa=t&rct=j&q=&esrc=s&source=web&cd=&ved=2ahUKEwjIu7 Lxs8_pAhVEPq0KHbjACVgQFjAEegQIBRAB&url=https%3A%2F%2Fwhc.unesco.org%2Fdocument%2F165027 &usg=AOvVaw2jgoLgIbngoL8FPlCSewCk.

c Bhadra Sharma and Kai Schultz, "New Everest Rules Could Significantly Limit Who Gets to Climb," *The New York Times*, August 14, 2019, accessed May 25, 2020, https://www.nytimes.com/2019/08/14/world/asia/everest-climbing-rules.html.

d Nepal, "Tourism and Change," 286.

e Sagarmatha Pollution Control Committee, "About Us," accessed May 25, 2020, https://www.spcc.org.np.

f Sanjay Nepal, "Everest Tourism Is Causing a Mountain of Problems," *The Conversation*, April 9, 2014, accessed May 25, 2020, https://theconversation.com/everest-tourism-is-causing-a-mountain-of-problems-23953.

g National Geographic Society, "Trash and Overcrowding at the Top of the World," October 1, 2019, accessed May 25, 2020, https://www.nationalgeographic.org/article/trash-and-overcrowding-top-world/.

h Rachel Graham, "The Environmental Cost of Climbing Mount Everest," *Euronews*, May 7, 2019, accessed May 25, 2020, https://www.euronews.com/living/2019/07/03/the-environmental-cost-of-climbing-mount-everest.

i Mark Jenkins, "Maxed Out on Everest," *National Geographic* 223, no. 6 (2013).

j Charlotte Edmond, "World's Highest Spring Clean Operation in Everest Turned Up 10 Tonnes of Trash," *World Economic Forum*, October 31, 2019, accessed May 25, 2020, https://www.weforum.org/agenda/2019/10/10-tonnes-of-trash-was-taken-down-everest-this-is-what-s-happened-to-it/.

k Nepal, "Everest Tourism."

l Graham, "The Environmental Cost."

m Nepal, "Tourism and Change," 286.

n Megan Spurrell, "Nepal Is Banning Single-Use Plastics on Mount Everest," *Condé Nast Traveler*, August 23, 2019, accessed May 25, 2020, https://www.cntraveler.com/story/nepal-is-banning-single-use-plastics-on-mount-everest.

o Pablo Figueroa, "Vanity, Pollution and Death on Mount Everest," *Our World*, July 15, 2013, accessed May 25, 2020, https://ourworld.unu.edu/en/vanity-pollution-and-death-on-mt-everest.

tourism. Untreated sewage is typically the largest source of water pollution from tourism. This is generally attributed to the fact that many international destinations around the world have either no sewage treatment and therefore discharge the sewage directly into the water supply, or an inadequate system and only a portion of sewage gets treated. In the case of Boracay, Philippines, nearly one-third of establishments were discharging wastewater into the sea. Bacteria levels were 47 times the standard for recreational water safety. As a result, the government shut down tourism for six months in 2018 to undertake cleanup efforts.[12] Cruise ships also constitute a significant source of tourism-related water pollution (see chapter 5). Other sources include fuels from recreational boats, chemical fertilizers, herbicides or pesticides used on resort properties and golf courses that leach into the groundwater or run off into water supplies, and even lotions and oils on the skin of tourists swimming in the water.

Polluted coastal waters may be an aesthetic detraction to tourists, but they can also have a negative impact on the tourism resources for the destination. The discharge of untreated sewage into water causes eutrophication, which is a process of nutrient enrichment. This stimulates algae growth, which has an unpleasant odor and can cause ecosystem damage, such as the suffocation of coral reefs. Visitors—as well as residents—would be at risk for contracting waterborne diseases like gastroenteritis, hepatitis A, dysentery, and typhoid. Likewise, water pollution can contaminate the food supply.

Air pollution is an increasing concern. One of the fundamental components of tourism is travel, which is dependent on the transportation that is available based on present technology. Where there is a dense concentration of vehicles for tourism, vehicle exhaust contributes to poor air quality. Although many urban destinations suffer from air pollution, tourism may not be the most significant cause. Tourists may be more likely to use public transportation due to restrictions on cars (e.g., emission controls) and traffic (e.g., taxes or permits for vehicles in inner-city zones or traffic-free zones) or other disincentives (e.g., limited parking areas, high parking fees, or confusing traffic patterns).

In contrast, natural places like the US National Parks have experienced increasing problems with pollution during high seasons. A 2019 National Parks Conservation Association study found that 96 percent of national parks suffered from significant air pollution problems that affect tourist visits, human health, and/or environmental health.[13] Tourists need personal cars to reach and get around at these destinations, but many parks have instituted policies to limit traffic congestion. Visitors may be required to park in designated areas and use dedicated transport within the park. According to the National Park Service, transportation accounts for over 30 percent of their annual greenhouse gas emission. The 2016 Green Parks Plan prioritizes reducing these emissions by transitioning to newer fuel-efficient vehicles and finding appropriate ways to encourage active transportation (e.g., walking and biking).[14]

Even when air pollution is not the direct result of tourism, it can have a negative impact on destinations. Air pollution adversely affects the health and quality of life of local residents. Tourists, particularly those with preexisting respiratory conditions such as allergies, asthma, or emphysema, can be affected by short-term exposure to environments with poor air quality. Although it often goes unacknowledged, tourists' psychological state, such as their mood or ability to handle stressors, can also be affected by air pollution in a destination.[15] Air pollution can adversely affect the quality of tourism resources. For example, air pollution has been cited as one of the greatest threats to ancient archaeological sites, such as the Parthenon in Athens, Greece. Related to air pollution, acid rain has the potential to damage forest resources, as has occurred in Germany's well-known Black Forest region.

The effects of noise pollution on destination residents was discussed in the last chapter. Increasing noise pollution from tourism also affects the patterns and behaviors of terrestrial and marine wildlife. Tourism-induced noise can affect satisfaction with destination experiences as well. Tourists visiting natural and/or sacred sites where a reverence for the environment is expected will be unhappy with the levels of noise from excessive numbers of tourists, air or road traffic, and others. As with air pollution, this has been a growing problem in some of the popular US National Parks. For example, scenic flights and helicopter tours are a key source of noise from Mount Rainier (Washington) to the Grand Canyon (Arizona).

Visual pollution results in a decline in the aesthetic quality of an environment. This may occur when landscapes are changed by tourism development. The construction of tourism infrastructure may be considered visual pollution if it seems out of place in that particular environment. This can refer to the location of a hotel on an otherwise undeveloped beach or a ski lift or ski slope on an otherwise forested mountainside. Visual pollution may also occur as landscapes are degraded by tourist activities. This can include trash, graffiti, or stacked rocks in natural areas that become an unexpected source of visual pollution for future generations of tourists expecting a more pristine environment or for locals interested in maintaining environmental quality (figure 10.3). In 2019, Granite Bay in Noosa National Park, Australia made headlines with pictures of the beach covered in messages, some of

**Figure 10.3.   Graffiti along a nature trail constitutes a source of visual pollution for locals and visitors alike. *Source*:** Velvet Nelson

which were offensive, spelled out with rocks. Local volunteers who organized the beach cleanup attributed the messages to a group of backpacking tourists.[16]

## LANDSCAPE DESTRUCTION

The various costs of tourism development and tourist activities can ultimately contribute to, or result in, the destruction of landscapes. In addition to changing the fundamental nature and appearance of the landscape, this can contribute to further environmental problems such as disruption of habitats, fragmentation of ecosystems, and reductions in biodiversity.

Much of the world's tourism development has taken place in coastal areas. There are several unique and specialized ecosystems in these areas—including sand dunes, coastal wetlands and mangroves, and coral reefs—all of which have been threatened by tourism development. Each of these ecosystems has a high level of biodiversity and helps protect the coastal land area from erosion and the potentially damaging effects of storm waves and tidal surges. However, sand dunes have been leveled and wetlands drained for beachfront hotel/resort development. This can lead to problems with erosion and beach loss, as well as an increased amount of silt in coastal waters, which will smother coral reefs. Tourists themselves may trample dunes and damage coral by touching it, standing on it, or taking pieces as souvenirs. The nature of the land may be lost to the construction of tourism infrastructure and facilities. In a forested environment, this contributes to local and global problems associated with deforestation, ranging from increased erosion to increased carbon dioxide in the atmosphere.

Environmental impacts can destroy habitats and disrupt the species that inhabit them. The destruction of an ecosystem for tourism development can contribute to a loss of biodiversity, while the destruction of parts of the landscape may fragment the wider habitat and affect species' migration patterns. Tourists who take things for souvenirs or move things can also have a negative impact on the landscape. For example, rock stacking can expose soil and contribute to erosion, disturb foraging and nesting areas for coastal birds, and eliminate shelter for reptiles or invertebrates.[17] The encroachment of tourism activities into these ecosystems can bring species into closer contact with people, both tourists and tourism industry workers. This can affect eating and breeding patterns, as well as endanger the health of animals (box 10.3).

## Box 10.3.   In-Depth: Wildlife Selfies

Wildlife tourism is a niche tourism product in which visitors seek opportunities to experience wildlife. People have long been interested in animals, and accordingly, wildlife tourism has been a topic of interest to understand the potential costs and benefits as well as strategies to ensure its sustainability. Recently, the trend of "wildlife selfies" has brought new attention to an already complicated issue.

Scholars remind us that tourist photography had an impact on wildlife prior to mobile technologies and selfies; however, social media has played a role in creating a demand for specific and unsustainable wildlife tourism experiences. Tourists often look for unusual experiences to photograph and share with friends and family, but celebrities and influencers have a global audience with millions of followers.[a] Sharing wildlife selfies normalizes the behavior, and tourists inspired by the photographs they see seek to recreate those experiences. A study found a 292 percent increase in the number of wildlife selfies posted on Instagram between 2014 and 2017. At least 40 percent of these photos showed a person in direct contact with wildlife (e.g., holding or hugging an animal) or interacting with wildlife that is baited, drugged, or restrained.[b]

Many animals are not easily seen in the wild, especially during the limited amount of time tourists may spend in a destination. To meet the demand for animal encounters, tour operators provide opportunities for viewing, interacting, and taking pictures with a variety of animals. While many countries have laws against removing animals from the wild and/or making money from captive wild animals, these laws are not always enforced. An investigation of 249 wildlife tourist attractions listed in Latin American countries found that over half offered direct contact with animals, and over 60 percent of the species identified in these experiences hold international legal protection by the Convention on the Trade in Endangered Species (CITES).[c] Beyond tour operators, individuals or families may keep animals to provide extra income from tourists.[d] Wildlife advocates express concerns about the ways in which animals are captured, kept, and handled that can take a physical and emotional toll on the animals. For example, when sloths are repeatedly handled by tourists, it can cause an increase in the animals' heart rates and lead to premature death.[e]

In addition to the ready-made photo-ops, tourists themselves try to create opportunities for interaction, often with serious consequences. In 2015, unauthorized tourists in Costa Rica swarmed an important nesting site for endangered olive ridley sea turtles to see, touch, and take selfies with the animals. Many of the animals returned to the ocean without laying eggs.[f] In the same year, a woman was injured at Yellowstone National Park after getting close to a bison and then turning her back on it to take a selfie. In response to the growing trend, the writer of a US National Park Service blog wrote, "Bison selfies are giving the impression that taking a picture in close proximity of a bison is a common activity, especially when there are limited negative consequences... Although these bison selfies might seem normal, there is a very real possibility that a bison-related injury could happen to you."[g]

In response to studies highlighting the negative effects of wildlife selfies, Instagram created a wildlife warning message in 2017 that pops up when a user searches or clicks on a hashtag like #slothselfie (figure 10.4).[h] Advocates hope that users will reflect on the issues before posting. However, as of 2020, there were over 22,000 posts with #slothselfie. In 2019, the Government of Costa Rica launched the #stopanimalselfies campaign to further raise awareness about animal welfare and the potential risks of animal encounters. The campaign encourages tourists to take photos when they are a safe distance from animals that are free to move about in their natural habitat. It recommends tourists avoid taking selfies with animals that are being held, restrained, or baited with food or those that could hurt them. Tourists are also encouraged to take pictures with stuffed animals with the caption "I don't harm wild animals for a selfie."[i] The hashtag garnered 1,700 posts by the time COVID-19 shut down travel in 2020.

*Discussion topic*: Do you think social media can be an effective tool for changing tourists' patterns of behavior with regard to wildlife selfies? Explain.

*Tourism online*: #stopanimalselfies, "Stop Animal Selfies," https://stopanimalselfies.org/en/home/

**Figure 10.4   In response to studies highlighting the negative effects of wildlife selfies, Instagram began using a wildlife warning message when users search or click on a hashtag like #slothselfie.**

[a] John Pearce and Gianna Moscardo, "Social Representations of Tourist Selfies: New Challenges for Sustainable Tourism," *Conference Proceedings of BEST EN Think Tank XV* (2015): 64.

[b] World Animal Protection, *A Close Up on Cruelty: The Harmful Impact of Wildlife Selfies in the Amazon* (London: World Animal Protection, 2017), accessed May 20, 2020, https://www.worldanimalprotection.org/sites/default/files/media/int_files/amazon_selfies_report.pdf.

[c] World Animal Protection, *A Close Up on Cruelty,* 21.

[d] Natasha Daly, "Special Report: The Amazon Is the New Frontier for Deadly Wildlife Tourism," *National Geographic,* October 3, 2017, accessed May 20, 2020, https://www.nationalgeographic.com/photography/proof/2017/10/wildlife-watch-amazon-ecotourism-animal-welfare/.

[e] Daly, "Special Report."

[f] L. Arias, "Mob of Tourists at Costa Rica's Ostional Beach Prevents Seat Turtles From Nesting," *The Tico Times,* September 9, 2015, accessed May 20, 2020, https://ticotimes.net/2015/09/09/crowd-tourists-costa-rica-prevent-sea-turtles-nesting.

[g] National Park Service, "Bison Bellows: A Case Study of Bison Selfies in Yellowstone National Park," November 2, 2017, accessed May 20, 2020, https://www.nps.gov/articles/bison-bellows-7-21-16.htm.

[h] Natasha Daly, "Exclusive: Instagram Fights Animal Abuse with New Alert System," *National Geographic,* December 4, 2017, accessed May 20, 2020, https://www.nationalgeographic.com/news/2017/12/wildlife-watch-instagram-selfie-tourism-animal-welfare-crime/.

[i] World Animal Protection, "Costa Rica Urges Tourists Not to Take Wildlife Selfies," November 13, 2019, accessed May 20, 2020, https://www.worldanimalprotection.org/news/costa-rica-urges-tourists-not-take-wildlife-selfies.

## CLIMATE CHANGE

As discussed in chapter 6, tourism resources and destinations are vulnerable to the effects of climate change. Yet, it is recognized among researchers and stakeholders that a two-way relationship exists: tourism is affected by, but also contributes to, climate change. A key UNWTO and United Nations Environment Programme report that estimated tourism was responsible for approximately 5 percent of the world's total greenhouse gas emissions in 2005 (table 10.1). This was broken down into tourism activities (4 percent), accommodations (21 percent), and transportation (75 percent). The latter category was further broken down into air (40 percent), car (32 percent), and other (3 percent).[18] It is worth noting that cruise ships were not included in this study.[19] More recent work argues that the 5 percent estimate should be considered conservative given the tremendous growth in tourism since the study was conducted. Based on adjusted predictions (prior to COVID-19), tourism-related greenhouse gas emissions will increase by 170 percent between 2010 and 2050.[20]

Attention is particularly focused on the transport sector, as it accounts for the largest proportion of tourism emission. Transport emissions from international tourism are predicted to increase by 45 percent from 2016 to 2030. Air transport is expected to continue

**Table 10.1.  Distribution of Greenhouse Gas Emissions in Tourism**

| Sector | Percent |
| --- | --- |
| **Transport** | **75%** |
| Air | 40% |
| Auto | 32% |
| Other | 3% |
| **Accommodations** | **21%** |
| **Activities** | **4%** |

to account for almost all interregional travel and a high proportion of intraregional travel. Europe is the primary exception, where arrivals by rail are predicted to more than double by 2030.[21] The dependence on and growth in air transport will continue to be a barrier in efforts to reduce the tourism sector's contributions to climate change.

In 2015, the global community created the Paris Agreement to work together toward the goal of keeping global temperature increase well below two degrees Celsius above preindustrial levels. As the agreement went into effect the following year, the UNWTO Secretary-General stated, "The tourism sector is both a vector and a victim of climate change and we are fully committed to contribute to reach the objectives set by the Paris Agreement."[22] While it is acknowledged that tourism stakeholders across the world have taken measures to reduce their greenhouse gas emission, there is still much work to be done. In one study, a tourism leader expressed concern about the lack of consistent and widespread actions in the tourism sector: "there [are] other industries that really start to put solid plans in place to reduce carbon emissions. It's increasingly obvious that our industry is not doing anything in a collective sense. … Tourism risks being considered a dirty industry, if it is not seen to be doing its share."[23]

Finally, tourism scholars remind us that the positive environmental effects of tourism, such as landscape or species preservation, may be outweighed by the negative environmental effects of climate change.[24]

# Factors in Environmental Effects

As with economic and social effects, there are some examples of how tourism directly affects the environment. This is particularly applicable when tourism activities are developed in environments where few or only small-scale human activities otherwise occur. The development of a ski resort in an undeveloped area involves considerable changes to the landscape: the removal of trees and boulders, the recontouring of the landscape to create runs, and the construction of roads, lifts, accommodation facilities, and more. This development alone—without considering the potential effects of operation—may contribute to or result in deforestation, habitat destruction, loss of biodiversity, destabilization of the slope, erosion, an increased risk of landslides and avalanches, and visual pollution. Yet, in many cases, it may be difficult to separate what effects directly result from tourism and what would have occurred as a result of residential and industrial activities undertaken by the local population. When tourism activities occur in already densely populated, highly urbanized, and/or industrialized areas, it can be hard to identify tourism's contribution to larger issues such as air or water pollution.

The specific environmental effects of tourism at a destination, and the extent of these effects, will vary. The factors that may determine these effects can include the quantity of tourists that visit the destination, the carrying capacity of the destination, the seasonality of tourism, the type of destination, the level of infrastructure, local environmental policies and regulations, and the nature of the environment at the destination.

As with social effects, it is often assumed that the larger the quantity of tourists, the greater the environmental effects. This can be true when the number of tourists visiting that destination exceeds its carrying capacity. Carrying capacity is a widely used concept in environmental geography, as well as related fields such as biology, to indicate the size of a species or population that an environment can support and sustain. Adapted and applied for our purposes, **tourism carrying capacity** refers to the number of tourists a destination or attraction can support and sustain. This helps the destination/attraction to understand its ability to withstand tourist use. Likewise, the destination must recognize that if the carrying capacity is exceeded, it is likely to result in varying degrees of damage that can diminish tourist satisfaction.

The tourism season can also be a factor in the nature and extent of effects. Large quantities of tourists during the high season may put extreme amounts of pressure on local resources. Many destinations have a low or off season during which the site will receive few visitors. This may provide enough time for the environment to recover. However, if the carrying capacity is greatly exceeded during this time, it may cause significant damage from which the environment of the destination will not be able to recover in the span of an off season. Stakeholders may need to shut the destination down for a longer period of time, as was seen in the case of Boracay.

Similarly, the type of destination and the level of infrastructure will also play a role in what environmental effects may occur. For example, mass tourism is associated with higher quantities of tourists; thus, the potential for negative environmental effects may be multiplied in comparison with small-scale niche tourism. Indeed, many long-standing, popular mass tourism destinations have experienced some of the worst environmental effects of tourism. An estimated eighteen million tourists visit Myrtle Beach, South Carolina each year. The destination has battled high levels of bacteria in the water and both long- and short-term swimming advisories for several sections of the beach due to the risk of gastrointestinal illnesses or skin infections.[25] Yet, other well-planned and developed mass tourism destinations may have the infrastructure in place to handle such quantities of tourists and strict regulations to control negative impacts.

In contrast, when a new and/or developing destination starts to receive more than just a few drifters, the infrastructure simply may not be in place yet to handle these numbers, even though they are still small compared to large-scale mass destinations. Moreover, even small numbers of tourists can have a negative impact on the destination's environment. For example, hikers in backcountry areas can cause considerable damage when they stray from prescribed paths, leave ruts or scars, disturb wildlife, pick plants, fell trees for firewood, light campfires carelessly, or improperly discard waste.

The nature of the environment at the destination can also determine the extent of effects from tourism. Fragile ecosystems, such as mountains, rain forests, or coral reefs, may be more vulnerable than others in that they are less able to withstand human use and recover from overuse. Likewise, historic and prehistoric sites are also vulnerable and need to be highly regulated to ensure that they are not adversely affected by increased exhaust from car traffic, wear and tear from foot traffic, dust and debris deposits, and careless or malicious behavior (e.g., vandalism and theft). Each of these environments has lower tourism carrying capacities. In some cases, the benefits of tourism may be negated when more of the visitor entrance fees must go toward combating the problems generated by tourism rather than restoring and/or preserving additional sites.

# Knowledge and Education

Education—of tourists, tourism industry workers, and local residents at a tourism destination—is an important means of preventing the negative environmental effects of tourism. In the case of tourists, ignorant and careless behavior can have a direct impact on the environment of the places they visit. Yet, tourists have little connection to these environments, and given the short-term nature of their experiences in these environments, they may not see the consequences of their behavior. For example, some tourists feel that they are paying for the services that a hotel or resort provides.[26] Thus, they will use the facilities as they see fit—whether it is having their linens laundered on a daily basis or leaving the room's lights, air conditioning, and/or appliances on when they are not in the room—without considering the implications of their wasteful resource consumption. Tourists may give little attention to their waste without considering that items left behind may alter the eating habits of local wildlife, cause some species to fall ill or die, or attract predators. While only a small subset of tourists travels specifically for educational purposes, the potential nonetheless exists for tourists to learn about the places they visit and to understand the consequences of their actions at that place.

Tourism industry workers play a key role in the implementation of mitigation strategies. A destination may have good intentions in devising a code of conduct or a sustainable development policy (see chapter 11); however, these strategies will fail if tourism industry workers are not properly informed of it and do not understand its rationale. For example, tourists have been made aware of water consumption issues use by hotel placards informing them of the destination's water resources and requesting that guests elect to reuse their linens. Many are willing to support this policy on the basis that they would not change their linens daily at home. However, it is too often the case that tourists find that their linens have been replaced by the housekeeping staff regardless of their decision. Similarly, tourists may be requested to separate their trash into designated bins for recycling, only to see staff dumping the bins together as waste. These tourists may become frustrated with the lack of follow-through and therefore ignore such requests in the future.

Finally, local residents must also understand the pertinent environmental issues of the destination and the strategies that are being undertaken to maintain its resources. Again, the best efforts of tourism stakeholders to develop activities with minimal environmental costs can be undermined by unsustainable activities undertaken by the local population. For example, the destination may seek to establish policies to conserve its resources—say sand or trees. However, if people in the local community have a basic need for these resources, or if they have little direct stake in tourism but can profit from the extraction of these resources, they will use them. This erodes the basis for tourism at the destination and contributes to a decline in the environmental quality and general quality of life in that place.

# Conclusion

Environmental geography is a vital component in the geography of tourism, as it represents the intersection of people and environment. Much of tourism involves direct interaction between tourists and the environments of the places that they visit that has the potential to affect the environment. Yet, tourism has wider environmental implications that must also be considered, from changes brought by tourism development to its contributions to climate change. These impacts largely result in negative consequences, but concerted efforts can be made by stakeholders at all scales (i.e., locally, nationally, and globally) to increase efforts to realize the benefits that tourism can have for the environment at the destination and to minimize the costs.

# Key Terms

- environmental geography
- protected area
- tourism carrying capacity

# Notes

1. The International Olympic Committee, *Report of the 2022 Evaluation Commission* (Lausanne: International Olympic Committee, 2015), accessed May 29, 2020, https://stillmed.olympic.org/Documents/Host_city_elections/ioc_evaluation_commission_report_sp_eng.pdf.

2. Personal communication.

3. UNESCO, "Cornwall and West Devon Mining Landscape," accessed May 28, 2020, http://whc.unesco.org/en/list/1215.

4. Seana Irvine and Erin Elliott, *Transformation: The Story of Creating Evergreen Brick Works* (Toronto: Evergreen Brick Works, 2012), accessed May 28, 2020, https://www.evergreen.ca/downloads/pdfs/Transformation-EBW.pdf.

5. Evergreen, "About Evergreen," accessed May 28, 2020, https://www.evergreen.ca/about/.

6. Columbus Zoo and Aquarium, "The Wilds—History," accessed May 28, 2020, https://thewilds.columbuszoo.org/home/about/about-the-wilds/history.

7. United Nations World Tourism Organization, *Compendium of Tourism Statistics Dataset [Electronic]* (Madrid: UNWTO, 2020).

8. Mandina Lodges, "Our Story," accessed May 29, 2020, https://www.mandinalodges.com/about-us/.

9. Yu-Fai Leung, Anna Spenceley, Glen Hvenegaard, and Ralf Buckley, *Tourism and Visitor Management in Protected Areas: Guidelines for Sustainability* (Gland: IUCN, 2018), accessed May 29, 2020, https://portals.iucn.org/library/sites/library/files/documents/PAG-027-En.pdf.

10. Claudio Milano, Joseph M. Cheer, and Marina Novelli, "Introduction: Overtourism: An Evolving Phenomenon," in *Overtourism: Excesses, Discontents and Measures in Travel and Tourism*, eds. Claudio Milano, Joseph M. Cheer, and Marina Novelli (Oxfordshire: CABI, 2019), 5.

11. Andrew Holden, *Environment and Tourism*, 2nd ed. (London: Routledge, 2008), 67.

12. Reil G. Cruz and Giovanni Francis A. Legaspi, "Boracay Beach Closure: The Role of the Government and the Private Sector," in *Overtourism: Issues, Realities and Solutions*, eds. Rachel Dodds and Richard W. Butler (Berlin: De Gruyter, 2019), 98.

13. National Parks Conservation Association, *Polluted Parks: How America Is Failing to Protect Our National Parks, People and Planet from Air Pollution* (Washington, DC: National Parks Conservation Association, 2019), accessed May 29, 2020, https://npca.s3.amazonaws .com/documents/NPCAParksReport2019.pdf.

14. National Park Service, *Green Parks Plan: Advancing Our Mission Through Sustainable Operations* (Washington, DC: National Park Service, 2016), accessed May 29, 2020, https:// www.nps.gov/subjects/sustainability/upload/NPS-Green-Parks-Plan-2016.pdf.

15. Ke Zhang, Yuansi Hou, Gang Li, and Yunhui Huang, "Tourists and Air Pollution: How and Why Air Pollution Magnifies Tourists' Suspicion of Service Providers," *Journal of Travel Research* 59, no. 4 (2020): 661.

16. Cailey Rizzo, "Tourists Are Writing Rude Messages in Rocks at this Australian Beach," *Travel + Leisure*, December 4, 2019, accessed June 1, 2020, https://www.travelandleisure.com/ travel-news/tourists-rock-grafitti-austrlia-beach-send-nudes.

17. Jesse Tabit, "These Seemingly Innocuous Tourist Behaviors Are Actually Incredibly Destructive," Fodor's Travel, August 19, 2019, accessed June 1, 2020, https://www.fodors .com/news/outdoors/these-seemingly-innocuous-tourist-behaviors-are-actually-incredibly-destructive.

18. Daniel Scott, Bas Amelung, Suzanne Becken, Jean-Paul Ceron, Ghislan Dubois, Stefan Gössling, Paul Peeters, and Murray C. Simpson, *Climate Change and Tourism: Responding to Global Challenges, Summary* (Madrid: World Tourism Organization and United Nations Environment Programme, 2007), 14 and 18.

19. C. Michael Hall, Girish Prayag, and Alberto Amore, *Tourism and Resilience: Individual, Organisational and Destination Perspectives* (Bristol: Channel View Publications, 2018), 6.

20. Stefan Gössling and Daniel Scott, "The Decarbonisation Impasse: Global Tourism Leaders' Views on Climate Change Mitigation," *Journal of Sustainable Tourism* 26, no. 12 (2018): 2072.

21. United Nations World Tourism Organization and International Transport Forum, *Transport-Related $CO_2$ Emissions of the Tourism Sector: Modelling Results* (Madrid: UNWTO, 2019), accessed May 30, 2020, https://www.e-unwto.org/doi/pdf/10.18111/9789284416660.

22. United Nations World Tourism Organization, "Tourism Committed to Fight Climate Change—COP22," November 14, 2016, accessed May 30, 2020, https://www.unwto.org/ archive/africa/press-release/2016-11-14/tourism-committed-fight-climate-change-cop-22.

23. Gössling and Scott, "The Decarbonisation Impasse," 2076.

24. Hall, Prayag, and Amore, *Tourism and Resilience*, 9–10.

25. Anna Young, "What Myrtle Beach Is Doing to Address Ocean Water Quality and How Much It Could Cost," *Myrtle Beach Online*, November 16, 2019, accessed June 1, 2020, https:// www.myrtlebeachonline.com/news/local/article237351879.html.

26. Velvet Nelson, "Investigating Energy Issues in Dominica's Accommodations," *Tourism and Hospitality Research* 10 (2010): 353.

# CHAPTER 11

# Sustainable Tourism Development

Over the past several decades, tourism has experienced extraordinary growth. With the sheer volume of people traveling both internationally and domestically, stakeholders around the world have been forced to look beyond the positive effects of this tourism to consider the present and future negative effects. At the same time, the concept of sustainable development has evolved into both a way of understanding the world and a way of working to solve key issues in the world. Thus, sustainable development has been used to understand how the effects of tourism already discussed—economic, social, and environmental—are interconnected and how to work toward sustainable tourism development. Sustainable tourism development requires a process of planning, development, and ongoing management to promote economic, social, and environmental objectives.

This chapter looks at the framework of sustainable development as well as the strategies used to promote sustainable tourism development. These strategies play an important role in determining the nature of a destination, the type of tourists that will visit, and the experiences they will have there. First, this chapter examines the concept of sustainable development, how it has been applied in tourism, and how it relates to the idea of resilience. The next section looks at models to help us understand the evolution of destinations considering sustainable development and resilience. The chapter then discusses some spatial management strategies that may be applied at destinations to maximize the economic, social, and environmental benefits of tourism and minimize its costs, to ensure long-term sustainability. Finally, it considers some of the practices that tourists can undertake to support sustainable tourism goals.

## Sustainable Development

Although now forty years old, sustainable development has been described as one of the most important concepts of our time.[1] The 1987 World Commission on Environment and Development Report titled *Our Common Future*, often referred to as the Brundtland Report after the chairperson of the commission, is widely recognized for its importance in shaping the concept and securing its place on the international political agenda. As defined in the report, sustainable development should be "development that meets the needs of the present without compromising the ability of future generations to meet their own needs."[2] This intergenerational idea of sustainable development resonated with many people throughout the world. It forced people to consider that the decisions made and the actions undertaken now may impact their ability, and their children's ability, to survive and thrive in the future. This prompted them to think about new ways of doing things.

The Brundtland Report laid the foundation for the United Nations Conference on Environment and Development that came to be known as the "Earth Summit" in Rio de Janeiro, Brazil in 1992. The purpose of this conference was to identify the principles of an agenda for action toward sustainable development, which continued to be viewed as development that would not threaten the needs of present and future generations. In the years that followed, however, this idea, while still important, was critiqued as being just an idea, not a practical approach that would help guide actions. By the 2002 United Nations World Summit on Sustainable Development in Johannesburg, South Africa, the focus had shifted to a holistic approach that linked economic development, social development, and environmental sustainability.

A typical conceptualization of this shows three overlapping circles, one each for economy, society, and environment. The middle of the diagram, where all three circles intersect, represents development that is sustainable (figure 11.1). That is the ideal we are working toward. In reality, development is often unbalanced, with emphasis placed on one or possibly two spheres at the expense of the other(s). However, sustainable development reminds us that they are all ultimately connected. Economic development cannot be maintained with a deteriorating environmental resource base, and the quality of the environment cannot be maintained in the face of poverty. The Rio+20 Summit further expanded upon this idea of interconnectedness. Sustainable development was viewed

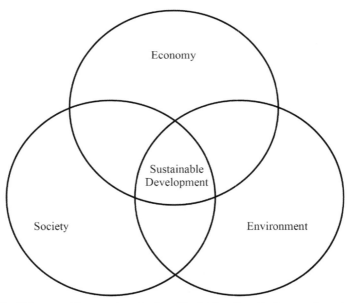

**Figure 11.1  This graphic representation illustrates the three overlapping components of sustainable development: economy, society, and environment. *Source:*** Velvet Nelson

as a process of promoting sustained, inclusive, equitable economic growth and social development that would reduce inequalities and raise basic standards of living as well as promoting integrated and sustainable management of natural resources and ecosystems.[3]

Although debate about the concept is ongoing, sustainable development is increasingly accepted as a means of trying to understand and work toward key issues. As such, various stakeholders are pushing the concept from an idea to an approach. At the global scale, world leaders took the opportunity to build upon the efforts started in 2000 with the creation of the Millennium Development Goals (MDGs). The MDGs were a set of eight goals, with related targets, primarily aimed at reducing extreme poverty in the less developed countries of the world over the course of a fifteen-year period.[4] As this period came to an end in 2015, the Sustainable Development Goals (SDGs) were established to focus efforts toward sustainable development over the next fifteen years all around the world, not just rural areas or less developed countries (table 11.1).[5]

**Table 11.1.  Sustainable Development Goals (SDGs)**

| SDGs |
| --- |
| Goal 1:  End poverty in all its forms everywhere |
| Goal 2:  End hunger, achieve food security and improved nutrition, and promote sustainable agriculture |
| Goal 3:  Ensure healthy lives and promote well-being for all at all ages |
| Goal 4:  Ensure inclusive and equitable quality education and promote lifelong learning opportunities for all |
| Goal 5:  Achieve gender equality and empower all women and girls |
| Goal 6:  Ensure availability and sustainable management of water and sanitation for all |
| Goal 7:  Ensure access to affordable, reliable, sustainable, and modern energy for all |
| Goal 8:  Promote sustained, inclusive, and sustainable economic growth, full and productive employment, and decent work for all |
| Goal 9:  Build resilient infrastructure, promote inclusive and sustainable industrialization, and foster innovation |
| Goal 10: Reduce inequality within and among countries |
| Goal 11: Make cities and human settlements inclusive, safe, resilient, and sustainable |
| Goal 12: Ensure sustainable consumption and production patterns |
| Goal 13: Take urgent action to combat climate change and its impacts |
| Goal 14: Conserve and sustainably use the oceans, seas, and marine resources for sustainable development |
| Goal 15: Protect, restore, and promote sustainable use of terrestrial ecosystems, sustainably manage forests, combat desertification, halt and reverse land degradation, and halt biodiversity loss |
| Goal 16: Promote peaceful and inclusive societies for sustainable development, provide access to justice for all, and build effective, accountable, and inclusive institutions at all levels |
| Goal 17: Strengthen the means of implementation and revitalize the global partnership for sustainable development |

# Sustainable Tourism Development

The applications for sustainable development in tourism have generated considerable interest, as well as additional debate. The UNWTO indicates that **sustainable tourism development** should be "tourism that takes full account of its current and future economic, social and environmental impacts, addressing the needs of visitors, the industry, the environment and host communities."[6] This definition is expanded into three points. Sustainable tourism should be a viable, equitable, long-term economic venture offering stable employment and reducing poverty. It should respect and conserve local cultural heritage and values and promote intercultural understanding and tolerance. Finally, it should use environmental resources efficiently, maintain ecological processes, and conserve natural heritage and biodiversity. Essentially, sustainable tourism development seeks to maximize the potential benefits discussed in the previous chapters.

Despite the general support for the ideas laid out above (and elsewhere), sustainability in tourism has been criticized as another buzzword used in government rhetoric and corporate public relations to generate a positive perception of the industry. Moreover, there have been different interpretations about how to apply these ideas in practice. One critique discussed three interpretations of the concept: the ability to maintain tourism over time, an approach to small-scale niche tourism, and a tool for sustainable development.[7]

In the first interpretation, sustainable tourism is approached from the typical definition of sustainable as "able to be maintained." Tourism stakeholders clearly have an interest in maintaining the industry over time. This perspective is criticized as placing an undue emphasis on economic interests. While social and environmental issues may be a lower priority, they must be considerations in the planning and maintenance of tourism nonetheless. Negative social and environmental effects from tourism have the potential to erode or destroy the foundation for tourism at a destination. Thus, to maintain the tourism industry, stakeholders must employ the holistic approach of sustainable development that encompasses economic development, social development, and environmental sustainability.

In the second interpretation, sustainable tourism is considered a response to the negative experiences of rampant mass tourism development. The concept is correlated to niche tourism, presented as an alternative to large-scale organized mass tourism. This is based on assumptions that small-scale niche tourism operators are more sensitive to social issues or environmental limits. Indeed, there are many scenarios that support this assumption. For example, local entrepreneurs who are members of the community and have a better understanding of, and relationship with, the social and natural environment of that place have a vested interest in working toward the betterment of that community. Likewise, ethically driven entrepreneurs are willing to invest in social and environmental initiatives that support their beliefs, even if it reduces their profit margin. However, there are also many scenarios where small-scale tourism operators do not have the time to devote to anything other than the day-to-day activities involved in running a business. They may not have the knowledge needed to properly plan and manage tourism or the capital needed to invest in sustainability strategies.

This perspective is also criticized because equating sustainable tourism with niche tourism implies that mass tourism cannot be undertaken sustainably. As underlined by the UNWTO, "Sustainable tourism guidelines and management practices are applicable to *all forms of tourism in all types of destinations*, including mass tourism and the various niche tourism segments."[8] It may be argued that it is especially important for sustainable practices to be implemented at mass tourism destinations because of the potential for negative consequences to be magnified by the large scale at which tourism takes place. There are certainly examples of unsustainable mass tourism development fueled by large, profit-driven corporations. However, in today's business environment, many companies have corporate responsibility programs that consider community relations and environmental impacts. Some even use a "triple bottom line" accounting framework that considers not only profit but also the social and environmental consequences of company policies and activities.

In the third interpretation, sustainable tourism is viewed as a tool that can be used to contribute to the goals of sustainable development. While this perspective is relatively well supported, the primary criticism is a lack of discussion or guidelines that would be of practical use in the development of such a sustainable tourism. The 2030 Agenda and the SDGs are helping to bring focus to this discussion. Sustainable tourism is specifically addressed in the targets for three of the SDGs, including SDG 8: promote sustained, inclusive, and sustainable economic growth, full and productive employment, and decent work for all; SDG 12: ensure sustainable consumption and production patterns; and SDG 14: conserve and sustainably use the oceans, seas, and marine resources for sustainable development. However, tourism has the potential to contribute to all of the goals.[9] The Tourism for SDGs platform serves as a resource on sustainable tourism, real-world tourism initiatives that support the SDGs, and suggestions for tourists who want to do their part.[10]

Additionally, the Global Sustainable Tourism Council (GSTC) created a set of criteria for destinations (i.e., public policy makers and destination managers) and the industry (i.e., hotel and tour operators) in 2013 and 2016, respectively. The GSTC Criteria provide global baseline standards for sustainable tourism using four pillars: sustainable management, socioeconomic impacts, cultural impacts, and environmental impacts. The criteria are used for education, policy-making, evaluation, and also certification through organizations such as EarthCheck for destinations (box 11.1), Travelife for tour operators, or Control Union for hotels.[11]

## Box 11.1.  Case Study: Toward Sustainable Tourism Development in the Azores

As well-known tourism destinations around the world face problems with overtourism, under-the-radar destinations have the opportunity to try to find a better path toward sustainable tourism development. The Azores, comprised of nine volcanic islands located in the middle of the Atlantic Ocean, is a Portuguese autonomous region (map 11.1). Due to the islands' remote locations and climate, the Azores has not experienced mass tourism development in

**Map 11.1.   The Azores, Portugal. The Azores became the world's first archipelago to be certified under the EarthCheck Sustainable Destination Program.**
***Source:*** Gang Gong

the same way as tropical island destinations.[a] Public services, fishing, livestock ranching, and the production of dairy products have been the primary economic activities on the island, but tourism has been growing.

Connections with the Azores were provided by two full-service carriers—TAP Air Portugal and SATA Airlines (now Azores Airlines)—as well as charter flights. Airfares were considered very high for visitors. In 2015, airline liberalization occurred, which allowed new airlines to service the islands, including low-cost carriers like Ryanair and easyJet. This increased competition led to reduced prices and an increase in tourist visits. Between 2014 and 2016, the number of visitors to the islands increased from 396,100 to 625,900.[b] In addition, Delta launched the first nonstop seasonal flight by a US airline to São Miguel, the largest island, in 2018. This brought a spike in North American tourists.[c] In 2019, the islands made Fodor's Go List. Citing the increase in low-cost flights, the editors encourage readers to "Go now before the rest of the planet stumbles upon the diverse landscapes [of] these nine Atlantic islands and the delightful local Portuguese flavor begins to change."[d]

Rather than reacting to this growth as it happens (or after), stakeholders have tried to be proactive. One tourism stakeholder noted, "We don't want to be 'the next Iceland.' It's a cautionary tale. You look at the stress that mass tourism has brought on to that country and you say, 'Okay, what can we do to not make those same mistakes?'"[e] Thus, sustainable tourism development is considered to be a high priority.[f]

Azores DMO was created in 2018 with the charge of planning, organizing, implementing, and monitoring the process of sustainable tourism development. Initiatives are coordinated with the public and private sectors, local residents, and applicable nongovernmental organizations. Recognizing the importance of physical resources for tourism, a key focus has been on the conservation of nature and protection of biodiversity. As a result, almost 25 percent of the archipelago's territory is classified as a protected area. Other initiatives work to maintain environmental quality across the islands, including managing air, water, noise, and light pollution.[g] Renewable energy development is prioritized with the goal of generating 80 percent of energy requirements from geothermal, solar, wind, and hydroelectric by 2030.[h] Finally, cultural sustainability is also considered with efforts to protect Azorean heritage and products.[i]

In 2019, the Azores became the world's first archipelago to be certified under the Earth-Check Sustainable Destination Program. Participating in international programs such as this helps the destination coordinate efforts among stakeholders and consistently monitor targets to maintain certification. In addition, it helps attract tourists who are interested in visiting sustainable tourism destinations as well as educating them about their own behaviors while traveling.

Despite these efforts, there are still some concerns about the sustainability of tourism in the archipelago. Growing visitor numbers have led to issues such as traffic congestion at popular attractions, particularly on the island of São Miguel. Hiking trails have required additional maintenance and even expanded infrastructure to accommodate increased use.[j] Some attractions have even begun limiting the number of visitors to the site at a time. One local guide noted that the tourists who visit the Azores are supposedly interested in nature but often do not consider their own actions at the destination. He cited tourists who left trash behind on nature trails or damaged infrastructure in their quest for a better picture.[k]

At present, visitor numbers are still relatively small (consider that Iceland, the destination to which the Azores was contrasted above, received 2.488 million visitors in 2018[l]). Tourism growth will continue to bring new challenges. With the established framework for sustainable tourism development, the Azores are well positioned to manage these challenges. However, maintaining sustainability will require continued coordinated stakeholder efforts and visitor education.

*Discussion topic*: Do you think tourism growth and sustainability can be compatible in destinations like the Azores?

*Tourism online*: Government of Açores, "Towards Sustainability," https://sustainable.azores.gov.pt/en/

[a] João Ponte, Gualter Cuoto, Pedro Pimentel, and André Oliveira, "Tourism Activities and Companies in a Sustainable Adventure Tourism Destination: The Azores," *Tourism & Management Studies* 14, no. 4 (2018): 25, 28.

[b] José Vieira, Gualter Câmara, Francisco Silva, and Carlos Santos, "Airline Choice and Tourism Growth in the Azores," *Journal of Air Transport Management* 77 (2019): 3.

[c] Sebastian Modak, "How the Azores Will Hold Off the Crowds and Stay a Natural Wonder," Condé Nast Traveler, October 24, 2018, accessed July 7, 2020, https://www.cntraveler.com/story/how-the-azores-will-hold-off-the-crowds-and-stay-a-natural-wonder.

[d] Fodor's Editors, "Fodor's Go List 2019," *Fodor's Travel*, November 12, 2018, accessed July 7, 2020, https://www.fodors.com/news/photos/fodors-go-list-2019.

[e] Modak, "How the Azores Will Hold Off the Crowds."

[f] Flavio Tiago, Artur Gil, Sara Temberger, and Teresa Borges-Tiago, "Digital Sustainability Communication in Tourism," *Journal of Innovation & Knowledge* (2020): https://doi.org/10.1016/j.jik.2019.12.002.

[g] Government of Açores, "Certification," accessed July 7, 2020, https://sustainable.azores.gov.pt/en/certification/#dmo.

[h] EarthCheck, "The Azores—the World's First Certified Archipelago," December 5, 2019, accessed July 7, 2020, https://earthcheck.org/news/2019/december/the-azores-the-worlds-first-certified-archipelago/.

[i] Government of Acores, "Certification."

[j] Tiago et al., "Digital Sustainability."

[k] Personal communication.

[l] United Nations World Tourism Organization, *Compendium of Tourism Statistics Dataset [Electronic]* (Madrid: UN-WTO, 2020).

# The Evolution of Destinations

Around the same time that the sustainable development concept was proposed, Richard Butler proposed the **tourist area life cycle** (TALC) model, sometimes also referred to as the resort life cycle.[12] Ever since, it has been widely discussed and applied to cases of tourism development around the world. Butler has argued that there was (and perhaps still is) a need to challenge the prevailing ideal that once a place was established as a tourist destination, interest in and visits to it would be maintained indefinitely.[13] In reality, few destinations can remain unchanged over time. Tourism is a dynamic system. With greater freedom to explore new, different, and unknown destinations, modern tourists have less place loyalty. A destination that does not respond to market trends will be perceived as outdated and unfashionable. Consequently, it will lose competitiveness in this highly competitive industry.

As a geographer, Butler's initial idea focused on the spatial implications of growth and development of tourism destinations. He argued that there are limits to growth. A destination that does not manage its tourism resources in light of the demands being placed on it will experience a decline in quality. This leads to a corresponding decline in the quality of tourists' experience and ultimately a decline in tourist visits. The TALC model provides a means of thinking about the development and evolution of destinations over the course of a series of stages. It describes changes in the character of the destination as well as in the types of tourists visiting and the nature of the effects from tourism there.

The first stage in the model is exploration. In this stage, tourists begin to be attracted to the destination for its inherent physical and/or human resources. Therefore, the primary attractions are most likely to be natural or human (not originally intended for tourism). The first tourists to "discover" the destination are typically adventurous, most likely categorized at the drifter end of the spectrum. With only a small number of tourists, the effects of tourism—positive or negative—are generally minimal. Given both the undeveloped nature of the destination and the type of tourists visiting in this stage, however, there is often a high level of interaction between tourists and local people.

The second stage is involvement. Following the arrival of the first tourists, local people begin to recognize the demand for tourism and develop new facilities. Subsequently, the public sector may offer some support, such as infrastructure development. The new stakeholders may begin to advertise the destination to encourage visits. Consequently, the destination experiences an increase in tourist numbers, more of whom would be characterized as explorers, and characteristics of the tourism industry in that place, such as season, become clearer. In this stage, the destination may experience some of the positive economic, social, and environmental effects of tourism.

The third stage is development. The number of tourists continues to increase, and more development occurs. Control over the tourism industry begins to pass from small business owners and local offices to a national governmental agency and large-scale, possibly even multinational, companies. With this continued development, individual mass tourists may begin to arrive. In this stage, the destination begins to experience many changes and an increase in the negative effects of tourism. For example, leakages will likely increase, tensions may build between locals and outsiders, and the overuse of resources may become apparent.

The fourth stage is consolidation. The tourism industry has become firmly established in that place, and the destination has become characterized by major multinational chain hotels and restaurants. A distinct central tourism district has emerged with a dense concentration of infrastructure and activities. However, many of the earliest facilities have become dated and may need to be upgraded. Tourism is the main economic contributor at the destination. With organized mass tourists visiting the destination, numbers are at a high, but the rate of increase begins to slow. In order to attract new markets, the destination may undertake widespread promotional campaigns.

The fifth stage is stagnation. The original natural and/or human attractions have been replaced by human-designed and artificial attractions. Consequently, the tourist area becomes divorced from the character of the place in which it is situated. The infrastructure has continued to deteriorate, and it experiences greater economic, social, and/or environmental consequences from the tourism industry. Although it is well known, it suffers from a poor reputation. The peak in tourism has been reached, and thus major promotion efforts must be undertaken. In addition, substantial discounts may need to be offered to maintain visitor numbers; however, cheap vacation packages will attract a new demographic of tourist that will further discourage earlier generations of tourists from returning.

The sixth stage can consist of decline, stabilization, or rejuvenation, depending on the decisions of destination stakeholders. If no action is taken, the tourist area will enter a period of decline. It may be immediate and drastic or slow and prolonged, but tourists will move on to other, newer destinations. The area will receive a smaller number of tourists from a more limited geographic area for weekend or daytrips. However, if minor adjustments are made and/or efforts are undertaken to better protect tourism resources, the tourist area may stabilize or perhaps see a limited amount of growth. If significant redevelopment projects are undertaken, the area can rejuvenate. This will involve investment in new facilities or upgrading existing ones. It may also involve creating new (human-designed) attractions, finding new ways to utilize previously untapped natural or human (not designed) attractions, and/or trying to attract new markets. If successful, this will create a new wave of growth.

TALC was created to be a general model of the tourism process. While it was intended to be applicable to destinations in various contexts around the world, not all will progress through the stages in the same way. The model has been criticized as being descriptive in nature, meaning that it is most useful in describing the process of development after it has occurred. Indeed, it can be difficult to identify and analyze the stages of a destination's development as it is taking place. Nonetheless, it can be predictive in the sense that it identifies what will happen if destinations are not appropriately planned, developed, and managed from the beginning. Although the concept of sustainable development had not been established when this model was proposed, the two are very closely related. As with sustainable development, TALC requires the acceptance of limits to development and necessitates a long-term perspective to minimize the negative effects of tourism.

In 2019, amidst growing complaints about overtourism in destinations around the world, Butler revisited this model. He reiterated that management of the resources on which tourism depends is essential. "Without such control, excessive development and loss of some or most of the basic attributes and attractions of these destinations would take place. Such a result is close to what is now known as overtourism."[14]

In an effort to advance theory in light of current discussions about sustainable tourism development and resilience, Patrick Holladay proposed an adapted model of destination development. He argues, "Understanding change is critically important in examining the conditions required to develop a resilient destination within the umbrella of sustainable tourism development."[15] Thus, the adapted model gives more attention to the later stages of destination development when change rendered the system vulnerable.

In this model, Holladay calls the first phase colonization. This brings together the first three phases of the TALC model with the slow increase in tourist visitation. Resilience is highest at this point. The second phase, maximality, generally equates to the consolidation phase of TALC, in which the capacity of the system is reached. Sustainable development of resources will begin to fail, economic returns will decline, and local people will become marginalized. The third phase is climax, characterized by mass tourism and peak visitor numbers. The system will become weak and vulnerable to shocks.

The fourth phase is certainty. In the TALC model, a destination can move into decline or rejuvenation; however, Holladay argues that with depleted social and ecological resources, rejuvenation is unlikely. The fifth phase is decline, or the complete loss of the destination. The sixth phase is surprise, as the system reorganizes and begins to rebuild resilience. From here, a destination could enter renewal, similar to the rejuvenation phase of TALC, in which reorganization creates the potential for a new system to develop. Escape is where some parts of the system break away, and regeneration represents the emergence of a new system with a higher level of resilience again. This encourages stakeholders to keep in mind that tourism systems are cyclical, fragile, and vulnerable to shocks. Thus, establishing destination resilience will support sustainable tourism development.[16]

# Planning, Developing, and Managing Destinations

Sustainable tourism development depends on good planning, development, and management to minimize the negative and maximize the positive effects of tourism. Many strategies, borrowed from the topical branches of geography and other fields, have been adapted and proposed as means of developing the spaces of tourism in ways that will achieve this goal. Among others, these include participatory planning, construction regulations, land management strategies, and carrying capacity analysis.

## PLANNING

Planning is fundamental to the development and management of sustainable tourism. Through this process, stakeholders must identify both goals (i.e., what they want as well as what they do not want from tourism) and strategies that will allow them to achieve those goals. This provides a framework to direct the efforts of various stakeholders to facilitate not only the tourism experience but also the sustainability of the industry. The planning process can be used to coordinate with stakeholders in other industries as well. Resources may need to be managed for multiple uses (e.g., maritime resources used in tourism and fishing) to prevent competition or conflict that could undermine one or both industries. Planning provides opportunities to create linkages that can benefit other industries as well. While planning is important prior to tourism development, it is important to remember that tourism is a dynamic system. Planning needs to be conducted periodically to reflect changing circumstances.[17]

Planning alone is not sufficient to maximize the benefits of tourism and to minimize its costs. It is important to consider who is involved, and how they are involved, in the planning process. Outsiders (e.g., corporate representatives or public sector officials) may take control of the process because they have knowledge and/or experience with tourism planning. However, they will not have the community's knowledge about the specific place in which the project will be developed. If only a select group of local stakeholders are consulted, the needs and perspectives of the remaining stakeholders may be ignored. In either scenario, the project is unlikely to be sustainable. Although the answers to these questions—who and how—will be contingent upon community dynamics and sociocultural norms, in general, the poorest segments of the population, minorities, and women are the ones who are most commonly excluded from the planning process. For tourism to support the goals of sustainable development, though, these are the groups who must be involved in planning to ensure that they are able to experience the benefits of tourism.

Participation in planning can occur to varying degrees. At a minimum, participation involves information sharing. This means that potential stakeholders should be informed, in advance, about a planned project. Stakeholders may be asked to provide information that will be used in the planning process. Taken a step farther, this information sharing can lead to consultation, where stakeholders are invited to participate in discussions about the proposed project and its implications. This gives stakeholders an opportunity to voice their opinions, but if the project is still controlled by outsider experts, or powerful insiders, they may have little influence over the process. The next step involves collaborative decision making. In this scenario, stakeholder groups are given the opportunity to use their local knowledge to determine what strategies are most likely to yield the greatest benefits. Finally, empowerment is the highest degree of participation, in which stakeholders assume a leading role in the planning process as well as project development and management.[18]

Participatory planning is intended to engage all potential stakeholders in the process, especially those whose voices have not previously been heard. This helps "flatten" power relations and promote equality. Participation allows people to share their knowledge and gain confidence about their role in the community and/or project. At the same time, tourism planners and developers gain insight into the local circumstances as well as what, exactly, are the needs and priorities of the community. Incorporated into the planning process, this will contribute to the sustainability of the project. Working together at this stage helps communities and tourism operators establish relationships, which will be more likely to translate into benefits later (e.g., hiring from the local community or creating linkages with local suppliers). Finally, stakeholders become invested in and assume ownership over the project and are motivated to work toward its success.[19]

This type of participatory planning can be time consuming and even contentious. Stakeholders will have different perspectives that may not be reconciled. Even efforts to try to engage all stakeholder groups in the process may not be successful. Existing power structures may be too strong to be overcome, which may prevent some groups from having a voice. Stakeholders may not trust each other to act with the community's best interests in mind as opposed to their own. Indeed, there are many challenges involved in the planning process, but the potential consequences are too great for it to be neglected.

## DEVELOPMENT

Various policies can be used to promote sustainable tourism development. For example, construction regulations on many island destinations around the world mandate that buildings must be no taller than or even shorter than the height of surrounding vegetation, typically palm trees. This equates to two or three stories. This type of regulation seeks to restrict the potential negative impacts of mass tourism development. Essentially, it prevents the development of the high-rise mega-resorts that dominate the coastal landscape of many popular 3 and 5S destinations. This limits the numbers of tourists in that space, as well as the amount of resources used and waste generated by those tourists. Similarly, development companies may be required to submit architectural designs for tourism infrastructure to ensure that it does not conflict with local styles and become a source of visual pollution.

**Spatial zoning** is a land management strategy that designates permissible uses of an area based on its resources and/or character. In tourism, zoning determines what tourism activities may be undertaken where. Typically, governmental regulatory agencies identify the resources within particular areas of a destination, as well as the demand for tourism opportunities in those areas. Then, officials determine which areas have the most appropriate resources to allow those activities. GIS is increasingly being used as a tool in this process. Each zone permits an increasing amount of human activity. This includes primary conservation areas with strictly controlled access, natural areas with minimal facilities, and recreation areas with the greatest access and opportunities for hiking, fishing, camping, picnicking, and more.

Zoning may be used to either spatially concentrate tourists or disperse them. **Preferred sites** are typically planned locations that attract visitors through advertisements and promotions; they have facilities like parking lots, restrooms, refreshments, picnic areas, designated paths, and/or information and interpretation centers. These sites spatially concentrate general visitors to ensure that their needs are met and to limit the effects of tourism to one particular area that is designed to handle it. The experience of these places may be enough for many visitors who do not feel the need to venture into other zones with less infrastructure and more fragile ecosystems (figure 11.2).

In contrast, tools like planned scenic drives or tourist routes may be used to disperse tourists. These routes take people away from pressure points and spread them out over a wider area so as to not exceed the carrying capacity in one particular place.

Figure 11.2  Managed natural areas may provide limited facilities for activities like camping, such as this space in Acadia National Park, Maine. This prevents users from environmentally destructive behavior as they attempt to create their own spaces. However, the majority of users will look for camping alternatives outside the park that have more amenities. *Source:* Kim Sinkhorn

Dispersal of tourists is often proposed as a strategy for places experiencing overtourism; however, this has proven challenging. It may be difficult to convince tourists that alternative areas have the same level of attractions. In addition, these areas must be willing and able to receive an increase in visitors.[20]

## MANAGEMENT

Stakeholders must take an active role in destination management to prevent the negative effects of tourism. This involves monitoring and regulating the use of attractions and facilities as well as managing patterns of visitor behavior. Carrying capacity analysis has been one technique for monitoring use. For the purposes of tourism, the carrying capacity concept has been used in different ways. Physical, environmental, perceptual, and social carrying capacities are some examples of the concept that are particularly useful in the geography of tourism.

**Physical carrying capacity** represents a somewhat literal interpretation of the concept in that it refers to the limits of a particular space. This may include things like the number of cars that a tourist site's parking area will hold or the actual number of people that the site can reasonably contain. As such, it is fairly straightforward and allows explicit restrictions to be put in place. **Environmental carrying capacity** refers to the extent of tourism that can take place at a site before its environment experiences negative effects. This can be more difficult to understand because it may not be based simply on the number of tourists but also on the type and accumulation of tourism activities.

**Perceptual carrying capacity** refers to the extent of tourism that can take place at a site before tourist dissatisfaction occurs. This carrying capacity will be reached when tourists decide that a site is too crowded and choose to go elsewhere.[21] Perceptual carrying capacity can also be difficult to determine because the perceived level of crowding is primarily based not only on individual preferences but also on cultural conventions. Indeed, an empty tourist attraction might be as off-putting for some visitors as a crowded attraction is for others.[22] Finally, **social carrying capacity** refers to the extent of tourism that can take place at a site before the local community becomes dissatisfied.[23] As with perceptual carrying capacity, social carrying capacity is contingent upon personal and social factors.

Aside from the physical carrying capacity, it can be extremely difficult to quantify capacity limits. There are often many different economic, social, and environmental factors that influence the carrying capacity in a particular place. Instead, carrying capacity analysis is considered one part of ongoing management strategies. Destination stakeholders should monitor sites for potential environmental impacts and pay attention to both tourist and community attitudes about the extent of visitation through surveys or social media reactions. Ultimately, setting capacity limits will involve a value judgment based on the available information.

After identifying impacts and limits of tourism in particular places, stakeholders may need to regulate the usage of these places through various entry restrictions and/ or fees. Only a certain number of visitors may be permitted at a site at any given time. This strategy has been implemented at numerous sites facing overtourism concerns. Visitor fees may also be imposed to keep visitor numbers low. Galápagos National Park has an adult foreign tourist entrance fee of US$100, and all visitors are required to travel with a certified guide. Not only does this promote a high-quality visitor experience with interpretation of the islands' natural features, it also ensures that park rules and regulations are enforced. With growing visitor numbers and concerns about the fragile natural environment, in 2019 the Ecuadorian government proposed increasing the fee to US$200 for adults spending three or more nights in mainland Ecuador before or after their visit to the park and US$400 for those spending only one or two nights.[24]

To tackle overtourism, popular European destinations have employed a variety of measures. Officials in Amsterdam, Netherlands felt that overcrowding in the city center had become hazardous. Amsterdam, home to 850,000 people, receives around 20 million tourists a year. Officials felt that this mass of tourists contributed to public costs, from keeping the city clean to maintaining security; thus they initiated a €3 per person per night tourist tax.[25] Rome announced a fine of €450 for sitting on the Spanish Steps, and Venice has implemented fines for tourists picnicking, leaning against storefronts, and standing still on bridges.[26] These measures have been described as draconian and anti-tourist rather than anti-tourism.[27] The media coverage of overtourism has brought attention to inappropriate and unsustainable tourist behaviors that should be avoided, but it is also worth raising awareness about sustainable tourist behaviors (see below).

# Sustainable Tourism Initiatives

There have long been examples of sustainable tourism initiatives in destinations around the world; however, a host of new projects and policies have taken off in recent years. In 2018, Six Senses Uluwatu opened in Bali, Indonesia with sustainability in mind. The facility was constructed from sustainably farmed timber, designed for minimal air conditioning to reduce energy consumption, and supplied with smart appliances to ensure energy efficiency (box 11.2). They have processes to separate waste for recycling, composting, or reusing. Food waste is used as a fertilizer for an on-site organic garden and kitchen oil is converted to biodiesel. Water is purified and made available to guests in reusable glass bottles.[28] In 2019, Natural Habitat Adventures ran the world's first zero-waste trip in Yellowstone National Park (US). From this experience, the operator learned about ways they could minimize waste in all of their tours and even created a guide for other tourism stakeholders.[29] Launched in 2020, Kisawa Sanctuary in Mozambique used local artisans, sand and seawater, and 3D printing technology to construct vacation bungalows with a minimal environmental footprint.[30]

---

## Box 11.2.  In-Depth: Climate Change Mitigation in Tourism

Box 5.2 introduced climate change mitigation as the technological, economic, and sociocultural changes that can lead to reductions in greenhouse gas emissions and offsetting travel-related emissions as one mitigation strategy. As more places move toward sustainable tourism development, stakeholders are experimenting with a range of strategies and approaches to lead to more sustainable resource consumption and reduce their contribution to climate change.

Because the tourism system encompasses a wide range of places, environments, service providers, business operators, and so on, there is no blueprint for climate change mitigation in tourism. Mitigation strategies may involve technological innovation, but they also depend on behavioral changes within the tourism system (i.e., both tourism stakeholders and tourists). In addition to offsetting emissions, tourism businesses and organizations can reduce greenhouse gas emissions by implementing strategies to reduce overall energy consumption, improve energy efficiency, and increase the use of renewable energy.

First, stakeholders should consider what kinds of emission-generating activities can be eliminated or avoided without significant disruption to the tourism product. In the transportation sector, a destination might invest in a well-developed public transportation system and encourage its use among tourists as opposed to the use of private cars. In the accommodation sector, hotel development should consider building design, positioning, material, and insulation to reduce the energy needed to keep rooms warm or cool. Technical options, such as key-card systems or shutoff systems, can be used to ensure that lights, appliances, and climate systems are not operating when the room is empty or the window/doors are open. In the food service sector, restaurants could create linkages with local producers to reduce the energy required to transport food to the destination.

Second, for emission-generating activities that cannot be avoided, stakeholders should ensure that energy is used efficiently. Transport operators can seek to maintain young fleets that are the most fuel efficient. Accommodations can install energy-efficient lighting and appliances. Restaurants can regularly maintain refrigerators and freezers to ensure a good seal, proper air circulation, and minimal frost buildup to maximize efficiency. Third, where possible, stakeholders should seek to increase the use of renewable energy. Transport fleets can be based on electric vehicles charged by renewable energy sources. Accommodations can use solar water-heating systems or solar environmental lighting.[a] Restaurants can also use solar power or get creative with local energy resources. For example, *cozido das Furnas* is a dish cooked in a geothermal chamber in the Azores (see box 11.1).

While some mitigation strategies require small behavioral changes, others may require a significant infrastructural (re)development. There has been a precedent set by some tourism stakeholders who have voluntarily adopted mitigation strategies, because it helps reduce costs, supports external certification, or is in line with personal philosophies on sustainability. However, for many small-scale tourism operators around the world, there are significant barriers to implementing mitigation strategies. Strategies based on technological innovations may require a major financial investment, from retrofitting facilities with energy-efficient technologies to purchasing renewable energy infrastructure. This may be beyond the means of small-scale tourism business owners. Other barriers include a lack of sufficient knowledge about mitigation strategies and even tourist resistance to strategies.[b]

Research has repeatedly shown that awareness of climate change does not mean that tourists will change their behavior to mitigate effects.[c] For example, tourists who are able to take one vacation per year are often unwilling to sacrifice their trip on the basis of environmental effects. Moreover, they may make choices to get the most from their experiences on vacation, like flying to get to the destination faster (versus bus or train) or leaving the air conditioning on in the room to ensure a cool and comfortable environment upon return. This behavior may even be contradictory to the tourists' behavior at home, but it is justified as short term and out of the ordinary.[d] As a vital part of the system, tourists must also be willing to make changes. Education about destination-specific climate change effects may help influence tourists' attitudes, but new policies may be needed to act as a catalyst for change.

*Discussion topic*: Find an example of a tourism project that has implemented one or more of these climate change mitigation strategies. Identify what actions have been taken and discuss the potential benefits of these actions.

---

[a] M. C. Simpson, S. Gössling, D. Scott, C. M. Hall, and E. Gladin, *Climate Change Adaptation and Mitigation in the Tourism Sector: Frameworks, Tools and Practices* (Paris: United Nations Environment Programme, University of Oxford, United Nations World Tourism Organization, and World Meteorological Organization, 2008): 68, 78–9.
[b] Velvet Nelson, "Investigating Energy Issues in Dominica's Accommodations," *Tourism and Hospitality Research* 10 (2010): 353.
[c] Peter Burns and Lyn Bibbings, "Climate Change and Tourism," in *The Routledge Handbook of Tourism and the Environment*, ed. Andrew Holden and David Fennell (London: Routledge, 2013), 413–4.
[d] Scott A. Cohen and James E. S. Higham, "Contradictions in Climate Concern: Performances at Home and Away," in *Tourism, Climate Change and Sustainability*, ed. Maharaj Vijay Reddy and Keith Wilkes (London: Routledge, 2013), 59.

---

Existing hotels are looking for ways to improve sustainability in their operations (figure 11.3). Hilton Worldwide set the goal of reducing the food waste that is sent to landfills by 50 percent by 2030 to support the 2030 Agenda. This includes sourcing food locally, composting, donating when safe, and creating ways to use food products that would normally be thrown away.[31] Marriott International announced that it is eliminating single-use toiletries bottles in their hotels around the world. The company estimates this will reduce plastic waste by 1.7 million pounds annually.[32]

Figure 11.3 This African lodge promotes sustainability by using recycled wine bottles filled with purified water in place of plastic water bottles and toiletries in reusable dispensers in place of single-use toiletries. *Source:* Velvet Nelson

# Sustainable Tourists

Governmental agencies, NGOs, tourism industry associations, and entrepreneurs have proposed guidelines or **codes of conduct** to help mitigate the negative effects of tourism. These codes may be targeted at any number of tourism stakeholders, including the industry and the local community but also tourists themselves. They help raise awareness about various issues, such as preservation of natural or cultural resources, with the aim of influencing patterns of behavior (figure 11.4).

The UNWTO adopted the Global Code of Ethics for Tourism in 1999. This code outlines principles intended to serve as a reference for sustainable tourism development that maximize the economic, social, and environmental benefits of tourism while minimizing the costs.[33] In concert with the International Year on Sustainable Tourism for Development in 2017, the UNWTO launched the Travel Enjoy Respect campaign with "tips for a responsible traveller," based on the Global Code of Ethics, to specifically educate tourists.

First, *honor your hosts and our common heritage* encourages tourists to research local customs and traditions, learn a few words of the local language, appreciate what makes a destination unique, and respect the privacy of local people. Second, *protect our planet* reminds tourists to avoid purchasing products made using endangered plants or animals, respect protected areas, and reduce resource consumption. Third, *support the local economy* asks tourists to buy locally made products, pay a fair price, and hire local guides with in-depth knowledge of the place. Fourth, *be an informed traveler*

**Figure 11.4   The coastal waters off British Columbia and Washington State offer excellent opportunities to see whales, orca, dolphins, seals, sea lions, and more. Tour operators must follow strict guidelines about their interactions with these species, such as how close they can get for viewing.** *Source:* Barret Bailey

recommends tourists research operators and experiences to support those that will provide local benefits and take appropriate health and safety precautions. Finally, *be a respectful traveller* requests tourists observe the laws and regulations of places visited, respect human rights, protect children from exploitation, support community projects, and promote positive experiences.[34]

Codes of conduct have limitations in that the information outlined often takes the form of broad principles rather than specific policies. Consequently, the target audience of such codes may not have the necessary knowledge, or perhaps even the capacity, to carry out their recommendations. For example, tourists are encouraged to buy locally made products, but they may have little means of distinguishing between those that are locally made and those that are not. In addition, the adoption of codes is voluntary rather than mandated. There may be little means of monitoring practices to ensure that the tourists are adhering to the codes.[35]

In 2019, the UNWTO identified "rising awareness on sustainability" as its key consumer travel trend, particularly with regard to zero plastic and climate change.[36] With this awareness, tourists are increasingly looking for ways that they can be more sustainable (box 11.3). Tourists can voluntarily make many small changes now, such as traveling with a refillable water bottle (including those with purification systems) as well as with reusable shopping bags, toiletry containers, straws, and utensils to avoid single-use plastics. Some destinations are already starting to require these changes with bans on certain products. In 2017, Kenya banned plastic bags. Tourists are required to pack with reusable bags and dispose of plastic bags from items purchased at a departing or connecting airport prior to arrival at the destination. In 2019, the San Francisco (California) airport stopped selling bottled water—a reduction of approximately four million plastic bottles per year. Tourists can fill their own bottles in the terminal at a filling station.[37]

Other changes can include using mobile travel documents instead of printed, packing lighter, walking at a destination instead of driving, reusing linens, and using reef-safe sunscreen. Tourists are increasingly encouraged to think about their food consumption, choose à la carte restaurants over buffets, and order only what they can eat to avoid food waste. It is estimated that approximately 1.3 billion tons of food is wasted each year, but it can be difficult to determine accurate estimates of food waste in tourism coming from institutional sources like restaurants, hotel buffets, and event catering and also from tourists using vacation rentals.[38]

These are actions that most tourists can reasonably take, but there is still much more that can be done. To continue moving toward sustainable tourism development, tourists must play their part.

---

## Box 11.3. Experience: Picking up Trash on the Big Island of Hawaii

*As the world pays greater attention to sustainability, tourists are beginning to consider the impacts of their actions while traveling. A quick online search will yield a host of articles, guides, and lists on how to be a more sustainable traveler. During a geography field course on the Big Island of Hawaii, Rachel had the opportunity to put some of these practices into action. However, she decided she wanted to go beyond minimizing her own footprint to doing her part to improve the environmental quality of the places she visited.*

Traveling has always been one of my favorite hobbies, but I didn't realize how hard it was to travel sustainably until I started studying environmental science. I have learned that some of the best ways a person can lower their traveling footprint is to do simple things like dispose of waste properly, recycle when possible, refuse single-use plastics, pack fewer items, and use public transit. I had the opportunity to practice some of these things when I was on the Big Island of Hawaii for a geography field course. On a few of our hikes, I noticed that there was litter sprinkled along the edges of the trails, and I decided that there was still more I could do. I could do my part to leave the island better than I found it. I came up with the idea to tie a trash bag to my waist, and when I came across trash, I would pick it up, store it, and then dispose of it properly (figure 11.5).

Initially, I was the only student in my class who did this, which is not surprising. Picking up trash was not something that we came to Hawaii to do. There were a few students who thought my trash bag was for their own personal use, a quick and easy way to get rid of their trash after we ate somewhere or stopped at a store. I explained to them that the whole point of the trash bag was to pick up the litter that had already been left behind and potentially affecting the environment or wildlife. If the bag was full of our own trash, then it left less room to make an impact. On one particular day, we hiked from South Point to Green Sand Beach. This remote, southern end of the island is prone to strong and twisting currents that deposit plastics, floating trash, rope, and nylon fishing lines ashore. I was shocked at how much trash accumulated in my trash bag. This time, it wasn't just me picking things up but everyone in my class and even a few bystanders who saw what we were doing. After this day, there were others in my class who joined in and carried a trash bag with them throughout our trip, and I believe it left a lasting impression on everyone.

Even though Hawaii has banned single-use plastics, there were still bits and pieces of plastic that we would pick up. Everything we gathered was human-made waste. As I picked

**Figure 11.5 When Rachel noticed litter along nature trails in Hawaii, she decided to carry a bag with her to pick up trash, store it, and dispose of it properly.** *Source:* Rachel Franklin and Valentina Rombado

up things like six-pack can rings, rope, forks, spoons, and fishing nets, I would think about the animals that I could potentially save from becoming entangled by the objects or choking on them after the animals mistook it for food. I remember my professor telling me that after picking up trash I was taking part in "malama 'aina" as they say in Hawaii (to respect and care for the land). In Hawaiian culture, there is a spiritual belief that you can obtain or lose power and strength depending on your choices and actions, kind of like karma. The thought of "malama 'aina" made me feel connected to the island while I was there in a way that I didn't expect. This made me want to treat the island as best I could. I quickly learned that Hawaii is a very spiritual place. Local people feel very strongly about taking care of the island and believe that if you take care of it, the island will take care of you.

The nature that you can find in Hawaii and the different ecosystems that you can immerse yourself in is what makes the island so beautiful. It is a biodiversity hotspot filled with many plants and animals that only exist on the islands of Hawaii. Unfortunately, many of Hawaii's unique creatures are endangered due to human activity and invasive species. As travelers, it's important to do our part to not only consider the other people around you on your trip but also consider the native wildlife that could be negatively impacted by your choices. It was an unforgettable experience to be in Hawaii, see the waterfalls, swim with the sea turtles, and watch the sunrises and sunsets but also to learn about the culture and find ways to integrate it into my own daily life. I hope that others will choose to make positive impacts on their trips and to try and leave their places of travel better than they found it.

*—Rachel*

# Conclusion

The framework of sustainable development helps us bring together our discussions of the economic, social, and environmental effects of tourism. Sustainable tourism development requires stakeholders to consider these potential effects in the planning and development of destinations as well as ongoing management as destinations evolve and effects begin to be realized.

Despite the considerable, and growing, attention given to sustainable tourism development over the past several decades, the modern, global tourism industry is not sustainable economically, socially, or environmentally. Researchers are often critical of and pessimistic about this. Progress is admittedly slow, but there are signs of change as well. This can lead to further change. Sustainable tourism experiences can provide a powerful lesson for tourists about what is being done and what can be done to make positive contributions to places, at home and while traveling.

# Key Terms

- code of conduct
- environmental carrying capacity
- perceptual carrying capacity
- physical carrying capacity
- preferred sites

- social carrying capacity
- spatial zoning
- sustainable tourism development
- tourist area life cycle

# Notes

1. Jeffrey D. Sachs, *The Age of Sustainable Development* (New York: Columbia University Press, 2015), 1.

2. World Commission on Environment and Development, *Our Common Future: Report of the World Commission on Environment and Development* (Oxford: Oxford University, 1987), 41.

3. Sachs, *The Age of Sustainable Development*, 5–6.

4. United Nations, "United Nations Millennium Development Goals," accessed July 9, 2020, http://www.un.org/millenniumgoals/.

5. United Nations, "SDGs: Sustainable Development Knowledge Platform," accessed July 9, 2020, https://sustainabledevelopment.un.org/sdgs.

6. United Nations World Tourism Organization, "Sustainable Development," accessed April 3, 2020, https://www.unwto.org/sustainable-development.

7. Jörn W. Mundt, *Tourism and Sustainable Development: Reconsidering a Concept of Vague Policies* (Berlin: Erich Schmidt Verlag, 2011), 121–2.

8. United Nations World Tourism Organization, "Sustainable Development," emphasis added.

9. United Nations World Tourism Organization, "Tourism in the 2030 Agenda," accessed July 9, 2020, https://www.unwto.org/tourism-in-2030-agenda.

10. United Nations World Tourism Organization, "Tourism for SDGs," accessed July 9, 2020, http://tourism4sdgs.org.

11. Global Sustainable Tourism Council, "The International Body for Sustainable Tourism Certification," accessed July 10, 2020, https://www.gstcouncil.org.

12. R. W. Butler, "The Concept of a Tourist Area Cycle Evolution: Implications for Management of Resources," *Canadian Geographer* 24, no. 1 (1980): 5–12.

13. Richard Butler, "The Resort Cycle Two Decades On," in *Tourism in the Twenty-First Century: Lessons from Experience*, ed. Bill Faulkner, Gianna Moscardo, and Eric Laws (London: Continuum, 2000), 288.

14. Richard W. Butler, "Overtourism and the Tourism Area Life Cycle," in *Overtourism: Issues, Realities and Solutions*, eds. Rachel Dodds and Richard W. Butler (Berlin: De Gruyter, 2019), 78.

15. Patrick J. Holladay, "Destination Resilience and Sustainable Tourism Development," *Tourism Review International* 22 (2018): 253.

16. Holladay, "Destination Resilience," 256–8.

17. Stephen Williams, *Tourism Geography* (London: Routledge, 1998), 128.

18. Peter Rogers, Kazi F. Jalal, and John A. Boyd, *An Introduction to Sustainable Development* (London: Earthscan, 2008), 230.

19. Heather Mair, "Trust and Participatory Tourism Planning," in *Trust, Tourism Development and Planning*, ed. Robin Nunkoo and Stephen L. J. Smith (London: Routledge, 2015), 58.

20. Rachel Dodds and Richard W. Butler, "Conclusion," in *Overtourism: Issues, Realities and Solutions*, eds. Rachel Dodds and Richard W. Butler (Berlin: De Gruyter, 2019), 264.

21. Williams, *Tourism Geography*, 116.

22. Buter, "Overtourism and the Tourism Area Life Cycle," 82.

23. Andrew Holden, *Environment and Tourism*, 2nd ed. (London: Routledge, 2008), 188.

24. Megan Spurrell, "Visiting the Galápagos Is About to Get a Lot More Expensive," *Condé Nast Traveler*, September 30, 2019, accessed July 9, 2020, https://www.cntraveler.com/story/visiting-the-galapagos-is-about-to-get-a-lot-more-expensive.

25. Jon Henley, "Overtourism in Europe's Historic Cities Sparks Backlash," *The Guardian*, January 25, 2020, accessed July 9, 2020, https://www.theguardian.com/world/2020/jan/25/overtourism-in-europe-historic-cities-sparks-backlash.

26. Louis Cheslaw, "What to Know about Venice's Strict Tourism Rules," *Condé Nast Traveler*, July 30, 2019, accessed July 9, 2020, https://www.cntraveler.com/story/what-to-know-about-venices-strict-tourism-rules; Louis Cheslaw, "You Could Be Fined $450 for Sitting on Rome's Spanish Steps," *Condé Nast Traveler*, August 8, 2019, accessed July 9, 2020, https://www.cntraveler.com/story/you-could-be-fined-dollar450-for-sitting-on-romes-spanish-steps.

27. Mark Ellwood, "The Other Side of Venice's Overtourism Problem," *Condé Nast Traveler*, October 24, 2018, accessed April 27, 2020, https://www.cntraveler.com/story/the-other-side-of-venices-overtourism-problem.

28. Six Senses Group, "Eco Resort in Bali," accessed July 10, 2020, https://www.sixsenses.com/en/resorts/uluwatu-bali/sustainability.

29. Natural Habitat Adventures, "The World's First Zero Waste Adventure," accessed July 10, 2020, https://www.nathab.com/zero-waste-adventure-travel/.

30. Kisawa Sanctuary, "Luxury Mozambique Resort," accessed July 10, 2020, https://kisawasanctuary.com.

31. Juliana Shallcross, "The World's Biggest Hotel Chains Are Turning Their Attention to Food Waste," *Condé Nast Traveler*, November 6, 2019, accessed July 10, 2020, https://www.cntraveler.com/story/the-worlds-biggest-hotel-chains-are-turning-their-attention-to-food-waste.

32. Kaitlin Menza, "How Do Little Hotel Toiletry Bottles Get Filled?" *Condé Nast Traveler*, October 10, 2019, accessed July 10, 2020, https://www.cntraveler.com/story/how-do-tiny-hotel-toiletries-get-filled.

33. United Nations World Tourism Organization, "Global Code of Ethics for Tourism," December 21, 2001, accessed July 9, 2020, https://webunwto.s3.eu-west-1.amazonaws.com/imported_images/37802/gcetbrochureglobalcodeen.pdf.

34. United Nations World Tourism Organization, "Travel Enjoy Respect," accessed July 9, 2020, http://www.travelenjoyrespect.org; United Nations World Tourism Organization, "Tips for a Responsible Traveller," accessed July 9, 2020, https://trello.com/c/X67eQzsh/1-english.

35. Peter Mason, *Tourism Impacts, Planning and Management*, 3rd ed. (London: Routledge, 2016), 199.

36. United Nations World Tourism Organization, *International Tourism Highlights 2019 Edition* (2019), 5, accessed March 5, 2020, https://www.e-unwto.org/doi/pdf/10.18111/9789284421152.

37. Louis Cheslaw, "What to Know About the San Francisco (SFO) Water Bottle Ban," *Condé Nast Traveler*, August 5, 2019, accessed July 10, 2020, https://www.cntraveler.com/story/san-francisco-airport-sfo-plastic-water-bottle-ban.

38. University of Eastern Finland, "Food Waste in Tourism Is a Bigger Issue Than Previously Thought," *ScienceDaily*, November 1, 2019, accessed July 10, 2020, https://www.sciencedaily.com/releases/2019/11/191101100142.htm.

# Part IV

# TOURISM AND PLACE

Destinations are the places of tourism. Just the idea of them is enough to captivate our imagination and create a demand for our experience of them. We formulate an idea in our minds of what we think it will be like and then, if we can, we try to turn these daydreams into reality. Given this opportunity, there are many factors that will shape our trip—from our expectations to the ways we choose to experience the destination. Most tourists do not conceptualize this in geographic terms, but the framework of geography provides a powerful means of thinking about these factors.

Geography is described as the study of places. In the geography of tourism, we can use the concept of place as a tool to help us understand the ways in which people think about tourism destinations, the ways in which they interact with them, and how they represent them to others. In this final section, we will use place to explore tourism as a geographic phenomenon. Chapter 12 discusses how various representations—from literature to promotions—create ideas about places as well as the experience of those places. Chapter 13 examines the role of social media in changing the ways tourists think about and interact with places. Finally, chapter 14 considers the ways in which tourists experience the places they visit.

# Tourism and Representations of Place

Place is a way of understanding the world. It refers to the parts of the earth that have been given meaning. Our understanding of places to which we have never been is shaped by the ways they are represented through media. There are few parts of the world that we have not been exposed to in one form or another. It may be easy to take these representations as accurate portrayals of reality, especially visual representations such as photographs and videos. However, as vivid as these images may be, they are nonetheless partial and selective. The audience becomes a passive observer who sees only what someone else has chosen for them to see. Still, representations of place are recognized to be extraordinarily important in tourism. As put by tourism scholar Dean MacCannell, "Usually, the first contact a sightseer has with a sight is not the sight itself but with some representation thereof."[1]

In this chapter, we will examine **place representations**. This describes the ways places are summarized and portrayed to an audience that then creates ideas and images about those places. This has implications for our discussion of the geography of tourism, as these ideas and images factor into tourists' decisions to visit a place and shape their expectations for their experiences there. First, this chapter takes a look at the types of media through which places are represented to various audiences and their relationship to tourism. Then it considers some of the issues associated with promoting places for tourism. These representations are intended to communicate specific meanings about a place to shape ideas about that place and ultimately to influence the decision to visit that place. We will first discuss place representations and place promotions, and then we will look at some of the strategies used to convey meanings about places. Finally, the chapter concludes by examining some of the consequences of representing and promoting places in travel and tourism.

## Place Representations

People have long represented other places through written descriptions and visual illustrations. Many of these representations have no overt connection to tourism and are not explicitly intended to encourage visitation to the place depicted. Other representations come from tourism experiences or provide information for potential tourists. All of these sources have the potential to create distinct impressions of places in the minds of their audience, which factors into demand for travel as well as destination choice.

## POPULAR MEDIA

Literature (e.g., plays, poetry, prose) was one of the earliest representations of other places to popular audiences. Far-off and exotic tropical islands frequently played an integral role in literature, not only providing the setting but also shaping the events of the story. William Shakespeare's *The Tempest* (early seventeenth century) was written at a time in which reports were coming back from parts of the world that were being "discovered," and his story contributed to the mythology of these places. Although the specific location is unclear, this is less important than the idea of the place represented to audiences who would never have any direct experience with the tropical island environment. Later, as tourism was expanding, literature played a role in creating a demand for experiences in places depicted. Authors such as Washington Irving and James Fenimore Cooper helped popularize the Hudson River Valley in New York state. Stories such as Irving's "Rip Van Winkle" (1819) and Cooper's *Last of the Mohicans* (1826) described real places that readers might know or be able to experience for themselves.

Avid readers will argue that written descriptions constitute some of the most powerful conceptions of place because they work in concert with their imagination; however, representations in film and serialized shows reach widespread audiences and play a significant role in creating demand for places (box 12.1). Searches for "Singapore" on Google and travel booking sites spiked following the release of *Crazy Rich Asians* (2018), and the destination saw a corresponding increase in visitors from the United States.[2] The first episode of *Game of Thrones* (2011–19) featured the Azure Window on the Maltese island of Gozo (figure 12.1), which could be visited until the natural structure collapsed in 2017. Other popular filming locations include Dubrovnik, Croatia's Old Town (King's Landing) and Kirkjufell, Iceland (Arrowhead Mountain). This has become such an important representation that tourism promoters seek to capitalize on the publicity that films and tourism generate. Since the release of the first *Lord of the Rings* (2001) film, New Zealand has been known as "The Home of Middle-Earth" and continues to actively promote Lord of the Rings tours on the destination's official tourism website.[3] However, the increase in demand attributed to these representations has been cited as a factor in some destinations' overtourism problems.

## Box 12.1.  Experience: Backpacking Tourism and the Idea of Westeros

*Films and shows exert a powerful influence on our imagination. Some tourists seek out the specific places they have already seen on screen, while others are inspired to seek out experiences. The popular series* Game of Thrones *has fueled a desire to do both. Kyle describes how the idea of Westeros shaped his experiences on a backpacking trip in Ireland.*

During my junior year as a college student, I took a leap of anxiety-driven faith and signed up for a three-week study abroad experience to Bedonia, Italy. Our small group of students was tasked with bringing a digital media presence to a mountain town encapsulated by tradition. We juxtaposed a commercialized town (i.e., Rome) to understand the pros and cons of each, and how we could promote Bedonia to draw tourism to it. I kept an eye and an ear out for the special things that a town like Bedonia could offer: the stories beneath the cobblestone streets, the slower pace of daily life, and the quality of the lives people lived. The essence of humanity that creates a place is far more fascinating than the amount of dollars it can provide. I realized that tourism needs to be focused on an experience, rather than a photo album backlogged on our phones and an artificial list to check off.

When I returned home that summer, I reached out to one of my professors who is a frequent traveler. Amidst our conversations of what I liked and disliked about my first trip abroad, we started discussing a "what if" scenario of an experimental course that involved traditional work throughout a semester, and that ended with a trip abroad to live within the words we were reading. Immediately, I suggested a trip to Ireland, focused on the idea of place and how words can create place as well as distinguish the idea of place for someone who hasn't been there. In the spring of 2017, that is exactly what happened. Led by two highly talented faculty members, as well as a group of nine students, we traveled from New Jersey to Dublin, Ireland to backpack the Wicklow Way and experience the history of oral tradition and spoken word.

Now, if we're being honest, Ireland has always been number one on my list of countries to visit for multiple reasons. The biggest, admittedly, is the world-renowned book/TV series *Game of Thrones*. While the beautiful landscapes of places such as Ireland, Scotland, Croatia, and even Spain paint the scene for a historical fantasy story, there is something special about a country dripping in history and experiencing it "off the beaten path." When the trip was coming to fruition, I was ecstatic to walk through castles, gaze at the horizon overlooking a quarry, or even walk through sunshine-deprived forests. I went into that trip with every intention for us to see Castle Ward, the site where *Game of Thrones* filmed a majority of the Winterfell scenes, or even the Dark Hedges, the infamous beech tree forest where they filmed the King's Road scenes. I wanted to live through that feeling, and even though we saw castles in the distance and walked through forests, I received the same expectations in an unexpected way.

We backpacked the entire way throughout our trip; while we didn't do the entire Wicklow Way, we managed to do 82 miles over the course of a week. During one of our twelve-mile days, it was lightly sprinkling when the sun finally peeked its head through the blanket of clouds. About an hour into our walking, the initial chatter of the day had ceased completely and everyone was alone with their thoughts. When we finally got up to a good pace, whoever was controlling the weather decided it was time to release the floodgates. Torrential downpours bombarded us from all sides, a curtain of rain in every direction you looked. Ideally, if we were all home we'd run to the closest store, or to our cars or homes, and wait for the storms to cease. Yet here we all were, eleven strangers halfway across the world, plastered in polyurethane jackets and no help in sight. We were our help. We were our own encouragement. Maybe walking twelve miles straight with 50 pounds on your back soaking wet doesn't sound appealing. Yet there I was, following the rhythm of my feet in the mud with no seeable end in sight, and I felt truly alone with myself for the first time in my life.

After scraping the dirt from our boots and peeling off the layers upon layers of clothes like an American onion, we all regrouped for a well-deserved meal after necessary showers at our final hotel. Sharing plates like family, an outsider would believe we did this all of the time. Once dinner was over, a local Irish folk band set up in the foyer of this small family-run hotel. Seated in dining chairs, some on egg crates, some standing close enough to the bar to pour a pint of Guinness between choruses, there were people everywhere. Then there I was, seated against the window of this crowded unfamiliar place. To this day I've never felt more at home than listening to those old men play their songs, surrounded by people all experiencing the same thing at the same time: life.

While I may have never sat upon the Iron Throne, or scaled the walls of a castle, I don't believe I would have gotten the same experience if I didn't use *Game of Thrones* as my grounding point. Stories and experiences don't come from fantastic sites and groundbreaking moments. They come from slowing down and taking yourself out of the bubble you've given yourself, and seeing the world for what it is; for what it has to offer. Moments of clarity. Friendship. Pride. Understanding. Things don't always have to be beautiful or important to be worthwhile. Yet when you can find meaning in the simplest of things, that's when you know you've truly won.

*—Kyle*

**Figure 12.1    Before the natural bridge collapsed, Malta's Azure Window was a frequently visited *Game of Thrones* film location. *Source:* Velvet Nelson**

An unflattering representation of a place in film or shows can also create negative ideas about specific or generalized places. A particular theme involves tourists getting caught up in local conflicts (e.g., *No Escape* [2015], in which an American family faces a violent uprising in an unspecified Southeast Asian nation). In other examples, the stark portrayal of a place in a film might contrast with generally glorified representations of that place. For example, Paris is typically associated with romantic imagery of lovers walking down the historic boulevards or kissing on a bridge over the Seine. However, the film *Taken* (2009) shows a much darker side of the city—and a much scarier idea of traveling abroad—when young American tourists are kidnapped to be sold in the sex trade.

## TRAVEL MEDIA

Few written records have been preserved from the earliest eras of travel; however, starting with the Age of Exploration in the Elizabethan Era, Western explorers and adventurers kept logs and journals of their journeys, some of which were later published. The primary purpose of published travel journals was to convey information and descriptions about the new places being explored. One of the most well-known examples of this type of account is Charles Darwin's *The Voyage of the Beagle: Journal of Researches into the Natural History and Geology of the Countries Visited During the Voyage of H.M.S. Beagle Round the World* (1839). In this text, Darwin described the geography, geology, biology, and anthropology of the places that he visited, including Brazil, the Galápagos Islands, New Zealand, Madagascar, and St. Helena.

As travel and tourism continued to evolve, a new type of text also evolved. Travelogues became a popular genre of English-language literature at this time, particularly in England but also in the United States. Some of the first examples came from established authors, including the likes of Charles Dickens and Mark Twain. Such writers sought out new places to experience and were among the first tourists to visit these places. Their books were informative about other places as well as entertaining stories. They helped fulfill the readers' sense of adventure and satisfy their curiosity about places they might not have had the opportunity to visit themselves. Yet, these narratives were also extraordinarily influential in generating new attitudes toward travel. The next generations of tourists who traveled for pleasure also kept journals, some of which were published. There was less need for these writers to provide the same extent of detailed, descriptive information. Instead, they gave greater emphasis to their experience of place and provided advice for potential future tourists based on what they did.

By the late nineteenth century, magazines were publishing not only special articles by travel writers but also dedicated travel columns that provided advice to potential tourists. For example, the British women's magazine *Queen* was one of the first to make "The Tourist" a featured column. As travel was just starting to become more accessible to women, many were uncertain about what to expect from their first experience, especially in foreign countries. The column offered practical advice on travel arrangements, suitable accommodations, expected patterns of dress, and etiquette, among other topics. This was intended to give women the confidence to travel and the ability to experience new places with pleasure rather than fear or anxiety.[4]

The lines between travel literature and place promotion began to blur as early tourism industry stakeholders began to "sponsor" writers. Railroad or steamship companies would provide them with complimentary trips using their services, which the tourists would then write about. For example, in the preface to the travel narrative *Back to Sunny Seas* (1905), Frank Bullen wrote:

> But I want to make it perfectly clear that I was the guest of the great Royal Mail Steam Packet Company, whose hospitality to me was more generous and farther-reaching than I could ever have dreamed of receiving. Yet I would like to make it clear too, if possible, that I have subdued my natural bias in favour of the Company, so that I have written only what I believe to be literally and exactly true.[5]

These companies were interested in creating demand for their services by creating a demand for experiences in the places they served.

These trends continued into the twentieth century. As the modern tourism industry was taking off after World War II, the travel industry became a leading source of advertising revenue for newspapers. In addition, tourism stakeholders began to offer paid trips to journalists to write about places or experiences in newspapers and magazines. While this journalistic practice would be considered unethical under other circumstances, it has long been accepted for travel. The rationale is that journalists and/or publications would not be able to afford to write about travel and places without the subsidies. Yet, unlike Bullen, American travel writers today are not required to disclose that tourism stakeholders paid for their travel.[6]

Travel-themed shows further blur the boundaries between popular media, travel media, and place promotions. Early shows highlighted different aspects of destinations and experiences in specific regions or around the world for viewers who might imagine themselves visiting those places. In a variation of this, *The Zimmern List* (2017–18) follows the former *Bizarre Foods* host Andrew Zimmern to explore places around the theme of food. However, travel-themed programming, such as *Expedition Unknown* (2015–present), has increasingly focused on the entertainment of extreme travel experiences that viewers have no ability to replicate.

## TRAVEL GUIDEBOOKS

With the development of the modern tourism industry, publishing companies began to produce explicit guidebooks for tourists. At the forefront of this industry, Thomas Cook put together a guidebook for his expeditions to describe the places that would be encountered and the sights seen during the course of the journey. On the other side of the Atlantic, Gideon Minor Davison has been credited with producing the first American guidebook. It described a specific route—termed the "fashionable tour"—that Davison intended readers to follow. One of the unique characteristics of this new book, however, was that it was small and cheaply printed. It was intended to be portable for the duration of the trip and disposable after the trip was completed.[7] As more tourists sought independent tourism experiences all over the world, guidebooks became a means of helping them confidently make their own travel decisions, prepare for their experiences, and navigate the destination efficiently.

Guidebooks long served, and to some extent continue to serve, as a pre-trip resource that shapes tourists' perceptions of places, their expectations for the destination, decisions about where to go, and ultimately their satisfaction with the experience.[8] In contrast with other forms of travel media, readers expect guidebooks to be comprehensive, practical, and objective. However, guidebooks are not a straightforward depiction of peoples and places but partial and selective representations. Guidebooks are intended to make places accessible to a diverse set of readers (i.e., different ethnic backgrounds, demographics, types of tourists). They reduce the complexity of places, and present only certain aspects of them, to avoid confusing potential tourists by presenting them with too much information. Authors make the decisions about which sites to include, which attractions are worthy of seeing and experiencing. This is partially a reflection of preexisting patterns in tourism, where representations reinforce the reputation and popularity of known attractions. It is also a reflection of the authors' perspectives, yet guidebooks typically provide little insight into who these authors are.[9]

Guidebooks have an incredible power to positively or negatively represent places. They can encourage visits to a place, identify new places, or recreate ideas about places that would allow them to be seen by potential tourists in a new light. Conversely, they can actively discourage visits or simply ignore places. With this type of passive representation, places may remain unknown, or potential tourists will infer that they are uninteresting or unattractive.[10] This not only shapes tourists' experiences but possibly even destination development. The overtourism crisis has added a layer of complexity to the representation of destinations. Authors must consider the potential consequences of continuing to represent places that are suffering from overcrowding and growing resident/visitor dissatisfaction as well as the potential outcomes of representing places that are less known and perhaps less equipped to handle a significant increase in tourists.

Companies such as Baedeker's, Fodor's, Frommer's, Lonely Planet, and Rough Guides are some well-known brands that produce guidebooks covering most destinations, at least at the regional scale. The nature of guidebooks is changing with technology. Potential tourists can browse information on guidebook company websites (e.g., Lonely Planet's Jordan travel page). They can also download the e-text version of guidebooks to their mobile devices as a convenient reference to be used throughout the trip. Yet, many travelers are now supplementing the guidebook with, or bypassing it in favor of, social media sites. These sites provide the most up-to-date information available and advice from "average" tourists like themselves as opposed to a professional (and possibly sponsored) travel writer.

# Place Promotion

Some representations are deliberately created with specific meanings to "sell" a place to external audiences. Tourism is a highly competitive global industry; therefore, the success of tourism destinations depends on the creation and promotion of clear and distinctive ideas about places. **Place promotion** is the deliberate use of marketing tools to communicate specific and selective ideas and images about a place to a target audience for the purpose of shaping perceptions of that place and ultimately influencing decisions. Because place promotion draws selectively upon the real nature of places and presents only those elements that will appeal to the target market segment, there may be many different representations of a destination. Each representation will highlight a different aspect of the destination, draw upon a different theme, and utilize different images to attract specific types of tourists.

Not all destinations use place promotion in the same way. Many destinations around the world are already widely represented in various media, and there is a preexisting suppressed demand (i.e., many people already believe they want to visit these places if/ when they have the opportunity). It may be more important that these destinations promote specific regions or places. This can help provide more detailed information about the unique resources and experiences available in different places and even to distribute tourists across the destination. However, for smaller and emerging destinations, place promotion is vital in raising awareness about the destination and what it has to offer.

## Box 12.2   Case Study: Place Branding in Slovenia

Brands are typically associated with consumer goods, but the concept has been applied to places as well. As such, "brand" is used as a metaphor for the ways in which places compete for a variety of purposes in the modern, global world.[a] The idea of place branding has been much debated. Some scholars were concerned that place branding would lead to the commodification of places, much like the commodification of culture discussed in chapter 9. Others dismissed the idea because there are significantly more challenges to branding a place than branding a product. Places are complex, and such a brand would have to encompass a diverse set of products and services. Moreover, there are countless public and private stakeholders who would have to be involved in the process of producing, promoting, and supporting the brand.[b] Nonetheless, scholars have identified place branding—the creation of a brand identity and communication of a brand image—as a powerful tool in place promotion.[c]

The European country of Slovenia has considerable tourism resources (map 12.1); however, it suffered from a weak image and low levels of awareness among international

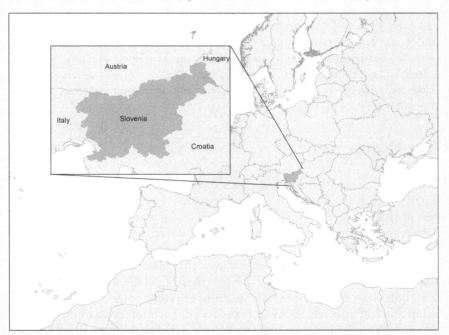

Map 12.1.  Slovenia. Due to a low level of awareness among international tourist markets, the Slovenian Tourist Board has worked to create and communicate a clear and consistent place brand. *Source:* Gang Gong

**Figure 12.2   Slovenia's Lake Bled, surrounded by the snow-capped mountains of the Julian Alps, is one of the most popular tourism destinations in the country. Such iconic images are often used in tourism promotions.** *Source:* Tom Nelson

tourist markets.[d] Initially, the Slovenian Tourist Board focused on promoting the destination as opposed to developing a clear brand. They started with slogan formation and logo design, but encountered various problems. The slogan "On the Sunny Side of the Alps" was intended to capitalize on both the country's physical resources for tourism—particularly attractive destinations in the Julian Alps like Lake Bled (figure 12.2)—and the preexisting positive tourism imagery associated with the larger Alpine region. However, Italy objected to this slogan and the perceived implication that, as Slovenia's neighbor, it was not physically and/or metaphorically "sunny." Consequently, Slovenia was forced to abandon the slogan. Another slogan, "Slovenia Invigorates," was poorly understood. In the 1990s and 2000s, the destination experimented with several different slogans and logos, which led to confusion and frustration.[e]

In the late 2000s, Slovenia undertook a new, more systematic brand-building effort. Unlike previous efforts that focused on the visual elements of tourism promotion (slogan and logo), this project was intended to be more holistic and reflective of the country's qualities and values. It was based on the perspectives of internal stakeholders from all elements of Slovenia's political, economic, and social spheres.[f] This process resulted in the formation of the "**I feel Slove**nia" brand. The corresponding "brand book" described the brand and offers a set of guidelines for various tourism stakeholders to ensure that the new brand was communicated consistently.

According to the brand book, the core of the "**I feel Slove**nia" brand is characterized by the following interrelated concepts: Slovenian green, pleasant excitement, and elemental.

> In Slovenia green is more than just a colour; it is "**Slovenian green**," express-
> ing the balance between the calm of nature and the tenacity of Slovenians…It
> symbolises a balance of lifestyle that joins the pleasant excitement with which we
> pursue personal desires with the common vision to move forward with nature.
> Slovenian green also describes our focus on the elemental, on what we feel under
> our hands. And finally, Slovenian green talks about the balance of all senses with
> which we experience Slovenia. We never remember Slovenia only through images.
> A memory of Slovenia combines the smell of a forest, a babbling brook, a surpris-
> ing taste of water, and the softness of wood. We feel Slovenia.[g]

The brand book recommends the use of green tones to characterize Slovenia. Using the small size of the country to its advantage, the brand promises that visitors will have the opportunity to truly experience the destination. Finally, the tremendous physical and cultural diversity of the country is also seen as an advantage, where visitors can have many different experiences in the course of one trip.

The process of place branding allows stakeholders to create a positive, recognizable, and unique identity that will distinguish the destination from others. Perhaps more importantly, this process helps stakeholders to develop a coherent brand identity that will help ensure they are promoting clear and consistent ideas about the place.[h]

*Discussion topic*: Create a place brand for the place in which you live. What are the key elements of this brand?

*Tourism online*: Slovenian Tourist Board, "The Official Travel Guide to Slovenia," https://www.slovenia.info/en

---

[a] Simon Anholt, *Places: Identity, Image and Reputation* (Houndmills: Palgrave Macmillan, 2010), 1.

[b] Maja Konecnik and Frank Go, "Tourism Destination Brand Identity: The Case of Slovenia," *Brand Management* 15, no. 3 (2008): 179.

[c] Simon Hudson and J. R. Brent Ritchie, "Branding a Memorable Destination Experience. The Case of "Brand Canada"," *International Journal of Tourism Research* 11, no. 2 (2009):

[d] Maja Konečnik, "Slovenia: New Challenges in Enhancing the Value of the Tourism Destination Brand," in *Tourism in the New Europe: The Challenges and Opportunities of EU Enlargement*, eds. Derek Hall, Melanie Smith, and Barbara Marciszweska (Oxfordshire: CABI, 2006): 86.

[e] Velvet Nelson, "Representations of a Destination Brand in Online Tourism Information Sources: The Case of Slovenia," *Tourism, Culture & Communication* 14 (2014): 44.

[f] Maja Konečnik, "Developing Brand Identity for Slovenia with Opinion Leaders," *Baltic Journal of Management*, 7, no. 2 (2012): 132.

[g] Pristop, *The Brand of Slovenia* (Ljubljana: Ministry of the Economy, 2007): 8.

[h] Nelson, "Representations of a Destination Brand," 43.

Poorly known destinations, often new or remote destinations, are perhaps the easiest to promote. Potential tourists have few ideas, positive or negative, about these places. Stakeholders have the opportunity to create and promote a desired image to shape potential tourists' ideas about that place. However, it can be very difficult and time consuming to change people's minds about a place for which ideas already exist.[11] A poor reputation may be based on serious past or present issues or events in the country or region of the country, including conflicts, political upheaval, acts of terrorism, human rights violations and/or atrocities, problems associated with the drug trade, crimes against tourists, disease outbreaks, and so on. Likewise, a poor reputation may be based on the destination's tourism industry, such as a poorly developed infrastructure, an unfriendly or hostile local population, and an overdevelopment of tourism.

Even places that have experienced positive changes may continue to receive less attention because of a poor reputation plagued by persistent stereotypes.

Some destinations with a poor reputation attempt to ignore the issue entirely in the creation of a new identity. For example, Detroit, Michigan, arguably has the worst reputation of any city in the United States based on reports of financial crisis, corruption, a decaying infrastructure, high crime rates, and more. However, the Detroit Metro Convention & Visitors Bureau's website resembles countless other destination websites with an emphasis on local food and drink (e.g., craft beer), place-specific attractions (e.g., Motown Museum), and culture (e.g., public art) without addressing concerns potential visitors might have.[12] Others choose to address issues head-on. In the case of Houston, Texas, media representations and promotions confirm the negative stereotypes about the city. Then they challenge those stereotypes and present readers with a different, but realistic, view of the city.[13]

Destinations perceived to be similar to others present a challenge for place promotion. The Caribbean is one such example. People often see the islands of the region as a collective. This becomes a problem when potential tourists think one island is the same as another. This not only affects the choice of specific destination but may also serve to discourage these tourists from returning and visiting another island because they think they have already had the "Caribbean experience." Consequently, each island tries to create and promote a distinctive place identity that plays up the resources that make them unique. St. Lucia capitalizes on its iconic landscape, the Twin Pitons. These volcanic spires have UNESCO World Heritage status. Trinidad is known for hosting the biggest annual party in the region: its version of Carnival.

Destinations at all geographic scales around the world have been involved in place promotion. Tourism boards or convention and visitors' bureaus (e.g., Las Vegas Convention and Visitors Authority) may be responsible for a local destination's image. Large destinations may have state- or regional-level agencies (e.g., Tourism Western Australia), while most countries now have some type of national tourism organization or association (e.g., Tourism Authority of Thailand). These organizations typically concentrate on creating a national tourism identity that can be promoted to an external or foreign audience, although there may be efforts to promote domestic tourism as well. Small and/or relatively similar destinations may work cooperatively through regional (i.e., supranational) tourism organizations to promote a specific destination region (e.g., Caribbean Tourism Organization, open to any country with a Caribbean coast). The resources available for place promotion vary widely based on the size of the destination, level of overall economic development, and the extent to which tourism development is a priority.

# Promotional Strategies

Place promotion allows destinations to create and communicate a clear, positive, recognizable, and distinctive place identity to differentiate themselves from others and maintain competitiveness. Yet, this task has become increasingly difficult. Destinations are no longer competing only with similar places in their region but with places around the world that claim the same kinds of attractions, such as beautiful landscapes or unique cultures.

Promotional strategies are intended to raise awareness about a place. They represent the characteristics of a place in simplified form as a concise means of identifying places that external audiences can easily recognize and remember. Destination logos, slogans, color schemes, and so on have long been seen as the signature elements of place promotion.[14] For example, the Caribbean island of Dominica has long been known as "the nature island" with a green logo featuring a face imposed on a mountain and waterfall landscape. While such tools might be easily dismissed as superficial marketing ploys, they can be significant nonetheless. When the government of Dominica entered into an agreement with Venezuela to build an oil refinery on the island, a local environmental organization and the Dominica Hotel and Tourism Association perceived the proposed project as a dual threat: the threat of environmental degradation that would destroy the quality and aesthetic appearance of the nature island and the threat that the *idea* of an oil refinery would have on the concept of Dominica as the "nature island."[15]

Place promotion is highly visual. Images capture the viewer's attention and create an impression of a place in his/her mind. This has long played a key role in potential tourists' decision-making processes.[16] Early tourism imagery included illustrations and black-and-white photographs; in today's digital media, it is dominated by eye-catching photographs and video files. These images depict characteristics of the place, including attractive landscape vistas and iconic scenes, as well as tourists participating in activities and enjoying themselves there—such as relaxing on the beach, hiking in the forest, or dining at sunset.

---

## Box 12.3.  In-Depth: Experiential Marketing

Destination stakeholders continuously look for innovative techniques to promote places. Traditional place promotion has primarily relied on visual imagery. Yet, tourism is an experiential product that involves all of the senses. Some destinations have experimented with various techniques to better incorporate these senses in promotions to communicate the experience of, and the feelings associated with, the consumption of place to potential tourists. **Experiential marketing** is intended to more fully engage potential tourists in the destination search. As it communicates the characteristics of a place, it appeals to readers' imagination,[a] inviting them to envision what their experience of that place would be like.

Rather than simply informing readers of attractive destination attributes, experiential marketing goes a step further by prompting readers to imagine they are actively having the experience described. Sights, scents, sounds, tastes, and touch all play a role in stimulating the imagination to create an overall feeling of the destination and an impression of the state of mind the visitor would have with such an experience. Research shows that the use of multiple senses in promotions contributes to clearer ideas about and generates interest in the place. It can even influence consumers' decision-making processes.[b] Humans experience the world through their senses, which are linked to memories and can stimulate emotion.[c] Thus, potential tourists become more emotionally invested in the idea of the experience and have a stronger desire to visit the place. This helps reduce the perceived risk involved in the purchase decision.

The sense of sight has long been the most important sense in tourism promotions. In the era of modern technology, potential tourists are exposed to many vivid visual images. However, written descriptions can also try to employ the use of sight to try to engage the reader. In one technique, a narrator assumes the role of travel guide and points out details to the reader, as if he or she were there, such as the variations of brightly colored fruits at a tropical market. To further engage the reader, sight can be used in combination with other senses. Sounds can imply particular types of experiences. If a narrator describes the array of sounds in an urban environment, it can prompt the reader to feel the activity and excitement of such a place, just as the soft sounds of nature can allow the reader to feel the stillness and peace.

Scents trigger memories and the emotions attached to those memories. Therefore, they can be used to create good feelings and even to reduce stress.[d] The narrator invites the reader to inhale the scent of fresh-baked bread or the aroma of fresh-brewed coffee. This has the potential to tap into the reader's memories, which can create pleasant feelings and associations. Moreover, it may prompt the reader to unconsciously inhale deeply, which has a calming effect. Taste is closely related to smell. As food and beverage experiences become a more important part of tourism, more destinations will promote the taste of place. In such cases, the narrator does not just identify key ingredients and distinctive dishes but describes the flavors, the sweetness, the crunchiness, and other characteristics of these products. Finally, touch is used to stimulate the imagination. The narrator encourages the reader to imagine what it is like to feel powdery sand underneath his or her toes or the cool breeze brushing across his or her skin.

Combined, all of the senses can be brought together in a destination's promotions to illustrate the feelings, emotions, and states of mind the reader could have if he or she were to visit that place.[e] If the reader becomes emotionally invested in this imagined experience, it will stimulate a demand for the actual experience. As a result, he or she will be likely to choose that destination over all others.

*Discussion topic*: Pick a destination and browse the official tourism website. Discuss the ways in which the website content appeals to each of the five senses. What content resonates with you the most?

---

[a] Simon Hudson and J. R. Brent Ritchie, "Branding a Memorable Destination Experience. The Case of 'Brand Canada'," *International Journal of Tourism Research* 11 (2009): 218.

[b] Dora Agapito, Patrícia Oom do Valle, and Júlio da Costa Mendes, "Sensory Marketing and Tourist Experiences," *Spatial and Organizational Dynamics* 10 (2012): 10.

[c] Annica Isacsson, Leena Alakoski, and Asta Bäck, "Using Multiple Senses in Tourism Marketing: The Helsinki Expert, Eckerö Line and Linnanmäki Amusement Park Cases," *Turismos: An International Multidisciplinary Journal of Tourism* 4, no. 3 (2009): 171.

[d] Isacsson, Alakoski, and Bäck, "Using Multiple Senses in Tourism Marketing," 171.

[e] Velvet Nelson, "Experiential Branding of Grenada's Spice Island Brand," in *Travel, Tourism, and Identity: Culture & Civilization, Volume 7*, ed. Gabriel Ricci (New Brunswick, NJ: Transaction Publishers), 123.

There are some consistent messages conveyed in place promotion as well as subtler messages. Themes appeal to touristic motivations such as fun and relaxation, excitement and adventure, tradition and timelessness, fantasy and romance, pristine and unspoiled, or exotic and different. A common tourism representation features an empty natural landscape like a quiet beach (figure 12.3) or an undisturbed forest.

**Figure 12.3  A common tourism representation features an empty natural land-scape like this quiet and secluded beach on the Caribbean island of Tobago.**
*Source:* Velvet Nelson

This emphasizes the naturalness and authenticity of the destination. It is targeted at potential tourists from crowded urban areas with a fast pace of life. Clearly, this plays upon the tourist inversions discussed in chapter 2 in terms of creating a sense of contrast with those places and activities that make up tourists' daily lives. Moreover, such representations invite potential tourists to imagine themselves in that place. This helps create a demand for the imagined experience and encourages tourists to visit that place for the purpose of turning fantasy into reality.

In 2019, the UNWTO identified "rising awareness on sustainability" as a key consumer travel trend.[17] A growing segment of tourism stakeholders are responding to this awareness not only through their actions (see chapter 11) but also in terms of their messages to potential consumers. Such messages may be used to communicate sustainable practices, encourage more widespread sustainable behavior among tourists, or specifically target a sustainably inclined tourist market that may lead to fewer negative effects.[18] Promoting sustainability is increasingly seen as important for maintaining competitiveness; however, consumers may be wary of "greenwashing." Preliminary studies on sustainability marketing in tourism have shown that textual messages are less effective. As with wider promotional strategies, visual imagery gains greater attention.[19] This is a relatively new area of tourism research, and more investigation of effective sustainability messages in tourism promotions is needed.[20]

# Promotional Media

Early tourism stakeholders relied on travelers' written accounts and word-of-mouth to promote both places and the services that would allow people to get to those places. Throughout much of the nineteenth century, rail companies in Britain did relatively little to advertise their services or the places they served. However, their American counterparts more quickly realized the value of generating tourism for the purpose of creating a steady market for the places they served. These companies, and later the British ones, produced abundant information and advertised in newspapers and magazines.

These patterns were perpetuated in the twentieth century. Travel service companies, also including airlines by this time, and national/regional tourism organizations continued to produce advertisements, pamphlets, brochures, and magazines to highlight the specific attractions of the destinations (figure 12.4). These materials could be distributed to potential tourists by mail or through travel agencies. In addition, stakeholders continued to adapt to new forms of media by using television advertisements as well. Television advertising is occasionally still used. For example, Tourism Australia aired a Crocodile Dundee-themed commercial featuring actor Chris Hemsworth during the 2018 Super Bowl.

With the rise of information technologies, the Internet emerged as the most important medium for place promotion. People learned about destinations, booked their travel arrangements, and formed expectations for their experiences via the Internet. The destination website, typically produced by national, regional, or local tourism organizations, served to raise awareness about the destination, provide contextual and logistical information, and create a demand for tourism to that place.

Websites were considered an improvement over print media in place promotion. They were more flexible in that they had the ability to provide a greater quantity of information. This information could also be customized for the market. For example, stakeholders could provide one representation of the destination for an American market when American English was selected as the language and a different representation for a Chinese market when Mandarin was selected. They could also provide information based on tourism product with different sections for ecotourism, cultural tourism, food and beverage tourism, and so on. Websites also offered a greater quantity and variety of media than was possible in printed materials, including more images as well as sound and video files. Social media has brought further changes in the way tourism stakeholders, as well as tourists themselves, represent places; however, this will be discussed in chapter 13.

# Place Demarketing

As places increasingly competed for tourists, place promotion became an important means of establishing and maintaining market position. Given this tradition, the idea of place demarketing may seem counterintuitive. The term demarketing was coined in the early 1970s and generally describes marketing strategies intended to manage

**Figure 12.4** New York's Bureau of State Publicity created advertisements, such as this one for the Catskill Mountains, to encourage some of the 15 million tourists attending the 1939 World's Fair in New York City to visit other destinations in the state during their trip. *Source:* New York State Archives. New York (State). Bureau of State Publicity. Advertising portfolio of state tourism promotions during 1939 World's Fair, 1939. Series A3324-78. Box 1, Volume 1.

excessive demand. **Demarketing** has been used in specific circumstances in tourism for many years and recently has gotten more attention as a means of trying to manage overtourism and reduce the negative effects of tourism.[21]

Applied to places, general demarketing refers to strategies to reduce demand for the experience of a place. Sites that are particularly vulnerable to tourist consumption (e.g., fragile ecological and archeological sites) frequently use these strategies to ensure that the carrying capacity is not exceeded. However, a range of destinations are now employing such strategies in an effort to maintain a quality environment and experience for both visitors and residents. Most destinations use a passive approach, which can be as simple as not actively seeking to raise awareness among new market segments.[22] In response to rapidly increasing visitor numbers, tourism officials for Amsterdam (the Netherlands) stopped promoting tourism to the city.[23] In other cases, destinations may stop promotional efforts during the high tourist season, while expanding promotions that encourage people to visit during the low season.

An active approach to general demarketing involves specifically asking visitors not to come. This is most commonly used in crises. For example, during the COVID-19 pandemic, the President and CEO of the Hawai'i Visitors and Convention Bureau wrote an open letter to the media:

> At this current juncture, amidst the uncertainty ushered forth by COVID-19, **we humbly ask that you and/or your publication(s) refrain from publishing any stories about Hawai'i that might encourage people to travel to the islands**. It is our responsibility to ensure the safety of visitors and residents alike, and therefore request that anything written about Hawai'i strongly discourages travelers from visiting Hawai'i until otherwise directed by our state officials.[24]

Selective demarketing refers to strategies to reduce demand for the experience of a place from certain market segments while promoting the destination to others. Destinations are likely to use these strategies when the negative effects of tourism are attributed to a type or group of tourists, and when stakeholders are concerned those tourists are a threat to the destination's reputation.[25] Consider the case of Mallorca, discussed in box 3.1. To reduce the problems associated with 5S tourism and change the destination's reputation, the Mallorca Tourism Foundation announced a plan in early 2020 to provide €750,000 in grants to promote "quality" tourism projects related to cultural and heritage tourism, food and beverage tourism, sports tourism, and MICE tourism—but not sun, sea, and sand.[26]

Demarketing can be a sensitive issue. Stakeholders in many destinations may feel that they cannot afford to reduce tourist numbers. To avoid angering these stakeholders who depend on tourism financially, demarketing may not be a formal policy. Yet, for extremely popular destinations that have experienced a backlash against overtourism, demand may be too strong for demarketing to be effective. Ultimately, destinations need to find a balance that will allow them to manage demand without destroying it altogether.[27]

# Consequences of Representations

Representations of place can be extraordinarily powerful in shaping ideas of and experiences in places; however, such representations need to be viewed critically. One of the most prominent scholars on the geography of place, Edward Relph, criticized place representations and particularly place promotion. He argued that these representations create superficial ideas of places, and their people, based on simplified, even exaggerated concepts that may be readily accepted by an external audience. These representations have little to do with the meanings that the place has for the people who live there.[28]

Place promotion must maintain a balance between tapping into generalized ideas of place that appeal to audiences and creating a sense of distinction among other destinations. Because destinations appeal to the same tourist motivations as others, promotions from places around the world draw upon the same themes. These places then run the risk of becoming "placeless." **Placelessness** is described as a loss of identity, in which one place looks and feels like other places, often as a result of the superficial, stereotypical images circulated by the media.[29] As tourism destinations, these places have the same experiences to offer. For instance, the idea of a tropical island paradise is important in tourism representations, but the stereotypical imagery could portray places in many different parts of the world. A destination needs to be able to not only attract potential tourists' interest with these general themes but also provide them with a reason to choose it over other destinations that may appeal to the same motivations or desires.

Scholars have argued that the early travel writers discussed above cannot be disconnected from empire. These writers were familiar with colonial discourses, and they reproduced them in their travel narratives. This refers to the ways people thought and talked about colonies and colonial peoples. For example, travel writers used the colonial rhetoric of conquest and achievement as they described overcoming the challenges of traveling in foreign places.[30] Places and peoples were viewed as the "other," and they were compared to those with which the travelers were familiar. This helped them to try to make sense of what they encountered, but it was nonetheless framed within preexisting ideas of what was right and superior.

Critics argue that travel writing today has changed little from these early narratives (see, for example, the short film *Bani Amor: Decolonizing Travel Culture*).[31] Travel writers continue to use authoritative voices to describe the other places and peoples, but it is based on their often-limited experiences as well as their own background and perspectives. From a critical perspective, this is predicated on the assumption that those peoples are unable to represent themselves. Indeed, for many destinations, the only representations audiences around the world receive come from outsiders (e.g., tourists or marketers).

The ethnicity, culture, and/or daily life one comes from are viewed as the norm, while everything else is the "other." Narratives of othering use descriptive words to highlight differences and emotional words to demonstrate surprise, confusion, or delight. These narratives are used to show readers that they had an out-of-the-ordinary experience and, accordingly, to gain social status from having had such experiences.[32] However, in the modern world, there are fewer opportunities for truly extraordinary experiences. Thus, even mundane aspects of life in that place can be romanticized and made exotic by the visitor. For example, local people on the Caribbean island of Grenada take buses every day for routine purposes, but for foreign tourists the brightly painted buses traveling winding roads at breakneck speed using Morse code horn signals can constitute an adventure and a story to be told.

Authenticity is measured by the extent of difference. Tourists may consider those places that have been exposed to global culture not "authentic." This not only diminishes the value of that place, its people, and its culture, but it also leads to a search for places further "off the beaten path." This search for the new and different is a process of discovery (and conquest) compared to that of earlier generations of explorers. However, tourists must consider what effect they have on the "authenticity" of such places. They may be responsible for bringing global culture to that place, even though they specifically came there because of its absence, or they may contribute to the process of museumization (chapter 9) as local people try to maintain tourist interest in their "traditional" culture.

Finally, representations of places through travel have been relatively narrow due to a general lack of diversity in the media. Travel personalities have typically been white, heterosexual males. Thus, the media continues to reproduce limited perspectives, which influences others' ideas about places and their peoples. In addition, it perpetuates ideas about barriers to travel for other individuals. The tools of social media are helping to create a shift in this norm, which will be discussed in the next chapter.

# Conclusion

Place is one of the core concepts in geography, and it is equally important in the geography of tourism. Tourism is an inherently place-based geographic phenomenon. It is important to consider the representations of places—from those in popular media to explicit place promotions—that shape ideas about places. This affects all parts of the tourism process, including our decisions about where to go, the experiences we have in those places, and even the way we represent those places to others. As we look to more responsible patterns of tourism, it is worth critically considering these issues.

# Key Terms

- experiential marketing
- demarketing
- placelessness
- place promotion
- place representation

# Notes

1. Dean MacCannell, *The Tourist: A New Theory of the Leisure Class* (New York: Schocken Books, 1976; reprinted with foreword by Lucy R. Lippard; Berkeley: University of California Press, 1999), 110. Citations refer to the California edition.

2. Eric Moya, "For Many Destinations, an Appearance in a Beloved Movie or TV Series can be an Enduring Enticement for Visitors," *Travel Weekly*, accessed June 2, 2020, https://www.travelweekly.com/Asia-Travel/Call-to-Action-Film-tourism.

3. Tourism New Zealand, "Lord of the Rings Trilogy," accessed June 2, 2020, https://www.newzealand.com/int/the-lord-of-the-rings-trilogy/.

4. Jill Steward, " 'How and Where to Go': The Role of Travel Journalism in Britain and the Evolution of Foreign Travel, 1840–1914," in *Histories of Tourism: Representation, Identity, and Conflict*, ed. John Walton (Clevedon: Channel View Publications, 2005), 44–5.

5. Frank T. Bullen, *Back to Sunny Seas* (London: Smith, Elder & Co., 1905), vii.

6. Elizabeth Becker, *Overbooked: The Exploding Business of Travel and Tourism* (New York: Simon & Schuster Paperbacks, 2013), 26–27.

7. Richard H. Gassan, *The Birth of American Tourism: New York, the Hudson Valley, and American Culture, 1790–1830* (Amherst: University of Massachusetts Press, 2008), 73–5.

8. Chak Keung Simon Wong and Fung Ching Gladys Liu, "A Study of Pre-Trip Use of Travel Guidebooks by Leisure Travelers," *Tourism Management* 32 (2011): 618.

9. Velvet Nelson, "The Construction of Slovenia as a European Tourism Destination in Guidebooks," *Geoforum*, 43 (2012): 1101.

10. Malin Zillinger, "The Importance of Guidebooks for the Choice of Tourist Sites: A Study of German Tourists in Sweden," *Scandinavian Journal of Tourism and Hospitality* 6, no. 3 (2006): 231–2.

11. Nigel Morgan, Annette Pritchard, and Roger Pride, "Tourism Places, Brands, and Reputation Management," in *Destination Brands: Managing Place Reputation*, 3rd ed., ed. Nigel Morgan, Annette Pritchard, and Roger Pride (Florence, KY: Routledge, 2011), 1.

12. Detroit Metro Convention & Visitors Bureau, "Visit Detroit," accessed June 3, 2020, https://visitdetroit.com.

13. Velvet Nelson, "Place Reputation: Representing Houston, Texas as a Creative Destination through Culinary Culture," *Tourism Geographies* 17, no. 2 (2015): 199.

14. Martin Boisen, Kees Terlouw, Peter Groote, and Oscar Couwenberg, "Reframing Place Promotion, Place Marketing, and Place Branding—Moving Beyond Conceptual Confusion," *Cities*, 80 (2018): 5.

15. Velvet Nelson, " "R.I.P. Nature Island": The Threat of a Proposed Oil Refinery on Dominica's Identity," *Social & Cultural Geography* 11, no. 8 (2010): 904.

16. Kelly J. MacKay and Daniel R. Fesenmaier, "Pictorial Element of Destination in Image Formation," *Annals of Tourism Research* 24, no. 3 (1997): 538.

17. United Nations World Tourism Organization, *International Tourism Highlights 2019 Edition* (2019), 5, accessed March 5, 2020, https://www.e-unwto.org/doi/pdf/10.18111/9789284421152.

18. Paul Hanna, Xavier Font, Caroline Scarles, Clare Weeden, and Charlotte Harrison, "Tourist Destination Marketing: From Sustainability Myopia to Memorable Experiences," *Journal of Destination Marketing & Management* 9 (2018): 37–8.

19. Xavier Font and Scott McCabe, "Sustainability and Marketing in Tourism: Its Contexts, Paradoxes, Approaches, Challenges and Potential," *Journal of Sustainable Tourism* 25, no. 7 (2017): 874.

20. Christina Tölkes, "Sustainability Communication in Tourism—A Literature Review," *Tourism Management Perspectives* 27 (2018): 10.

21. Marco Martins, "Tourism Planning and Tourismphobia: An Analysis of the Strategic Tourism Plan of Barcelona 2010–2015," *Journal of Tourism, Heritage & Services Marketing* 4, no. 1 (2018): 4.

22. Dominic Medway, Gary Warnaby, and Sheetal Dharni, "Demarketing Places: Rationales and Strategies," *Journal of Marketing Management* 27, nos. 1–2 (2011): 125–7.

23. CNT Editors, "How Technology Can Help Us Tackle Overtourism," *Condé Nast Traveler*, March 25, 2019, accessed June 4, 2020, https://www.cntraveler.com/story/how-technology-can-help-us-tackle-overtourism.

24. John Monahan, "Request to Suspend Hawaii Travel-Focused Editorial Coverage," April 6, 2020, accessed June 4, 2020, https://www.hawaiitourismauthority.org/media/4424/request-to-suspend-hawaii-travel-focused-editorial-coverage.pdf.

25. Víctor Quiñones Cintrón, Jonathon Von Hack, Myra Mabel Pérez Rivera, Angely Yomara Medina Velázquez, and José Davis Pellot, "The Evolution of Demarketing Literature," *Fórum Empresarial* 22, no. 1 (2017): 80.

26. "Majorca Offers Tourism Subsidies," Majorca Daily Bulletin, February 22, 2020, accessed June 4, 2020, https://www.majorcadailybulletin.com/news/local/2020/02/22/63079/majorca-financial-aid.html.

27. Rachel Dodds and Richard W. Butler, "Conclusion," in *Overtourism: Issues, Realities and Solutions*, eds. Rachel Dodds and Richard W. Butler (Berlin: De Gruyter, 2019), 265–6.

28. Edward Relph, *Place and Placelessness* (London: Pion, 1976), 58.

29. Relph, *Place and Placelessness*, 90.

30. Mary Louise Pratt, *Imperial Eyes: Travel Writing and Transculturation*, 2nd ed. (London: Routledge, 2008), 146.

31. The Bruno Brothers, "Bani Amor: Decolonizing Travel Culture," accessed June 4, 2020, https://vimeo.com/190281078.

32. Carmela Bosangit, Juline Dulnuan, and Miguela Mena, "Using Travel Blogs to Examine Postconsumption Behavior of Tourists," *Journal of Vacation Marketing* 18, no. 3 (2012): 214.

# CHAPTER 13

# Tourism, Representations of Place, and Social Media

Information technologies play an important, and evolving, role in all aspects of tourism today. The Internet brought about a shift in the provision of tourism services from "high street" travel agents to online booking tools (chapter 4). It also brought about a shift in the media of tourism representations from print to digital with the creation of destination websites (chapter 12). In this Web 1.0 era, tourism stakeholders were primarily responsible for generating and publishing content that was viewed by potential visitors. Now, Web 2.0 is bringing changes faster than many tourism stakeholders—let alone tourism research—can keep up.

Web 2.0 provides the platform for social media applications in which users themselves are involved in creating and exchanging content.[1] This user-generated content (UGC) takes various forms: blogs (e.g., TravelBlog), microblogs (e.g., Twitter), photos (e.g., Instagram), videos (e.g., YouTube), posts (e.g., Facebook), and reviews (Tripadvisor). The ubiquity of such content in tourism has led some scholars to describe the current situation as **Travel 2.0**. This refers to the interactive approach in which tourists are both consumers and producers of travel information online.

Consider, for example, how social media play a role in each of the stages of the tourism process (chapter 2). Tourists are increasingly using social media for information and inspiration during the pre-trip stage. In the movement stage, tourists may use crowdsourcing apps like Waze to find the most efficient route to their destination, in addition to posting social media updates regarding their progress. During the experience stage, social media allow visitors to be more flexible by accessing information or getting feedback while they are at the destination,[2] as well as posting updates. For those tourists who have not already shared photos, reactions, and/or reviews during the experience stage, they can do so in the post-trip stage. The process becomes cyclical when other tourists use this content for their information and inspiration in the pre-trip stage (figure 13.1).

Social media are highly dynamic, and each new development produces many changes throughout the tourism system. This chapter will consider some of these changes related to tourism representations. The first section will pick up where the last chapter left off with place promotions. Social media have created new challenges

**Figure 13.1. Social media have become a part of every stage of the tourism process.** *Source:* Velvet Nelson

for destination stakeholders but also new opportunities. The second section will look at tourists' uses of social media, and the chapter concludes by examining some of the evolving consequences of social media representations of places in travel and tourism.

# Place Promotion

Social media are changing the nature of marketing. Millennials and Gen Zers do not respond to traditional marketing. Instead, these audiences generally perceive social media content to be more relevant, up-to-date, and credible than information available from other sources.[3] However, this presents a distinct challenge for place promotion. A destination marketing organization is now only one of many sources of ideas and information about places and tourism products, assuming this source is considered at all. Social media representations may contradict the place brand destination stakeholders worked to cultivate. These representations may show the destination in a negative light, which can contribute to a poor reputation that may be hard to overcome. Yet, these representations can also provide unprecedented access into what tourists are looking for from their experiences and what factors affect their satisfaction with the destination.

## ADAPTING TO SOCIAL MEDIA

Tourism stakeholders were slow to understand the power of social media and even slower to act.[4] Some were unconvinced of the potential for social media to be used as a marketing tool. Others believed that social media users were not their target audience (e.g., social media were only used by young people who lacked the power to make travel decisions or the financial resources to travel). Even as social media's influence grew, many tourism stakeholders remained unsure how to make social media work for them and simply did not have the human resources to be able to devote the time and energy required to develop social media capabilities. The first stakeholders to use social media essentially maintained existing marketing strategies by replicating website content on various social media platforms. However, it quickly became clear that tourism stakeholders needed to find new ways of communicating with and engaging their audiences or risk lacking a critical competitive advantage.[5]

First, destination marketing organizations adapted tourism websites to move away from the one-way communication model of Web 1.0 to incorporate more social media content within the sites. Some destinations drew from personal travel blogs. The first-person narrative style of blogs allows the writer to convey information while engaging audiences with stories about people, places, and experiences.[6] Destinations such as Luxembourg include a blog on their official tourism website that provides information on specific topics (e.g., best picnic spots) or special events (e.g., holiday festivities).[7] Destination stakeholders may recruit local residents to write a blog post about their favorite places to go or things to do. This could help potential visitors get an insider perspective on the destination and a sense of a more authentic experience of place. In another approach, stakeholders might use visitor stories to give others an idea of what their own experience might be like.

Additionally, traditional destination website image galleries have been replaced with linked Instagram photos. Gold Coast, Queensland is one of Australia's most-visited destinations with 5.3 million overnight (domestic and international) visitors and another 8.3 million day-trip visitors.[8] On the Destination Gold Coast website, photos replicate the promotional images that are posted to the destination's official Instagram.[9] In a very different destination on the other side of the world, Cleveland, Ohio long suffered from a poor reputation. Stakeholders knew that it would be difficult to try to change peoples' ideas on their own, so they let others do it for them through popular and social media representations. Thus, the gallery on the This is Cleveland website features a compilation of visitors' Instagram photos from places around the city.[10] While promotional images might be viewed with skepticism, actual visitor photos may be seen as more representative and authentic.

Destination stakeholders have increasingly recognized the importance of the "Instagrammability" of places. This is not only about how well the place will look in photos posted on social media but also how the traveler's life appears online. A market study of UK-based Millennial travelers further found that 40 percent of respondents reported that Instagrammability was their highest priority when evaluating potential destinations.[11] Likewise, the UNWTO identified "travel to show" as a top consumer travel trend in 2019, including "'Instagrammable moments', experiences and destinations."[12] Tapping into this motivation, the Enjoy Illinois website highlights the most Instagrammable spots in the state, from the iconic Cloud Gate sculpture in Chicago's Millennium Park to the natural landscapes of Shawnee National Forest. The site encourages potential visitors to "do it for the 'gram'" and reminds them to use #Enjoy Illinois when they share their photos.[13]

Beyond the destination website, stakeholders now have a presence on most social media platforms with access to audiences worldwide. As with the destination website, stakeholders have to move away from one-way communication to engagement. Engagement starts with a click but increases when users consume content (e.g., destination photos or videos) and react to it through likes, favoriting, rating, and/or leaving a comment. To encourage engagement, stakeholders may use a question-and-response approach, such as "what is your favorite place at destination X?" Stakeholders can learn from users' answers, but these answers can also promote the destination to other users by identifying and highlighting aspects they might not be aware of. This can prompt further discussion among users, which can be effective in generating a "buzz" about the destination.[14] Stakeholders might also ask questions about what types of experiences or services that potential and/or actual visitors would like to see provided to develop relationships with visitors and enhance satisfaction with the destination.

Further engagement involves following, in which users are more consistently exposed to content rather than just through a specific pre-trip information search. This increases awareness about the destination and helps to create a demand for its experience. With this engagement, stakeholders seek to maintain an active presence to keep the destination in the minds of potential visitors without annoying followers by bombarding them with content.[15] Finally, users contribute through sharing their own content that promotes the destination.[16] Through these interactions, potential visitors become more connected to and invested in the destination, which creates a competitive advantage. Additionally, those who visit are more likely to be satisfied with the experience of the destination.[17]

Social media have especially been an asset for lesser-known destinations and tourism businesses.[18] These platforms allow them to raise awareness among potentially limitless audiences, which would have been virtually impossible in the past due to logistical and financial constraints. In addition, such stakeholders can better leverage **word-of-mouth** (WOM) to give potential visitors the confidence to take a chance on an unknown entity. The risk associated with the destination decision-making process is considered higher than for other types of products because the purchase is made prior to the experience, and the experience cannot be returned if it is not satisfactory. Traditionally, WOM involved person-to-person communication in which individuals relied on the experiences of family or friends to help them make an informed pre-trip decision. Today, **electronic word-of-mouth** (eWOM or "word of mouse") gives individuals access to the opinions of more tourists and about more places.[19]

## LEARNING FROM SOCIAL MEDIA

Social media provide tourism stakeholders with insight into tourists' perceptions, preferences, expectations, experiences, and reactions (box 13.1). Online reviews specifically highlight the features of the destination that visitors like or dislike, which helps stakeholders to understand their strengths and weaknesses. Personal travel blogs offer a deeper understanding of the destinations' tourists as well the tourism process. This might include information such as how visitors learned about the destination, how they arrived there, what they did, what they thought about it, and what they want to tell others. This allows managers to understand their tourists and even to identify areas of potential within the destination environment.

---

### Box 13.1.   Case Study: Reactions to Bonaire's Slave Huts in Tripadvisor Reviews

Tourism is often associated with fun and relaxation, but destinations around the world are increasingly integrating sites associated with dark pasts into their tourism offer. Much attention has been focused on high-profile dark sites such as the Auschwitz concentration camp in Poland. Visitors to this site have the opportunity to prepare themselves for the experience, even if they ultimately find their expectations and/or preparation inadequate. But what about dark sites that are simply one part of, and perhaps even a contrast to, a larger tourist experience? These places can present a stark contrast, physically and/or emotionally, to tourists' vacation experiences, and therefore provoke strong reactions.[a]

Social media has the potential to yield insight into these reactions. While blogs offer detailed narratives of how some tourists make sense of their experiences, the "small stories" told on various platforms offer a wider view of tourists' perspectives. Tripadvisor claims to be the world's largest travel platform boasting 463 million average monthly visitors and 860 million reviews of 8.7 million accommodations, airlines, experiences, and restaurants in 2019.[b] One study examined Tripadvisor reviews to better understand the reactions of tourists, who were neither heritage tourists nor dark tourists, to the unexpected encounter of a dark heritage site: slave huts on the Caribbean island of Bonaire (map 13.1).[c]

Like many places in the region, tourism is a significant economic activity on Bonaire. In 2019, the destination received 605,800 visitors, over three-fourths of whom arrived by cruise ship.[d] Scuba diving, snorkeling, and water sports are among the most popular tourist activities. Despite the presence of heritage resources, heritage tourism, and slavery heritage in particular, is a minor part of tourism for Bonaire. The Dutch brought enslaved Africans to the island in the seventeenth century to work in the salt pans. In 1863, enslaved Africans in the Dutch possessions were emancipated.

Today, there are several sites with "slave huts" that are easily accessible from the main road on the southwestern part of the island. These very small structures located along the coast provided sleeping quarters for enslaved individuals working in the salt pans. Tourism Corporation Bonaire identifies the huts as a tourist attraction,[e] although there is little in the

**Map 13.1.   Bonaire, Dutch Caribbean. While the majority of tourists to Bonaire are interested in the Caribbean destination's white sand beaches and coral reefs, the island's slave huts constitute a dark heritage site.** *Source:* Gang Gong

**Figure 13.2.  Bonaire's slave huts offer visitors insight into the dark history of slavery on the island while also serving as the entry to a popular dive site.** *Source:* Velvet Nelson

way of tourist infrastructure at the sites. The sites are considered a scenic attraction, with picturesque views of both the ocean with bright turquoise water and the distinctive landscape of the salt pans, and they mark popular dive sites (figure 13.2).

Tourists from all over the world visited the slave huts, although only a small minority indicated in their review that they planned to go to the site. Most noted that their visit was one stop on a driving tour of the island, primarily shore excursions from cruise ships or in between dives, or something they simply stumbled upon. Reviewers described the setting of the slave huts in overwhelmingly positive terms such as beautiful, picturesque, idyllic, tranquil, and peaceful. For some, this made the dark aspect of the site all the more disconcerting. Regarding the huts themselves, reviewers particularly focused on the small size, trying to give others a sense of perspective by comparing them to their height or to the size of a dog house.

A key theme in reviews was the emotional response to the site. Although the environment was similar to what they had experienced elsewhere on the island, the "feel" of this site was different. "What I will remember about this stop is the feeling I got when I was there. For me, there was a somberness about the place in spite of its beauty" (US visitor). For some, that beauty turned threatening. "You can only imagine the grueling conditions that the slaves had to endure here, with the salt, sun and trade winds only adding to the discomfort and inhuman treatment they got in the first place" (UK visitor). Many reviewers noted that they tried to imagine, or they encouraged readers to imagine, what conditions were like for the enslaved, but around 20 percent still found their imagination to be inadequate.

Following the moments spent at the slave huts, visitors continued their vacation. Some struggled with the idea of returning to a carefree vacation after their experience. For one reviewer, visiting the slave huts put his/her experiences in perspective. While this individual conceived his/her vacation on Bonaire as "heaven," s/he drew upon the empathetic response to the experience of the slave huts and imagined that the enslaved would have conceived the same place as "hell." Yet, this was not the case for all reviewers. One wrote: "They are really cute little huts. We saw them in 2 locations not too far apart…Go during sunset! They are awesome!" (US visitor). These very different responses created a source of tension.

> Wow. Honestly, if you visit these without taking the time to contemplate why they are here and what they are, you are TOTALLY missing the point and should get back on the cruise ship bubble you may have come from. It would be like visiting the Anne Frank house in Amsterdam and coming away with "it was cozy" or Auschwitz near Kraków and thinking it was "so spacious" (US visitor).

One limitation to the use of social media in tourism studies is the lack of contextual data. More nuanced information about reviewers could yield greater insight into responses, such as why some were affected by the experience and others were not. Nonetheless, social media posts shed light on visitors' experiences and, in this case, their emotional responses (or lack thereof) to an unexpected encounter with dark heritage.[f]

*Discussion topic*: Read the Tripadvisor reviews for a selected destination or attraction. What can you learn about the experience of this place? What questions do you still have about the experience?

*Tourism online*: Tourism Corporation Bonaire, "Bonaire Official Site," at https://www.tourismbonaire.com

---

[a] Velvet Nelson, "Liminality and Difficult Heritage in Tourism," *Tourism Geographies* 22, no. 2 (2020): 311–2.

[b] Tripadvisor, "About Tripadvisor," November 2019, accessed June 18, 2020, https://tripadvisor.mediaroom.com/us-about-us.

[c] Nelson, "Liminality and Difficult Heritage in Tourism."

[d] Statistics Netherlands, "Tourism on Bonaire and Saba up in 2019," April 21, 2020, accessed June 18, 2020, https://www.cbs.nl/en-gb/news/2020/17/tourism-on-bonaire-and-saba-up-in-2019.

[e] Tourism Corporation Bonaire, "Slave Huts & Obelisks," accessed June 18, 2020, https://www.tourismbonaire.com/sightseeing/slave-huts-obelisks.

[f] Nelson, "Liminality and Difficult Heritage in Tourism."

Analyzing social media comments and conversation allows stakeholders to effectively "listen" to visitors and to make improvements, in service provision and/or place promotion, accordingly. This can increase visitor satisfaction, which will be reflected in social media, contribute to a positive destination reputation, and potentially promote visitor loyalty. Staying attuned to social media helps stakeholders be responsive to changes, whether it is a new type of tourist to the destination or new patterns of behavior among today's tourists. Stakeholders can further use social media as an opportunity to enhance customer relationship management. For example, they can express appreciation to users who post positive pictures and experiences or to reviewers who provide positive feedback.

Whereas complaints about tourism experiences were once private matters, they are now public via social media. Consistent negative feedback that is unaddressed or poorly addressed is problematic and can damage a destination's reputation. However, stakeholders' response to complaints can, in fact, result in positive engagement. Stakeholders can respond promptly and politely, provide explanations or solutions as appropriate, and demonstrate that they are taking the complaint seriously and working to remedy the issues raised. Assuming the user making the complaint is looking for a resolution, such a response should be satisfactory. In addition, stakeholders may be able to build trust with other users who see that the individual making the complaint was treated courteously.[20]

Finally, given the present importance of Instagram, destination stakeholders should monitor Instagrammers' photos and adapt management and marketing strategies accordingly. For example, one study from Montevideo, Uruguay found that official promotional materials highlighted a much smaller number of attractions in the city than the attractions visited, photographed, and posted by tourists. At the same time, at least 10 percent of the attractions featured in the promotional materials were not represented in Instagram photos.[21] Thus, the attractions destination stakeholders think should be of interest to visitors may not be. In addition, stakeholders may need to develop resources into attractions along with the appropriate infrastructure. Another study from Stellenbosch, South Africa compared promotional images from the region's winelands with those posted on social media (i.e., Flickr and Instagram). While promotional images focused on the experience (e.g., a group of young people enjoying a wine tasting), social media images overwhelmingly focused on the landscape.[22]

# Place Representations

As in the early days of tourism, tourists are once again key producers of information about the places and experiences of travel. Some of this content is intended for and shared with select audiences, such as family, friends, and members of closed groups. However, much travel-based social media content is publicly available for audiences around the world, and, indeed, some users actively cultivate large numbers of followers.

## SOCIAL MEDIA USERS

In 2020, there were 3.8 billion active social media users around the world, with platforms such as Facebook and Instagram accounting for 2.5 and 1.0 billion active monthly users, respectively.[23] Travel and tourism are popular themes on both platforms, with Facebook Business reporting that 68 percent of Millennials find ideas for trips on Facebook and 60 percent on Instagram.[24] Instagram in particular has a high proportion of content related to travel. At the time of writing (June 2020), #travel is used in 469.7 million posts with another three million specifically aimed at inspiration (e.g., #travelinspiration, #travelinspo, #travelinspired). Posts such as these, among others, now play a substantial role in creating a demand for travel in general as well as a demand for the experience of particular places. Place holds a central position in these posts as they show beautiful beaches, colorful cities, vast natural landscapes, famous monuments, and iconic wildlife species.

As discussed above, tourists are increasingly interested in how their vacations—as well as their lives—will look on social media. Travel is seen as an important part of the identity for many people on social media. They may experience something along the

**Figure 13.3. Travel is an extraordinarily popular theme on social media, which can inspire others or create a sense of envy.** *Source:* Amber Fisher

lines of Facebook or Instagram envy when they see friends post travel pictures, and many seek to create that response in others with their own social media posts (figure 13.3).[25]

Travel-specific social media follow a similar model as platforms like Instagram with the aim of building a community of like-minded travelers. Mapify allows users to upload pictures, identify locations, and optionally to tell the story of their experience in that place to provide others with information and inspiration. Travelstoke allows users to create profiles and spots that can document their own trips as well as serve as a resource for others in the community who might be interested in visiting the same places.

Blogs and vlogs provide another option for social media. Travel-themed blogs can be found on any general blog hosting site, and YouTube is the primary site for travel vlogs. As with early travel writers (chapter 12), users provide more in-depth descriptive information about the places visited and often practical advice for their audience. Many users also tell stories, personal narratives of their experiences, their thoughts, and their emotions.[26] Tourists undertaking extraordinarily trips, such as a gap year, blog primarily to document their experiences in the different places visited as well as to update family and friends on their activities. Others specifically seek to gain a following (see below). Regardless, blogs and vlogs are generally publicly available. Thus, they are among the representations of place that may be encountered in a potential tourist's pre-trip search and even "pinned" on Pinterest for later reference.

Finally, online reviews are a part of decision-making today. Users do not know online reviewers, but eWOM is often perceived to be more trustworthy compared to place promotion.[27] However, these representations are an individual's interpretation of places and experiences, and there are many factors that can influence this. Some studies have found that there are higher levels of dissatisfaction in tourism than in other services industries. Tourists may be more sensitive because they are outside of their usual surroundings and comfort zones.[28] In the past, tourists were more likely to recount their experiences during the post-trip stage. Although stories told in this stage were based on memory (and forgetting), tourists had time to process their thoughts and to contextualize them within the circumstances of the experience and of the trip as a whole. Today, the real-time nature of mobile technologies has the potential to affect tourists' representations. For example, the in-the-moment reviews of tourists who are tired, angry, hungry, or intoxicated may represent the destination or experience in a very different way than it would if those same tourists reflected and posted later.

## SOCIAL MEDIA INFLUENCERS

Influencer marketing is a practice that capitalizes on social media users with a significant following. Such individuals have the ability to shape the attitudes and decision-making processes of their followers in favor of a particular brand or concept. Influencer marketing was initially successful in beauty and fashion, but the practice is now widespread. In particular, this type of marketing is more likely to reach Millennials and Gen Zers than traditional marketing; however, different approaches are often required for different audiences.[29] Mega-influencers are typically celebrities with over one million followers. These influencers allow brands to reach the largest number of people; however, that does not mean that those people will be interested in the product. Micro-influencers have a smaller base of followers in a particular niche, but marketing generally has a higher level of resonance and engagement.[30] Although nano-influencers have the smallest base of followers, they are most likely to resonate with Gen Zers because they are seen as more authentic and trusted.

In 2019, the influencer marketing industry was worth US$8 billion. Before COVID-19, that number was projected to increase to US$15billion by 2022.[31] In tourism, international hotel brands were some of the earliest adopters of influencer marketing, while destinations have again been slow to adapt. Particularly for lesser-known destinations, influencer marketing presents an opportunity to raise awareness, reach wider audiences, and promote positive images.[32] In 2015–16, New Zealand's South Island saw significant tourism growth. Local stakeholders attributed this to concerted efforts to partner with Instagram influencers who, through their photos and posts, created a demand for the destination.[33]

Influencers use travel blogs to further develop their brand. For example, *The Catch Me If You Can* blog allows readers to follow travel influencer Jessica Nabongo on her journey to become the first documented black woman to visit every country in the world (completed in 2019).[34] Posts feature eye-catching photographs and provide information about places while making specific recommendations for where to stay, what to do, and what to eat. Her content serves as a resource and an inspiration for travel, and her high-profile status has allowed her to create her own travel company. Others use their blogs to sell products, such as boutique clothing or affiliate-linked travel supplies.

During COVID-19 when travel was almost entirely shut down, the tenuousness of influencer marketing was exposed. Influencers reported that social media engagement had increased while stay-at-home orders were in place, but website traffic from people researching and booking travel fell. In addition, most tourism marketing budgets were cut, resulting in the majority of influencer campaigns being postponed or canceled altogether.[35]

Social media content has been trending toward more visual and live content with short video stories.[36] YouTube has over two billion average monthly users who watch over a billion hours of video a day.[37] While a majority of every generation uses YouTube regularly, the percentages are very high for the younger generations. Video offers richer, more diverse content than photos and text.[38] Particularly Gen Zers are looking for the real experiences of other like-minded tourists, as opposed to a staged promotional video.[39] Thus, individual travel vlogs sharing experiences on YouTube have become an important representation of place, and some vloggers have attained a high level of followers. For example, the YouTube channel for travel vlogger Louis Cole, FunForLouis, has two million subscribers, while the posted videos have nearly 320 million views.

Social media users can also gain influential status through high levels of engagement on review sites. For example, Tripadvisor's TripCollective is a program in which contributors receive points for content that equate to a certain level of reviewer status as well as badges that show other users their level of expertise.[40] Since the proliferation of online reviews can create problems with information overload, users may look to those reviewers with higher contributor or helpfulness status. This gives individuals considerable power to shape the ideas and expectations of others.

# Consequences of Representations

As discussed in the previous chapter, representations of place play an important role in shaping ideas of and experiences in places. These representations should be viewed critically to understand the perspective or motives of those creating these representations and their potential consequences. Social media increases the complexity of these issues with both negative and positive implications.

## AUTHENTICITY

Authenticity is a subject that has long been discussed in the tourism literature, but some authors argue that we need to give it renewed attention in this time characterized by "fake news."[41] In particular, social media have facilitated the proliferation of fake news, or fabricated content presented in a way that mimics news media without the editorial norms or processes that ensured the accuracy and credibility of information.[42] As discussed above, consumers are looking for authenticity, and the nature of social media and user-generated content have been seen as a means of providing this. Yet, there are significant questions about authenticity in social media representations.

A key issue in authenticity directly pertains to influencers' representation of places. Some critics argue that, despite the apparent significance of the destination, place has become secondary to the portrayal of the influencer's travel lifestyle. Furthermore, as more Instagrammers post similar content, users become desensitized to the unique characteristics of places.[43] Instagram content, where one place looks like another due to superficial images, runs the risk of creating a sense of placelessness just the same as place promotion (chapter 12).

Users looking for Insta-fame and marketing contracts must make even ordinary places or mundane experiences look extraordinary. The locations of photographs are deliberately chosen and carefully framed for the best angles. An influencer may even obtain access to parts of a site that are normally off limits to visitors. The timing of the shots may be highly selective. He may spend several days in a location waiting for the weather to cooperate to get a perfect sunset photo. She may get up extraordinarily early in the morning to be the first at a site to get a photo with an unimpeded view or to capture herself in solitary reflection. Users may capitalize on sophisticated editing software to push the "wow" factor even further. In an extreme example, a cultural site in Bali that became a popular Instagram attraction was exposed to be a contrived photo op.[44] For the average visitor to such places, the experience of these places may have little in common with what they saw online. For those visitors who save up for trips or perhaps even a once-in-a-lifetime trip, such unrealistic expectations lead to disappointment.

As with the critiques of travel writing, scholars argue that Instagram representations replicate colonial ideology of conquest. Beyond aesthetics, erasing other tourists from scenes suggests the exclusivity of the experience. Local people are rarely included; when they are, they are often presented as symbols of the authenticity of the experience. Depictions of empty landscapes imply a place that exists for the tourist's consumption as opposed to other local uses.[45]

Consumers of social media content have often found it difficult to distinguish between posts related to influencer marketing campaigns and those that are not.[46] In recognition of this, the US Federal Trade Commission issued a disclosure guide for social media influencers receiving payment for posts as well as free or discounted products and services. Influencers are reminded to ensure disclosures are clearly located in the endorsement message, photo, video, or live stream and to avoid vague language such as "sp" in lieu of "sponsored."[47]

Similarly, there are concerns about the veracity of travel reviews. The news media has reported stories of business owners who pose as customers to write positive reviews of their services or negative reviews of their competitors.[48] In response, some sites claim to have verified reviews; for example, a hotel booking site may only post reviews from customers who made reservations through their site and had a confirmed stay. However, this policy does not preclude reviews from individuals with a vested interest in the business. Reports have also questioned whether sites filter or suppress reviews, thereby offering a selective sample of customer opinions.

## CONTRIBUTING TO AND COMBATTING OVERTOURISM

Popular media has linked Instagram influencers and overtourism. Many tourists have a desire to take pictures of the iconic places that have been seen so many times before. While this contributes to problems of overtourism in major European cities, it is especially concerning for nature destinations. Visitors interested in enjoying nature are increasingly expressing their frustration at the commercialization of places with people jockeying for the best shot, promoting products, and even live streaming their experience. Moreover, when influencers put remote natural locations that have not been managed for tourism "on the map," these places cannot handle the often-dramatic increase in demand (box 13.2).

---

### Box 13.2.  In-Depth: Geotagging

In 2018, the Jackson Hole Travel & Tourism Board launched a campaign to raise awareness about the potential effects of geotagging, or adding geospatial information to, social media photos and videos.

> In Jackson Hole, our lands are highly "grammable" because of a tradition of preserving the wild. Unfortunately, every time someone tags the precise location in an epic nature photo, it brings excess traffic that's harmful to the environment. As champions of conservation, we ask that you share your photos using a generic location tag: Tag Responsibly, Keep Jackson Hole Wild.[a]

This campaign stemmed from a dramatic increase in visitors to Delta Lake, attributed to influencer photographs on social media. In the past, only one or two people would make the nine-mile hike on an unofficial, unmarked, non-maintained trail that has a "difficult" rating to visit the lake each day. This number grew to over 100 people per day.[b] The landscape suffered from erosion and trampled vegetation as a result of the increased foot traffic. In addition, those who were drawn to the lake because of the geotag were often not prepared for the difficulty of the hike. As a result, visitors got lost and were injured and required local rescue support.[c] The request to "tag responsibly" is now listed as one of the steps to promote sustainable tourism at the destination.

Due to the destination's response, this case is frequently cited in the ongoing debate about geotagging and its potential contributions to overtourism; however, there are countless other examples. In particular, off-the-beaten-path places like Delta Lake do not have the infrastructure to support a significant increase in visitors, whether that is one hundred tourists or several thousand tourists. For example, there may be insufficient road access or parking facilities, resulting in traffic congestion, decreased air quality, and/or resident frustrations. There may be insufficient paths, toilet facilities, waste bins, or maintenance, resulting in degraded landscapes, sanitation issues, and/or health and safety problems. Critics have also raised concerns that criminal organizations could make use of geotagged tourism photos. Poachers could use location data embedded in photos taken on safari to track rare and endangered wildlife, especially those in areas that are not formally protected. Likewise, human traffickers could use the data to identify potential victims.

Along with the Jackson Hole tourism board, organizations such as the Leave No Trace Center for Outdoor Ethics have issued social media guidelines that recommended users think before using specific geotags, and some users have even promoted the hashtag #nogeotag.[d]

However, the hard stance of the #nogeotag movement generated pushback by those who argue that it is a form of gatekeeping in which tourists who are privileged enough to travel to spectacular places have the power to decide who has the right to visit them.[e]

As long as tourists are influenced by what they see of others' patterns of travel and behavior, social media users do have power. Some users clearly have more influence than others, but the effects of social media posts cannot always be predicted. Thus, the advice to "tag responsibly" is worth bearing in mind. In other words, visitors should consider the circumstances of the place before they decide to tag—or not. If possible, visitors should look to local stakeholders as a guide. In particular, failing to respect the wishes of private property owners and residents has been a problem. In contrast, destination planners and business owners may be actively trying to develop tourism; therefore, they may support or even encourage geotagging for its potential to raise the destination's profile.[f]

Visitors should also consider the potential consequences of increased visitation to that place and candidly discussing the reality of the places tagged. In the case of wildlife photos, a photographer might discuss the type of lens used to allow him/her to take pictures from a distance while cautioning others about the disruptive and potentially harmful effects of getting too close to the animals to try to get a similar shot on a phone camera. In the case of remote or hard-to-reach places, visitors should consider candidly discussing the reality of the places tagged. This could include the type of preparation required, the duration of the trip, and the level of physical difficulty. This information could help followers make an informed decision about whether to visit and how to do so in a way that does not endanger themselves or other people.[g]

While Instagram shaming has highlighted unsustainable behaviors, there has been relatively little engagement with followers about social and environmental impacts on places visited. Perhaps even discussing the issues associated with geotagging presents an opportunity for social media users to demonstrate and promote sustainable travel behaviors.

*Discussion topic*: Choose a travel photo. What factors would you consider when deciding whether to geotag this photo on social media? Does this photo present any opportunities to engage with sustainable tourism?

*Tourism online*: Responsibly Wild, "Sustainability," at https://www.visitjacksonhole.com/sustainability

---

[a] Responsibly Wild, "Sustainability," accessed June 9, 2020, https://www.visitjacksonhole.com/sustainability.

[b] Stacey Leasca, "How Your Instagram Geotag Might Be Putting Wild Animals and Natural Areas at Risk Around the World," *Travel + Leisure*, March 22, 2019, accessed June 9, 2020, https://www.travelandleisure.com/travel-news/geotagging-bad-for-safari.

[c] Joana Haugen, "Generic Geotagging: An Opportunity for Influencers to Rethink their Impact," *Adventure Travel News*, January 29, 2019, accessed June 9, 2020, https://www.adventuretravelnews.com/generic-geotagging-an-opportunity-for-influencers-to-rethink-their-impact.

[d] Alisa Walsh, "New Social Media Guidance," *Leave No Trace Center for Outdoor Ethics*, June 8, 2018, accessed June 9, 2020, https://lnt.org/new-social-media-guidance/.

[e] Tyler Moss, "The Geotagging Debate Is Really about Gatekeeping in the Outdoors," Condé Nast Traveler, November 18, 2019, accessed June 9, 2020, https://www.cntraveler.com/story/the-geotagging-debate-is-really-about-gatekeeping-in-the-outdoors.

[f] Haugen, "Generic Geotagging."

[g] CNT Editors, "How Technology Can Help Us Tackle Overtourism," Condé Nast Traveler, March 25, 2019, accessed June 9, 2020, https://www.cntraveler.com/story/how-technology-can-help-us-tackle-overtourism.

In addition to contributing to overcrowding, social media are considered to influence tourist behaviors at destinations. Too often, this is irresponsible behavior that leads to negative social and environmental effects. In March 2019, due to optimal climatic conditions, Southern California experienced a "super bloom" of wildflowers. Thousands of people flocked to the area every day, creating massive traffic jams and parking problems. Driven to get the ideal shot in this scene, tourists attempted steep trails in high-heeled shoes, strayed from designated walking paths, trampled the flowers, laid down in the flowers, picked flowers, and more. After a particularly crowded weekend, the city of Lake Elsinore temporarily declared a public safety emergency.[49]

With social pressure for better and better photos, tourists have also engaged in antisocial (figure 13.4) and even dangerous behaviors. Also in March 2019, a viral photo featured a pair of Instagram influencers hanging out of a moving train in Sri Lanka. A Fodor's Travel contributor wrote:

> Hello! This is an open letter to Instagram influencers. Here's the whole letter: Stop endangering your own lives, as well as those around you, to take a "daring" travel photo for the internet. It is not impressive, you don't look worldly, and no one is benefiting from this. In fact, by posting this photo, you are absolutely (consciously or not—doesn't matter which!) putting other people's lives at risk—those people who are actually on this train with you and those who see this photo and think, 'Hey, maybe I should try something like that!'[50]

This is not an exaggeration; there are many examples of tourists who have been hurt or killed in their quest for a better photo.

**Figure 13.4.  Tourists are going to greater lengths for Insta-worthy photos.** *Source:* Velvet Nelson

Increasingly, writers argue that influencers (or the more benign "content creators") have an obligation to use their influence to model and promote responsible travel behaviors. Such behaviors include respecting the rights of property owners and the privacy of individuals as well as demonstrating courtesy to other visitors and not adversely affecting their experience of place. Likewise, behaviors should not adversely affect the quality of places, the protection of historic monuments, or the preservation of natural environments.

In light of overtourism, influencers are encouraged to be honest about the reality of places, including whether they are overcrowded or if there are local anti-tourist movements. Provided alternate destinations are interested in and capable of receiving an increase in visitors, influencers can re-direct attention to these places and potentially alleviate some of the pressure on overcrowded places.

## Box 13.3.  Experience: Rethinking Expectations and Social Media Representations of Paris, France in the Wake of the *Charlie Hebdo* Shooting

*Our ideas about places come from many sources, from literature to social media; however, various factors can cause our experiences to be quite different from our expectations. In January 2015, armed men entered the Parisian offices of* Charlie Hebdo, *a French satirical magazine, and killed seventeen people. Ali visited the city in the wake of that event. She reflects on her expectations, experiences, and her own social media representations.*

Paris, France is so often mythologized as a literary oasis of progressive ideas, creativity, and free speech. As a kid who dreamt about growing up and becoming a writer, I always saw the city as a utopia for artists, and frequently fantasized about traveling there one day to write the next great novel. But after traveling to Paris only a few weeks after the *Charlie Hebdo* shooting—a physical security threat that put into question freedom of speech—I was forced to confront my romanticized views of the city and consider the difficult social and political issues it was facing.

In the Spring of 2015, I traveled to Paris on a faculty-led, study abroad trip with my professor and five other students from my department. Our itinerary was stacked with visits to museums and historical landmarks frequented by literary giants. I always gravitated toward the work of twentieth-century expatriate writers like Gertrude Stein, Ernest Hemingway, and F. Scott Fitzgerald—writers who left the US to make this literary capital their home—and now here I was, about to explore the city that inspired so many pieces of art and works of literature that had been instrumental to my own academic research.

I stepped off the plane naively thinking we would be greeted by men and women in chic outfits and beautiful architecture—an aesthetic visual I had created for myself based on films I had seen, and images posted by friends and influencers on social media. After leaving the airport, however, we were instead greeted by a heavy presence of French military and police. Although a few weeks had passed since the attack, men and women in full combat gear were actively posted at all major transportation stations and landmarks for increased security, and the slogan "Je Suis Charlie" was prominently graffitied on walls and the sides of buildings all over the city.

Experiencing the city in the aftermath of the *Charlie Hebdo* shooting shattered my idea of Paris as a safe, romantic space to be a writer and forced me to think about important very real social and political issues. I had imagined traveling to a free-spirited city that celebrated diversity, but this Paris was disconcerting and filled with growing racial tension over immigration. Although I enjoyed visiting the various museums and literary hubs I had set out to see, it was impossible not to fixate on the military and police personnel toting weapons throughout the city. As someone who had never traveled outside of the US, I was excited to share my experiences with friends and family. But, after the militarized Paris I experienced, I became wary of sharing my visits to major landmarks like Notre Dame, the Eiffel Tower, and the Arc de Triomphe in real time, out of fear they would worry for my safety.

While *Charlie Hebdo*'s satirical cartoons about Islamic leaders were considered to be the motive for the January 2015 attack, the slogan that arose from it, "Je Suis Charlie," was quickly adopted as a global expression of freedom of speech and a symbol of solidarity for the publication. The hashtag #jesuischarlie was used on social media to create a discourse between journalists and non-journalists about censorship, violence against journalists, and anti-Islamic behavior—topics that my peers and I found difficult not to discuss throughout our trip. Being in Paris at this particular moment in time started a dialogue between my classmates and me. It led us to meaningful conversations about the purpose of art and literature and sparked healthy debates over the roles and responsibilities that writers and artists must take on.

I'd be lying to you if I said I went to Paris with zero intention of posting about my trip on social media, but after the Paris I experienced had dismantled my individual, preconceived notions of the city, I felt it was important to share my visit as authentically as possible. I began posting images of the militarized Paris I witnessed, attempting to capture the disruption I had felt during my visit with the juxtaposition of beautiful architecture and military and police. These photos not only provided a genuine representation of my visit but continued to generate conversations with friends and family members long after I returned, who weren't aware of Paris's then climate, and wanted to hear more about my trip specifically in the wake of this event.

Traveling to Paris ended up being both an eye-opening and influential experience for me. It inspired me to continue pursuing a career in media and advocacy, and perhaps more importantly, made me think deeply about how performative travel can be on social media. If staged photos online can influence our ideas of places, then social media can most certainly be co-opted to share authentic travel experiences that lead to larger, more significant cultural conversations.

—*Ali*

## VIRTUAL COMMUNITIES

If travel personalities have generally been middle-aged white males, social media influencers are often described as "the beautiful blonde dressed in a breezy couture dress staring wistfully over the dazzling sea."[51] Nonetheless, social media has allowed people of all ages, genders, ethnicities, religions, and sexual orientations to add their voices to the growing conversation about travel and tourism in the modern world. Influencers, bloggers, and vloggers provide examples for others who identify with them, while virtual communities provide a forum for people to share ideas, fears, and inspirations.

Travel has long held challenges for African Americans, such as the Jim Crow laws discussed in chapter 4. According to a black travel blogger, "Though that dark chapter of our history has passed, the woes of being a black traveler haven't completely disappeared. There is still much anxiety felt around being a black person and visiting a new state for the first time."[52] Yet, the African American travel market has been growing, accounting for US$63 billion in 2018.[53] Influencers like Jessica Nabongo (above) and vlogger Phil Calvert (Phil Good Travel) provide visibility for black travelers, while social media allow individuals to share information, advice, and stories—both good and bad—as a sort of new Green Book. A research study found that #TravelingWhileBlack on Twitter is used to discuss occurrences of racism, awareness of being black while traveling, and meaningful experiences traveling while black.

> [S]haring their lived narrative provides a pathway to strengthen and empower the Black travel movement. Positive experiences are shared and discussed as a way to uplift the community, whereas negative ones can help inform future travelers. These experiences can be isolating, and they are part of what draws Black travelers to the movement emerging on social media.[54]

Virtual communities, like Nomadness Travel Tribe with over 20,000 members, provide a dedicated platform for these discussions. As these communities grow, they also have the potential to exert greater influence on the industry.

The LGBTQIA+ community also presents a significant tourist market segment. Travel blogs like Dopes on the Road and Nomadic Boys not only chronicle the authors' travel experiences but serve as a resource for other travelers. Safety and acceptance while traveling are key concerns, and significant research may be required to understand the culture, openness, and inclusiveness of destinations. Virtual communities can help travelers learn from the experiences of others and gain confidence to try different destinations. Additionally, it may be difficult to identify businesses that are owned by or support the LGBTQIA+ community to visit while traveling. Online platforms like Eat Queer provide a community-driven resource in which local people highlight their favorite places to eat and drink. Queering the Map allows community members to post personal place-based stories. Described by one travel writer:

> A pin in Athens denotes a queer neighborhood and another a gay bar. The history of gay emperor Hadrian is pinned in Rome, as well as poignant moments like a lesbian couple being harassed in the metro and defended by a local. These memories would never be included in traditional guidebooks— much less in history books—but continue a tradition of queer storytelling. It infuses a place with queerness in a way that makes a queer traveler, like me, feel less alone, less different in a new place.[55]

These are just two examples of the virtual communities in which people can connect with like-minded travelers: solo travelers, female travelers, plus-size travelers, travelers with disabilities, travel photographers, digital nomads, and many more. While these voices are primarily heard within their own communities, they are gaining wider attention. As more readers and viewers are exposed to diverse ideas and viewpoints, we would hope to see a shift away from the colonial discourses of the past to a more self-critical awareness of how we understand, engage with, and represent the places and peoples of our travels.

# Conclusion

Stakeholders in places all over the world are engaged in place promotion to raise awareness among external audiences, create positive perceptions, and encourage people to visit their place over any other. However, with the growing role of social media, the ability of these stakeholders to shape place reputation is limited. There has been a steep learning curve for stakeholders to try to adapt and researchers to understand the fast-paced changes in the ways today's tourists use social media. This will continue to be an ongoing challenge in the years to come.

# Key Terms

- electronic word-of-mouth
- Travel 2.0
- word-of-mouth

# Notes

1. Kyung-Hyan Yoo and Ulrike Gretzel, "Use and Creation of Social Media by Travellers," in *Social Media in Travel, Tourism and Hospitality: Theory, Practice and Cases*, ed. Marianna Sigala, Evangelos Christou, and Ulrike Gretzel (Ashgate: Surrey, 2012), 198.

2. Ulrike Gretzel, "The Role of Social Media in Creating and Addressing Overtourism," in *Overtourism: Issues, Realities and Solutions*, eds. Rachel Dodds and Richard W. Butler (Berlin: De Gruyter, 2019), 64.

3. Gretzel, "The Role of Social Media," 64.

4. Stella Kladou and Eleni Mavragani, "Assessing Destination Image: An Online-Marketing Approach and the Case of TripAdvisor," *Journal of Destination Marketing & Management* 4 (2015): 189.

5. Stephanie Hays, Stephen John Page, and Dimitrios Buhalis, "Social Media as a Destination Marketing Tool: Its Use by National Tourism Organization," *Current Issues in Tourism* 16, no. 3 (2013): 213.

6. Daniel Leung, Rob Law, Hubert van Hoof, and Dimitrios Buhalis, "Social Media in Tourism and Hospitality: A Literature Review," *Journal of Travel & Tourism Marketing* 30 (2013): 11.

7. Visit Luxembourg, "Blog," accessed June 12, 2020, https://www.visitluxembourg.com/en/blog.

8. Destination Gold Coast, "Annual Report 2018–19," accessed June 12, 2020, https://www.destinationgoldcoast.com/Portals/0/Documents/Corporate/AboutUs/AnnualReports/2018-19/DGC_ANNUALREPORT19_WEB.pdf.

9. Destination Gold Coast, "Official Tourism Website for the Gold Coast in Queensland, Australia," accessed June 12, 2020, https://www.destinationgoldcoast.com.

10. This Is Cleveland, "Cleveland, Ohio," accessed June 12, 2020,https://www.thisiscleveland.com.

11. Lee Hayhurst, "Survey Highlights Instagram as Key Factor in Destination Choice among Millennials," *Travolution*, March 24, 2017, accessed June 12, 2020, https://travolution.com/articles/102216/survey-highlights-instagram-as-key-factor-in-destination-choice-among-millennials.

12. United Nations World Tourism Organization, *International Tourism Highlights 2019 Edition* (2019), 5, accessed March 5, 2020, https://www.e-unwto.org/doi/pdf/10.18111/9789284421152.

13. Illinois Office of Tourism, "The Most Instagrammable Spots in Illinois," accessed June 12, 2020, https://www.enjoyillinois.com/plan-your-trip/most-instagrammable-places.

14. Stephanie Hays, Stephen John Page, and Dimitrios Buhalis, "Social Media as a Destination Marketing Tool: Its Use by National Tourism Organization," *Current Issues in Tourism* 16, no. 3 (2013): 221.

15. Khaldoon Nusair, Mehmet Erdem, Fevzi Okumus, and Anil Bilgihan, "Users' Attitudes toward Online Social Networks in Travel," in *Social Media in Travel, Tourism and Hospitality: Theory, Practice and Cases*, ed. Marianna Sigala, Evangelos Christou, and Ulrike Gretzel (Ashgate: Surrey, 2012), 219.

16. Kevin Kam Fung So, Ceridwyn King, Beverley A. Sparks, and Ying Wang, "The Role of Customer Engagement in Building Consumer Loyalty in Tourism Brands," *Journal of Travel Research* 55, no. 1 (2016): 64.

17. Paul Harrigan, Uwana Evers, Morgan Miles, and Timothy Daly, "Customer Engagement with Tourism Social Media Brands," *Tourism Management* 56 (2017): 597–8.

18. Evangelos Christou, "Introduction to Part 2," in *Social Media in Travel, Tourism and Hospitality: Theory, Practice and Cases*, ed. Marianna Sigala, Evangelos Christou, and Ulrike Gretzel (Ashgate: Surrey, 2012), 69.

19. Leung et al., "Social Media in Tourism and Hospitality," 8.

20. Rebecca Dolan, Yuri Seo, and Joya Kemper, "Complaining Practices on Social Media in Tourism: A Value Co-Creation and Co-Destruction Perspective," *Tourism Management* 73 (2019): 36.

21. Daniel Paül I Agustí, "Characterizing the Location of Tourist Images in Cities. Differences in User-Generated Images (Instagram), Official Tourist Brochures, and Travel Guides," *Annals of Tourism Research* 73 (2018): 108.

22. Louise A. Bordelon and Sanette L.A. Ferreira, "Tourist Photographs and Destination Imagery on Social Media: Reading the Stellenbosch Winelands through a Tourist Lens," *Tourism Review International* 21 (2017): 326.

23. Dave Chaffey, "Global Social Media Research Summary 2020," Smart Insights, April 17, 2020, accessed June 15, 2020, https://www.smartinsights.com/social-media-marketing/social-media-strategy/new-global-social-media-research/.

24. "Reach Travelers When They're Deciding Where to Go with Trip Consideration," *Facebook Business*, March 6, 2018, accessed June 10, 2020, https://www.facebook.com/business/news/reach-travelers-when-theyre-deciding-where-to-go-with-trip-consideration.

25. Gretzel, "The Role of Social Media," 69.

26. Ana María Munar and Jens Kr. Steen Jacobsen, "Motivations for Sharing Tourism Experiences through Social Media," *Tourism Management* 43 (2014): 47.

27. Agustí, "Characterizing the Location of Tourist Images in Cities," 103.

28. Dolan et al., "Complaining Practices on Social Media in Tourism," 36.

29. Francisco Femenia-Serra and Ulrike Gretzel, "Influencer Marketing for Tourism Destinations: Lessons from a Mature Destination," in *Information and Communication Technologies in Tourism 2020*, eds. J. Neidhardt and W. Wörndl (Springer International Publishing: Chaim, 2020), 65.

30. Ulrike Gretzel, "Influencer Marketing in Travel and Tourism," in *Advances in Social Media for Travel, Tourism and Hospitality: New Perspectives, Practices and Cases*, eds. Marianna Sigala and Ulrike Gretzel (Routledge: New York, 2018), 149.

31. Audrey Schomer, "Influencer Marketing: State of the Social Media Influencer Market in 2020," *Business Insider*, December 17, 2019, accessed June 12, 2020, https://www.businessinsider.com/influencer-marketing-report.

32. Femenia-Serra and Gretzel, "Influencer Marketing for Tourism Destinations," 66.

33. Charlie Mitchell, "Instagram Thanked for South Island Tourism Boom," *Stuff*, March 26, 2016, accessed June 12, 2020, https://www.stuff.co.nz/travel/news/78274433/instagram-thanked-for-south-island-tourism-boom.

34. Jessica Nabongo, "About," accessed June 11, 2020, https://thecatchmeifyoucan.com/about.

35. Carole Rosenblat, "Love 'Em or Hate 'Em, Influencers Have Nowhere to Travel Right Now—How Are They Surviving?" *Fodor's Travel*, May 1, 2020, accessed June 15, 2020, https://www.fodors.com/news/coronavirus/love-em-or-hate-em-influencers-have-nowhere-to-travel-right-now-how-are-they-surviving.

36. Gretzel, "The Role of Social Media," 63.

37. YouTube, "Press," accessed June 15, 2020, https://www.youtube.com/about/press/.

38. Jessica Baron, "The Key to Gen Z is Video Content," *Forbes,* July 3, 2019, accessed June 15, 2020, https://www.forbes.com/sites/jessicabaron/2019/07/03/the-key-to-gen-z-is-video-content/#53921db53484.

39. Sofia Reino and Brian Hay, "The Use of YouTube as a Tourism Marketing Tool," *Travel and Tourism Research Association: Advancing Tourism Research Globally* 69 (2016): 8.

40. Tripadvisor, "TripCollective FAQs," accessed June 15, 2020, https://www.tripadvisor.com/vpages/tripcollective_faqs.html.

41. Jane Lovell and Chris Bull, *Authentic and Inauthentic Places in Tourism: From Heritage Sites to Theme Parks* (Routledge: Abingdon, 2018): 1.

42. David M. J. Lazer, Matthew A. Baum, Yochai Benkler, Adam J. Berinsky, Kelly M. Greenhill, Filippo Menczer, Miriam J. Metzger, Brendan Nyhan, Gordon Pennycook, David Rothschild, Michael Schudson, Steven A. Sloman, Cass R. Sunstein, Emily A. Thorson, Duncan J. Watts, and Jonathon L. Zittrain, "The Science of Fake News," *Science* 359, no. 6380 (2018): 1094–5.

43. James Asquith, "Have Instagram Influencers Ruined Travel for an Entire Generation?" *Forbes*, September 1, 2019, accessed June 16, 2020, https://www.forbes.com/sites/jamesasquith/2019/09/01/have-instagram-influencers-ruined-travel-for-an-entire-generation/#2e52df3c1e30.

44. Anneta Konstantinides, "Visitors Have Discovered That a Bali Tourist Attraction Popular with Instagram Influencers Is Actually a Fake Photo Op," *Business Insider*, July 9, 2019, accessed June 16, 2020, https://static1.businessinsider.com/bali-tourist-spot-popular-instagram-fake-photo-op-2019-7?jwsource=cl.

45. Sean P. Smith, "Instagram Abroad: Performance, Consumption and Colonial Narrative in Tourism," *Postcolonial Studies* 21, no. 2 (2018): 172–191.

46. Alice Audrezet, Gwarlann de Kerviler, and Julie Guidry Moulard, "Authenticity Under Threat: When Social Media Influencers Need to Go Beyond Self-Presentation," *Journal of Business Research* (2019) https://doi.org/10.1016/j.jbusres.2018.07.008.

47. Federal Trade Commission, "Disclosures 101 for Social Media Influencers," November 2019, accessed June 16, 2020, https://www.ftc.gov/system/files/documents/plain-language/1001a-influencer-guide-508_1.pdf.

48. Raffaele Filieri, Salma Alguezaui, and Fraser McLeay, "Why Do Travelers Trust TripAdvisor? Antecedents of Trust towards Consumer-Generated Media and Its Influence on Recommendation Adoption and Word of Mouth," *Tourism Management* 51 (2015): 175.

49. Caitlin Morton, "Tourists Are Already Destroying California's Super Bloom," *Condé Nast Traveler*, March 19, 2019, accessed June 16, 2020, https://www.cntraveler.com/story/how-to-see-californias-super-bloom.

50. Audrey Farnsworth, "Instagram Influencer Behavior Has Got to Change—They're Ruining Travel and Risking Lives," *Fodor's Travel*, March 7, 2019, accessed June 16, 2020, https://www.fodors.com/news/travel-tips/instagram-influencer-behavior-has-got-to-change-theyre-ruining-travel-and-risking-lives.

51. Barbara Noe Kennedy, "These Are the 11 Best and Worst Travel Trends of the Past Decade," *Fodor's Travel*, October 25, 2019, accessed May 1, 2020, https://www.fodors.com/news/photos/these-are-the-11-best-and-worst-travel-trends-of-the-past-decade.

52. Briona Lamback, "The 6 Best US Travel Destinations for Black Travelers in 2019," *Matador Network*, May 20, 2019, accessed June 16, 2020, https://matadornetwork.com/read/best-travel-destinations-black-travelers/.

53. Eben Diskin, "African-Americans Spent $63 Billion on Travel in 2018," *Matador Network*, December 26, 2018, accessed June 16, 2020, https://matadornetwork.com/read/african-americans-spent-billion-travel-2018/.

54. Alana K. Dillette, Stefanie Benjamin, and Chelsea Carpenter, "Tweeting the Black Travel Experience: Social Media Counternarrative Stories as Innovative Insight on #TravelingWhile Black," *Journal of Travel Research* 58, no. 8 (2019): 1359.

55. Melissa Kravitz Hoeffner, "This Mapping Tool Collects Queer Sites and Memories," *Condé Nast Traveler*, August 15, 2019, accessed June 16, 2020, https://www.cntraveler.com/story/queering-the-map-collects-queer-sites-and-memories.

# CHAPTER 14

# Experiences of Place in Tourism

Experiences of place in tourism vary widely depending on the characteristics of place, the circumstances of the visit, and who we are. The geography of tourism is well suited to our examination of these factors. We can apply a long tradition of geographic research on concepts such as place, placelessness, and sense of place to understand the nature of places and how our relationships with places shape tourism experiences. We can also use the contemporary framework of powerful geography to try to better understand and work to address the factors that will affect tourism experiences for particular demographics.

In this chapter, we blend these perspectives—old and new—to conclude our examination of the interrelationships between place and tourism. The first section discusses the ways in which tourism shapes the character of places, while the second section looks at the factors that shape how tourists experience the places they visit. The final section considers some of the ways in which technology is changing the experience of place.

## Places and Tourism

In the previous chapters, we saw how important representations of places are in shaping the ways in which people think about tourism destinations. The character of a place is important in attracting and maintaining tourism. Yet, the unique character of a place may ultimately be affected by tourism.

One of the most influential works on the geography of place has been Edward Relph's *Place and Placelessness* (1976). In this work, Relph defines a geography of places that are unique and full of meaning; these places create a world that is rich and varied. He contrasts this with a placeless geography. Non-places have few characteristics that situate them in their location or distinguish one from another, and they lack meanings beyond certain stereotypical ideas. Thus, in a placeless geography, the character of the setting is devoid of significant or unique features, and people do not recognize that places are different. Consequently, placelessness involves both a look and a feel of sameness.

For example, the tropical beach has been described as a non-place. These beaches feature the same, typically stereotyped characteristics (e.g., sunny skies, palm trees, white sands, clear waters, possibly umbrellas and lounge chairs), regardless of their actual location in the tropical world (see figure 12.3). In fact, even when such a place is visited, there may be few readily apparent features that would distinguish it from other, similar places or indicate the wider character of the place in which it is situated. These beaches are loaded with superficial meanings, such as fun, relaxation, and escape, but they often lack the depth of meaning associated with places that are unique.

Relph is particularly critical of tourism and argues that it plays a key role in creating placelessness: "Tourism is an homogenizing influence and its effects everywhere seem to be the same—the destruction of the local and regional landscape that very often initiated tourism, and its replacement by conventional tourist architecture and synthetic landscapes and pseudo-places."[1] In other words, tourism destinations are prone to becoming non-places. This is often attributed to the standardization of mass tourism. Multinational companies that build resorts and restaurants in the same style and offer the same services regardless of location tend to characterize mass tourism destinations. These multinational companies reflect the demands of organized mass tourists that the places they visit—even if they are foreign places—have at least certain elements of home that are familiar and comfortable. Thus, there is a certain sameness to mass beach destinations in many parts of the world.

Another variation of placelessness refers to places that are artificial, contrived, and have little relationship to the history and/or reality of the places in which they are situated. Relph describes this as a process of "Disneyfication" in which the synthetic world of the theme park affects the character and development of other places.[2] Scholars have applied this concept to various places, including existing places that have been subject to Disneyfication, such as New Orleans, as well as places that have been developed in this way, such as Las Vegas.

Although there is some truth in the relationship between tourism and placelessness, tourism has also contributed to processes of localization. In the face of standardization as a result of global processes, some places have made a conscious effort to reassert local interests, traditions, and distinctiveness. This helps reinforce, or possibly recreate, a unique sense of identity and character for places that might otherwise be lost. This has the distinct advantage of giving that place a competitive advantage among tourists (or place consumers) who are looking for a unique experience of place.

## Box 14.1.  Case Study: Creative Tourism in Portugal

Destinations are always looking for ways to stay competitive. Tourists are increasingly looking for new ways to experience places. Creative tourism is a growing niche product that has the potential to promote tourism to specific places, diversify the tourism offer, take advantage of existing resources, and support sustainable tourism for destination stakeholders. At the same time, creative tourism provides engaging and memorable experiences for tourists.[a]

According to UNESCO, creative tourism involves "travel directed toward an engaged and authentic experience, with participative learning in the arts, heritage, or special character of a place, and it provides a connection with those who reside in this place and create this living culture."[b] Creative tourism is not a passive process of listening and observing. Tourists are co-creators in the experience; they actively apply what they learn, tap into their own creativity, and gain new skills. Those who are interested in creative tourism are typically interested in smaller, immersive experiences, but there is no single type of creative tourist.[c] Participants may be singles, couples, families with children, or groups of friends. They may be independent tourists or part of an organized tour group.

Creative tourism activities, ranging from learning traditional folk dances to how to make chocolate, allow visitors to gain insight into local skills, traditions, and the distinctive characteristics of the places they visit.[d] In addition, visitors participating in creative tourism often have the opportunity to get closer to the back regions of the destination. For example, a tourist who attends a flamenco show in Spain is likely to do so at a hotel, restaurant, or theater in the main tourist area. In contrast, to participate in a workshop at a flamenco school, a tourist may have to venture into a local neighborhood.[e] Thus creative tourism is an expression of the trend to "live like a local."

In Portugal, the Creative Tourism Destination Development in Small Cities and Rural Areas (Creatour) initiative was developed to be an incubator for creative tourism. The pilot projects across the country (map 14.1) seek to capitalize on and revitalize local tangible (e.g., industrial areas) and intangible cultural heritage resources (e.g., traditional knowledge). Projects include folklore, dance, art, weaving, pottery, beekeeping, food production, and more. The development of these resources into creative tourism products is intended to immerse visitors in local culture while providing unique, place-based experiences. In addition, it is intended to bring economic (e.g., income), social (e.g., cultural preservation and pride), and environmental (e.g., natural preservation) benefits to participating communities.[f]

Pilot projects in the Alentejo region are rooted in the area's traditional products and processes, such as cooking and winemaking. The experience might look something like this: participants take a walking tour of the small historic city of Évora, the capital of the region. The tour ends in a small neighborhood at a local chef's home. As opposed to a more passive experience of learning about or sampling the regional cuisine, participants are immediately immersed in the process of preparing foods, such as chopping vegetables, grilling meats, or making sauces (figure 14.1). Throughout the process, the chef talks about the ingredients and where they come from, traditional recipes and methods of cooking, and the distinctive qualities of the regional cuisine. Dishes are prepared in stages, so participants are able to sample while they work before sitting down to a communal meal with the chef.

Participants then transfer to the countryside to visit a local winery. They might take a tour of the vineyards and wine-making facilities similar to a standard winery tour, but the main departure lies in the wine tasting. In this creative experience, participants are given several local varietals of wine, a beaker, and a worksheet to make their own wine blend. Participants taste the varieties to determine what proportions of each they want to use in their blend, then measure and mix the wines. They can taste again to see if they like their blend and try a different combination if desired. When they determine their preferred blend, winery staff will help them mix, bottle, and cork the wine to enjoy after they return home.

Creative tourism experiences such as this will not appeal to all types of tourists, but demand for these products is growing. Many destinations around the world are looking to meet this demand, to attract tourists to new places, and to foster meaningful interactions between tourists and local people and promote a more sustainable form of tourism.

*Discussion topic*: Using the tangible and/or intangible tourism resources of your area, describe a potential creative tourism project.

*Tourism online*: Creatour, "Overview," https://creatour.pt/en/about/overview/

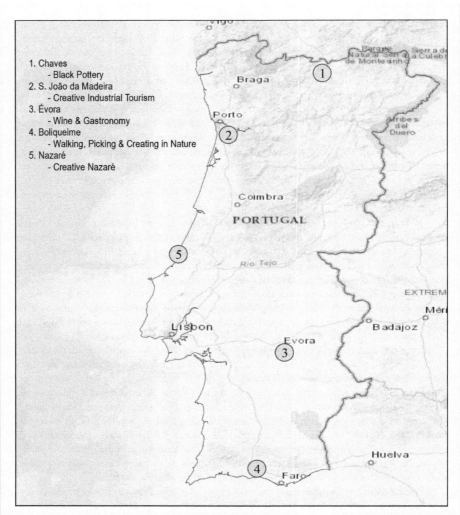

**Map 14.1.   Creatour Projects, Portugal. This map shows just a sample of the diverse projects developed under Portugal's Creative Tourism Destination Development in Small Cities and Rural Areas initiative. *Source:* Gang Gong**

[a] Nancy Duxbury and Greg Richards, "Towards a Research Agenda for Creative Tourism: Developments, Diversity, and Dynamics," in *A Research Agenda for Creative Tourism*, eds. Nancy Duxbury and Greg Richards (Cheltenham: Edward Elgar Publishing, 2019): 1–2.

[b] United Nations Educational, Scientific, and Cultural Organization, "Towards sustainable strategies for creative tourism: Discussion report of the planning meeting for 2008 international conference on creative tourism Santa Fe, New Mexico, USA October 25–27, 2006.

[c] Siow-Kian Tan, Shiann-Far Kung, and Ding-Bang Luh, "A Model of 'Creative Experience' in Creative Tourism," *Annals of Tourism Research* 41 (2013): 154, 156.

[d] Tan et al. "A Model of 'Creative Experience'," 155.

[e] Greg Richards, "Creativity and Tourism: The State of the Art," *Annals of Tourism Research* 38, no. 4 (2011): 1235.

[f] Creatour, "Overview," accessed June 23, 2020, https://creatour.pt/en/about/overview/.

**Figure 14.1.** In this creative tourism experience in Évora, Portugal, local chefs engage participants in learning about, preparing, and eating distinctive local dishes. *Source:* Velvet Nelson

# Sense of Place

**Sense of place** refers to the association with and emotional attachment to places based on the meanings given to those places. It is one of the ways in which we are connected to the world and therefore an integral part of the human experience.[3] A sense of place is developed by experience in and a relationship with a place. In particular, geographer Yi-Fu Tuan argued that "sense of place is rarely acquired in passing. To know a place well requires long residence and deep involvement."[4] Thus, the places of our everyday lives are those that hold the most meaning for us and therefore are the ones to which we are most attached. However, sense of place can also contribute to our understanding of the geography of tourism.

The relationship with and feelings we have toward the places of our everyday lives can play a role in the demand for tourism. In addition to affection and attachment, the familiarity of these places can generate feelings of complacency or even hostility if we begin to perceive that we are tied to or imprisoned there. Even though we know that these are the places to which we will always return, we may still feel the need for a temporary change of place. Tourism provides us with this opportunity.

Tourism is a means of experiencing new places and places in new ways. Unfamiliar places are experienced differently than familiar ones. While we take certain aspects of a familiar place for granted, everything in a new place is different and unknown. We may have a greater sense of curiosity and excitement. Activities that seem mundane in our daily lives—driving from one place to another, taking a walk up the street, going to the store, finding something to eat—can suddenly turn into an adventure. As we have the potential to encounter new things, we tend to observe more carefully. Since we typically have a greater sense of security in the places that we consider our own, we may even be challenged to pay more attention to our surroundings in a new place to find what we need or to keep ourselves safe.

Finally, experiences in new places often cause us to reflect on our experiences in those places most familiar to us, those that constitute the setting of our daily lives. In some cases, the sudden absence of those aspects of a place that we take for granted may prompt us to appreciate them more upon our return, at least for a little while. We may find that there are aspects of a place we would rather see changed, to be more like that of a place visited. In essence, experiences in other places may cause us to refine our sense of place.

# Experience of Place

There are countless factors that can affect tourists' experience, ranging from poor infrastructure to the presence of pests. Perhaps one of the greatest factors that has a distinct impact on tourists' experiences is the weather conditions of a place at the time of a trip.[5] Nothing is likely to ruin a tourist's experience more than unexpected and undesirable weather conditions that prevent them from seeing or doing the things they had planned. While it may be an unusual—perhaps even unprecedented—occurrence for that place, it may be the only experience tourists have with that place. Other factors may be unrelated to the place but will affect the tourists' experience nonetheless. For example, tourists who are sick during their vacation may not be able to participate in certain activities, and they are likely to enter into their experiences with far less enthusiasm than they would have otherwise.

Interactions with the people at a destination can play an important role in tourists' experience of that place. In a new place, we may not know where to go, how to act, or whom to trust. Tourists are often wary of being taken advantage of or cheated—in some cases, rightly so. Tourists may have little knowledge of how much things should cost or the way things work; consequently, they are at the mercy of tourism stakeholders and local people to deal with them fairly. Encounters with local people who are honest and friendly, or those who go out of their way to help strangers, can have an extraordinarily positive impact on tourists' experience. Conversely, encounters with even a few people at the destination who are dishonest, unhelpful, hostile, or harassing can shape the way tourists forever think about that place.

Personal factors, such as previous experiences and personality, play a role in the way an individual experiences a place. We approach experiences with different attitudes. Some tourists feel apprehension, anxiety, or even fear, perhaps from the very moment they leave home, at the unknown of experiencing a new place. For tourists who have little experience with new and different places, this should lessen with time, as they become more comfortable. In contrast, other tourists may experience a sense of euphoria at being in a place where everything is new. This, too, can lessen with time as the novelty of the experience begins to wear off.

Tourists have different logistical options for experiencing a destination. The following sections discuss guided tours and independent travel as two options and how each shapes the experience of place.

## GUIDED TOURS

Tourists can experience a destination or destinations through a guided tour. There is an endless variety of experiences that range from a complete package trip to a day-long excursion as one part of a larger trip, from a group with dozens of participants to a one-on-one experience. Tourists might choose this experience for a number of different reasons, reflecting the type of tourist, the desired tourism product, the choice of destination, or the motivations for the trip. Essentially, guided tours can serve different purposes and provide different types of experiences of place.

Organized mass tourists are often interested in the convenience of a package trip, such as a coach tour of major European cities. The itinerary is preplanned (e.g., what places to visit and for how long), and all of the logistical arrangements have already been made (e.g., how to travel, where to stay, where to eat). This creates a "worry-free" holiday for tourists who do not have the time or interest in planning a trip and do not want any surprises. Although these tours are tremendously popular, they are criticized for minimizing the experience of place. There is little need to come to the destination with any knowledge of the place, as all arrangements have already been made and guides provide necessary information along the way. With a set itinerary, there is little opportunity for exploration and interaction with the place or its people. The spontaneity of the tourism experience is eliminated, and tourists are reduced to passive observers of place through the windows of a climate-controlled bus. In response to such complaints, some tour providers have expanded their range of itineraries, increased flexibility and free time, and offered high-quality experiences based on local knowledge.[6]

Guided tours may also be used to facilitate certain types of special-interest tourism, such as those that require specific skills. Tourists may be interested in participating in an activity at the destination—such as rock climbing, scuba diving, or horseback riding—but have little previous experience with that activity. As such, a tour provides them with instruction, necessary equipment, and a guide to help them along the way and ensure their safety. Likewise, special-interest tourism may require in-depth local knowledge. Tourists interested in bird watching, wildlife photography, or fishing may require a local guide who will know when and where they will have the greatest opportunities for these activities.

Guided tours may be necessary to allow tourists to visit places they would not otherwise know about or have access to (figure 14.2). This can include places not generally made known to outsiders, such as an unmarked hiking trail, or those places not open to outsiders except on a tour because of logistical or safety reasons (e.g., the subterranean passages of the Seattle Underground). Some destinations impose such specific regulations on tourists that a guide is necessary to ensure that proper procedures are followed; some of the strictest controlled destinations actually require that tourists travel with a guide. This is the case in places like Tibet, Bhutan, and North Korea.

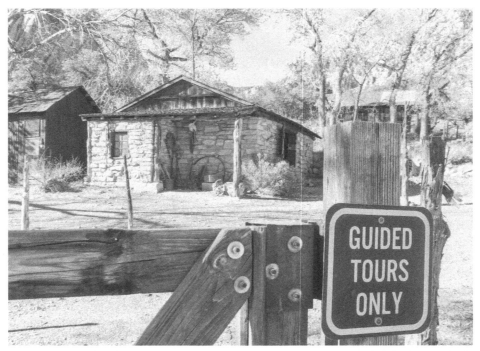

**Figure 14.2.   Guided tours may be necessary to allow tourists to visit places, such as this part of Spring Mountain Ranch State Park, Nevada.** *Source:* Velvet Nelson

Thus, while the types of tourists who visit these "off-the-beaten-track" destinations are fairly adventurous explorers and drifters looking for a unique experience, they must travel in a different manner than they would normally.

The existence of tour guides dates back to the earliest eras of tourism. Tour guides played an important role in the Grand Tour era, before the tourism industry and infrastructure were developed. With little in the way of guidebook information, maps, signs, or other features that facilitate tourism, outsiders were dependent on guides. Guides would literally guide tourists in places that were unfamiliar, inaccessible to outsiders, and in which they would be met with suspicion or hostility by the local population. These guides would also metaphorically guide tourists in the process of personal development that was intended to accompany an experience such as the Grand Tour.[7]

Modern tour guides continue to serve a variety of functions. In addition to taking care of logistical arrangements, guides are responsible for the safety and well-being of tourists during the course of the trip. They are responsible for ensuring that tourists are familiar with and abide by local customs and policies. Tour guides are expected to have a good knowledge of the places visited. While some tour itineraries are preplanned, others are flexible, and it is up to the guide to determine the course of the trip/excursion to reflect the interests of tour participants. The guide may be expected to find routes that will yield the best opportunities to encounter desired points of interest. This is particularly applicable on special interest tours where those points are moving targets (e.g., wildlife). In addition, guides must be able to convey their knowledge of a place to participants. This must be done in a way that is easily understood by visitors, which may require translating or interpreting things that might seem strange or unusual to outsiders.

Guides must balance providing information about places and entertaining tourists on holiday. Increasingly, the traditional roles of guide as presenter and entertainer and tour group as the audience is not sufficient. Tourists are looking for more engaging and interactive experiences that will be more meaningful.[8] Some tours integrate more stories of peoples and places into the script, to better connect with visitors and to create a sense of a distinctly localized experience.[9] Other tours focus on the co-creation of experiences in which visitors are active participants in the tour. In the Parks Canada "Québec by Lantern Light" tour (Québec City, Canada), visitors are transformed into newly arrived Irish immigrants. Costumed guides representing a variety of characters acquaint these immigrants with the city and educate them on how to survive.[10]

Tour guides may be required to have certain skill sets, such as fluency in multiple languages, and some knowledge of the tourists' culture to understand what their interests are, what type of experience they want, and how to best represent the places visited. Some tourists may want information about the places, while others may be more interested in myths or personal stories. In some cases, tourists may not want any interpretation at all; the guide is simply intended to facilitate travel and highlight sights to be seen and/or photographed. Guides must be flexible and accommodating to meet the needs of tour participants as they arise.

Tour guides can have a highly important role to play in tourists' experiences of a place. They constitute another form of representation; they represent local peoples and places to tourists. As such, they have tremendous power in determining what is important and will be seen—and, conversely, what will not—and shaping what tourists think about those places and their experiences. Guides are considered an essential interface between tourists and the destination.[11] However, they are not entirely autonomous; they may be required to represent the aspects and stories of the place that are officially sanctioned. In other words, they may be limited by what places the government will allow guides to take tourists and what topics they can discuss.[12]

Tourists place a great deal of trust in their guides to be honest, give them accurate information, and generally deal with them fairly. Of course, this is not always the case. Guides may fabricate information, advise them to purchase inauthentic souvenirs, or require them to pay additional "fees" that line their pockets or those of their acquaintances. However, tour companies depend on their reputation, and social media allows dissatisfied customers to spread the word about any problems they had with a tour. Moreover, because tour guides play such an important role in representing the destination, governments frequently implement regulations and/or require licenses for tour guides. Nonetheless, unlicensed guides operating in the informal sector of the economy are common in many destinations around the world, and experiences with them vary widely.

## INDEPENDENT TRAVEL

Many tourists prefer to experience a place on their own. Just as organized package tours are criticized for minimizing tourists' experience of place, independent explorations are often considered to provide the greatest opportunities for tourists to develop a sense of place. Of course, a deeper experience of a place does not necessarily translate into a positive one, and there can be both advantages and disadvantages of going it alone at the destination.

Those who prefer independent travel value the flexibility to set their own itinerary. Based on their interests and priorities, they can choose what places they want to visit and what sights to see. These may be primary attractions, but one of the advantages of independent travel is the ability to get off the traditional tourist track and experience more of the place than the front regions. For example, tourists come en masse to visit Piazza dei Miracoli, the main tourist complex in Pisa, Italy, featuring the famous Leaning Tower. This is a well-known primary attraction and one that all kinds of tourists to Tuscany are likely to see. However, those on a guided tour will likely only experience this part of Pisa, while those traveling independently have the potential to explore other parts of the historic city if they choose.

Likewise, tourists who travel independently are not bound by a strict schedule, unless they set it for themselves. They have the flexibility to linger at a site that they find enjoyable or interesting without feeling rushed, and conversely, they are free to move on to the next attraction if they decide they have done all they wanted in that place. Consequently, tourists can feel that they had the fullest experience of a place with little perceived wasted time (e.g., waiting at rendezvous points).

Those who travel by personal vehicle may be subject to the same criticisms as those who travel by tour bus: their only experience of other places is from a distance and in passing. However, personal vehicles can be used as a means of getting *to* a destination but not the primary means of *experiencing* it. Independent travelers may choose to walk or use public transportation at the destination, which will provide opportunities for interactions with local people, access to back regions, and insight into the lived experience of the place.

This more flexible style of travel allows for greater spontaneity in the experience of place. Independent travel does not always go as planned; in fact, it frequently does not. For many tourists, their most memorable and rewarding experiences of a place are those that were stumbled upon by accident in the course of exploring on their own. These are the experiences where they met interesting local people, found a great restaurant, saw places they never would have encountered otherwise, and observed or participated in a unique local event.

Of course, not all unexpected experiences are pleasant ones. For many tourists, the prospect of traveling without a guide and facing the unexpected alone are great sources of stress. Tour participants benefit from operators who scout out the best attractions, accommodations, or restaurants. Tourists who plan their own trips, on the other hand, must make selections from their best guess based on whatever information is available. Traveler reviews are seen as a means of avoiding the worst experiences, but they cannot prevent us from running into problems that require solving.

Tour participants benefit from dedicated transportation that takes them directly to points of interest. In contrast, those who rely on public transportation may be frustrated by restrictive schedules and an inability to get to tourist sites not served by transportation systems. Independent tourists also run the risk of getting lost. For some, this is an adventure and creates opportunities, but for others, it is a source of stress. These tourists face the potential frustration of not reaching the desired attractions or the anxiety of finding themselves in undesirable, possibly unsafe, locations.

Independent tourists may not always have access to the same extent of information about the places and attractions visited. Sites have varying degrees of information available to independent tourists. Some highly developed attractions have self-guided audio tours via mobile phone and well-annotated displays or interactive monitors. However, less developed or local attractions with fewer resources may provide little information about the site or use only the local language in guides and displays. This information is also typically limited to basic facts without providing the level of detail or richer stories that a good tour guide might have to offer.

Finally, tour guides act as a middleman between tourists and local people. These guides should speak the local language and understand local customs and therefore be able to help tourists navigate foreign destinations. Even the most conscientious tourists who try to familiarize themselves with the local culture and speak some basic words of the language can run into problems with miscommunication and misunderstanding when they have to manage various situations on their own. The stress, frustration, and/or dissatisfaction that arise from any of these aspects of a trip can affect tourists' attitudes toward the place and their experience of it.

## TOURIST DEMOGRAPHICS

Although it is recognized that tourists are not a single, homogenous group that will experience places in the same ways, tourism research has not always given these differences much consideration. Feminist geography has particularly led the way in examining the factors that cause women to experience places differently than men. However, research into the factors that affect other demographics of tourists has been slower to develop. As we saw in the last chapter, virtual communities on social media have played an important role in starting the conversation about the factors that shape tourists' experiences of places.

## SOLO INDEPENDENT FEMALE TOURISTS

Solo independent tourists travel without a companion or an organized tour group. In the past, solo tourists were often considered among the most adventurous tourists and outside the norm, but these attitudes have shifted. With increased demand for travel, tourists are choosing to travel when and how they can. Many solo tourists have partners who may not be interested in traveling or may not be able to travel at the same times. One study identified a 42 percent increase in solo tourist bookings between 2015 and 2018 and a 45 percent increase among solo female tourists in particular. Another study found a 600 percent increase in searches for solo travel on Pinterest between 2017 and 2018.[13]

Although there are examples of female travelers throughout history, travel was long seen as the province of men. Throughout the early eras of tourism, only a small percentage of women had the time, money, and social standing to be able to travel. The prevailing sociocultural attitude was that it was inappropriate for respectable women to travel extensively and simply unacceptable for them to travel by themselves. Those who did were viewed by society as eccentric at best; at worst, they faced a ruined reputation.

Today, women are frequent travelers, yet attitudes toward them traveling—especially abroad and alone—remain antiquated. After announcing their intentions to travel alone, women are frequently subject to reactions from family and friends that may range from surprise (e.g., "Are you sure that's safe?") to disapproval (e.g., "I don't think that's a good idea.") and even outrage (e.g., "How could you think of doing something like that?").[14] These reactions may be well intentioned, as they reflect a concern for the woman's well-being, but they also reproduce and reinforce the perception that women are vulnerable and thus solo independent travel is unwise.

The prospect of negotiating an unfamiliar place can be scary for anyone, but these fears are magnified by tourism industry guidelines for female travelers (e.g., dos and don'ts lists or security warnings) and media stories. Take, for example, the 2019 *New York Times* article "Adventurous. Alone. Attacked." The article reads: "The number of female solo travelers has skyrocketed, but amid Instagram-worthy escapades are tales of violence and death, raising questions about how the world is greeting women who travel alone."[15]

Perceptions of acceptable behavior for women and toward women vary widely around the world. Solo independent female tourists may be judged by the sociocultural norms of the destination and subject to the reactions of local people. In some places, the idea of a woman traveling alone may still be unacceptable. When traveling to other culture regions, women often report feeling conspicuous, receiving unwanted attention, sensing hostility, experiencing some form of harassment, and feeling insecure or unsafe. In particular, women traveling without a male companion may be viewed as sexually available. For example, in some culturally conservative destinations, it may be unusual for a woman to appear in public unaccompanied, and those who do—including foreign tourists—will be thought of as sex workers. Conversely, in destinations that have received female sex tourists, all foreign women may be perceived to be looking for that sort of relationship and approached accordingly.

All of these factors affect women's travel patterns and the ways they experience other places. They affect whether or not a woman decides to travel alone; if she does travel, they affect where she goes or where she stays, including the neighborhood in which an accommodation is located and the level of security it affords.[16] These factors affect the places she visits at the destination and the type of activities she participates in. She may feel safest within a certain part of the destination, perhaps the front region where there are other people (especially other tourists) who make her feel less noticeable and less of a target. Some types of places perceived to be less safe than others (e.g., large urban areas with high crime rates or remote, isolated forested areas) may be avoided. A woman might feel comfortable in a particular place during the day, when it is well lit and populated by other women and children, but less comfortable at night when she might be more likely subjected to harassment. As a result, she may choose to stay in at night instead of experiencing aspects of life at the destination.

In addition, a woman may make other sorts of adjustments during a trip in an effort to minimize the risk of encountering problems while traveling alone. She may modify her patterns of behavior to be more in line with what is acceptable for women in that place. She may change her patterns of dress to fit local norms (e.g., covering her hair in conservative Muslim countries, figure 14.3), to be more conservative (e.g., longer sleeves or higher necklines) so that she attracts less unwanted attention and/or incorrect assumptions. If she is not married, she may wear a band on her ring finger to send the message that, although she is not traveling with a man, she should not be seen as "available."

Given real and perceived security issues, a woman may feel that it is her responsibility to not put herself in unsafe places or dangerous situations. Consequently, she has to be constantly aware of her surroundings. This can increase the level of stress associated with travel, which can generate frustration because she is unable to relax and enjoy the experience. Moreover, she may feel that she has an incomplete experience of place because there are certain areas of the destination where she is not comfortable going, typically back regions where she would be conspicuous. Likewise, there may be certain activities that she would like to participate in but does not feel like she can.

**Figure 14.3. This American tourist wore a headscarf while she was in Senegal, a predominantly Muslim West African country.** *Source:* Pamela Rader

These constraints play a real role in shaping women's travel patterns. Not all women will approach travel and experience destinations in the same ways. For some women, these issues may generate suppressed demand. Many women will acknowledge that places at home can also be unsafe, and the experiences faced by solo independent female travelers can also happen to single women at home. However, women at home typically understand the situation and know how to best respond, whereas this is not always the case in foreign environments. As one travel writer notes,

> due to circumstances amplified in fish-out-of-water situations, I can't necessarily respond the way I might in my familiar element (i.e. rudely). I might not be able to articulately dissent—or scarier, still, be understood in good faith…And there's cultural relevance to consider, as well: his workplace or even culture may have different social norms, and I am in his 'home.'[17]

Many female tourists find that solo independent travel is empowering and fulfilling, as they gain confidence in themselves and a sense of accomplishment for overcoming constraints.[18] Many feel freer to enjoy their experiences in new places when they travel with others. Still others navigate their experiences one at a time, assessing situations and their comfort level as they go. Regardless of the approach, the tourism industry is taking notice of this demographic and starting to consider factors that affect female tourists' experiences.[19]

## BLACK TOURISTS

Tourism RESET is a network of scholars working on issues of race, ethnicity, and social equity in tourism. The project was founded by geographer Derek Alderman, and geographers are well represented among the group's research fellows. Their work has helped bring greater attention to the issues, past and present, that shape black tourists' experiences.[20]

For example, Jeffrey Finney and RESET fellow Amy Potter examine the case of Tybee Island, Georgia. Nearly thirty years after Civil Rights activists held wade-ins on the island to push for desegregation of public beaches, access to these beaches was once again called into question with the beginning of Orange Crush in 1988, an annual end-of-year beach party for predominantly African American college students. Throughout the event's now thirty-year history, local officials have looked for a way to prevent it from taking place without impacting other events (e.g., Fourth of July celebrations). Businesses such as hotels and restaurants close during the weekend of the event, and police presence is traditionally high. In an interview with the authors in 2016, one of the event organizers said,

> These are thousands of college students coming from wherever they are educated, young leaders of tomorrow being looked at as if they are naturally criminals when they are not…It just makes you feel like we're not moving forward at times we are moving backwards. And that's sad. That's honestly very sad.[21]

Another RESET fellow, Perry Carter, argues that we need to consider the legacy of racial discrimination as we seek to understand present patterns of travel for African Americans. In his work, he found that African Americans, in comparison to white Americans, were more likely to travel in large groups, visit destinations recommended by people they know, follow a preset itinerary, and avoid unfamiliar things. Although places are no longer segregated, they are still racialized, and African Americans may still be perceived as out of place in "white" spaces, including popular tourism destinations. Such places and experiences become more stressful than relaxing.[22]

At the time of writing (June 2020), the Black Lives Matter movement is raising awareness about racism and violence against people of color. We need to keep these conversations going in the arena of tourism as well.

## AND MORE

Although these two demographics have been topics in tourism research, the factors that affect the experiences of many others are also worth consideration (box 14.2). As with the above groups, LGBTQIA+ tourists often face greater considerations about where and how to travel. These tourists may have to spend more time researching potential destinations to understand their legal rights but also the culture. They may not feel like they can be themselves or openly show affection with their partner because they do not know what peoples' reactions will be. This can increase the stress of travel.

However, as discussed in the previous chapter, social media are helping tourists to learn from the experiences of others and find welcoming local businesses. In addition, more places are becoming open and accepting, which increases both opportunities for and the enjoyment of travel.

## Box 14.2.  Experience: Big and Tall Travel

*As individuals, we all have certain things that we consider in our pre-trip planning and factors that affect our experiences in the places we visit. This is based on our personalities, past experiences, and worldviews—but it is also based on things like our age, gender, race, ethnicity, religion, sexual orientation, and even physical characteristics. Like many geography students, Jesse is interested in experiencing other places, but his size creates challenges to travel that not everyone experiences. In this box, he shares his perspective on the struggles he faces as well as what about travel makes it worth it.*

I have always wanted to travel, to experience new places, to meet new people, and to try new foods. I thought the last reason was a little silly, but the more I talk to people about travel, the more I realize that food is a big attraction for many of us. I want to try local foods and to taste new things that are not commercialized or Americanized.

I am a big guy. Taking an airplane (or any other form of public transportation) to get to where I want to go is uncomfortable for me, to say the least. For most of my experiences, I would say that I am a square peg trying to fit inside a triangle-shaped hole. When I get onboard, I am numb to the looks I get walking down the narrow passageway to get to my seat way in no man's land, otherwise known as economy. Once I finally make it to my seat, I have to let the flight attendant know that I need a second buckle. I don't even attempt to close it the first time so that I can avoid the same disappointed feeling I get from my favorite sports team that extends as far as they can go but still miss the goal by a lot.

If you are remotely big, and heaven-forbid tall like I am, you know to pick an aisle seat to save yourself hours of leg torture. I can take up at least one-and-one-third seats. If I get really lucky, on that flight there will be a place with two seats available so that I can spread out. Most of the time, I don't have to ask to be moved. Flight attendants are usually on the ball and will ask me, sometimes before takeoff, if I want to change seats. For that, I am always grateful. But if seats are not available, all I can say is that I know the meaning of up close and personal. I have tried hanging out in the aisle, but there are flight attendants and passengers constantly moving around. In my seat, the moment I am about to get comfortable, someone bumps into me or I have to move so that the snack cart can go by, or the drink cart, or the trash cart. As a result, I don't fall asleep on an airplane. I just can't. Flying is still the fastest and most convenient way to travel long distances, so I do it over and over again. Plus, you can also meet interesting people on a plane, myself included.

I think it is important to be intentional when you travel, take the opportunity to discover something new, and get to know local people. In Spain, I had an adventure. I got lost and met all sorts of people along the way. Fortunately, I can speak Spanish, so I did make it back to the hotel. I was just a little cold and hungry, but that set the stage for a great meal. I tried lots of different foods on that trip, but I could not bring myself to eat the snails. Morocco was like stepping into a completely different world. The food was amazing, and I even ate sheep brains here. We stayed in a *riad* while we were there, which is a sort of Moroccan house. It was comfortable and cozy, but the narrow passageways could be tight. I could still fit through these passageways, but sometimes I had to walk sideways. In Hawaii, I wanted to see how beautiful it was. I wanted to see how ancient societies had thrived on an island in the middle of the ocean. However, I was not ready for the mountains. My visit to the Big Island nearly killed me. But, I also ate some of the biggest and best testing fruit I have ever had, and if you haven't tried butterfish, you are not living life.

Travel is not always easy. You have to be able to adjust to any hardships that arise along the way. Like when I was coming home from Spain and our flight was cancelled and no one told us about it. Suddenly, we were spending a night in Iceland. It is always hard to find a relatively safe spot to try to sleep in an airport. If you are big, it is even harder. Still, getting to travel allowed me to live and to experience a new place. It also gave me a sense of accomplishment. As I write this, I find that it is fun recalling all of the good times I had—and even some of the struggles. I will travel again, and maybe I will finally have those snails.

*—Jesse*

Tourists with disabilities often have the same desires to travel as able-bodied people, but travel can range from inconvenient to virtually impossible. Invisible disabilities such as hearing difficulties or chronic pain can pose challenges for travel that are compounded by the fact that other people do not see or understand the problem.[23] These tourists may face resistance from overprotective families, and they themselves may experience anxiety about the unknown. Again, these tourists are likely to have to invest more time in pre-trip research to understand the accessibility of an attraction, and the presence or absence of accessible infrastructure (e.g., appropriate parking facilities, paths, ramps, toilets) will distinctly shape the experience.[24] More places are working to accommodate tourists with disabilities. In 2019, a travel company launched the first wheelchair-accessible tour of the UNESCO World Heritage Site Machu Picchu (Peru).[25] However, there is still much work to be done to increase accessibility for all types of tourists.

# Consumption of Places

As a fundamentally place-based activity, places are the primary object of consumption in tourism. Sociologist John Urry described the process of visual consumption as the tourist gaze. The **romantic tourist gaze** is a private or personal experience, where the tourist can gaze in peace and feel as though he or she formed a connection with that place. This is typically undertaken in natural tourist sites (e.g., scenic vistas) and spiritual places (e.g., religious temples). Tourists who prefer the romantic gaze may think the experience is "ruined" by the presence of others. In contrast, the **collective tourist gaze** depends on the presence of people. This occurs in public places that are at least partially characterized by the people found there. The main square or plaza in an urban area may be a tourist attraction, not just for the architecture of the buildings that define the space, but also for the activity there (box 14.3).[26]

# Box 14.3.   In-Depth: When the Romantic Gaze Becomes a Collective One

It is now an iconic Instagram travel photo: a lone traveler standing atop Roy's Peak, taking in the spectacular scene that the viewpoint in New Zealand provides in solitude. In November 2018, one such photo went viral. It looked much the same as the others, except it was posted along with a second shot. This one showed the long line of tourists waiting for their turn to take the very same photo.[a]

If you are not yet familiar with Roy's Peak, there are countless other examples. We can all imagine classic, awe-inspiring scenes such as Half Dome (US), Machu Picchu (Peru), Stonehenge (England), Victoria Falls (Zambia and Zimbabwe), Angkor Wat (Cambodia), or the Great Wall (China). Some are purely spectacular natural environments; others combine tremendous human heritage with a dramatic setting. Still others are mystical in ways we cannot always explain. When presented with these images, we cannot help but imagine ourselves there, taking in the gaze. With few, if any, people present in the typical representations, we can picture ourselves standing alone and simply appreciating the scene. Perhaps we might even feel an overwhelming awe at being able to immerse ourselves in these exceptional places—in other words, the romantic gaze.

Yet, the experience of these places has become decidedly collective as millions of tourists visit every year. Cars, RVs, and tour buses require extensive parking facilities located near the site or viewing area for convenience. Both tour groups and independent tourists roam the site and accumulate in key spots. The concentration of tourists can also attract vendors selling a range of products, as well as pickpockets and hustlers looking for opportunities. This mass of people affects the physical quality of the site by trampling paths, accumulating waste, increasing noise levels, and leaving graffiti or vandalizing property. These changes detract not only from the view but also the sensory experience of the gaze and the relationship that the tourist has with the object of the gaze.

As more and more places around the world become victims of their own popularity, the much-anticipated romantic gaze is fundamentally changed to a collective one. When a tourist is expecting a romantic gaze but gets a collective one instead, he or she is likely to be frustrated and dissatisfied with the experience. In reaction to the Roy's Peak photo, a social media user commented, "This really upsets me. What is wrong with these people? If I hiked all the way up and finally got to this view, I would just stare and cry and be thankful I got to see it."[b] Some tourists will avoid these popular, and increasingly overcrowded, sites. Instead, they will look for other places that may be considered secondary or tertiary attractions (i.e., less sought-after) but continue to offer the more personal experience of the romantic gaze.

For those classic sites that have a distinct hold on our imagination, however, countless tourists will still visit. Because they are the "must-see" or "bucket list" places, these tourists will still visit even if they know that they will not have that quiet, solitary experience with the place. Some tourists will not even be bothered by the absence of the romantic gaze. Nonetheless, many of these same tourists will also try to create a photo that gives the appearance of the romantic gaze, as in the case of Roy's Peak.

The average tourist to countless historic and/or scenic sites around the world today will not experience these places in solitude and stillness, as both popular and social media images tend to show. Other tourists are very much a part of the experience of these places today, yet we try to erase them from that experience by waiting for and/or staging a "clear" photograph, free of people. If we are willing to accept that our experience of these sites will involve a collective gaze rather than a romantic one, we are more likely to be satisfied with our experience. In addition, we might find that there is more of interest in the collective gaze if we are willing to approach it with good nature and a little humor.

*Discussion topic*: Why do you think tourists have such a strong motivation to photograph places based on the romantic gaze when the experience is based on the collective gaze?

*Tourism online:* Tourism New Zealand, "Roy's Peak Track," https://www.newzealand.com/au/feature/roys-peak-track/

[a] Sean P. Smith, "Landscapes for 'Likes': Capitalizing on Travel with Instagram," *Social Semiotics* (2019) DOI: 10.1080/10350330.2019.1664579.
[b] Victoria Park, "Form an Orderly Queue: Recreating the Perfect Instagram Photo in New Zealand," *BBC News*, November 28, 2018, accessed June 23, 2020, https://www.bbc.com/news/blogs-trending-46342915.

For most tourists, it is not just about seeing the sights; it is also about recording them. Scholars Mike Robinson and David Picard argue, "To be a tourist, it would seem, involves taking photographs. Whilst photography is clearly not the exclusive preserve of tourists, it is nonetheless one of the markers of *being* a tourist."[27] Tourists have long sought to "capture" the scene and bring it home with them as evidence of having been there and a tool to remember the experience. In the earliest eras of tourism, tourists would sketch the places visited or purchase paintings and replicas of famous sites. This practice became even more firmly embedded in tourism with the development of small, portable, easy-to-use personal cameras. While the camera became a symbol of "the tourist," most were nonetheless willing to endure potential derision to be able to record the places they visited as well as themselves in those places.

Today, mobile phones have become the preferred camera for tourists, and the perceived need to document one's experiences is even stronger. This desire to record can ultimately shape the ways tourists experience the destination. Based on Urry's original concept of the tourist gaze, scholars have proposed the social media tourist gaze, in which the ritualized act of taking and posting photos frames the tourist experience. It is no longer a matter of "I was here" but "I am here."[28] Moreover, with the social media tourist gaze, tourists are aware of their audience and organize their experience in such a way that will best be received by this audience.[29]

The itineraries of both group and independent tours are often structured around stops at locations that have been predetermined to offer the best photographic opportunities. Thus, the first and perhaps the only thing tourists do at these locations is take a picture. These tourists may not even be aware of what they are taking pictures of or why. Tourists are often so focused on taking pictures that they lose the opportunity to really explore the places. While such tourists have visual evidence of the places they visit, they do not really see or experience them through their other senses. They are, in a sense, merely "collecting" places. One study described a "photo-taking impairment effect" when tourists who took photos of museum exhibits did not remember them as well as those who simply observed them.[30]

Selfies further shape the gaze by directing it toward the screen and away from the place and the experience (figure 14.4).[31] There is no shortage of examples of selfie deaths in recent years. Some argue that tourists simply are not paying attention to

**Figure 14.4.** "Selfies" are a part of modern tourism. *Source:* Velvet Nelson

their surroundings as they try to capture the perfect shot. Others cite social media as a factor driving tourists to undertake more risks for the rewards of likes and comments. In response to the death of a college student who lost his footing and fell to his death at the Cliffs of Moher in 2019, a member of Ireland's Department of Health proposed creating "selfie seats" at the site to allow tourists to safely position themselves as they try to capture their shot.[32]

# Virtual Experiences of Place

As virtual reality (VR) and augmented reality (AR) continue to develop, we are starting to see more applications in tourism. At the destination, these technologies have the potential to change the ways tourists experience place. AR applications project information on the users' immediate surroundings to add to visitor experiences. AR applications can overlay digital content onto the real environment. This can help minimize disruption to vulnerable heritage sites in contrast with adding physical infrastructure such as interpretive signage, while providing information in a more engaging format. Overlaid content can help visitors better visualize what a site looked like in a different time period. Destinations can even use AR gaming applications to send tourists on a quest to learn about the place and its history in an active and novel way.[33]

VR applications are increasingly common for the marketing of places. This allows potential visitors to get a feel for the destination to help them decide if they want to visit that place in person. As with the experiential marketing strategies discussed in chapter 12, VR is a way of promoting a greater interest in and attachment to the experience.[34] In light of problems with overtourism and possible restrictions on visitor numbers to vulnerable places, like the Galápagos, VR has been suggested as a means of allowing people to experience these places.[35] Finally, during the COVID-19 shutdowns, VR provided the only means of experiencing other places.

# Conclusion

Tourist experiences have been considered the realm of related fields in tourism studies, such as psychology and sociology; geography has been a less significant approach to this topic. As a fundamentally place-based activity, there is much potential for cross-fertilization between the geography of tourism and the geography of place. Just as representations of place are an extraordinarily important part of tourism, so is the experience of places. Yet, we must always remember, as John Urry wrote in *The Tourist Gaze*, "There is no universal experience that is true for all tourists at all times."[36]

# Key Terms

- collective tourist gaze
- romantic tourist gaze
- sense of place

# Notes

1. Edward Relph, *Place and Placelessness* (London: Pion, 1976), 93.
2. Relph, *Place and Placelessness*, 95.
3. Relph, *Place and Placelessness*; Edward Relph, "Sense of Place," in *Ten Geographic Ideas That Changed the World*, ed. Susan Hanson (New Brunswick, NJ: Rutgers University Press, 1997).
4. Yi-Fu Tuan, "Place: An Experiential Perspective," *Geographical Review* 65 (1975): 164.
5. Jelmer H. G. Jeuring and Karin B. M. Peters, "The Influence of the Weather on Tourist Experiences: Analysing Travel Blog Narratives," *Journal of Vacation Marketing* 19, no. 3 (2013): 209.

6. Anthony Peregrine, "Why You're Wrong about Coach Tours—They Are the Greatest Way to Travel," *The Telegraph*, June 12, 2019, accessed June 24, 2020, https://www.telegraph .co.uk/travel/tours/escorted-tours-why-you-are-wrong-about-coach-holidays/?WT.mc_ id=tmg_share_em.

7. Erik Cohen, "The Tourist Guide: The Origins, Structure, and Dynamics of a Role," *Annals of Tourism Research* 12 (1985): 5–8.

8. Betty Weiler and Rosemary Black, "The Changing Face of the Tour Guide: One-Way Communicator to Choreographer to Co-Creator of the Tourist Experience," *Tourism Recreation Research* 40, no. 3 (2015): 364–5.

9. Jeroen Bryon, "Tour Guides as Storytellers—From Selling to Sharing," *Scandinavian Journal of Hospitality and Tourism* 12, no. 1 (2012): 29.

10. Parks Canada, "Québec by Lantern Light," May 25, 2020, accessed June 25, 2020, https://www.pc.gc.ca/en/lhn-nhs/qc/fortifications/activ/videovisite/lanterne-lantern.

11. John Ap and Kevin K. F. Wong. "Case Study on Tour Guiding: Professionalism, Issues, and Problems," *Tourism Management* 22 (2001): 551.

12. Heidi Dahles, "The Politics of Tour Guiding: Image Management in Indonesia," *Annals of Tourism Research* 29, no. 3 (2002): 787–8.

13. Katherine Lagrave, "Solo Travelers Aren't Being Punished Anymore," *Condé Nast Traveler*, January 31, 2019, accessed June 25, 2020, https://www.cntraveler.com/story/solo-travelers-arent-being-punished-anymore.

14. Erica Wilson and Donna E. Little, "The Solo Female Travel Experience: Exploring the 'Geography of Women's Fear,'" *Current Issues in Tourism* 11, no. 2 (2008): 174.

15. Megan Specia and Tariro Mzezewa, "Adventurous. Alone. Attacked." *The New York Times*, March 25, 2019, accessed June 25, 2020, https://www.nytimes.com/2019/03/25/travel/ solo-female-travel.html.

16. Erica Wilson and Donna E. Little, "A 'Relative Escape'? The Impact of Constraints on Women Who Travel Solo," *Tourism Review International* 9 (2005): 165–6.

17. Rachel Levitt, "A Feminist Shares Her Un-Feminist Trick for Staying Safe While Traveling," *Fodor's Travel*, November 28, 2018, accessed June 25, 2020, https://www.fodors.com/ news/travel-tips/a-feminist-shares-her-un-feminist-trick-for-staying-safe-while-traveling.

18. Fiona Jordan and Heather Gibson, "'We're Not Stupid … But We'll Not Stay Home Either': Experiences of Solo Women Travelers," *Tourism Review International* 9 (2005): 205.

19. Lale Arikoglu, "For Better Hotels, Hilton's Kellyn Smith Kenny Talks to Women about Every Detail," *Condé Nast Traveler*, December 6, 2019, accessed June 25, 2020, https://www. cntraveler.com/story/kellyn-smith-kenny-hilton.

20. Tourism RESET, "Tourism RESET," accessed June 25, 2020, https://www.tourismreset .com.

21. Jeffrey R. Finney and Amy E. Potter, "'You're Out of Your Place': Black Mobility on Tybee Island, Georgia from Civil Rights to Orange Crush," *Southeastern Geographer* 58, no. 1 (2018): 117.

22. Perry L. Carter, "Coloured Places and Pigmented Holidays: Racialized Leisure Travel," *Tourism Geographies* 10, no. 3 (2008): 266–7, 278, 281.

23. Julia Buckley, "How I Travel with My Invisible Disability," *Condé Nast Traveler*, August 19, 2019, accessed June 25, 2020, https://www.cntraveler.com/story/how-i-travel-with-my-invisible-disability.

24. Ayse Nilay Evcil, "Barriers and Preferences to Leisure Activities for Wheelchair Users in Historic Places," *Tourism Geographies* 20, no. 4 (2018): 701–2.

25. Katherine Lagrave. "Machu Picchu Is Wheelchair Accessible for the First Time," *Condé Nast Traveler*, February 4, 2019, accessed June 25, 2020, https://www.cntraveler.com/story/ machu-picchu-is-wheelchair-accessible-for-the-first-time.

26. John Urry, *The Tourist Gaze* (London: Sage, 1990); John Urry, *Consuming Places* (London: Routledge, 1995), 131.

27. Mike Robinson and David Picard, "Moments, Magic, and Memories: Photographic Tourists, Tourist Photographs, and Making Worlds," in *The Framed World: Tourism, Tourists, and Photography*, ed. Mike Robinson and David Picard (Farnham: Ashgate, 2009), 1.

28. Michael James Walsh, Raechel Johns, and Naomi F. Dale, "The Social Media Tourist Gaze: Social Media Photography and Its Disruption at the Zoo," *Information Technology & Tourism* 21 (2019): 393.

29. Andrew Duffy, "Two-Way Street: How Smartphones and the Social Web Impact the Traveller's Liminal Gaze," *Mobile Media & Communication* 7, no. 1 (2019): 62.

30. Allie Jones, "Are Vacations Better When You Don't Take a Single Photo?" *Condé Nast Traveler*, November 19, 2019, accessed June 25, 2020, https://www.cntraveler.com/story/are-vacations-better-when-you-dont-take-a-single-photo.

31. Ulrike Gretzel, "The Role of Social Media in Creating and Addressing Overtourism," in *Overtourism: Issues, Realities and Solutions*, eds. Rachel Dodds and Richard W. Butler (Berlin: De Gruyter, 2019), 69.

32. Jesse Tabit, "These Places Could Be Getting 'Selfie Seats' Because People Are Dying," *Fodor's Travel*, February 13, 2019, accessed June 25, 2020, https://www.fodors.com/news/news/these-places-could-be-getting-selfie-seats-because-people-are-dying.

33. M. Claudia tom Dieck and Timothy Jung, "A Theoretical Model of Mobile Augmented Reality Acceptance in Urban Heritage Tourism," *Current Issues in Tourism* 21, no. 2 (2018): 154–6.

34. Tom Griffin and Meghan Muldoon, "Exploring Virtual Reality Experiences of Slum Tourism," *Tourism Geographies* (2020): DOI: 10.1080/14616688.2020.1713881.

35. CNT Editors, "How Technology Can Help Us Tackle Overtourism," *Condé Nast Traveler*, March 25, 2019, accessed June 4, 2020, https://www.cntraveler.com/story/how-technology-can-help-us-tackle-overtourism.

36. Urry, *The Tourist Gaze*, 1.

# Glossary

**accessibility.** The relative ease with which one location may be reached from another

**acculturation.** The process of exchange that takes place when two groups of people come into contact over time

**affect.** To act on or produce a change in something

**back region.** The part of a destination that is not intended for, or is closed to, tourists

**biogeography.** The study of living things

**climate change adaptation.** The technological, economic, and sociocultural changes that are intended to minimize the risks and capitalize on the opportunities created by climate change

**climate change mitigation.** The technological, economic, and sociocultural changes that can lead to reductions in greenhouse gas emissions

**climatology.** The study of climate

**code of conduct.** A set of voluntary principles intended to inform patterns of behavior among tourism stakeholders and tourists to minimize the negative environmental effects of tourism

**collective tourist gaze.** The visual consumption of public places that are characterized by the presence of other people

**commodification.** The transformation of something of intrinsic value into a product that can be packaged and sold for consumption

**cultural geography.** A broad topical branch in human geography that studies various issues pertaining to how societies make sense of, give meaning to, interact with, and shape space and place

**deferred demand.** Those people who wish to travel but do not because of a problem or barrier at the desired destination or in the tourism infrastructure

**demarketing.** Strategies to reduce the demand for the experience of a place among tourists in general or specific market segments

**demonstration effect.** Changes in attitudes, values, or patterns of behavior experienced by local people as a result of observing tourists

**direct economic effect.** The introduction of tourist dollars to the local economy

347

**discretionary income.** The money that is left over after taxes and all other necessary expenses have been taken care of

**domestic tourism.** The activities of a resident visitor within their own country on a tourism trip

**drifter.** A type of tourist that seeks out new tourism destinations, utilizes local infrastructure, and immerses himself or herself in the local culture

**economic development.** A process of change that creates the conditions for improvements in productivity and income of the population

**economic geography.** The study of the spatial patterns of economic activities, including locations, distributions, interactions, and outcomes

**ecotourism.** (the International Ecotourism Society definition). Responsible travel to natural areas that conserves the environment, sustains the well-being of local people, and involves interpretation and education

**effect.** Something that is produced by an agency or cause; a result or a consequence

**effective demand.** Those people who wish to and have the opportunity to travel

**electronic word-of-mouth.** The sharing of information using Web 2.0 technologies

**environmental carrying capacity.** The extent of tourism that can take place at a site before its environment experiences negative effects

**environmental geography.** A topical branch of geography that lies at the intersection of physical geography and human geography and is concerned with the ways in which the environment affects people and people affect the environment

**experience stage.** The primary stage of the tourism process, in which tourists participate in a variety of activities at a destination

**experiential marketing.** Marketing that uses multiple senses in such a way that will prompt the audience to imagine the experience and become emotionally invested in it

**explorer.** A type of tourist that travels for more than pleasure or diversion, utilizes a combination of tourist and local infrastructure, and seeks interaction with local people

**front region.** The part of a destination that has been entirely constructed for the purpose of tourism

**geomorphology.** The study of landforms

**geotourism.** (National Geographic Society definition). Tourism that sustains or enhances the geographical character of a place, including its environment, culture, aesthetics, heritage, and the well-being of its residents

**globalization.** The increasing interconnectedness of the world

**historical geography.** The study of the geography and geographic conditions of past periods and the processes of change that have taken place over time to better understand the geography of the present

**human geography.** One of the two main subdivisions of geography, which focuses on the study of the patterns of human occupation of the earth

**hydrology.** The study of water

**inbound tourism.** The activities of a nonresident visitor within the destination or country on a tourism trip

**indirect economic effect.** The second round of spending, in which recipients of tourist dollars pay the expenses of and reinvest in their tourism business

**individual mass tourist.** A type of tourist that travels for pleasure and seeks experiences different from those that may be obtained at home without straying too far from his or her comfort zone

**induced economic effect.** An additional round of spending after the recipients of tourist dollars pay the government, employees, suppliers, and so on; money spent by these new recipients for their own purposes

**interchange.** A node within a transportation network

**international tourism.** The activities of resident visitors outside their country on a tourism trip

**last-chance tourism.** A recent trend in tourism in which tourists seek environments that are experiencing fundamental changes and might ultimately "disappear"

**leakages.** The portion of the income from tourism that does not get reinvested in the local economy; occurs with each round of spending

**leisure time.** The free time left over after necessary activities have been completed, in which an individual may do what he or she chooses

**lingua franca.** A language used for the purpose of communication between people speaking different languages

**linkages.** The connections formed between tourism and other local economic sectors that can support tourism and help provide the goods and services demanded by tourists

**mass tourism.** The production of standardized experiences made available to large numbers of tourists at a low cost

**meteorology.** The study of weather

**movement stage.** The stage of the tourism process in which tourists use some form of transportation to reach the destination and to return home; may be a means to an end or a part of the experience stage

**multiplier effect.** A ratio of the additional income generated by the indirect and induced economic effects from the respending of tourist dollars in the local economy

**niche tourism.** The production of specialized experiences for relatively small markets based on a particular resource at the destination or a specific tourism product

**no demand.** Those people who do not travel and do not wish to travel

**organized mass tourist.** A type of tourist that travels purely for diversion, in which place is less important than experience, and is entirely dependent on the tourism infrastructure

**outbound tourism.** The activities of a resident visitor outside the destination or country on a tourism trip

**overtourism.** (from the United Nations World Tourism Organization definition). The impact of tourism on a destination, or parts thereof, that excessively influences perceived quality of life of citizens and/or quality of visitors experiences in a negative way

**perceptual carrying capacity.** The extent of tourism that can take place at a site before tourist dissatisfaction occurs

**physical carrying capacity.** The limits of a particular space, such as the number of tourists a site can contain

**physical geography.** One of the two main subdivisions of geography, which focuses on the study of the earth's physical systems

**place.** A unit of the earth's surface that has meaning based on the physical and human features of that location

**placelessness.** A loss of identity where one place looks and feels like other places, often as a result of the superficial, stereotypical images circulated by the media

**place promotion.** The deliberate use of marketing tools to communicate both specific and selective ideas and images about a particular place to a desired audience for the purpose of shaping perceptions of that place and ultimately influencing decisions

**place representation.** The way places are summarized and portrayed to an audience that then creates ideas and images about those places

**political geography.** The study of the ways states relate to each other in a globalized world

**post-trip stage.** The final stage in the tourism process after the tourists return home, in which they relive their trip through memories, pictures, and souvenirs

**potential demand.** Those people who wish to travel and will do so when their circumstances change

**preferred sites.** Planned locations that have sufficient tourist facilities to spatially concentrate visitors, thereby limiting the environmental effects of tourism to a particular area

**pre-trip stage.** The first stage in the tourism process, in which potential tourists evaluate their travel options, make decisions, and complete all arrangements for a trip

**pro-poor tourism.** (Pro-Poor Tourism Partnership definition). Tourism that results in increased net benefits for poor people and ensures that tourism growth contributes to poverty reduction

**protected area.** (International Union for Conservation of Nature definition). A clearly defined geographical space recognised, dedicated, and managed, through legal or other effective means, to achieve the long-term conservation of nature with associated ecosystems and cultural values

**pull factor.** Something in the destination environment that attracts people to visit that place over another

**push factor.** Something impels people to temporarily leave their usual environment to travel somewhere else

**region.** A unit of the earth's surface that is distinguished from other areas by certain characteristics

**regional geography.** An approach in geography that studies the varied geographic characteristics of a region

**relative location.** The position of a place in relation to other places

**resilience.** The ability of a system to absorb shocks and disturbances and recover

**romantic tourist gaze.** A private, personal experience in which tourists feel they form a connection with a place through the visual consumption of that place

**rural geography.** The study of contemporary rural landscapes, societies, and economies

**scale.** The size of the area studied

**sense of place.** The association with and emotional attachment to places

**social carrying capacity.** The extent of tourism that can take place at a site before the local community becomes dissatisfied

**social geography.** The topical branch of geography concerned with the relationships between society and space, such as space as a setting for social interaction or the ways in which spaces are shaped by these interactions

**spatial zoning.** A land management strategy that designates permissible uses of an area based on its resources and/or character—that is, what tourism activities may be undertaken where

**suppressed demand.** Those people who wish to travel but do not

**sustainable tourism development.** (United Nations World Tourism Organization definition). Tourism that takes full account of its current and future economic, social, and environmental impacts, addressing the needs of visitors, the industry, the environment, and host communities

**terminal.** A node where transport flows begin and end

**topical geography.** An approach in geography that studies a particular geographic topic in various place or regional contexts

**tourism.** (from the United Nations World Tourism Organization definitions). The activities of visitors or travelers taking a trip to a destination outside of their usual environment for less than a year for any purpose (business, leisure, or other personal purpose) other than to be employed in the country or place visited

**tourism attractions.** Aspects of places that are of interest to tourists and can include things to be seen, activities to be done, or experiences to be had

**tourism carrying capacity.** Refers to the number of tourists a destination or attraction can support and sustain

**tourism demand.** The total number of persons who travel, or wish to travel, to use tourist facilities and services at places away from their places of work and residence

**tourism products.** The increasingly specialized types of experiences provided in the supply of tourism

**tourism resource.** A component of the destination's physical or cultural environment that has the potential to facilitate tourism or provide the basis for a tourism attraction

**tourism resource audit.** A tool that can be used by destination stakeholders to systematically identify, classify, and assess all of those features of a place that will impact the supply of tourism

**tourism stakeholders.** The various individuals and/or organizations that have an interest in tourism

**tourism supply.** The aggregate of all businesses that directly provide goods or services to facilitate business, pleasure, and leisure activities away from the home environment

**tourist area life cycle.** A model proposed to explain the process of development and evolution of tourism destinations over six stages, including exploration, involvement, development, consolidation, stagnation, and an undetermined post-stagnation stage

**tourist dollars.** The money that tourists bring with them and spend at the destination on lodging, food, souvenirs, excursions, and other activities or services

**tourist-generating regions.** The source areas or origins for tourists

**tourist inversions.** The theory that the experience that a tourist seeks in his or her temporary escape is one of contrasts and involves a shift in attitudes or patterns of behavior away from the norm to a temporary opposite

**tourist-receiving regions.** The destination areas for tourists

**tourist typology.** An organizational framework to identify categories of tourists based on motivations, behavior, demographic characteristics, or other variables

**transport geography.** The topical branch of geography concerned with the movement of goods and people from one location to another, including the spatial patterns of this movement and the geographic factors that allow or constrain it

**transportation mode.** The means of movement or type of transportation; generally air, surface, or water

**transportation network.** The spatial structure and organization of the infrastructure that supports, and to some extent determines, patterns of movement

**transportation node.** An access point on a transportation network

**travel account.** The difference between the income that the destination country receives from tourism and the expenditures of that country's citizens when they travel abroad

**Travel 2.0.** The interactive approach in which tourists are both consumers and producers of travel information online

**urban geography.** The study of the relationships between or patterns within cities and metropolitan areas

**vulnerability.** A system's sensitivity or susceptibility to shocks and disturbances

**word-of-mouth.** The passing of information, typically through person-to-person communication, that shapes ideas about places and influences travel decisions

# Bibliography

Adgate, Brad. "An Advanced Media Ad Campaign for Puerto Rico Tourism." *Forbes*, February 5, 2019. Accessed March 20, 2020. https://www.forbes.com/sites/bradadgate/2019/02/05/an-advanced-media-ad-campaign-for-puerto-rico-tourism/#13c0e5492820.

Agapito, Dora, Patrícia Oom do Valle, and Júlio da Costa Mendes. "Sensory Marketing and Tourist Experiences." *Spatial and Organizational Dynamics* 10 (2012): 7–19.

Airbnb Help Center. "What Is Open Homes?" Accessed May 15, 2020. https://www.airbnb.com/help/article/2340/what-is-open-homes.

Airbnb Newsroom. "Fast Facts." Accessed March 18, 2020. https://news.airbnb.com/fast-facts/.

Air Transport Action Group. "Beginner's Guide to Sustainable Aviation Fuel, Edition 3," November 2017. Accessed April 15, 2020. https://aviationbenefits.org/media/166152/beginners-guide-to-saf_web.pdf.

Albalate, Daniel, and Germà Bel. "Tourism and Urban Public Transport: Holding Demand Pressure under Supply Constraints." *Tourism Management* 31 (2010): 425–33.

Albalate, Daniel, Javier Campos, and Juan Luis Jiménez. "Tourism and High Speed Rail in Spain: Does the AVE Increase Local Visitors?" *Annals of Tourism Research* 65 (2017): 71–82.

Alderman, Derek H. "Surrogation and the Politics of Remembering Slavery in Savannah, Georgia (USA)." *Journal of Historical Geography* 36, no. 1 (2010): 90–101.

Alderman, Derek H., and Rachel M. Campbell. "Symbolic Excavation and the Artifact Politics of Remembering Slavery in the American South: Observations from Walterboro, South Carolina." *Southeastern Geographer* 48, no. 3 (2008): 338–5.

Alderman, Derek H., and Joshua Inwood. "Toward a Pedagogy of Jim Crow: A Geographic Reading of The Green Book in Teaching Ethnic Geography in the 21st Century." In *Teaching Ethnic Geography in the 21st Century*, edited by Lawrence E. Estaville, Edris J. Montalvo, and Fenda A. Akiwumi, 68–78. Washington, DC: National Council for Geographic Education, 2014.

American Association of Geographers. "AAG 2019 Annual Meeting – Washington, DC." Accessed March 11, 2020. https://www2.aag.org/aagannualmeeting/AAGAnnualMeeting/AAG2019DC.aspx.

———. "AAG to Facilitate Virtual Meeting." Accessed March 23, 2020. https://www2.aag.org/aagannualmeeting/.

American Shore and Beach Preservation Association. "National Beach Nourishment Database." Accessed April 20, 2020. https://gim2.aptim.com/ASBPANationwideRenourishment/.

Andrews, Hazel. "Feeling at Home: Embodying Britishness in a Spanish Charter Tourists Resort." *Tourist Studies* 5, no. 3 (2005): 247–66.

Andriotis, Konstantinos. *Degrowth in Tourism: Conceptual, Theoretical and Philosophical Issues,* Oxfordshire: CABI, 2018.

Anholt, Simon. *Places: Identity, Image and Reputation.* Houndmills: Palgrave Macmillan, 2010.

Ap, John, and Kevin K. F. Wong. "Case Study on Tour Guiding: Professionalism, Issues, and Problems." *Tourism Management* 22 (2001): 551–63.

Arias, L. "Mob of Tourists at Costa Rica's Ostional Beach Prevents Seat Turtles From Nesting." *The Tico Times,* September 9, 2015. Accessed May 20, 2020. https://ticotimes. net/2015/09/09/crowd-tourists-costa-rica-prevent-sea-turtles-nesting.

Armstead, Myra B. Young. "Revisiting Hotels and Other Lodgings: American Tourist Spaces through the Lens of Black Pleasure-Travelers, 1880–1950." *The Journal of Decorative and Propaganda Arts* 25 (2005): 136–59.

Ashley, Caroline, Charlotte Boyd, and Harold Goodwin. "Pro-Poor Tourism: Putting Poverty at the Heart of the Tourism Agenda." *Natural Resource Perspectives* 51 (2000): 1–6.

Ashley, Caroline, Dilys Roe, and Harold Goodwin. "Pro-Poor Strategies: Making Tourism Work for the Poor." *Pro-Poor Tourism Report* 1 (2001). Available at https://www.odi.org/sites/ odi.org.uk/files/odi-assets/publications-opinion-files/3246.pdf

Arikoglu, Lale. "For Better Hotels, Hilton's Kellyn Smith Kenny Talks to Women About Every Detail." *Condé Nast Traveler,* December 6, 2019. Accessed June 25, 2020. https://www.cn-traveler.com/story/kellyn-smith-kenny-hilton.

Asquith, James. "Grounded Flight Attendants are Being Redeployed to Hospitals in Coronavirus Battle." *Forbes,* March 30, 2020. Accessed May 15, 2020. https://www.forbes.com/sites/ jamesasquith/2020/03/30/grounded-flight-attendants-are-being-redeployed-to-hospitals-in-coronavirus-battle/#139f05a74eb6.

———. "Have Instagram Influencers Ruined Travel for an Entire Generation?" *Forbes,* September 1, 2019. Accessed June 16, 2020. https://www.forbes.com/sites/jamesasquith/ 2019/09/01/have-instagram-influencers-ruined-travel-for-an-entire-generation/#2e52df3c1e30.

Audrezet, Alice, Gwarlann de Kerviler, and Julie Guidry Moulard. "Authenticity Under Threat: When Social Media Influencers Need to Go Beyond Self-Presentation." *Journal of Business Research* (2019) https://doi.org/10.1016/j.jbusres.2018.07.008.

Awwad, Ramadan A., T. N. Olsthoorn, Y. Zhou, Stefan Uhlenbrook, and Ebel Smidt. "Optimum Pumping-Injection System for Saline Groundwater Desalination in Sharm El Sheikh." *WaterMill Working Paper Series 11* (2008). Accessed October 26, 2011. http://www. unesco-ihe.org/WaterMill-Working-Paper-Series/Working-Paper-Series

Badcock, James. "Spain's Hotel Chambermaids 'Las Kellys' Fight for Fair Pay." *BBC News,* October 18, 2017. Accessed May 8, 2020. https://www.bbc.com/news/world-europe-41650252.

Bali Discovery Tours. "Strong Start to 2019 for Foreign Tourist Arrivals to Bali." Accessed April 20, 2020. https://balidiscovery.com/news/strong-start-to-2019-for-foreign-tourist-arrivals-to-bali.

Banerjee, Sukanya, Siddhartha Sankar Nath, Nilanjan Dey, and Hjime Eto. "Global Medial Tourism: A Review." In *Medical Tourism: Breakthroughs in Research and Practice,* 1–19. Hershey, PA: IGI Global, 2018.

Baron, Jessica. "The Key to Gen Z is Video Content." *Forbes,* July 3, 2019. Accessed June 15, 2020. https://www.forbes.com/sites/jessicabaron/2019/07/03/the-key-to-gen-z-is-video-content/#53921db53484.

Basu, Paul. "Route Metaphors of 'Roots-Tourism' in the Scottish Highland Diaspora." In *Reframing Pilgrimage: Cultures in Motion,* edited by Simon Coleman and John Eade, 150–74. London: Routledge, 2004.

Battour, Mohamed and Mohd Nazari Ismail. "Halal Tourism, Concepts, Practises, Challenges and Future." *Tourism Management Perspectives* 19 (2016): 150–54.

Baum, Tom. "Images of Tourism Past and Present." *International Journal of Contemporary Hospitality Management* 8, no. 4 (1996): 25–30.

Beaven, Katherine Alex. "A Futurist Predicts How You'll Be Traveling After Coronavirus." *Fodor's Travel*, April 1, 2020. Accessed April 13, 2020. https://www.fodors.com/news/coronavirus/a-futurist-predicts-how-youll-be-traveling-after-coronavirus.

Becker, Elizabeth. *Overbooked: The Exploding Business of Travel and Tourism*. New York: Simon & Schuster Paperbacks, 2013.

Beckerson, John, and John K. Walton. "Selling Air: Marketing the Intangible at British Resorts." In *Histories of Tourism: Representation, Identity, and Conflict*, edited by John Walton, 55–68. Clevedon, UK: Channel View Publications, 2005.

Benjamin, Stefanie, Alana Dillette, and Derek H. Alderman. "'We Can't Return to Normal': Committing to Tourism Equity in the Post-Pandemic Age." *Tourism Geographies* DOI: 10.1080/14616688.2020.1759130.

Blake, Eric S. "The 2017 Atlantic Hurricane Season: Catastropic Losses and Costs." *Weatherwise* 71, no. 3 (2018): 28–37.

Blázquez-Salom, Macià, Asunción Blanco-Romero, Jaume Gual Carbonell, and Ivan Murray. "Tourist Gentrification of Retail Shops in Palma (Majorca)." In *Overtourism: Excesses, Discontents and Measures in Travel and Tourism*, edited by Claudio Milano, Jospeh M. Cheer, and Marina Novelli, 36–69. Oxfordshire: CABI, 2019.

Boeing. "Pilot & Technician Outlook 2019–2038." Accessed April 15, 2020. https://www.boeing.com/commercial/market/pilot-technician-outlook/.

Boisen, Martin, Kees Terlouw, Peter Groote, and Oscar Couwenberg. "Reframing Place Promotion, Place Marketing, and Place Branding—Moving Beyond Conceptual Confusion." *Cities*, 80 (2018): 4–11.

Boniface, Brian, and Chris Cooper. *Worldwide Destinations: The Geography of Travel and Tourism*. 4th ed. Amsterdam: Elsevier Butterworth Heinemann, 2005.

Boorstin, Daniel J. *The Image: A Guide to Pseudo-Events in America*. New York: Vintage Books, 1961; 50th Anniversary Edition, 2012.

Bordelon, Louise A., and Sanette L. A. Ferreira. "Tourist Photographs and Destination Imagery on Social Media: Reading the Stellenbosch Winelands through a Tourist Lens." *Tourist Review International* 21 (2017): 317–29.

Borunda, Alejandra. "See How Much of the Amazon is Burning, How It Compares to Other Years." *National Geographic*, August 29, 2019. Accessed April 20, 2020. https://www.nationalgeographic.com/environment/2019/08/amazon-fires-cause-deforestation-graphic-map/.

Bosangit, Carmela, Juline Dulnuan, and Miguela Mena. "Using Travel Blogs to Examine Postconsumption Behavior of Tourists." *Journal of Vacation Marketing* 18, no. 3 (2012): 207–19.

Brady, Sasha. "Self-Driving Hotel Suites Could Dramatically Change the Way We Travel." *Lonely Planet*, November 23, 2018. Accessed May 4, 2020. https://www.lonelyplanet.com/articles/self-driving-hotel-suites.

The Bruno Brothers. "Bani Amor: Decolonizing Travel Culture." Accessed June 4, 2020. https://vimeo.com/190281078.

Bryon, Jeroen. "Tour Guides as Storytellers—From Selling to Sharing," *Scandinavian Journal of Hospitality and Tourism* 12, no. 1 (2012): 27–43.

Buckley, Julia. "How I Travel With My Invisible Disability." *Condé Nast Traveler*, August 19, 2019. Accessed June 25, 2020. https://www.cntraveler.com/story/how-i-travel-with-my-invisible-disability.

Bullen, Frank T. *Back to Sunny Seas*. London: Smith, Elder & Co., 1905.

Burgen, Stephen. "Spanish Hotel Cleaners Seek Tripadvisor's Help to Fight Exploitation." *The Guardian*, July 2, 2018. Accessed May 8, 2020. https://www.theguardian.com/world/2018/jul/02/spanish-chambermaids-seek-tripadvisor-help-to-fight-exploitation?CMP=Share_iOSApp_Other.

Butler, Alex. "Millennials Would Rather Take Shorter Trips Than One Long Vacation, Says Survey." *Lonely Planet*, May 9, 2016. Accessed March 19, 2020. https://www.lonelyplanet.com/articles/millennial-vacation-trips.

Butler, David L. "Whitewashing Plantations." *International Journal of Hospitality & Tourism Administration* 2, no. 3–4 (2001): 163–75.

Butler, David L., Perry L. Carter, and Owen J. Dwyer. "Imagining Plantations: Slavery, Dominant Narratives, and the Foreign Born." *Southeastern Geographer* 48, no. 3 (2008): 288–302.

Butler, James A. "Tourist or Native Son: Wordsworth's Homecomings of 1799–1800." *Nineteenth-Century Literature* 51, no. 1 (1996): 1–15.

Butler, R. W. "The Concept of a Tourist Area Cycle Evolution: Implications for Management of Resources." *Canadian Geographer* 24, no. 1 (1980): 5–12.

Butler, Richard. "The Resort Cycle Two Decades On." In *Tourism in the 21st Century: Lessons from Experience*, edited by Bill Faulkner, Gianna Moscardo, and Eric Laws, 284–99. London: Continuum, 2000.

Butler, Richard W. "Overtourism and the Tourism Area Life Cycle." In *Overtourism: Issues, Realities and Solutions*, edited by Rachel Dodds and Richard W. Butler, 76–89. Berlin: De Gruyter, 2019.

———. "Overtourism in Rural Settings: The Scottish Highlands and Islands." In *Overtourism: Issues, Realities and Solutions*, edited by Rachel Dodds and Richard W. Butler, 199–213. Berlin: De Gruyter, 2019.

Butler, Richard, and Wantanee Suntikul. "Tourism and War: An Ill Wind?" In *Tourism and War*, edited by Richard Butler and Wantanee Suntikul, 1–11. London: Routledge, 2013.

Buzinde, Christine N., and Carla Almeida Santos. "Interpreting Slavery Tourism." *Annals of Tourism Research* 36, no. 3 (2009): 439–58.

Cai, Wenjie, Brad McKenna, and Lena Waizenegger. "Turning It Off: Emotions in Digital-Free Travel," *Journal of Travel Research*, https://doi.org/10.1177/0047287519868314.

Campbell, Charlie. "Otto Warmbier's Death May Spell the End of American Tourism to North Korea. Sadly, That's About It." *Time*, June 22, 2017. Accessed April 29, 2020. https://time.com/4824670/north-korea-otto-warmbier-kim-jong-un-torture/.

Caribbean Tourism Organization. *Caribbean Vacation Planner*. Coral Gables, FL: Gold Book, 2002.

Carter, Perry L. "Coloured Places and Pigmented Holidays: Racialized Leisure Travel," *Tourism Geographies* 10, no. 3 (2008): 265–84.

Chaffey, Dave. "Global Social Media Research Summary 2020." *Smart Insights*, April 17, 2020. Accessed June 15, 2020. https://www.smartinsights.com/social-media-marketing/social-media-strategy/new-global-social-media-research/.

Champion Traveler. "One SpaceX Rocket Launch Produces the Equivalent of 395 Transatlantic Flights Worth of CO2 Emissions." Accessed April 10, 2020. https://championtraveler.com/news/one-spacex-rocket-launch-produces-the-equivalent-of-395-transatlantic-flights-worth-of-co2-emissions/.

Chang, Brittany. "32 Cruise Ships around the World Have Been Affected by the Coronavirus So Far, Leaving Passengers Infected, Dead, or Stranded—See the Full List." *Business Insider*, March 25, 2020. Accessed April 13, 2020. https://www.businessinsider.com/cruises-that-have-been-affected-by-coronavirus–2020–3.

Chang, T. C., and Shirlena Huang. "Urban Tourism: Between the Global and the Local." In *A Companion to Tourism*, edited by Alan A. Lew, C. Michael Hall, and Allan M. Williams, 223–34. Malden, MA: Blackwell, 2004.

Chappell, Bill. "Family Trust Wins Supreme Court Fight against Bike Trail." *NPR*, March 10, 2014. Accessed April 27, 2020. https://www.npr.org/sections/thetwo-way/2014/03/10/288584936/family-trust-wins-supreme-court-fight-against-bike-trail.

Cheer, Joseph M., Leigh Mathews, Kathryn E. van Doore, and Karen Flanagan. *Modern Day Slavery and Orphanage Tourism*. Oxfordshire: CABI, 2020.

Cheslaw, Louis. "Gen Z Are Pressuring the Travel Industry in All the Right Ways." *Condé Nast Traveler*, July 29, 2019. Accessed March 20, 2020. https://www.cntraveller.com/article/gen-z-travel-industry.

———. "What to Know About the San Francisco (SFO) Water Bottle Ban." *Condé Nast Traveler*, August 5, 2019. Accessed July 10, 2020. https://www.cntraveler.com/story/san-francisco-airport-sfo-plastic-water-bottle-ban.

———. "What to Know About Venice's Strict Tourism Rules." *Condé Nast Traveler*, July 30, 2019. Accessed July 9, 2020. https://www.cntraveler.com/story/what-to-know-about-venices-strict-tourism-rules.

———. "You Could be Fined $450 for Sitting on Rome's Spanish Steps." *Condé Nast Traveler*, August 8, 2019. Accessed July 9, 2020. https://www.cntraveler.com/story/you-could-be-fined-dollar450-for-sitting-on-romes-spanish-steps.

Chhabra, Deepak, Robert Healy, and Erin Sills. "Staged Authenticity and Heritage Tourism." *Annals of Tourism Research* 30, no. 3 (2003): 702–19.

Christou, Evangelos. "Introduction to Part 2." In *Social Media in Travel, Tourism and Hospitality: Theory, Practice and Cases*, edited by Marianna Sigala, Evangelos Christou, and Ulrike Gretzel, 69–71. Ashgate: Surrey, 2012.

Chung, Jin Young, and Taehee Whang. "The Impact of Low Cost Carriers on Korean Island Tourism." *Journal of Transport Geography* 19 (2011): 1335–40.

Churchill Downs Incorporated. "What to Expect at the Kentucky Derby." Accessed March 11, 2020. https://www.kentuckyderby.com/visit/what-to-expect.

Cintrón, Víctor Quiñones, Jonathon Von Hack, Myra Mabel Pérez Rivera, Angely Yomara Medina Velázquez, and José Davis Pellot. "The Evolution of Demarketing Literature." *Fórum Empresarial* 22, no. 1 (2017): 77–108.

Claval, Paul. "Regional Geography: Past and Present (A Review of Ideas, Approaches and Goals)." *Geographia Polonica* 80, no. 1 (2007): 25–42.

"Climate Change Could Bring Tourists to UK—Report." *The Guardian*, July 28, 2006. Accessed April 20, 2020. https://www.theguardian.com/travel/2006/jul/28/travelnews.uknews.climatechange.

CNT Editors. "How Technology Can Help Us Tackle Overtourism." *Condé Nast Traveler*, March 25, 2019. Accessed June 4, 2020. https://www.cntraveler.com/story/how-technology-can-help-us-tackle-overtourism.

Coca-Stefaniak, Andres, and Alastair M. Morrison. "City Tourism Destinations and Terrorism—A Worrying Trend for Now, But Could It Get Worse?" *International Journal of Tourism Cities* 4, no. 2 (2018): 409–12.

Cohen, Erik. "Toward a Sociology of International Tourism." *Social Research* 39, no. 1 (1972): 164–82.

———. "Authenticity and Commoditization in Tourism." *Annals of Tourism Research* 15 (1988): 371–86.

———. "The Tourist Guide: The Origins, Structure, and Dynamics of a Role." *Annals of Tourism Research* 12 (1985): 5–29.

Cohen, Scott A., and Debbie Hopkins. "Autonomous Vehicles and the Future of Urban Tourism." *Annals of Tourism Research* 74 (2019): 33–42.

Cole, Sam. "Space Tourism: Prospects, Positioning, and Planning." *Journal of Tourism Futures* 1, no. 2 (2015): 131–40.

Cole, Stroma. "Introduction: Gender Equality and Tourism—Beyond Empowerment." *In Gender Equality and Tourism: Beyond Empowerment*, edited by Stroma Cole, 1–11. Oxfordshire: CABI, 2018.

Columbus Zoo and Aquarium. "The Wilds—History." Accessed May 28, 2020. https://thewilds.columbuszoo.org/home/about/about-the-wilds/history.

Cook, Matthew R. "Counter-Narratives of Slavery in the Deep South: The Politics of Empathy Along and Beyond River Road." *Journal of Heritage Tourism* 11, no. 3 (2016): 290–308.

Cormack, Bill. *A History of Holidays, 1812–1990*. London: Routledge, 1998. "Coronavirus: 'Unprecedented' Crowds in Wales Despite Warnings. BBC News, March 22, 2020. Accessed May 18, 2020. https://www.bbc.com/news/uk-wales–51994504.

"Coronavirus: 'Unprecedented' Crowds in Wales Despite Warnings," BBC News, March 22, 2020, accessed May 18, 2020, https://www.bbc.com/news/uk-wales-51994504.

Cranley, Ellen. "The 29 Riskiest Countries for Americans to Travel to." *Business Insider*, June 12, 2019. Accessed April 29, 2020. https://www.businessinsider.com/travel-warnings-us-state-department–2019–6.

Creatour. "Overview." Accessed June 23, 2020. https://creatour.pt/en/about/overview/.

Creegan, Chris, and Kieran Guilbert. "Slavery Risk for Young Brits taking Mallorca Seasonal Party Jobs." *Global Citizen*, June 1, 2018. Accessed March 9, 2020. https://www.globalcitizen.org/en/content/britons-modern-slavery-uk-mallorca-party-jobs/.

Cresswell, Tim. *Place: A Short Introduction*. Malden, MA: Blackwell, 2004.

Cruise Lines International Association. "2020 State of the Cruise Industry Outlook." Accessed April 13, 2020. https://cruising.org/-/media/research-updates/research/state-of-the-cruise-industry.pdf.

Cruz, Reil G., and Giovanni Francis A. Legaspi. "Boracay Beach Closure: The Role of the Government and the Private Sector." In *Overtourism: Issues, Realities and Solutions*, edited by Rachel Dodds and Richard W. Butler, 95–110. Berlin: De Gruyter, 2019.

Cultural & Natural Heritage Tours—Galapagos. "20% Growth in Land-Based Tourism Last Year—Can this Continue?," February 1, 2019. Accessed April 14, 2020. https://www.cnhtours.com/news/2019/2/1/20-growth-in-land-based-tourism-last-year-can-this-continue/.

Dahles, Heidi. "The Politics of Tour Guiding: Image Management in Indonesia." *Annals of Tourism Research* 29, no. 3 (2002): 783–800.

Daly, Natasha. "Exclusive: Instagram Fights Animal Abuse with New Alert System." *National Geographic*, December 4, 2017. Accessed May 20, 2020. https://www.nationalgeographic.com/news/2017/12/wildlife-watch-instagram-selfie-tourism-animal-welfare-crime/.

———. "Special Report: The Amazon Is the New Frontier for Deadly Wildlife Tourism." *National Geographic*, October 3, 2017. Accessed May 20, 2020. https://www.nationalgeographic.com/photography/proof/2017/10/wildlife-watch-amazon-ecotourism-animal-welfare/.

Davie, Tim. *Fundamentals of Hydrology*. 2nd ed. London: Routledge, 2002.

De Freitas, C. R. "Tourism Climatology: Evaluating Environmental Information for Decision Making and Business Planning in the Recreation and Tourism Sector." *International Journal of Biometeorology* 48 (2003): 45–54.

deRios, Marlene Dobkin. "Drug Tourism in the Amazon." *Anthropology of Consciousness* 5, no. 1 (1994): 16–19.

Destination Gold Coast. "Annual Report 2018–19." Accessed June 12, 2020. https://www.destinationgoldcoast.com/Portals/0/Documents/Corporate/AboutUs/AnnualReports/2018-19/DGC_ANNUALREPORT19_WEB.pdf.

———. "Official Tourism Website for the Gold Coast in Queensland, Australia." Accessed June 12, 2020. https://www.destinationgoldcoast.com.

Detroit Metro Convention & Visitors Bureau. "Visit Detroit." Accessed June 3, 2020. https://visitdetroit.com.

Diab, Atef M. "Bacteriological Studies on the Potability, Efficacy, and EIA of Desalination Operations at Sharm El-Sheikh Region, Egypt." *Egyptian Journal of Biology* 3 (2001): 59–65.

Dillette, Alana K., Stefanie Benjamin, and Chelsea Carpenter. "Tweeting the Black Travel Experience: Social Media Counternarrative Stories as Innovative Insight on #TravelingWhile-Black." *Journal of Travel Research* 58, no. 8 (2019): 1357–72.

Diskin, Eben. "African-Americans Spent $63 Billion on Travel in 2018." *Matador Network*, December 26, 2018. Accessed June 16, 2020. https://matadornetwork.com/read/african-americans-spent-billion-travel–2018/.

Dixon, Emily. "Bali Volcano: Flights Canceled after Mount Agung Erupts." *CNN Travel*, May 25, 2019. Accessed April 20, 2020. https://www.cnn.com/2019/05/25/asia/indonesia-bali-volcano-eruption-intl/index.html.

Dodds, Rachel, and Richard W. Butler. "Conclusion." *In Overtourism: Issues, Realities and Solutions*, edited by Rachel Dodds and Richard W. Butler, 262–76. Berlin: De Gruyter, 2019.

———. "Enablers of Overtourism." *In Overtourism: Issues, Realities and Solutions*, edited by Rachel Dodds and Richard W. Butler, 6–21. Berlin: De Gruyter, 2019.

———. "Introduction." *In Overtourism: Issues, Realities and Solutions*, edited by Rachel Dodds and Richard W. Butler, 1–5. Berlin: De Gruyter, 2019.

Dogru, Tarik, Elizabeth A. Marchio, Umit Bulut, and Courtney Suess. "Climate Change: Vulnerability and Resilience of Tourism and the Entire Economy." *Tourism Management* 72 (2019): 292–305.

Dolan, Rebecca, Yuri Seo, and Joya Kemper. "Complaining Practices on Social Media in Tourism: A Value Co-Creation and Co-Destruction Perspective." *Tourism Management* 73 (2019): 35–45.

Dominica Hotel and Tourism Association. *Destination Dominica*. North Miami, FL: Ulrich Communications Corporation, 2003.

Dowling, Ross, and David Newsome. *"Geotourism: Definition, Characteristics and International Perspectives."* In *Handbook of Geotourism*, edited by Ross Dowling and David Newsom, 1–22. Cheltenham: Edward Elgar Publishing, 2018.

Duffy, Andrew. "Two-Way Street: How Smartphones and the Social Web Impact the Traveller's Liminal Gaze." *Mobile Media & Communication* 7, no. 1 (2019): 60–75.

Duncan, James, and Derek Gregory. "Introduction." *In Writes of Passage: Reading Travel Writing*, edited by James Duncan and Derek Gregory, 1–13. London: Routledge, 1999.

Duxbury, Nancy, and Greg Richards. "Towards a Research Agenda for Creative Tourism: Developments, Diversity, and Dynamics." In *A Research Agenda for Creative Tourism*, edited by Nancy Duxbury and Greg Richards, 1–16. Cheltenham: Edward Elgar Publishing, 2019.

Edmond, Charlotte. "World's Highest Spring Clean Operation in Everest Turned Up 10 Tonnes of Trash." *World Economic Forum*, October 31, 2019. Accessed May 25, 2020. https://www.weforum.org/agenda/2019/10/10-tonnes-of-trash-was-taken-down-everest-this-is-what-s-happened-to-it/.

Eichstedt, Jennifer L., and Stephen Small. *Representations of Slavery: Race and Ideology in Southern Plantation Museums*. Washington, DC: Smithsonian Institution Press, 2002.

Ellwood, Mark. "How Chinese Tourists are Changing the Travel Landscape." *Condé Nast Traveler*, November 2, 2018. Accessed April 24, 2020. https://www.cntraveler.com/story/chinese-tourists-changing-travel.

———. "The Other Side of Venice's Overtourism Problem." *Condé Nast Traveler*, October 24, 2018. Accessed April 27, 2020. https://www.cntraveler.com/story/the-other-side-of-venices-overtourism-problem.

Eugenio-Martin, Juan L., and Federico Inchuasti-Sintes. "Low-Cost Travel and Tourism Expenditures." *Annals of Tourism Research* 57 (2016): 140–59.

Evergreen. "About Evergreen." Accessed May 28, 2020. https://www.evergreen.ca/about/.

Exchange Initiative. "About TraffickCam." Accessed March 10, 2020. https://traffickcam.com/about.

Expedia and The Center for Generational Kinetics. *Generations on the Move: A Deep Dive into Multi-Generational Travel Trends and How Their Habits Will Impact the Future of the Industry*, January 2018 (2017). Accessed March 20, 2020. https://viewfinder.expedia.com/wp-content/uploads/2017/12/Expedia-Generations-on-the-Move.pdf.

Fair Trade Tourism. "About Us." Accessed May 9, 2020. http://www.fairtrade.travel/About-Us/.

Farmaki, Anna, and Dimitrios Stergiou. "Impacts of P2P Accommodation: Neighbourhood Perspectives." *e-Review of Tourism Research* 16, no. 2/3 (2019): 43–52.

Farnsworth, Audrey. "Instagram Influencer Behavior Has Got to Change—They're Ruining Travel and Risking Lives." *Fodor's Travel*, March 7, 2019. Accessed June 16, 2020. https://www.fodors.com/news/travel-tips/instagram-influencer-behavior-has-got-to-change-theyre-ruining-travel-and-risking-lives.

———. "No One Wants to Hang Out at an Airport – So Stop Trying to Make it a Thing." *Fodor's Travel*, September 4, 2019. Accessed March 11, 2020. https://www.fodors.com/news/airlines/no-one-wants-to-hang-out-an-airport-so-stop-trying-to-make-it-a-thing.

Federal Trade Commission. "Disclosures 101 for Social Media Influencers," November 2019. Accessed June 16, 2020. https://www.ftc.gov/system/files/documents/plain-language/1001a-influencer-guide-508_1.pdf.

Feifer, Maxine. *Tourism in History: From Imperial Rome to the Present*. New York: Stein and Day, 1986.

Femenia-Serra, Francisco, and Ulrike Gretzel. "Influencer Marketing for Tourism Destinations: Lessons from a Mature Destination." In *Information and Communication Technologies in Tourism 2020*, edited by J. Neidhardt and W. Wörndl, 65–78. Springer International Publishing: Chaim, 2020.

Fennell, David A. *Ecotourism*. 4th ed. London: Routledge, 2015.

Figueroa, Pablo. "Vanity, Pollution and Death on Mount Everest." *Our World*, July 15, 2013. Accessed May 25, 2020. https://ourworld.unu.edu/en/vanity-pollution-and-death-on-mt-everest.

Filieri, Raffaele, Salma Alguezaui, and Frazer McLeay. "Why Do Travelers Trust TripAdvisor? Antecedents of Trust towards Consumer-Generated Media and Its Influence on Recommendation Adoption and Word of Mouth." *Tourism Management* 51 (2015): 174–85.

Finer, Daisy. "Biomarkers, Sweat Lodges, and Shamans: Today's Wellness Retreats Go Far Beyond a Detox." *Condé Nast Traveler*, August 26, 2019. Accessed March 16, 2020. https://www.cntraveler.com/story/whats-next-for-destination-spas-and-wellness-retreats.

Finney, Jeffrey R., and Amy E. Potter. "'You're out of Your Place": Black Mobility on Tybee Island, Georgia from Civil Rights to Orange Crush." *Southeastern Geographer* 58, no. 1 (2018): 104–214.

Firshein, Sarah. "All the Ways the Travel Industry Is Helping with Coronavirus." *Condé Nast Traveler*, March 26, 2020. Accessed May 15, 2020. https://www.cntraveler.com/story/how-the-travel-industry-is-helping-amid-coronavirus.

Florida, Richard. *The Rise of the Creative Class, Revisited*. New York: Basic Books, 2012.

Font, Xavier, and Scott McCabe. "Sustainability and Marketing in Tourism: Its Contexts, Paradoxes, Approaches, Challenges and Potential." *Journal of Sustainable Tourism* 25, no. 7 (2017): 869–83.

Francis, Justin. "Overtourism: It's Time for Some Answers." In *Overtourism: Issues, Realities and Solutions*, edited by Rachel Dodds and Richard W. Butler, v–vi. Berlin: De Gruyter, 2019.

Freytag, Tim, and Michael Bauder. "Bottom-Up Touristification and Urban Transformations in Paris," *Tourism Geographies* 20, no. 3 (2018): 443–60.

Froude, James A. *The English in the West Indies or the Bow of Ulysses*. London: Longmans, Green and Co., 1909.

Fullagar, Simone, Erica Wilson, and Kevin Markwel. "Starting Slow: Thinking Through Slow Mobilities and Experiences." In *Slow Tourism: Experiences and Mobilities*, edited by Simone Fullagar, Kevin Markwell, and Erica Wilson, 1–8. Bristol: Channel View Publications, 2012.

Gajanan, Mahita. "The FAA Just Banned Flights over Iranian Air Space. Here's What Fliers Need to Know." *Time*, June 21, 2019. Accessed April 10, 2020. https://time.com/5611991/faa-iran-air-space-tensions-ban/.

Garau-Vadell, Joan B., Desiderio Gutiérrez-Taño, and Ricardo Díaz-Armas. "Residents' Support for P2P Accommodation in Mass Tourism Destinations." *Journal of Travel Research* 58, no. 4 (2019): 549–65.

Gassan, Richard H. *The Birth of American Tourism: New York, the Hudson Valley, and American Culture, 1790–1830*. Amherst: University of Massachusetts Press, 2008.

Gay, Kathlyn. *African-American Holidays, Festivals, and Celebrations: The History, Customs, and Symbols Associated with Both Traditional and Contemporary Religious and Secular Events Observed by Americans of African Descent*. Detroit: Omnigraphics, 2007.

Gelbman, Alon. "Tourism, Peace, and Global Stability." In *Handbook of Globalisation and Tourism*, edited by Dallen J. Timothy, 149–60. Cheltenham: Edward Elgar Publishing Limited, 2019.

Gerulaityte, Egle. "Can #MeToo Help Stop Sex Tourism?" *Equality Now*. Accessed March 10, 2020. https://www.equalitynow.org/can_metoo_help_stop_sex_tourism?locale=en.

Gibson, Chris. "Locating Geographies of Tourism." *Progress in Human Geography* 32, no. 3 (2008): 407–22.

Global Sustainable Tourism Council. "The International Body for Sustainable Tourism Certification." Accessed July 10, 2020. https://www.gstcouncil.org.

Godfrey, Kerry, and Jackie Clarke. *The Tourism Development Handbook: A Practical Approach to Planning and Marketing*. London: Cassell, 2000.

Goeldner, Charles R., and J. R. Brent Ritchie. *Tourism: Principles, Practices, Philosophies*. 9th ed. Hoboken, NJ: Wiley, 2006.

Gómez-Martin M. Belén. "Weather, Climate, and Tourism: A Geographical Perspective." *Annals of Tourism Research* 32, no. 3 (2005): 571–91.

González-Pérez, Jesús M. "The Dispute over Tourist Cities. Tourism Gentrification in the Historic Centre of Palma (Majorca, Spain)." *Tourism Geographies* 22, no. 1 (2020): 171–91.

Good, Rana. "5 Cool Eco-Friendly Features on the New Celebrity Flora." *Forbes*, July 29, 2019. Accessed August 14, 2020. https://www.forbes.com/sites/ranagood/2019/07/29/eco-friendly-features-celebrity-flora/#5fd890c623f3.

Government of Nepal. "State of Conservation Report Sagarmatha National Park (Nepal) (N120)," November 2017. Accessed May 25, 2020. https://www.google.com/url?sa=t&rct=j&q=&esrc=s&source=web&cd=&ved=2ahUKEwjIu7Lxs8_pAhVEPq0KHbjACVgQFjAEegQIBRAB&url=https%3A%2F%2Fwhc.unesco.org%2Fdocument%2F165027&usg=AOvVaw2jgoLgIbngoL8FPlCSewCk.

Gössling, Stefan, and Daniel Scott, "The Decarbonisation Impasse: Global Tourism Leaders' Views on Climate Change Mitigation." *Journal of Sustainable Tourism* 26, no. 12 (2018): 2071–86.

Graburn, Nelson. "The Anthropology of Tourism." *Annals of Tourism Research* 10 (1983): 9–33.

Graham, Rachel. "The Environmental Cost of Climbing Mount Everest." *Euronews*, May 7, 2019. Accessed May 25, 2020. https://www.euronews.com/living/2019/07/03/the-environmental-cost-of-climbing-mount-everest.

Greater Houston Partnership. "Houston Facts 2019." Accessed March 18, 2020. https://www.houston.org/sites/default/files/2019-08/Houston%20Facts%202019%20Final_3.pdf.

Green, Victor H. *The Negro Motorist Green Book*. New York: Victor H. Green & Co., Publishers, 1949.

Gregory, Derek. "Scripting Egypt: Orientalism and the Cultures of Travel." In *Writes of Passage: Reading Travel Writing*, ed. James Duncan and Derek Gregory, 114–50. London: Routledge, 1999.

Gregory, Derek, Ron Johnston, and Geraldine Pratt. *Dictionary of Human Geography*. 5th ed. Hoboken, NJ: Wiley-Blackwell, 2009.

Gretzel, Ulrike. "Influencer Marketing in Travel and Tourism." In *Advances in Social Media for Travel, Tourism and Hospitality: New Perspectives, Practices and Cases*, edited by Marianna Sigala and Ulrike Gretzel, 147–56. Routledge: New York, 2018.

———. "The Role of Social Media in Creating and Addressing Overtourism." In *Overtourism: Issues, Realities and Solutions*, edited by Rachel Dodds and Richard W. Butler, 62–75. Berlin: De Gruyter, 2019.

Griffin, Tom, and Meghan Muldoon. "Exploring Virtual Reality Experiences of Slum Tourism." *Tourism Geographies* (2020): DOI: 10.1080/14616688.2020.1713881.

Gross, Sven, and Louisa Klemmer. *Introduction to Tourism Transport*. Oxfordshire: CABI, 2014.

Gunn, Clare A., and Turgut Var. *Tourism Planning: Basics, Concepts, Cases*. 4th ed. New York: Routledge, 2002.

Guttentag, Daniel. "Airbnb: Disruptive Innovation and the Rise of an Informal Tourism Accommodation Sector," *Current Issues in Tourism* 18, no. 12 (2015): 1192–217.

Haddouche, Hamed, and Christine Salomone. "Generation Z and the Tourist Experience: Tourist Stories and Use of Social Networks." *Journal of Tourism Futures* 4, no. 1 (2018): 69–79.

Halewood, Chris, and Kevin Hannam. "Viking Heritage Tourism: Authenticity and Commodification." *Annals of Tourism Research* 28, no. 3 (2001): 565–80.

Hall, Derek R. "Conceptualising Tourism Transport: Inequality and Externality Issues." *Journal of Transport Geography* 7 (1999): 181–8.

Hall, Michael C., and Alan Lew. *Understanding and Managing Tourism Impacts: An Integrated Approach*. New York: Routledge, 2009.

Hall, Michael C., Girish Prayag, and Alberto Amore. *Tourism and Resilience: Individual, Organisational and Destination Perspectives*. Bristol: Channel View Publications, 2018.

Halladay, Patrick J. "Destination Resilience and Sustainable Tourism Development." *Tourism Review International* 22 (2018): 251–61.

Hanna, Paul, Xavier Font, Caroline Scarles, Clare Weeden, and Charlotte Harrison. "Tourist Destination Marketing: From Sustainability Myopia to Memorable Experiences," *Journal of Destination Marketing & Management* 9 (2018): 36–43.

Hanna, Stephen P. "Placing the Enslaved at Oak Alley Plantation: Narratives, Spatial Contexts, and the Limits of Surrogation." *Journal of Heritage Tourism* 11, no. 3 (2016): 219–34.

Hanson, Susan. "Thinking Back, Thinking Ahead: Some Questions for Economic Geographers." In *Economic Geography: Past, Present, and Future*, ed. Sharmistha Bagchi-Sen and Helen Lawton Smith, 25–33. London: Routledge, 2006.

Harrigan, Paul, Uwana Evers, Morgan Miles, and Timothy Daly. "Customer Engagement with Tourism Social Media Brands," *Tourism Management* 56 (2017): 597–609.

Hayhurst, Lee. "Survey Highlights Instagram as Key Factor in Destination Choice among Millennials." *Travolution*, March 24, 2017. Accessed June 12, 2020. https://travolution.com/articles/102216/survey-highlights-instagram-as-key-factor-in-destination-choice-among-millennials.

Hays, Stephanie, Stephen John Page, and Dimitrios Buhalis. "Social Media as a Destination Marketing Tool: Its Use by National Tourism Organizations." *Current Issues in Tourism* 16, no. 3 (2013): 211–39.

Henley, Jon. "Overtourism in Europe's Historic Cities Sparks Backlash." *The Guardian*, January 25, 2020. Accessed July 9, 2020. https://www.theguardian.com/world/2020/jan/25/overtourism-in-europe-historic-cities-sparks-backlash.

Higgins, Charlotte. "Art in the Countryside: Why More and More UK Creatives Are Leaving the City." *The Guardian*, August 26, 2013. Accessed April 27, 2020. https://www.theguardian.com/artanddesign/2013/aug/26/art-countryside-uk-creatives.

Holden, Andrew. *Environment and Tourism*. 2nd ed. London: Routledge, 2008.

Holland, Mary. "The Cruise Ship That Could Preserve the Galapagos Islands." *Condé Nast Traveler*, August 30, 2019. Accessed April 14, 2020. https://www.cntraveler.com/story/the-cruise-ship-that-could-preserve-the-galapagos-islands.

Horng, Jeou-Shyan, Hsuan Hsu, and Chang-Yen Tsai. "An Assessment Model of Corporate Social Responsibility Practice in the Tourism Industry," *Journal of Sustainable Tourism* 26, no. 7 (2018): 1085–104.

Hose, Thomas A. "Selling the Story of Britain's Stone." *Environmental Interpretation* 10 (1995): 16–17.

Hosney Fahmy, Faten, Ninet Mohamed Ahmed, and Hanaa Mohamed Farghally. "Optimization of Renewable Energy Power System for Small Scale Brackish Reverse Osmosis Desalination Unit and a Tourism Motel in Egypt." *Smart Grid and Renewable Energy* 3 (2012): 43–50.

Hudson, Simon, and J. R. Brent Ritchie. "Branding a Memorable Destination Experience. The Case of 'Brand Canada.'" *International Journal of Tourism Research* 11 (2009): 217–28.

Huffman, Jennifer. "National Publicity About Fires and Blackouts Has Impact on Napa Tourism." *Napa Valley Register*, November 1, 2019. Accessed April 20, 2020. https://napavalleyregister.com/news/local/national-publicity-about-fires-and-blackouts-has-impact-on-napa-tourism/article_19b31892-7bb8-5666-be78-a25255b3049d.html.

Hughes, Emma, and Regina Scheyvens. "Corporate Social Responsibility in Tourism Post-2015: A Development First Approach." *Tourism Geographies* 18, no. 5 (2016): 469–82.

Human Rights Watch. "Migrant Workers' Rights on Saadiyat Island in the United Arab Emirates: 2015 Progress Report," February 10, 2015. Accessed May 9, 2020. https://www.hrw.org/report/2015/02/10/migrant-workers-rights-saadiyat-island-united-arab-emirates/2015-progress-report#page.

———. "Qatar: Urgently Investigate Migrant Worker Deaths," October 10, 2019. Accessed May 9, 2020. https://www.hrw.org/news/2019/10/10/qatar-urgently-investigate-migrant-worker-deaths#.

Hyundai Motor Manufacturing Alabama. "About HMMA." Accessed May 7, 2020. http://www.hmmausa.com/our-company/about-hmma/

i Agustí, Daniel Paül. "Characterizing the Location of Tourist Images in Cities. Differences in User-Generated Images (Instagram), Official Tourist Brochures, and Travel Guides." *Annals of Tourism Research* 73 (2018): 103–15.

Illinois Office of Tourism. "The Most Instagrammable Spots in Illinois." Accessed June 12, 2020. https://www.enjoyillinois.com/plan-your-trip/most-instagrammable-places.

"India Orders Tourists to Leave Kashmir over 'Terror Threat'." *BBC News*, August 3, 2019. Accessed April 29, 2020. https://www.bbc.com/news/world-asia-india-49222571.

Inglis, Fred. *The Delicious History of the Holiday*. London: Routledge, 2000.

International Air Transport Association. "Deeper Revenue Hit from COVID-19," March 24, 2020. Accessed April 15, 2020. https://www.iata.org/en/pressroom/pr/2020-03-24-01/.

International Darky-Sky Association. "International Dark Sky Places." Accessed March 12, 2020. https://www.darksky.org/our-work/conservation/idsp/.

The International Ecotourism Society. "What Is Ecotourism?" Accessed March 10, 2020. https://ecotourism.org/what-is-ecotourism/.

The International Olympic Committee. "How Do We Know That Rio 2016 Was a Success." Accessed March 11, 2020. https://www.olympic.org/news/how-do-we-know-that-rio-2016-was-a-success.

———. *Report of the 2022 Evaluation Commission* (Lausanne: International Olympic Committee, 2015). Accessed May 29, 2020. https://stillmed.olympic.org/Documents/Host_city_elections/ioc_evaluation_commission_report_sp_eng.pdf.

Ioannides, Dimitri, and Kristina Zampoukous. "Exploring the Geographic Dimensions of Tourism Work and Workers." In *A Research Agenda for Tourism Geographies*, edited by Dieter K. Müller, 89–98. Cheltenham: Edward Elgar Publishing, 2019.

Irvine, Seana, and Erin Elliott. *Transformation: The Story of Creating Evergreen Brick Works* (Toronto: Evergreen Brick Works, 2012). Accessed May 28, 2020. https://www.evergreen.ca/downloads/pdfs/Transformation-EBW.pdf.

Isacsson, Annica, Leena Alakoski, and Asta Bäck. "Using Multiple Senses in Tourism Marketing: The Helsinki Expert, Eckerö Line and Linnanmäki Amusement Park Cases." *Turismos: An International Multidisciplinary Journal of Tourism* 4, no. 3 (2009): 167–84.

Islas Travel Guides. "Welcome to Our Guide to Magaluf." Accessed March 9, 2020. http://www.majorca-mallorca.co.uk/magaluf.htm

Ivanov, Stanislav, and Craig Webster. "Conceptual Framework for the Use of Robots, Artificial Intelligence and Service Automation in Travel, Tourism, and Hospitality Companies." In *Robots, Artificial Intelligence, and Service Automation in Travel, Tourism and Hospitality*, edited by Stanislav Ivanov and Craig Webster. London: Emerald Publishing, 2019.

———. "Economic Fundamentals in the Use of Robots, Artificial Intelligence and Service Automation in Travel, Tourism, and Hospitality." In *Robots, Artificial Intelligence, and Service Automation in Travel, Tourism and Hospitality*, edited by Stanislav Ivanov and Craig Webster. London: Emerald Publishing, 2019.

Ivanovic, Milena. *Cultural Tourism*. Cape Town: Juta, 2008.

Jamal, Tazim, Blanca Camargo, Jennifer Sandlin, and Romano Segrado. "Tourism and Cultural Sustainability: Towards an Eco-Cultural Justice for Place and People." *Tourism Recreation Research* 35, no 3 (2010): 269–79.

Japan National Tourism Organization. "Sakurajima." Accessed April 20, 2020. https://www.japan.travel/en/spot/603/.

Jasne-Verbeke, Myriam, and Wanda George. "Reflections on the Great War Centenary: From Warscapes to Memoryscapes in 100 Years." In *Tourism and War*, edited by Richard Butler and Wantanee Suntikul, 273–87. London: Routledge, 2013.

Jenkins, Mark. "Maxed Out on Everest." *National Geographic* 223, no. 6 (2013).

JetBlue. "JetBlue Prepares Its Business for a New Climate Reality," January 6, 2020. Accessed April 15, 2020. http://blueir.investproductions.com/investor-relations/press-releases/2020/01-06-2020–131859289.

Jeuring, Jelmer H. G., and Karin B. M. Peters. "The Influence of the Weather on Tourist Experiences: Analysing Travel Blog Narratives." *Journal of Vacation Marketing* 19, no. 3 (2013): 209–19.

Jones, Allie. "Are Vacations Better When You Don't Take a Single Photo?" *Condé Nast Traveler*, November 19, 2019. Accessed June 25, 2020. https://www.cntraveler.com/story/are-vacations-better-when-you-don't-take-a-single-photo.

Jones, Calvin, and ShiNa Li. "The Economic Importance of Meetings and Conferences: A Satellite Account Approach." *Annals of Tourism Research* 52 (2015): 117–33.

Joppe, Marion. "The Roles of Policy, Planning and Governance in Preventing and Managing Overtourism," In *Overtourism: Issues, Realities and Solutions*, edited by Rachel Dodds and Richard W. Butler, 250–61. Berlin: De Gruyter, 2019.

Jordan, Fiona, and Heather Gibson. "'We're Not Stupid … But We'll Not Stay Home Either': Experiences of Solo Women Travelers." *Tourism Review International* 9 (2005): 195–211.

Jover, Jaime, and Ibán Díaz-Parra. "Who Is the City for? Overtourism, Lifestyle Migration and Social Sustainability." *Tourism Geographies* DOI: 10.1080/14616688.2020.1713878 (2020).

Kaplan, David H., Steven R. Holloway, and James O. Wheeler. *Urban Geography*. 3rd ed. Hoboken, NJ: Wiley, 2014.

Kershaw, Steve. *Oceanography: An Earth Science Perspective*. Cheltenham, UK: Stanley Thornes, 2000.

Kevan, Simon. "Quests for Cures: A History of Tourism for Climate and Health." *International Journal of Biometeorology* 37 (1993): 113–24.

Khair, Tabish, Martin Leer, Justin D. Edwards, and Hanna Ziadeh. *Other Routes: 1500 Years of African and Asian Travel Writing*. Bloomington: Indiana University Press, 2005.

Kingsley, Charles. *At Last: A Christmas in the West Indies*. New York: Harper & Brothers Publishers, 1871.

Kisawa Sanctuary. "Luxury Mozambique Resort." Accessed July 10, 2020. https://kisawasanctuary.com.

Kladou, Stella, and Eleni Mavragani. "Assessing Destination Image: An Online Marketing Approach and the Case of TripAdvisor." *Journal of Destination Marketing & Management* 4 (2015): 187–93.

Knight, David W. "An Institutional Analysis of Local Strategies for Enhancing Pro-Poor Tourism Outcomes in Cuzco, Peru." *Journal of Sustainable Tourism* 26, no. 4 (2018): 631–48.

Knight, David W., and Stuart P. Cottrell. "Evaluating Tourism-Linked Empowerment in Cuzco, Peru," *Annals of Tourism Research* 56 (2016): 32–47.

Knight, David Warner. "Poverty Alleviation Through Tourism? Community Perceptions of Intrepid Travel in Peru's Sacred Valley," *Intrepid Travel*. Accessed May 6, 2020. https://www.intrepidtravel.com/sites/intrepid/files/teal/1.%20Peru%20Research%20Summary%2C%20David%20W%20Knight.pdf.

Knowles, Richard D. "How the Journal of Transport Geography Has Evolved since 1993." *Journal of Transport Geography* 81 (2019): 1–4.

Konečnik, Maja. "Developing Brand Identity for Slovenia with Opinion Leaders." *Baltic Journal of Management*, 7, no. 2 (2012): 124–42.

———. "Slovenia: New Challenges in Enhancing the Value of the Tourism Destination Brand." In *Tourism in the New Europe: The Challenges and Opportunities of EU Enlargement*, edited by Derek Hall, Melanie Smith, and Barbara Marciszweska, 81–91. Oxfordshire: CABI, 2006.

Konecnik, Maja, and Frank Go. "Tourism Destination Brand Identity: The Case of Slovenia." *Brand Management* 15, no. 3 (2008): 177–89.

Konstantinides, Anneta. "Visitors Have Discovered That a Bali Tourist Attraction Popular with Instagram Influencers Is Actually a Fake Photo Op." *Business Insider*, July 9, 2019. Accessed June 16, 2020. https://static1.businessinsider.com/bali-tourist-spot-popular-instagram-fake-photo-op-2019-7?jwsource=cl.

Koster, Rhonda L. "Why Differentiate Rural Tourism Geographies?" In *Perspectives on Rural Tourism Geographies: Case Studies from Developed Nations on the Exotic, the Fringe and the Boring Bits in Between*, edited by Rhonda L. Koster and Doris A. Carson, 1–13. Cham: Springer, 2019.

Kravitz Hoeffner, Melissa. "This Mapping Tool Collects Queer Sites and Memories." *Condé Nast Traveler*, August 15, 2019. Accessed June 16, 2020. https://www.cntraveler.com/story/queering-the-map-collects-queer-sites-and-memories.

Kyte, Simon, David Goodger, and Helen McDermott. "'No-Deal' Brexit to Knock 2% off Travel and Tourism GDP," *Oxford Economics*, December 6, 2018. Accessed May 2, 2020. https://www.oxfordeconomics.com/recent-releases/fdf4ac5f-5d3b-49c0-87a7-1b9578093b96.

Lagrave, Katherine. "Machu Picchu Is Wheelchair Accessible for the First Time." *Condé Nast Traveler*, February 4, 2019. Accessed June 25, 2020. https://www.cntraveler.com/story/machu-picchu-is-wheelchair-accessible-for-the-first-time.

———. "Solo Travelers Aren't Being Punished Anymore." *Condé Nast Traveler*, January 31, 2019. Accessed June 25, 2020. https://www.cntraveler.com/story/solo-travelers-arent-being-punished-anymore.

Lamback, Briona. "The 6 Best US Travel Destinations for Black Travelers in 2019." *Matador Network*, May 20, 2019. Accessed June 16, 2020. https://matadornetwork.com/read/best-travel-destinations-black-travelers/.

Lanegran, David A., and Salvatore J. Natoli. *Guidelines for Geographic Education in the Elementary and Secondary Schools*. Washington, DC: Association of American Geographers, 1984.

Las Vegas Convention and Visitors Authority. "Las Vegas Historic Tourism Statistics." Accessed April 20, 2020. https://assets.simpleviewcms.com/simpleview/image/upload/v1/clients/lasvegas/Historical_1970_to_2019_ada0164b-b599-4fac-8f7a-eb26bfe17187.pdf.

Lazer, David M. J., Matthew A. Baum, Yochai Benkler, Adam J. Berinsky, Kelly M. Greenhill, Filippo Menczer, Miriam J. Metzger, Brendan Nyhan, Gordon Pennycook, David Rothschild, Michael Schudson, Steven A. Sloman, Cass R. Sunstein, Emily A. Thorson, Duncan J. Watts, and Jonathon L. Zittrain. "The Science of Fake News," *Science* 359, no. 6380 (2018): 1094–6.

Lemelin, Raynald Harvey, Emma Stewart, and Jackie Dawson. "An Introduction to Last Chance Tourism." In *Last Chance Tourism: Adapting Tourism Opportunities in a Changing World*, edited by Raynald Harvey Lemelin, Jackie Dawson, and Emma J. Stewart, 3–9. London, Routledge, 2012.

Leung, Daniel, Rob Law, Hubert van Hoof, and Dimitrios Buhalis. "Social Media in Tourism and Hospitality: A Literature Review." *Journal of Travel & Tourism Marketing* 30 (2013): 3–22.

Leung, Yu-Fai, Anna Spenceley, Glen Hvenegaard, and Ralf Buckley. *Tourism and Visitor Management in Protected Areas: Guidelines for Sustainability* (Gland: IUCN, 2018). Accessed May 29, 2020. https://portals.iucn.org/library/sites/library/files/documents/PAG-027-En.pdf.

Levitt, Rachel. "A Feminist Shares Her Un-Feminist Trick for Staying Safe While Traveling." *Fodor's Travel*, November 28, 2018. Accessed June 25, 2020. https://www.fodors.com/news/travel-tips/a-feminist-shares-her-un-feminist-trick-for-staying-safe-while-traveling.

Lew, Alan, and Bob McKercher. "Modeling Tourist Movements: A Local Destination Analysis." *Annals of Tourism Research* 33, no. 2 (2006): 403–23.

LG Electronics. "LG Airport Robots Take Over Korea's Largest Airport," July 21, 2017. Accessed May 4, 2020. https://www.lg.com/sg/press-release/lg-airport-robots-take-over-koreas-largest-airport.

Löfgren, Orvar. *On Holiday: A History of Vacationing*. Berkeley: University of California Press, 1999.

Lomine, Loykie. "Tourism in Augustan Society (44 BC–AD 69)." In *Histories of Tourism: Representation, Identity, and Conflict*, edited by John Walton, 69–87. Clevedon, UK: Channel View Publications, 2005.

Lovell, Jane, and Chris Bull. *Authentic and Inauthentic Places in Tourism: From Heritage Sites to Theme Parks*. Routledge: Abingdon, 2018.

Lumsdon, Les, and Stephen J. Page. "Progress in Transport and Tourism Research: Reformulating the Transport-Tourism Interface and Future Research Agendas." In *Tourism and Transport: Issues and Agenda for the New Millennium*, edited by Les Lumsdon and Stephen J. Page, 1–28. Amsterdam: Elsevier, 2004.

Lund, Tommy. "Sweden's Air Travel Drops in Year When 'Flight Shaming' Took Off." *Reuters*, January 10, 2020. Accessed April 15, 2020. https://www.reuters.com/article/

us-airlines-sweden/swedens-air-travel-drops-in-year-when-flight-shaming-took-off-idUSK-BN1Z90UI.

Lupiani, Joyce, and Jordan Gartner. "Las Vegas Sands to Pay Employees Amid Venetian, Palazzo Closures." *KTVN Las Vegas*, March 18, 2020. Accessed May 7, 2020. https://www.ktnv.com/news/las-vegas-sands-closing-the-venetian-and-palazzo-hotel-casinos.

MacCannell, Dean. "Staged Authenticity: Arrangements of Social Space in Tourist Settings." *American Journal of Sociology* 79, no. 3 (1973): 589–603.

———. *The Tourist: A New Theory of the Leisure Class*. New York: Schocken Books, 1976. Reprinted with foreword by Lucy R. Lippard. Berkeley: University of California Press, 1999.

MacKay, Kelly J., and Daniel R. Fesenmaier. "Pictorial Element of Destination in Image Formation." *Annals of Tourism Research* 24, no. 3 (1997): 537–65.

MacLeod, Nicola. "Cultural Tourism: Aspects of Authenticity and Commodification." In *Cultural Tourism in a Changing World: Politics, Participation, and (Re)presentation*, edited by Melanie K. Smith and Mike Robinson, 177–90. Clevedon, UK: Channel View Publications, 2006.

Mahrouse, Gada. "War-Zone Tourism: Thinking Beyond Voyeurism and Danger." *ACME: An International Journal for Critical Geographies* 15, no. 2 (2016): 330–45.

Mair, Heather. "Trust and Participatory Tourism Planning." In *Trust, Tourism Development and Planning*, edited by Robin Nunkoo and Stephen L. J. Smith, 46–63. London: Routledge, 2015.

"Majorca Offers Tourism Subsidies." *Majorca Daily Bulletin*, February 22, 2020. Accessed June 4, 2020. https://www.majorcadailybulletin.com/news/local/2020/02/22/63079/majorca-financial-aid.html.

Mak, Athena H. N., Margaret Lumbers, and Anita Eves. "Globalisation and Food Consumption in Tourism." *Annals of Tourism Research* 39, no. 1 (2012): 171–96.

Mamaghani, Farrokh. "Impact of E-Commerce on Travel and Tourism: An Historical Analysis." *International Journal of Management* 26, no. 3 (2009): 365–75.

Mandina Lodges. "Our Story." Accessed May 29, 2020. https://www.mandinalodges.com/about-us/.

Martin, Geoffrey J. *All Possible Worlds: A History of Geographical Ideas*. New York: Oxford University Press, 2005.

Martins, Marco. "Tourism Planning and Tourismphobia: An Analysis of the Strategic Tourism Plan of Barcelona 2010–2015," *Journal of Tourism, Heritage & Serivces Marketing* 4, no. 1 (2018): 3–7.

Maruyama, Naho, and Amanda Stronza. "Roots Tourism of Chinese Americans." *Ethnology* 49, no. 1 (2010): 23–44.

Mason, Peter. *Tourism Impacts, Planning and Management*. 3rd ed. London: Routledge, 2016.

Mathieson, Alister, and Geoffrey Wall. *Tourism: Economic, Physical, and Social Impacts*. London: Longman, 1982.

Maude, Alaric. "Applying the Concept of Powerful Knowledge to School Geography." In *The Power of Geographical Thinking*, edited by Clare Brooks, Graham Butt, and Mary Fargher, 27–40. Chaim: Springer, 2017.

———. "What Might Powerful Geographical Knowledge Look Like?" *Geography* 101 (2016): 70–6.

Maxcy, Kylie. "Actually Cool Things to Do When You Visit London." *Thrillist*, November 28, 2018. Accessed April 26, 2020. https://www.thrillist.com/travel/london/things-to-do-in-london.

May, Kevin. "How 25 Years of the Web Inspired the Travel Revolution." *The Guardian*, March 12, 2014. Accessed March 30, 2020. https://www.theguardian.com/travel/2014/mar/12/how-25-years-of-the-web-inspired-travel-revolution.

McKnight, Tom, and Darrel Hess. *Physical Geography: A Landscape Appreciation*. Upper Saddle River, NJ: Prentice Hall, 2000.

McLaughlin, Karl. "Anti-Tourism Attacks in Spain: Who Is Behind Them and What Do They Want?" *The Conversation*, August 9, 2017. Accessed April 29, 2020. https://theconversation.com/anti-tourism-attacks-in-spain-who-is-behind-them-and-what-do-they-want–82097.

McNamara, Karen Elizabeth, and Bruce Prideaux. "A Typology of Solo Independent Women Travellers." *International Journal of Tourism Research* 12 (2010): 253–64.

McVeigh, Tracy. "Magaluf's Days of Drinking and Casual Sex Are Numbered—Or So Mallorca Hopes." *The Observer*, April 18, 2015. Accessed March 9, 2020. https://www.theguardian.com/travel/2015/apr/18/vodka-sex-magaluf-tourists-spain-mallorca-shagaluf.

Medway, Dominic, Gary Warnaby, and Sheetal Dharni. "Demarketing Places: Rationales and Strategies." *Journal of Marketing Management* 27, no. 1-2 (2011): 124–42.

Menza, Kaitlin. "How Do Little Hotel Toiletry Bottles Get Filled?" *Condé Nast Traveler*, October 10, 2019. Accessed July 10, 2020. https://www.cntraveler.com/story/how-do-tiny-hotel-toiletries-get-filled.

Mervosh, Sarah. "Carnival Cruises to Pay $20 Million in Pollution and Cover-Up Case." *The New York Times*, June 4, 2019. Accessed April 13, 2020. https://www.nytimes.com/2019/06/04/business/carnival-cruise-pollution.html.

Milano, Claudio, Joseph M. Cheer, and Marina Novelli. "Introduction: Overtourism: An Evolving Phenomenon." In *Overtourism: Excesses, Discontents and Measures in Travel and Tourism*, edited by Claudio Milano, Joseph M. Cheer, and Marina Novelli, 1–17. Oxfordshire: CABI, 2019.

Milano, Claudio, Marina Novelli, and Joseph M. Cheer. "Overtourism and Tourismphobia: A Journey Through Four Decades of Tourism Development, Planning and Local Concerns." *Tourism Planning & Development* 16, no. 4 (2019): 353–7.

Miley, Jessica. "Japanese Hotel Fires Robot Staff after They Annoy Human Staff and Guests." *Interesting Engineering*, January 17, 2019. Accessed May 4, 2020. https://interestingengineering.com/japanese-hotel-fires-robot-staff-after-they-annoy-human-staff-and-guests.

Minihane, Joe. "What Brexit Will Mean for Travelers." *CNN Travel*, January 31, 2020. Accessed May 2, 2020. https://www.cnn.com/travel/article/post-brexit-travel-advice/index.html.

Mitchell, Charlie. "Instagram Thanked for South Island Tourism Boom." *Stuff*, March 26, 2016. Accessed June 12, 2020. https://www.stuff.co.nz/travel/news/78274433/instagram-thanked-for-south-island-tourism-boom.

Monahan, John. "Request to Suspend Hawaii Travel-Focused Editorial Coverage," April 6, 2020. Accessed June 4, 2020. https://www.hawaiitourismauthority.org/media/4424/request-to-suspend-hawaii-travel-focused-editorial-coverage.pdf.

Monterrubio, Carlos, Maribel Osorio, and Jazmín Benítez. "Comparing Enclave Tourism's Socioeconomic Impacts: A Dependency Theory Approach to Three State-Planned Resorts in Mexico." *Journal of Destination Marketing & Management* 8 (2018): 412–22.

Morgan, Nigel, Annette Pritchard, and Roger Pride. "Tourism Places, Brands, and Reputation Management." In *Destination Brands: Managing Place Reputation*, 3rd ed., edited by Nigel Morgan, Annette Pritchard, and Roger Pride, 3–20. Florence, KY: Routledge, 2011.

Morris, Hugh. "Majorca and Ibiza Ban Pub Crawls and 'Happy Hour' in New Crackdown on Boozy Tourists." *The Telegraph*, January 20, 2020. Accessed March 9, 2020. https://www.telegraph.co.uk/travel/news/alcohol-laws-magaluf-ibiza/.

Morrison, Alastair M., Xinran Y. Lehto, and Jonathon G. Day. *The Tourism System*, 8th edition. Dubuque: Kendall Hunt Publishing, 2018.

Morton, Caitlin. "Tourists Are Already Destroying California's Super Bloom." *Condé Nast Traveler*, March 19, 2019. Accessed June 16, 2020. https://www.cntraveler.com/story/how-to-see-californias-super-bloom.

———. "Would You Stay in a Hotel Room That Cleans Itself?" *Condé Nast Traveler*, February 26, 2019. Accessed May 4, 2020. https://www.cntraveler.com/story/would-you-stay-in-a-hotel-room-that-cleans-itself.

Moscardo, Gianna, Philip Pearce, Alastair Morrison, David Green, and Joseph T. O'Leary. "Developing a Typology for Understanding Visiting Friends and Relatives Markets." *Journal of Travel Research* 38, no. 3 (2000): 251–9.

Mowforth, Martin, and Ian Munt. *Tourism and Sustainability: Development, Globalisation and New Tourism in the Third World*, 4th ed. Abingdon: Routledge, 2016.

Moya, Eric. "For Many Destinations, an Appearance in a Beloved Movie or TV Series Can Be an Enduring Enticement for Visitors." *Travel Weekly*. Accessed June 2, 2020. https://www.travelweekly.com/Asia-Travel/Call-to-Action-Film-tourism.

Moynihan, Ruqayyah, and Thomas Giraudet. "Richard Branson Wants Virgin Galactic to Send People to Space Every 32 Hours by 2023." *Business Insider*, September 10, 2019. Accessed April 10, 2020. https://www.businessinsider.com/branson-virgin-galactic-people-space-every-32-hours-2019-9?r=US&IR=T.

Müller, Dieter K. "Tourism Geographies: A Bibliometric Review." In *A Research Agenda for Tourism Geographies*, edited by Dieter K. Müller, 7–22. Cheltenham: Edward Elgar Publishing, 2019.

Munar, Ana María, and Jens Kr. Steen Jacobsen. "Motivations for Sharing Tourism Experiences through Social Media." *Tourism Management* 43 (2014): 46–54.

Mundt, Jörn W. *Tourism and Sustainable Development: Reconsidering a Concept of Vague Policies*. Berlin: Erich Schmidt Verlag, 2011.

Nabongo, Jessica. "About." Accessed June 11, 2020. https://thecatchmeifyoucan.com/about.

National Geographic Society. "Crown of the Continent: About the Region." Accessed March 17, 2020. https://crownofthecontinent.natgeotourism.com/info/about-the-region/cote7f04525dd3fbc235.

———. "Geotourism." Accessed March 2, 2020. https://www.nationalgeographic.com/maps/geotourism/.

———. "Waterton-Glacier International Peace Park." Accessed March 17, 2020, https://crownofthecontinent.natgeotourism.com/content/waterton-glacier-international-peace-park/cot4c671f8692e2cf66a.

———. "Trash and Overcrowding at the Top of the World," October 1, 2019. Accessed May 25, 2020. https://www.nationalgeographic.org/article/trash-and-overcrowding-top-world/.

National Parks Conservation Association. *Polluted Parks: How America is Failing to Protect Our National Parks, People and Planet from Air Pollution* (Washington, DC: National Parks Conservation Association, 2019). Accessed May 29, 2020. https://npca.s3.amazonaws.com/documents/NPCAParksReport2019.pdf.

National Park Service. "Bison Bellows: A Case Study of Bison Selfies in Yellowstone National Park," November 2, 2017. Accessed May 20, 2020. https://www.nps.gov/articles/bison-bellows-7-21-16.htm.

———. "Glacier National Park: Climate Change." Accessed March 17, 2020. https://www.nps.gov/glac/learn/nature/climate-change.htm.

———. *Green Parks Plan: Advancing Our Mission Through Sustainable Operations* (Washington, DC: National Park Service, 2016). Accessed May 29, 2020. https://www.nps.gov/subjects/sustainability/upload/NPS-Green-Parks-Plan-2016.pdf

Natural Habitat Adventures. "The World's First Zero Waste Adventure." Accessed July 10, 2020. https://www.nathab.com/zero-waste-adventure-travel/.

Nelson, Velvet. "The Construction of Slovenia as a European Tourism Destination in Guidebooks." *Geoforum*, 43 (2012): 1099–107.

———. "Experiential Branding of Grenada's Spice Island Brand." In *Travel, Tourism, and Identity: Culture & Civilization, Volume 7*, edited by Gabriel Ricci, 115–26. New Brunswick, NJ: Transaction Publishers, 2015.

———. "Investigating Energy Issues in Dominica's Accommodations." *Tourism and Hospitality Research* 10 (2010): 345–58.

———. "Place Reputation: Representing Houston, Texas as a Creative Destination through Culinary Culture." *Tourism Geographies* 17, no. 2 (2015): 192–207.

———. "Representations of a Destination Brand in Online Tourism Information Sources: The Case of Slovenia." *Tourism, Culture & Communication* 14 (2014): 41–52.

———. " 'R.I.P. Nature Island': The Threat of a Proposed Oil Refinery on Dominica's Identity," *Social & Cultural Geography* 11, no. 8 (2010): 903–19.

Nepal, Sanjay. "Everest Tourism Is Causing a Mountain of Problems." *The Conversation*, April 9, 2014. Accessed May 25, 2020. https://theconversation.com/everest-tourism-is-causing-a-mountain-of-problems–23953.

Nepal, Sanjay K. "Tourism and Change in Nepal's Mount Everest." In *Mountain Tourism: Experiences, Communities, Environments and Sustainable Futures*, edited by Harold Richins and John S. Hull, 285–94. Oxfordshire: CABI, 2016.

Nilay Evcil, Ayse. "Barriers and Preferences to Leisure Activities for Wheelchair Users in Historic Places." *Tourism Geographies* 20, no. 4 (2018): 698–715.

Noe Kennedy, Barbara. "These Are the 11 Best and Worst Travel Trends of the Past Decade." *Fodor's Travel*, October 25, 2019. Accessed May 1, 2020. https://www.fodors.com/news/photos/these-are-the-11-best-and-worst-travel-trends-of-the-past-decade.

Nusair, Khaldoon, Mehmet Erdem, Fevzi Okumus, and Anil Bilgihan. "Users' Attitudes toward Online Social Networks in Travel." In *Social Media in Travel, Tourism and Hospitality: Theory, Practice and Cases*, edited by Marianna Sigala, Evangelos Christou, and Ulrike Gretzel, 207–24. Ashgate: Surrey, 2012.

Office of the High Commissioner for Human Rights. "Combatting Child Sex Tourism," April 10, 2013. Accessed March 10, 2020. https://www.ohchr.org/EN/NewsEvents/Pages/ChildsexTourism.aspx.

O'Hare, Maureen. "Henley Index: Japan Tops 2020 List of World's Most Powerful Passports." *CNN Travel*, January 7, 2020. Accessed April 28, 2020, https://www.cnn.com/travel/article/henley-index-world-best-passport-2020/index.html.

Oktoberfest. "The Official Oktoberfest Review 2019." Accessed March 11, 2020. https://www.oktoberfest.de/en/magazine/oktoberfest-news/2019/the-official-oktoberfest-review–2019.

Ohio Sauerkraut Festival. "About." Accessed March 11, 2020. https://sauerkrautfestival.waynesvilleohio.com/about/history-of-the-sauerkraut-festival–4/.

Omondi, Rose Kisia, and Chris Ryan. "Sex Tourism: Romantic Safaris, Prayers and Witchcraft at the Kenyan Coast." *Tourism Management* 58 (2017): 217–27.

Ong, Lei Tin Jackie, Donovan Storey, and John Minnery. "Beyond the Beach: Balancing Environmental and Socio-Cultural Sustainability in Boracay, the Philippines," *Tourism Geographies* 13, no. 4 (2011): 549–69.

Oppermann, Martin. "Sex Tourism." *Annals of Tourism Research* 26, no. 2 (1999): 251–66.

Opray, Max. "Tourist Boom for Ayahuasca a Mixed Blessing for Amazon." *The Guardian*, January 24, 2017. Accessed March 11, 2020. https://www.theguardian.com/sustainable-business/2017/jan/24/tourist-boom-peru-ayahuasca-drink-amazon-spirituality-healing.

Pacific Asia Travel Association. "About PATA." Accessed March 6, 2020. https://www.pata.org/about-pata/.

Page, Stephen, and Joanne Connell. "Transport and Tourism." In *The Wiley Blackwell Companion to Tourism*, edited by Alan A. Lew, C. Michael Hall, and Allan M. Williams, 155–67. Malden, MA: Wiley Blackwell, 2014.

Pain, Rachel, Michael Barke, Duncan Fuller, Jamie Gough, Robert MacFarlane, and Graham Mowl. *Introducing Social Geographies*. London: Arnold, 2001.

Pappas, Nikolaos. "UK Outbound Travel and Brexit Complexity." *Tourism Management* 72 (2019): 12–22.

Park, Victoria. "Form an Orderly Queue: Recreating the Perfect Instagram Photo in New Zealand." *BBC News*, November 28, 2018. Accessed June 23, 2020. https://www.bbc.com/news/blogs-trending-46342915.

Parks Canada. "Québec by Lantern Light." May 25, 2020. Accessed June 25, 2020. https://www.pc.gc.ca/en/lhn-nhs/qc/fortifications/activ/videovisite/lanterne-lantern.

Pearce, John, and Gianna Moscardo. "Social Representations of Tourist Selfies: New Challenges for Sustainable Tourism." *Conference Proceedings of BEST EN Think Tank XV* (2015): 59–73.

Peregrine, Anthony. "Why You're Wrong About Coach Tours—They Are the Greatest Way to Travel." *The Telegraph*, June 12, 2019. Accessed June 24, 2020. https://www.telegraph.co.uk/travel/tours/escorted-tours-why-you-are-wrong-about-coach-holidays/?WT.mc_id=tmg_share_em.

Peter, Sarah. "Hurricanes Cost Caribbean $1 Billion in Tourism: Industry Group." *Reuters*, June 14, 2018. Accessed March 20, 2020. https://www.reuters.com/article/us-storm-tourism/hurricanes-cost-caribbean-1-billion-in-tourism-industry-group-idUSKBN1JA2IA.

Peters, F. E. *The Hajj: The Muslim Pilgrimage to Mecca and the Holy Places*. Princeton: Princeton University Press, 1994.

Pile, Tim. "Seven Tourist Stereotypes—Which One Fits You?" *Post Magazine*, August 23, 2017. Accessed March 18, 2020. https://www.scmp.com/magazines/post-magazine/travel/article/2107837/seven-tourist-stereotypes-which-one-fits-you.

Port of San Diego. "Chula Vista Bayfront Project." Accessed April 26, 2020. https://www.portofsandiego.org/projects/chula-vista-bayfront.

Pristop. *The Brand of Slovenia*. Ljubljana: Ministry of the Economy, 2007.

Puckett, Jessica. "EasyJet Will Now Pay for Carbon Offsets on All Its Flights." *Condé Nast Traveler*, November 19, 2019. Accessed April 15, 2020. https://www.cntraveler.com/story/easyjet-will-now-pay-for-carbon-offsets-on-all-its-flights.

———. "New Airbus Planes Will Track Your Every Move through the Cabin." *Condé Nast Traveler*, September 13, 2019. Accessed May 4, 2020. https://www.cntraveler.com/story/new-airbus-planes-will-track-your-every-move-through-the-cabin.

———. "What Spending a Night at a Space Hotel Looks Like." *Condé Nast Traveler*, September 6, 2019. Accessed April 10, 2020. https://www.cntraveler.com/story/what-spending-a-night-at-a-space-hotel-looks-like.

Pratt, Mary Louise. *Imperial Eyes: Travel Writing and Transculturation*. 2nd ed. London: Routledge, 2008.

Pratt, Stephen, and Anyu Liu. "Does Tourism Really Lead to Peace? A Global View." *International Journal of Tourism Research* 18 (2016): 82–90.

Prideaux, Bruce. "The Role of the Transport System in Destination Development." *Tourism Management* 21 (2000): 53–63.

"Reach Travelers When They're Deciding Where to Go with Trip Consideration." *Facebook Business*, March 6, 2018. Accessed June 10, 2020. https://www.facebook.com/business/news/reach-travelers-when-theyre-deciding-where-to-go-with-trip-consideration.

Reddy, Maharaj Vijay, Mirela Nica, and Keith Wilkes. "Space Tourism: Research Recommendations for the Future of the Industry and Perspectives of Potential Participants." *Tourism Management* 33 (2012): 1093–102.

Reilly, Jennifer, Peter Williams, and Wolfgang Haider. "Moving towards More Eco-Efficient Tourist Transportation to a Resort Destination: The Case of Whistler, British Columbia." *Research in Transportation Economics* 26 (2010): 66–73.

Reino, Sofia, and Brian Hay. "The Use of YouTube as a Tourism Marketing Tool." *Travel and Tourism Research Association: Advancing Tourism Research Globally* 69 (2016): 1–12.

Relph, Edward. *Place and Placelessness*. London: Pion, 1976.

———. "Sense of Place." In *Ten Geographic Ideas That Changed the World*, edited by Susan Hanson, 205–26. New Brunswick, NJ: Rutgers University Press, 1997.

Richards, Greg. "Creativity and Tourism: The State of the Art." *Annals of Tourism Research* 38 (2011): 1225–53.

Rickly, Jillian M. "Overtourism and Authenticity." In *Overtourism: Issues, Realities and Solutions*, edited by Rachel Dodds and Richard W. Butler, 46–61. Berlin: De Gruyter, 2019.

Rivera, Lauren A. "Managing 'Spoiled' National Identity: War, Tourism, and Memory in Croatia." *American Sociological Review* 73 (2008): 613–34.

Rizzo, Cailey. "Tourists Are Writing Rude Messages in Rocks at this Australian Beach." *Travel + Leisure*, December 4, 2019. Accessed June 1, 2020. https://www.travelandleisure.com/travel-news/tourists-rock-grafitti-austrlia-beach-send-nudes.

Roberts, Margaret. "Powerful Knowledge and Geographical Education." *The Curriculum Journal* 25 (2014): 187–209.

Robinson, Mike, and David Picard. "Moments, Magic, and Memories: Photographic Tourists, Tourist Photographs, and Making Worlds." In *The Framed World: Tourism, Tourists, and Photography*, edited by Mike Robinson and David Picard, 1–38. Farnham, UK: Ashgate, 2009.

Rodrigue, Jean-Paul, Claude Comtois, and Brian Slack. *The Geography of Transport Systems*. 4th ed. London: Routledge, 2017.

Rogers, Peter, Kazi F. Jalal, and John A. Boyd. *An Introduction to Sustainable Development*. London: Earthscan, 2008.

Rosenblat, Carole. "Love 'Em or Hate 'Em, Influencers Have Nowhere to Travel Right Now—How Are They Surviving?" *Fodor's Travel*, May 1, 2020. Accessed June 15, 2020. https://www.fodors.com/news/coronavirus/love-em-or-hate-em-influencers-have-nowhere-to-travel-right-now-how-are-they-surviving.

Ross, Winston. "Holland's New Marijuana Laws Are Changing Old Amsterdam." *Newsweek*, February 22, 2015. Accessed March 11, 2020. https://www.newsweek.com/marijuana-and-old-amsterdam-308218.

Saarinen, Jarkko. "Not a Serious Subject?! Academic Relevancy and Critical Tourism Geographies." In *A Research Agenda for Tourism Geographies*, edited by Dieter K. Müller, 33–41. Cheltenham: Edward Elgar Publishing, 2019.

Sabre Corporation. "The Sabra Story." Accessed March 30, 2020. https://www.sabre.com/files/Sabre-History.pdf.

Sachs, Jeffrey D. *The Age of Sustainable Development*. New York: Columbia University Press, 2015.

Sagarmatha Pollution Control Committee. "About Us." Accessed May 25, 2020. https://www.spcc.org.np.

Saha, Shrabani, and Ghialy Yap. "The Moderation Effects of Political Instability and Terrorism on Tourism Development: A Cross-Country Panel Analysis." *Journal of Travel Research* 53, no. 4 (2014): 509–21.

Sampson, Hannah. "What Does America Have Against Vacation?" *The Washington Post*, August 28, 2019. Accessed March 19, 2020. https://www.washingtonpost.com/travel/2019/08/28/what-does-america-have-against-vacation/.

Sandford, Alasdair. "Post-Brexit Guide: Where Are We Now – and How Did We Get Here?" *Euronews*, March 24, 2020. Accessed May 2, 2020. https://www.euronews.com/2020/02/11/brexit-draft-deal-first-of-many-hurdles-to-a-smooth-exit.

Santich, Barbara. "The Study of Gastronomy and Its Relevance to Hospitality Education and Training." *Hospitality Management* 23 (2004): 15–24.

Scheyvens, Regina. *Tourism and Poverty*. New York: Routledge, 2011.

Scheyvens, Regina, and Gabriel Laeis. "Linkages between Tourist Resorts, Local Food Production and the Sustainable Development Goals." *Tourism Geographies* (2019). DOI: 10.1080/14616688.2019.1674369.

Schomer, Audrey. "Influencer Marketing: State of the Social Media Influencer Market in 2020." *Business Insider*, December 17, 2019. Accessed June 12, 2020. https://www.businessinsider.com/influencer-marketing-report.

Scott, Daniel. "Climate Change Implications for Tourism." In *The Wiley Blackwell Companion to Tourism*, edited by Alan A. Lew, C. Michael Hall, and Allan M. Williams, 466–78. Malden, MA: Wiley Blackwell, 2014.

Scott, Daniel, Bas Amelung, Suzanne Becken, Jean-Paul Ceron, Ghislan Dubois, Stefan Gössling, Paul Peeters, and Murray C. Simpson. *Climate Change and Tourism: Responding to Global Challenges, Summary*. Madrid: World Tourism Organization and United Nations Environment Programme, 2007.

Scott, Daniel, and Christopher Lemieux. "The Vulnerability of Tourism to Climate Change." In *The Routledge Handbook of Tourism and the Environment*, edited by Andrew Holden and David Fennell, 241–58. London: Routledge, 2013.

Seongseop Kim, Samuel, and Bruce Prideaux. "Tourism, Peace, Politics and Ideology: Impacts of the Mt. Gumgang Tour Project in the Korean Peninsula." *Tourism Management* 24 (2003): 675–85.

Sequera, Jorge, and Jordi Nofre. "Debates Shaken, Not Stirred: New Debates on Touristification and the Limits of Gentrification." *City* 22, nos. 5–6 (2018): 843–55.

Seraphin, Hugues. "Natural Disaster and Destination Management: The Case of the Caribbean and Hurricane Irma." *Current Issues in Tourism* 22, no. 1 (2019): 21–8.

Seraphin, Hugues, Vanessa Gowreesunkar, Mustafeed Zaman, and Stéphane Bourliataux-Lajoinie. "Community Based Festivals as a Tool to Tackle Tourismphobia and Antitourism Movements." *Journal of Hospitality and Tourism Management* 39 (2019): 219–23.

Shaffer, Marguerite. *See America First: Tourism and National Identity, 1880–1940*. Washington, DC: Smithsonian Institution Press, 2001.

Shallcross, Juliana. "The World's Biggest Hotel Chains Are Turning Their Attention to Food Waste." *Condé Nast Traveler*, November 6, 2019. Accessed July 10, 2020. https://www.cntraveler.com/story/the-worlds-biggest-hotel-chains-are-turning-their-attention-to-food-waste.

Sharma, Bhadra, and Kai Schultz. "New Everest Rules Could Significantly Limit Who Gets to Climb." *The New York Times*, August 14, 2019. Accessed May 25, 2020. https://www.nytimes.com/2019/08/14/world/asia/everest-climbing-rules.html.

Sharpley, Richard. "Tourism and the Countryside." In *A Companion to Tourism*, ed. Alan A. Lew, C. Michael Hall, and Allan M. Williams, 374–81. Malden, MA: Blackwell, 2004.

Shaw, Gareth, and Allan M. Williams. *Critical Issues in Tourism: A Geographical Perspective*. 2nd ed. Malden, MA: Blackwell, 2002.

Sheeler, Jason. "How to Fly Private Without Breaking the Bank." *Condé Nast Traveler*, January 10, 2020. Accessed April 14, 2020. https://www.cntraveler.com/story/how-to-fly-private-semi-private-jets.

Shepherd, Robert. "Commodification, Culture, and Tourism." *Tourist Studies* 2, no. 2 (2002): 183–201.

Simmons, Jack. "Railways, Hotels, and Tourism in Great Britain, 1839–1914." *Journal of Contemporary History* 19 (1984): 201–22.

———. "Thomas Cook of Leicester," *The Leicestershire Archeological and Historical Society, Transactions* 49 (1973): 18–32.

Simonsen, Morten, Stefan Gössling, and Hans Jakob Walnum. "Cruise Ship Emissions in Norwegian Waters: A Geographical Analysis." *Journal of Transport Geography* 78 (2019): 87–97.

Simpson, Murray C., Stefan Gossling, Daniel Scott, C. Michael Hall, and Elizabeth Gladin. *Climate Change Adaptation and Mitigation in the Tourism Sector: Frameworks, Tools and Practices*. Paris: UNEP, University of Oxford, UNWTO and WMO, 2008.

Sims, Shannon. "How Could Travel Giant Thomas Cook Fail?" *The New York Times*, September 23, 2019. Accessed March 26, 2020. https://www.nytimes.com/2019/09/23/travel/why-thomas-cook-travel-collapsed.html.

Six Senses Group. "Eco Resort in Bali." Accessed July 10, 2020. https://www.sixsenses.com/en/resorts/uluwatu-bali/sustainability.

Skeete, Ryan. "CTO Caribbean Tourism Performance Report 2018 & Outlook for 2019," February 13, 2019. Accessed April 22, 2020. https://www.onecaribbean.org/wp-content/uploads/Ryan-Skeete-CTO-State-Industry-Report-2019.pdf.

Smith, Sean P. "Instagram Abroad: Performance, Consumption and Colonial Narrative in Tourism." *Postcolonial Studies* 21, no. 2 (2018): 172–91.

———. "Landscapes for 'Likes': Capitalizing on Travel with Instagram," *Social Semiotics* (2019) DOI: 10.1080/10350330.2019.1664579.

Smith, Stephen L. J. "Defining Tourism: A Supply Side View." *Annals of Tourism Research* 15, no. 2 (1988): 179–90.

So, Kevin Kam Fung, Ceridwyn King, Beverley A. Sparks, and Ying Wang. "The Role of Customer Engagement in Building Consumer Loyalty in Tourism Brands." *Journal of Travel Research* 55, no. 1 (2016): 64–78.

Sönmez, Sevil F. "Tourism, Terrorism, and Political Instability." *Annals of Tourism Research* 25, no. 2 (1998): 416–56.

Specia, Megan, and Tariro Mzezewa. "Adventurous. Alone. Attacked." *The New York Times*, March 25, 2019. Accessed June 25, 2020. https://www.nytimes.com/2019/03/25/travel/solo-female-travel.html.

Spencer, Andrew. *Travel and Tourism in the Caribbean: Challenges and Opportunities for Small Island Developing States*. Cham: Plagrave Macmillan, 2019.

Spurrell, Megan. "Nepal Is Banning Single-Use Plastics on Mount Everest." *Condé Nast Traveler*, August 23, 2019. Accessed May 25, 2020. https://www.cntraveler.com/story/nepal-is-banning-single-use-plastics-on-mount-everest.

———. "Visiting the Galápagos Is About to Get a Lot More Expensive." *Condé Nast Traveler*, September 30, 2019. Accessed July 9, 2020. https://www.cntraveler.com/story/visiting-the-galapagos-is-about-to-get-a-lot-more-expensive.

Steiger, Robert. "Tourism and Climate Change." In *A Research Agenda for Tourism Geographies*, edited by Dieter K. Müller, 138–48. Cheltenham: Edward Elgar Publishing, 2019.

Stephens, Ronald J. *Idlewild: The Black Eden of Michigan*. Charleston: Arcadia, 2001.

Steward, Jill. " 'How and Where to Go': The Role of Travel Journalism in Britain and the Evolution of Foreign Travel, 1840–1914." In *Histories of Tourism: Representation, Identity, and Conflict*, edited by John Walton, 39–54. Clevedon, UK: Channel View Publications, 2005.

Stone, Philip R. "A Dark Tourism Spectrum: Towards a Typology of Death and Macabre Related Tourist Sites, Attractions and Exhibition." *Tourism* 54, no. 2 (2006): 145–60.

Stone, Philip R., and Richard Sharpley. "Consuming Dark Tourism: A Thanatological Perspective." *Annals of Tourism Research* 35, no. 2 (2008): 574–95.

Strahler, Alan. *Introducing Physical Geography*, 6th edition. Hoboken: John Wiley & Sons, Inc., 2013.

Strasdas, Wolfgang. "Ecotourism and the Challenge of Climate Change: Vulnerability, Responsibility, and Mitigation Strategies." In *Sustainable Tourism & the Millennium Development Goals: Effecting Positive Change*, edited by Kelly S. Bricker, Rosemary Black, and Stuart Cottrell, 209–30. Burlington: Jones & Bartlett Learning, 2013.

Stylianou-Lambert, Theopisti, Nikolaos Boukas, and Marina Christodoulou-Yerali. "Museums and Cultural Sustainability: Stakeholders, Forces, and Cultural Policies." *International Journal of Cultural Policy* 20, no. 5 (2014): 566–87.

Swarbrooke, John. *The Development and Management of Visitor Attractions*. 2nd ed. Burlington, MA: Butterworth-Heinemann, 2002.

Tabit, Jesse. "These Places Could Be Getting 'Selfie Seats' Because People are Dying." *Fodor's Travel*, February 13, 2019. Accessed June 25, 2020. https://www.fodors.com/news/news/these-places-could-be-getting-selfie-seats-because-people-are-dying.

———. "These Seemingly Innocuous Tourist Behaviors Are Actually Incredibly Destructive." *Fodor's Travel*, August 19, 2019. Accessed June 1, 2020. https://www.fodors.com/news/outdoors/these-seemingly-innocuous-tourist-behaviors-are-actually-incredibly-destructive.

Tan, Siow-Kian, Shiann-Far Kung, and Ding-Bang Luh. "A Model of 'Creative Experience' in Creative Tourism." *Annals of Tourism Research* 41 (2013): 153–74.

Texas Bluebonnet Wine Trail. "Welcome to the Texas Bluebonnet Wine Trail." Accessed March 18, 2020. https://www.texasbluebonnetwinetrail.com.

Thiessen, Tamara. "Australia Bushfire Burns Tourism Industry: $4.5 Billion as Holidayers Cancel." *Forbes*, January 20, 2020. Accessed April 20, 2020. https://www.forbes.com/sites/tamarathiessen/2020/01/20/australia-bushfires-hit-tourism-industry-as-holidayers-cancel/#1556876672c5.

This Is Cleveland. "Cleveland, Ohio." Accessed June 12, 2020. https://www.thisiscleveland.com.

"Thomas Cook Blames Heatwave for Profit Warning." *BBC News*, September 24, 2018. Accessed April 20, 2020. https://www.bbc.com/news/business–45624215.

Thompson, Paul. "Blarney Stone 'Most Unhygienic Tourist Attraction in the World.'" *Daily Mail*, June 16, 2009. March 20, 2020. https://www.dailymail.co.uk/news/article-1193477/Blarney-Stone-unhygienic-tourist-attraction-world.html.

Timothy, Dallen J. "Cross-Border Partnership in Tourism Resource Management: International Parks Along the US-Canada Border." *Journal of Sustainable Tourism* 7, nos. 3&4 (1999): 182–205.

———. "Tourism, War, and Political Instability: Territorial and Religious Perspectives." In *Tourism and War*, edited by Richard Butler and Wantanee Suntikul, 12–25. London: Routledge, 2013.

Tölkes, Christina. "Sustainability Communication in Tourism – A Literature Review." *Tourism Management Perspectives* 27 (2018): 10–21.

tom Dieck, M. Claudia, and Timothy Jung. "A Theoretical Model of Mobile Augmented Reality Acceptance in Urban Heritage Tourism." *Current Issues in Tourism* 21, no. 2 (2018): 154–74.

Tourism New Zealand. "Lord of the Rings Trilogy." Accessed June 2, 2020. https://www.newzealand.com/int/the-lord-of-the-rings-trilogy/.

Tourism RESET. "Tourism RESET." Accessed June 25, 2020. https://www.tourismreset.com.

Towner, John. "The Grand Tour: A Key Phase in the History of Tourism." *Annals of Tourism Research* 12 (1985): 297–333.

———. "What Is Tourism's History?" *Tourism Management* 16, no. 5 (1995): 339–43.

Tripadvisor. "TripCollective FAQs." Accessed June 15, 2020. https://www.tripadvisor.com/vpages/tripcollective_faqs.html.

Tuan, Yi-Fu. "Place: An Experiential Perspective." *Geographical Review* 65 (1975): 151–65.

Uber Elevate. "Uber Air." Accessed April 27, 2020. https://www.uber.com/us/en/elevate/uberair/.

UK Inbound. "Two out of Three Tourism Businesses Fear Immigration Reforms May Cause Closures," October 10, 2019. Accessed May 2, 2020. https://www.ukinbound.org/

advocacy-news/two-out-of-three-tourism-businesses-fear-immigration-reforms-may-cause-closures/.

United Nations. "SDGs: Sustainable Development Knowledge Platform." Accessed July 9, 2020. https://sustainabledevelopment.un.org/sdgs.

———. "United Nations Millennium Development Goals." Accessed July 9, 2020. http://www.un.org/millenniumgoals/.

———. "Transforming Our World: The 2030 Agenda for Sustainable Development." Accessed May 5, 2020. https://sustainabledevelopment.un.org/post2015/transformingourworld.

United Nations Educational, Scientific, and Cultural Organization. "The Criteria for Selection." Accessed March 11, 2020. https://whc.unesco.org/en/criteria/.

———. "Cornwall and West Devon Mining Landscape." Accessed May 28, 2020. http://whc.unesco.org/en/list/1215.

———. "List of UNESCO Global Geoparks (UGGp)." *Earth Sciences.* Accessed March 2, 2020. http://www.unesco.org/new/en/natural-sciences/environment/earth-sciences/unesco-global-geoparks/list-of-unesco-global-geoparks/.

———. Towards Sustainable Strategies for Creative Tourism: Discussion Report of the Planning Meeting for 2008 International Conference on Creative Tourism. Santa Fe, New Mexico, USA October 25–27, 2006.

———. "UNESCO Global Geoparks and Their Contribution to the Sustainable Development Goals." *Earth Sciences.* Accessed March 2, 2020. http://www.unesco.org/new/en/natural-sciences/environment/earth-sciences/unesco-global-geoparks/sustainable-development-goals/.

United Nations Office of the High Representative for the Least Developed Countries, Landlocked Developing Countries, and the Small Island Developing States. "About the Small Island Developing States." Accessed May 9, 2020. http://unohrlls.org/about-sids/

United Nations World Tourism Organization. *Compendium of Tourism Statistics Dataset [Electronic].* Madrid: UNWTO, 2020.

———. "Global Code of Ethics for Tourism," December 21, 2001. Accessed July 9, 2020. https://webunwto.s3.eu-west-1.amazonaws.com/imported_images/37802/gcetbrochureglobalcodeen.pdf.

———. *Global Report on Women in Tourism, Second Edition, Key Findings* (2019). Accessed May 7, 2020. https://www.e-unwto.org/doi/pdf/10.18111/9789284420407.

———. "Glossary of Tourism Terms." Accessed March 5, 2020. https://www.unwto.org/glossary-tourism-terms.

———. "International Tourism Growth Continues to Outpace the Global Economy," January 20, 2020. Accessed May 2, 2020. https://www.unwto.org/international-tourism-growth-continues-to-outpace-the-economy.

———. *International Tourism Highlights 2019 Edition* (2019). Accessed March 5, 2020. https://www.e-unwto.org/doi/pdf/10.18111/9789284421152.

———. "Sustainable Development." Accessed April 3, 2020. https://www.unwto.org/sustainable-development.

———. "SDG 1—No Poverty." Accessed May 5, 2020. http://tourism4sdgs.org/sdg-1-no-poverty/.

———. "Tips for a Responsible Traveller." Accessed July 9, 2020. https://trello.com/c/X67eQzsh/1-english.

———. *Tourism and Culture Partnership in Peru—Models for Collaboration between Tourism, Culture and Community.* Madrid: UNWTO, 2016.

———. "Tourism for MDGs." Accessed July 9, 2020. http://tourism4sdgs.org.

———. "Tourism in the 2030 Agenda." Accessed July 9, 2020. https://www.unwto.org/tourism-in-2030-agenda.

———. "Tourism Committed to Fight Climate Change—COP22," November 14, 2016. Accessed May 30, 2020. https://www.unwto.org/archive/africa/press-release/2016-11-14/tourism-committed-fight-climate-change-cop-22.

———. "Travel Enjoy Respect." Accessed July 9, 2020. http://www.travelenjoyrespect.org.

United Nations World Tourism Organization and International Transport Forum. *Transport-Related CO$_2$ Emissions of the Tourism Sector: Modelling Results*. Madrid: UNWTO, 2019. Accessed May 30, 2020. https://www.e-unwto.org/doi/pdf/10.18111/9789284416660.

United States Census Bureau. "Urban and Rural." Accessed April 26, 2020. https://www.census.gov/programs-surveys/geography/guidance/geo-areas/urban-rural.html.

United States Department of State. "Birth Tourism Update," January 23, 2020. Accessed March 12, 2020. https://travel.state.gov/content/travel/en/News/visas-news/20200123_birth-tourism- update.html.

———. "Global Level 4 Health Advisory – Do Not Travel." Accessed March 20, 2020. https://travel.state.gov/content/travel/en/traveladvisories/ea/travel-advisory-alert-global-level-4-health-advisory-issue.html.

University of Eastern Finland. "Food Waste in Tourism Is a Bigger Issue Than Previously Thought." *ScienceDaily*, November 1, 2019. Accessed July 10, 2020. https://www.sciencedaily.com/releases/2019/11/191101100142.htm.

Uriely, Natan, and Yniv Belhassen. "Drugs and Tourists' Experiences." *Journal of Travel Research* 43 (2005): 238–46.

Urry, John. *Consuming Places*. London: Routledge, 1995.

———. *The Tourist Gaze*. London: Sage, 1990.

Vacanti Brondo, Keri. "The Spectacle of Saving: Conservation Voluntourism and the New Neoliberal Economy on Utila, Honduras." *Journal of Sustainable Tourism* 23, no. 10 (2015): 1405–25.

The Venetian Las Vegas. "Human Resources." Accessed March 31, 2011. http://www.venetian.com/Company-Information/Human-Resources

Visit Luxemborg. "Blog." Accessed June 12, 2020. https://www.visitluxembourg.com/en/blog.

Visit Scotland. "Climate & Weather in Scotland." Accessed April 20, 2020. https://www.visitscotland.com/about/practical-information/weather/.

Visser, Gustav. "The Challenges of Tourism and Urban Economic (Re)Development in Southern Cities." In *A Research Agenda for Tourism Geographies*, edited by Dieter K. Müller, 107–16. Cheltenham: Edward Elgar Publishing, 2019.

Vodeb, Ksenija. "Cross-Border Regions as Potential Tourist Destinations along the Slovene Croatian Frontier." *Tourism and Hospitality Management* 16 (2010): 219–28.

Waitt, Gordon, and Chris Gibson. "Tourism and Creative Economies." In *The Wiley Blackwell Companion to Tourism*, edited by Alan A. Lew, C. Michael Hall, and Allan M. Williams, 230–9. Malden, MA: Wiley Blackwell, 2014.

Waldek, Stefanie. "You Can Soon Vacation in Space for $35,000 Per Night." *Condé Nast Traveler*, June 10, 2019. Accessed April 10, 2020. https://www.cntraveler.com/story/you-can-soon-vacation-in-space-for-dollar35000-per-night.

Walsh, Michael James, Raechel Johns, and Naomi F. Dale. "The Social Media Tourist Gaze: Social Media Photography and its Disruption at the Zoo." *Information Technology & Tourism* 21 (2019): 391–412.

Walton, John K. "Prospects in Tourism History: Evolution, State of Play, and Future Development." *Tourism Management* 30 (2009): 783–93.

Wang, Sean H. "Fetal Citizens? Birthright Citizenship, Reproductive Futurism, and the 'Panic' over Chinese Birth Tourism in Southern California." *Environment and Planning D: Society and Space* 35, no. 2 (2017): 263–80.

Ward, Julian. *Xu Xiake (1587–1641): The Art of Travel Writing*. London: Routledge, 2001.

Ward-Perkins, David, Christina Beckmann, and Jackie Ellis. *Tourism Routes and Trails: Theory and Practice*. CABI: Oxfordshire, 2020.

Watson, C. Scott, and Owen King. "Everest's Thinning Glaciers: Implications for Tourism and Mountaineering." *Geology Today* 34, no. 1 (2018): 18–25.

"Wave of Terror Attacks in Turkey Continue at a Steady Pace." *The New York Times*, January 5, 2017. Accessed April 29, 2020. https://www.nytimes.com/interactive/2016/06/28/world/middleeast/turkey-terror-attacks-bombings.html?_r=0.

Wearing, Stephen. *Volunteer Tourism: Experiences That Make a Difference*. Wallingford, UK: CABI, 2001.

Webber, Derek. "Space Tourism: Its History, Future and Importance." *Acta Astronautica* 92 (2013): 138–43.

Weed, Julie. "Book Your 'Bud and Breakfast,' Marijuana Tourism Is Growing in Colorado and Washington." *Forbes*, March 17, 2015. Accessed March 11, 2020. https://www.forbes.com/sites/julieweed/2015/03/17/book-your-bud-and-breakfast-marijuana-tourism-is-growing-in-colorado-and-washington/#33a7884864d4.

Weiler, Betty, and Rosemary Black. "The Changing Face of the Tour Guide: One-Way Communicator to Choreographer to Co-Creator of the Tourist Experience." *Tourism Recreation Research* 40, no. 3 (2015): 364–78.

Wheeler, Tony. "Foreword." In *Overtourism: Excesses, Discontents and Measures in Travel and Tourism*, edited by Claudio Milano, Joseph M. Cheer, and Marina Novelli, xv–xvii. Oxfordshire: CABI, 2019.

Williams, Stephen. *Tourism Geography*. London: Routledge, 1998.

Wilson, Antonia. "UK Tourism Industry Set to Struggle under Post-Brexit Immigration Plans." *The Guardian*, November 4, 2019. Accessed May 2, 2020. https://www.theguardian.com/travel/2019/nov/04/uk-tourism-industry-struggle-post-brexit-immigration-plans.

Wilson, Erica, and Donna E. Little. "A 'Relative Escape'? The Impact of Constraints on Women Who Travel Solo." *Tourism Review International* 9 (2005): 155–75.

———. "The Solo Female Travel Experience: Exploring the 'Geography of Women's Fear'." *Current Issues in Tourism* 11, no. 2 (2008): 167–86.

Wong, Chak Keung Simon, and Fung Ching Gladys Liu. "A Study of Pre-Trip Use of Travel Guidebooks by Leisure Travelers." *Tourism Management* 32 (2011): 616–28.

Wong, Maggie Hiufu. "India's New Pakyong Airport Opens in Incredible Himalayan Surroundings." *CNN Travel*, September 25, 2018. Accessed April 20, 2020. https://www.cnn.com/travel/article/pakyong-airport-india/index.html.

Woods, Michael. *Rural Geography*. London: Sage, 2005.

World Animal Protection. *A Close Up on Cruelty: The Harmful Impact of Wildlife Selfies in the Amazon*. London: World Animal Protection, 2017. Accessed May 20, 2020. https://www.worldanimalprotection.org/sites/default/files/media/int_files/amazon_selfies_report.pdf.

———. "Costa Rica Urges Tourists Not to Take Wildlife Selfies," November 13, 2019. Accessed May 20, 2020. https://www.worldanimalprotection.org/news/costa-rica-urges-tourists-not-take-wildlife-selfies.

The World Bank. "Peru: Easing Business Regulations in One of the World's Most Famous Tourist Destinations," November 1, 2016. Accessed May 6, 2020. https://www.worldbank.org/en/results/2016/11/01/peru-easing-business-regulations-in-one-of-the-worlds-most-famous-tourist-destinations.

World Commission on Environment and Development. *Our Common Future: Report of the World Commission on Environment and Development*. Oxford: Oxford University, 1987.

World Tourism Organization, *"Tourism Highlights 2000, 2nd ed.,"* August 2000. Accessed March 27, 2020. https://www.e-unwto.org/doi/pdf/10.18111/9789284403745.

World Travel Awards. "2019 Winners – World Travel Awards." Accessed March 11, 2020. https://www.worldtravelawards.com/winners/2019.

World Travel & Tourism Council. "Home." Accessed March 20, 2020. https://www.wttc.org.

———. "WTTC Now Estimates Over 100 Million Jobs Losses in the Travel & Tourism Sector and Alerts G20 Countries to the Scale of the Crisis," April 24, 2020. Accessed May 8, 2020. https://wttc.org/News-Article/WTTC-now-estimates-over-100-million-jobs-losses-in-the-Travel-&-Tourism-sector-and-alerts-G20-countries-to-the-scale-of-the-crisis.

Xie, Philip Feifan. *Authenticating Ethnic Tourism*. Bristol: Channel View Publications, 2011.

Xu, Honggang, and Tian Ye. "Tourist Experience in Lijiang—The Capital of Yanyu." *Journal of China Tourism Research* 12, no. 1 (2016): 108–25.

Yeginsu, Ceylan, and Michael Wolgelenter. "Thomas Cook Travel Company Collapses, Stranding Thousands." *The New York Times*, September 23, 2019. Accessed March 26, 2020. https://www.nytimes.com/2019/09/23/travel/thomas-cook-airline-collapse.html.

Yoo, Kyung-Hyan, and Ulrike Gretzel. "Use and Creation of Social Media by Travellers." In *Social Media in Travel, Tourism and Hospitality: Theory, Practice and Cases*, edited by Marianna Sigala, Evangelos Christou, and Ulrike Gretzel, 189–205. Ashgate: Surrey, 2012.

Young, Anna. "What Myrtle Beach Is Doing to Address Ocean Water Quality and How Much It Could Cost." *Myrtle Beach Online*, November 16, 2019. Accessed June 1, 2020. https://www.myrtlebeachonline.com/news/local/article237351879.html.

YouTube. "Press." Accessed June 15, 2020. https://www.youtube.com/about/press/.

Zander, Kerstin K., Angelica Saeteros, Daniel Orellana, Veronica Toral Granda, Aggie Wegner, Arturo Izurietah, and Stephen T. Garnett. "Determinants of Tourist Satisfaction with National Park Guides and Facilities in the Galápagos." *International Journal of Tourism Sciences* 16, nos. 1–2 (2016): 60–82.

Zarroli, Jim. "Boeing 737 Max Grounding Takes Toll on Airlines and Passengers." NPR, July 29, 2019. Accessed April 15, 2020. https://www.npr.org/2019/07/29/746345317/boeing-737-max-grounding-takes-toll-on-airlines-and-passengers.

Zhang, Ke, Yuansi Hou, Gang Li, and Yunhui Huang. "Tourists and Air Pollution: How and Why Air Pollution Magnifies Tourists' Suspicion of Service Providers." *Journal of Travel Research* 59, no. 4 (2020): 1–13.

Zillinger, Malin. "The Importance of Guidebooks for the Choice of Tourist Sites: A Study of German Tourists in Sweden." *Scandinavian Journal of Tourism and Hospitality* 6, no. 3 (2006): 229–47.

# Index

# About the Author

**Velvet Nelson** received her BS in business administration from West Liberty University, her MA in geography with a concentration in rural development from East Carolina University, and her PhD in geography from Kent State University. She joined the Department of Geography and Geology at Sam Houston State University in Huntsville, Texas, in 2006 and is currently a full professor. She is a human geographer with interests in cultural geography and sustainable development, but her primary research focus has been on tourism. She has conducted archival research on historical patterns of tourism in the Caribbean, as well as fieldwork on islands such as Dominica, Grenada, and St. Vincent to examine current issues. In 2010, she received a Fulbright Fellowship to conduct research and teach in the Faculty of Humanities and Social Sciences at the University of Primorska in Slovenia. Since then, she has been invited back to the university as a visiting scholar in the Faculty of Tourism three times. Her most recent research examines the city of Houston, Texas, as an emerging food and beverage destination. She has published her research in peer-reviewed journal articles and presented it at regional, national, and international conferences both within geography and in the interdisciplinary field of tourism studies. In addition, she is a member of the *Tourism Geographies* and *Journal of Cultural Geography* editorial boards and the *Tijdschrift voor Economische en Sociale Geografie* international advisory board. She is also a member of the Commission on the Geography of Tourism, Leisure, and Global Change of the International Geographical Union and the International Research and Scholarship Exchange committee of the American Association of Geographers. She strongly believes in direct experience through travel as a means of learning about new places. As such, she travels at every opportunity.

# EXPLORING GEOGRAPHY

**Series Editor: David H. Kaplan**